ID646387

THE CANADIAN HOCKEY ATLAS

THE CANADIAN HOCKEY ATLAS

STEPHEN COLE

AN ANGEL EDITION FOR

DOUBLEDAY CANADA

Acknowledgements

I would like to thank the following for their assistance and support in the assembly of this book:

For their invaluable research assistance, thanks to Paul Patskou, Normand Pawluck, Alex Obal, Jacquie McNish, Jeff Keats, Ernie Fitzsimmons, Craig Campbell and everyone at the Hockey Hall of Fame, the Nova Scotia, New Brunswick and Saskatchewan Sports Halls of Fame, along with the good folks at the Toronto Reference Library and the (Toronto) Beaches Library. The Society for International Hockey Research website (SIHR) proved invaluable in the creation of city team lists.

For her incredible editorial work, thanks to Joanna Freedman (who checks closer than Bob Gainey, a flattering reference I hope she now understands), and Patricia Holtz for her detailed copy edit.

For creative direction and production; thanks to Sara Angel's entire crew at Angel Editions—Sara herself and Amy Hick, along with Bao-Nghi Nhan (picture research); thanks also to John Pylypczak and Jordan Poirier of Concrete Design Communications Inc.

Thanks to Maya Mavjee, Brad Martin, and Amy Black at Doubleday Canada.

Thanks to my agent, Dean Cooke, and everyone at The Cooke Agency, for tea and sympathy.

Previous Spread: The first McGill hockey team, 1881.
Opposite: Sher-Wood hockey sticks.

Text copyright © 2006 Stephen Cole
Caption, design and compilation copyright © 2006 Angel Editions Inc.

All rights reserved. The use of any part of this publication, reproduced, transmitted in any form or by any means electronic, mechanical, photocopying, recording or otherwise, or stored in a retrieval system without the prior written consent of the publisher—or, in the case of photocopying or other reprographic copying, a license from the Canadian Copyright Licensing Agency—is an infringement of the copyright law.

Doubleday Canada and colophon are trademarks.

Library and Archives Canada Cataloguing in Publication

Cole, Stephen
The Canadian hockey atlas / Stephen Cole.

ISBN-13: 978-0-385-66093-8
ISBN-10: 0-385-66093-6

1. Hockey players — Canada.
2. Hockey — Canada — History.
3. Canada — History, Local. I. Title.

GV848.4.C3C63 2006   796.962'0971   C2006-900768-3

Printed and bound in Singapore

Published in Canada by
Doubleday Canada, a division of
Random House of Canada Limited

Visit Random House of Canada Limited's website: www.randomhouse.ca

10   9   8   7   6   5   4   3   2   1

For Jacquie McNish

TABLE OF CONTENTS

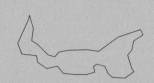

PROVINCE
NOVA SCOTIA

38

PROVINCE
NEW BRUNSWICK

60

PROVINCE
QUEBEC

76

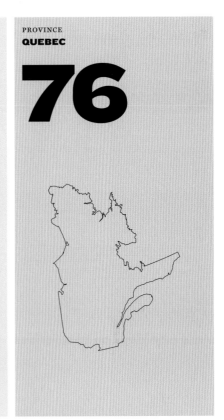

PROVINCE
ALBERTA

282

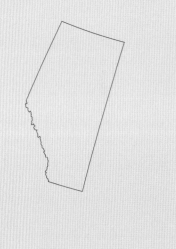

PROVINCE
BRITISH COLUMBIA

326

THE TERRITORIES
YUKON, NORTHWEST TERRITORIES
& NUNAVUT

368

Town and Country

I tricked myself into writing the book you have in your hands, after I was asked by a publisher if I'd be interested in putting together an international hockey atlas, a book examining the sport from England to Ukraine.

I could only listen politely for so long, and then, finally, I interrupted. "'Hockey is the Canadian specific'—British Columbia poet Al Purdy said that.

"Why not a Canadian hockey atlas? Everywhere else, hockey is a sport. But here, it's a way of life. What's that old expression, If life gives you a lemon, make lemonade? Life gave much of Canada five-month-long winters, and so in response we came up with the sport of hockey. Why not talk about the sport from the perspective of our towns and cities? Let's, at last, have a record of where our players come from. Record the names of the teams and the players who have made hockey special. Tell their stories. Tell our story."

"A Canadian hockey atlas? Sounds great—let's go for it," the publisher responded.

A few days later, panic set in. How in Bobby Hull had I ever let myself be roped into writing something as big as all of Canada's outdoors? It's easy enough to decide where to start writing about hockey in this country. But where do you stop? A more crucial problem—how to find those records of "where our players came from."

Fortunately, my primary researcher, Paul Patskou—one of Canada's foremost hockey archivists—was able to solve the latter problem, obtaining from his colleague Normand Pawluck a 2,900-name list that documented the birthplace of every Canadian player who had skated as little as a single shift in the National Hockey League between 1917 and 2006.

The Canadian Hockey Atlas is more than a record of Canadian NHL accomplishments, though. Junior, senior and women's teams, as well as players, are profiled here; as are many city clubs that achieved international glory, from the Dunlops of Whitby, Ontario ("Go Dunnees!"), to the Smoke Eaters of Trail, British Columbia. This hockey atlas also includes the tale of a Maritime hockey rivalry so fierce that the federal government was once called upon to intercede, as well as the story of how Josiah Flintabbatey Flonatin left his imprint on Manitoba.

Ever since Foster Hewitt, famed broadcaster for the NHL's Toronto Maple Leafs, first hunched over a *Hockey Night in Canada* microphone (on 12 November 1931), and shouted out his soon-to-be-famous cry—"Hello Canada! And hockey fans in the United States and Newfoundland...", the National Hockey League has enjoyed a mystical place in the Canadian imagination. Whenever a player is introduced to fellow Canadians as having played in the NHL, the one-word response is always the same: "Wow!"

For this reason, "Native-born NHL players" are listed, place by place, among the more than 100 civic entries and 300 stories included in this volume. A list of famous local teams and a brief chronology of how the towns and cities came into being also form part of these introductory sections. I wish that there could have been room for more entries, more stories. But had any more been included here, the result would have been a coffee table book that looked...well...that looked like Kramer's actual coffee table-sized book on that famous episode of *Seinfeld*.

In addition, however, to the more than 100 Canadian towns and cities profiled here, close to 1,000 Canadian towns and cities and the NHL players that brought them to our attention are fully listed in an appendix at the back of the atlas.

The decision as to which towns and cities to profile in this collection was not based on size. Vancouver, Calgary, Toronto, Ottawa and Montreal are here; but so are Cupar, Saskatchewan—Eddie Shore's hometown (population 591)—and Port Hood, Nova Scotia (835 citizens), where Al MacInnis turned the family barn black with the imprint of tens of thousands of drilled pucks.

The goal, in selecting which stories to tell was the same, in either case—to help define our hockey experience, while providing a Canadian geographical hockey history.

The outcome of this odyssey, then, is *The Canadian Hockey Atlas*. Good luck to the brave cartographer who tries to chart the English and Ukrainian hockey experiences. Although every hockey enthusiast should know that the best Ukrainian hockey players, Johnny Bucyk, Vic Stasiuk and Bronco Horvath—the famous NHL Uke Line from the late 1950s—were born in Canada.

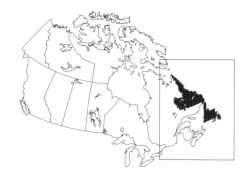

Opening Spread:
St. John's native
Michael Ryder of the
Montreal Canadiens.

T he history of Newfoundland hockey is the story of coming, warring and going—not always in that order.

In the 16th century, French, Portuguese and Basque fishermen battled for control over the Island's resource-rich Grand Banks before disappearing entirely, leaving behind only the exotic names of fishing ports. Similarly, many Newfoundland players and teams—even some towns—that once competed for the symbol of provincial hockey supremacy, the Herder Memorial Trophy, have all but vanished.

Senior hockey became a ruling passion in Newfoundland following the end of World War II. Players were imported from elsewhere in Canada to fight on ice for the Island's mining, fishing, and pulp-and-paper towns. For years, the name of one of the first senior teams, the Buchans Miners, was pronounced like a curse in other parts of the region. The team was born in the 1920s, when an abandoned ore shack was remodelled into an arena to provide a base for entertainment in the central Newfoundland mining town.

Bob's Our Uncle

According to childhood friends, when Bob Cole played hockey as a youth in St. John's he barked out play-by-play commentary of the unfolding action in the precise, impassioned style of Maple Leafs broadcaster Foster Hewitt. In 1954, on a lark, Cole and a few classmates made a mock broadcast tape that impressed disc jockeys at the radio station VOCM (Voice of the Common Man). Cole soon won a part-time DJ job, reading the news and spinning records. When he was asked to broadcast a local hockey game, his bustling, homey commentary earned him a job broadcasting games out of the old St. John's Memorial Stadium every winter night.

Mustering his courage, the young announcer made a pilgrimage to Toronto and asked broadcast legend Foster Hewitt to critique one of his tapes. Hewitt took Cole into his office and broke down a hockey game, not as sport but as a drama. "Don't try to yell for a full 60 minutes," Hewitt told Cole. "There is a voice level for a game-winning goal, that's your top level, and you have to build to it."

The lessons from Hewitt stuck. Like his mentor, Cole learned to interpret the game as national theatre. Hockey became folk melodrama—news of warring tribes brought to families waiting at home.

Cole also had a quality that was rooted forever in the time and place he became a broadcaster—Newfoundland in the 1950s, a time when hockey was more a way of life than an entertainment choice. Arriving at *Hockey Night in Canada* in 1973, he would provide a valuable link to hockey broadcasting's golden era, a time before expansion and cable TV, when hockey was as simple as two teams and one channel.

By 2000, Cole may have sounded old-fashioned compared to the upbeat smoothies who were broadcasting sporting events. For instance, his trademark shout, "Oh, baby!", was something Frank Sinatra might have used in one of his ring-a-ding-ding recording sessions in 1950's. But his avuncular pipe-and-slipper manner only served to make Bob Cole even more valuable. Cole has been a welcome guest in our living rooms for more than 30 years. Bob is, indeed, our uncle; a down-home voice who knows the game inside out. Watching hockey with him is always a pleasure.

Bob Cole, with Dave Warren,
at Memorial University, 1958.

Technically, the Buchans Miners were amateurs, but by the late 1940s players were being compensated, with cushy jobs, by the town's mining company. Soon, other Newfoundland businessmen began recruiting hockey stars, in the hopes of building more competitive teams and bolstering community spirit. Frank Moores, a future provincial premier and the son of a wealthy Conception Bay fishing magnate, was instrumental in forming the Conception Bay CeeBees senior hockey team in the late '50s by luring players with the offer of local jobs.

Ironically, while senior Newfoundland teams imported talent from the mainland, the best young Newfoundlanders were going elsewhere to learn their craft. Recent National Hockey Leaguers from the Rock, Michael Ryder, Jason King and Darren Langdon, joined the exodus of young people leaving the province in search of better-paying jobs elsewhere. The search for opportunity had similarly lured the parents of NHL great Gary Roberts from Twillingate, Newfoundland (mentioned in the classic Newfoundland folk song "I's the B'y") to Toronto a few months before the hockey star was born.

Hockey players who remained in Newfoundland—described as "the best and most comfortable place on earth" by the province's first NHL export, Bishop's Falls native Alex Faulkner—had the pleasure of competing for a trophy that local players considered to be Newfoundland's Stanley Cup. The Herder Memorial Trophy was created in 1935, in memory of William Herder, owner of Newfoundland's *Evening Telegram*. Faulkner, who fought for both provincial and National Hockey League trophies, recalls that the battles in the '60s between the Conception Bay CeeBees and the St. John's Capitals were every bit as passionate as the struggles between the more famous central Canadian NHL rivals, Montreal and Toronto:

> When I was with the CeeBees, which played out of Harbour Grace, I felt like I was on Newfoundland's team. We'd go play exhibition games, the fans would be cheering us more than their own team sometimes. The games between us and St. John's were wars. See, the CeeBees represented small-town Newfoundland. We were from "down around the bay," as we say here. Grand Falls, Harbour Grace, Bay Roberts, Bell Island, Bishop's Falls. The townies kind of looked down their noses at us. And we loved nothing more than beating them.

Alex Faulkner and his brothers, George and Jack, though, were rare "home-brew" stars, who ultimately skated their way out of Newfoundland by playing for a variety of professional and amateur teams in Canada and the United States. So pronounced, in fact, was the departure of local hockey talent that when the Corner Brook Royals defeated the Stephenville Jets, 7–6, in a Herder playoff in 1986, only a single goal, by the legendary Andy Sullivan, was authored by a Newfoundlander.

Predictably, the escalating costs of importing talent proved unsustainable for the province's struggling small towns. In 1989, the Newfoundland Senior Hockey League was $500,000 in debt, and teams began to collapse. The Herder Memorial Trophy went uncollected in 1991. A new league, comprised of local amateurs, however, began competing for the trophy again in 1992, rekindling community pride. The province's hockey fortunes were still so shaky in 2004, though, that the Newfoundland Hockey Hall of Fame in Corner Brook ran out of cash and was headed for bankruptcy until a last-minute bailout saved the centre.

While efforts to keep hockey and the economy vibrant in this province have been an enduring struggle, Alex Faulkner is convinced that "all Newfoundlanders would stay home if you give them a good job. There's a feeling here, I don't know how to describe it, but it's a good, safe place. Friendlier than anywhere else you'll go." The hockey player's sentiments are echoed by St. John's politician and former federal cabinet minister John Crosbie, who once remarked, "You can always tell the Newfies in heaven. They're the only ones who want to go home."

Once Upon a Mine

The discovery, in the early 1900s, of rich lead, zinc and copper deposits in Buchans, Newfoundland, made a fortune for the American Smelting and Refining Company, but few of the profits were shared with the town's hard-working miners. By the 1940s, workers were so fed up with 14-hour workdays, meagre wages averaging 37 cents an hour and vermin-infested bunkhouses that they went on strike. The brief strike ended when a slim wage hike was granted, and ASARCO sought to smooth frayed labour relations by upgrading the town's scrappy hockey team with mainland talent.

The senior team's biggest fan was mine manager, George Thomas, who in 1950 imported ringers from a sister mining team in Kirkland Lake, Ontario, with the offer of salaried jobs at the mine. Armed with these mainland stars, the Buchans Miners went on a five-year rampage, winning four Herder Memorial Trophies, the province's highest hockey honour. In 1952, the team humbled Corner Brook, 27–3 and 28–3, in the playoffs. Home contests were civic celebrations.

But the victory parties didn't go on forever. By the 1970s, the Buchans mine was running out of ore, and ASARCO began winding down its operations. The shrinking town could no longer support a hockey team, and when the mine was closed officially, in 1984, only a few hundred residents remained.

Although the Buchans team is long gone, its descendants have yielded a legacy of riches that no player-miner could have imagined. In the 1990s, Chris Verbiski, son of former Buchans Miners hockey import Mort Verbiski, was struggling to make a living prospecting for minerals in northern Labrador. In 1993, he and his partner Albert Chislett discovered, along the barren coast, a rusting outcrop of rock that proved to be the cap of one of the world's richest nickel deposits, now known as Voisey's Bay.

BISHOP'S FALLS

FOUNDED
Located 12 miles east of Grand Falls-Windsor, on the banks of the Exploits River, Bishop's Falls derives its name from Nova Scotia-based Anglican bishop John Inglis, who visited the area in 1827. The town was not officially founded until 1909, when a pulp mill and hydroelectric generating station were erected near the river. The town expanded again in the 1920s, when it served as a major service centre for the Newfoundland Railway Company and its Newfie Bullet train.

NATIVE-BORN NHL PLAYERS
Alex Faulkner

FAMOUS LOCAL TEAMS
Senior-pro: Bishop's Falls Flyers, Bishop's Falls Kinsmen, Bishop's Falls Woodsmen

CURRENT POPULATION
3,688

ALEX FAULKNER'S STORY:

"Imagine a Newfoundland Boy in the NHL"

On 7 December 1961 Alex Faulkner became the first Newfoundlander to play in the National Hockey League. Faulkner was born in Bishop's Falls, a town outside Grand Falls, in 1936. He provided this oral history in January 2005.

My father was a railroad engineer—coal, oil, diesel; he worked 'em all. He'd go from Bishop's Falls to Corner Brook, stay the night at the staff house, then return next day. Everyone else in town worked in lumber. They'd grind the wood here in Bishop's Falls, then pump it through a tube to the mill in Grand Falls, 10 miles away. Couldn't put it on the river—river went the other way.

I'll tell you, there were no rinks in the '40s; we played on two ponds. Shallow one—you fell through, you were up to your knees. Week later, big pond froze; we hopped over there. By November, we'd be dying to play on the Exploits River. My father's rule, and we didn't dare cross him, was we couldn't go on the ice until it was thick enough for horses to cross. Day they did, oh, boy, was better than Christmas.

I learned hockey on that river. All the strategy, George and I, my other brothers, we figured out ourselves. Never had a coach or saw a real game. We played all day. We even played in the house Saturday night, listening to Foster Hewitt in the kitchen. We'd roll a sock up, fire it at the doorway. Broke some lights, but my father didn't mind. My mother was a great cook. We had lots of energy.

We were Leaf fans. Funny thing was my father got us Rangers sweaters. That's why when George came back from playing in the Montreal organization to play and coach the Conception Bay CeeBees, they wore Rangers colours.

I came into my own in 1958. I'd played 30 matches my whole life; now I was playing all the time. The CeeBees worked at Frank Moores' fish plant, but hockey was our job. Once, Montreal Juniors came to town—[future NHLer] Jacques Laperriere on defence. We were down one, late, when their coach, Claude Ruel, went to two lines; beat us, 10–6. How'd I do? Ah, not bad. Six goals.

King Clancy [of the Maple Leafs] scouted me, when he was here visiting

Depends If You Like Apples or Oranges

Montreal has the Richard brothers; Viking, Alberta, has the Sutters; and Bishop's Falls boasts the Faulkners. Alex, George, Jack and their nephew Gene have all been inducted into the Newfoundland and Labrador Hockey Hall of Fame. Conventional wisdom has it that Alex Faulkner, who made it to the National Hockey League, was the family's (and perhaps the province's) best player, but the former Toronto Maple Leafs and Detroit Red Wings forward isn't so sure. "Depends if you like apples or oranges. I had more luck around the net, but [my brother] George was better all 'round. Problem was he got stuck in the Montreal system in the '50s. Look what he did in 1966, in his mid-thirties, playing for Canada in the Olympics—he was the best tournament defenceman and led Canada in goals. Overall, he was better by a country mile."

Howie Meeker. I played for the Leafs' farm team in Rochester and got called up in Montreal. What a feeling. A fellow from Newfoundland in the NHL! And look, over there was [Maurice] Richard, Doug Harvey and Jacques Plante.

People said to me when I went to Detroit, boy, it must've been sweet to score those goals in the Cup against Toronto. Not at all. They were a great bunch. My wife was working in Toronto. When we played the Leafs, I'd fly back with them. I'd just skate by the Leaf bench past [trainer] Bobby Haggart in warm-up and he'd nod. They'd wait for me and give me a lift home with them. Even gave me a ride one night I scored against them. Great fellas, as I said. We'd get to the airport, they offered me a lift into town. Usually, I helped Bobby unpack the Leafs bags—here me, a Red Wing now, and off I'd go with Bobby.

Anyway, the 1963 playoffs was my most memorable hockey moment—scored three goals [for Detroit] against Chicago, two more [in] one game to beat Toronto. They had me on *Hockey Night in Canada* after that game. Bobby Hull interviewed me, asked me about fishing back home—on camera.

Leafs finally beat us [in the finals], but [then Newfoundland premier] Joey Smallwood closed the schools in the province and gave us a parade, when my wife and I come home. Bumper to bumper from Bishop's to Grand Falls. Put my wife and I in a fire truck. I didn't speak as long as Mr. Smallwood, I tell you. I was numb. Whole thing felt like it was happening to someone else in a storybook.

Alex Faulkner became the first Newfoundlander to play in the NHL, joining the Toronto Maple Leafs on 7 December, 1961.

Six-Week Blaze

Corner Brook-born rookie Jason King captured the attention of the National Hockey League in the fall of 2003 with a barrage of early goals—10 in his first 17 games—for Canada's other coast's team, the Vancouver Canucks. King's debut was so successful that it prompted a heavy metal tribute, "The Corner Brook Kid," from Vancouver musician Heavy Eric Holmquist:

The Corner Brook kid from the Maritimes,
Wears 17 when he hits the ice.
The Corner Brook kid, he's skated miles,
The kid's on fire tonight!

The Sedins set him up, he's eager to score
And when he does, the whole place roars.
He does double duty up and down the wing,
When he fills the net, Heavy Eric sings,

Jason King—number 17—he plays the wing.
Go Canucks—arrghhhhh!

CORNER BROOK

FOUNDED
Corner Brook's history dates back thousands of years to a time when two Aboriginal groups, the Beothuks and the Maritime Archaic people, lived on the shores of western Newfoundland. British explorer James Cook surveyed and recorded the area's geography in 1767, but for the next 160 years Corner Brook was sparsely populated. Its primary residents were a few dozen hardy families whose fathers and sons fished in the summer and worked on nearby lumber camps in the winter. The town barely grew until the mid-1920s when a pulp-and-paper mill was built. Today, Corner Brook is Newfoundland's second largest city, with a variety of lumber- and fishing-related industries.

NATIVE-BORN NHL PLAYERS
Keith Brown, Doug Grant, Jason King, Joe Lundrigan

FAMOUS LOCAL TEAMS
Junior: Corner Brook Royals;
Senior-pro: Corner Brook Aces, Corner Brook Monarchs, Corner Brook Royals

CURRENT POPULATION
20,013

A Royal Flush

Defeating the opposition was only one of the hurdles faced by Newfoundland hockey teams. Sometimes a bigger challenge was getting to the game.

Even though the Corner Brook Royals won the very first provincial championship, the Herder tournament, triumphing over the Guards of St. John's with relative ease, at least one member of the Royals team was defeated simply by the trip. The back-and-forth train ride across Newfoundland in 1935 might have thwarted even Hannibal's troops. The Royals had to travel for 32 grinding hours to reach St. John's. Star player Hal Power promptly succumbed to appendicitis and was replaced by manager Gerry Edens. Two wins later, with Power sewed up again, the team boarded the train for the day-and-a-half plow back to Newfoundland's west coast through snowdrifts that dwarfed the engine.

Travel cost the team in other ways. The Royals continued to dominate Newfoundland hockey well into the 1980s, but the cost of building and transporting the team to compete outside the province made a mockery of budgets. Unpaid debts forced the Royals to withdraw from senior hockey in the 1982–83 season.

The team was rescued a year later by Cliff Gorman, whose dedication to the Royals dates back to the 1950s. An engineer, Gorman staked his career on tackling some of Newfoundland's steepest challenges. He helped the U.S. Air Force develop an early-warning radar system in remote regions of the province and oversaw survey teams for the construction of the massive Churchill Falls hydroelectric project.

For all his engineering skills, Gorman is best remembered in Newfoundland for his contributions to hockey, a game he never played. Mr. Hockey, as he was known locally, devoted most of his spare time to serving as general manager of the Corner Brook Royals. When the team was crushed by its debts in the early 1980s, Gorman spearheaded the fundraising drive that put the team back in business.

After Mr. Hockey revived the Royals, the team went on to win the province's Herder Memorial Trophy in 1985. Many believed that the Royals were poised to

Regal companions: the Corner
Brook Royals, 1935.

grasp the national senior prize, the Allan Cup, after the team won its first three
games in a championship duel with the Thunder Bay Twins. Alas, Corner Brook
would cede the next four games to its Ontario opponent, with the final defeat
coming at home before an army of grieving fans.

The following season, the same Corner Brook team made a triumphant
return to the Allan Cup competition, coming from behind to force a seventh game
against the Ontario champs, the Flamboro Mott's Clamatos, a Brantford team
stocked with former National Hockey Leaguers (Rocky Saganiuk, Stan Jonathan),

The Royals' quixotic chase for the Allan Cup came at an enormous cost.

along with Blake Hull, the son of superstar Bobby Hull. Though the final game
was played in Brantford, Corner Brook supporters made all the noise, a delegation
of fans from back home buttressed by a thousand displaced Newfoundlanders
living in Toronto.

Led by Sheldon Currie, Robbie Forbes, Tim Cranston, Todd Stark, Dan
Cormier, Steve McKenzie and goalie Dave Matte, the Royals made every one of
their fans happy, winning, 8–5, and so continuing on to the Allan Cup finals,
facing the Nelson Maple Leafs on the road in Nelson, British Columbia. The '86
championship finals were a Royal flush, with Corner Brook winning four straight,
capping the series with a 7–0 shutout by Matte. When the Royals returned to
Corner Brook with the province's first Allan Cup triumph, they were feted like
war heroes. The noisy motorcade that escorted the team home from the airport
at one point stretched all the way from Stephenville to Corner Brook.

The Royals' quixotic chase for the Allan Cup came at an enormous cost, unfortunately, and once again the team struggled to stay afloat. With Mr. Hockey,
Cliff Gorman, still watching over Corner Brook's most beloved sporting franchise,
however, the Corner Brook Royals would be revived later in the 1990s, and in
2002 they achieved their 10th Herder win.

Plaque celebrating the
Corner Brook Royals'
win of the Herder Cup
in 1985.

DEER LAKE

FOUNDED

Deer Lake got its name in the 1800s, when European explorers came upon migrating caribou and mistakenly identified them as deer. The first settlers to arrive here were loggers and lumbermen from Cape Breton, Nova Scotia, who were drawn to the region's heavy forests. Deer Lake became a company town in 1922, when the Newfoundland Power and Paper Company built a hydroelectric plant at the lake's edge to supply power to a nearby pulp-and-paper plant. Overnight, campsites and paper shacks were set up to accommodate close to 3,000 workers, hired to build the massive project.

NATIVE-BORN NHL PLAYERS
Darren Langdon

FAMOUS LOCAL TEAMS
Senior-pro: Deer Lake Red Wings

CURRENT POPULATION
4,060

Deer Lake's own, Darren Langdon.

Free Beer in Deer Lake!

In his first National Hockey League game, in 1995, New York Rangers forward Darren Langdon leaped in front of Montreal Canadiens goalie Patrick Roy to screen the netminder's view of the play. Sure enough, the puck whistled past the two players and tugged the back of the net. As the Montreal crowd groaned, referee Paul Stewart called out Langdon's number. "Never touched it," Langdon informed the hockey official.

Disinterested in more paperwork, Stewart smiled. "Aw it's your first game. Yes, you did." Afterward, Rangers captain Mark Messier took the Deer Lake native out and bought him a suit to celebrate.

This gracious inauguration into the NHL might explain why goal-scoring always puts Langdon in a charitable mood. When the winger opened his Deer Lake bar, Langer's, in the late '90s, he announced that patrons would receive a free beer every time he scored a goal.

Only problem with that offer was that Langdon mysteriously stopped scoring. In his first four NHL seasons Langdon collected 14 markers; but after the bar opened he scored a single goal in five seasons, while playing for the Carolina Hurricanes, the Vancouver Canucks and the Montreal Canadiens.

Finally, during the Stanley Cup playoffs of 2004, the dry spell ended when Montreal coach Claude Julien threw out Langdon to fire up his team, down three games to two and losing game six, 1–0, to the Boston Bruins. Circling the Bruins' net, Langdon neatly redirected a short pass from teammate Yanic Perreault behind Bruins goalie Andrew Raycroft—a goal that simultaneously blew the roofs off Montreal's Bell Centre and, a time zone away, Deer Lake's most famous sports bar, Langer's. "It was great. I scored early because out on the Rock the kids would still be up," Langdon commented to reporters after the game. He then mentioned that he was glad to spring for a round in his bar, allowing that the free beer offer "hasn't cost much until now."

During the NHL labour dispute of 2005, Langdon returned to Deer Lake to play with his hometown Red Wings. In the small-town arenas of Newfoundland, the NHLer rediscovered his long-dormant scoring skills and led the Red Wings to the province's senior hockey championship, where they triumphed over the Conception Bay CeeBees and won the 2005 Herder Memorial Trophy.

ST. JOHN'S

Where the rubber meets
the ice: A St. John's
Capitals puck.

FOUNDED

The city got its name in 1497, when Italian explorer John Cabot sailed into the large, protected harbour on the feast day of St. John the Baptist and named the haven after the first saint of the Catholic church. For hundreds of years, Basque, French, British and Dutch fishing and naval forces battled for control of the valuable harbour and of its nearby fishing grounds, until the British recaptured it for the last time from the French in 1762. By the late 1700s, some intrepid workers had chosen to build permanent homes in St. John's and in nearby outports. Even so, the population grew slowly because of the hardships involved in fishing Newfoundland's stormy seas and farming its rocky shores. Dominated by fishing merchants, St. John's did not elect its first municipal government until 1888. As other mining and forest resources were discovered in the province, St. John's emerged as Newfoundland's commercial and government centre.

NATIVE-BORN NHL PLAYERS

Ryan Clowe, Harold Druken, Jason Morgan, Dwayne Norris, Terry Ryan, Michael Ryder, John Slaney, Harry "Moose" Watson

FAMOUS LOCAL TEAMS

Junior: Saint John's Caps, Saint John's Fog Devils, St. John's Jr. Guards; **Senior-pro:** St. Bon's, St. John's All-Stars, St. John's Blue Caps, St. John's Capitals, St. John's Fieldians, St. John's Guards, St. John's Maple Leafs, St. John's Navy, St. John's Royals, St. John's Shamrocks, St. John's Shamrocks-Capitals

CURRENT POPULATION

128,000

Townies Go to War!

That St. John's hockey was founded by soldiers, bankers and churchmen is somehow fitting, for the sport truly became both a religious and class war that would last the better part of the 20th century.

The city's first "hockeyists" were British soldiers, stationed here during the War of 1812, who combatted boredom and cold by playing the popular English sport of hurley on the natural ice rinks of Quidi Vidi Lake and St. John's Harbour.

The Great Fire of 1892 in St. John's, which ravaged the city, brought builders from "away"—as Newfoundlanders like to say of outsiders—to reconstruct its churches. And the bank crash of 1894 attracted Montreal financiers, who endeavoured to impose both more conservative lending practices and more formal and gentlemanly hockey rules.

Despite such efforts to foster better sportsmanship, violent rivalries characterized the early days of St. John's hockey. The antagonism could be traced to the teams' recruiting practices. Membership in the city's first league, founded in 1899, was determined by religious, national and, in some instances, economic affiliations. The Victorias recruited Canadian players (Newfoundland did not join Confederation until 1949). The names of other teams left little doubt among locals as to the players' cultural and religious associations. There were the Bankers, the Fieldians (Anglican), the St. Andrew's (Presbyterian), the Star of the Sea Society (Catholic) and the St. Bon's (more Catholics), along with one team that was simply called The City Team.

Fog Clears, Devils Arrive

St. John's hockey is always as complicated as a snarled tackle line on a fishing rod. The St. John's Fog Devils joined the Quebec Major Junior Hockey League (QMJHL) in the fall of 2005, but only after a lively public skirmish that saw the team's owners, local business titans Derm and Craig Dobbin, face off against civic proprietors of St. John's Mile One Stadium.

Both the city and the Dobbins had applied for a new entry in the Quebec league. But when the QMJHL awarded the franchise to the Dobbin family ownership group, the city-operated St. John's Sports and Entertainment Department voted unanimously at first not to lease Mile One Stadium to a competitive bidder. A financial accommodation was eventually worked out after a fractious public debate.

The Fog Devils made a local boy their first choice in the Quebec league expansion draft, selecting 19-year-old St. John's forward Scott Brophy, a former player for the Gatineau Olympiques.

Sometimes not even individuals within teams got along. As reported in St. John's *Evening Telegram*, the very first St. Bon's practice, in early 1899, was marked by arguments and a nosebleed:

> The rule of "offside" was frequently violated, and on more than one occasion the points—and goalkeepers would be found in [a] scuffle at the off end of the rink, but this did not appear to matter much. The goals obtained were so numerous that it was difficult to keep count—both sides appear to have won. At the commencement of the second half [St. Bon's] President [Greene] who had been playing brilliantly, got an ugly blow between the eyes from the puck and had to retire.

Perhaps predictably, the first "away" game involving a St. John's team ended badly, when in 1913 a local businessman and sports enthusiast, Jack Tobin, assembled an all-star caravan of hockey players, intending to cross Portugal

I've been to war and I've played for the Stanley Cup, but I've never seen anything more intense than a hockey playoff in Newfoundland.

Cove to meet a Bell Island squad. Unfortunately, Tobin's party had to turn back because an ice floe they were hoping to cross on drifted past the target town.

The following decades of hockey in St. John's continued to bring excitement, religious discord and, occasionally, misadventure. Teams were still formed on the basis of church affiliations, which heightened civic rivalries at a time when "mixed marriage" could mean the union of a Catholic named Riley and an Anglican named Scott. Moreover, because St. John's was the cultural, political and economic centre of the province, the city's ruling class presumed an elevated social status within the province. While St. John's natives looked down their noses at nonresidents, Newfoundlanders who lived outside the capital city took a different view. The rest of the province figured that the "townies" were a tad self-important, and when hockey was introduced to the picture all these latent prejudices found a savage purpose.

Consequently, provincial battles for the amateur senior championship, the Herder Memorial Trophy, became all-out war. St. John's, often represented by the stalwart St. Bon's, fared well in these tournaments until the '50s, at which point Newfoundland mining towns began hiring workers more for their ability to put a puck in the net than for their skill in extracting minerals from the earth's surface. Protesting what they called the "shamateur" tactics of their rivals, St. John's senior teams pulled out of the Herder competition for a few years in the mid '50s.

St. John's return to the provincial contest may have signalled a truce between long-standing adversaries, but the underlying hostilities between the various teams had not abated. With religious, business and civic groups continuing to play a major role in the formation of Newfoundland teams in the '60s and '70s, antagonism on the ice was almost inevitable.

Ex-Maple Leafs player Howie Meeker offers a valuable outsider's perspective on the province's hockey turbulence. Meeker arrived in St. John's in the late 1950s as a high-priced coach for the United Church Athletic Association, which gave him a front-row seat to view the city's hockey holy wars. Recalling his Newfoundland years, Meeker said, "I've been to war and I've played for the Stanley Cup, but I've never seen anything more intense than a hockey playoff game in Newfoundland."

73–1

Michael Ryder wears number 73 for the Montreal Canadiens—a fitting designation, it might seem, for the odds of Ryder making it to the National Hockey League were probably 73–1. The Bonavista, Newfoundland, native played only nine games of midget hockey and was still well behind other players his age while playing for the Hull Olympiques (Quebec Major Junior Hockey League). This somewhat slow start might explain why he was selected 216th in the 1998 NHL Entry and so began his pro career 20,000 leagues under the sea, playing for the East Coast Hockey League's Tallahassee Tiger Sharks. By 2003, however, the scoring star had graduated to the Montreal Canadiens, where he proceeded to slap in 25 goals and 38 assists during his first season with the team. Ryder's success is explained by his ability to find empty slivers of the net and by his enduring belief in self. Recently, his mother found an old grade-school questionnaire. Under ambition, Michael had replied simply, "Hockey player."

Meeker Inherits Newfoundland

On World War II manoeuvres in England, Howie Meeker bellied up to a stone fence only to be blown skyward by an explosion. Still in mid-air, Meeker spotted the cause of his misfortune, a fellow Canadian from a rival platoon, staring up in wonder. Later, in the hospital, Meeker promised a visiting officer, "When I get back, if you still have that corporal there, I'll kill him, stone dead. That idiot threw a live hand grenade over the fence."

Meet Howie Meeker—only 5'9", 165 pounds, yet among the top 10 in penalties, his first National Hockey League season (1946–47). In 1951, the Maple Leafs player took a second job as Tory MP for Waterloo South. Canada's prime minister at the time, Quebecer Louis Stephen St. Laurent, needled Meeker whenever Montreal beat Toronto. Once, after the Leafs finally won, Meeker was ready: "Prime Minister," he cackled, "Leafs played Canadiens last night and whipped their ass, 6–2. Could you please explain this for us, sir?"

Meeker gave up parliament and, later, Toronto, after his short tenure as the Leafs general manager ended in 1957, following a heated exchange with Leafs president, Stafford Smythe. "He shoved me, and I popped him between the eyes," Meeker later recalled.

After that, Meeker moved to St. John's, Newfoundland, where he coached senior hockey, opened a sporting goods store, and provided radio and TV commentary. A trip to Montreal, in 1968, led to an appearance on *Hockey Night in Canada* (HNIC) and the start of a 30-year broadcasting career. That first night in Montreal, Meeker revealed the extent to which his time on the Rock had improved his gift for gab:

> Look at Beliveau—moving around Pelyk like a hoop around a barrel. Where's Walton? Looking in the stands for pretty girls? Hey-hey, the big fellow puts it home, easy as picking strawberries.

"Howie was a sensation," recalled HNIC executive Ralph Mellanby. "He was from Newfoundland and he didn't owe the [National Hockey] league anything. If Beliveau had a bad game, he said it. No broadcaster changed TV hockey more than Howie."

A DIVINE SPORT

Wayne Johnston, a native of St. John's, captures in his richly comic family novel, *The Divine Ryans*, how hockey served as a battleground in the city's religious wars. In the novel, a priest is concerned that nine-year-old Draper Doyle has become obsessed with hockey. He asks Doyle if he knows what the CH stands for on Montreal's jerseys. Canadiens and Habitants, the boy replies. The priest winces. For the man of the cloth, hockey is religion, and religion is everything. "C and H are the first and last letters in church," he says, "but you know the word [church] means nothing unless U R in it."

Opening Spread:
Tampa Bay Lightning
star, and Murray Harbour
native, Brad Richards,
gets ready to hit the ice.

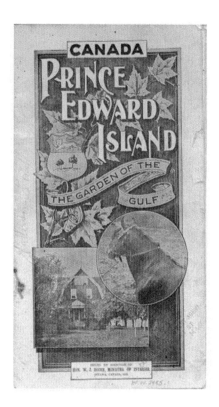

Cover of a brochure advertising
Prince Edward Island as The Garden
of the Gulf, 1912.

F or more than a century, the only sure things about winter in Prince Edward Island have been bad weather and the Charlottetown-Summerside hockey rivalry. Come to think of it, bad weather characterizes the Charlottetown-Summerside rivalry, as well.

In fact, a disregard for the winter climate may be the only issue upon which the civic rivals would be prepared to agree. Their ongoing feud dates back to the first time the cities met to discuss a provincial senior championship, on 31 March 1897: The participating clubs couldn't come to terms on an impartial island referee, and so they had to import a Mr. Pyke from Halifax.

With this matter settled, the Charlottetown Abegweits, also known as the Abbies, soon delighted fans by taking the first three island championships. The team, which took its name from the Mi'kmaq term for Prince Edward Island, "cradled on the waves," found losing hard, however. In 1900, when the Summerside Crystals finally emerged victorious, the Abegweits insisted that their rivals sign a legal document declaring that the Crystals had merely won that particular year and did not own the resulting trophy in perpetuity.

Despite growing acrimony, the teams resumed conflict every winter, if for no other reason than playing elsewhere proved dangerous. In 1907, the Abbies travelled to St. John's, Newfoundland, for a March tournament against local senior teams. The entire trip normally would have taken five days, but when the team was returning home aboard the SS *Stanley*, the ship—while crossing the Northumberland Strait—became snared in a gathering ice floe, which threatened to crush the 60-passenger carrier. Fretting family members of the team spent a grim 48-hour vigil at the Charlottetown wireless office, waiting for news of the ship's fate. The *Stanley*'s hull withstood the ice, however, and the Abbies hiked to Pictou Island for provisions. In April, the floe broke up into huge bobbing ice cubes, and the team finally made it back to Charlottetown—32 days after the players had left P.E.I.

The most recent battle between the long-standing city rivals occurred in junior hockey, in 1997. This competition took place on a national stage, as that spring Summerside was scheduled to host the Royal Bank Tier II Canadian national junior championship. If Summerside triumphed in the provincial finals, the team would have a chance to achieve a national championship in its own hometown. But if Charlottetown won and then went on to vie for the big prize in its rivals' home rink... No, the prospect was too grim for Summerside to consider.

Making this hockey event more dramatic still, the Crystals—now the Western Capitals, or the Caps, and now a junior team—were coached by Summerside hockey legend Gerard Gallant, a former National Hockey League all-star. For the first time in memory, the team was a heavy favourite to beat the Abbies, also now a junior team, in a provincial playoff. After all, the Caps had gone undefeated in 11 regular season games with Charlottetown. But the Abbies had their own hometown NHL-hero coach, fiery Forbes Kennedy, not to mention a tradition of success in big games. As Charlottetown mayor Tex MacDonald crowed to local newsmen, "Historically, Charlottetown has been successful against Summerside during the past 50 years. And history has a tendency to repeat itself."

MacDonald sure hoped so. The cities had an ongoing wager. An Abbies loss meant he'd have to ferry Summerside mayor Basil Stewart around in a wheelbarrow during that city's July Lobster Carnival. A Charlottetown win meant that Mayor Stewart would taxi MacDonald around during Charlottetown's August Gold Cup parade.

Sure enough, the underdog Abbies went up 1–0 during the first game. Coach Gallant didn't know what was worse, the score or a visiting lady from Charlottetown who sat in a corner of the stadium harassing the Caps with slurred catcalls from a plastic horn.

In the dressing room, after the first period, Gallant's eyes were glowing coals. "Boys, I am tired of hearing that horn over there yelling and laughing at us, saying we have no heart," he told the players. Driven by their coach's outrage, the Capitals scored two quick goals, ultimately triumphing in a 4–3 win. Afterward, Gallant deflected credit for his motivational skills, advising reporters, "That lady with the horn woke us up."

After that initial game, mother winter put P.E.I. to sleep, dumping a fat blanket of snow on the province. P.E.I. and the hockey series were shut down for three days. When the playoffs continued, the teams would have to play six games in as many nights.

And what games! At home, Abbies goalie Chris MacDonald put up a historic stand, making 46 saves in a 3–1 win. Back in Summerside, Charlottetown continued to up the ante with its captain, Craig Hodge, netting three goals in a 6–4 win. Afterward, Gallant decided against talking to the Caps players, but he made his feelings clear, pounding a map of fury onto the dressing room wall that separated him from the team. The fourth game, in Charlottetown, was more charged still. The Abbies went up 4–1 and 6–3, only to see the Caps rally to tie the score. Fans' nerves became more frayed with every goal. Fights spread into the stands. From their benches, coaches Kennedy and Gallant swore at each other. And Charlottetown won—again. Final score: 8–6. The underdogs were now up three games to one, and needed only one more win to ruin Summerside's winter.

When the Caps, back at home, rebounded with a tidy 4–2 win, everyone knew that game six, in Charlottetown, would be decisive. Summerside regained their form, pushing to a 4–2 lead. The team scored again in the third period—game

Abegweit day! Poster for the Charlottetown Abegweits, 1922–23.

The Summerside Crystals, 1899.

over. But wait, the goal was disallowed. More than 3,000 fans, including the Abbies' female horn section, roared approval. Charlottetown responded with a furious counterattack, peppering Harlin Hayes, a wall in Summerside's net. Finally, the Abbies broke through with a goal. The score was now 4–3 and Kennedy's team continued to press.

The last minutes of the game brought the ice drama to a peak. Abbies forward William Hubloo had a breakaway but was hauled down by the opposition. No penalty. The crowd, then Coach Kennedy, went crazy when, minutes later, Charlottetown received a major penalty, ensuring a Summerside victory. Ready to fight, the teams spilled from the benches onto the rink with the coaching staffs close behind. In the battleground of the Charlottetown Civic Centre, the city's finest jumped between the warring teams, paying particular attention to the health of the referees and linesmen—the very men responsible, the Abbies believed, for what was now a tied series. These officials, Kennedy complained to reporters afterward, wanted the Capitals to win so that the team might play in the national tournament, hosted by Summerside, in a month's time. Where was Referee Pyke from Halifax when P.E.I. needed him most?

Summerside won that seventh game of the playoffs, 8–4, surviving a late scare that had the tenacious Abbies trailing by a single goal with a half-period remaining. After 50 years of losing to their rivals, Summerside now emerged as provincial champion.

Five weeks later, the Summerside Western Capitals went on to take the Canadian Tier II finals in a dramatic, come-from-behind victory over British Columbia's South Surrey Eagles. Still, winning the national championship somehow seemed anticlimactic to the team's devoted fans—probably because in finally beating Charlottetown, Summerside already felt as if it had conquered the world.

The 1905 Summerside Alphas.

Skirting the Issue

The first recorded women's hockey game in Prince Edward Island was played between the Summerside Alphas and the Charlottetown Micmacs on 4 February 1905. The Alphas won, 4–2, in double overtime. A *Charlottetown Guardian* reporter noted that "skirts seemed an awkward dress sometimes, but they were convenient for stopping the puck." Another women's team from Summerside, the Crystal Sisters, would become one of the great women's teams in Canada during the '20s and '30s. By then, female players were no longer required to play in dresses.

CHARLOTTETOWN

FOUNDED
Like the province of Prince Edward Island, Charlottetown came under British rule following the Treaty of Paris in 1763. The city was named after Queen Charlotte, wife of King George III of the United Kingdom.

LOCAL-BORN NHL PLAYERS
Dave Cameron, John Hughes, Tyler Larter, Al MacAdam, Shane MacEachern, Garth MacGuigan, Billy MacMillan, Bob MacMillan, Gary "The Cobra" Simmons, Bob Stewart, Wes "Bucko" Trainor, Bob Whitlock

FAMOUS LOCAL TEAMS
Junior: Charlottetown Abbies, Charlottetown Abegweits, Charlottetown Royals, Prince Edward Island Rocket; **Senior-pro:** Charlottetown Abegweits, Charlottetown All Stars, Charlottetown Holmans, Charlottetown Islanders, Charlottetown Legionnaires, Charlottetown Navy, Charlottetown Parkdale Royals, Charlottetown Primroses, Charlottetown Victorias, Charlottetown West End Rangers, Charlottetown Wildcats

CURRENT POPULATION
65,000

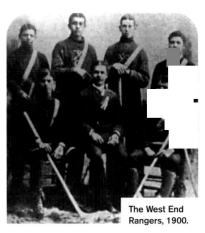

The West End Rangers, 1900.

Charlottetown and Country

Prince Edward Island hockey legend Billy MacMillan first put skates to ice on his grandfather's farm in Gurnsey Cove, 45 miles from MacMillan's boyhood residence in Charlottetown. In 1970, upon signing his first National Hockey League contract with the Toronto Maple Leafs for $15,000 (with a $5,000 signing bonus), he bought a farm outside Charlottetown. "I'd died and gone to heaven," MacMillan says of the day he put down lasting roots in his native soil.

This move is typical of P.E.I. hockey, where "hometown hockey hero" is a lasting designation. Billy's hockey-playing brother, Bobby, also returned to Charlottetown when his NHL career was over, as did fellow NHLers Al MacAdam, Gerard Gallant and Forbes Kennedy.

Although Billy MacMillan did his first pirouette on skates on a frozen pond at his grandfather's farm, he actually learned to play hockey behind his own house in Charlottetown on a 25-by-150-foot two-backyard rink devised by his father. The house next door belonged to the Whitlocks. "Bobby Whitlock, a cousin, went on to play in the NHL, just like [my brother] Bobby and me," MacMillan recalls.

At night, MacMillan dreamed that his backyard rink might lead to Maple Leaf Gardens. "I remember, clear as day, picking up *Weekend* magazine as a kid and reading a story by Andy O'Brien about St. Michael's grads that ended up in the NHL," MacMillan says, referring to a Toronto secondary school famous for its hockey program. "There were 40 pictures of 'em all. Soon as I saw that story, something clicked."

After a free and easy novice career, starring in paperweight, peewee, bantam and midget hockey in Charlottetown, the budding athlete's life was disturbed

Champions of Government Pond

The Charlottetown West End Rangers, formed in 1899—in an era of racial segregation in sports—were residents of the Bog, a district inhabited by impoverished Charlottetown blacks and whites. The Rangers, the only black hockey team in Prince Edward Island, played against other "coloured" teams in Halifax, Truro and New Glasgow, Nova Scotia. The Charlottetown team used sticks whittled from tree limbs and played on Government Pond, the natural ice surface that was lost when further government buildings were constructed on the site in 1960. Famed for their fast, furious play, the Rangers won the coloured hockey championship of the Maritimes in 1920. A Charlottetown newspaper of the day celebrated the team's combative style with the following poem:

> It's all very well—to talk
> about the Abbies;
> And it's all very well—to talk
> about the Vics.
> But for tough old hockey
> fightin'—
> The kind we take delight in,
> Yer orter see the Rangers
> use their sticks.

by tragedy. His father died of a heart attack at the age of 37. "You don't get over something like that, ever," MacMillan says with evident sadness.

John Ready, a teacher at Queen Charlotte High School, took MacMillan under his wing and arranged for a Toronto Maple Leafs scout to watch him play. MacMillan passed the audition and was soon bound for Toronto. "I just had a burning desire to play hockey at the time," he says, in explaining his zeal to impress the Leafs scout. "Looking back, I don't know if it was healthy. I just thought about hockey all the time. It was an obsession, you could say."

MacMillan excelled in hockey while at St. Michael's, playing under legendary hockey coach and teacher, Father David Bauer. In 1963, the Maple Leafs, reigning Stanley Cup champions, tendered the young player a minor league contract, but as much as MacMillan wanted to fulfill his childhood dream, he also had family business to attend to. "After my father died, the five [kids in the family] decided

"I could hear people singing the national anthem for the first time ever."

we were all going to go to university. It was a commitment, you could say. And right then, St. Dunstan's [now the University of Prince Edward Island] offered me a scholarship to play hockey and get an education back home. My wife, Marge, taught at St. Dunstan's. I couldn't say no. Pro hockey would have to wait."

A chance meeting with Father Bauer at a Maritime hockey function two years later changed MacMillan's life again. "He told me he was putting together a national program in Winnipeg. I could continue my education and play for Canada against the best teams from Europe. I'd be able to see the world, maybe go to the Olympics. And I'd be playing with friends from St. Mike's—Terry O'Malley, Barry Mackenzie."

MacMillan saw all these hopes come to fruition, helping Canada to win a bronze medal in the 1968 Olympics in Grenoble. He also took part in the little-discussed Canadian Miracle on Ice—when the Canadian national team, the Nats, with the help of ex-NHL star Carl Brewer and the vocal support of Prime Minister Lester Pearson, battled back from 2–0 and 3–1 deficits to defeat Russia, 5–4, thereby taking the 7 January 1967 Centennial Cup in Winnipeg.

MacMillan scored the winning goal that night, but he exhibits characteristic P.E.I. reserve in elaborating on his own heroics: "Oh, I don't know. I shot it from the blue line and somehow it went in."

His memory improves significantly when asked how he celebrated afterward. "It was centennial year, remember. And the Russians were a fantastic team. You know when I saw them in 1972, I thought the '67 team might have been better. Anyway, they were beating everybody, including us. But we always come close. We played a strong defensive system.

"And that night we had the crowd behind us. We knew everyone was watching on TV. Carl Brewer was fantastic—he wasn't afraid of the Russians at all. And he could control the play, slow the game and then speed it up with a good pass. We battled all night and won. And in the end, when they played the national anthem, I looked up and I could hear people singing the national anthem out loud for the first time ever. Just here and there, not everywhere. But they were singing. And to see Father Bauer after the game so happy—we'd won, finally. What a way to kick off centennial year!"

What made the victory particularly special for MacMillan was that he'd brought part of Charlottetown with him that night. "I'd arranged to have my mom and brother Bobby at the game. Bobby was 15, going to school in

Forbes Kennedy, on the right, getting something started for the Detroit Red Wings.

Former Abbies Player Starts World War III

One of the toughest customers ever to step through a National Hockey League saloon door, Forbes Kennedy, was born in Dorchester, New Brunswick, where his father worked at a correctional institute. Those early roots and Kennedy's subsequent unruly behaviour led future foes to comment mischievously that his mother was doing time when she had him. Not true, although the Charlottetown Abbies graduate (1951) and future coach would spend more than 16 hours in NHL penalty boxes.

Good enough and tough enough to spend nine seasons in the pre-expansion NHL, Kennedy went out with a series of bangs in his last big league game in 1969. His then team, the Toronto Maple Leafs, was losing, 10–0, to the Boston Bruins in an April playoff game. Even so, the Boston crowd was in an ugly mood after Toronto's Pat Quinn flattened Bruins god Bobby Orr. With the game lost, and Toronto being pummelled by the biggest and baddest of the Bruins, Leafs coach Punch Imlach rousted Kennedy from the bench with three words of encouragement: Get something started. With those instructions, Kennedy planted himself in front of the Boston net and took on every Bruin on the ice, including "Terrible" Teddie Green and equally tough Johnny "Pie" McKenzie. When more Bruins jumped off the bench, Kennedy took them on, too. The referee gave him an NHL-record 48 minutes in penalties, plus a game misconduct—the hockey equivalent of two life sentences.

After he made it through a rioting crowd, Kennedy was met in the dressing room by Coach Imlach, who whispered in his ear, "Forbie, when I said get something started, I didn't mean World War III."

Winnipeg at the time, staying with me. We all went back to our apartment to celebrate—just the family. It's a great, great memory."

There would be others: Winning the bronze Olympic medal; finally playing for the Leafs and scoring 22 goals in 1970; going on to play for and help coach the 1980 New York Islanders to the Stanley Cup; and eventually returning to Charlottetown to coach at his old alma mater, the University of Prince Edward Island, taking the men's hockey team, the Panthers, to the semifinals of the 1991 college championship.

The return to P.E.I. was a fitting end to MacMillan's career, he acknowledges. "I don't know how to put it, except to say this is home. And I know Bobby and some of the other NHLers from Charlottetown feel the same way," MacMillan says. "Maybe if you've been around the world a bit, you learn to appreciate it here—the weather, the people, I don't know, just the comfortable feel of the place."

MURRAY HARBOUR

FOUNDED
Eight immigrant families from
Scotland arrived at this windswept
outpost in 1806. Nearby Cape Bear
Lighthouse, which was constructed in
1881, was the first land station to hear
of the sinking of the *Titanic* in 1912.

NATIVE-BORN NHL PLAYERS:
Brad Richards

FAMOUS LOCAL TEAMS
Not applicable

CURRENT POPULATION
354

Murray Harbour at dawn; for many locals,
the workday is already underway.

Casting a Different Net

Sometimes a small-town dreamer can make a whole province's fantasy come true.
Certainly Brad Richards fulfilled every hope of Prince Edward Island hockey
fans in becoming the hero of the 2004 Stanley Cup finals.

Born in 1980, Brad grew up in Murray Harbour, a fishing village east of
Charlottetown. Just over 350 people live in the town, with maybe half as
many still around after dawn's first light. Brad's dad, Glen Richards, leaves
home at 4 a.m. every day except Sunday to attend to lobster traps buried
40 fathoms deep, miles from shore. Some days, when the ocean is calm and
the sky scrubbed free of clouds, Glen Richards figures he has the best job
in the world. But then there are the "dirty days," when the sun doesn't bother
with Murray Harbour. Glen has to go out then, too.

Glen named his gleaming white 46-foot boat *Brad and Paige*, after his
children, and he figured Brad would eventually take over for him. Fishing is what
the Richardses have done for four generations.

Brad Richards, however, wanted to have his father's previous job, playing
junior goalie for the Charlottetown Abbies. Dad wouldn't hear of it. "He said
it was the worst position," the hockey player once explained. "He said you can't
win playing goal, and if anything goes wrong it's your fault."

This was enough to turn Richards away from goaltending, but not from
hockey itself. And Glen Richards could see that his son was a natural. From age
two, his father says, "he stepped onto the rink and he just kind of took off."
He excelled quickly, too. One thing about growing up in a small town, when
there are often only 10 or 11 on a team, is that players get plenty of ice time.
By the time Brad was 13, though, Glen Richards knew that if his son was to
make it in hockey he would have to leave the boats of Murray Harbour for good.

At first, 14-year-old Brad cried every night at Notre Dame College in
Saskatchewan (see page 277). He didn't intend to be a fisherman, but that
didn't mean that he wanted to be thousands of miles away from the sea and
from his home.

At least he got along with his Montreal roommate, Vincent Lecavalier.
Before long, the two young teenagers became fast friends and confidants. Together
they could laugh off the day's events—what this teacher said and that kid did.
They began to talk about how great it would be to play junior together—maybe
even make the NHL?

The next spring the friends watched the Stanley Cup playoffs on TV, punch-
ing each other in the arm after impressive plays. Afterward, they imagined
how maybe one day they'd overcome heroic obstacles to themselves win the Cup.

Millions of young players have such dreams. But Brad Richards and Vincent Lecavalier would one day prove that fantasies sometimes do come true.

The two athletes were the only grade nine students to make Notre Dame's competitive bantam team. In 1996, Lecavalier, a rangy centreman with evident star skills, went on to play in the Quebec Major Junior Hockey League for the Rimouski Oceanic. A year later the team's general manager asked Lecavalier if his old roommate and linemate might fit in. Would he ever, came the reply.

Remarkably, both young men were drafted by the Tampa Bay Lightning in 1998. Lecavalier jumped to the pros, while Richards, the less-experienced winger, continued to mature in junior, still playing for the Oceanic. And improve he did. By his Most Valuable Player and Memorial Cup winning year in the Quebec league, Brad was a P.E.I. hero, with Islander cars crowding the Confederation Bridge on their way to Halifax or Moncton to see him play.

That first taste of success was nothing, however, compared to the heights that he would reach four years later in the 2004 playoffs.

That post-season, Brad led all his fellow players in goals and assists, as he and Lecavalier carried their team to series wins over New York, Montreal, Philadelphia and—after an enormous struggle—the Calgary Flames. During these playoffs Brad produced the winning goals, often in heroic fashion, in seven different games. In Murray Harbour and elsewhere across Prince Edward Island, hockey fans sometimes felt as if they were asleep, dreaming. As indeed they should have been. The overtime games in Calgary sometimes went on well into the middle of the night for Islander audiences, time zones away.

Glen Richards, Brad's dad, was already at work on his boat when his son

Brad Richards takes the Stanley Cup home to Murray Harbour.

scored the only goal in Tampa's 1–0 game four win in Calgary. The star left winger made sure, however, that his father would see the decisive seventh game in Tampa: Brad bought flights to the match for 26 family members. The rest of Murray Harbour drove to Murray River to watch the game on closed-circuit TV in the Northumberland Arena. Five hundred people sat at banquet tables laid across the arena's concrete floor, with kids—well past their bedtime—in Brad Richards uniforms running around the adults' feet.

When the real Brad Richards and best friend Vincent Lecavalier won the Stanley Cup, the Northumberland Arena exploded with a shout that just about lifted the roof beams. A thousand miles away, Brad left the Tampa Bay dressing room early to throw himself into a scrum of jubilant Richardses. In Murray Harbour, meanwhile, the family lobster boat bobbed in its mooring. For one of the few times in 150 years, there would be no Richards boat going out to sea on a good work morning, the following day.

The Summerside Crystals, looking dapper on a road trip in 1925.

SUMMERSIDE

FOUNDED
United Empire Loyalists first arrived in Summerside in 1785. The town was named after Summerside House, an inn, founded by early settler Joseph Green, which was said to be on the sunny side of the island. Summerside was incorporated as a city in 1994.

NATIVE-BORN NHL PLAYERS:
Chuck Cahill, John Chabot, Gerard Gallant, Doug MacLean (NHL coach), Steve Ott, Kent Paynter, Maynard Schurman, Erroll Thompson

FAMOUS LOCAL TEAMS
Junior: Summerside Western Capitals, Summerside Crystals;
Senior-pro: Summerside Crystals, Summerside Pioneers, Summerside RCAF

CURRENT POPULATION
16,200

Loose Moose

Everett "Moose" MacDonald, a native of Prince Edward County, Prince Edward Island, was unarguably the most colourful figure ever to wear (or not wear) a Summerside Crystals uniform. Before joining this senior team, the forward toiled in the 1920s for the Alberton Regals of the province's Intermediate League, once showing up for a game in Kensington, P.E.I., without equipment. Regardless, MacDonald skated out for the third period of the game, wearing only skates and long johns, proclaiming, "The Moose is loose." Another story has Moose playing on his wedding night, scoring 14 goals for the old senior O'Leary Maroons before bringing his antlers on home to be with the missus.

The Winter Side of Summerside

Islanders like to boast that Prince Edward Island has more ice surfaces per capita than any other place in the world. This province of 135,000 inhabitants has 37 rinks, 27 of them covered. And that number does not take into account the many frozen football fields that are also sometimes pressed into service.

Summerside is home to the most famous of these rinks, Cahill (formerly Civic) Stadium, a squat aluminum-sided barn erected by local men, most of them off-duty fishermen, in a month-long rush during 1952. Except for National Hockey Leaguer Errol Thompson, who escaped from P.E.I. to Halifax, Nova Scotia, to play junior before making his name with the Toronto Maple Leafs, nearly every Summerside native to make it in hockey graduated from Cahill Stadium.

Gerard Gallant, the Summerside-born NHL star and coach, grew up a two-minute walk away from the legendary stadium and played there whenever he could. But rinks have public hours, and Gerard and his friends had an appetite for shinny that knew no timetable. What to do?

"Every winter we'd flood the high school football field," Gallant once remembered. "It was huge—big enough to get a couple or three games going on at the same time. The only problem was that the boards they put up around the ice had absolutely no give to them. Now you weren't supposed to check each other, but guys would slip up and forget about that every once in a while. That was a big deal for us, though. They'd turn the lights on and we had some great games well into the night."

Gallant's recollection of this period of his youth pretty well sums up the winter side of Summerside, where the appetite for hockey is insatiable, the

"Almost every good childhood memory I have comes from that rink."

players, rough, and the community spirit—witness the volunteer-built Cahill Stadium (named for ex-NHLer George Cahill)—indomitable.

Gallant played as a junior in Cahill Stadium for the Summerside Crystals before going on to star for the Detroit Red Wings alongside superstar Steve Yzerman for nine seasons. Gallant's best season was 1988–89, when he counted 39 goals, 54 assists and 230 penalty minutes—good enough to be deemed an NHL all-star. Upon retiring in 1996, Turk, as old teammates called him, returned home to P.E.I., coaching the Summerside Western Capitals, the junior team that would follow the Crystals, to the Royal Bank 1997 Tier II Canadian National Junior Championships. Best of all, under Gallant, the Capitals beat their provincial rivals, the Charlottetown Abbies, during the winning run.

Long-time NHL coach and general manager Doug MacLean also grew up a rink rat in Cahill Stadium during the 1960s. Afterward, he returned to Summerside, teaching high school and coaching the Western Capitals. In 1985, he graduated to NHL coaching ranks, and in 1996, as head coach of the Florida Panthers, MacLean took the team to the Stanley Cup finals. Two seasons later, he became the general manager of the Columbus Blue Jackets.

For all his travels and NHL successes, MacLean is still affected by the hold that Summerside's Cahill Stadium has over him. "No one could have greater memories of a place than I have of [Cahill Stadium]. Almost every good childhood memory I have comes from that rink," MacLean told Scott Russell for the sports writer's book *The Rink*. Reminiscing further about the building's character—and characters—MacLean, referring to his coaching days at Cahill in the '80s, recalled, "The stadium was so cold, but everybody smoked back then." Two veteran regulars in the corner stands unfailingly brought a radio. "I supposed they were listening to play-by-play on CJRW [a Summerside radio station]. One day I asked to see the radio and started turning the dials, which, of course, came off. I found out the radio was really a flask and these two old codgers had been drinking vodka just to keep warm."

MacLean never let go of Cahill or Summerside. After his Panthers reached the Stanley Cup finals in 1996, he held the team's training camp in his hometown stadium that summer.

And in the same way that close to a hundred Summerside fishermen got together to build a local rink one summer in 1952, five Islanders got together in 1999 to build a hockey franchise in Ohio. Shortly after getting the job as general manager of the Columbus Blue Jackets, MacLean hired assistant general manager Jim Clark, coach Gerard Gallant, radio broadcaster George Matthews and team services co-ordinator Jim Rankin. All five men had grown up within six blocks of each other in Summerside.

Heroines of Summerside

In 1904, the Summerside Alphas became the town's first female hockey team. That same year, celebrated author Lucy Maud Montgomery, born in nearby Clifton, Prince Edward Island, created her most famous fictional character, Anne of Green Gables, when she jotted down these words in a notebook: "Elderly couple apply to orphan asylum for a boy. By mistake a girl is sent them."

As imagined by author Montgomery, Anne Shirley would one day become the principal of Summerside High School. Meanwhile, real-life Summersiders, the hockey-playing Alphas, would gain heroic distinction as being the best women's hockey team in the Maritimes in 1932. That same year, the team tied the Canadian champions, the Montreal Maroon Sisters, 2–2, in an exhibition match. Players in that memorable game included Martha Nicholson, Zilpha Linkletter, Irene Linkletter (captain), Margaret Gallant, Minnie Boswell, Helen Montgomery, Pat MacLellan, Lillian Dickie, Alice Noonan and Irene Silliphant. And while there wasn't an Anne of Green Gables, the team did boast an Anne Green.

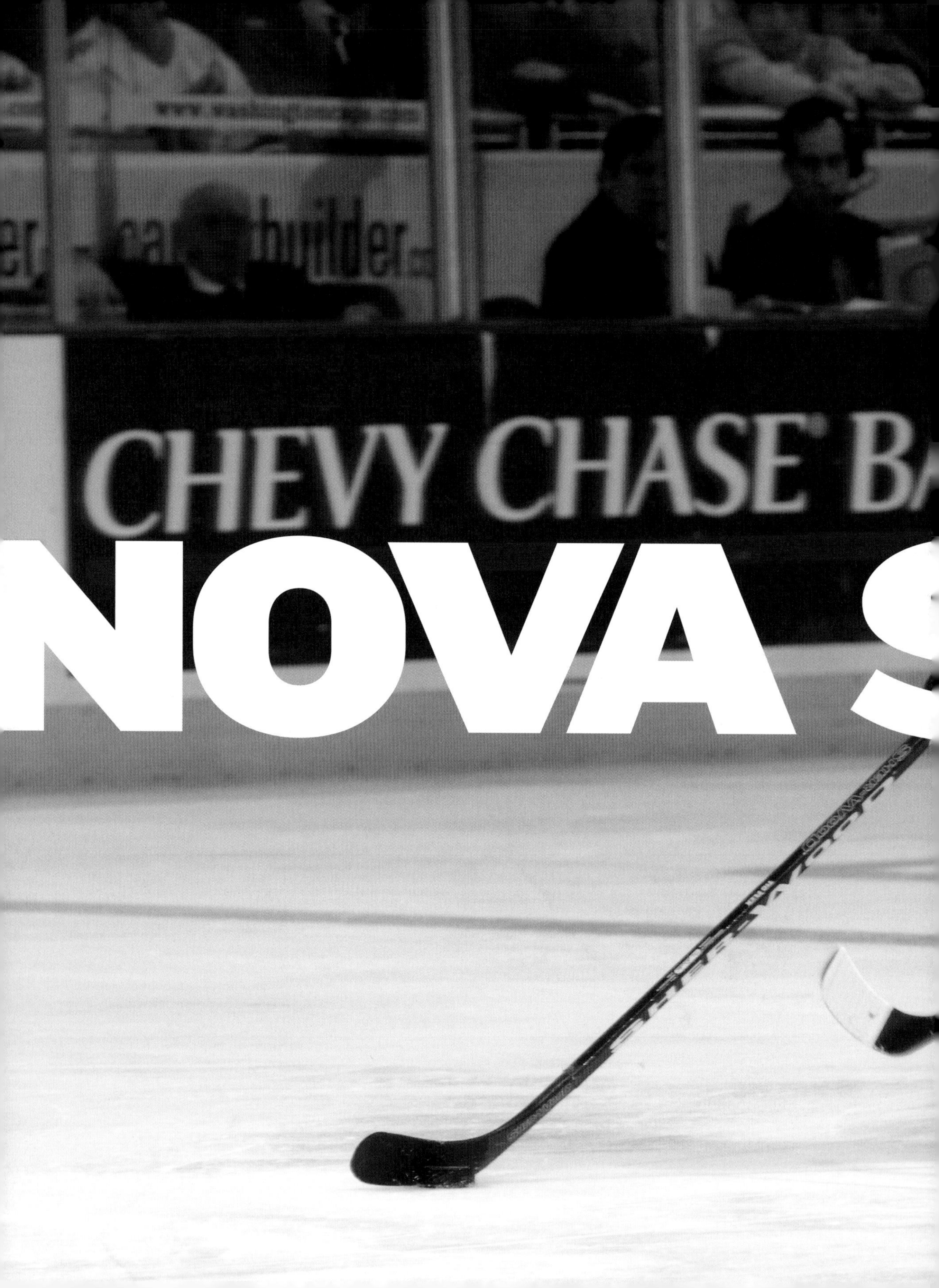

NOVA S

H

Now at ricket with hurlies some dozens of boys
Chase the ball o'er ice, with a deafening noise.
–The Acadian Magazine (Halifax, January 1827)

alifax-based author Hugh MacLennan captured the passions and prejudices that have characterized nearly two centuries of Nova Scotia hockey when he wrote about the sport in his 1954 novel, *Two Solitudes.* "To spectator and player alike, hockey gives the release that strong liquor gives a repressed man. It is the counterpoint of Canadian self-restraint, it takes us back to the fiery blood of Gallic and Celtic ancestors who found themselves minorities in the cold, new environment and had to discipline themselves as all minorities must."

Cape Breton Island, the mountainous northern end of Nova Scotia, is Canada's toughest neighborhood. French, Scottish and Irish immigrants fled war, persecution and poverty in the 1700s and 1800s to settle here. By the 1940s, their scrappy descendants were eking out a marginally better living in the region's coal mines and steel mills. And anyone who ever visited the old Glace Bay Forum in the '50s to watch the Glace Bay Miners take on the Sydney Millionaires bore witness to the explosive rivalries that MacLennan wrote about.

Games in the regional senior league began in an orderly fashion. Queues were civil. Fans had players' names and abilities memorized, although some dreamers purchased programs for a chance to win the $35 door prize. Everyone stood straight, fedoras held to their chests during the singing of "God Save the King":

Confound their politics/ Frustrate their knavish tricks/
On Thee our hopes we fix/Oh, save us all.

And then—war. Maritime hockey rivalries have always been fierce, but contests between the Miners and Millionaires—maybe it was the class warfare implied by their team names—went beyond passionate.

In one famously tense battle in the 1950s, Glace Bay fans inched forward in their seats, nervously chain-smoking, leaping to their feet with hoarse shouts of encouragement when the Miners pressed the game to their advantage. Without much luck, it turns out. For Sydney Millionaires goalie Nick Pidsodney, was playing like, well, like a million bucks that night. By the third period, a blue cloud of cigarette smoke engulfed the upper stands. With the game still in question, restless partisans stole through the haze to settle matters.

Antigonish coaching legend and amateur hockey historian John Brophy takes the story over from here: "In Glace Bay one night, they threw a bucket of piss on [Pidsodney]. A bucket of piss, for God's sake. That's what it was like when Sydney and Glace Bay played." Other fans remember the bare-headed goalie taking the dunking in Charlottetown, Prince Edward Island, where a south-end balcony in the old Forum used to extend over the goal crease. Perhaps the incident happened in both places, which would explain why Pidsodney moved back to Ontario in 1954 to play for the Senior Hamilton Bulldogs.

Cape Breton was not the only place in Nova Scotia where hockey was a matter of combustible pride. After World War II, management of senior league teams in Windsor, Nova Scotia, kept a well-worn 78-rpm copy of "God Save the King" to play at full volume over loudspeakers whenever referees had trouble stopping fights. Upon hearing the music, players would immediately desist, jumping

Opening Spread: Sidney Crosby, the 2005 number one draft pick for the Pittsburgh Penguins.

Hot Stove Leagues

Dalhousie graduate Hugh MacLennan was a lifelong hockey fan. In 1954, he wrote about the hockey days of his Nova Scotia youth for *Holiday* magazine:

On clear afternoons when frigid air pinched the nostrils and made noses run, when the sky changed from deep blue through pale blue to aquamarine and rose, those rinks were a focus for the yells of all the kids in town. You could see their bright-coloured jerseys weaving in and out, toques or peaked hats on their heads, and always there were one or two who would hold your eye. They were the ones who made their shoulders swerve one way while their feet went the other, who sliced through a melee with their heads up and the puck controlled, as if their sticks were extensions of their arms.

Often there was a shack nearby where skates could be changed and hands warmed beside a hot stove. The stove was tended by a bad-tempered man in galluses who sold chocolate bars and soft drinks. The air was hot and foul, and the old man's perpetual refrain was, 'Shut thet door—and keep it shut!' To this day there are millions of Canadians who can't see a potbellied, rusty old stove without feeling nostalgia for a happy youth.

The Sydney Millionaires, 1913.

to attention until the anthem died out—after which they would return to throwing punches.

Sometimes, not even patriotism worked. In 1936, Haligonians jeered the Canadian Olympic team in a match against a local team, the Halifax Wolverines. Some threw refuse. The fans had cause to be unhappy. A strong argument could have been made that the Wolverines, the 1935 winners of

Crosby played with extra dash and ingenuity that had Nova Scotia fans celebrating with military cheers.

the amateur hockey championship, the Allan Cup, were unfairly stripped of their right to represent Canada in the Olympics because of the Canadian Amateur Hockey Association's strict interpretation of players' residency requirements.

Nova Scotia hockey is more than just fights and fury, however. And everyone who was in the Halifax Metro Centre on 15 January 2005, to see the junior hockey team Rimouski Oceanic play the Halifax Mooseheads, experienced the play of emotions that stirs a Nova Scotia hockey crowd. Sidney Crosby, who played centre for the Quebec team, was a Halifax-area boy who had jilted locals by playing hockey elsewhere. He had been booed in his hometown before. But not on this particular night. The nimble 17-year-old phenom, who had just led Canada to a gold medal win at the world junior hockey championship, was greeted with a standing ovation in a pregame ceremony. Sensing the crowd's shifting mood, Crosby played with extra dash and ingenuity, engineering six goals on the way to an 8–4 win that had Nova Scotia fans from Bridgetown to Tatamagouche celebrating with military cheers.

But only when we take a look at the list of locals who have made their careers in the upper ranks of professional hockey, do we come to understand the unequivocal pride and toughness that characterize Nova Scotia players. John Brophy, Dennis Bonvie and Frank "Never" Beaton all hail from Antigonish.

VEE IS FOR VICTORY

Probably the best hockey team ever to play out of the Maritimes, the Halifax-based Nova Scotia Voyageurs—the "Vees"—won the Calder Cup in 1972, 1976 and 1977. The Vees, of the American Hockey League, were the Montreal Canadiens' farm team—players included Larry Robinson, Steve Shutt, Rod Langway, Bob Gainey and Guy Carbonneau.

Brophy and Bonvie, who toiled chiefly in the minors, hold penalty records, respectively, for the Eastern Hockey League and the American Hockey League. Beaton, who played with a variety of leagues, culminating in a two-year stint with the New York Rangers in the late 1970s, earned his nickname for ruining his fists on the chin of every hockey heavyweight contender within swinging distance. More recent Nova Scotia toughs include such current and retired NHLers as forward Doug Doull from Glace Bay; left winger Eric Boulton, right winger David Ling and defenceman Cam Russell from Halifax; as well as defenceman Kevin Morrison and gritty two-way power forward Mike McPhee, both from Sydney. New Glasgow boasts the accomplishments of rock-solid Colin White, the powerful New Jersey Devils defenceman.

The pride with which locals take to the ice is understandable. After all, Nova Scotia—and particularly the cities of Windsor and Halifax-Dartmouth—is where the gathering tribes of Irish, Scottish and English settlers along with the Mi'kmaq First Nation helped to build Canada's national sport. And so, the fervent hockey players and fans of this province carry on in the tradition of those "dozens of boys" who first chased "the ball o'er ice, with a deafening noise."

Mi'kmaq craftsmen carving hockey sticks. For more than 50 years the best hockey sticks in the world were made in Nova Scotia.

Micmacs

Master carvers and enthusiastic hockey players, the Mi'kmaq, a First Nations people living in Nova Scotia, New Brunswick, Prince Edward Island, the Gaspé Peninsula and northeastern New England, skated with bones strapped to their moccasins. In the mid-19th century, Mi'kmaq craftsmen whittled hockey sticks from hornbeam trees. For decades, their one-piece sticks were the most durable and effective ever made. Starr Manufacturing of Dartmouth, N.S., a famed producer of skates, took over the making and distribution of the sticks—labelled Micmacs—in the 1860s. Micmacs were sold across North America until the company ceased making them during the Great Depression.

ANTIGONISH

FOUNDED

Antigonish was originally a Mi'kmaq settlement. Acadians, of French origin, settled in the area in 1755, followed in the 1770s by Scots fleeing oppressive conditions in western Scotland. Irish Loyalists who fought with the defeated British army in the American War of Independence were awarded land surrounding Antigonish Harbour in 1784. They first named the region Georgetown, then Dorchester, and then, finally, Antigonish, a name derived from the Mi'kmaq language.

NATIVE-BORN NHL PLAYERS

Frank "Never" Beaton, Dennis Bonvie, Craig MacDonald, John McGibbon, Dean Melanson

FAMOUS LOCAL TEAMS

Junior: Antigonish Bulldogs;
Senior-pro: Antigonish Bulldogs

CURRENT POPULATION

5,200

John Brophy smiling. He must be near a hockey rink.

The Antigonish Bulldog

Then there was the time, in 1983, when the Nova Scotia Voyageurs, the "Vees," of the American Hockey League, had played a bad game and showed up the next morning for practice to find coach John Brophy on a chair at centre ice, his face reddening under the familiar Q-tip cap of white hair. "Skate!" Brophy ordered, still in his chair, nursing a coffee in the breeze of his players' toil. Later, he asked trainer Brian Patafie for a refill, then barked at the Vees, "Now, other way—move!"

Five coffees later, players were skating on their knees. When Brophy quit the arena, forward Jeff Brubaker stormed the dressing room and destroyed his coach's coffee-maker with his stick.

That tale is just one of a thousand Brophy stories, and who knows how many are true? What can be certain is that John Brophy is the personification of Antigonish hockey. Antigonish is derived from the Mi'kmaq word *nalegitkunech*, meaning "where branches are torn off." Long ago, wild bears wandered freely in

Setting up the rink, Antigonish County, 1930s.

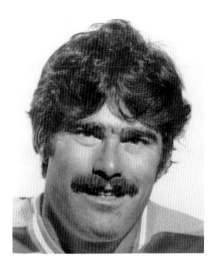

MACLEAN HITS 100

Though born in France, military brat Paul MacLean grew up across Canada, settling early on in Antigonish, where as an adolescent he fussed with radio frequencies in an attempt to pull in night games from New York and Boston. A decade later he was playing in these cities—for the National Hockey League. An All-Star in the 1984–85 year, MacLean scored a career-high 41 goals and 101 points for the Winnipeg Jets, the team with which he spent seven seasons.

this region, ripping down branches in search of beechnut sweets. Tearing down anything that stands in the way of a win, Brophy has brought a lot of *nalegitkunech* to every arena in which he has played or coached.

A hockey vagabond who left his Antigonish school during a grade-five fire drill, never to return, Brophy began as a player with the Halifax St. Mary's junior team in 1950, and ended his hockey career, 55 years later, as coach of the hometown Junior A Antigonish Bulldogs. In between those moments in time are enough towns to fill a train schedule.

Like many old soldiers, Brophy likes war tales to be told by fellows who were there. Nobody else laughs in the right places.

Brophy was born in a farmhouse in Antigonish County, in 1933. His mother died when he was young, and his father went west to work on the railway, farming out eight kids to relatives. At nine, John was fishing with his uncle 10 miles out in the Atlantic. He followed an adored older brother, Tom, a successful footballer, around St. Francis Xavier University. John gravitated to the rink, however. Someone was always short a player in intramural games. He put in eight-hour hockey days before catching on with the Halifax Saint Mary's Juniors in the late 1940s. There, Brophy earned a reputation as a ferocious defenceman and, in 1952, he was recruited into senior hockey by the Moncton Hawks. For the next 21 years, he played and coached with teams in the Eastern Hockey League.

Here is where the train schedule starts—while in the Eastern Hockey League, Brophy played for Troy, Long Island, Baltimore, Charlotte, Philadelphia and New Haven. He set a record amount of work for referees in the EHL: over 3,600 minutes in infractions, two and a half days in the penalty box.

But it was as a coach, first in the EHL and later in the National Hockey League that Brophy became a legend. He was the second coach, after Scotty Bowman, to win 800 professional games. His greatest string of victories came in the 1990s, coaching the East Coast Hockey League's Hampton Roads Admirals to three championships (1991, 1992 and 1998).

For all the wins, Brophy generated even more tall tales. His only comment after one loss was to deposit team sticks in a garbage can. While coaching the Toronto Maple Leafs from 1986 to 1989, he once entered the dressing room and muttered, "You guys are playing like you're asleep." Then he shrugged and turned off the lights.

In the mid-1970s, screenwriter Nancy Dowd asked her brother, Ned, who played for Brophy in the minor leagues, to sneak a tape recorder onto the team bus. Dowd began compiling Brophy anecdotes, which she eventually turned into the scheming player-coach played by Paul Newman in the film *Slap Shot*.

That Brophy once threw a tape of *Slap Shot* off a team bus shouldn't come as a surprise. Like many old soldiers, Brophy likes war tales to be told by fellows who were there. Nobody else laughs in the right places. Nobody else understands that you have to get the punches and punchlines just right because, in the end, laughter and stories are a hockey player's true pension.

Fifty years after leaving his hometown to play minor league hockey, Brophy was back in Antigonish, a thousand stories richer. He had been everywhere. Worked in the off-season as an ironworker on the DEW (distant early warning) Line in the far north; handled a lug wrench, constructing New York office

"Never"...oops!... "Seldom" Beaton

Frank "Never" Beaton was a branch ripped from the same Antigonish hockey tree that produced John Brophy. Sometimes a character player, sometimes merely a character, Beaton forged a lengthy minor-league career with his shoulders and fists. After a cup of coffee, no sugar, with the National Hockey League's New York Rangers, he played alongside Gilles "Bad News" Bilodeau, Dave Hanson and Steve Durbano on the infamous 1977–78 Birmingham Bulls of the World Hockey Association (WHA). The quartet racked up 21 goals...and 1,062 penalty minutes.

For years, Frank the Fighter went undefeated—although WHA Edmonton teammates once had to smuggle him out of the rink in an equipment bag, to protect him from angry fans. Then he lost a fight. Hockey can be an unforgiving sport: After that defeat, the scrappy player's nickname was Frank "Seldom" Beaton.

Paul Newman played a character based on John Brophy in the 1977 film, *Slap Shot*. To his right, Vancouver-born actor Michael Ontkean.

towers. And in the process, Brophy had helped hundreds of players. Jeff Brubaker of the Vees, in fact, registered a career high in goals the season that he destroyed Brophy's coffee machine.

Wherever his travels took him, though, Brophy always came back to Nova Scotia. When, in the '80s, Montreal offered him the job of coaching the American Hockey League's Halifax Voyageurs, he had to stop himself from dancing upon leaving general manager Irving Grundman's office. And in December 2004 the 72-year-old Brophy brought his hockey career full circle by volunteering to coach Antigonish's junior hockey club. When contacted by Antigonish Bulldogs general manager Danny Berry, Brophy's opening line was, "When can I start?"

Halifax Rules

James Power, a sports reporter for the old *Halifax Herald*, wrote down the rules of hockey as played in the Halifax-Dartmouth area in the 1860s. Many of his rules still apply in modern hockey.

The Halifax Rules:

1 The game was played with a wooden puck.
2 The puck was not allowed to leave the ice.
3 Stones marking the goal were placed parallel to side boards.
4 No slashing was allowed.
5 No lifting the stick above the shoulder was permitted.
6 Teams changed ends after every goal.
7 Players had to keep "on side" of their sticks.
8 Forward passes were permitted.
9 Players played the entire game.
10 There was a no-replacement rule for penalized players.
11 The game had two 30-minute periods with a 10-minute break.
12 Goalies stood for the entire game.
13 Goals were decided by umpires, who stood at the goalmouth and rang a handbell.

HALIFAX-DARTMOUTH

FOUNDED

Originally called Chebucto—meaning "biggest harbour"—by the Mi'kmaq, Halifax was founded in 1749 as a military outpost. The city was named after George Montague-Dunk, second Earl of Halifax. Dartmouth, on the eastern side of Halifax harbour, was founded in 1750 and is believed to have been named after Sir William Legge, Earl of Dartmouth. Ferry service between Halifax and Dartmouth was established in 1972, and it is now the oldest running saltwater ferry service in North America.

NATIVE-BORN NHL PLAYERS

Eric Boulton, Sidney Crosby (born in Cole Harbour, NS), Ryan Flinn, Bert Hirschfield, Jack Ingram, David Ling, Ian MacNeil, Peter Marshall, Wayne Maxner, Glen Murray, Eldon "Pokey" Reddick, Cam Russell, Wendell Young

FAMOUS LOCAL TEAMS (DARTMOUTH)

Junior: Cole Harbour Colts, Dartmouth Arrows, Dartmouth Fuel Kids, Dartmouth Oland Exports, Scotia Dairy Queen Blizzard;
Senior-pro: Dartmouth Chebuctos, Dartmouth Lakers, Dartmouth Mounties, Dartmouth RCAF

FAMOUS LOCAL TEAMS (HALIFAX)

Junior: Halifax Atlantics, Halifax Jr. Canadians, Halifax Colonels, Halifax Lions, Halifax Mooseheads, Halifax Oland Exports, Halifax Team Pepsi;
Senior-pro: Halifax Army, Halifax Atlantics, Halifax Crescents, Halifax Navy, Halifax RCAF, Halifax Socials, Halifax St. Mary's, Halifax Wanderers, Nova Scotia Voyageurs

CURRENT POPULATION

276,200

STARR MAKERS

Once a nail factory, Dartmouth's Starr Manufacturing began to make skates in 1863. The company produced over 11 million skates before the Great Depression. For decades, all competitive hockey players wore Starr's "Halifax" skates, branded with the city's name on the blades.

Canadian Idol

Youth is a time for experimenting. And that is exactly what 16-year-old Sidney Crosby was doing one night, in a 2003 Quebec Major Junior Hockey League game, when he figured he would try something he had been fooling around with in practice. Half squatting, Crosby lowered the shaft of his stick and scooped the puck up, lacrosse style, onto the tape of his blade. Number 87 then crept to the side of the net, and extending the cradled puck behind the unsuspecting goalie, he snuck the puck into the top corner.

Ha, it worked! Overcome with delight, Crosby raced out for a clear patch of ice and a toboggan ride on his knees.

On the bench, his Rimouski Oceanic teammates reacted as if they had seen a UFO land. A delighted shiver went through the Quebec crowd. *Est-çe que tu as vu, ha?*

Halifax-Dartmouth—indeed, all of Nova Scotia—has waited almost two centuries for Sidney Crosby. Many natives believe the province to be the birthplace of hockey. Nova Scotia is where the tools of the game—sticks and skates—were first manufactured. The Halifax-Dartmouth area has produced many good players and championship teams, but Sidney Crosby of Cole Harbour, a suburb of Dartmouth, is something else: He is potentially the next Great One, a much-hoped-for Maritime heir to Lemieux, Gretzky, Lafleur, Orr, Hull, Howe and Richard. Already, Crosby's "lacrosse" goal in junior is hockey history, and it will forever take its place beside other magic plays—such as the time Fred "Cyclone" Taylor, a whirlwind scorer in the early 1900s, allegedly skated in backward from centre to score a goal.

But matters aren't so simple, nowadays. Crosby's goal was instantly part of the day's news cycle—shown after headline news and before the weather. Then, we all saw the clip repeated on TV sports highlight shows. With each replay, the goal seemed more remarkable, and yet also somehow more...showy.

That Saturday on *Hockey Night in Canada*, commentator Don Cherry came out of his "Coach's Corner" swinging. "I like [Crosby]," he began. "I see the way he plays and everything. But I've seen him now after goals. He slides on the ice on his knees."

As the famous goal was replayed, Cherry continued. "Everybody thinks, 'Oh, this is super.' This is a hot-dog move! Quebec Remparts will remember [that] the next time they play.... They're going to grab the mustard and put it all over him."

Within weeks, Crosby's private pantomime was fast-moving merchandise, as the Oceanic began selling DVDs with promised footage of *le fameux but du 87*—87's famous goal—for a price that played on the youngster's number ($8.69).

All this attention, it should be noted, happened when Sidney Crosby was 90 days past his 16th birthday. Months later, after leading all Canadian juniors with 135 points in 59 games, he would turn down a $7 million contract to play in Hamilton, Ontario, for the fledgling World Hockey Association. At 17, more fame and fury followed: In 2005, Crosby played on the top line in Canada's gold-medal world junior championship win, and then had his Team Canada jersey stolen (and later returned) by an Air Canada baggage handler. Such are the perils and rewards of winning hockey's "Canadian idol" competition.

Crosby, in fact, has been a famous hockey player for almost all his life. Just as Wayne Gretzky had a backyard rink, Crosby, at age two, had a basement hockey playground, which his dad, Troy, a 1984 Montreal Canadiens goalie draft pick, painted ice white, with red and blue lines. Sidney was skating at three and

Sidney Crosby was hockey's most famous apprentice from 2003–05, playing for the Rimouski Oceanic of the Quebec junior league.

Wolverines Tossed to the Wolves

Once again Central Canada has sunken its iron talons into these seaward provinces and made us like it.
—Halifax Chronicle, 1936

For years, winners of the Allan Cup, the senior amateur hockey championship, represented Canada in the Olympics. Then again, the Olympic candidate invariably came from central Canada, home of the fuss-budget Canadian Amateur Hockey Association.

Sticklers for rules, the CAHA could inflame teams and their fans with its decisions. No one was more infuriated than the rough-and-tumble Halifax Wolverines, who captured the Canadian senior hockey crown in 1935 by defeating Ontario's Port Arthur Bearcats in a 4-3 win. The Allan Cup victory meant that the Halifax team would represent Canada in the Olympics, a rare cause for Maritime celebration during the Depression.

Swelling hearts were soon broken, alas. The CAHA stripped the Wolverines of their Olympic status after it ruled that some of the team's players had violated the association's local residency requirements, a stipulation that had not been enforced for years. The Port Arthur team was handed the Olympic berth, instead, a stinging reversal that was greeted in the Maritimes as a sign of Canadian bias against the region. This setback, coupled with a harsh economic climate, forced the Wolverines to disband.

The CAHA ultimately agreed to let Wolverines "Chummie" Lawlor, Vince Ferguson, Ernie Mosher and goalie Sylvester "Daddy" Bubar join the Port Arthur team for the Olympic bid. But shortly before the team was to leave for Halifax to sail to Germany and the 1936 Olympics, the CAHA threw the Wolverines to the wolves, expelling the Haligonians for allegedly requesting living allowances while overseas. The players denied the charge. Mosher even swore an oath to that effect. The CAHA was not swayed, however, and refused to hold a hearing on the matter. League official E.A. Gilroy claimed he was suffering from pleurisy and was in no condition to see the players.

Later, when the Bearcats arrived in Halifax for a pre-Olympics match against the Wolverines, the CAHA refused to let the four disqualified stars play in the game for their home team. The Olympic team was subsequently booed and pelted with bottles and other refuse by the infuriated Halifax crowd. The *Halifax Chronicle* also aimed a few brickbats at the CAHA. "Once again central Canada has sunken its iron talons into these seaward provinces and made us like it," the paper fumed.

outplaying everyone two years older by the age of five; he gave his first newspaper interview at seven.

Don Cherry's remarks aside, Crosby has the kind of talent that turns veteran hockey observers into gushing admirers. "In terms of skill, he's as good as I've seen," enthused Edmonton Oilers executive Kevin Prendergast. "He could stick-handle inside a phone booth."

As promised, Sidney Crosby emerged from that phone booth looking like Superman when he turned pro with the Pittsburgh Penguins, emerging as the team's top performer during the 2005–06 National Hockey League season.

NEW GLASGOW

FOUNDED
A long-time Aboriginal settlement, the city of New Glasgow was established in 1798, shortly after the discovery of coal in nearby Pictou County. The area's first foreign-born settlers came from Glasgow, Scotland.

NATIVE-BORN NHL PLAYERS
Lowell MacDonald, Jon Sim, Derrick Walser, Colin White

FAMOUS LOCAL TEAMS
Junior: New Glasgow Bombers, New Glasgow Jr. Panthers, Weeks Crushers; **Senior-pro:** New Glasgow Black Foxes, New Glasgow Bombers, New Glasgow Chevrolets, New Glasgow Colts, New Glasgow Cubs, New Glasgow Panthers, New Glasgow Rangers, New Glasgow Tigers

CURRENT POPULATION
9,467

Frank Morrison of the New Glasgow Cubs.

STUDENT ATHLETES

New Glasgow's Lowell MacDonald overcame a career-threatening knee injury, in 1971, to play in the 1973 National Hockey League all-star game, thereby winning the Bill Masterton Memorial Trophy, which honours perseverance, sportsmanship and dedication to hockey. He also showed stamina in other ways—attending Halifax's St. Mary's University in the off-season for 12 years, in order to earn a bachelor's degree. Later, he obtained his master's. In 1989, MacDonald's son Lane won the Hobey Baker Award for best U.S. college hockey player of the year while he attended Harvard University.

Cubs Wander into Trouble

Every winter for over a century, New Glaswegians have felt the surge of patriotism that comes when hometown heroes skate forth in local colours to do battle. Citizens walk around with britches hitched a little higher, if the local team has defeated rivals from Trenton, Pictou or Stellarton the previous evening. The city has also served continually as the site of international and regional matches, playing host to the world under-17 championship, the Air Canada midget championships, and the Irving Oil Challenge Cup celebrating Atlantic Canada's Bantam AAA championship. As well, NHL-championship winners hailing from New Glasgow—in 1999, Jon Sim of the Dallas Stars, and in 2001 and 2003, Colin White of the New Jersey Devils—have brought the Stanley Cup home to thousands of cheering fans, lining the streets to celebrate their local heroes.

Ah, but there was once a time when not just a single player but an entire team of New Glasgow natives played for the world championship of hockey. Before the National Hockey League, before even the National Hockey Association (1911–17), the Stanley Cup was won or lost on the basis of civic challenges. Trustees determined who the worthy opponents were. In 1906, these decision-makers decreed that the Montreal Wanderers, an itinerant team that wandered through several leagues and had won the first of three Stanley Cup championships earlier that year, had to defend its crown against the champions of the Nova Scotia Hockey League, the New Glasgow Cubs.

The intrepid Cubs made the arduous 1,200-mile train ride into Montreal.

This trip gave them more than enough time to dwell on what had happened in 1900 to the Halifax Crescents. That year, the Crescents, the last Nova Scotia team to travel to Montreal in quest of "silver," had been crushed by the Montreal Shamrocks, who slapped in a combined 21 goals to the Crescents' two, during back-to-back games.

That tale of defeat seemed ancient history, however, as the Cubs skated onto the ice for a Christmas-season match against the Montreal powerhouse. The crowd at the old Montreal Arena let out a wounded sound in the very first minute of play, as Cubs coverpoint Marks raced down the ice to score against legendary Wanderer goalie Riley Hern. The Wanderers retaliated for a quick goal, and the two teams battled through a penalty-filled half that had the champion Montrealers up, 4–2.

After that, however, the Wanderers found their more customary poise and élan, outscoring the visitors, 6–1, in the second 30 minutes for a final score of 10–3. The Cubs fared no better in the second match of the two-game series, losing, 7–2. As the *Halifax Chronicle* glumly reported after the second defeat, "Unfortunately [the Cubs] lost control of the puck every time they were permitted to bring it close to the Wanderers' net."

Despite the drubbing, the Montreal papers acknowledged that New Glasgow had put in a game effort, and even the *Chronicle*'s last words on the feisty Cubs were, "They died fighting...and when the gong rang for the finish of the match, they said they were going to come back and try again."

New Glasgow Cubs players included Morrison, goal; Musick, point; Marks, coverpoint; McDonald, rover; Williams, right wing; and Lennon, left wing.

Dude, I had no idea it was the Stanley Cup

Ninety-odd years after the Cubs made their skate for glory, New Glasgow native Colin White, defenceman for the champion New Jersey Devils, brought the Stanley Cup to his hometown for summer block parties, in 2000 and 2003.

The 2003 affair was particularly spirited. The day began with White and friends competing in a ball hockey tournament that had been planned at a party the night before. Later, more than 10,000 revellers crowded city streets to watch White and his wife parade the Stanley Cup through town. The procession began at New Glasgow Stadium, and before long the skirl of bagpipes and mural of congratulatory signs overcame White. "Man, some of those folks drove from New Brunswick," he said at one point. "Some of those folks are in from Newfoundland."

Afterward, White stopped at a fitting locale for any day that had begun with a ball hockey game—a drive-through McDonald's. White placed his order, but the delivery was slow as staff crowded around the takeout window to ogle the three-foot cup riding in his convertible. After a while, an impatient driver behind him barked, "Come on, let's go!"

White twisted around and heaved the cup over his head.

"Dude, I'm sorry," the driver quickly apologized. "I had no idea it was the Stanley Cup. Stay as long as you want."

PORT HOOD

FOUNDED
First called Keg-weom-kek ("sandy shoal") by the Mi'kmaqs, and then Juste-au-Corps by the French, in 1786 the settlement was renamed Port Hood in honour of Samuel Viscount Hood, the British commander in chief of North America.

NATIVE-BORN NHL PLAYERS
Al MacInnis

FAMOUS LOCAL TEAMS
Not applicable

CURRENT POPULATION
835

The Big Shot

As a teenager, in the 1970s, Al MacInnis spent his summer mornings lifting lobster crates, developing heavy ropes of muscle on his shoulders and fore-arms. Come afternoon, when family and friends were off to Port Hood's warm and shallow beach, he, too, pulled off his shirt, but worked on his slapshot instead of a tan.

Putting down a skinned plywood launching pad in front of the family barn, the son of a Cape Breton coal miner would bring out a pail of pucks and begin his own particular set of farm chores:

Slap—bang!

Slap—bang!

After several years, the MacInnis barn was black with the bruises of a thousand pucks, and young Al could shoot harder than all but a few National Hockey League players. The tiny coal-mining town of Port Hood was about to graduate its most famous citizen.

Ironically, it wasn't a slapshot that got MacInnis noticed by scouts. That moment came when he was 15 and a defenceman for the Nova Midgets, playing in the provincial junior championships against the Cape Breton Colonels. The Midgets were down a goal with 13 seconds left, when they received a penalty shot. Coach Donnie MacIsaac had better players but chose his young defenceman, saying later that he could tell by his eyes that he wanted the puck.

Many of the 2,500 fans in attendance swear MacInnis waved to them as he swooped to pick up the puck at centre ice. He disagrees. There can be no question, however, of what happened next.

MacInnis hurried in on net and drew back to shoot, sending the goalie flopping, then threw the puck quickly to his forehand, from where he lifted it into the net—all as fast as the mark of Zorro.

After finishing off the Colonels, MacInnis and the Novas travelled to Winnipeg, Manitoba, for the 1979 Air Canada Cup midget championship. There, scouts noticed Al's fast hands and extraordinary shot. He caught on with Saskatchewan's junior Regina Blues, then transferred to Ontario's junior Kitchener Rangers, breaking Bobby Orr's point-scoring record for a defence-man, before arriving as the centrepiece of the great Calgary team of the 1980s.

Now, MacInnis was ripping apart barns all across the NHL. Just as true baseball fans showed up early at the ballpark to see Mickey Mantle or Mark McGwire hit during batting practice, hockey enthusiasts arrived at the rink well before Calgary Flames games just to see (and hear!) "The Chopper" shoot a puck. In one 1984 game, MacInnis took a memorable shot from outside the opposition blue line before hurrying off for a line change. The blast toppled St. Louis Blues goalie Mike Liut—cracking his mask—and then dribbled past the unconscious goalie into the net.

In 1989, the towering defenceman helped lead Calgary to the Stanley Cup and won the Conn Smythe Trophy as most valuable player of the playoffs. MacInnis was also a key contributor to Canada's 2002 gold-medal Olympic team. In between these events, he won the Norris Trophy as the best NHL defenceman of 1999, as well as six "hardest shot" competitions at league all-star games.

But the shot MacInnis remembers best came long before Port Hood celebrated its only NHL star with a Home of Al MacInnis sign. "Every so often I think about what would have happened if I didn't make that penalty shot," he told a *St. Louis Post-Dispatch* reporter in 2003, referring to his long-ago Nova Midgets goal against the Cape Breton Colonels. "I'm sure everybody can look back and find somewhere, when they got the break they needed. It was kind of meant to be."

Al MacInnis broke Bobby Orr's junior point-scoring record for a defenceman while playing for the Kitchener Rangers.

A view of Sydney, 1784.

SYDNEY

FOUNDED
Sydney was settled, in 1785, by Col. Joseph Frederick Wallet DesBarres and United Empire Loyalists from New York. A second wave of settlers, from the Scottish Highlands, arrived two decades later.

NATIVE-BORN NHL PLAYERS
Paul Boutilier, Nelson Burton, Norm Ferguson, John Hanna, Fabian Joseph, Parker MacDonald, Don MacLean, Al MacNeil, Mike McPhee, Kevin Morrison

FAMOUS LOCAL TEAMS
Junior: Cape Breton Metros, Cape Breton Screaming Eagles, Sydney Bruins, Sydney Flyers, Sydney Shipyards; **Senior-pro:** Cape Breton Oilers, Cape Breton Miners, Sydney AAA, Sydney Millionaires, Sydney Nationals, Sydney Navy, Sydney Socials

CURRENT POPULATION
33,000

PARK IT RIGHT THERE

A Sydney Millionaire in 1949, Parker MacDonald would go on to play in the National Hockey League for 14 years. In the 1962–63 season, he tallied 33 goals for the Detroit Red Wings, playing left wing alongside Gordie Howe and Alex Delvecchio.

Millionaires Sink Leaky Boates

Sydney is the birthplace of a number of hockey greats: Danny Gallivan, the famous play-by-play voice of the Montreal Canadiens; Parker MacDonald, a National Hockey League winger who played alongside superstar Gordie Howe; Stanley Cup winner Mike McPhee, of the 1986 Montreal Canadiens; and long-time NHL coach and executive Al MacNeil. Still, the city's greatest contribution to hockey lore would have to be Cape Breton's most famous and illustrious team, the Sydney Millionaires.

Who wanted to be a Millionaire in the '40s? Just about any hockey player who wasn't in the military or playing in the NHL, that's who. Together, Sydney, North Sydney, Glace Bay and New Waterford—the coal and steel towns of Cape Breton—formed an important engine in Prime Minister Mackenzie King's war effort. The region boasted full employment. Young men with hockey skills were pulled here with the promise that local mining and steel companies would give them paying jobs that left them plenty of time to participate in the most spirited games played anywhere.

Lou Medynski, a Stonewall, Manitoba, native, settled in Sydney, playing for the Millionaires. "It was an ideal set-up," he told author Bill Boyd. "A three-team league—Sydney, Glace Bay and North Sydney. We slept in our own beds every night. And the rinks were usually packed. They loved hockey here. And I was at the steel plant for 25 years."

Actually, Sydney players were only treated like Millionaires by fans. Many athletes, such as Medynski, had day jobs. Still, Millionaires were working-class heroes at a time just after the Great Depression, when "work" and "heroes" both had been in short supply.

The Sydney heroes' most important job, they knew, was beating the Glace Bay Miners. There were reasons for the feud. Glace Bay was a mining town with a puck-sized chip on its shoulder, in regard to its wealthier steel-city foe. As well, bloody labour disputes from back in the '20s had turned many Cape Breton sister communities into "us and them" rivals.

It was a flush, feverish time, and hockey was an expression of community

Maritime Champions

Jack Atchison

Doug Fritz

Ray Powell

Tony Graboski

Tic Williams

Jack Fritz

Remi Van Daele

Harry Whebby

Bill Gill

Bun MacEachern

Keith Langille

Ralph Anderson

Art Bennett

Bill Dickie

Vern Buckles

The 1940 Sydney Millionaires.

Sydney Millionaires 1940

Danny Gallivan, microphone at the ready.

pride and prejudice. When Glace Bay and Sydney played, there were fights on the ice, in the stands and on the way in and out of the stadium. Players were careful not to be noticed parking their cars in rival cities, because fans sometimes put sugar in the fuel tanks.

In 1941, the Millionaires seemed a cinch to sweep their division and move on to the Allan Cup, the senior amateur hockey championship, especially since Glace Bay had previously been charged with having more than the allowed four paid players on its team. The Miners' top goalie and a star forward had to go to meet the requirements.

Miners owner Marty MacDonald schemed his way out of the club's predicament, however. A wartime rule allowed for the replacement of any player who joined the services. MacDonald went to the team's remaining goalie, Earl "Leaky" Boates, with a proposition. "I'll give you $200 to join the army," he said.

Boates didn't want to go. MacDonald made a second offer. "Here's $100 and a train ticket to Montreal. Get lost for a while."

With Boates gone, MacDonald hired a netminder with a more promising nickname, Bill "Legs" Fraser—a Winnipegger renowned for his lightning-fast kick saves. With Fraser in net, Glace Bay won the first three games in the best-of-seven series, 4–1, 1–0 and 5–4.

The losses enraged the Sydney team, which demanded that the games be washed out. The Nova Scotia Hockey Association agreed. In response, Glace Bay citizens set up roadblocks, preventing any goods from moving the 20 miles between the two cities. With Mackenzie King's war engine suddenly minus one of its pistons, Ottawa finally intervened—threatening to send troops, if Glace Bay didn't lift the blockade. The city had no choice, especially since Leaky Boates had bobbed back to the surface in Truro, Nova Scotia, where he was spotted by a reporter.

The series began again in Glace Bay, days later. Living up to his "leaky" billing, Boates allowed in nine goals as the Miners took a thrashing from the Millionaires. Glace Bay forfeited the remaining games, sensing the inevitable.

The Sydney team moved on to the Allan Cup, which they lost to the Regina Pats. The Saskatchewan team, alas, featured a goaltender who also lived up to his nickname—future NHL great, "Sugar" Jim Henry.

Danny Boy

Hockey's greatest lyricist, Danny Gallivan, actually wanted to be a baseball pitcher. The "about middle" son of 13 children born to a Sydney coal miner was good, too—with a buggy-whip arm that won him an invitation to the St. Louis Cardinals training camp in the late 1930s. A throwing injury ended his baseball hopes, however.

After a two-year stint with the Canadian army during World War II and a degree from St. Francis Xavier University in Antigonish, Nova Scotia, where he debuted on the campus radio station (CJFX), Gallivan moved to Halifax. There, his love of sports and language flourished, as he found work broadcasting hockey on local radio station CJCH and teaching Latin. While covering a junior hockey playoff game in Montreal between the Halifax St. Mary's and the Montreal Royals, Gallivan's lilting baritone brought him to the attention of the National Hockey League's Canadiens, who, in 1953, made him the English-language voice of the team.

Over three decades, first on radio, and then on television, Gallivan's ecstatic wordplay changed how we talked about hockey. Generations of hockey street urchins mimicked his signature phrases. Toqued attackers spoke of "stepping gingerly over the blue line" and threatening Canadian Tire nets with "cannonading drives." Shinny players lost bald tennis balls "in the paraphernalia" of a goalie's equipment, meaning that the balls were stuffed somewhere in the goalie's baggy corduroy trousers.

Because Gallivan loved language as much as sport, he managed to "sing" what is true and wonderful about hockey. Dick Irvin, who broadcast alongside Gallivan from the Montreal Forum, once marvelled at how the game possessed his partner:

"To get to the English broadcast booth in the Forum, you had to travel past [fellow announcer] René Lecavalier and the French booth. And the thing I remember about Danny is he was so loud I don't think I ever heard René…. And once you got beside him, well, that's when the show began. Because Danny would swing over to the right if a long pass changed the direction of the play. Back he'd jump a few seconds later. And he'd leap out of his seat if something exciting happened. He was right into the game."

TRURO

FOUNDED
Inhabited first by the Acadians in the early 1700s, and then, in the 1750s, by Scottish and Irish settlers arriving from New England, the settlement changed its name from Cobequit to Truro, in 1760. The town was incorporated in 1875.

NATIVE-BORN NHL PLAYERS
Lyle Carter, Gord "Doggie" Kuhn

FAMOUS LOCAL TEAMS
Junior: Truro Bearcats;
Senior-pro: Truro Bearcats

CURRENT POPULATION
12,000

Bearcats Forever

Apart from their periodic hibernations, the Truro Bearcats have kept the hockey history of this town alive for over 100 years.

Junior A and B Bearcats, as well as senior Bearcats, have played in at least six different leagues. The senior Bearcats—led by winger Doggie Kuhn, who later would play for the National Hockey League's New York Americans—won the provincial championship in 1925 and went on to challenge unsuccessfully the Ontario Port Arthur Bearcats for the Allan Cup. Then, in 1935, a junior Bearcats team captured the provincial championship. And we mustn't forget about midget hockey: Truro's Art Dorrington, the first black player to sign with an NHL team, led the 1946 Bearcats to the Nova Scotia midget championship. Later on, there were the junior B Bearcats, which won five junior B titles between 1968 and 1974 before folding. In 1997, the Bearcats re-emerged as a Junior A team. But it was a senior Truro Bearcats team that in 1998 would reward local citizens with the 20th century's finest Bearcats victory.

In April 1998, the senior Truro Bearcats concluded the province's 70-year courtship of the Allan Cup with a satisfying 6–1 home victory over the London Admirals. The senior hockey championship was hosted at a riotously happy Colchester Legion Stadium in Truro. Local hero Sandy MacKenzie counted two goals for the Bearcats. "The Allan Cup is for the love of the game, and these guys love it more than anybody," he said. The Truro win was Nova Scotia's first Allan Cup since the Halifax Wolverines snatched the title in 1935. For the Bearcats, the 1998 victory was a last hurrah. The team disbanded at the end of the season.

The 1926 Truro Bearcats.

The 2005–06 junior Truro Bearcats.

WINDSOR

FOUNDED

French-speaking Acadians arrived in Windsor in 1684, and in 1749 a British settlement was established there. When war loomed between the British and the French in 1755, four ships expelled 1,000 Acadian French for the sake of settlement security. In 1878, Windsor was incorporated as a town.

NATIVE-BORN NHL PLAYERS

Nick Greenough

FAMOUS LOCAL TEAMS

Junior: Windsor Royals; **Senior-pro:** Windsor Avonians, Windsor Maple Leafs, Windsor Swastikas

CURRENT POPULATION

3,725

Where Hockey Grew

While Nova Scotia provided a crucial link in the development of modern hockey, it is impossible to declare that the sport was invented in Windsor, as some have claimed. Hockey historians can more accurately say that the city's biggest skating rink—Long Pond—is the frozen delta where hockey grew into a modern sport.

Minutes after inventing the ball, it seems, humans developed the creeping urge to whack this object with a stick. In the 19th century, archaeologists discovered a bas-relief depicting a faceoff from ancient Greece. Furthermore, Roman soldiers later took a game not unlike hockey with them north to the British Isles.

After the Romans got the puck rolling, a Scottish version of the sport became shinty, meaning "commotion" or "brawl." Ireland, too, developed a similarly brawling sport known as "hurley." In 1527, in order to combat growing savagery in the game, "the horling of a litill ball with sticks and staves" was prohibited in Ireland by the Galway Statutes. And in England, in the 1400s, King Edward III banned stickball because it threatened to eclipse the more militarily useful sport of archery.

Something like hockey was being played by Aboriginal Canadians around the same time. Old Joe Cope, an elder of the Mi'kmaq tribe, recalled in the 1940s, "Long before the pale faces strayed to this country, [we] played two ball games, a field [hockey] game and an ice game."

As it happens, the Mi'kmaq, as well as the shinty- and hurley-playing descendants of the Irish, Scottish and English, converged in Windsor, Nova Scotia, in the late 18th century. In winter, each of these cultures took to the glassy ice of the city's Long Pond, where something like hockey became popular.

Documentation of the sport's earliest origins is provided by T.C. Haliburton (1796–1865), author of such phrases as "the early bird gets the worm" and "don't look a gift horse in the mouth." In 1844, Haliburton wrote fictionally about his schoolboy days at Windsor's King's College: "And you boys let out racin', yelpin', hollerin', and whoopin' like mad with pleasure, and the playground, and the game at bass in the fields, or hurly on the long pond on the ice…" This reference to "hurly on the long pond" has long been thought to be the first written reference to hockey on ice in Canada. A subsequent mention of the sport was made in an 1876 edition of the *Windsor Mail*, by an anonymous writer who recalled seeing a skater "having his front teeth knocked out with a hurley."

Armed with information such as this, many Nova Scotia hockey historians have declared that hockey was first played at Long Pond by the students of King's College, Windsor, in and around 1800. As the story goes, the sport spread quickly from

The Windsor
Swastikas, 1910.

Windsor Royalty

Before gaining lasting ignominy as the badge of Nazi oppression and racism, the swastika was considered a symbol of hope. Romans regarded the mark as a sign of peace. Up until the 1930s, the swastika was simply an arrangement of four L's celebrating Luck, Light, Love, and Life.

For Maritime hockey fans in the early 20th century, however, the swastika was largely a symbol of hockey skill and grace. The Windsor Swastikas were, perhaps, Nova Scotia's most popular team in the decade prior to World War I. In addition to winning a provincial senior title in 1910, the team went on barnstorming tours of other provinces and was particularly admired in Newfoundland, where the Swastikas players were received as sports royalty.

Part of the team's appeal was its fashion sense. The Swastikas were early proponents of dark-and-light jerseys so that they could always be distinguished from their opponents. The team also had an off-ice dress code—a collegiate look that favoured wool-knit overcoats and Donegal-tweed slouch hats. Coaches and managers were partial to breast-pocket puffs and vest-pocket gold watch chains. Such stylishness came naturally to the team: the Swastikas were the sons of Windsor aristocracy and would retire to positions as department store, clothing and dry goods merchants.

Swastikas players were known for more than good breeding and elegant attire. Nova Scotia invented the "rover" position—a flashy Bobby Orr-type who played the entire rink. And two Swastikas rovers would gain local and international acclaim: Lew Shaw was a legendary scorer, who translated his celebrity into a popular local pool hall, while Blaine Sexton continued his success on the rink, taking his skates and equipment with him to England during World War I. There, he would organize the London Ice Hockey Team, earning the nickname "Mister Hockey" during a decade-long reign as European scoring champion.

Long Pond to Fort Edward—again, located in Windsor—and was then brought by soldiers to the iced-over ponds and frozen harbour inlets of Dartmouth and Halifax.

The problem with Windsor's claim, however, is that there are stories of a sport similar to hockey being played elsewhere earlier. One report has residents of Stoney Brook (now Princeton, New Jersey) playing hockey in the winter of 1786.

Perhaps, though, the greatest proof of Nova Scotia's claim to being the birthplace of hockey is that this province is the place where the tools of the game were developed and first marketed. In 1866, the Starr Manufacturing Company of Dartmouth created the first patent on hockey skates. Uniform wooden pucks originated in Nova Scotia, as well. And the province's Aboriginal Mi'kmaq carvers perfected the first one-piece hockey sticks.

While it would be too strong a statement to insist that modern hockey was created in Windsor, we can fairly say that Nova Scotia is where the sport grew into the popular enterprise we know today and that Windsor is the birthplace of hockey in the Maritimes.

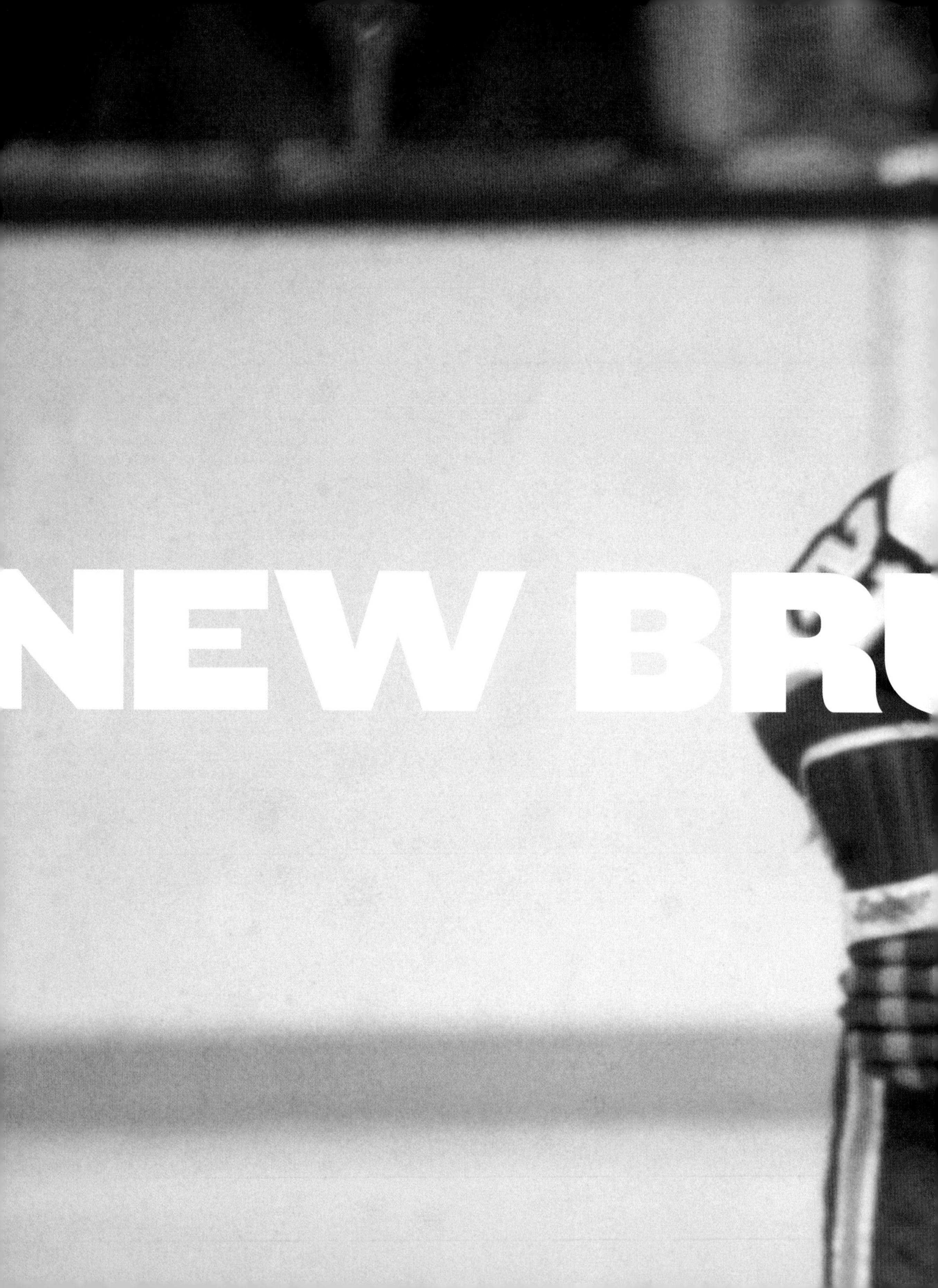

NEW BR

Opening Spread: New Brunswick hockey great Danny Grant, playing for the Minnesota North Stars, 1974.

A skating craze captivated New Brunswick in the 1850s, transforming winter from a time of sleepy hibernation into a major social season.

Acme skates, imported from Dartmouth, found their way onto Saint John's Lily Lake. Suddenly, the kids' game of tag took on fantastic dimensions—becoming faster, longer, wider, and subject to daring turns, not to mention spectacular crashes.

Skating men moved fast as racehorses. Inevitably, crowds pulled together along makeshift 100- to 600-yard courses to determine who was fastest. To increase public interest, prize stakes of £50 sterling were put up for big weekend races. Competitors such as Leo and Steve Gerow, Bob Bustin and Albert Lyon became local legends—the Maritime equivalent of Wild West gunslingers.

Skates also did Cupid's bidding. An afternoon stroll on "sailing shoes" was better than ballroom dancing, as the adventure of skating allowed for both real and pretend falls, which could only be corrected with a swift embrace.

Some strutting peacocks preferred to perform figure eights and showy "pigeon wings," for the amusement of gathering crowds. Accomplished "fancy skaters," such as Oliver Goldsmith and Samuel Gardner, could actually carve their names with pride on the frozen white canvas of Lily Lake.

Last, but certainly not least, were the hurley players: boisterous youngsters who showed up in the morning to claim the lake's best surfaces—broad patches of polished ice blown free of snow by the wind. Occasionally, players alarmed passing strangers by swatting cricket balls into their midst, then chasing into the crowd after them bearing hurleys—long wooden sticks curled up at the end like elves' boots.

Ice hurley took off because Acme skates made the game affordable and relatively easy to perform. Still, the first popular skate was, by today's standards,

Miramichi Creed

"We were all going to make the NHL, when I was 10 or 11," writes New Brunswick author David Adams Richards in *Hockey Dreams*, his finely observed reminiscence of growing up on skates in Miramichi, a town on the province's northeast coast. "In those years, long ago, the weather was always more than it is now. There was more of it—more snow, more ice, more sky—more wind. More hockey."

The most stirring moment in the memoir comes when Richards offers up the definitive Canadian hockey creed:

> If you think that you are a Canadian, then my boy I will show you I am a Canadian, too—if they check me from behind I will get up, if they kick and slash I will get up. If we play three against five for 15 minutes I will get up. I, too, am a Canadian. They will not take this away from me. Nor, can I see, will they ever take it away from you. At the moment they think we are defeated we will have just begun. I will prove forever my years on the river, on the back rinks, on the buses, on the farm teams. I will prove forever that this is what has shaped me.

Skating on Lily Lake in St. John, 1900.

The 1934 Allan Cup-winning Moncton Hawks.

Putting the boot to winter blues: Starr "Acme Club" self-fastening skates, patented in 1863.

New Brunswick Beats Canada to Win Olympic Gold

After taking the senior Moncton Hawks to Allan Cup wins in 1933 and 1934, coach Percy Nicklin escaped the endless bickering over amateur hockey eligibility in Canada by moving to England. Prior to the 1936 Olympics, he scouted his old homeland in search of British-born Canadians who could help form the British team. His prize was Glasgow-born Moncton Hawks star, Jimmy Foster. After the Canadian Amateur Hockey Association disqualified Canada's national champions, the Halifax Wolverines, from representing Canada in the 1936 Olympic Games, their replacement, Ontario's Port Arthur Bearcats, faced Nicklin's British team at the games. In an ironic upset, Canada lost the gold medal to Nicklin's team, which was stacked with Canadian-British all stars.

an unwieldy contraption—sword pontoons that were attached to boots with screws and leather straps. Putting on skates required the use of a tightening gimlet. According to the marvelous history of Saint John sporting life, *Saint John: A Sporting Tradition*, "Can I borrow your gimlet?" was the phrase heard most often on Sunday afternoon skating outings.

A letter to the editor in the 26 January 1863 edition of *The Morning News*, a Saint John newspaper, makes it clear just how common hurley, speed skating and "fancy" skating—not to mention plain skating—had become:

Sir,

[The skating craze] affects all classes and conditions: high, low, rich and poor are visited with it. It is contagious also, passing from house to house until the residents moved en masse, skates in hand, to Lily Lake. The hills leading to this beautiful resort are covered with people every fine afternoon. It is a pleasant walk from town, and one feels well repaid as you approach the lively scene [on the lake]. You begin to think the world is on skates...

Months later, Saint John's leading citizens began dreaming out loud about an ice palace that would provide a more refined skating setting. More than $15,000

The most fabulous ice surface in its day, the Victoria Skating Rink served as a temporary shelter for the homeless after the Great Fire of Saint John, in 1877.

was collected to build the Victoria Skating Rink, which, when it opened on 5 January 1865, was touted as the most fabulous ice palace in the world, drawing interest from across North America and eliciting a rapturous report in New York's *Scientific American*.

The architectural wonder was located on City Road at the site upon which the Colonial Inn now stands. More than 160 feet in diameter and 80 feet high, the arena boasted a roof—like a wide umbrella—supported by ribcage beams, and a rising spiral staircase that housed platforms for musicians and onlookers. A handsome showcase during the day, the rink became even more dazzling at night, as flickering gaslights suspended from the rafters made the roof come alive in a celestial blaze. Saint John's best families took to the ice during "fancy dress" carnival weekends, as characters out of Shakespeare and nursery rhymes flew past each other on the oval rink, while more mature folk enjoyed the view from the galleries and terraces.

As Romeo and Old Mother Hubbard danced, sheltered from the wind's torment at Saint John's "Vic," local skaters, travelling on New Brunswicker James A. Whelpley's just-patented Long Reach Speed Skates, took the excitement of the sport with them to distant cities. Skaters soon discovered that the razor-sharp 17-inch blades of the famous Long Reachers were ideal for speed skating and long-distance racing. By 1870, tireless "river men" took to the Saint John River after breakfast and, seven hours later, could arrive in time for supper 80 miles away in Fredericton.

And so, the winter sport of skating spread quickly throughout New Brunswick. Lily Lake remained the epicentre of the province's skating world. By the 1890s, and lasting into the 1930s, as many as 20,000 skaters would show up to watch big races on Saint John's favourite winter playground.

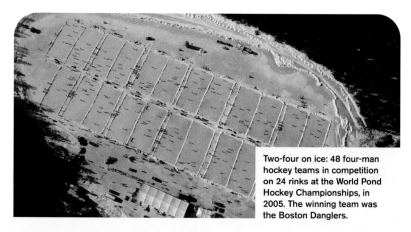

Two-four on ice: 48 four-man hockey teams in competition on 24 rinks at the World Pond Hockey Championships, in 2005. The winning team was the Boston Danglers.

On Olden Pond

Every February since 2002, the town of Plaster Rock, New Brunswick, has doubled in size when up to 100 four-person hockey teams arrive, sticks in hand, to compete in the World Pond Hockey Championship on the thick black ice of nearby Lake Roulston. Here is hockey as Lord Stanley intended—no neutral zone traps or fretting coaches. Pond hockey games don't even have any goalies! Teams come from across Canada and the U.S., ranging from college buddies in their 30s to house-league immortals pushing 60. The names of the competitors say it all: The Skateful Dead, 4-Play, Raggedy Ass River Boys. The tournament is played on a cluster of 24 rinks. Nets are two yards wide and one foot high. Games remind us of how hockey was played 100 years ago.

FREDERICTON

FOUNDED

Settled by the French in 1692, Fredericton came under British influence after the fall of Louisburg in 1758. It became a Loyalist landing upon the end of the American Revolution in 1783. The settlement was named Fredericstown in 1785, in honour of Prince Frederick, the second son of King George III.

NATIVE-BORN NHL PLAYERS

Danny Grant, Fred "Buster" Harvey, Fred McLean, Rollie McLenahan, Willie O'Ree

FAMOUS LOCAL TEAMS

Junior: Fredericton Bears, Fredericton Chevvies, Fredericton Falcons, Fredericton Hawks, Fredericton Jr. Capitals, Fredericton Jr. Red Wings, Fredericton Lions; **Senior-pro:** Fredericton Alpines, Fredericton Army, Fredericton Canadiens, Fredericton Capitals, Fredericton Express, Fredericton Merchants, Fredericton Red Wings, University of New Brunswick Varsity Reds

CURRENT POPULATION

54,068

Danny Grant: best shot (and sideburns!) in hockey in the '70s.

Grant Routs Sittler at Showdown

"Who is the shooting star of the NHL? The finest goalie? It's anyone's guess. Watch for the answer on 'Showdown,' a Hockey Night in Canada *special."*

With those words, along with footage of a strangely hooded mystery skater stealing in on a goalie, "Showdown" began. Hosted by Brian McFarlane, with chirping commentary from Howie Meeker, this *Hockey Night in Canada* (HNIC) intermission feature of the mid-1970s awarded $15,000 to forwards who could outpoint rivals in three events—first a target shoot; then, a rink-long dash around pylons; and finally, a nerve-racking penalty-shot competition. The series, shot in Maple Leaf Gardens before training camp in August, ran on HNIC throughout the season. Each week, another star would be extinguished.

In the 1975–76 season, the round-robin event attracted, among others, such National Hockey League greats as Phil Esposito, Bobby Clarke and Le Blond Demon, Guy Lafleur. Because he was only a fair skater, Danny Grant, a Fredericton native who had just come off a 50-goal year with the Detroit Red Wings, was considered a long shot. Nevertheless, there he was, up against Leafs hero Darryl Sittler, for the grand finale (which aired during the Philadelphia-Montreal Stanley Cup finals).

Little did Sittler and the rest of Canada know, however, that Grant had spent his entire childhood getting ready for this competition. As a kid growing up in Barker's Point (now part of Fredericton), he set up tires outside his house for target practice, firing literally thousands of pucks at Dunlop bull's eyes. Perhaps coyly alluding to this training, Grant—pulling on his Father of Confederation sideburns—told HNIC host Brian McFarlane before the final competition, "The shooting part of the game is going to have to do it for me." And indeed, the Fredericton underdog won the target shoot, smoking the top-left Styrofoam Frisbee to outpoint Sittler.

Number 27 for the Leafs, however, rebounded during the skating competition, throwing himself through the pylons like a downhill skier. As Grant laboured

AM I BLEU?

French is the first language of almost 35 percent of the population of New Brunswick, Canada's only officially bilingual province. The province's universities have won the University Cup, awarded annually to the best college hockey team in Canada, four times. The Université de Moncton's Aigles Bleus, coached by former National Hockey League coach Jean Perron, was the first university team east of Ontario to win the honour, triumphing in both 1980 and 1981. The team also won the trophy in 1995. In 1998, the University of New Brunswick in Fredericton took the cup.

Willie O'Ree with the Boston Bruins, 1960.

Colour-Blind Ambition

The Coloured Hockey League of the Maritimes was founded in 1895 in Halifax and quickly expanded to neighbouring provinces. Made up of sons and grandsons of runaway American slaves who had found safe harbour along Canada's eastern coast, "coloured" teams included the Halifax Eurekas, Africville Seasides, Dartmouth Jubilees, Truro Victorias and Charlottetown Rangers.

Black hockey was a fast-paced game that helped to modernize a sport largely regarded at the time as the pastime of Victorian gentlemen. Black goalies were the first to drop to the ice and to roam free of the goal. And coloured league forward Eddie Martin was reputedly winding up for slapshots in 1902. (Bernie "Boom Boom" Geoffrion would popularize the slapshot in the National Hockey League, but not until the 1950s.)

The Maritime league collapsed in 1920, as the practice of segregation began to crumble and black players were allowed into other leagues. Black stars slowly emerged, such as Fredericton's Manny McIntyre, who played alongside black Torontonians Herb and Ossie Carnegie on the Les Noirs line for the Quebec senior hockey Sherbrooke Saints in the 1948–49 season.

This trio of black Canadians was not invited to play, however, in the exclusively white National Hockey League. Fredericton's Willie O'Ree learned that black athletes such as himself were not supposed to play hockey, period, from an unlikely source. The athlete went with his championship youth baseball team to visit New York on a field trip in 1947. During a visit to Brooklyn's Ebbets Field, he met major league baseball's first black player, Jackie Robinson. O'Ree told Robinson that he intended to play professional hockey.

"There aren't any black hockey players," Robinson told him.

O'Ree would have to overcome an obstacle even greater than racial prejudice, though, to make it to the NHL. A deflected puck deadened his right eye in the juniors. "You'll never be able to play hockey again," a doctor told him.

O'Ree disagreed. No doctor could see inside him. He had been playing hockey since his father hosed the family's Fredericton backyard to make a rink when O'Ree was three. Changing his playing position from left wing to right wing so that he could accept passes with his good eye, the skater turned pro with Jean Beliveau's old minor league team, the Quebec Aces, in 1957.

The following year, O'Ree became the first black person to play in the NHL, suiting up with the Boston Bruins in a game at the Montreal Forum. After being sent down, O'Ree returned to Boston in 1960, scoring his first goal in the NHL against Canadiens goaltender Charlie Hodge on New Year's Eve. "I can't tell you what I had for breakfast, but I can remember that goal like it was yesterday," O'Ree told reporters. "I dove into the net after that puck."

O'Ree would go on to play hockey for 21 more seasons, almost all of them in the minors, where he would win a number of scoring championships. He would also run into Jackie Robinson years later at a civil rights banquet. Robinson remembered him with a smile. "You ever make it in hockey?" he asked. O'Ree's response made both men very happy.

through the same obstacle course, commentator Meeker sighed, "Danny's taking the long way home."

With Sittler enjoying a one-goal lead and Grant down to his final penalty shot, the Leafs' offensive star seemed poised to win the shootout. "C'mon Danny," Meeker exhorted as Grant coasted in on goalie Rogie Vachon. Until then, everyone had tried to beat the dancing acrobat by shooting, much to Meeker's surprise. As the announcer pointed out, the diminutive Los Angeles Kings goalie was coming out so far, the net was no more than a rumour behind him. This time in, however, Grant froze Vachon with a forehead shiver, then tucked a neat backhand past the goalie's spreading pad. "We're going to overtime," Howie cackled, again, showing his Maritime sympathies (see page 23).

 From that point on, both luck and Danny Grant seemed to be against Sittler. His next time in on Vachon, the Leafs forward aimed a shot between the goalie's legs only to have the puck carom off the inside of the post. Darryl poked in the rebound, but referee Art Skov waved off the goal. The next visit, Sittler fired a bullet to the top corner, which Vachon deflected high with his wrist.

Now it was Grant's turn. Would he try to go high, glove side, taking advantage of Vachon's throbbing hand? The little goalie seemed to think so, pulling far out of his crease ever so slightly to the left, inviting Grant to attack his stick side. Danny faked a shot—going for an instant to his backhand, pulling Vachon with him—and then dipped back to the collapsed goalie's stick side, bulging the net with a snap shot.

"Fifteen thousand dollars'll buy a lot of lobster!" Meeker cheered, applauding Grant's brilliant manoeuvre.

"Danny's hands are so quick," HNIC's McFarlane remarked, analyzing the goal, "that he could steal cheese from a mouse trap."

A member of the Stanley Cup-winning Montreal Canadiens in 1968 and NHL rookie-of-the-year with the Minnesota North Stars the following season, the "Showdown" champion (and Detroit Red Wings star) would return to Maritime rinks after injuries shortened his playing career. He coached the Fredericton Capitals to the New Brunswick intermediate title in 1980–81 and later took the Fredericton Red Wings to the 1988–89 Atlantic midget championship. He also coached the University of New Brunswick Varsity Reds in the 1990s. When the school began to require that all coaches be university-trained teachers, Grant volunteered to be an assistant coach—helping to take the team to the CIAU finals in 1997.

Not many former NHL stars would be content to serve as an assistant coach for a university team, but Grant has always been true to his Maritime roots. After his "Showdown" moment of glory, he shrugged off the congratulations of the HNIC announcers with the comment, "Ah, that's an old move I brought with me from a rink in the Maritimes. I was saving it for a while."

Black Kat Crosses New Brunswick's Path

Born in Miramichi, New Brunswick, Greg Malone moved to Fredericton for school and led the Fredericton High School Black Kats to the provincial varsity hockey championship in 1973. That season, he counted 35 goals and 41 assists in 23 games. He later went on to average 20 goals a season in an 11-year National Hockey League career with the Pittsburgh Penguins, Hartford Whalers and Quebec Nordiques. His son, Ryan Malone, followed in the path of his father's skates, playing with the Pittsburgh Penguins.

MONCTON

FOUNDED
Acadians arrived in the area in the early 1600s. British soldier Lt. Col. Robert Monckton, after whom Moncton was named, led the capture of nearby Fort Beauséjour in 1755. Moncton was incorporated as a town in 1855.

NATIVE-BORN NHL PLAYERS
Ron Anderson, Charlie "Boo Boo" Bourgeois, Rick Bownass, George Carroll, Gordie Drillon, Scott Fraser, Dick Gamble, Gary Geldart, Rollie "the Goalie" Melanson

FAMOUS LOCAL TEAMS
Junior: Moncton Alpines, Moncton Athletics, Moncton Beavers, Moncton Bruins, Moncton Flyers, Moncton Hawks, Moncton Wheelers, Moncton Wildcats; **Senior-pro:** Moncton Alpines, Moncton Athletics, Moncton Bears, Moncton Flyers, Moncton Golden Flames, Moncton Hawks, Moncton Maroons, Moncton RCAF, Moncton Victorias, New Brunswick Hawks

CURRENT POPULATION
90,359

WINTER CARROLLING

"Carroll's got the puck. Over to Carroll. Back to Carroll, who slides it to Carroll. There's a line change and Carroll, Carroll and Carroll hop over the boards."

That's how a broadcaster might have described the play-by-play in an extraordinary 1923 exhibition match between the Moncton Victorias, finalists in the Maritime Semi-Pro Championships, and the Carroll Brothers Hockey Team. The eight sons of Mr. and Mrs. Frederick Carroll—Harold, Blair, Jack, Cecil, George, Fred, Ken and Tom—won the series three-zip (8–4, 6–2, 2–1).

The Carrolls were offered National Hockey League contracts with Boston, New York and major Canadian centres, but except for George, who played for the Montreal Maroons and the Boston Bruins, the brothers preferred life in sunny Sunny Brae, a suburb of Moncton. An arena was named in their honour there. While the rink is no longer in operation, the family name has been transferred to one of four new rinks built as part of Moncton's new hockey complex, the Tim Hortons 4 Ice Centre.

Easy as Tying Your Laces

A trusting child once sent a letter to Leafs star Gordie Drillon. He glued a newspaper photo of Drillon onto an envelope—no name or address—and assumed the letter would find its way to his hero.

It did—every postal worker from Moncton to Toronto knew Gordie's Maple Leaf Gardens home.

Hockey Night in Canada broadcaster Foster Hewitt made Moncton-born Drillon famous in the hard, late days of the Great Depression. Drillon did his part, too, leading the National Hockey League in scoring in 1937–38. But it was the way he scored that captured Foster's (and so, the public's) fancy. Hewitt liked to plot out goals as a singer would map a song, carefully building to a crescendo. But Gordie never gave him the chance. His goals seemed to come out of nowhere, giving Hewitt heart palpitations. As a consequence, radio listeners were jolted off their sofas by Drillon's artistry.

Playing on the rink his dad created at the family's McAllen Lane home in Moncton, and then, later, setting records with the local junior team, the Moncton Athletics (1930–31), Gordie Drillon wasn't like most other budding stars. His style was not to navigate an entire team before blasting one home, but rather to steal into an unoccupied patch of ice anywhere near the net and redirect a pass into the bottom corner of the cage before anyone quite realized what had happened. The player's seemingly effortless style didn't go over well in Maple Leaf Gardens, where only gold-seat patrons could appreciate his craft. But on the radio, Foster Hewitt's astonished cry—"Apps over the line... *Drillon scores!*"—made Gordie's name synonymous with excitement.

It helped that Hewitt liked Gordie. "Thing was, Foster had an office in the Gardens. He ate with us, lived with us..." the player later told reporter Allan Abel. Journalist Wes McKnight liked Drillon, too: Drillon frequently guested on McKnight's widely syndicated "BeeHive" sports radio show. (Fifteen dollars a visit and all the corn syrup you could carry home.)

Then again, everybody outside Toronto liked hockey's first famous Drillon, a big (6'2"), gracious Maritimer who loved to play and talk hockey. He palled around with boxing legend Jack Dempsey in New York and with tavern regulars in Montreal. When the Leafs travelled out west for an exhibition series, his was the friendly hand everyone wanted to shake.

In Toronto, however, Gordie's popularity was not a given. Leafs owner Conn Smythe didn't appreciate the forward's relaxed manner on the ice. And everybody in Toronto knew the owner's sentiments, probably because Smythe shouted his disapproval from a steel bunker atop Maple Leaf Gardens. Eventually, the Gardens crowd joined in.

The "real" Dick Gamble, 1951.

The pride of Moncton, Gordie Drillon was the last Toronto Maple Leaf to win an NHL scoring championship (1937–38).

The Tin Man

No hockey player appeared in more games, worked longer shifts or endured more childish arguments than Dick "Grumps" Gamble. After helping the junior 1945 Moncton Bruins win the Maritime junior championship, Moncton-born Gamble became a 23-goal scorer for the National Hockey League's Montreal Canadiens in 1951–52, and counted a dozen 20-goal seasons in the American Hockey League with Buffalo and Rochester. A solid career, for sure, but that was only his night job.

In the daytime, Gamble was the ubiquitous tin man of Pro Hockey, the first table hockey game to employ miniature NHL facsimiles. Gamble was the Montreal Canadiens—that's right, the whole team. His image appeared on every tin defenceman and forward, even on the figure of the goalie. Pro Hockey debuted at a Montreal toy fair in 1954 and it was immensely popular. Gamble never missed a shift for decades.

Good-natured Drillon didn't complain. He never did. Years earlier, when reporters continually misspelled his name, he simply had it changed from Drillen to Drillon.

Regardless of the player's non-confrontational attitude, Drillon's problems with Smythe worsened during the 1942 playoffs. The Leafs winger had a good first series, contributing five points in six games. But he stalled in the finals against Detroit. The Leafs went down three games before Smythe ordered Drillon benched in favour of Don Metz, who sparked the Leafs' historic Cup-winning comeback. After that, Smythe sold the last Leaf to win the scoring championship to Montreal for $30,000.

True to character, Drillon did not let the trade get him down. In his first season with the Canadiens (1942–43), the pride of Moncton counted a career-high 28 goals. The following year brought greater glory when, at the peak of his career, Gordie Drillon enlisted in the war. Always a fan favourite, he was now a folk hero, too.

After his time in the service, Drillon scouted and coached intermittently, returning for one last hurrah with the 1949–50 senior Saint John Beavers, tapping in 48 goals in 49 games—easy as tying your laces. As a scout, he lobbied hard for Maritimers, getting Moncton's Dick Gamble and Prince Edward Island's Errol Thompson NHL jobs. Nova Scotia-born broadcaster Danny Gallivan, a Drillon admirer, returned the favour, pulling a few skate laces to get Drillon into the NHL Hall of Fame in 1975.

In retirement, Drillon lived quietly in Moncton, returning to Toronto for Hall of Fame ceremonies. Before going home again afterward, he would drop by Montreal to visit former Canadiens teammate Toe Blake at his tavern.

At Blake's bar, the hockey "war stories" flew faster than the beer. Gordie particularly enjoyed recounting Conn Smythe tales—like the time the bald skinflint "Conned" Drillon with a signing bonus, handing over bundle after bundle of money, bound in rubber bands. Smythe's package contained a thousand bills—all of them ones. Still Drillon was happy. It was hard to offend Depression-era NHLers. "I'd never seen so much money in all my life," he remembered to Allan Abel. "I walked to the bank looking over my shoulder. I was sure 15 guys were after me."

Drillon never got too carried away, though, with being a folk hero. In the 1940s, he won an award for being the most popular player in the NHL. He kept the big trophy on his Moncton back porch, next to his tools.

Hawks Capture Calder

Memories of the great Moncton Hawks senior team were revived in 1978 when a new pro team, called the New Brunswick Hawks, began play in the American Hockey League. Memorable moments from the team's first year include coach Ed Johnston and Pat Quinn (former skipper for the Maine Mariners) getting into a coat-ripping Laurel and Hardy-style brawl, and the boisterous play of defenceman-forward-showman Mel Hewitt. (The Saskatoon native was a frequent visitor to the penalty box and would eventually adopt a number that made it appear he was behind bars—111.) Three and a half years later, the Hawks were on top of the AHL world, defeating the Nova Scotia Voyageurs to win the 1982 Calder Cup.

Sure sign of winner: The Université de Moncton Aigles Bleus, another celebrated Moncton team, has won the C.I.A.U. championship four times. Here they celebrate their 1982 win.

SAINT JOHN

FOUNDED

Saint John was discovered by Samuel de Champlain on St. Jean Baptiste Day in 1604. The town was seized by the British in 1758 and destroyed in the American Revolution, later to be rebuilt by United Empire Loyalists. In 1785, Saint John became Canada's first incorporated city.

NATIVE-BORN NHL PLAYERS

Hilliard Graves, Paul Higgins, Bob Joyce, Jackie Keating, Andrew McKim, Neil Nicholson, Yvon Vautour

FAMOUS LOCAL TEAMS

Junior: Saint John Beavers, Saint John Schooners, Saint John Sea Dogs, Saint John St. Petes; **Senior-pro:** Saint John Beavers, Saint John Flames, Saint John Fusiliers, Saint John Oilers, Saint John Pontiacs, Saint John Schooners, Saint John St. Peters, Saint John Victorias, Saint John Vitos

CURRENT POPULATION

90,762

Harbouring a Grudge

Sticks and stones break bones in Cape Breton hockey rivalries, but in late 19th-century contests between Saint John, New Brunswick, and Halifax, Nova Scotia, names were what really hurt.

Indoor hockey, as opposed to pond free-for-alls, was a gentleman's pursuit at the time. Ice polo, played with a mallet and ball, had been the big sport in New Brunswick in the 1880s, and the snooty patrician names chosen by clubs playing out of the Lansdowne Rink, located on Charlotte Street, betrayed city sportsmen's delusions of aristocratic grandeur—Carleton, Wellington, Bluenose.

When the Saint John Hockey League—importing a rulebook from Montreal—was formed in 1894, the elitism that had characterized ice polo continued. For instance, in 1894, a local ice polo/hockey club hesitated to accept a challenge from a team employing a working-class player, George Logue, a deckhand on a river steamer. Players feared the loss of social standing would prevent them from being accepted by the bank and insurance professionals who filled the ranks of other clubs.

While local matches excited significant interest, only when teams began accepting outside challenges in 1895—putting the New Brunswick port city's pride on the line—did hockey surpass ice polo as a spectator sport.

Teams from Halifax, another port city, were natural rivals. And Saint John's first hockey stars, Frank and Andy Tuft of the Saint John All Stars, became civic heroes when the team downed an All-Halifax team in an 1896 challenge match. (Although it could be argued that weather as much as the Tuft brothers did in the Halifax team that year, as the Nova Scotia club shipped in from Digby during a storm, showing up for play on legs still wobbly from rough seas.)

Rubbing its victory in with sea salt, Saint John began calling its all-star team the C.W.P.s—Canada's Winter Port hockey team. A name that was sure to rile natives of Halifax.

Saint John newspapers argued that the matter wasn't debatable. New Brunswick's harbour was free from ice year round, and Halifax's wasn't. Not true, Haligonians insisted. The matter was settled in Saint John's favour by the C.W.P.s, although not in a manner you might expect.

Saint John harbour scene, with steamships at berth.

SEAL OF APPROVAL

The Saint John Sea Dogs entered the Quebec Major Junior Hockey League in the fall of 2005. Sea Dog is a common local term for harbour seals, and the club's logo features a seal emerging from the water. The name was chosen in a city-wide name-the-team contest. Defenceman Alex Grant, from Antigonish, Nova Scotia, was the first Sea Dog chosen in the 2005 amateur draft.

While playing in Halifax one frigid February, Saint John team members looked outside and saw a sheet of ice stretching from the harbour out to Georges Island. Thinking fast, the players hired a photographer to take pictures of men walking atop the frozen water—none of them Jesus. The photos were then given prominent display, accompanied by mocking headlines, in Saint John newspapers.

These chilly exchanges formed the backdrop for the next big series between the Maritime rivals, held in Halifax in 1898. The C.W.P.s hit the ice to calls of "fog eaters!" and worse. The Saint John players were evidently rattled by their reception as the all-star team lost consecutive games to the Halifax Crescents, All-Halifax and Halifax Wanderers.

Halifax newspapers serenaded the Saint John team on the boat back home with a specially arranged variation of the then-popular tune "Sweet Bye and Bye":

> The scene was changed. 'Twas in the rink.
> The play was strong and quick.
> A well-fought game; yet "Crescents" won,
> The "Ports" felt kind of sick.
> "Oh, never mind, we'll win the next,"
> St. John's was heard to say.
> But, sad to tell, "All Halifax"
> Won by their brilliant play...

In March 1898, 1,500 Saint John fans crammed into Singer Rink for a two-game rematch between the C.W.P. team and the Halifax Crescents. Neither team had scored late into the first game, although the Crescents held an advantage in play, with several Halifax players enjoying close-in chances. Outmanoeuvring C.W.P. goalie Frank "Little" Tuft, however, was like trying to elude your own image in a mirror.

Saint John ultimately scored the breakthrough goal when, with seconds remaining, forward W.S. Dunbrack solved the Crescents goalie, Bishop. With the winning goal, the New Brunswick rink erupted with shouts of glad relief.

The Stompin' Game

From broadcasters Danny Gallivan to Howie Meeker to Bob Cole, no region has contributed more to the sound of hockey than Atlantic Canada. So it comes as no surprise that a Maritimer supplied our national hockey anthem.

In Saint John, 1936, Charles Thomas "Stompin' Tom" Connors was born in the dead of winter to an unwed teenager. He grew up in orphanages, foster homes and on the high seas (working illegally as an underage seaman). The musician began writing songs at age 11 but did not start singing them until he was a nickel short of a 40-cent beer in Timmins, Ontario, in 1964.

Everyone who has ever been in a Canadian arena with a sound system knows the first-, second-, and third-period verses to Tom's "The Hockey Game" ("the best game you can name"). Although first released in 1972, the song did not become a hockey anthem until the National Hockey League's Ottawa Senators began playing the spirited tune in 1993 during breaks in games.

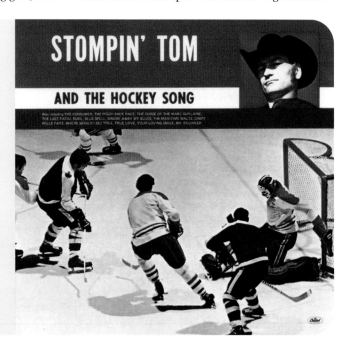

Coach Jackie Keating, with his 1946 Maritime Senior Champion Saint John Beavers.

Dance with the Girl That Brung Ya

John "Jackie" Keating was born in 1908, to a working-class family, in what was once Newcastle, New Brunswick, but is now officially part of the city of Miramichi. "Times were tough," he once said. "There was one pair of skates in our family."

Before long, however, it seemed as if there was only one real pair of skates in all of Miramichi. Though only 136 pounds, Keating was the region's best "hockeyist." Playing for the senior Saint John Fusiliers, he led the Maritimes in both scoring and penalty minutes in 1926–27. (He also won a senior baseball batting crown at that time, lining drives between infielders to compile a .389 average.)

Jackie took the Fusiliers and then the Saint John Beavers to the Allan Cup senior national championships in 1926 and 1927, before eventually accepting a 1931 offer from the National Hockey League's New York Americans. In contract negotiations with the team's general manager, Eddie Gerard, Keating showed characteristic grit, holding out until he got twice the club's original $2,500 offer.

After two seasons in the NHL (1931–33), Keating played in a variety of American minor league hockey cities. After World War II, he returned to New Brunswick, where he achieved lasting glory as coach of the senior Saint John Beavers. Although the Beavers were just moderately successful in the 1945–46 regular season, the club surprised everyone in the senior provincial playoffs, knocking off the league-leading Moncton Maroons.

After this victory, the Beavers moved on to the Maritime senior championship, facing the powerhouse Halifax Navy, the Nova Scotia champions. Halifax jumped to a 2–1 game lead, with the final matches to be played in Nova Scotia. Several Beavers were injured, and there was civic pressure for coach Keating to call upon the runner-up Maroons for player help.

Keating chose, instead, to "dance with the girl that brung ya." The Beavers deserved the chance to decide their own fate, he decreed.

The coach's decision was met with some derision. At one point, an airily confident naval officer moved through the Halifax crowd, $20 in hand, drawing guffaws by offering up a bet to all takers—20:1 odds. A Beaver fan obliged, perhaps only to shut the gambler up.

The officer would lose $400 as Keating's Beavers stunned the Navy in a dramatic two-game sweep, with "Smiling Bill" Giggey turning in a heroic goaltending display. More than 7,000 fans greeted the Saint John players when they returned in a freshly painted victory bus. Standing at the front of the line, his pants hitched high, was Jackie Keating—ready to go again.

The second game had more of a carnival atmosphere as the emboldened Saint John team built on an early lead. Andy "Big" Tuft scored two for the C.W.P.s, and his brother Frank was, again, a wall in net. As the 5–0 shellacking rolled to an easy conclusion, the jubilant crowd sang out a chant that was only too familiar to opponents during the team's many civic challenge match victories:

Big Tuffy, Little Tuffy, Old Tuffy's son
Big Tuffy shot a goal—Saint Johns won.

The once "gentlemanly" Saint John practitioners of the sport of hockey had evidently learned to drop their gloves.

QUE

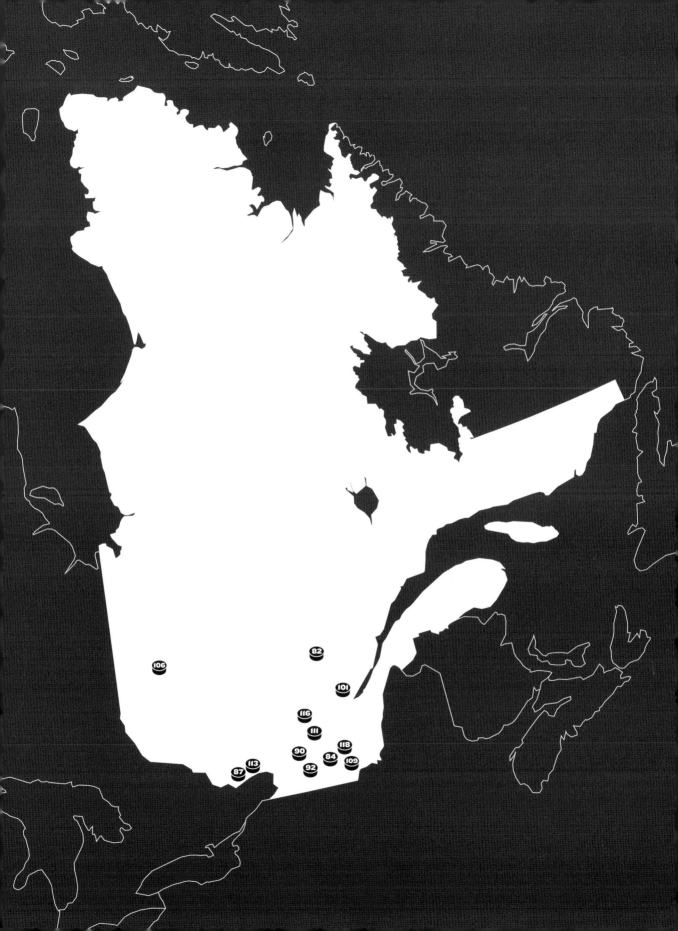

Opening Spread: Le Block Quebecois—goalie Patrick Roy with the Montreal Canadiens.

It has often been written of Georges Vezina (1887-1926) that he sired 24 children. But in another way, the goalie, whose cool and calm demeanor earned him the nickname the Chicoutimi Cucumber, has over 120 descendants.

By 2005, 734 Quebecers had played in the National Hockey League. Of those players, 121—or over 16 percent—tended goal. No other province comes close to matching this number. Newfoundland, Prince Edward Island, New Brunswick, Nova Scotia, Manitoba, Saskatchewan, Manitoba, Alberta and British Columbia have, combined, produced 125 NHL goalies.

Recently Quebec has been even more prolific in the netminding department. Since 1955, the province has contributed 26 names to the Vezina Trophy, awarded to the NHL's best goalie, compared to runner-up Ontario (14 names). And although the NHL now recruits goalkeepers from around the world, 20 percent of the 82 goalies to appear in the 2002–03 season were from Quebec.

Why has Quebec given birth to so many talented netminders? It would be fun to suggest that the province's (and the Montreal Canadiens') historic status as a besieged French minority within Confederation—and within the NHL—led to a royal succession of historic defenders. And there is some truth to this. Georges Vezina, Jacques Plante and in particular Patrick Roy (le Roi) were immensely stylish, stirring goalies—saviours in every sense.

But it is perhaps more accurate to say that Quebec hockey is a tale of glory. The Flying Frenchmen have always been forwards with florid, inspirational nicknames—The Rocket, Le Gros Bill, Boom Boom, The Flower, Super Mario. Even Quebec junior hockey is a goal-scoring paradise, attracting virtuoso marksmen from as far away as Nova Scotia (Sidney Crosby) and Missouri (Pat LaFontaine).

Quebec's junior goalies, therefore, receive rigorous apprenticeships. Those who succeed become heroes—idols who uphold a historic legacy. Jacques Plante's sister lived next to Bernie Parent's family in Montreal, and whenever Vezina winner Jacques visited his sibling, future Vezina winner Bernie would attach himself to the off-duty goaltender in hopes of learning more about his chosen profession.

Patrick Roy also worshipped a Quebec goaltending master. While growing up, Roy so admired Quebec Nordiques goalie Daniel Bouchard that he slept with a stick the Nordiques star had given him. Roy would, in turn, become a dream

Montreal-born Lorne "Gump" Worsley. The nickname came from a comic book character of the same name.

Shawinigan Falls' Jacques "Jake the Snake" Plante, the inventor of modern goaltending, demonstrates the need for goalie masks.

Stop in the Name of Love

The following Quebecers have won their home province everlasting goaltending glory. Not all these goalies are French Canadians. In their time, English Quebecers "Paddy" Moran, Gump Worsley, Eddie Johnston and Gerry McNeil would also carve their names on the Stanley Cup with pride:

Jean-Sebastien Aubin	Claude Cyr	Michel "Bunny" Laroque	Michel Plasse
Marco Baron	Jean-Francois Damphousse	Jean-Louis Levasseur	Jason Pomminville
Stephane Beauregard	Denis DeJordy	Gord Laxton	Felix Potvin
Yves Belanger	Marc Denis	Pascal Leclaire	Claude Pronovost
Michel Belhumeur	Philippe DeRouville	Claude Legris	Andre Racicot
J.C. Bergeron	Conrad Dion	Reggie Lemelin	Alain Raymond
Daniel Berthiaume	Michel Dion	Mario Lessard	Herbert Rheaume
Paul Bibeau	Tom Draper	Percy "Peerless Percy" LeSueur	Manon Rheaume [female]
Marc-Andre Binette	Michel Duman	Roberto Luongo	Vincent Riendeau
Martin Biron	Claude Evans	Gordon McRae	Fern Rivard
Dan Blackburn	Eric Fichaud	Gerard "Gerry" McNeil	Roberto Romano
Gilles Boisvert	Stephane Fiset	Gilles Meloche	Dominic Roussel
Daniel Bouchard	Marc-Andre Fleury	Jean Marois	Patrick Roy
Martin Brochu	George Gardner	Corrado Micalef	Danny Sabourin
Martin Brodeur	Mathieu Garon	Paddy Moran	Bob Sauve
Richard "King Richard" Brodeur	Gilles Gilbert	Olivier Michaud	Richard Sevigny
Frank Brophy	Jean-Sebastien Giguere	Hal Murphy	Bob Sneddon
Mario Brunetta	Andre Gill	Phil Myre	Christian Soucy
Jacques Caron	Mario "Goose" Gosselin	Jean-Guy Morissette	Sam St. Laurent
Sebastien Caron	Gilles Gratton	Mike O'Neill	Kim St. Pierre [female]
Frederic Cassivi	Pierre Hamel	Maxime Ouellet	Jocelyn Thibault
Frederic Chabot	Denis Herron	Ted Ouimet	Jose Theodore
Lorne "Sad Eyes" Chabot	Charlie Hodge	Paul Pageau	Vincent Tremblay
Bob Champoux	Bob Holland	Marcel Paille	Rogatien "Rogie" Vachon
Sebastien Charpentier	Jim Hrivnak	Bernie Parent	Georges Vezina
Mathieu Chouinard	Joseph Ironstone	Rich Parent	Gilles Villemure
Dan Cloutier	Eddie Johnston	Lester "The Silver Fox" Patrick	Jimmy Waite
Jacques Cloutier	Patrick Labrecque	Marcel Pelletier	Derek Wilkinson
Jim Corsi	Jean-Francois Labbe	Steve Penney	Bernie Wolfe
Maurice Courteau	Charline Labonte [female]	Robert Perreault	Lorne "Gump" Worsley
Marcel Cousineau	Patrick Lalime	Jacques "Jake the Snake" Plante	Matthew Yeats

hero and inspire generations of Quebec hockey players. "When Patrick Roy came up to the Montreal Canadiens, I was nine years old," Montreal native and Columbus Blue Jackets netminder Marc Denis once recalled. "I loved the Montreal Canadiens and Patrick Roy won the Stanley Cup for them all by himself as a young rookie [in 1986]. Every kid in Montreal, forget if he was a goalie, he wanted to be Patrick."

Roy's strong positional play and imposing style—pads hugging the ice to seal the lower net, chest and shoulders puffed out like a cobra—was then formalized into the "Quebec goaltending style," as taught by the Allaire brothers, Francois and Benoit, in their suddenly world-famous Montreal goaltending academy. "It creates lots of pride in the province that there are so many goaltenders," Francois Allaire commented in 2003. "I think there are 11 or 12 starting goalies from a league of 30 teams that come from Quebec, so it is the news every week. One day, it is Brodeur did this, and the next it is Roy broke this record. Then it's Theodore this and Denis that. The kids [in Quebec] are reading about it every day. I always say to my [students], 'We're better technically and we have our own style of goaltending and it's well known. We don't play like Europeans or Americans.' And the players like that and they just want to get better."

By the 1990s, Quebec's best hockey players, it seems, had gravitated entirely to scoring or stopping goals—the glamour positions. Few mastered defence. Who wanted to be co-pilot on a plane?

CHICOUTIMI

FOUNDED

The Jesuits established a mission here in 1782. The name Chicoutimi is derived from the Montagnais First Nation phrase meaning "as far as it is deep," a reference to the Saguenay River. The town of Chicoutimi was established in 1845 and became known for its pulp-and-paper mills in the 20th century.

NATIVE-BORN NHL PLAYERS

Michel Bergeron, Luc Dufour, Germain Gagnon, Johnny "Black Cat" Gagnon, Leo Gaudreault, Fern Gauthier, Alain Langlais, John Smrke, Georges Vezina

FAMOUS LOCAL TEAMS

Junior: Chicoutimi Sagueneens, Chicoutimi-Granby; **Senior-pro:** Chicoutimi Bluets, Chicoutimi Carabins, Chicoutimi Comets, Chicoutimi Sagueneens, Chicoutimi Volants

CURRENT POPULATION

60,000

Georges "The Chicoutimi Cucumber" Vezina didn't learn to skate until he was 18. The goalie learned to play in his boots.

One Cucumber, Two Cats

Chicoutimi is still served by sisters from 10 Catholic orders, though their numbers are dwindling. Back when Georges Vezina made the city famous, however, Chicoutimi was the first bead in the Quebec Catholic rosary.

Born in 1887, Vezina was a model citizen: diligent, religious and obviously civic-minded. After all, he volunteered to patrol nets for the city's senior hockey team, the Sagueneens, when they faced the Montreal Canadiens during the pro team's exhibition tour of the province in 1910. The imperturbable Vezina made a better impression on the Habs than the Canadiens did on Chicoutimi locals that night, shutting down the visiting pros with a remarkable economy of motion.

Vezina was the Canadiens goalie the following season and never missed a game in 15 years (367 games in a row), leading the team to Stanley Cups in 1916 and 1924. His style was unique. Perhaps because he didn't learn to skate until he was 18, the goalie relied on his stick, a weapon he learned to wield with the skill of a Jedi warrior. And he never fell to the ice. Goalies weren't allowed to do so in those days, so he simply didn't—ever.

"I...remember him as the coolest man I ever saw, absolutely imperturbable," forward Frank Boucher remembered. "He simply played all his shots in a standing position. Vezina was a pale narrow-featured fellow, almost frail looking, yet remarkably good with his stick. He'd pick off more shots with it than he did with his glove."

After deflecting an avalanche of rubber (78 of 79 shots) during one championship game against Ottawa, reporters and fans began calling Vezina the Chicoutimi Cucumber, although his French nickname, *l'Habitant silencieux* (the silent habitant,) was maybe a better fit.

Vezina was deeply religious. He and his wife, Marie, had 24 children, 20 of whom died shortly after birth. He toiled through personal troubles and work-related injuries without comment. Even when he arrived at the Canadiens camp in the fall of 1925 looking wan and a great deal underweight, he said nothing. In the Canadiens' first regular season game that year, he waved away every shot the Pittsburgh Pirates directed his way during the first 20 minutes but left the ice

Black Cat Crosses Forum

A lightning-fast elf with a Brylcreemed skullcap of black hair, Johnny "Black Cat" Gagnon played right wing on the pinball-quick Joliat-Morenz-Gagnon line that lifted Montreal's spirits during the Depression. His route to the National Hockey League wasn't easy. Papa Gagnon thought that hockey was a waste of time and used his son's sticks for kindling. So Johnny Gagnon would scour local rinks for parts of broken sticks, which he cobbled together as best he could.

After playing a season for the Chicoutimi Bluets, the teenager lit off for Trois-Rivières, then for Quebec City. He was playing for the Quebec City Sons of Ireland when he tried out for the Montreal Canadiens. After spending a season between Quebec City and Providence, he was promoted to the big club, which was in search of a skater who might keep up with forwards Howie Morenz and Aurel Joliat. Gagnon was an immediate sensation, earning the nickname The Black Cat of Chicoutimi for his darting manner and the gleaming eight-ball shine of his black hair.

His native city and disapproving father were always with him, though. Johnny was playing in the Cup finals in 1930 when he received word in Chicago that his father had died. Gagnon took a series of trains home for the funeral, then returned to the Forum, where he played his best hockey ever. The Black Cat scored four goals in three games, including the Cup-winner, to give the Canadiens their fourth championship.

at the end of the first period inexplicably bleeding from the mouth. Vezina insisted on returning after the first intermission, but he soon collapsed, falling to the ice.

Vezina had played his last hockey game. Doctors diagnosed him as having an advanced case of tuberculosis. He was ordered home to recuperate and returned to his place in the Laurentians outside Chicoutimi. Vezina died there four months later at the age of 39.

How much the world had changed since Vezina's start in professional hockey became apparent with two subsequent Chicoutimi natives to make it big in hockey. Diminutive Johnny "Black Cat" Gagnon introduced himself to Canadiens general manager, Leo Dandurand, at Vezina's funeral and, immediately, went into a sales pitch, suggesting that he could help the Canadiens.

"How big are you?" Dandurand asked the skinny youngster.

"One hundred fifty," Gagnon responded quickly.

Dandurand was skeptical but issued the player an invitation to attend the team's training camp. Sure enough, Gagnon weighed in at 150. At least five of those pounds, however, were rocks that Johnny had distributed evenly in his pockets. Gagnon went on to have a splendid National Hockey League career.

The next Chicoutimi native to make his mark in hockey didn't have the talent to measure up to Vezina or Gagnon, but Michel Bergeron had more brass than a marching band. After his long, mostly minor league career was over, le Petit Tigre became the hero-coach of the Quebec Nordiques in the 1980s, then later an unfailingly provocative hockey analyst on *La Soirée du hockey*, the French-language version of *Hockey Night in Canada*.

During his youth, Bergeron demonstrated the same fearlessness that would later make him a successful coach and commentator. In 1967, as a teenager, he was a catcher in Havana, Cuba, with the touring Canadian national baseball team. The country's leader, Fidel Castro, suited up for Cuba one particular day. And when the Cuban dictator strayed a little off third base, Bergeron jumped to his feet and faked a snap throw to third. El Presidente dove back to the bag, eating a little dirt on the way. Then he stood up and glared at Bergeron, who glared right back. To hell with Castro: Le Petit Tigre wanted to win!

Chicoutimi, c. 1900.

The best NHL hockey player never to win the Stanley Cup: Marcel Dionne.

DRUMMONDVILLE

FOUNDED

Named after Sir George Drummond, the first Canadian-born Governor of Canada, Drummondville was founded in 1815. At first, a British military post, Drummondville would grow into a city following the construction of electric power dams on the François River and the Hemming Rapids in the early 1900s. Drummondville is located 68 miles east of Montreal.

NATIVE-BORN NHL PLAYERS

Serge Boisvert, Sebastien Charpentier, Yvan Cournoyer, Gilbert Dionne, Marcel Dionne, Ray Fortin, Alan Haworth, Gord Haworth, Claude Houde, Yvon Lambert, Eric Messier, Lester Patrick, Marcel Pelletier, Leo Thiffault

FAMOUS LOCAL TEAMS

Junior: Drummondville Diggers, Drummondville Olympique, Drummondville Rangers, Drummondville Voltigeurs; **Senior-pro:** Drummondville Eagles, Drummondville Intrepids, Drummondville Maroons, Drummondville Rockets

CURRENT POPULATION

46,599

Hey, Jack Pot

The Drummondville Voltigeurs entered the Quebec Major Junior Hockey League in 1982. The team is named after the city's famous infantry brigade, the Voltigeurs Canadiens, who helped turn back a much larger American force headed to capture Montreal in the 1813 Battle of Châteauguay. This historic victory explains the hockey team's logo, an infantry-man wielding a hockey stick. Voltigeurs hockey infantrymen have included National Hockey Leaguers Steve Duchesne and Daniel Briere.

In 1991, the Voltigeurs, with Ian Laperriere and Patrice Brisebois on defence, lost to the Spokane Chiefs in the Memorial Cup finals, despite having a much better fight song:

The Voltigeurs' JACK POT
(translation from French)

You work hard, sweat on
your brow
You live the rhythm of
your passions
On the long road to victory
You use your elbows,
you win the war
(Chorus)
Hey, Jack Pot
Effort is rewarded
To those who give everything
And fight until the very end
Tattooed on the heart —
Voltigeurs

The Homecoming

Maybe Marcel Dionne started feeling the pressure of great expectations when he first looked up to see his father, a former lumberjack. Gilbert Dionne was 6'1", 230 pounds, while Marcel Dionne was among the smallest kids at St-Zephirin, a two-rink elementary school across the street from his house in Drummondville.

Marcel would spend his early years on those rinks, arriving first thing in the morning, still chewing his breakfast, eager to shovel away the night's snow. He skated all day and would even fall asleep at night playing his favourite sport. He and his brother Renald had a hockey game they'd play after lights out.

"Numéro sept, D'troit?"

"Norm Ullman."

"Quatorze, T'ron-to?"

"Dave Keon."

National Hockey League names were the only English the two brothers knew. Still, Marcel Dionne dreamed about exotic teams as other kids imagined pirates. Maybe he'd play in a foreign city some day. He was certainly a great little player. At eight, he could drop into a crouch and pedal untouched through a scrum at the school rink.

Uncle Gilles got him on a peewee team, even though the boy was underage. The first game went badly. The young Dionne was always offside. He didn't know the rules. He ran home crying afterward. Within weeks, though, he was the best player in the league.

Though small, Dionne had great balance, blinding speed and endless ener-gy—skills he built on during his summer job. The Dionne family grocery store sold beer, and Marcel Dionne spent his youth peddling cases of Laurentide and Brador all over Drummondville on the handlebars of his bike.

Many of his customers were in attendance when Marcel Dionne took to the ice in 1967 for the Drummondville Rangers, the city's new junior franchise. His family and their friends were also at the game cheering, and when the 16-year-old got home, everyone was crowded into his house, discussing the game, talking about him. Marcel, everyone agreed, was the best player to come out of Drummondville since Yvan Cournoyer, then a power-play specialist for the Canadiens.

Some players welcome attention, a town behind them rooting for their success. But for Marcel Dionne, hockey was supposed to be an adventure, not a duty. He would tell biographer, Ted Mahovlich, "I felt trapped... During one game, I remember it was third period, I got up and left. I went to the dressing room, took off my equipment and thought, 'That's it. I'm done.'"

Dionne would return, though, leading the Rangers to the provincial championship. Still he felt that he had to get out of Drummondville. After the season, the 16-year-old came home from school one day to find that the St. Catharines Black Hawks had called. The Black Hawks! That sounded better than Rangers. St. Catharines was where number 9, Bobby Hull, started. And 21, Stan Mikita.

The Ontario city adopted Marcel Dionne with open arms. He enjoyed working with his teammates, mastered English and met the woman who would become his wife. In his second and third seasons, Marcel Dionne led Ontario junior hockey in points.

Then came an ugly homecoming. The time was 1971—a year after the militant Quebec separatist organization, the Front de libération du Québec, had murdered Quebec labour minister Pierre Laporte, leading prime minister Pierre Trudeau to invoke the War Measures Act. At the same time Quebec was experiencing a hockey renaissance, with the emergence of heroes Guy Lafleur and Gilbert Perreault. Dionne, however, had left for Ontario and for an English-speaking city.

In the spring of 1971, political tensions entered the hockey arena, when Marcel and the Black Hawks faced off against Lafleur's Quebec Remparts for the right to represent eastern Canada in the Memorial Cup, the junior national hockey championship. In the very first game, played on the Black Hawks' rink, a St. Catharines fan threw frogs on the ice. The teams split the first games, with Dionne outplaying Lafleur.

King of Drummondville

Marcel Dionne says his favourite hockey moment came the day after he saw brother Gilbert win the Stanley Cup in Montreal and took a 45-minute drive east to the old hometown to find his dad in front of the house, beaming. "Son," the father said, gathering Dionne in his arms, "we finally won the Cup." Gilbert scored six goals, including a game-winner in the Canadiens' 1993 playoff march.

That Stanley Cup marked Gilbert Dionne's independence day. He had always been proud of his talented older brother Marcel. As a boy, the younger Dionne was the only kid in the neighbourhood to wear the mustard yellow jersey of his brother's team, the Los Angeles Kings. But Gilbert Dionne also wanted to be a hockey player in his own right. In Drummondville, that aspiration meant being placed against a measuring stick that reached to the Hall of Fame. Like his brother, Gilbert Dionne felt compelled to pursue hockey for a junior hockey team in Ontario. In Kitchener, he somehow never got around to telling people that he was Marcel Dionne's brother. After winning the Stanley Cup, he didn't have to.

Gilbert Dionne.

Hitting the Hay

Yvan Cournoyer was nicknamed "The Roadrunner" after the cartoon character. His dad, a Drummondville machinist, advised him that National Hockey League coyotes were more wily than the one his namesake faced in Warner Brothers cartoons. In the pros, Yvan would need an edge. So his father fashioned 10 steel pucks. "Practise with these," he told his son, only to come home and find a demolished basement.

Hay bales were brought downstairs next, for use in target practice. "I would shoot at the hay," Cournoyer remembered. "Wrist shot—10 right, then 10 left, then 10 backhand. I would do this every day for hours." In time, Cournoyer could fire a puck on the fly, past flinching goalies, from outside the circle. Thanks to his basement work, the naturally left-handed scooter sometimes even scored right-handed.

A Canadiens forward his entire career, Cournoyer was Most Valuable Player of the 1972 playoffs and made such an impact on Russian audiences in the 1972 Summit Series that he was the lone Canadian to be invited to Moscow in 2002 to celebrate the 30th anniversary of the Russian-Canadian series.

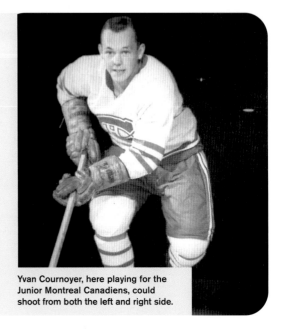

Yvan Cournoyer, here playing for the Junior Montreal Canadiens, could shoot from both the left and right side.

But Quebec City had been greatly angered by the widely reported frogs episode. And French fans taunted Dionne with vile curses upon his return to Quebec for the next pair of games. "That's not swearing to them," he told teammates. "In the French language, you swear against the church." But he knew better. The second match played in Quebec was worse. Dionne's family received death threats—trouble his parents didn't need, what with a new baby in Marcel Dionne's old room. And after the game, 2,500 rioting Remparts fans surrounded the Black Hawks' bus, smashing windows. Marcel slept between beds at the team's motel that night, as if waiting for a bomb. Dionne was now a villain in his own province, an English-Canadian sellout—Joe Frazier to stay-at-home French hero Guy Lafleur's Muhammad Ali.

St. Catharines returned home, down three to one. The Black Hawks won game five, but parents wouldn't let the players return to Quebec. St. Catharines defaulted.

Back in Drummondville, fans soon lost interest in Dionne's old team, the junior Rangers, and the club folded. By then, Dionne was an NHLer, playing for the Detroit Red Wings. Detroit, as fervent a hockey town as there is in the U.S., was a trial for Marcel—great expectations, a bad team. Everyone was expecting him to be a saviour, just as they had in Drummondville.

Then the Los Angeles Kings came calling. The Kings! That option sounded even better than being a Red Wing. Dionne flourished in L.A., where he took to the ice with the joyous abandon he had brought to the St-Zephirin rink thousands of mornings earlier. In L.A., on a team that never came close to winning the Stanley Cup, he was free just to play hockey. For a dozen years, Dionne was magnificent. Nine of those seasons were spent on the Triple Crown line with Charlie Simmer and Dave Taylor—a remarkable unit that seemed to play with a dozen arms and a single pair of eyes. At one time, Marcel was the second highest point-getter in NHL hockey history. He remains the most productive Quebec forward ever.

Sometimes life works out. Junior hockey returned to Drummondville. The Voltigeurs now play—where else?—at the Marcel Dionne Arena. And the name Dionne finally did make its mark on the Stanley Cup. Gilbert Dionne, the baby who came into the world shortly before Marcel's unhappy homecoming in 1971, would later help the Montreal Canadiens win the Stanley Cup in 1993.

GATINEAU-HULL

FOUNDED

Located on the west bank of the Gatineau River and on the north shore of the Ottawa River, Hull was founded in 1800 by Philemon Wright, who named a lumber camp there after his original home in Britain, Kingston-upon-Hull. For decades the Ottawa River, as seen from Hull, appeared on the Canadian one-dollar bill. In 2002, the Quebec government amalgamated the cities of Hull, Gatineau, Aylmer, Buckingham and Masson-Angers into what is now called Gatineau.

NATIVE-BORN NHL PLAYERS

Gatineau: Daniel Briere, Francois Guay, Eric Landry, Steve Martins, Christian Soucy; **Hull:** Michel Larocque, Guy Larose, Christian Masse, Rob Murphy, Denis Potvin, Jean Potvin, Stephane Richer, Dominic Roussel, Guy Trottier

FAMOUS LOCAL TEAMS

Junior: Gatineau L'Intrepide, Gatineau Olympiques, Gatineau Selectes, Hull Excelsiors, Hull Festivals, Hull-Ottawa Canadiens, Hull Volants; **Senior-pro:** Hull-Ottawa Canadiens, Hull Volants

CURRENT POPULATION
226,696

Denis Potvin.

The Incredible Hull-k

Defenceman Denis Potvin is listed in most reference books as being born in Ottawa, Ontario, where indeed the National Hockey Leaguer first achieved fame as a wunderkind for the barber pole-striped junior 67's. But Denis, born in 1953, grew up on the Quebec side of the Ottawa River in what was then Hull. Even when his family moved to Vanier, a French-speaking enclave within Ottawa, Denis still felt as if he were in Quebec. Most of his neighbours were French. And Denis spent Saturday nights in front of the TV, watching René Lecavalier and *La Soirée du Hockey* on channel nine—the French channel.

Lecavalier spoke the language of hockey beautifully. And the Canadiens were almost always led to victory by Denis's idol, the supremely poised Jean

Doug Harvey's game wasn't the same after being traded from Montreal to the Quebec Aces.

The End of the Line

Montreal Canadiens players didn't just start off in Hull. Some ended here, too. In 1946, Doug Harvey, a Montreal native, won a baseball batting championship, hitting .351 for the Hull-Ottawa AA team. He'd also won a heavyweight boxing championship in the Canadian Navy during World War II. But hockey and the Montreal Canadiens (1947–61) were what he made his life's pursuit.

A record 10-time first team National Hockey League all-star, the defenceman could slow down or speed up a game at will, sometimes both in a matter of seconds—slipping behind his net, waiting for opponents to drift into an inattentive languor, then speeding a crisp pass to a breaking winger. Harvey loved hockey, especially playoff crusades in foreign cities—rattling back to Montreal in a train with snoring teammates while the Canadian National Railways (CNR) whistle announced another Habs victory at every stop on the way home.

Traded from Montreal in 1961, Harvey's career wound down the hard way. And so when Tommy Gorman, ex-president of the Canadiens, offered him a job and free lodgings at Connaught Park Raceways in Hull in the early '80s, Harvey jumped at the opportunity. Maybe the accommodations were what lured him—a vintage CNR sleeping car, restored to its original green-and-black colour scheme, nestled in the backyard of Gorman's mansion home.

Memorable Coaches

Theoretically, the junior Hull-Ottawa Canadiens existed to groom playing talent for the parent Montreal team. And indeed the 1958 junior team, which defeated the Canadiens' top western club, the Regina Pats, to win the Memorial Cup, was loaded with future Habs, including captain Ralph Backstrom, Bobby Rousseau and J.C. Tremblay (Bruce Gamble, an Ontario Hockey Association interleague loan from Guelph, was in nets). But as it turns out, the most important members of the '58 graduating class were general manager Sam Pollock and coach Scotty Bowman. Pollock won nine championships in his 14 years in Montreal (1965–78). Bowman earned the same total for three different teams (Montreal/Pittsburgh/Detroit).

Hull would become a magnet for exceptional executives. The most famous personalities involved with the Hull Olympiques, the 1986 Memorial Cup finalists, were Luc Robitaille (forward), Pat Burns (coach) and Wayne Gretzky (owner). The 1997 Hull Olympiques, who would win the Memorial Cup at home, were coached by Claude Julien, another future National Hockey League leader. Coach Benoit Groulx would lead the Olympiques to the finals of the Memorial Cup in 2003 and 2004, where the team bowed out to the Kitchener Rangers and the Kelowna Rockets.

View of Hull, 1830.

Beliveau. There was, however, a persistent storm front in heaven—the hated Toronto Maple Leafs. Denis took it as a personal affront when gangling George Armstrong or that pagan Eddie Shack interfered with Beliveau's divine right of passage.

Potvin also kept a watchful eye on English-speaking kids (likely Leafs fans) when friends congregated on rue Vincent Massey. Altercations were frequent and Denis was always there, first in line, when snowballs or punches were thrown. Later, with the junior Ottawa 67's of the Ontario Hockey League, Potvin chafed at coach Bill Long's habit of checking that French-speaking players such as Bunny Laroque and Pierre Jarry were in their rooms on road trips while the team's English players were left alone. Regardless of these tensions, Denis was loved in Ottawa, where he stayed with the 67's from ages 13 to 20, long enough to draw a pension.

In fact, the Hall of Fame defenceman epitomized the cross-cultural spirit of the Gatineau-Ottawa region. There are federal workplaces on both sides of the Ottawa River. Thousands of locals are employed in one city and live in the other. Many are bilingual. Some areas of Gatineau are English-speaking—Shawville, for instance. Some areas of Ottawa, such as Vanier, are French.

Denis Potvin embodied all the hyphens in the national capital region. He was, after all, a Hull-Ottawa, French-English-speaking kid. But it was more than that. The pressure of straddling the border of Leafs-Canadiens, French-English territory was evidently too much. Perhaps some Hulk-like change in Potvin's on-ice personality was caused by watching those brutal Toronto-Montreal play-off wars in the '60s. Whatever it was, Potvin became a classic French-Canadian player—beautiful to watch, endlessly creative with the puck, as poised as his hero Jean Beliveau. But when upset or wronged, Potvin would turn into something neither definably English nor French—the Incredible Hull-k, violent, strong and as vindictive as an Ottawa taxman.

In junior, playing for the 67's across the Chaudière Bridge from his birthplace, he was equally feared and admired. In his final season with the junior team, the defenceman collected 123 points and 232 penalty minutes. At age 15, he fought an older boy, Fran McKay, who angered him with the taunt, "Hey Potvin, why doncha get your coach to change your diapers?" When McKay regained conscious-ness, the 6'4" St. Catharines winger had a fractured skull, a broken collarbone and two blackened eyes. By the end of his junior career, Potvin's open-ice body-checks were almost like watching a car wander into a suddenly busy train crossing. Stretchers were frequently needed to cart the victims away.

Doug Harvey, the first great Quebec defenceman, said of Potvin after playing

Denis Potvin, playing in the OHL for the Ottawa 67's.

him in a local exhibition game in 1968, "He's going to be as good as he wants to be." At the time, Potvin was 15; Harvey, 44. Harvey was almost always right in hockey matters. Though Montreal's general manager Sam Pollock tried everything he could think of to make Potvin a Canadiens team member, Potvin was selected first overall by the New York Islanders in the 1973 NHL player draft. Playing with his older brother Jean, he would lead the Islanders to four Stanley Cups before the decade was over.

Frequently, Denis Potvin was the most gifted, talented player on the ice. In the 1976 Canada Cup, the defenceman led the tournament in scoring. But every so often, in the heat of battle, anger would turn to rage, and the Incredible Hull-k would re-emerge.

Hull of a Joke

Vermont industrialist Ezra Butler Eddy, self-proclaimed "matchmaker to the world," moved his match factory to Hull in 1851. (He was mayor of the city through much of the 1880s.) E.B. Eddy's eventually expanded to produce a great number of paper products including, by the 1960s, toilet-roll dispensers marked Eddy Hull. Eddy Hull? Every hockey fan knew it was Bobby Hull and Eddie Shack. So in schools across central Canada, jokers would write under Eddy Hull the name Bobby Shack just to make the dispenser joke, well…indispensable.

Mario Lemieux, playing for another Laval team, the Laval Voisins.

THE LAVAL TITAN

The career of arguably the most accomplished French-Canadian hockey player of all time, Mario Lemieux, officially began in Laval, where he starred for the Laval Titan from 1981 to 1984. In his final year there, he established a record for Canadian junior hockey, scoring 133 goals and 149 assists in 70 games. Once he set up a goal by making a blind pass to a trailing winger. On the bench, the coach asked Lemieux how he knew the player was there. "I could tell by the sound of his skates," Mario shrugged.

LAVAL

FOUNDED
Laval was established as a seigneury and granted to the Jesuits in 1636, six years before neighbouring Montreal was established. The city of Laval was officially incorporated in 1965.

NATIVE-BORN NHL PLAYERS
Donald Audette, Mathieu Chouinard, Pascal Dupuis, J.F. Fortin, Martin Grenier, Patrick Labrecque, Daniel Laperriere, Eric Perrin, Martin St. Louis, Jose Theodore

FAMOUS LOCAL TEAMS
Junior: Laval Laurentide, Laval Laurentides, Laval Leafs, Laval National, Laval Saints, Laval Titan, Laval Voisins;
Senior-Pro: Laval Chiefs

CURRENT POPULATION
350,000

Little Big Men

Laval's Eli Sherbatov created a sensation at the world under-18 division tournament in Bulgaria in early 2005, scoring four goals and five assists in leading Israel to a bronze medal. What caught everyone's attention, though, was the player's size. At 13, Eli was 4'8", barely 90 pounds—easily a foot smaller and half the weight of many of his competitors.

Fantastic, a lot of people in Eli's Montreal suburb smiled, figuring that was the end of his story even if the kid declared his hope to play one day in the National Hockey League. One of Sherbatov's neighbours, however, told Eli's father not to worry about size because talent is what counts. That man was Normand St. Louis, father of 2003–04 NHL most valuable player, scoring leader and Stanley Cup star, Martin St. Louis.

Monsieur St. Louis would know. He'd seen Marty and best friend Eric Perrin play ball hockey with the mob out on Duranty Street. The two boys were wizards with a hockey stick and tennis ball. And no one could get the puck away from them at Samson Arena, Couvrette Park and Florent Park.

The best friends still wanted to play hockey after high school, but they figured that Quebec hockey had no place for them. They were small—St. Louis, 5'7"; Perrin, 5'9"—in contrast to the standard bearer for Laval hockey, Mario Lemieux, the 6'4" NHL centreman who once starred for the Laval Titan in junior. The time of the Little Big Man in hockey seemed to have passed.

Marty and Eric went to the University of Vermont, where their friendship deepened. As did that of their parents, who exchanged news of their kids' school careers every Thursday night at regular double-date dinners at Laval's Jardino's or Palma Italian.

And what news! Marty set a record for point scoring (267) in his four-year career in Burlington, while Eric established the school's record for goals (107). Neither was drafted by NHL teams, but Marty caught on with the Calgary Flames, played intermittently and was bought out of his contract in 2000. Too small, again, was the verdict. Eric, meanwhile, drifted into the minors.

Marty once more had to move south to find ice time. Allowed plenty of playing time for the Tampa Bay Lightning, he began to flash the skills that once had fans jumping to their feet in Burlington and Laval. Greased Lightning, they

A still from the film
Les Boys.

Les Boys Will Be Boys

In Quebec, two sequels have followed from the 1977 Paul Newman hockey bur-
lesque, *Slap Shot*. *Les Boys*, a three-film comedy series about a slapshot-happy
amateur team who are always getting into mischief, has made almost $20 mil-
lion in Quebec since 1997. Then there are the Laval Chiefs, an amateur pro team
who play in the Quebec Hockey League. The Chiefs are actually named after
the Charlestown Chiefs in *Slap Shot*. They play like it, too. There are up to 10 fights
a period, not including the dust-ups in the stands. A game with hated crosstown
rivals, the Verdun Chiefs, once drew a full house at the Montreal Bell Centre,
not to mention 20 police cars, four fire trucks and four paddy wagons.

called him in Tampa. No one could accelerate faster. And his hummingbird dips
inside the enemy blue line left defenders grasping at air. He'd pass off to an open
winger or fire away himself, taking advantage of a quick release and an unfailingly accurate shot.

By the fall of 2003, no seat was to be found at Laval's Bar Chez Hervé for
Lightning games, for Martin was suddenly the best player not only in Laval but
anywhere in the world. The facts were right there in *Le Journal de Montréal*'s
sports pages every week—Martin St. Louis leading the NHL in scoring!

St. Louis achieved the ultimate victory in 2003–04—taking his team to first
place, making the all-star team, winning the NHL scoring race, then helping
Tampa Bay to knock off Montreal, Philadelphia and Calgary to win the Stanley
Cup. More incredible still, his best friend since 1985, Eric Perrin, was there
with him, having been called up by the Lightning late in the season.

After they won the Stanley Cup, Martin and Eric took the trophy to Burlington,
Vermont, to show their college friends, before bringing it home to Laval. Now
everyone at Chez Hervé, indeed all across Montreal and Canada, was forced to con-
cede that yes, hockey had a place for Little Big Men. Look at Marcel Dionne,
look at Yvan Cournoyer, look at Henri Richard. Look at Martin St. Louis.

MONTREAL

FOUNDED

The Algonquin, Wyandot (Huron) and Haudenosaunee (Iroquois) inhabited the area around what is now known as Montreal for 8,000 years prior to the arrival in 1535 of Jacques Cartier. The French explorer renamed the Haudenosaunee village of Hochelaga, calling the settlement Mount Royal. Missionaries led by Paul de Chomedey de Maisonneuve helped establish a local mission in 1642, erecting a wood cross on Mount Royal. The settlement quickly became a centre for the growing fur trade and a port of entry into what was then called New France. The Treaty of Paris in 1763 ceded all of New France, including Montreal, to Great Britain. American Revolutionaries took control of the city briefly in 1775. Montreal was incorporated as a city in 1832, and by the late 19th century, the growing metropolis was the undisputed economic centre of Canada. The Canadian Pacific Railway established its headquarters here in 1880. The bilingual city alternated between French and English mayors at the turn of the 20th century. The practice ended in 1914, after the annexation of neighbouring French villages made Montreal a predominantly francophone city once again. Montreal celebrated its 350th birthday in 1992. It is now Canada's second largest city, after Toronto.

NATIVE-BORN NHL PLAYERS (MONTREAL):

Ramzi Abid, Shawn Anderson, Jean-Sebastien Aubin, Marco Baron, Serge Beaudoin, Marc Bergevin, Bob Berry, John Bethel, Paul Bibeault, Andre Binette, Dan Blackburn, Sylvain Blouin, Patrick Boileau, Mike A. Boland, Marcel Bonin, Mike Bossy, Emile Bouchard, Joel Bouchard, Andre Boudrias, Conrad Bourcier, Jean Bourcier, Ray Bourque, Neil Brady, Patrice Brisebois, Connie Broden, Martin Brodeur, Paul Brousseau, Steve Brule, Ralph Buchanan, Ron Buchanan, Hy Buller, Fred Burchell, Robin Burns, Walt Buswell, Larry Carriere, Ronald Carter, Sebastien Centomo, Lorne Chabot, Dennis Chasse, Enrico Ciccone, Ogilvie Cleghorn, Sprague Cleghorn, Rey Comeau, Bert Connolly, Roger Cormier, Mark Cornforth, Jim Corsi, Daniel Corso, Yves Courteau, Corey Crawford, Maurice Croghan, Glen Currie, Claude Cyr, Alexander Daigle, J.J. Daigneault, Vincent Damphousse, Dan Daoust, Eric Daze, Johnny Denis, Marc Denis, Jacques Deslauriers, Gary Dineen, Jason Doig, Bobby Dollas, Gord Donnelly, Andre Dore, Graham Drinkwater, Steve Dubinsky, J.P. Dumont, Norm Dupont, Yanick Dupre, Edward Emberg, Bob Errey, Arthur Farrell, Stephane Fiset, Gerry Fleming, Reg Fleming, Steven Fletcher, Bryan Fogarty, Peter Folco, Dave Forbes, Connie Foley, Steve Gainey, Michel Galarneau, Garry Galley, Simon Gamache, Jimmy Gardner, Denis Gauthier, Jean Gauthier, Jean-Guy Gendron, Bernie Geoffrion, Danny Geoffrion, Jean-Sebastien Giguere, Rod Gilbert, Bob Girard, Daniel Goneau, Benoit Gosselin, Jean-Luc Grand-Pierre, Mike Grant, Benoit Gratton, Terry Gray, Richard Grenier, Jocelyn Guevremont, Ben Guite, Pierre Hamel, Walter Harnott, Doug Harvey, Paul Haynes, Gerry Heffernan, Bob Holland, Greg Holst, Eric Houde, Mike Hough, Jim Hrivnak, Ryan Hughes, Harry Hyland, Gord Hynes, Bruno Jacques, Pierre Jarry, Brian Johnson, Ernie Johnson, Eddie Johnston, Ross Johnstone, Steve Kasper, Gordon Keats, Mike Krushelnyski, Moe L'Abbe, Daniel Lacroix, Eric Lacroix, Ernest Laforce, Roger Lafreniere, Serge Lajeunesse, Bobby Lalonde, Chris Langevin, Jean-Marc Lanthier, Ian Laperriere, Guy Lapointe, Georges Laraque, Francis Larivee, Mario Larocque, Phil Latreille, Dominic Lavoie, Gord Laxton, Patrice Lefebvre, Yannick Lehoux, Alain Lemieux, Mario Lemieux, Robert Lemieux, Gaston Leroux, Jean-Yves Leroux, Francis Lessard, Normand Leveille, Bob Logan, Dave Logan, Matthew Lombardi, Roberto Luongo, Donald MacIver, Fleming Mackell, John Mahaffy, Tom Manastersky, Jimmy Mann, Sylvio Mantha, Dan Marois, Gilles Marotte, Randy McKay, Tony McKegney, Ron Meighan, Scott Mellanby, Eric Meloche, Gilles Meloche, Corrado Micalef, Sergio Momesso, Hartland Monahan, Michel Mongeau, Jim Montgomery, Dick Moore, Stephane Morin, Jim Morrison, Kenneth Mosdell, Hal Murphy, Alain Nasreddine, Buddy O'Connor, Gates Orlando, James Orlando, Paul Pageau, Bernie Parent, Rich Parent, Mike Parizeau, Rollie Paulhus, Cory Pecker, Roger Pelletier, Joel Perreault, Jimmy Peters, Noel Picard, Robert Picard, Roger Picard, Michel Plasse, Adrian Plavsic, Jason Pominville, Yves Preston, Claude Provost, Jean Pusie, Paul Raymond, Mel Read, Mike Ribeiro, Henri Richard, Maurice Richard, David Ritchie, Claude Robert, Earl Robinson, Luc Robitaille, Ernest Roche, Roberto Romano, Bobby Rousseau, Guy Rousseau, Roly Rousseau, Joe Rullier, Ernie Russell, Bernie Saunders, Reggie Savage, Serge Savard, Richard Sevigny, Daniel Shank, Frank Sheppard, Martin Simard, Bob Sirois, Bob Sheddon, Martin St. Amour, Bruno St. Jacques, Nelson Stewart, Gaston Therrien, Gilles Thibaudeau, Jocelyn Thibault, Mario Thyer, Patrick Traverse, Harry Trihey, Ian Turnbull, Nick Vachon, Carol Vadnais, Randy Velischek, Phil Watson, Peter White, Archibald Wilcox, Bernie Wolfe, Lorne Worsley, Ross Yates, Larry Zeidel

NATIVE-BORN NHL PLAYERS (LACHINE):

Billy Bell, Kelly Burnett, Frank Eddolls, George Gardner, Mike Gaul, Phil Goyette, Charlie Hodge, Francois Lacombe, Claude Lapointe, George Mantha, Pete Morin, Reg Sinclair, Claude Verrett

NATIVE-BORN NHL PLAYERS (VERDUN):

Normand Baron, Jim Bartlett, Eric Charron, Guy Charron, Ed Courtenay, Jean Cusson, Denis Cyr, Polly Drouin, Ron Harris, Gord Hollingworth,

Claude Legris, Fern Majeau, Don Marshall, Rick Martin, Jim Peters, Les Ramsay, Jean Savard, Dollard St. Laurent, Dan Vincelette, Wally Weir, Moe White

FAMOUS LOCAL TEAMS

Junior: Montreal Bleu-Blanc-Rouge, Montreal Comets, Montreal Jr. Canadiens, Montreal Jr. Royals, Montreal Juniors, Montreal Lafontaine, Montreal NDG Monarchs, Montreal St. Pats;

Senior-pro: Montreal AAA, Montreal Army, Montreal Bell Telephone, Montreal Canadiens, Montreal CNR, Montreal Cyclones, Montreal Eurekas, Montreal Montagnards, Montreal Maroons, Montreal Nationals, Montreal Navy, Montreal Royals, Montreal Shamrocks, Montreal Sr. Canadiens, Montreal Victorias, Montreal Wanderers

CURRENT POPULATION
3,426,350

McGill students enjoy a game on campus, c.1910.

Les Glorieux

Civic leaders had feared that something like the Richard Riot, the city's infamous 17 March 1955 insurrection, might happen in Montreal if hockey grew from a gentlemanly recreation into a public sport.

The first hockey clubs in Halifax, Nova Scotia, and St. John's, Newfoundland, were elite fraternities, reflecting the prevailing belief that hockey might be too dangerous a thrill for the masses. The idea of uniformed players (armed with clubs!) firing up large crowds terrified authorities. As long ago as the 14th century, English parliament had decreed that landowners would be sentenced to three years in prison for allowing property to be used for "banned ball," or "bandy," as the edict called it. In the Anglo-Irish Maritimes, despite official efforts to contain bandy's grandson, hockey, the sport spread easily to soldiers and workers and soon became universal.

Just as in the Maritimes, hockey was played in early 19th-century Montreal. In Montreal, however, a mutually accepted boundary existed between the two solitudes—the minority English Protestant elite and the French Catholic majority. The Montreal *Gazette* confirms that in 1837, the year of the rebellions in Upper and Lower Canada, a less serious skirmish took place between the Uptown Canadians, a French-speaking team, and the Irish Catholic Dorchester Uptowns at the corner of what is now boulevard René-Lévesque and rue Bleury.

Still the popular outdoor sport, whether played by French- or English-speaking Montrealers, was not welcome at the city's famous, subscribers-only Victoria skating rink until much later. Tellingly, the first game was organized by a Halifax interloper, a 25-year-old McGill University student named James Creighton, who arrived at the rink on 3 March 1875, with a bundle of Micmac sticks from back home. After Creighton explained Halifax Rules (see page 48) to the "nines" (teams of nine), uniformed players dashed off to play the first-ever indoor hockey game under the watchful gaze of 40 friends and a Montreal *Gazette* reporter who would explain the sport to his audience: "The game is like lacrosse in one sense—the block [of wood] having to go through flags placed about eight feet apart in the same manner as a rubber ball—but in the main, the old country game of shinty gives the best idea of hockey... The game was concluded about half past nine and the spectators then adjourned well-satisfied with the evening's entertainment."

Hockey flourished at McGill in the years after Creighton convened that first game. The university organized a hockey team and published the rules of the sport in the Montreal *Gazette* on 27 February 1877. Over the next decade McGill students shaped field hockey laws to the needs of the evolving ice sport. And a

Dominion Square, Montreal, c. 1910.

McGill's first hockey team,1881. Many believe that the university club was hockey's first organized team.

student team won hockey's first ever intercity challenge match, defeating the Montreal Victorias and tying a Quebec City team in the 1883 Montreal Winter Carnival championship, which was played on the St. Lawrence River.

Montreal and Quebec City teams could even be said to have first perfected the game. When the Dartmouth Chebuctos from Nova Scotia toured Quebec in 1889 for the first encounter between hockey's two founding cultures, the hosts prevailed by a 23–3 margin.

After the Stanley Cup was put in play (see page 159), English Montreal men's clubs dominated, winning the trophy fifteen times between 1893 and 1910. During this period, the city boasted an Irish team, the Shamrocks; a Scottish team, the Victorias; and an English team, the Wanderers. A French-Canadian club, however, would not emerge until 1903–04, when, first, the Montreal Nationals, and, then, the Montreal Montagnards formed teams that were a scalding embarrassment to French-speaking fans. The Nationals lost their first four games, defaulted the next six, then folded. The Montagnards lost every game one season and were humiliated by Brockville, 26–0, the following year.

Le Club athlétique Canadien, salvation of French Montreal hockey, was formed in the 1909–10 season. A National Hockey Association rule the following season prevented other teams, including the Montreal Wanderers, from using French-speaking players, thus making the Canadiens the exclusive club for the best French-Canadian talent. Under the sure hand of general managers George Kennedy and then Leo (m'sieu Léo) Dandurand, a Franco-American from Bourbonnais, Illinois, the Canadiens became known as the Flying Frenchman, winning a Stanley Cup in 1916 with Les Trois Mousquetaires—Georges Vezina, Jack Laviolette and Didier Pitre.

The following decade, Dandurand's great find, Howie Morenz, ("l'Homme éclair," or the "Stratford Streak," as he was known in English), turned the Canadiens into the most famous hockey team in the world. That the Canadiens' first two superstars—Georges Vezina and Howie Morenz—were taken from the club in tragic fashion, Vezina succumbing suddenly to tuberculosis, Morenz crashing horribly into the boards and then perishing in hospital from a resulting embolism, offered certain proof of the histrionic nature of what was now, beyond doubt, Montreal's hockey team.

Forum Hat Trick

Named after a roller-skating rink that had previously stood on the same site, the Montreal Forum was constructed for $1,500,000 in 1924. But it could be truly said that the rue Ste-Catherine shrine was built by players and fans who worshipped hockey there for 70 winters. The game's architects, Morenz, Richard, Beliveau and Lafleur, created the arena's ambience. And the army chorus that alerted referees of opposition infractions with a booming "Heyyyyy!" were ghosts of fans who renewed their season tickets in the Great Beyond.

Montreal author Mordecai Richler remembered entering the Forum as a kid in the '40s: "I only got to see the great Richard twice. Saving money earned collecting bills for a neighbourhood butcher on Sunday mornings, my friends and I bought standing-room tickets for the millionaires section. And then, flinging our winter caps ahead of us, we vaulted barriers, eventually working our way down to ice level. Each time we jumped a barrier, hearts thumping, we tossed our hats ahead of us, because if an officious usher grabbed us by the scruff of the neck, as often happened, we could plead, teary-eyed, that some oaf had tossed our cap down and we were only descending to retrieve it."

The Montreal Wanderers in 1905.
The Wanderers won the Stanley Cup
four times between 1906 and 1910.

The '30s brought more bad news for Montreal hockey. The Great Depression killed the city's popular English-speaking team, the Maroons. Talk even arose of the Canadiens moving to Cleveland and of turning the "Fabulous Forum", the team's home, into a streetcar barn. But in 1942 the Canadiens found a hero who would lead the team to everlasting glory.

Maurice Richard represented Montreal even before he joined the Canadiens. He once juggled playing hockey for five local teams under assumed names (Maurice Rochon, for instance). Winter was in his blood, it seemed. As a child, he would leave home wearing skates and play four-hour shifts at nearby La Fontaine Park, returning for meals that were taken with dripping skates still strapped to his feet. When ice at the park wasn't available, Maurice flew along the Back River. It was forbidden—the water was too fast, the ice never thick enough. He didn't notice or care.

Richard played in his sleep, dreaming about scoring, he once admitted. Constantly tense when awake, the Montreal Canadiens rookie frightened and intrigued coach Dick Irvin Sr., who said he had never met a player so obsessed with scoring and winning. After practice, Richard would scatter a bucket of pucks onto the ice and then disconnect the black dots, sweeping them with equal force backhand and forehand—he was ambidextrous—into the corners of the net.

The Rocket and the Pocket Rocket: Maurice and Henri Richard.

Soon, he had memorized the net from every patch of ice within scoring distance at the Forum.

Richard was six feet tall and, in his prime, a swift, well-packed 180 pounds. Inside the blue line, he was faster and stronger still, able to cast aside defenders with a swimmer's backstroke. "Boy, he went in there like a rocket," gasped an onlooker watching Richard elude defenders one practice. Sportswriter Dink Carroll overheard the comment and began calling Maurice "The Rocket."

After battling crippling injuries early on, The Rocket exploded in his second National Hockey League season, pouring 12 goals into the net in nine playoff matches to win Montreal the Stanley Cup in 1943, then obliterating scoring records by counting 50 goals in as many games the following season. In the subsequent playoffs, he scored his team's every goal in a 5–1 victory over Toronto and was named all three stars.

Richard was a folk hero now. Fans brought notebooks and pencils to games to preserve the memory of his goals, like the time he emerged bloodied from the dressing room with seconds left in a playoff game, suffering from a concussion—he was in a trance, really—then fought through the Boston team to score the winning goal. In restaurants, citizens approached "Ree-charr" with offerings of money—tithes for Montreal's hockey king.

Author Roch Carrier recorded what it was like on Quebec rinks during the

Hockey Night in Ville-Émard

Six National Hockey League scoring championships, two Stanley Cups and an Olympic gold medal later, it seems hard to believe that the best French-Canadian hockey player of all time began his career stickhandling bottle caps through piano legs on a make-believe basement rink in Ville-Émard, a west-end suburb of Montreal. More incredible still, Mario Lemieux (French for "the best") wasn't *le mieux* Lemieux on the basement tile floor. That honour went to older brother (by three years) Alain, who later played in the NHL, as well. Richard Lemieux (a year senior to Mario) was also involved in the basement league. Schedules went on forever—the Lemieux played every night, all night, year after year, graduating eventually to real sticks and a plastic puck. The basement floor held out, but the piano legs were whittled to kindling by slashing sticks. A Hall of Fame hockey mom, Madame Lemieux sometimes wore bandages on her fingers when she played splintered piano keys. And Mr. Lemieux, a construction worker, sometimes had to repair the ceiling after the boys pitchforked the tiles celebrating a goal.

Mario played on ice, too, of course, and first gained neighbourhood attention when Alain Lemieux's coach asked him to jump down from the stands to play in an exhibition match with nine- and 10-year-olds. Before long, the six-year-old had collected a goal and an assist. In junior, the youngest Lemieux was a sensation, scoring 133 goals and 149 assists playing for the Laval Titan. Later with the Pittsburgh Penguins and with Canadian national teams, the 6'4" centre was one of the most beautiful sights in hockey—elegant, powerfully swift, with an anaconda-like grace that allowed him to glide past grasping defenders. And that six-year-old who had learned to thread passes between piano legs grew into a master tactician who could sneak the puck through an army of legs to an open winger or convert a pass anywhere into the net. He was a magician. He was Mario the Magnificent!

HAPPY WANDERERS

The Montreal Wanderers earned their team name travelling the country in defence of the Stanley Cup, which they won in 1906, 1907, 1908 and 1910. Always controversial, the team raided other clubs and ignored directions from league officials, dropping out of the Stanley Cup in 1904, for instance, because they were unhappy with officials. After winning the Cup in 1907, the team left the trophy at a photo shoot. It was stolen, but the Wanderers ignored ransom demands. (The frustrated thief finally returned it to the photographer.)

The team featured 16 Hall of Famers, including Sprague Cleghorn, Lester Patrick, Art Ross and Hod Stuart. Montreal's first English team went out with a blaze—if not a blaze of glory—folding in 1918, when their Westmount Arena mysteriously burned down seven games into the NHL season.

Montreal's English team:
the Montreal Maroons, 1933.

The S Line

Though only a part of the National Hockey League for 14 seasons (1924–38), the Montreal Maroons captured the hearts of English Montrealers as well as two Stanley Cups (1925, 1932), produced the game's first 300-goal scorer (Nels Stewart), and were the first proprietors of the Montreal Forum. The club had hoped to retake the name of the Montreal Wanderers, but the team's purple-red sweaters were such a hit that the team soon became the Maroons. The club also boasted the NHL's best line in the early '30s, the S Line—two boys from Toronto's Beaches (Nels Stewart and Reginald Smith), along with Albert Siebert. The trio were so good they were all accorded individual nicknames—"Ol' Poison" Stewart scored; "Hooley" Smith checked; and "Babe" Siebert lugged the puck.

Richard era in *The Hockey Sweater*: "When the referee dropped the puck, we were five Maurice Richards taking it away from five other Maurice Richards. We were 10 players; all of us wearing with the same blazing enthusiasm the uniform of the Montreal Canadiens. On our backs, we all wore the famous number 9."

Predictably, a great number of Montreal kids soon joined Richard on Forum ice. By the late 1950s, more than half the Canadiens—including stars Doug Harvey, "Boom Boom" Geoffrion, Maurice's younger brother Henri Richard, and Dickie Moore—were Montrealers. By comparison, only two players on the Leafs 1959–60 club were Torontonians.

For Richard's Canadiens, hockey was ecstasy or disgrace. Perhaps not surprisingly, the team's most lasting achievement was a mature and forward-looking response to the Rocket's greatest humiliation. Richard was on the verge of winning his first scoring title in the spring of 1955 when his legendary temper overtook him in Boston. Hal Laycoe, an ex-teammate, clipped him with an errant stick. Rising in a fury, Richard felt blood on his face and threw himself at the Bruins defender. Linesman Cliff Thompson twice grabbed number 9 and was thrown aside. The third time he reached for Richard, The Rocket turned and dropped Thompson like a plank.

Two days after Richard attacked the linesman, NHL president Clarence Campbell suspended The Rocket for the final three games of the season and for the playoffs. The city of Montreal suffered an immediate breakdown. When a local bus driver learned of Campbell's action he drove through a flashing railroad crossing, nearly killing everyone on board. The NHL offices, then in Montreal's Sun Life Building, were besieged with crank calls. Some fans simply cried into the telephone. NHL referee Red Storey remembers a radio announcer's comment the morning of Montreal's last regular season home game: "Is this St. Patrick's Day or Blow Up the Sun Life Building Day?" This was indeed the moment that Edward III, in outlawing bandy in the 14th century, and every subsequent leader who worried about hockey, had feared.

At the Montreal Forum, on rue Ste-Cathérine, more than 600 protesters arrived prior to the start of Montreal's final home game of the regular season—some chanting "Kill Campbell." Inside the Forum, the mood was equally charged. A glum Richard watched from a goal judge's booth as the Detroit Red Wings made easy work of his deflated teammates. Arriving late with his secretary-fiancée and two female friends, Clarence Campbell became the target of verbal, then physical abuse. During the first intermission a youth sprang toward Campbell, decorating his suit with ripe tomatoes. Campbell rose, pointing to his assailant. But the police were handling trouble elsewhere in the arena: a mob of protesters had pressed in, bent on revenge. Then, a tear-gas bomb went off, sending Campbell's persecutors scrambling for the exits. A Montreal detective would tell *Maclean*'s magazine, "The bomb thrower protected Campbell's life by releasing it at precisely the right moment."

The Montreal Forum in the 1920s.

La Sainte-Flanelle

Although the Canadiens' sweater, *la Sainte-Flanelle*, has not changed much in 70 years, hockey's most famous uniform required decades of refinement. The Canadiens' first 1909 sweater was dark blue with white trimming. The centre of the jersey contained a six-inch-high white letter C. Pants were white, stockings red. George Kennedy owned the Canadiens in 1910–11 and called the team le *Club athlétique Canadien*. The sweater was changed to red and initially sported a white gothic C superimposed on a green maple leaf. The following season, the team adopted something closer to the now-familiar red "barber pole" jersey. A narrow white stripe separated the wider red and sky blue bands. The crest, however, read CA. In November 1917 the club joined the brand-new National Hockey League and changed its name to *le Club de hockey Canadien*, adding the now famous CH to sweaters. *La Sainte-Flanelle* has undergone minor additions and subtractions over the years. In 1921, the H changed from blue to white. In 1925 and 1926, team jerseys had a globe on the front to signify winning the Stanley Cup. In the fall of 1935, crests disappeared off the arm bands and a darker blue was introduced to make a more dramatic colour scheme. The red sweater was now perfect. The white version of the Canadiens' uniform would be introduced in the fall of 1946.

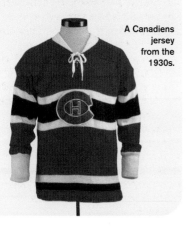

A Canadiens jersey from the 1930s.

But just as The Rocket had not been contained by officials earlier that week in Boston, the crowd gathered around the Forum would not be tamed by police. The Richard Riot was under way. Stores were ransacked, fires set. By next morning, rivers of broken glass extended for miles in every direction around the Forum.

Richard and the Canadiens would respond to the worst moment in franchise history with characteristic resolve, and also with a new, hard-won wisdom. Richard went on the radio and asked for public calm. The player made a pledge to accept his punishment and come back next year to help the team win the Stanley Cup.

Months later, the Canadiens hired the team's first bilingual coach, Toe Blake. What followed was the greatest period in franchise history. The Canadiens won a record number of games (45) the following season, with Richard, successfully fighting age and injuries, scoring 38 goals. Montreal won the Stanley Cup in 1956 and would not let it go for the rest of the decade, winning an unprecedented five Stanley Cups in a row. In the spring of '57, with everyone watching on *Hockey Night in Canada*, the Rocket led all playoff scorers with 11 goals in 10 games.

The glory years had arrived. Between 1955 and 1979, the team that Richard made great would win the Stanley Cup 14 times. The Canadiens were exalted heroes now, as the sudden profusion of patriotic nicknames would suggest—*les Glorieux, la Sainte-Flanelle, le bleu-blanc-rouge, le Tricolore*. And everywhere the Canadiens travelled in Canada, whether it was Toronto, Winnipeg, Edmonton, Calgary or Vancouver, local fans showed up in Montreal jerseys. No longer simply the heroes of Montreal, the Canadiens were now regarded as the standard bearers of all that was best in Canadian hockey. The player and the team some had feared might destroy Montreal had united a hockey nation.

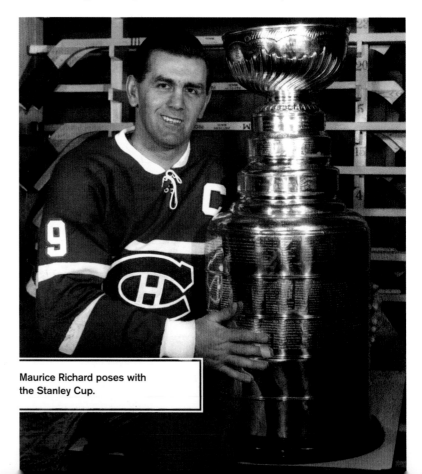

Maurice Richard poses with the Stanley Cup.

QUEBEC CITY

FOUNDED

Canada's oldest city, Quebec City was founded in 1608 by explorer Samuel de Champlain. By 1666, the settlement's population was a scant 547, and only after France increased incentives for settlers did the population begin to expand and its importance as a trading centre flourish. As the town grew, so did its significance as a military base, prompting the French to fortify their stronghold with a magnificent Citadel. The fortification offered little protection when the British surprised the French in 1759, defeating their militia on the Plains of Abraham. What had been intended as the capital of New France would become a hub in the expanding British North American empire. From 1859 to 1865, Quebec City was the capital of Canada, the last before Confederation. Quebec City famously hosted two vital World War II conferences, in 1943 and 1944. The first was attended by Franklin Delano Roosevelt, Winston Churchill and Prime Minister Mackenzie King. In 2002, Quebec City and 12 neighbouring municipalities merged to form an eight-borough megacity.

NATIVE-BORN NHL PLAYERS

Joel Baillargeon, Marty Barry, Fred Bergdinon, Steve Bernier, David Brisson, Mario Brunetta, Guy Chouinard, Jean-Philippe Cote, Sylvain Cote, Maurice Courteau, Xavier Delisle, Rene Drolet, Gord Dineen, Kevin Dineen, Mario Doyon, Rene Drolet, Gaetan Duchesne, Donald Dufresne, Len Fontaine, Eric Germain, Alexander Giroux, Camille Henry, Michel Lachance, Pierre Lacroix, Simon Lajeunesse, Jack LeClair, Reggie Lemelin, Percy LeSueur, Cliff Malone, Joe Malone, Jean Marois, Bert McInenly, Mike McMahon, Gerard McNeil, Patrick Moran, Dave Morissette, James Pollock, Marc-Antoine Pouliot, Pascal Rheaume, Jacques Richard, Pierre Rioux, Mario Roberge, Serge Roberge, Jean-Marc Routhier, Patrick Roy, Derek Smith, Nils Tremblay, Vincent Tremblay, Alain Vigneault

FAMOUS LOCAL TEAMS

Junior: Quebec A's, Quebec Baronet, Quebec Citadelle, Quebec Frontenacs, Quebec Remparts, Quebec Sons of Ireland, Quebec Victorias; **Senior-pro:** Quebec Aces, Quebec Bulldogs

CURRENT POPULATION

682,757

Le Gros Bill: Jean Beliveau with the Montreal Canadiens.

ACE SPY

Alfred Hitchcock made his film *I Confess* in Quebec City in 1951. Perhaps he should have made a thriller about Jean Beliveau's best friend in Quebec City, Emile Couture, a future Quebec Aces functionary, but in 1943 a sergeant in the Royal 22nd Regiment of Quebec. Couture was one of thousands employed to keep the Quebec Conference, a wartime summit involving Winston Churchill, Franklin Roosevelt and Mackenzie King, quiet and safe. While Canadian destroyers patrolled the St. Lawrence and warplanes circled above the Château Frontenac, Couture secured the meeting room after leaders quit for the day. Clearing up one afternoon, he found a red binder and took it with him to dispose of later. That night, he brought out the binder and discovered detailed plans for the Normandy Invasion. He returned them immediately to shocked, wary officials, who ordered him kept under military surveillance until D-Day. Couture later received a British Empire Medal.

Château Beliveau

Perhaps we should start Jean Beliveau's story in Trois-Rivières, his birthplace, or in Victoriaville, where he first played hockey. We might even place him in Nova Scotia. The first Beliveau to arrive in the New World—Antoine—settled in Port Royal in 1642. Jean Beliveau's ancestors lived in what is now Annapolis Royal for generations before being expelled, along with thousands of other Acadians, in the 18th century.

But Jean Beliveau's story really starts in Quebec's capital, for he and Quebec City hockey came of age together. The sport had been played here before, of course. The Quebec Bulldogs were established in 1888, and famed forward Joe Malone helped the Bulldogs win the Stanley Cup in 1912 and 1913. But if Malone was a superstar, Beliveau was a folk hero, an athlete whom children adored and powerful politicians strove to please.

Born in Trois-Rivières in 1931, Beliveau grew quickly and well. At 16, he was

Jean Beliveau celebrates a hat trick.

already larger-than-life (6'3"), altar-boy shy, with a classic profile that gave promise of noble intention. He led Quebec junior hockey in both goals (94) and tall tales his first two seasons with the Victoriaville Tigers (1947–49). The 16-year-old fired a pair past Verdun's Lorne Worsley in his debut, then weeks later, in Quebec City, he beat a wandering goalie to a puck with his extension-ladder reach, guiding the puck past startled Citadelle netminder Jacques Plante into an empty cage.

Quebecers called the Victoriaville sensation "Le Gros Bill" after the folk song "Le Voilà le gros Bill" ("Here Comes Big Bill"). But the player would not stay in Victoriaville for long. For in 1949, fate intervened, as it will on behalf of heroes.

Beliveau was a national figure now— heir to The Rocket

Quebec City's Coliseum burned down and the Victoriaville franchise folded. Beliveau's rights went to the Quebec Citadelle, who built a gleaming white palace grand enough to accommodate Beliveau, Le Colisée—or as it would soon be known, Château Beliveau.

Beliveau was still a kid when he arrived in Quebec's capital city in 1949, just months removed from raising rabbits in his Victoriaville backyard. And he could only really express himself on the hockey rink and the baseball diamond (where his crackling fastball brought pro offers). Though lonely at first, Beliveau feasted on his new home, wandering the ancient Upper Town for hours at night.

The city loved him. He enjoyed free steaks at Cartier Street restaurants. Laval Dairy paid him a working man's salary to hand out ice cream from a roving truck. He conquered his shyness by talking to kids on a province-wide Saturday children's radio show, broadcast on CHRC. Good fortune seemed to follow him everywhere. Beliveau fell for a local girl, won a Quebec Junior Hockey League scoring championship, and helped the Citadelle capture the Quebec provincial junior championship all in the same year.

The Montreal Canadiens beckoned. The Aces, Quebec City's semi-pro team, offered Beliveau $15,000 to sign, twice the amount that National Hockey Leaguers were making in 1951. Hearing this, a bagman for Premier Duplessis who had invited himself to the salary negotiations cleared his throat. Beliveau was promptly offered $20,000 by the Quebec Aces. With that bid accepted, the 19-year-old became the highest-paid hockey player in the world.

Beliveau was a national figure now—heir to The Rocket (with the Aces, he wore Richard's famous number 9). Toronto and Montreal newspapers printed "Wanted" signs speculating what the Canadiens would pay as reward for the star's capture. But Jean was happy in Quebec City. After games, he and his sweet-heart (Élise Couture) left Le Colisée for Old City nightspots, slipping through a side entrance to their regular table. Thousands of local fans followed Beliveau on the road. Sunday afternoon games at the Forum against the senior Montreal Royals were sold out, with half the onlookers having been bused in from Quebec City.

Perhaps the adulation of Quebec City fans was so keen because they knew that Beliveau would eventually have to test his talent with the National Hockey League. Finally, in the fall of 1953, he left Château Beliveau for Montreal. His going-away party would prove to even Maurice Duplessis that Le Gros Bill had grown too large for the Quebec City stage. In 1952, the premier held a public christening for a local highway. That same day, a crony of Beliveau's started up a new restaurant on boulevard Ste-Anne, promising an appearance by the Aces

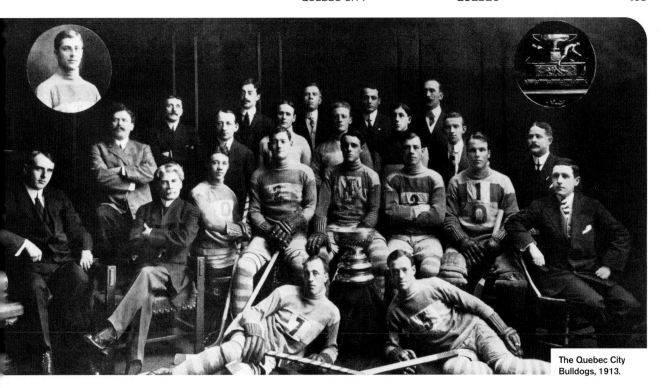

The Quebec City
Bulldogs, 1913.

British Bulldogs

The Bulldogs' name gave away the English nature of Quebec City's first great hockey franchise. The team took the 1912 Stanley Cup with the help of Hall of Fame goalie Paddy Moran's equipment. Moran anticipated another larger-than-life Quebec City goalie, Patrick Roy, by wearing oversized sweaters that draped like bat wings under the arms. But the team's true star was another Quebec City native, Joe "The Phantom" Malone, a gliding skater who earned his nickname by disappearing—poof!—in the attacking zone and materializing in front of the net to slam home another goal. Malone provided much of the offence in the Bulldogs' 1912 and 1913 Cup wins and then vanished to Waterloo, Ontario, for a season before joining the Montreal Canadiens. He scored five goals in the Canadiens' first-ever National Hockey League game, a 19 December 1917 win against the Ottawa Senators. He went on that year to chalk up an incredible 44 goals in 20 games, a record that held until Maurice Richard scored 50 in 1943–44. The Phantom owns one NHL record, though, that has withstood the test of time. Back with the Bulldogs again in 1920, playing against the Toronto St. Pats, the Phantom of the Colisée scored seven goals in one game.

star. Only dutiful reporters showed up for the road opening. Big Jean, meanwhile, was mobbed by over 7,000 gleeful fans.

With the Canadiens, Beliveau continued to fulfill his heroic destiny, leading the team to glory in three separate decades. He would also crown his Quebec City successor in 1962. While convalescing from an injury, he ventured back to his old hometown to take in the city's famous winter carnival, where he watched in amazement as an underage player (wearing Beliveau's Montreal Canadiens number 4!) made the Quebec City international peewee hockey tournament famous. This young dynamo scored 30 of his team's 48 goals—blazing slapshots into the top corner from inside the blue line one shift, then slaloming through entire teams for an artful tip-in the next—leading his peewee team to a tournament win. After scoring three goals one game, the beaming 10-year-old was presented to Beliveau, who confirmed the hat trick by crowning Guy Lafleur with a proper *chapeau* for a newspaper photo shoot.

A scout for the Quebec Aces (now a junior team) wrote in his notebook of

Le Roi—the King

The only goalie whose expression could be read from behind a mask, Patrick Roy, once responded to chiding by enemy forward Jeremy Roenick with the comment, "I can't hear, Jeremy, I've got two Stanley Cup rings plugging my ears."

Always, Roy did things his way, although like any kid, the Quebec City youngster had his heroes—first Rogie Vachon, then Quebec Nordiques' Dan Bouchard, a villainous trickster who painted the inside of his pads white to make shooters believe there was a gaping hole between his legs. Patrick's American-born mother, Betty, a swim coach, secured an autographed Bouchard stick for her son, which read, "See you in the NHL." At first, that dream hardly seemed likely. Patrick didn't make a local midget team and so left town for Granby, where he was tortured for three seasons on the defenceless junior Bisons by the likes of Mario Lemieux and Pat LaFontaine. Being left to his own devices did, however, allow Patrick the freedom to develop his own style—low to the ice, using paddle and pads to seal the bottom third of the net in scrambles.

Surviving target practice for Quebec Major Junior Hockey League firing squads also left the teenager with an unmistakable swagger. He arrived at age 19 in the National Hockey League with puck-sized chips on both shoulders. Montreal Canadiens' coach Jacques Lemaire didn't like the way Roy flopped around and once offered him a pillow in practice, asking if he wanted to sleep. Months later, when the coach finally called his number, the goalie didn't respond to Lemaire and, instead, asked a teammate, "Did he just mention my name?"

The following season, 1985–86, Roy was up with the Canadiens for good, living in teammate Lucien Deblois' basement. New coach Jean Perron decided to go with the 20-year-old in the playoffs. The rest is NHL history. Roy disposed of Boston, Hartford, New York and Calgary in the journeymen Canadiens' miraculous Stanley Cup run. He repeated the Cup-winning trick in 1993, and *Hockey Night in Canada* cameras caught him winking at Tomas Sandstrom in the finals after stealing a goal away from the Los Angeles winger.

Given Roy's temperament, there were predictable rough patches. Three years after his 1993 victory, he suffered Granby-era flashbacks in an 11–1 Montreal Forum shellacking at the hands of the Detroit Red Wings. Pulled after nine goals, Roy fixed coach Mario Tremblay with a gelid stare, then walked to nearby club president Ronald Corey and said, "That's my last game in Montreal."

Even in Denver, where he played net for the Colorado Avalanche (formerly the Quebec Nordiques), helping the team to Stanley Cups in 1996 and 2001, Roy remained Quebec's goalie. By then, the Allaire brothers had opened a successful Montreal goaltending camp that featured, as part of its course load, an hour-long video of Patrick Roy at work. Early students included Martin Brodeur, Robert Luongo, Jose Theodore and Patrick Lalime. Soon, the province was flooded with Roy clones, although no one could erase the memory of number 33 in net—rotating his head as if to resolve a crick in his neck during a lull in play, arguing with goal posts, and on the rare occasions opponents scored, searching his overabundant sweater and pads for security breaches.

Retiring in 2003, Roy was asked at a press conference what NHL shooter he feared the most. "To be honest, no one," he said. Then he laughed, adding, "I guess things have not changed, eh?" The following season, the King returned to his Quebec throne, becoming general manager of the junior Quebec City Remparts at Le Colisée. He named himself coach of the team in 2005.

the Thurso native's play, "Lafleur, Guy. Excellent skater. Strong and accurate right-handed shot. Interesting style of play. Can fake right or left. Excellent forward, can also play defensively." Five years later, in Canada's centennial year, Lafleur was playing for Le Gros Bill's Quebec Aces in Le Colisée. The teenager continued to wear Beliveau's number 4.

The two stars were different players, however. While Beliveau performed with an almost magisterial calm, Lafleur played with pitched emotion, racing like a burning fuse down the wing. Fans loved him. "Le Blond Demon"

"Lafleur, Guy. Excellent skater. Strong and accurate right-handed shot."

was Quebec City hockey from 1967 to 1971, scoring 130 goals in his final season to lead the local junior team, now called the Quebec Remparts, to the Memorial Cup.

During those years, Quebec City's ardour for hockey was unmatched in Canada. Lafleur graduated to the Canadiens and to further glory in the fall of 1971. The city, meanwhile, won a World Hockey Association (WHA) franchise in 1972, the Quebec Nordiques, and offered Beliveau a cool million to return to the scene of his first triumphs. Big Jean declined, but Maurice Richard accepted the head coaching job—for the first week anyway. (With no physical outlet for his hockey passions, Richard found coaching unbearable and quit after the first game.)

The Quebec Nordiques were an artistic and a financial success, as fans crowded into Le Colisée to watch the team—led by the ineffably cool Marc Tardif and puppy-dog Reggie Houle—challenge annually for the WHA's Avco Cup, which the team won in the spring of 1977. A year and a half later, the Nordiques joined the NHL, making life miserable for the Canadiens.

The team reeled off three shrewd picks—Remparts star Michel Goulet, feisty Dale Hunter and Czech rookie Anton Stastny—with its first NHL draft and, then, with a move that might have formed the basis for a John le Carré thriller, snatched Anton's older brother Peter, in a surreptitious raid behind the Iron Curtain. Goalie Dan Bouchard came next. (A Quebec City teenager at the time, Patrick Roy studied Bouchard with the discerning eye of a master apprentice.)

The Nordiques' playoff battles with the Canadiens in the '80s were, along with the Edmonton-Calgary wars in Alberta, the quintessential pro hockey rivalries of the era. Every spring, Le Colisée and the Montreal Forum became the scene of dark, dangerously thrilling playoff struggles. What made these Cain and Abel affairs so intense and exhausting for Quebec City fans was that native sons—first Remparts star Lafleur, and then local hero Patrick Roy—were employed by the rival Canadiens. The torture became too much when the Nordiques left town for Denver in 1995, becoming the Colorado Avalanche; then promptly acquired Roy in a trade with Montreal; and finally won the Stanley Cup in the team's very first year outside Quebec City.

All was not lost, however. The junior Remparts, who folded in 1985 (a victim of the success of the Nordiques), would return in the early 1990s. And just as Guy Lafleur came home to finish his NHL career with the Nordiques (1989–91), Patrick Roy returned to Quebec City after completing his NHL career and was named vice president of Remparts Hockey Operations in 2003. The house that Beliveau made and Guy Lafleur paid for—Le Colisée—successfully hosted the Memorial Cup that spring. The following year, the Remparts drew more than 200,000 fans, a post-Lafleur record.

Pee Wees' Big Adventure

The Quebec international peewee hockey tournament began, in 1960, as a peewee hockey showcase to complement February's Quebec City Winter Carnival. Eleven-year-old Brad Park from the Scarborough Lions created a stir that first tourney (and would later go on to a Hall of Fame career as a National Hockey League defenceman). Two years later, Guy Lafleur electrified the Colisée. With Lafleur, the Quebec international tournament became an institution. Subsequent hockey stars to debut there included Wayne Gretzky, Gilbert Perreault, Mark Howe, Mario Lemieux and Eric Lindros. Today, the event attracts teams from as far away as South Africa and is very much a community event. Five hundred families billet visiting players and local companies donate food. Over six million fans have visited the Colisée to watch the games. That number includes many former players—some who return for non-peewee-related reasons. Quebec City defenceman Sylvain Cote once said that he returned as a teenager because "it was a good place to meet chicks."

ROUYN-NORANDA

FOUNDED

In 1911, Ontario prospector Edmund Horne ventured into the lake-strewn wilderness that is now Rouyn-Noranda. Three years later, he would discover gold there. The resulting mineral stampede resulted in two towns—Rouyn and Noranda—amalgamated in 1986.

NATIVE-BORN NHL PLAYERS

Bob Blackburn, Christian Bordeleau, J.P. Bordeleau, Paulin Bordeleau, Jacques Caron, Jacques Cloutier, Roland Cloutier, Wayne Connelly, Jacques "Coco" Cossete, Eric "Rico" Desjardins, Chris Hayes, Rejean Houle, Dave Keon, Jacques Laperriere, Steve Larouche, Jean Lemieux, Jean-Louis Levasseur, Pit Martin, Stephane Matteau, William McDonagh, Ted Ouimet, Andre Racicot, Andre St. Laurent, Bob Sullivan, Dale Tallon, Pierre Turgeon, Sylvain Turgeon

FAMOUS LOCAL TEAMS

Junior: Noranda Aces, Noranda Copper Kings, Rouyn Aces, Rouyn Flashes, Rouyn-Noranda Alouettes, Rouyn-Noranda Huskies

CURRENT POPULATION

28,270

Dave Keon ended his career with the Hartford Whalers.

Hockey Boom Town

Rouyn-Noranda has produced a wealth of gold and copper, but undoubtedly the northern Quebec mining town's most famous export is hockey players. Although the twin towns' combined population has hovered around 30,000 for decades, this area has given birth to more National Hockey Leaguers than some provinces—28 players in all, most notably gold-standard '60s-era Hall of Famers Dave Keon and Jacques Laperriere, but also a continual vein of silver-grade performers from the '70s (Dale Tallon and Reggie Houle) right up to the present day (schoolboy pals Pierre Turgeon, Stephane Matteau, Rico Desjardins and Andre Racicot).

And while Rouyn-Noranda is probably best known for its butter-smooth forwards, the city has also produced an elbows-up intimidator who once stared down Dave "The Hammer" Schultz. The intimidator was Canada's first female sports columnist, Christie Blatchford. (Her dad, Ross Blatchford, ran the Noranda Recreation Centre, "the Rec," in the 1950s.)

One theory to explain why northern Quebec and Ontario have produced so many hockey players is that the mines in these regions imported minor-league baseball and hockey stars between the wars to stock competitive semipro industrial league teams in both sports—clubs such as the Noranda Copper Kings (hockey) and the Thetford Mines Miners (baseball). The competitive zeal

Head Games

In addition to all his hockey achievements, Jacques Laperriere enjoyed 15 minutes of fame in the '60s as a TV pitchman for Instantine aspirins. A sinister English adman littered Jacques's copy with a minefield (for the French tongue) of "h" sounds, but the defencemen stickhandled his way through the piece with characteristic brio. The ad went something like this: "Allo, am Jacques Laperriere for Instant'n. N 'ockey, the 'edache is an occupational 'azard. When I get the 'edache, I ritch for Instant'n."

Pierre Turgeon with the
Montreal Canadiens.

Dave Keon with the Stanley Cup.

created by these teams was contagious, the explanation goes. And so after gold
and copper strikes in the area, a hockey boom was inevitable, given that hockey
is Rouyn-Noranda's favourite winter sport and that winters here are never less
than six months long.

Evidence of that boom first arrived in the early '60s when Dave Keon and
Jacques Laperriere graduated to the fabled Toronto Maple Leafs and Montreal
Canadiens. Being from Quebec, Keon obviously didn't grow up in Leafs country,
but he was a candidate for the blue-and white-by virtue of his language and faith.
His mother and father, both originally from the Ottawa Valley, were faithful
English Catholics who performed the rosary every night after supper. A local

Jacques Laperierre.

sensation with the Noranda Juveniles, Keon passed an audition to a Detroit junior camp at age 15, but his parents refused to let him go. Legendary Leafs scout Bob Davidson managed to sign the youth, however, with the offer of a proper Catholic education from the Basilian fathers at St. Michael's College School, a private secondary school in Toronto.

The St. Mike's juniors were a powerful bargaining chip at the time. Indeed, enemy NHL teams used to complain about the difficulty of competing with Toronto for Catholic players, since the Maple Leafs had a scout in every parish in Canada.

One priest at the school made an immediate impact on Keon. St. Mike's hockey coach Father David Bauer saw right away that the Noranda youngster was a wonderful, graceful skater. One little hop on his back skate and he was off. Sometimes it looked as if Keon was a sailing vessel in a lake full of rowboats. But Keon was also slight and tended to linger outside scrums, waiting for play to

Fans used to joke that players hid in front of the net when Laperierre wound up.

come to him. Father Bauer told the teenager that he would never make the NHL unless he used his speed to check. He had to learn to play without the puck.

Keon was a fast learner. By the time he arrived in the NHL with the Leafs in 1960, he was maybe the most gifted checker in hockey. Not only could the bilingual centreman keep up in conversation with the Canadiens' Flying Frenchmen, but he could skate with them, too.

Maybe the most striking quality about Keon's work was his discipline. During the '60s, he led the Leafs, a team built on defence, to four Stanley Cups, winning the Conn Smythe Trophy as the most valuable performer in the 1967 playoffs. Every game that decade he went one-on-one with Beliveau, Richard, Mikita, Esposito, Ullman and Delvecchio—all future Hall of Famers who were inevitably foiled by Keon's relentless attention. Further proof of the miracle of his craftsmanship was that during all those Mission Impossible assignments, he recorded a mere 36 minutes in penalties from 1960–69.

For Montreal Canadiens rearguard, Jacques Laperierre, the 1960s was also a decade crowded with accomplishment—a rookie of the year award (1964) and a best NHL defenceman award (1966), along with four all-star appearances. Laperriere would also match Keon with four Stanley Cup wins in his first six seasons.

The Rouyn native was an unlikely superstar—tall, seemingly all arms and legs, with a curiously upright, egg-beater skating style. Still, no forward could get around him. His extension-ladder reach and bony elbows made the left side of the Canadiens defence as thorny as a bramble bush. "Lappy," as he was called, was a superb passer as well, with a hard, if sometimes erratic, shot. (Fans used to joke that players hid in front of the net when Laperriere wound up.) A threat on power plays, he could also headman the puck and connect with long-bomb passes to breaking wingers with the best of his defensive contemporaries.

Laperriere's talents could be readily appreciated by young working-class fans who congregated to watch the sainted Canadiens in Rouyn-Noranda bars that were as rough as Lappy's elbows, with names such as the Maroon Lounge, the Moulin Rouge and the Radio Hotel. But perhaps the Rouyn native's game was best understood by the game's accountants. In 1972–73, NHL statisticians determined that Jacques Laperriere had the greatest plus-minus record of any player in the league.

All Four One

Rouyn-Noranda natives can often play two sports as well as speak two languages. In 1981, the city finished third in the Canadian Little League baseball championships. The following year, the same team reached the Little League world series in Williamsport, Pennsylvania, where the club was beaten 8–4 in the semifinals by Taiwan. Incredibly, the baseball team was led by four friends who would all, one day, make their mark in the National Hockey League. Pierre Turgeon was the team's slugging first baseman, while Stephane Matteau played catcher, Andre Racicot played shortstop and Eric Desjardins patrolled the outfield. Desjardins, Racicot and Turgeon would all end up playing for the Montreal Canadiens. And all four would work at a hockey school run by, you guessed it, Rouyn-Noranda hero Jacques Laperriere.

SHERBROOKE

FOUNDED
Located at the confluence of the St-François and the Magog Rivers, Sherbrooke was first settled in 1793 by United Empire Loyalists. Though established by English settlers, it is now predominantly a French-speaking community. The city grew substantially on 1 January 2002, with the amalgamation of the cities of Sherbrooke, Ascot, Bromptonville, Deauville, Fleurimont, Lennoxville, Rock Forest and St-Élie-d'Orford.

NATIVE-BORN NHL PLAYERS
Eric Belanger, Pierre-Marc Bouchard, Dan Chicoine, Mathieu Dandenault, Christian Dube, Gilles Dube, Norm Dube, Marc Fortier, Bill Heindl, Jean-Francois Labbe, Gordon McRae, Yanic Perreault, Gerry Plamondon, Bob Rivard, Stephane Robidas, Claude St-Sauveur, Jimmy Waite

FAMOUS LOCAL TEAMS
Junior: Sherbrooke Braves, Sherbrooke Beavers, Sherbrooke Faucons, Sherbrooke Indians;
Senior-pro: Sherbrooke Canadiens, Sherbrooke Cantons, Sherbrooke Castors, Sherbrooke Jets, Sherbrooke Randies, Sherbrooke Red Raiders, Sherbrooke St-Francois, Sherbrooke Saints, Sherbrooke St. Xavier

CURRENT POPULATION
141,200

Sher-Wood hockey sticks.

Stick Work

The other big question that Canadian kids ask their parents—"Where do hockey sticks come from?"—has a simple answer.

Sherbrooke, Quebec, of course.

Thirteen National Hockey Leaguers have found their way to the NHL from this part of the Eastern Townships. Sherbrooke is also where amateur sensation Herb Carnegie had his best season in the 1940s. As well, the city has sponsored teams that run the gamut from Beavers to Jets to Randies to Saints. Still, when it comes to shinny, Sherbrooke is most famous for producing that whippy, brightly decorated instrument of sporting pleasure, the modern hockey stick.

A local company, Sher-Wood Drolet Corp., is the biggest manufacturer of sticks in the world. Thirty percent of NHLers use Sher-Woods. Because of exclusive contracts with minor league teams, so does every Manitoba Moose (American Hockey League) and Roanoke Valley Viper (United Hockey League). In fact, many people reading this have probably handled a stick from Sher-Wood's 650,000-square-foot plant—using it, most likely, to whack around one of the millions of pucks the company has dropped into the marketplace.

Sherbrooke wasn't always synonymous with hockey gear. A nearby Quebec town, St-Jean d'Iberville (manufacturers of CCM equipment), succeeded Dartmouth, Nova Scotia (producer of Micmac sticks), as the hockey stick capital of Canada. But in 1949, a local hardware clerk, Leo Drolet, speculated on the money to be made in something as popular and as impermanent as a hockey stick.

At the time, hockey sticks were made of ash (for the shaft) and elm (for the blade). The quality of the black ash grown around Sherbrooke was inferior, so Drolet bought from wood suppliers in nearby Scotstown and Cowansville,

Migrating Beavers

The Sherbrooke Beavers were the best junior team in Quebec during the mid-1970s, winning the playoff championship in 1975, 1977 and 1982. (Rick Vaive, Richard Sevigny and Jere Gillis were three of the stars during this era.) The team represented Canada in the 1976 world junior championships, finishing second. The most valuable player on that team was coach Ghislain Delage who saw that other countries were represented by national teams and suggested that Canada adopt a winter training camp and scouting unit to select a better-prepared team. His recommendations led to the Canadian junior hockey program.

The Beavers left Sherbrooke in 2003 for Lewiston, Maine, where the French-speaking team became the Lewiston MAINEiacs. Ironically, Lewiston had been a popular destination for the 900,000 Quebecers who had left the province over a six-decade period that ended with the Great Depression.

Quebec, and even from Maine and New Hampshire across the border in the U.S. For elm, he scouted Ontario. Indeed, he spent much of that early period searching for good suppliers, discovering bad ones the expensive way. (Once a dissatisfied customer surprised Drolet outside church with a cord of Sher-Wood kindling.)

Drolet spent the 1950s and 1960s learning the retail business. One successful promotional strategy was to limit supply for a new line, explaining, with a

The right winger scored on the next shift, then twice later in the game. From then on, Lafleur was a Sher-Wood man.

shrug, that the product was selling out elsewhere. Retailers sold their meagre allotment, of course, and inevitably put in fat orders for the next year.

In the late '60s, the National Hockey League expanded from six to 12 teams and from one to three weekly TV broadcasts—in addition to the familiar Saturday night *Hockey Night in Canada* broadcasts (CBC), there also were televised games on Wednesday nights (CTV) and Sunday afternoons (CBS) now. Sher-Wood responded by tailoring its gear to maximize increased exposure after a Sher-Wood executive, Georges Guilbault, was struck by a thunderbolt while watching the 1971 NHL playoffs. That spring Montreal Canadiens rookie goalie Ken Dryden created a sensation, stopping everything the Boston Bruins and Chicago Blackhawks threw at him, then hopping to his feet at the edge of the crease, loafing contentedly on his upright Sher-Wood as he watched play drift to the other end. Why not increase the size of the Sher-Wood lettering on Dryden's stick? Guilbault thought, after seeing the goalie turn away another scoring rush. Think of the free publicity!

Soon the company was aggressively romancing NHL players. In the mid-1970s, Guilbault had Sher-Wood customize a stick to Guy Lafleur's specifications. (At the time, The Flower was using a Finnish KOHO.) Guilbault then secured an audience with Lafleur through Canadiens team trainer, Pierre Meilleur, and watched in horror one practice as Guy destroyed stick after stick with the powerful swing of his slapshot. "*Fort comme un boeuf*," the executive marvelled. ("Strong as a bull.")

Sher-Wood came back with a fortified model. Lafleur feigned disinterest but allowed a few Sher-Woods to be added to his game quiver. Guy was in a rare slump at the time and broke his KOHO early in one game. Returning to the bench, he asked Meilleur for a Sher-Wood. The right winger scored on the next shift, then twice later in the game. From then on, Lafleur was a Sher-Wood man.

With player endorsements and custom design came increased prices and profits. In the early '60s, the prevailing industry wisdom was that no one would pay more than $5 for a hockey stick. Hey, they can break. A dozen years later, kids were paying $25 for a good piece of wood. Sher-Wood's profits rose from $46,900 in 1949 to $1,739,000 in 1969. Today, the company is one of the biggest businesses in Sherbrooke and the largest partner in a $40,000,000 global hockey equipment industry.

The modern Sher-Wood stick can be made out of graphite, carbon fibre or aluminum. Even wooden sticks are made of cheap lightweight aspen reinforced with fibreglass. And though a better name for today's product might be Sher-not-Wood, the hockey sticks are still made in Sherbrooke, Quebec, by the company that Léo Drolet founded on a $500 loan from his family.

THE PUCKS START HERE

Sher-Wood's sister company, Sherbrooke-based InGlasCo Corporation, keeps the world well supplied with pucks, although the company outsources much of the manufacturing. National Hockey League souvenir pucks are made in Buchov, Slovakia.

InGlasCo has imported over four million units since 1989. NHL official game pucks, however, are made in a plant outside Montreal. Each NHL club buys 5,000 pucks from InGlasCo annually. These pucks are made of rubber and carbon or coal dust. Carbon or coal gives a puck its colour and density, while sulfur vulcanizes the rubber—making it more elastic. The ingredients are mixed in a giant blender; rolled into soft, flat sheets; then baked for 20 minutes in molding presses. *Et voilà!*

SOREL-TRACY

Logo of the
Sorel Eperviers.

FOUNDED
Canada's fourth oldest city was established at the mouth of the Richelieu River on the south bank of the St. Lawrence River in 1642. An early commander of French troops, at what was then called Fort Richelieu, was Pierre de Saurel, after whom Sorel was named. Sorel-Tracy was amalgamated in 2000.

NATIVE-BORN NHL PLAYERS
Francois Beauchemin, Michel Belhumeur, Claude Cardin, Frederic Cassivi, Michel Deziel, Marc-Andre Fleury, Andre Gill, Claude Laforge, Wildor Larochelle, Pierre Mondou

FAMOUS LOCAL TEAMS
Junior: Sorel Black Hawks, Sorel Eperviers, Sorel Royaux; **Senior-pro:** Sorel Dinosaures, Sorel Royaux, Sorel-Tracy Mission

CURRENT POPULATION
34,194

Christmas Presents

Two particular winters loom large in Sorel history. The first was the winter of 1781, when German immigrant Baroness Riedesel invited British and German soldiers from what was then Fort Richelieu to a Christmas Eve party at her house, where she served bread pudding in the dining room by the dazzling play of lights from a towering, candlelit fir tree. The German soldiers, on loan from the Duke of Brunswick to help defend Canada, were familiar with a decorated tree, a tradition in their homeland for almost 100 years. But British soldiers were thrilled by the sight of what is accepted to have been North America's first Christmas tree. The custom soon spread through the Sorel community, which was then a small military town—surrounded by millions of potential Christmas trees.

Quebec's head start with Yuletide celebrations might partly explain why the province produces almost 25 percent of Canada's six million annual Christmas trees. (The North American tree business would really take off in the middle of the 19th century after Queen Victoria's German husband, Prince Albert, lit up a Christmas tree at Windsor Castle.)

Sorel's second great Christmas present arrived almost two centuries later when its junior hockey team, the Sorel Black Hawks, distinguished itself during what was Quebec's renaissance hockey period, the superstar '70s. During the 1973–74 season, the club established a Canadian junior hockey record for points in a 70-game schedule, accumulating 117 points on 58 wins, 11 losses and a tie.

Better yet for locals, the Quebec Major Junior Hockey League team performed the feat in the most crowd-pleasing of all fashions, filling the opposition net at a fast, frantic pace. Three players on the 1973–74 team flirted with 100-goal seasons. The number one line boasted the devilishly handsome Pierre "Lucky" Larouche, later a 50-goal scorer in the National Hockey League with Pittsburgh and Montreal, Michel Deziel and Jacques "Coco" Cossette, who contributed 94, 92 and 97 goals respectively. The Black Hawks' secondary lines offered no reprieves for opposition goalies, for additional forwards included Pierre Mondou and Michel "Le Petit Tigre" Bergeron (both with 62 goals). Every game was Christmas Day that season as locals crowded into the Colisée

Silver Butterfly

Born in 1984, Marc-Andre Fleury grew up beside a Sorel cornfield, in a house built by his carpenter father, playing a style of goaltending constructed from the careful study of Quebec legends Patrick Roy and Martin Brodeur. The youngster has Roy's hands and Brodeur's legs, on the bottom of which dangle original butterfly goalie Glenn Hall's flashing feet. The Fleurys rented goalie equipment for him early on, and seeing his promise, Marc-Andre was allowed to attend the prestigious Montreal goaltending school run by Patrick Roy disciple, Francois Allaire.

At 15, Fleury exhibited a Roy-like swagger while playing in Cape Breton. After allowing two soft goals, he was summoned to the bench by the coach, who weighed him down with a clipboard. Fleury returned the sheet with the message, "I'm not a statistician, I'm a goalie."

Three years later in 2003, the goalie was drafted first overall by the Pittsburgh Penguins, who made him a millionaire at age 18. Fleury earned the reward by shaking off the flu at the 2003 junior championships in Halifax to lead Canada to a silver medal finish—the same colour he would dye his hair after receiving one of his first big league cheques.

Pierre "Lucky" Larouche
with the Canadiens.

Cardin on rue Victoria to unwrap all the gift goals the Black Hawks would score as a result of dizzying passing manoeuvres. Hat tricks were as common as coughing on these winter nights. The team scored an average of nine goals a game. And to top it all off, two of the stars—the crafty Deziel and dipsy-doodling Pierre Mondou—were Sorel boys.

Christmases always end, unfortunately. After the team's record regular-season rampage, the Black Hawks lost in the playoffs to arch enemy, the Quebec Remparts.

Two seasons later, in the fall of 1976, the fans of Sorel received another temporary prize when a quiet 16-year-old defenceman from Montreal joined the Black Hawks for the first campaign in what would be a Hall of Fame career. The kid's name was Raymond Bourque. Much to the despair of Sorel's hockey lovers, the Black Hawks flew the coop in Bourque's second season, relocating to the Montreal suburb of Verdun.

Today, the amalgamated town of Sorel-Tracy is represented locally by the Mission, a team in the semi-pro North American Hockey League, and in the NHL by Sorel-born goalie sensation Marc-Andre Fleury.

THURSO

FOUNDED
Located on the Ottawa River, the village of Thurso sprang up around the same time as Hull. The town, which for decades was a lumber camp, received an economic boost with the arrival of a Singer sewing-machine factory in 1925.

NATIVE-BORN NHL PLAYERS
Guy Lafleur

FAMOUS LOCAL TEAMS
Senior-pro: Thurso Lumber Kings

CURRENT POPULATION
682

The Flower in Spring

In the 1970s, Quebec singer Robert Charlebois looked into a Montreal audience and saw Guy Lafleur everywhere—or at least he spotted hundreds of fans wearing Lafleur's number 10 jersey. "Do you like Guy Lafleur?" he inquired.

The crowd erupted, some chanting, "Guy! Guy! Guy!"

"I like him, too," Charlebois smiled. "In the winter, he replaces the sun."

Everybody loved Guy Lafleur. In native Thurso, a factory town 30 miles east of Ottawa, Guy served five years as an altar boy in the parish church. When the youngster, at 14, decided to move to Quebec City for hockey, the family received a visit from an astonished priest. The cleric had always believed that Lafleur wanted to join the priesthood.

People saw what they wanted to in Guy. The only son of a welder, he grew up a golden boy. On Sundays the family would travel to Rejean Lafleur's parents for weekly dinners involving 50 cousins. Guy was the child everyone enjoyed— easy smiling, naturally open and so graceful when he ran that it looked as though he'd been carried away by the wind.

More than just nature was at work here. A brother at l'École Ste-Famille told Guy's class that to succeed you had to devote yourself to a task early on, as local songwriter legend Paul Anka had proven. Anka, a Fisher Park student from nearby Ottawa, had played the Chaudière nightclub in Hull—the Chaud—when he was just 11, before making it big with the love song "Diana," written for his babysitter, which went on to sell nine million records.

Guy didn't want to become a crooner or a priest; he hoped to play hockey for the Montreal Canadiens, just like his idol Jean Beliveau. Still Lafleur took his teacher's message to heart. At age nine, in 1960, he went into training, running circles around Thurso, past the old English cemetery and the rink, a gift from Singer Sewing, the town's chief employer. Some days, the boy ran up to 10 miles. He also volunteered for work at a friend's farm, strengthening his wrists milking cows.

Lafleur practised hockey, too, of course. His dad welded goal cages out of discarded pipes, which were then dressed with potato sacking. Kids congregated for weekend-long hockey marathons at the Lafleur rink. Winter weekdays, Guy arrived at l'École Ste-Famille an hour before classes for morning games. The youngster played again at noon, then stayed for a longer match after school. Rejean Lafleur sometimes went into his son's room late Friday night and found Guy asleep in bed, fully costumed—pads on and everything—ready for hockey the next morning.

Guy Lafleur with the Stanley Cup.

At first no one knew how good Guy was, because he played among older boys. But his talent announced itself when he joined a real league at age 10. He was no bigger than anyone else, skinnier perhaps, but somehow sufficiently coordinated to fire slapshots from the blue line that rang off the crossbar with an alarm-bell chime. Some parents refused to let their children play in nets against him. But in 1962, Guy's talent was enough to take him from Thurso to the Franco-Ontarian town of Rockland, where he was made an honorary citizen in order to play as an underage peewee in the Quebec City international peewee tournament. (Thurso didn't have a peewee team of its own to compete in Quebec City.)

Lafleur returned from the tournament as an Ottawa Valley legend. In towns such as Hawkesbury, Gatineau and Buckingham, kids who played against him or knew someone who knew someone who played against him talked about Guy

Like many heroes, Guy had an essential mystery about him.

in hushed whispers. "There's this kid, eh, 10 years old, he can shoot the puck like Bobby Hull. No, no—I seen it. Name's Guy La-flew-er."

Graduating to junior hockey in Quebec City, Lafleur became another kind of star. The media noticed the English translation of his surname ("the flower") and the blond flag of hair that flew in his wake. Finally, numbers were available to gauge his talent. He scored 103 goals one season, then 130 the next, leading the Quebec City Remparts to the Memorial Cup in 1971.

Maybe he wouldn't have been as big a star in Montreal if he had been as good as everyone had hoped right away. But Lafleur was entirely mortal his first three years with the Canadiens, scoring goals like everyone else—on a rebound or a pass-out. Montreal, the best hockey city in the world, and Lafleur, the great prodigy, almost seemed shy around each other.

Then, in the fall of 1973, Guy took off his helmet to play. Like a scene in a movie where a reclusive girl takes off her glasses and shakes loose her hair to reveal a beautiful woman, Guy was immediately everything Montreal wanted him to be—a right winger as glamorous and deadly as Maurice Richard, "*Le blond démon*". Lafleur would score more than 50 goals in six straight seasons. And in every one of those years, he led the league in lifting fans from their seats. No one could shoot on the fly like Guy.

Lafleur was loved everywhere—in Quebec City and Montreal, but also in Toronto and Edmonton where transplanted Montrealers showed up at Maple Leaf Gardens or at Northland Coliseum, every one of them wearing number 10, it seemed. Whenever Lafleur grabbed hold of the puck, the chant would begin: "Guy! Guy! Guy! Guy!" Lafleur was the rare superstar who could inspire both teams to elevate their game—he made hockey a better sport. Fans were thrilled by the way he exploded down his wing, moving with the controlled fury of a downhill ski racer.

Like many heroes, Guy had an essential mystery about him. He would show up for night games in the early afternoon and sit in the dressing room, fully dressed, skates tight, chain-smoking, waiting to play. Once he admitted to keeping clocks and watches stashed, tick-tick-ticking, in drawers in his house. "When I open the drawer I can feel seconds, minutes, hours marching by," he told biographer, Georges-Hébert Germain. "And I tell myself that everything passes—things, people, even nature—and that you can never go backwards, or stop, or prevent time from carrying us away."

Time, it turned out, would take away Lafleur's talent too soon. At age 30, he somehow became disconnected from his gift. For three seasons, he was a Guy

Guy Lafleur in action, with his blond hair flying like a flag.

Lafleur impersonator as opposed to Le blond démon. La Sainte-Flanelle became unbearably heavy. He retired from the Canadiens at age 33.

The following day a member of Parliament, Lorne Nystrom, offered the following testimonial in the House of Commons: "It may be that everywhere else in the world the ascendance of Flower Power began and ended in the sixties, Mr. Speaker, but in Montreal it began in 1971 and ended yesterday when Guy Lafleur retired."

The House stood and applauded the hockey player. A few even offered up the now famous chant: "Guy! Guy! Guy!"

Gilles Villemure with the New York Rangers.

TROIS-RIVIÈRES

FOUNDED
Trois-Rivières was founded in 1634 by the famed explorer Samuel de Champlain and was named for the three channels found at the confluence of the St. Lawrence and St. Maurice rivers.

NATIVE-BORN NHL PLAYERS
Steve Begin, Jean Beliveau, Pierre "The Fleeting Frenchman" Bellefeuille, Gilles Boisvert, Edmond Bouchard, Marc Bureau, Marc Dufour, Andre "Moose" Dupont, Red Goupille, Andre Hinse, Robert Perreault, Rene Robert, Normand Rochefort, Pierre Sevigny, Jacques Toupin, Gilles Villemure

FAMOUS LOCAL TEAMS
Junior: Trois-Rivières Draveurs, Trois- Rivières Ducs, Trois-Rivières Flambeaux, Trois-Rivières Leafs, Trois-Rivières Reds; **Senior-pro:** Trois-Rivières Caron & Guay, Trois-Rivières Laviolettes, Trois-Rivières Leafs, Trois-Rivières Lions, Trois-Rivières Millionaires, Trois-Rivières Renards, Trois-Rivières Volants, Trois-Rivières Voltigeurs

CURRENT POPULATION
46,264

Hot to Trot

A left-handed goalie, Gilles Villemure began confounding shooters as a junior with the Trois-Rivières Reds in 1959. He was small (5'8") and a disciplined player of angles, with a bright crown of red hair.

Like most players in the 1960s, Villemure also had a summer job, although his occupation was unique among hockey players: he rode trotters back home in Trois-Rivières. Villemure would climb to the top of both professions. He led the American and Western Hockey Leagues in shutouts three times before being brought up by the National Hockey League's New York Rangers for the 1970–71 season, during which he won the Vezina Trophy with fellow Rangers netminder Eddie Giacomin. In addition to goaltending in Madison Square Garden, Villemure raced at New York's famed Meadowlands Racetrack.

Seventeen Minutes of Fame

Trois-Rivières is most famous for its goalies. Native son Gilles Villemure was an "original six" National Hockey League goalie and the winner of a Vezina Trophy. But another city netminder—here for only seventeen minutes, really—made Trois-Rivières the centre of the hockey world one night in 1991.

That goalie, born in Lac Beaufort, Quebec, began like others in the profession, trying to keep up with the older kids, all of whom dreamed of being scoring sensations. Inevitably, it was the littlest kid who would receive the order, "You play nets." This goalie, though tiny, was very good. Good enough at age five to play goalie in an organized league in Lac Beauport—over the howling protests of dad. Good enough to take a Beauport team to the peewee tournament in nearby Quebec City in 1983. That event was what made the goalie become famous, for the goalie was a girl (playing against boys!)—unheard of at the time.

Manon Rheaume, the talented female goaltender, grew older and improved, garnering the attention of the Canadian woman's hockey program. Younger brother Pascal Rheaume also made a name for himself, winning a position as a forward for the Trois-Rivières Draveurs ("the raftsmen") in the Quebec Major Junior Hockey League. (He would eventually play in the NHL for a number of teams.)

At 19, Manon Rheaume visited her brother and mentioned to Draveurs coach,

Gaston Drapeau, that she hoped to play for the Canadian woman's hockey team. Could she maybe practise with the Draveurs? Drapeau invited her to try out. Six goalies were invited to camp. Only three made it, including Manon, who stopped all 14 shots in her first exhibition game.

Great legs, the coaches said. The comment didn't come with wolf whistles. Number 33 (like her idol Patrick Roy) had fast feet. A good glove, too. At first, she was kept on the team's farm club in Louisville, Quebec, outside Trois-Rivières. Then a Draveurs goalie, Jean-Francois Labbe, was injured. Manon was called up.

Nobody anticipated the resulting furor. Trois-Rivières was suddenly the capital of the hockey world. Coach Drapeau phoned Patrick Roy's agent to get a PR firm to handle media. Every newspaper and every TV broadcast carried another story about Our Lady of the Nets. "Be ready," Drapeau advised Manon—the goalie teammates called "Tom Boy"—the day before the Granby Bisons visited.

The next day, the Draveurs' starting goalie, Jocelyn Thibault, had a rough

Manon Rheaume.

"I want to see how much better I can become. If I do not do this, I will never know."

game against the Bisons, letting a 4-1 lead melt away. The crowd at the Trois-Rivières Colisée was calling for Rheaume now: "Manon, Manon, Manon." The rookie goalie's legs were nervous pistons under her pads. Then Coach Drapeau tapped her on the shoulder.

Rheaume was finally out there on the ice, the first female to play junior hockey. The Trois-Rivières crowd jumped to its feet screaming. The next hour, which stretched over the second and third period, was adrenaline-fuelled bedlam. Seventeen minutes of hockey—10 saves, 3 goals, a thousand screams. The drama required and received a dramatic conclusion. A slapshot from nowhere found its way through a weaving scrum.

This is what Manon lived for—why she competed.

"I do this because I love to play hockey," she would explain. "Hockey is my passion. To face shots at 100 miles per hour… I do not do this because I am the first woman. I want to see how much better I can become. If I don't do this, I will never know."

This slapshot destroyed Manon's mask, bending the fibreglass into her eyebrow—knocking her out on her feet, really. There was blood in her eye, blood wetting her face. She didn't fall. She wanted to stay in. But Manon needed stitches. She left the game to a standing ovation.

Manon would lead Canada to women's world championships in 1992 (winning the tournament's Most Valuable Player designation) and 1994. She helped her country to a silver medal in 1998. Manon Rheaume would also be the first woman to play in an NHL game, an exhibition match between the Tampa Bay Lightning and the St. Louis Blues. She served a period, allowing two goals, one of which, a Brendan Shanahan one-timer, could have happened to anyone.

Trois-Rivières would witness other historic hockey moments. Forward Rene Robert, a locally born star with the town's junior Maple Leafs in the 1960s, would play in the NHL as part of the Buffalo Sabres' famed French Connection. In addition, goalie Jacques Cloutier took the Draveurs to two Memorial Cups in 1978 and 1979. And the city's university team, the Trois-Rivières Patriotes, would win the CIS University Cup in 1991, 2001 and 2003. But Trois-Rivières would never know another night like 26 November 1991, when a female Draveur—truly, a raftsman—rode her way into hockey history.

Trick Shot

Trois-Rivières native Rene Robert was a perfect blend of the skills of Gilbert Perreault and Richard Martin, Robert's Quebec linemates on the National Hockey League's Buffalo Sabres. Robert could shoot, skate and pass, as could other members of the famous French Connection (see page 119). But he could also scheme, as he proved one night in upstate New York, when on 20 May 1975 he unleashed hockey's most famous trick shot.

A fog had drifted into Buffalo's Memorial Auditorium shortly after a Stanley Cup finals playoff game had begun between the Sabres and the Philadelphia Flyers. Teams were sent out to speed around the rink in an effort to fan away settling fog banks. But by overtime the haze in the Aud was as thick as wool. Goalie Bernie Parent had been unbeatable in close during these playoffs. But Robert had a better idea—he wouldn't try to get near Parent to score. Stopping inside a fog bank inside the Philly blue line, Robert wound up for a slapshot no one saw until it bulged the net behind Parent. "I never saw the puck go in," the forward would say later. "No one did. Only when the red light go on did we know we'd won."

The Victoriaville Tigers, 2002.

Sleeping Tiger

Junior and senior editions of the Victoriaville Tigers have represented Victoriaville for more than 70 years. Jean Beliveau was a Tiger during the team's first junior incarnation. The 1968 senior team, featuring the services of "Gypsy Joe" Hardy of Kenogami, who later played with the National Hockey League's California Golden Seals, won the Allan Cup. And a 2002 junior edition of the Tigers challenged for the Memorial Cup, thanks to the inspired play of defence-man Danny Groulx. The Tigers are now partly owned by the city's most famous citizen, Gilbert Perreault, who also coached the team for two seasons. "I enjoyed coaching, but the owner and coach couldn't get along," he would joke.

The most famous recent Tigers alumnus would be Montreal-born Alexandre Daigle. Movie-star hand-some and a gifted scorer, Daigle packed Victoriaville's modest Colisée des Bois-Francs in the early '90s for Tigers games. The Ottawa Senators thought they were getting the next Guy Lafleur, bypassing top junior defenceman Chris Pronger to take Alexandre "The Great" first in the 1993 NHL draft, then signing the forward to a $13 million contract. Alas, Daigle's most memorable accomplishment during his years with Ottawa would be dating actress-celebrity Pamela Anderson (the pride of Ladysmith, British Columbia). The former Tigers player partially redeemed himself in 2003–04, putting in a solid 20-goal NHL season with the Minnesota Wild.

VICTORIAVILLE

FOUNDED
This farming community on the Nicolet River in southern Quebec became a town in 1860, choosing the name Demersville to honour the internationally famous Catholic cleric Modeste Demers. A year later the name was changed to Victoriaville, after Queen Victoria.

NATIVE-BORN NHL PLAYERS
Rene Corbet, Eric Lavigne, Real Lemieux, Gilbert Perreault, P.J. Stock

FAMOUS LOCAL TEAMS
Junior: Victoriaville Bruins, Victoriaville Panthers, Victoriaville Tigres (Tigers); **Senior-pro:** Victoriaville Tigres

CURRENT POPULATION
25,000

The French Connection

All the uncles of Gilbert Perreault claimed to have played with Jean Beliveau, the city's star before Gilbert Perreault came along. Perreault loved Beliveau, too. He wore number 4, Big Jean's numeral, on his peewee sweater. And his coaches under-stood that Perreault would play centre, as Beliveau had, by virtue of his evident skills. Other kids turned; Gilbert swooped. Nobody had more moves.

Remarkably, every city in Quebec seemed to have a peewee Perreault back then. By 1960, the province had created tournaments to celebrate the sudden bonanza of hockey talent. "Marcel [Dionne] was playing for Drummondville and I was playing for Victoriaville, which are about a half-hour, forty-five minutes apart," Perreault would remember. "At the time we were eight years old, we didn't know each other personally. And as we got older it just kept going, always competing against each other. It was the same with Guy Lafleur. We all went to the peewee tournament. I was there with Victoriaville. Marcel with Drummondville. And Lafleur with Thurso. So that's how we got to know each other... Quebec City had the peewee tourna-ment, Montreal had the big bantam tournament, and Drummondville had the big midget tournament. Year after year, we were in these tournaments."

Victoriaville's most famous team, the senior Tigers, won the Allan Cup in 1968 when Gilbert was playing for the Montreal Junior Canadiens. Perreault him-self would win two Memorial Cups for the Junior Habs in 1969 and 1970.

Those trophies offered further proof that Quebec was experiencing a hockey renaissance—a phenomenon that would be evident in the next 15 years during the National Hockey League's annual draft. Victoriaville's Perreault was chosen number one in the 1970 sweepstakes. And four out of five of the following season's top picks were French Canadians: Thurso's Lafleur (number one), Drummondville's Dionne (number two), Montreal's Jocelyn Guevremont (number three), and Verdun's Richard Martin (number five). In 1972, Quebec City's Jacques Richard was ranked number two. In 1973, Hull-born Denis Potvin was selected first. Sylvain Turgeon (Rouyn-Noranda), Ian Turnbull (Montreal), Pierre Larouche (Taschereau), Andre Savard (Temiscamingue), Ray Bourque (Montreal), Pierre Mondou (Sherbrooke), Denis Savard (Pointe Gatineau), Michel Goulet (Peribonka) and Kevin Lowe (Lachute) would all distinguish themselves as top draft picks before 1984, the year that Mario Lemieux (Montreal) and Patrick Roy (Quebec City) put double exclamation marks on the province's second golden era of hockey.

The first Quebec renaissance took place in the late 1950s, as evidenced by all those Cups won by the homegrown Canadiens. But by 1970, the NHL had changed draft rules. The Canadiens no longer enjoyed the feudal right to the best Quebec juniors. Though the Canadiens managed to secure enough Quebec talent to win five Cups in the 1970s, much of the local talent escaped. In fact, the decade's best Quebec line, Perreault, Martin and Trois-Rivières' Rene Robert, would play for the Buffalo Sabres.

Writer Ross Brewitt interviewed Perreault during his first NHL season with the Sabres, in 1970–71. Perreault couldn't speak English yet. An interpreter,

Gilbert Perreault, here with the Montreal Junior Canadiens.

With those words, hockey had its most famous line of the 1970s. Bobby Orr pronounced Perreault the most exciting player in hockey.

veteran Phil Goyette, tagged along. Brewitt asked Perreault if he practised his astonishing array of feints and dodges. Perreault frowned and then entered into a spirited debate with his interpreter. Finally, Goyette turned to Brewitt: "He says, 'How do I know what I'm going to do until I get there?'"

In the fall of 1971, Perreault showed up at Buffalo's training camp overweight. Coach Punch Imlach, who had once tutored Beliveau in Quebec City, took speedy rookie Richard Martin aside and said, "Get on Perreault's left side and make the f—— skate. I don't care what you do, but make him skate."

Finally, Perreault had someone who knew what he was going to do before he got there. Martin had been in the Junior Canadiens with Perreault, although on the second line (Marc Tardif and Reggie Houle had teamed with Perreault). Perreault-Martin shone that season in Buffalo. And in the spring of 1972, Imlach traded Eddie Shack to Pittsburgh for right wing Rene Robert, who had matched wits with Perreault in junior while playing as a centre for the Trois-Rivières Maple Leafs.

The trio, initially dubbed "The French Line," clicked immediately. All three players had skated together as teenagers and had played vintage Quebec-style fire-wagon hockey. In the fall of 1972, one of the linemates scored and Buffalo's Memorial Auditorium erupted twice—first after the goal, then seconds later when Lee Coppola, who ran the message board, posted the comment "The French Connection Strikes Again." (The crowd enjoyed the topical reference. *The French Connection*, a crime drama, had won an Academy Award for Best Picture earlier that spring.)

With those words, hockey had its most famous line of the 1970s. Bobby Orr pronounced Perreault the most exciting player in hockey. Martin was maybe its hardest shooter. Robert approximated both linemates' talents—he could skate and shoot with Martin and pass and think with Perreault. The French Connection connected for 738 goals over seven seasons. The fire wagon bumped the Montreal Canadiens out of the playoffs on the Sabres' way to the Stanley Cup finals in 1975 and trampled the Soviet Red Army team, 12–6, in a 1976 exhibition game. The French Connection were beautiful to watch, a Quebec hockey touring company that worked out of upstate New York.

And when the three linemates finished their NHL careers, they eventually returned home to Quebec to receive their due. In 1988, Perreault became a part owner and coach of the Victoriaville Tigers, the junior team he had never managed to play for. Not that this new proprietary status mattered—Gilbert Perreault had "owned" Victoriaville hockey his entire life.

Opening Spread:
Mississauga-born
forward, Jason Spezza
emerged as an Ontario
hockey star with the
Ottawa Senators in the
2005–06 season.

Victorious: The Toronto Maple Leafs
celebrate their 1964 Stanley Cup win.

ockey is Canada's sport and Ontario's obsession. According to the Canadian Amateur Hockey Association, almost 45 percent of the 505,000 kids playing amateur hockey in this country today come from Ontario. And according to the most recent edition of the hockey encyclopedia *Total Hockey*, Ontario has given birth to more National Hockey League players (1,999) than the next four most productive provinces—Quebec, Alberta, Saskatchewan and Manitoba—combined (1,996 players).

Ontario is also Canada's hockey trophy case. Donated by Lord Stanley, governor general of Canada (1888–93), the Stanley Cup was first awarded (to the Montreal AAA) in Ottawa in 1893. The Memorial Cup, emblematic of Canadian junior hockey supremacy, was created by the Ontario Hockey Association, in 1919, as a tribute to Canadians who had died overseas during World War I. And the Allan Cup, which Montreal business tycoon Sir H. Montague Allan earmarked for senior hockey, with the hope that the trophy would mean to amateurs "what the Stanley Cup now represents to the professionals, with the undesirable features eliminated," became almost exclusively the possession of Ontario teams during the '20s and the '50s.

As of 2005, Ontario cities had won 44 Memorial Cups and 47 Allan Cups. In piling up a treasure trove of silverware, the province contributed some of the game's most compelling performers, players who would become synonymous with their birthplaces: Stratford's Howie Morenz, "The Stratford Streak"; Parry Sound's Bobby Orr; Point Anne's Bobby Hull; and Brantford's Wayne Gretzky. Indeed, the hockey talent pool in Ontario is so rich that in the years before the NHL universal draft (1969) an NHL team might put together an entire forward line out of a single Ontario town. The NHL Boston Bruins performed just such a trick, recruiting The Kraut Line (Milt Schmidt, Woody Dumart and Bobby Bauer) from Kitchener in the late 1930s, and subsequently winning Stanley Cups in 1939 and 1941. The Toronto Maple Leafs performed a similarly successful grab in the World War II years, filling a depleted roster with The Flying Forts, three teenage kids from Fort William (now Thunder Bay)—Gaye Stewart, Gus Bodnar and Bud Poile.

All this homegrown talent bred significant community interest. As everywhere else in Canada, local teams became standard bearers for the community. Ontario team owners, however, had fatter wallets than some others, and a fixation on winning. Renfrew lumber baron M.J. O'Brien, for instance, bankrolled the Renfrew Millionaires, the most expensive pro team in hockey in the first decade of the 20th century.

The Millionaires never won a championship, but they did inspire their fans to engage in epic bouts of gambling. A group of Renfrew fans bet $5,000 on a game between the Millionaires and the Montreal Maroons in 1908. (The Millionaires lost.) Hockey betting was an epidemic throughout Ontario at the time. That same year, Charlie Chittick, an Ottawa hockey referee, told Toronto sportswriter Milt Dunnell that while loitering in a Haileybury, Ontario, hotel before a 1908 senior game between the home team and Cobalt, he saw $40,000 wagered in less than 20 minutes.

Indeed, gambling and hockey fever were inextricably linked in the creation of the Toronto Maple Leafs, the franchise that, in the 1930s, became English-speaking Canada's national hockey team. In 1926, Toronto construction magnate Conn Smythe placed a $10,000 bet on the University of Toronto hockey team, in a game against

McGill. Coming out on top, he then rode all his winnings on the underdog Toronto St. Pats in a contest with another NHL team, the Ottawa Senators. Lo and behold, the St. Pats won, thus giving Smythe a bankroll sufficient to buy the team, whose name he immediately changed to the Toronto Maple Leafs.

Conn Smythe holds a unique place in Canadian sports, but the story of Ontario hockey is also rich with other tales of gambling adventurers who would travel the province's long winter highways on team buses, eager to win glory for their town. In his 1985 letter to the *Globe and Mail*, Timmins actor Cec Linder, who played CIA agent Felix Leiter in the 1964 James Bond film, *Goldfinger*, shared his memory of one of those bus rides:

> In 1951 and 1952, I used to travel, along with Rex Stimers, Tommy Garriock and Jackie Gatecliff, with the St. Catharines Teepees junior hockey team, as a staff member of Radio Station CKTB, to do the "Industrial Story of the Night" after the second period, on behalf of the Chamber of Commerce, who sponsored the hockey broadcasts.
>
> We're on the bus heading for Barrie for a game one night against the Flyers. When he tired of telling his hilarious stories—we never tired of listening—[St. Catharines coach Rudy] Pilous turned to a few key players, and began goading them that Barrie would, to use his words, "beat the s——" out of them that night. Before you know it, he had a $10 bet with each of his three pivotal men, Pierre Pilote, Hank Ciesla and Hughie Barlow.
>
> So having coerced his top players into putting their money where their mouths were, Pilous smugly returned to his storytelling, and the bets were on. Needless to say, the Teepees beat the Barrie Flyers, 6–2, that night. But what the players didn't know was that the wily Pilous had a $200 bet with Hap Emms, coach of the Barrie Flyers, that his beloved Teepees would beat the Flyers. How's that for motivation?

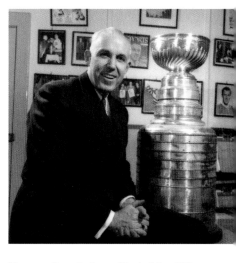

Clarence Campbell, president of the NHL, with Lord Stanley's Cup in 1957.

Ontario Hockey Trophy Case

Memorial Cup Winners:

2005	London Knights
2003	Kitchener Rangers
1999	Ottawa 67's
1993	Sault Ste. Marie Greyhounds
1990	Oshawa Generals
1986	Guelph Platers
1984	Ottawa 67's
1982	Kitchener Rangers
1981	Cornwall Royals
1980	Cornwall Royals
1979	Peterborough Petes
1976	Hamilton Fincups
1975	Toronto Marlboros
1973	Toronto Marlboros
1972	Cornwall Royals
1968	Niagara Falls Flyers
1967	Toronto Marlboros
1965	Niagara Falls Flyers
1964	Toronto Marlboros
1962	Hamilton Red Wings
1961	Toronto St. Michael's Majors
1960	St. Catharines Teepees
1958	Ottawa-Hull Canadiens
1956	Toronto Marlboros
1955	Toronto Marlboros
1954	St. Catharines Teepees
1953	Barrie Flyers
1952	Guelph Biltmores
1951	Barrie Flyers
1948	Port Arthur West End Bruins
1947	Toronto St. Michael's
1945	Toronto St. Michael's
1944	Oshawa Generals
1940	Oshawa Generals
1939	Oshawa Generals
1936	West Toronto Nationals
1934	Toronto St. Michael's
1933	Newmarket Reds
1932	Sudbury Wolves
1929	Toronto Marlboros
1927	Owen Sound Greys
1924	Owen Sound Greys
1922	Fort William War Veterans
1920	Toronto Canoe Club
1919	University of Toronto Schools

Allan Cup Winners:

2005	Thunder Bay Twins
1989	Thunder Bay Twins
1988	Thunder Bay Twins
1987	Brantford Mott's Clamatos
1985	Thunder Bay Twins
1984	Thunder Bay Twins
1983	Cambridge Hornets
1981	Petrolia Squires (Sarnia)
1979	Petrolia Squires
1977	Brantford Alexanders
1975	Thunder Bay Twins
1974	Barrie Flyers
1973	Orillia Terriers

1971	Galt Hornets
1969	Galt Hornets
1963	Windsor Bulldogs
1961	Galt Terriers
1960	Chatham Maroons
1959	Whitby Dunlops
1958	Belleville McFarlands
1957	Whitby Dunlops
1955	Kitchener-Waterloo Dutchmen
1953	Kitchener-Waterloo Dutchmen
1952	Fort Frances Canadians
1951	Owen Sound Mercurys
1950	Toronto Marlboros
1949	Ottawa Senators
1943	Ottawa Commandos
1942	Ottawa RCAF
1940	Kirkland Lake Blue Devils
1939	Port Arthur Bearcats
1937	Sudbury Tigers
1932	Toronto Nationals
1929	Port Arthur Bearcats
1927	Toronto Varsity Grads
1926	Port Arthur Bearcats
1925	Port Arthur Bearcats
1924	Sault Ste. Marie Greyhounds
1923	Toronto Granites
1922	Toronto Granites
1921	University of Toronto
1919	Hamilton Tigers
1918	Kitchener Hockey Club
1917	Toronto Dentals

1910	Toronto St. Michael's
1909	Kingston Queen's University
1908	Ottawa Cliffsides

Stanley Cup Winners:

1967	Toronto Maple Leafs
1964	Toronto Maple Leafs
1963	Toronto Maple Leafs
1962	Toronto Maple Leafs
1951	Toronto Maple Leafs
1949	Toronto Maple Leafs
1948	Toronto Maple Leafs
1947	Toronto Maple Leafs
1945	Toronto Maple Leafs
1942	Toronto Maple Leafs
1932	Toronto Maple Leafs
1927	Ottawa Senators
1923	Ottawa Senators
1922	Toronto St. Pats
1921	Ottawa Senators
1920	Ottawa Senators
1918	Toronto Arenas
1914	Toronto Blueshirts
1911	Ottawa Senators
1910	Ottawa Senators
1909	Ottawa Senators
1907	Kenora Thistles
1906	Ottawa Silver Seven
1905	Ottawa Silver Seven
1904	Ottawa Silver Seven
1903	Ottawa Silver Seven

BARRIE

Barrie, seen from Allandale, c. 1863.

FOUNDED

For centuries, Barrie, on the western shore of what is now known as Kempenfelt Bay, was a stopping place for First Nations people making the portage between Lake Simcoe and the Nottawasaga River to Lake Huron. During the War of 1812, Barrie became an important military transport centre. The town took its name from British Admiral Sir Robert Barrie in 1832. The railroad joined Barrie to York (Toronto) in 1865, and when Highway 400 connected the two cities in 1950, the self-proclaimed Beautiful City by the Bay became a popular summer tourist destination.

NATIVE-BORN NHL PLAYERS

Perry Anderson, Steve Chiasson, Shane Corson, Joe DiPenta, Leighton "Hap" Emms, Bruce Gardiner, Jim Hamilton, Mike Hoffman, Greg Johnston, Brian Kinsella, John Madden, Dan Maloney, Terry Martin, Garry Monahan, Hugh Plaxton, Glen Richardson, Darren Rumble, Wayne Rutledge, Darryl Shannon

FAMOUS LOCAL TEAMS

Junior: Barrie Athletic Club, Barrie Canoe Club, Barrie Colts, Barrie Flyers; **Senior-pro:** Barrie Athletic Club, Barrie Colts, Barrie Flyers

CURRENT POPULATION

125,000

The Big Emms

If the rumour is true that Leighton Emms only smiled after winning a hockey game, he would still appear to have lived a contented life, for the Ontario junior coaching legend led six teams to the Memorial Cup, winning four national championships.

Emms grew up on a farm outside Barrie, the youngest of 13 children. As a teenager, Emms always had a brooding air about him, and so became known by the derisive nickname "Hap," short for "happy."

Emms learned hockey in a church league, then graduated to the Barrie Colts in junior (1921–24). Starting in 1926, the big defenceman (6', 195 lbs) played 11 seasons in the NHL—mostly with the New York Americans—before drifting into the minors. After serving in World War II, he returned to his hometown to create the fabled junior Barrie Flyers franchise.

"There is no substitute for hard work, gentlemen," Emms told players. And Emms' teams practised harder and were in better condition than their opponents. Emms liked to think that his players were in superior moral shape as well: A devout United churchgoer, he wouldn't allow his teams to play on Sunday, enforced 9:30 p.m. curfews, and prohibited drinking, smoking and swearing. (The F-word prompted an automatic 50-cent fine.) Even in the swinging sixties, Emms never loosened up. Upon hearing that Derek Sanderson—who played for the Flyers from 1963 to 1966—had pulled a groin muscle, Emms insisted that the player get rid of his girlfriend. "Tell her you're married to hockey," were his final words on the subject.

Emms' style and temperament particularly suited postwar Barrie, a conservative farming and lumber community that wasn't so sure about its growing economic relationship with nearby Toronto. Adding to Emms' popularity, were his service in the war and his status as a hockey hero; he was the first local to

COLTS FEVER

Barrie began another memorable chapter in junior hockey in 1995, when the Barrie Colts began playing out of the Barrie Molson Centre. (What would teetotaling coach Hap Emms think? A hockey rink, in his hometown, named after a beer company.) The team finished first, overall, in the junior Ontario Hockey League in 1999–2000.

make it in the NHL, and he carried himself with the gruff assurance of a small-town world-beater. People liked him, sour mug and all. And they loved the Flyers even more.

"The Flyers were like the New York Yankees at the time," recalled Don Cherry, the renowned *Hockey Night in Canada* broadcaster, who once was a defence-man for the Barrie Flyers. "It was the best team money could buy. Old Hap Emms went out and bought all the best players from the other towns." The big line on the 1950–51 Barrie team consisted of future NHLers Real Chevrefils, Jerry Toppazzini and Leo Labine, who came from Timmins, Copper Cliff and Haileybury, Ontario, respectively.

Emms not only knew how to pick his players; he also knew how to get results from them. Cherry, a Kingston boy, was once the object of a classic coaching lesson from the one-time Barrie farm boy. "[Emms] could sure get the message across to the players, how to play the game," Cherry explained. "One night against the Toronto Marlies, Eric Nesterenko, who was a junior hotshot, came down against me. I watched the puck, instead of him, and he passed it through my digestive tract to score a goal. For the next 10 days I had to wear a puck around my neck on a skate lace, like the chicken's head on the dog that killed it."

Emms toughened and trained two Memorial Cup-winning teams in Barrie, defeating the Winnipeg Monarchs in 1951 and the St. Boniface Canadiens in 1953. The victories were widely celebrated in Barrie, although both the city and Emms seemed almost more satisfied with the Ontario provincial tournament wins over Toronto junior teams, which qualified the Flyers for the nationals. "Hap couldn't have been happier than he was in '53, when we beat [Toronto] St. Mike's and [Toronto] Marlies to win Ontario," Cherry recalled. "He was the best I ever saw at getting under the other team's skin. Late in a key game against St. Mike's, Hap sent a gift-wrapped package to their bench… Charlie Cerre was the coach, and there were some priests behind the bench, too. There was Lloyd Percival's book on how to coach hockey. It really upset them, and Bill Dineen, who was [St. Mike's] captain, tried to come into our bench after Emms. We won the game." After the Flyers' win over the Toronto Marlies, Hap was happier still.

In 1960, Emms moved the Flyers to Niagara Falls, where the team won Memorial Cups in 1965 and 1968. In the 1970s, he owned the junior St. Catharines Black Hawks franchise. A trophy in his honour, the Hap Emms Memorial Trophy, is awarded annually to the best goalie in the Canadian national junior championships.

Stern as a preacher and tough as a drill sergeant, "Hap" Emms (seen here with the New York Americans in 1934) turned the Barrie Flyers into the best junior hockey franchise in Canada in the early 1950s.

Bless Me Leo, For I Have Sinned

In addition to running the Barrie Flyers, Hap Emms also owned an electrical company in town. He frequently employed players to help out during the off-season. One of Emms' crews was working in a local church when a penitent entered the building. "I was [rewiring] the confessional booth," recalled Leo Labine, a star with the Flyers (1950–51) and later with the Boston Bruins, when "suddenly a guy comes in and sits on the other side. So I'm there and he's saying, 'Father, I haven't been up to par' and went on for a while. So I say, 'Go say five Our Fathers and five Hail Marys and I'm quite sure you'll look after yourself a little better from now on.'"

Emms, who had been watching the confessional exchange, hurried over to Labine after the greatly unburdened confessor left the church. "What are you doing?" Emms asked.

"I was in there, so what could I do? I just said what the priest tells me."

BRANTFORD

FOUNDED

In 1784, Captain Joseph Thayendanegea Brant, a Mohawk chief, relocated his people from upper New York to the Grand River basin in southwestern Ontario. The settlement site was purchased from the Six Nations people in 1839. City fathers chose to locate Brantford on the historic spot where Brant had forded the Grand River. Brantford is often called The Telephone City, for this is where Alexander Graham Bell conceived the idea of the telephone. Today, however, the city is more often referred to as the birthplace of Wayne Gretzky.

NATIVE-BORN NHL PLAYERS

Shawn Antoski, Bill Cook, David Gans, Chris Gratton, Dan Gratton, Josh Gratton, Gerry Gray, Brent Gretzky, Wayne Gretzky, Len Hachborn, Pat Hickey, Fred Hunt, Jim Jamieson, Doug Jarvis, Don Johns, Keith Jones, Barry Long, Paul MacKinnon, Dan Mandich, Mike Posavad, Chris Pusey, Jeff Reese, Len Ronson, Jack Shewchuk, Greg Stefan

FAMOUS LOCAL TEAMS

Junior: Brantford Alexanders, Brantford Classics, Brantford Lions, Brantford Redmen, Brantford Tri-Colour; **Senior-pro:** Brantford Alexanders, Brantford Blast, Brantford Indians, Brantford Mott's Clamatos, Brantford Nationals, Brantford Penguins, Brantford Professionals, Brantford RCAF, Brantford Redmen, Brantford Smoke, Brantford Tri-Colour

CURRENT POPULATION

90,195

THE OTHER ONE

A second family graduate of the Walter Gretzky backyard flying school, Brent Gretzky, has been lucky enough to make a living playing the game he loves everywhere from Austria to Asheville, North Carolina—where he played for the Asheville Smoke, a United Hockey League team coached and managed by brother Keith, between 1998 and 2000. In the early 1990s, he suited up for the National Hockey League's Tampa Bay Lightning, where, in 1993, the centreman faced off against brother Wayne. Their father, Walter, who was in the crowd that evening, was just glad that the two athletes didn't fight. "The two can't play a game of cards without fighting about something," he said at the time.

If You Build It, He Will Come

Hockey fans may be shocked to discover that the magical abilities of winter's prodigy, Wayne Gretzky, extended into the summertime. Bill Byckowski, a Toronto Blue Jays scout, played against Gretzky's Brantford team in a bantam baseball tournament. "He was [regularly] a shortstop, but he pitched a 5-0 no-hitter against us," Byckowski would recall. "Later in the tournament, he was warming up left-handed as a pitcher. He used to switch pitching arms. He was a right-hander against us. He had a knuckleball, a curveball—and he could throw strikes."

Wayne Gretzky didn't grow up to be a baseball player, though—hockey called him first. In fact, the suspicion remains that Gretzky was a phenomenon made inevitable by a magic winter garden. For just as Ray Kinsella, protagonist of *Field of Dreams*, the film inspired by Edmonton author W.P. Kinsella's novel, brought the translucent ghost of Shoeless Joe Jackson to life by carving a handsome ballpark out of an Iowa cornfield, surely, Walter Gretzky, father of Wayne, helped conjure up "The Great One" by creating the perfect ice surface in the backyard of the family's Brantford home.

As parents know, no easy kit to make a rink can be bought at Canadian Tire. The procedure takes time, a steady hand, dogged footwork and the ability to shuffle in place for hours to ward off frostbite.

Walter Gretzky began before winter even arrived, cutting his backyard lawn to a hobo's stubble. And when first freeze came, he employed his trade secret. Most dads stand ankle deep in snow to hose down a rink. Not Walter. He figured

Brantford's hockey prodigy would go on to represent Canada on the world stage as both a player and a manager.

such a manoeuvre would leave frozen glacial tides. Instead, he kept a sprinkler on overnight, creating an ice surface that was absolutely flat and blemish-free. And then, he put another coat on the next night...and the night after that. By the time Walter Gretzky pronounced the job done, ice on the 20-by-36-foot rink was seven inches thick and the boards true as a father's love.

Brantford didn't have a hockey league for children under 10 in the '60s, but Wayne, who started skating at age two, played hundreds of games a month on

Soon, hockey wouldn't be able to stop talking about Wayne.

what neighbourhood kids called the Wally Coliseum. Walter also devised special practice runs, arranging empty detergent containers in a button-on-a-shirt pattern, then sending kids—including Wayne's younger brother Brent, who also enjoyed a pro hockey career—swooping full speed through the course.

After years at his father's backyard flight school, Wayne took off as a Brantford peewee in 1971: The 4'4" 11-year-old won national fame by scoring 378 goals in 69 games. He couldn't stop thinking about hockey. "I spent most of Grade 8 with [Wayne's] bony elbow resting on my desk," remembered Carolyn Leitch, now a Toronto business reporter. "We were classmates at Greenbrier Public School in Brantford and our homeroom teacher put me between Wayne and the other jocks, in a vain attempt to keep them from talking hockey nonstop."

Soon, hockey wouldn't be able to stop talking about Wayne. At 16, he successfully auditioned for the legendary junior team, the Peterborough Petes. The following year, he was a sensation for the Sault Ste. Marie Greyhounds, doubling league attendance in Ontario junior hockey wherever he went.

Interest in hockey in Brantford also increased. The Brantford Alexanders, a senior team, won the Allan Cup in 1976. A junior team, also called the Alexanders, played here from 1978 to 1984. In 1987, another Brantford team, the Mott's Clamatos, won another Allan Cup.

Wayne, meanwhile, kept moving. In the spring of 1977, at 17, he led all scorers at the world junior hockey tournament in Montreal. That fall, he turned pro with Indianapolis in the World Hockey Association, enrolling for a brief time at David Letterman's high school there.

Eight games later, Wayne was sold—along with Peter Driscoll and Ed Mio—to the Edmonton Oilers. "We didn't learn of the sale until late in the day and we flew, in a Lear jet, to Edmonton," Driscoll recalled. "Because Wayne was the smallest and youngest, we stuck him in the jump seat at the back of the plane. A little while later, we found out that he was petrified of flying. Wayne surrounded himself with hockey sticks on the trip. I think he thought they would protect him."

That they did and more. Number 99 would arguably become the most famous player in hockey history. In Edmonton, he won everything—eight scoring titles in a row (1980–87), four Stanley Cups, three 200-plus point seasons and an array of scoring records that won't be broken unless the National Hockey League resorts to soccer nets.

Wayne Gretzky may have been the hockey hero of a generation, but he was not blessed with obvious talents. He couldn't skate particularly fast, he wasn't strong, and he didn't shoot hard. His talent, sportswriter E.M. Swift once observed, "was all in his head." How Wayne did it, not even his best friends on the Oilers knew for sure. "The one thing that sticks with me is when he scored

Alexanders Answer Bell

The great inventor Alexander Graham Bell moved with his family from Scotland to Brantford, Ontario, in 1870. While lolling atop his "dreaming place," the leafy yard of the family's Tutela Heights estate overlooking the Grand River, Bell was visited by an idea for what would be the telephone. One hundred years later, the city would name its junior and senior hockey teams after Bell.

The senior Brantford Alexanders, with playing coach John McMillan and hard-shooting winger Jack Egers (formerly a 20-goal scorer with the St. Louis Blues), defeated the Spokane Flyers in the Allan Cup finals to help celebrate the city's centennial, in 1977. A decade afterward, another local senior club, the Brantford Mott's Clamatos ("The Motts," to locals), again won the trophy that recognizes Canadian senior hockey supremacy. That Allan Cup-winning team included Blake Hull (son of superstar Bobby) along with former National Hockey Leaguers Don Edwards (goal), Rocky Saganiuk, Stan Weir, Fred Boimistruck and Stan Jonathan.

the nine goals in [two games,] to get 50 in 39 games [in 1982]," says ex-teammate Paul Coffey. "I remember we played back-to-back games. Then one day he says, 'I think I'm going to get four tonight.' Well he goes out and gets four. The next morning, on the way to breakfast, he says, 'I think I'm going to get five tonight.' I say, 'Yeah, whatever.' And he got five goals. It always sticks out in my mind, how amazing that was."

Maybe a Brantford backyard hockey rink explains the legendary player's greatness. "If you build it, he will come," God said to Ray Kinsella in *Field of Dreams*. Perhaps He made the same offer to Walter Gretzky.

CAMBRIDGE-GALT

FOUNDED
Originally Cambridge-Galt was Shade's Mills, a planned agricultural community created in 1816. The site of the original town was the juncture where Mill Creek flows into the Grand River. In 1825, the settlement became Galt, in honour of John Galt, the Scottish novelist and land developer who had established Guelph, Ontario. Galt would soon become a manufacturing centre and it was the industrial capital of the Waterloo region before being over-taken by Kitchener early in the 20th century. The city of Galt would become amalgamated with the nearby towns of Preston and Hespeler, to form Cambridge, in 1973.

NATIVE-BORN NHL PLAYERS
Cambridge: Louis DeBrusk, Trevor Gillies, Brad Shaw, John Tanner, Matt Walker, Scott Walker; **Galt:** Alexander "Lex" Chisholm, Joe Contini, Alex Forsyth, Ray Getliffe, Norm Himes, Red Laurence, Mike Moffatt, Jim Schoenfeld, Wiggie Wylie

FAMOUS LOCAL TEAMS
Cambridge Junior: Cambridge Winterhawks; **Cambridge Senior-pro:** Cambridge Hornets; **Galt Junior:** Galt Black Hawks, Galt Garrison, Galt Kists, Galt Rangers, Galt Red Wings, Galt Rockets, Galt Terrier Pups; **Galt Senior-pro:** Galt Hornets, Galt Pros, Galt Terriers

CURRENT POPULATION
120,000

Rask, Rask

CBC radio host and author Peter Gzowski learned to play hockey growing up in Galt, in the 1950s, an experience he recaptured with evident passion in his 1981 book, *The Game of Our Lives*:

> Weekends were the best. I would wake early Saturday morning [and hurry] into my clothes: warm corduroy trousers, a plaid shirt and heavy socks. Down the stairs [I'd go] where my skates and outer clothing had steamed overnight on the radiator. I would lace on the skates, stretching out my leg with each eyehole to get the laces tight enough to stop circulation... If I was lucky I would get to the rink before anyone else. Then I could move around by myself, reveling in the clean air and the early light, and the untrammeled free-dom I would feel as my body swayed with the rhythm of my strides. My hockey stick was an extension of my body, swinging back and forth in front of me as I moved. Counterclockwise I went at first, moving on the right wing along the boards and down along the end, making ever longer strides as I built up speed, digging in with each pushing foot, hearing the rask, rask, as I glided into each step.

348 wins, 2 losses

Although women's hockey only became an Olympic sport in 1998, many women's hockey teams played like Olympians in the decades beforehand. The team to beat in the 1930s was the Preston Rivulettes, and many tried. In the decade prior to the war, the Rivulettes won 348 times, lost twice and tied three times.

Preston would later be incorporated into Cambridge, along with Galt. In 1961, the senior Galt Terriers won the Allan Cup. Gordie Howe was hidden on the junior Galt Red Wings for a year. In addition, a local journalist, Peter Gzowski, would write one of the two or three classic hockey books of all time, *The Game of Our Lives*.

Still, the tale of the Preston Rivulettes is a story that grows better and better with every passing season. The Rivulettes started off as a softball team: nine girls who, instead of making cookies, enjoyed baking themselves in the sun, whacking fly balls into far pastures, firing the ol' pill around the bases and set-tling into a collective friendship—becoming a team. But that only took care of the summer.

Then, one night in 1930, some of the girls were at the old Lowther Street

TERRIERS RUN TABLE

Coach Harry Neale's Galt Terriers took the Allan Cup in a hurry, in 1961, winning 19 of their last 20 senior league games, then sweeping the Amherst Ramblers and the Rouyn-Noranda Alouettes in the playoffs. The Cup came with a 5–1 win over the Winnipeg Maroons at the Galt Arena. The team consequently represented Canada with distinction in the 1962 world championships, finishing second to Sweden. Neale would coach in the National Hockey League and he became a valuable member of the *Hockey Night in Canada* broadcast team. The Terriers changed their name to the Galt Hornets later in the decade and won two more Allan Cups, in 1969 and 1971.

Where's Gordie?

Gordie Howe, of Floral, Saskatchewan, was signed by the National Hockey League's Detroit Red Wings at age 16 and was assigned to the team's Ontario junior club, the Galt Red Wings. The only problem was that the Saskatchewan junior league refused Howe's transfer to Galt. "I got some news for you, kid, and you're not going to like it," Red Wings coach Al Murray told him. "You're not going to be able to play with the team, just practise." Murray tutored Howe during the winter of 1944–45. The hockey player spent most of his days in Galt, though, working at the Galt Art Metal Company. A little over a year later, Howe was starring in the NHL.

Arena, discussing the coming season and their efforts to stay in shape. Someone suggested, "We should start a hockey team." A bystander laughed. Baseball was one thing, but hockey?

That laugh would be all the competitive Rivulettes needed. Hilda and Nellie Ranscombe, Marm and Helen Schmuck, Marg Gabbitass, Myrtle Parr, Toddy Webb, Pat Marriot and Helen Sault made up that first hockey team, which played other women's clubs from nearby Kitchener, Guelph, Hamilton, Stratford, Port Dover and Toronto.

The Preston team was invincible from the start. Hilda Ranscombe had played hockey growing up, and years of thumping a cowhide ball out of the park had made her stronger and more competitive still. She quickly became the team's star, a right winger who could blast around the defence and fool a goalie with a practised bob and weave. (Indeed, she would outmanoeuvre famed National Hockey League netminder Terry Sawchuk with this very move in an exhibition display at the Galt Arena in the 1950s.)

The Rivulettes took the Ontario Ladies Hockey Association championship in 1930, winning the Bobby Rosenfeld Trophy. Led by Ranscombe, the team would prevail over its competitors for the next nine years, winning the Ontario championship every year until 1940. The team also claimed 10 Eastern

"The team was the most valuable player," she insisted.

Canadian and six national, or "Dominion," titles. (The arrival of World War II and the call for women factory workers triggered the shutdown of the women's league in the early 1940s.)

One of Preston's very few losses came against Edmonton, in the 1930s, when the Rivulettes were under the weather. "[Their] girls were good," Ranscombe would allow afterward, "but three of our girls were sick. All I did on the ice was cough."

"Sorry, I couldn't let you win," referee (and future NHL commissioner) Clarence Campbell told the Preston team in the dressing room after the game with a wink, hoping to lighten their mood.

Despite being devastated by the flu, the Rivulettes never would have attempted to have that game postponed. The Great Depression had made them tough, as Hilda Ranscombe would again prove five decades later, in 1998, when she was inducted into the Cambridge Sports Hall of Fame. The event's organizers had feared that she might not make it because both her legs had recently been amputated. But Ranscombe could never say no to a hockey engagement, and so she arrived in a wheelchair.

The Rivulettes' other great strength came across when someone mentioned to Ranscombe that she had been the most valuable member of her old team. That claim wasn't true, she said, looking back on the decade that the Preston Rivulettes had ruled hockey rinks and baseball diamonds. "The team was the most valuable player," she insisted.

The Rivulettes' top scorer, Hilda Ranscombe.

The Preston Rivulettes were queens of the rink in the 1930s, winning the Ontario women's hockey championship every year that decade.

Edouard "Newsy" Lalonde earned his nickname working on the hometown newspaper as a kid. He became big news in hockey, leading the NHL in scoring as a Montreal Canadien in 1918–19 and 1920–21.

CORNWALL

FOUNDED

Cornwall was first settled, in 1784, by United Empire Loyalists, led by Lt. Col. Sir John Johnson, who were escaping the American Revolution. The city was originally called New Johnstown, but it was soon renamed Cornwall, for Prince George, the Duke of Cornwall.

NATIVE-BORN NHL PLAYERS

Billy Carter, Bob Charlebois, Alain Chevrier, Carson Cooper, Corrie D'Alessio, Corbett Denneny, Cy Denneny, Chad Kilger, Newsy Lalonde, Blair MacDonald, John Markell, Scott Pearson, Steve Poapst, Bruce Racine, Steve Seguin, Donald Smith, Orval Tessier, Ron Ward, John Wensink

FAMOUS LOCAL TEAMS

Junior: Cornwall Colts, Cornwall Royals; **Senior-pro:** Cornwall Aces, Cornwall Army, Cornwall Calumets, Cornwall Canadians, Cornwall Chevvies, Cornwall Cookies, Cornwall Cougars, Cornwall Flyers, Cornwall

CURRENT POPULATION

57,581

Double Lives

Given that Cornwall is a bilingual Ontario-Quebec border town, it seems fitting that the city's most famous athlete was a master of two sports. The greatest hockey player in the first quarter of the 20th century, Edouard Charles "Newsy" Lalonde inspired the term "Flying Frenchman" while performing for the Montreal Canadiens. But for a while, he was better known (and better paid) as a lacrosse player.

Called Newsy because he had once worked as a printer for the *Cornwall Freeholder*, Lalonde created his own hockey club as a young man, organizing a team called the Sweepers, whose players paid for ice time by agreeing to keep rinks free of snow. All that shovelling left Newsy with powerful legs and a mean disposition. He quickly won a reputation for having the fastest skates (and quickest temper) in the Ottawa Valley.

He also had a sense of humour and enjoyed telling the story of how, in 1907, he broke into professional hockey for Sault Ste. Marie. "I left Cornwall by train one evening, rode all night, and arrived in the Soo at eight o'clock the next evening," he told Bill Roche for the author's collection, *The Hockey Book*. "I had not eaten since early morning. I had had to sit up all night in a day coach, since a berth was not included in the one-way transportation... The Soo team won the game, 3–1, and I scored two goals. But how did I score those goals? That's the question... Old-timers will remember that, in those days, the strategy of lifting the puck out of the defence area from one end of the rink to the other, instead of carrying it out, was just passing from existence. But Pittsburgh, the team we were playing, was still using the old backhand for clearing.

"Well, twice in that game, when we had forced the play into Pittsburgh's end, I saw one of their players start a clearing lift-shot just a few feet away. I scooted over...flipped around on my skates and turned my back to him. The rising puck landed in the seat of my pants and dropped to the ice just behind me. I flipped around again, nabbed the loose puck and waltzed in and scored. Just two bum shots, as it were, but they put me right into pro hockey to stay."

A Cornwall hockey team, 1905.

Fastest Ever

Although hockey experts will never be able to determine who the swiftest skater has been, reliable evidence suggests that Corb Denneny was the fastest hockey player on land. After turning pro as a lacrosse player for Cornwall at age 14, in 1908, he moved to Toronto to play both sports, in 1914. Taking part in an exhibition track meet at the Canadian National Exhibition two years later, he tied the world record for the 100-yard dash, running the race in 9.6 seconds.

Newsy became a star with the Toronto Professionals in 1908–09, scoring 29 more conventional goals in nine games. The following season, he joined the inaugural edition of the Montreal Canadiens, leading the brand new National Hockey Association with 28 goals in 12 games, first with the Canadiens and, then, with the Renfrew Millionaires (see page 173).

But hockey was only Newsy's winter job. He devoted his summers to professional lacrosse, which was then the more popular sport in central Canada. Cornwall competed in a circuit against another team from Ottawa and clubs from Toronto and Montreal.

A peerless attacker, with magical hands and a confounding array of shivers and head fakes, Newsy was far and away the greatest lacrosse player of his era.

In 1911, Newsy made front page news for becoming the highest-paid athlete in North America, accepting $6,500 to play 16 games for a lacrosse team in Vancouver. He played hockey for a third of that pay in the same city for the Vancouver Millionaires.

Newsy would return to the Montreal Canadiens, a team he eventually led to its first Stanley Cup, in 1916—collecting $238 in bonus money. Throughout the second decade of the 20th century, Newsy was the embodiment of French-Canadian hockey—a lightning-fast forward who flew across the ice, playing with conspicuous élan. When Canadiens general manager Leo Dandurand traded the player, in 1922, to the Saskatoon Sheiks for Aurel Joliat, a Swiss Protestant from Ottawa, the Montreal executive had the foresight to have his phone disconnected.

In 1950, Newsy Lalonde's double life was permanently recognized, when he was named the best Canadian lacrosse player of the half-century and a few months later was elected to the Hockey Hall of Fame.

The dual nature of Cornwall's sporting life would also be reflected in other ways. The city's most famous team, the Cornwall Royals, would win a Memorial Cup, in 1972, in the Quebec junior league and, then, in 1980 and 1981, in the Ontario junior league. And the city's most famous female hockey player, Albertine Lapensee, star forward on the women's Cornwall Victorias from 1917 to 1919, also lived a dual existence. Her career with the women's team ended when she returned from a trip to New York as a man—Albert Smith.

Royal Flush

Despite playing in two provincial leagues for three coaches between 1972 and 1981, the Cornwall Royals reigned supreme in Canadian junior hockey that decade, winning three Memorial Cups. During those years, winter air that was normally soured by local pulp mills somehow smelled sweet as candy. First, in 1972, the Royals, a Quebec league blue-collar team that toiled out of the old Water Street Arena, took the junior crown for its coach, local hockey legend Orval Tessier. Eight years later, in 1980, the Royals had become an Ontario junior team, with Doug Carpenter at the helm. The team was stacked with talent—Scott Arneil, Fred Boimistruck, and the always sensational Dale Hawerchuk. The team won again, knocking off the Peterborough Petes, just as Tessier's team had done. The following season, though, the Royals had their best-ever team, with Arneil, Boimistruck and Hawerchuk returning, along with additions Marc Crawford (captain) and Doug Gilmour, who would score the winning goal against Kitchener. The coach, that season, was Bob Kilger, who would later represent Cornwall as a federal member of parliament for the Liberal party.

In 1992, the Royals franchise moved to Newmarket, Ontario.

GUELPH

FOUNDED
Guelph was established by Scottish novelist and civic planner John Galt in 1827, when the location was chosen as the headquarters of the Canada Company, a British-based land-development firm for whom Galt was the Canadian superintendent. Guelph, named by Galt for the German ancestors of then-reigning king George IV, was consequently known as the "Royal City." Guelph officially became a city in 1879, and in the 1880s it was the 10th largest community in Canada.

NATIVE-BORN NHL PLAYERS
Arthur Brooks, Paul Brydges, Tony Cassolato, Lloyd Finkbeiner, "Leapin'" Lou Fontinato, Harry "Yip" Foster, Mike Hudson, Greg Jacina, Brian MacLellan, Kirk Maltby, George McPhee, Gord McTavish, Ron Scott, Bill Sweeney

FAMOUS LOCAL TEAMS
Junior: Guelph Biltmores, Guelph Indians, Guelph Junior B's, Guelph Leaflets, Guelph Mad Hatters, Guelph Maple Leafs, Guelph Platers, Guelph Royals, Guelph Storm;
Senior-pro: Guelph Biltmores, Guelph Mad Hatters, Guelph Maple Leafs, Guelph Nationals, Guelph Pros, Guelph OAC, Guelph Regals

CURRENT POPULATION
106,170

Hat Tricks

A college town, set on the not-so-frantic Speed River and surrounded by richly quilted farmland, Guelph is one of southern Ontario's most genteel communities. So it is perhaps fitting that the city's most famous hockey team was named after the elegant, locally crafted Biltmore hat.

One out of three Canadian hat wearers wore Biltmore products in the decade following World War II—even metal rapper Kid Rock wears one today. And certainly, in the 1950s, everyone in hockey knew who the Guelph Biltmores were. In the 1951–52 season, the Guelph junior team won the Memorial Cup in convincing fashion, sweeping the western champions, the Regina Pats, in a four-game series by a collective score of 30–8.

Coach Alf Pike's team opened that series in the brand new 4,247-seat Guelph Memorial Gardens, with scalpers charging up to $3 for a seat. The Biltmores won, 8–2, that first night, outshooting the Pats, 46–10. (Subsequent games in the series would be played at Maple Leaf Gardens.)

A New York Rangers farm club, the Biltmores famously graduated six players to the National Hockey League parent team the following season, including captain Andy Bathgate and defenceman Harry Howell (both of whom would go on to Hall of Fame careers), along with Aldo Guidolin, Ron Murphy, Dean Prentice and Bill McCreary. (Guelph's own "Leapin'" Lou Fontinato would make the Rangers a few seasons later.) The star of the 1951–52 team, however, was Ken Laufman, who established a junior Ontario scoring record that year (counting 53 goals and 86 assists), but who would turn down a New York Rangers job offer, opting instead to return to his hometown, Kitchener, where he played—for more money, he insisted—on Bobby Bauer's Allan Cup-winning senior teams that represented Canada in the Olympics in 1956 and 1960.

None of those accomplishments, though, compared to winning it all for the

Winnipeg's Andy Bathgate suffered a major knee injury his first shift with the Guelph Biltmores. Though restricted to a knee brace, he enjoyed a stellar career, leading the Biltmores to a Memorial Cup in 1952 and winning the NHL's most valuable player award with the New York Rangers in 1959.

Look Before You Leap

A Guelph hockey broadcaster gave "Leapin'" Lou Fontinato his nickname, referring to the furious high-jumping tantrums the Biltmores defenceman engaged in after being called for a penalty. Following his junior years with the Guelph Biltmores, Fontinato enjoyed a nine-year National Hockey League career with the New York Rangers and the Montreal Canadiens (1954–63) before retiring to a cattle farm in nearby Rockwood, in Wellington County, Ontario.

Well, the defenceman probably did not enjoy one famous moment of his pro career. On 1 Febuary 1959 Fontinato sought out Gordie Howe behind the Rangers' net, to settle an old score with the big winger. "I must have thrown 10 punches before he threw one," Fontinato would later tell a Guelph *Mercury* reporter, Richard Hutton. The one big punch Gordie did throw, however, caught Lou square on the nose, whereupon the big defenceman went down like lemonade on a hot day. "It looked like a train hit me," he conceded.

Eddie Shack with a classic "Mickey Spillane" '50s brushcut. Shack sold Guelph Biltmore hats out of the back of his car trunk long into his pro career with the Toronto Maple Leafs.

Biltmores, Laufman told a Guelph *Mercury* reporter in 2002, at a 50th anniversary banquet honouring the team's Memorial Cup win. Guelph was a city of 28,000 at the time, and it had had to defeat Montreal and Toronto to make it to the finals. "We had a big tickertape parade through the city, and planes were flying overhead," Laufman remembered. "We all sat in convertibles, with our names on the sides of the cars. It was really quite something."

The Biltmores, who were also called the Mad Hatters sometimes, would acquire their best salesman when the most forward of forwards, Eddie Shack, joined the team in 1952: "When I was in Guelph, I used to buy hats from the Biltmore hat factory," Shack told writer Charles Wilkins. "And I'd carry them around in my car. At that time I had a convertible—I'd have hats in the back seat, hats in the trunk...maybe 50 hats in all. I'd come up to a guy and say, 'A man is not properly dressed without a hat.' I wore one all the time... Bought 'em for three bucks, sold them for 10. I'd sell to my teammates, too. I'd say, 'Boys have I got some great deals, boom, let's have 'er, guys!' And I'd get cash. When I went home to Sudbury I'd always take a load. Even when I played for the Maple Leafs, I'd head out to Guelph and get a load of hats."

Shack was not the maddest hatter ever to represent the Royal City. In 1899, Cooney Shields, a member of the city's senior team, the Guelph Nationals, removed a glass eye during games to put off his opponents.

HAMILTON

FOUNDED

In 1784, the British purchased shore land on the western edge of Lake Ontario from Mississauga Aboriginals to provide homes for Loyalists fleeing the United States. The city was named after George Hamilton, a local settler and politician who helped build a thriving community in what is now the eastern part of the city. Hamilton's proximity to Niagara Escarpment limestone, Canadian Shield iron ore and flourishing shipping and railway transportation routes in the Great Lakes area made Hamilton an important iron-and-steel producer in the late 1800s. Hamilton's blue-collar roots are reflected in its many colourful nicknames: "Steel City," "The Hammer" and "Lunchbucket City."

NATIVE-BORN NHL PLAYERS

Dave Andreychuk, Walt Atanas, Bob Barlow, Paul Beraldo, Allan Bester, Andy Brown, Frank Caprice, Joe Cirella, Ian Cushenan, Herb Dickenson, Dave Dryden, Ken Dryden, Blake Dunlop, Cecil "Babe" Dye, Don Edwards, Darren Eliot, Nelson Emerson, Ed Gilbert, Todd Harvey, John Holota, Harry Howell, Ron Howell, Al Jensen, Jay Johnston, Stan Kemp, Derek King, Blair MacKasey, Adam Mair, Ken Mann, Jay Mazur, Rick McCann, Al McDonough, Brian McGratton, Doug McKay, Marty McSorley, Ron Murphy, Ric Nattress, Murray Oliver, George Owen, Geoff Peters, Pat Quinn, Wayne Rivers, Nick Smith, Rick Smith, Steve Staios, John Tonelli, Dennis Ververgaert

FAMOUS LOCAL TEAMS

Junior: Hamilton Aerovox, Hamilton Beavers, Hamilton Bengal Cubs, Hamilton Fin Cups, Hamilton Hawks, Hamilton Huskies, Hamilton Lloyds, Hamilton Red Wings, Hamilton Rowing Club, Hamilton Szabos, Hamilton Tiger Cubs, Hamilton Tigers, Hamilton Victorias, Hamilton Whizzers; **Senior-pro:** Hamilton Beavers, Hamilton Bulldogs, Hamilton Canucks, Hamilton Dofascos, Hamilton Majors, Hamilton Pats, Hamilton Rowing Club, Hamilton Steelhawks, Hamilton Tiger Cats, Hamilton Tigers

CURRENT POPULATION

502,000

Sudbury's Shorty Green starred for the Hamilton Tigers, both as a junior and as an NHL star.

Strike One, You're Out

Professional hockey is a money-making affair. The promoters are in the game for what they can make out of it, and the players wouldn't be in the game if they didn't look at matters in the same light.
—Shorty Green, Hamilton Tigers, 1925

The home of Stelco and Dofasco steelworkers, Hamilton has seen many union conflicts over the years. The city was also the site of the first-ever professional sports strike in North America, a dispute that cost the Steel City a chance at the Stanley Cup.

Hamilton already had a senior team named the Hamilton Tigers, an Allan Cup winner in 1919, when the Abso-Pure Ice Company, which had cornered the refrigeration and ice-delivery market in the city, decided it needed another tenant in its new 3,800-seat artificial-ice rink, the Barton Street Arena. So Abso-Pure purchased the last-place National Hockey League Quebec Bulldogs for $5,000 at the end of the 1919 20 season, changing the team's name to the Tigers.

For the next five seasons Hamilton had two Tigers in the Barton Street tank. At first, the senior team outdrew the NHLers—not surprising when you consider that the NHL Tigers, who boasted a goalie named "Holes" Lockhart, finished dead last their first four years in the four-team league (Toronto St. Pats, Ottawa Senators and Montreal Canadiens rounding out the competition).

Despite the NHL club's losing record, general manager Percy Thompson was in the midst of a successful team renovation, bringing in Jake Forbes from

Suddenly, and without warning, the Tigers were the best club in hockey.

the St. Pats to replace "Holes" Lockhart and signing star Billy Burch from the New Haven Westminsters of the United States Amateur Hockey Association in 1922, then trading the team's lone star, Joe Malone, to the Canadiens for tough-as-he-sounds defenceman Bert "Pig Iron" Corbeau in 1923. The next season, Thompson went on a one-stop shopping spree in northern Ontario, picking up brothers Shorty and Red Green along with Alex McKinnon and Charlie Langlois from the Sudbury Wolves.

Suddenly, and without warning, the Tigers were the best club in hockey. Shorty Green was a particular favourite with Hamiltonians, who remembered him from his previous stay in the Steel City, when he had helped the 1919 senior Tigers to the Allan Cup. In the midst of the NHL Tigers' giddy 1924–25 run, the Hamilton *Herald* ran a big photo spread of Green with a cutline challenge to the hockey world: "Find his equal!"

The Tigers remained in first place that entire season, an expansion year that saw the league jump from four to six teams (adding the Boston Bruins and Montreal Maroons) and from 24 to 30 games. Attendance was flourishing at the Barton Street Arena. But while everything was Abso-Perfect in the Tigers' accounting books, the players were far from happy.

Other NHL teams offered pay raises and generous Christmas bonuses, to acknowledge the increase in regular season games, plus an extra round of play-offs, what with the NHL winners now having to face the western Canadian hockey champions for the Stanley Cup. The first-place Tigers received not a dollar more for a month's extra work.

Only a storm, grumbling through a canyon, picks up sound like a hockey team that figures it's being screwed. The last game of the season was a war in Montreal that left every Tigers player "decorated to some extent in the hectic struggle with the Frenchmen," according to the *Hamilton Spectator*. At one point in the game, a "Frenchwoman" even leaned over the glass and clubbed forward Alex McKinnon over the head. On the train ride back to Hamilton, the unhappy first-place team advised general manager Percy Thompson that they wouldn't play another game that season, not even for the Stanley Cup, without receiving a $200 bonus. And that was that.

But it wasn't that simple. Shorty Green and Billy Burch met with NHL commissioner Frank Calder a few days later. Calder was flabbergasted at the players' demands, particularly when the athletes grumbled about not seeing any of the $15,000 expansion fees the NHL teams received from the new entries in Montreal and Boston. In a grim precursor of the contract disputes that would ruin NHL hockey 80 years later, the two sides argued about capital risk versus labour sweat.

Then, that Friday, Calder issued an ultimatum: The players had until high noon the following day to back down, or else they would all be suspended.

First Tims in Canada

The Canadian winter weekend morning ritual of driving your kid to hockey practice at dawn—eyes pried open with Tim Hortons coffee—began in Steel City. Tim Horton, a famous 1960s defence man with the Toronto Maple Leafs, opened his first coffee shop in 1964, at 64 Ottawa Street North in Hamilton. More than 1,500 more Tim Hortons would open across the country during the next 40 years. Horton himself created Canada's breakfast of champions—the Dutchie, a square no-hole glazed doughnut studded with raisins.

Tim Horton was always big on customer satisfaction. Once, when he was playing for the New York Rangers in the 1970s, he complained to a hotel desk clerk about the soft drink dispenser on his floor, which was robbing him of quarters. When no one hurried to the scene, Horton wrestled the fridge-sized dispenser into the elevator and brought it down to the front desk in person.

Power Player

Hamilton-born winger Dave Andreychuk ended his local apprenticeship with the Hamilton Hawks, in 1980, at age 16. From that team, he went on to play junior with the Oshawa Generals for two seasons before embarking on a quarter-century career in the National Hockey League. Everywhere he went, the 6'4" forward was a power-play specialist, a guy who used his boarding-house reach to tap in, deflect and shovel home goals around the crease. In 2002, he tallied his 250th power-play goal to surpass Phil Esposito as the all-time leader in that category. Andreychuk was captain of the 2003–04 Stanley Cup champion Tampa Bay Lightning.

The Tigers players refused. Calder suspended them, ruling that the athletes wouldn't be allowed back to the NHL until every striking Tigers player paid a $200 fine. Meanwhile, the Montreal Canadiens were declared the NHL champions and then were clobbered by the Pacific Coast Hockey League's Victoria Cougars in the finals, a great embarrassment to the NHL.

Within weeks, the Abso-Pure Ice Company got out of the hockey business at an enormous profit, raffling off a few players, then selling the franchise for $75,000 to New York bootlegger Big Bill Dwyer. Dwyer turned the team into the New York Americans and rewarded Shorty Green and Billy Burch with enormous raises (Green's salary went from $3,000 to $5,000).

Everybody won, except Hamilton hockey fans, who lost an NHL team and maybe the city's only chance at a Stanley Cup. Not that Steel Town's blue-collar fans begrudged the striking Tigers their defiant stand. Shorty Green remained a hero in the Ontario city. In fact, Hamilton kids took to calling the stubby, cast-iron, soon-to-be-green drinking fountains that went up throughout the Hamilton downtown in the 1920s, "shorty greens." The nickname is still used today.

KENORA

FOUNDED
Kenora originated as Rat Portage, a fur-trading post on the Lake of the Woods in northwestern Ontario. The city became a transportation centre in the final two decades of the 19th century, a vital link in the westward-moving Canadian Pacific Railway. In 1905, Rat Portage changed its name to the more pleasant-sounding Kenora. In 1907, the Kenora Thistles won the Stanley Cup, becoming the smallest city (7,000 at the time) ever to win the trophy.

NATIVE-BORN NHL PLAYERS
Bob Bailey, Gary Bergman, Tim Coulis, John Gallagher, Henry Harris, Tom Hooper, Charles McVeigh, Dennis Olson, Don Raleigh, Mike Richards, Neil Strain

FAMOUS LOCAL TEAMS
Junior: Kenora Boise, Kenora Thistles, Kenora Muskies;
Senior-pro: Kenora Canadians, Kenora Thistles

CURRENT POPULATION
15,838

Rink Rats

Kenora wasn't always Kenora. At the turn of the 19th century, the northwestern Ontario town had a more richly descriptive and (then more appropriate) name—Rat Portage.

The city sprang to life in the 1870s, as the transcontinental railway muscled its way past the Lake of the Woods toward Manitoba. Suddenly, a small settlement occupied by card-playing Hudson Bay trappers was besieged by itinerant railway workers looking to kill their off-hours with whiskey and sin, a circumstance that prompted the Canadian Pacific Railway to prohibit brothels and saloons within seven miles of the city.

That restriction only encouraged criminals to take to nearby islands. By 1880, the region had almost as many stills as muskrats. Eight hundred barrels of whiskey made it into the port every month, often hidden within barrels of coal oil. Then gold was discovered in the nearby area, swelling the city further, but also—eventually—bringing police and responsible government to Rat Portage.

Sport became an important local winter diversion in the 1890s, with the arrival of the hockey-happy Hardisty family from Winnipeg. Rat Portage held a contest to decide on a name for the town's newly formed team. Bill Dunsmore, a local carpenter and loyal Scot, suggested the winning entry—the Thistles.

Enthusiasm for hockey found a focal point in 1895, when the Princess Rink, a boxlike arena with humming electric lights, was built. Now the red-on-white senior Thistles became the city's leading ambassadors, competing regularly with teams from Brandon, Winnipeg and Portage la Prairie.

Before long, hockey became a governing passion of local kids, rink rats who spent winters playing and dreaming the sport. The junior Thistles, some of whom were as young as 12, felt ready to take on the world and so decided to challenge the town's senior team. The youngsters—a group that included future Hockey Hall of Famers Tommy Phillips, Tom Hooper, Billy McGimsie and Silas Griffis—overwhelmed the seniors that night, harassing their elders into a damp heap. Ten years later, the kids had matured into a senior team that could hold its own with the best hockey clubs in Canada.

That initial upset of the town seniors defined how the new edition of the Thistles went about business, for the team always played as if trying to run the opposition off the rink. They skated hard and worked in tandem, moving the puck up the ice with crisp passes, whereas other hockey teams relied on individual rushes. Rat Portage changed how hockey was played, by bringing both defencemen up on offensive rushes. (Before this, teams always kept one player back.) An impressed *Montreal Star* reporter suggested that the 1905 edition of the Thistles "were the fastest (team) that has ever been seen anywhere on ice."

Still, the team was deprived of the Stanley Cup, in 1903 and 1905 losses to the Ottawa Silver Seven. Then, in 1907, the team conducted a successful chemistry experiment, importing "Bad" Joe Hall from Brandon, Manitoba. Montreal's Art Ross joined the team by way of Winnipeg. And star Tommy Phillips recruited goalie Eddie Giroux from the Toronto Marlboros. The town of 7,000 also had something of a public relations makeover, changing its name from Rat Portage to the more mellifluous Kenora.

Neither of these moves hurt, as the Kenora Thistles edged out the Montreal Wanderers to capture the 1907 Stanley Cup, making Rat Por...er...Kenora, the smallest city ever to win hockey's grandest prize.

Future Hall of Famer Tommy Phillips ended his career with the Vancouver Millionaires of the Pacific Coast Hockey Association. He only played for a year, 1911–12, but still managed to score 17 goals in as many games.

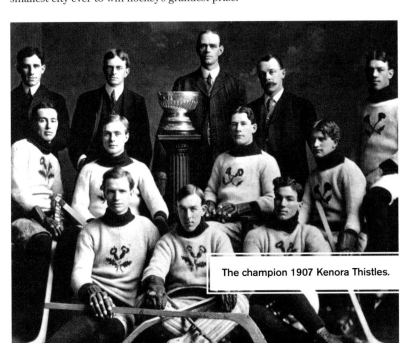

The champion 1907 Kenora Thistles.

KINGSTON

Modern skaters commemorate the first Kingston hockey game with a yearly re-enactment on Kingston harbour.

FOUNDED

The French-built Fort Frontenac was ceded to the British in the 1760s, and the growing settlement was renamed King's Town, in honour of King George III. A vital stopping point for lake and river transport, Kingston grew quickly, becoming the colony's largest town in the early 1800s. Between 1841 and 1843, it served briefly as the capital of what was then known as the Province of Canada. It has gradually emerged as one of the country's leading educational centres, the home of Queen's University and of the Royal Military College.

NATIVE-BORN NHL PLAYERS

Bryan Allen, Scott Arniel, Cam Botting, Kip Brennan, Fred Brown, Rob Brown, Jack Caffery, Wayne Cashman, Dick Cherry, Don Cherry, Tony Cimellaro, Chris Clifford, Brandon Convery, Alex Cook, Frederick "Bun" Cook, Bob Dailey, Allan Davidson, Peter Dineen, Jim Dorey, Pete Driscoll, John Erskine, Shawn Evans, Doug Gilmour, Hank Goldup, Hugh Harvey, Todd Hawkins, John Hendrickson, Scott Hollis, Dennis Kearns, Nick Knott, Guy Leveque, Ken Linseman, Jay McClement, Jay McKee, Mike Meeker, Kirk Muller, Bob Murray, Mike Murray, Fred O'Donnell, Don O'Donoghue, Rick Paterson, Pat Patterson, Rob Plumb, Ron Plumb, Kenneth Randall, Nathan Robinson, Mike Rowe, Brit Selby, Mike Smith, Trevor Steinburg, Thomas Thurlby, John Tripp, Marty Walsh, James Walsh

FAMOUS LOCAL TEAMS

Junior: Kingston AAC, Kingston Canadians, Kingston Frontenacs, Kingston Jr. Lions, Kingston Raiders, Kingston Saints, Kingston Vics, Kingston Voyageurs; **Senior-pro:** Kingston Aces, Kingston Army, Kingston Combines, Kingston Frontenacs

CURRENT POPULATION

146,838

The Old College Try

Kingston is the birthplace of *Hockey Night in Canada*'s clothes horse and provocateur Don Cherry; surefire Hall of Famer Doug Gilmour; and, according to some local historians, the sport of hockey itself.

Like Windsor, Nova Scotia, another city that takes credit as the home of Canada's national sport, Kingston was first a military and university town. In fact, the Royal Canadian Rifles were stationed in both Windsor and Kingston in the early 19th century. One Kingston officer, Arthur Henry Freeling, provided what many believe to be the first recorded mention of the word "hockey," scrawling in his January 1843 diary: "Began to skate this year, improved quickly and had great fun at hockey on the ice." In 1846, local diarist Edwin Horsey wrote, "Most of the boys were quite at home on skates. They could cut the figure eight and other fancy figures, but 'shinny' was their delight. Crowds would be placed at the Shoal Tower and Point Frederick, and 50 or more players on each side would be in a game."

According to Capt. Jim Sutherland, who became president of the Ontario Hockey Association in 1915, during the 1850s, Kingston's Royal Canadian Rifles would split into two divisions and battle it out on the town's frozen harbour. Skaters sometimes outnumbered spectators in these affairs, with as many as

100 bustling, steam-breathing combatants taking to the ice at any one time. (Presumably, there were no offsides.)

Despite this evidence of long-ago hockey in Kingston, other historical records suggest that the game started earlier in Nova Scotia. In 1844, author Thomas Chandler Haliburton of Nova Scotia (see page 58) wrote about boys during his school days "racin', yellin', hollerin' and whoopin'," while playing hurley on Windsor's Long Pond around the year 1800. Based on this evidence, historians can presume that Kingston began playing a game like hockey shortly after. Then again, Haliburton doesn't mention "skatin'" in his writing, just "racin'."

Montreal—with Maritimer James Creighton's help—is an easier call in terms of establishing the sport of hockey (see page 93), as an indoor hockey game with rules and a trophy was played there in the Victoria Rink in 1875. Here again, though, Kingston was not far behind. Queen's University students played an organized one-hour contest against cadets from the Royal Military College on 10 March 1886. The game took place on Kingston harbour ice, near Victoria or Shoal Tower. (It is still replicated in late February every year, weather permitting, by historical re-enactors.)

One of Kingston's earliest hockey triumphs occurred in 1909, when the Queen's University team beat the Ottawa Cliffsides to take the second-ever Allan Cup, the Canadian senior championship title. *The Daily British Whig* (later, the *Kingston Whig-Standard*) would celebrate the victory with a series of headlines and subheads that were stacked like pancakes:

An octagonal puck, cut from a lacrosse ball, and believed to be the oldest of its kind in the world, and a handcrafted hockey stick used in an 1888 game between Queen's University and the Royal Military College.

QUEEN'S WON

The Sir Montague Trophy Comes Here

STRENUOUS GAME

TWENTY MINUTES OVERTIME HAD TO BE PLAYED

Queen's Led in the Scoring, But Cliffsides Managed to Keep Up With the Calvinists—There Was Much Excitement During the Vigorous Game

The "vigorous game" was played in Ottawa in front of 4,500 fans and two distinguished sportsmen: Sir Montague Allan, who donated the senior hockey championship cup, was present, and Governor General Earl Grey, who gave his name to the Canadian Football League Grey Cup, performed the ceremonial "facing of the puck"—the ceremonial dropping of the puck.

The regular contest was played in two 30-minute halves and ended tied at four goals each, a situation that sent referee Blair Russell and the "judge of play," S. Macpherson, both of Montreal, into a worried huddle. These were still the early days of hockey; the Ottawa Cliffsides had won the year before but had never even received a trophy, as the award was just now being completed. Perhaps the officials hadn't finished the rule book, either.

Russell finally decreed that an overtime session would be played. And it was during this final period of the game that Queen's players first exemplified the sharp-edged temper that came to characterize local players. Kingston-born Wayne Cashman, for example, a junior Kingston Frontenacs grad who played sheriff for the National Hockey League's Boston Bruins from 1968 to 1983, once responded to the trade of friend and teammate Phil Esposito to New York by throwing a TV out of his hotel window onto the parking lot below, then ordering and charging 100 sandwiches from room service. Don Cherry, long-time NHL coach and broadcaster, has always gone about his business with an evident temper. Once, on the radio, he exploded when someone alluded to a metric measurement. "How come, you go in a supermarket, you're looking for hamburger, it's in metric or something,"

The Queen's hockey team, 1886.

The Queen's Women's hockey team, 1917.

WHO IS THAT MASKED WOMAN?

Queen's University hockey player Elizabeth Graham was the first-ever goaltender to wear a hockey mask, sporting a fencing mask for an intercollegiate game in 1927. The *Montreal Daily Star* reported that Graham "gave the fans a surprise when she stepped into the nets and then donned a fencing mask." Legend has it that Graham's father insisted his daughter adopt extra protection after she'd had extensive dental work done.

Tailored for Success

Don Cherry's father was a Kingston amateur baseball star, a strapping centrefielder with iron wrists, who, in addition to his electrician's job, made a little extra dough by dropping into the bar at the Royal Canadian Horse Artillery Club, throwing $10 on the table and challenging the room to a test of strength. Don's mother was a military tailor who fashioned uniforms for Royal Military College cadets. The marriage of the tailor and baseball star made for some interesting innings. Once, Delmer Cherry arrived home grousing about his wife's cooking. How come she never made anything fancy—creamed onions, for instance? Maude Cherry said nothing, but the next day she prepared the requested dish for dinner. Her husband, who had had a bad day at work, sniffed at the food and announced, "I don't like creamed onions." Maude poured the dish over Delmer's head, and he never complained about his wife's cooking again.

The Cherrys would produce two hockey-playing sons. Dick Cherry enjoyed more success as a player, completing two full seasons for the National Hockey League's Philadelphia Flyers (1968–70). Older brother Don, however, managed to transform a lengthy stay in the minor leagues (and one 1955 playoff game for the Boston Bruins) into an extraordinary coaching and broadcasting career.

As it happened, Don would make use of a tailor to draw attention to himself, favouring three-inch collars and flashy ties for his weekly appearances, from 1980 onward, on *Hockey Night in Canada*. Sartorial overkill only served to make Cherry's plain virtues more apparent. His thunderous exclamations and complaints transported two generations of fans from their living rooms to Thunder Bay and Medicine Hat taprooms, hockey's parish churches. Cherry became a hero to millions of average Delmers and Maudes across Canada.

Killer

Doug Gilmour was often described as 5'11" and 175 pounds, yet when he stood beside a reporter who was 5'10" and 165 pounds, the scribe seemed taller and wider at the shoulders. Whatever Gilmour's actual size, tenacity was what made the National Hockey Leaguer the biggest player on the ice. And his drive to give more than he had in every game was evident in the 1989 Stanley Cup finals between the Calgary Flames and the Montreal Canadiens. Killer, as Gilmour's Flames teammates called him, scored the empty-net Cup-clinching goal against the Canadiens in game six, but he passed at a chance to hoist the Cup for a skate around the Forum afterward. He was just too tired to lift the trophy.

The player, who started his career with the minor hockey Kingston Legionnaires and the Kingston junior B Voyageurs, returned from Alberta to Ontario as a member of the Maple Leafs in 1992 and almost succeeded in taking the Leafs to the Stanley Cup finals two seasons later. Although Gilmour spent only six of his 20 NHL seasons in Toronto, he remains one of the most popular players ever to wear a Leafs crest.

he once asked. "But then, say, a killer is loose, and then it's OK for the press to say he's 6'2", 200 pounds. That metric stuff drives me nuts."

What was driving the Queen's hockey team into a fury, in 1909, was the play of a hummingbird-quick attacker for the Cliffsides, a Mr. Henry, who had scored two goals and still looked dangerous in overtime. Pennock, the Queen's coverpoint (a defensive position), decided to eliminate Ottawa's most persistent threat by lambasting Mr. Henry against the boards, drawing not only a penalty but also a stretcher for the no-longer-dangerous Cliffsides forward.

Queen's survived the ensuing power play, then went on the attack. At one point, a Queen's player fired a loose puck at the net. The Ottawa goalie made the save, but the Kingston forwards, growing more hotly determined by the second, joined in a rugger scrum, pushing the goalie backward into the net. Fearing the worst, a Cliffsides defender moved the finishing line back, lifting the net away. He was given a one-minute penalty and Queen's pressed its advantage further. An unnamed *British Whig* correspondent described how the Kingston team would go on to achieve its winning goal: "Dobson found the fair-haired Queen's wing man [Campbell], waiting for a chance. Dobson slipped the puck to Campbell as both Merrill and Hall rushed at him, expecting a shot, and Campbell, with no one upon him, steadied himself and sent in a fine shot."

Queen's fans jumped the boards and carried away the new champions on their shoulders. "The news of Queen's victory was received here about 11:20 o'clock," the *Whig* continued, "and at several places where the hockey fans had gathered to hear the bulletins, there was great rejoicing. Queen's students were out in force, and bands of them paraded Princess Street...hurling their Gaelic yell, and cheering for their hockey representatives, who had won the highest amateur hockey honor in Canada."

In its report about the Allan Cup victory, the Kingston newspaper included one ungracious comment: "Everything favoured the Cliffsides at Ottawa. They were at home on the ice and the crowd was with them. Hence, Queen's victory, though secured in overtime and by a margin of one goal, is really greater than it appears. Had the season been earlier, home and home matches would have been played, and it is pretty certain that Queen's would have defeated the interprovincial champions here by four or five goals." Max Jackson, sports voice of Kingston's CKWS Radio and Television from the late '50s to the early '80s, would have had a response to such unseemly gloating. As Max used to say in his signature sign-off, "If you don't play a sport, be one."

Wayne Cashman with the Boston Bruins.

Ted Lindsay, ready and eager for another of a thousand hockey battles.

DEAR MOM, I SAW BARCLAY TODAY...

A referee was needed at the dinner table, to stop Barclay, Bob and Bill Plager's fight over second helpings. The Kirkland Lake boys only really started to get along when they all played together for the St. Louis Blues of the National Hockey League, in the late 1960s. The worst family fight, before their NHL years, took place in Guelph. At the time, Bob was a member of the Guelph Biltmores and Barclay played as a defenceman for the Peterborough Petes. The two junior hockey players fought on the ice, then twice more, in the corridor, as they headed to the dressing room to have their wounds stitched. Cops had to break them up. After the game, the brothers bumped into each other at a local restaurant. Bob jumped up from the table, ready to go again, but Barclay had just dropped by to remind his brother to write home to Ma in Kirkland Lake.

KIRKLAND LAKE

FOUNDED

Kirkland Lake was founded in 1911, after gold was discovered in the region. The first strike was made by William Wright, who invested some of his new wealth in Toronto's *Globe and Mail*. The town's most famous prospector was Harry Oakes, who arrived penniless and left with an enormous fortune that eventually earned him a British peerage. Within a decade, the city was the second biggest gold producer in Canada. At its economic peak in the 1940s, the city was known as "the hub of the north."

NATIVE-BORN NHL PLAYERS

Ralph Backstrom, Don Blackburn, Buddy Boone, Dick Duff, Murray Hall, Chuck Hamilton, Earl Heiskala, Larry Hillman, Wayne Hillman, Willie Marshall, Bob Murdoch, Claude Noel, Barclay Plager, Bill Plager, Bob Plager, Daren Puppa, Dick Redmond, Mickey Redmond, Mike Walton, Dave Watson, Tom Webster

FAMOUS LOCAL TEAMS

Junior: Kirkland Lake Blue Devils, Kirkland Lake Legion, Kirkland Lake Hargreaves, Kirkland Lake Lion Cubs; **Senior-pro:** Kirkland Lake Blue Devils, Kirkland Lake Lakers, Kirkland Lake Millionaires, Kirkland Lake Prospectors, Kirkland Lake Wright-Hargreaves

CURRENT POPULATION

8,616

Underground Heroes

Twenty-two million ounces of gold and 21 National Hockey League players came out of Kirkland Lake during the city's mining and hockey boom. From 1948 to 1973, a local representative was in all but six Stanley Cup finals, a circumstance that prompted broadcaster Foster Hewitt to remark that Kirkland Lake was "the town that made the NHL famous." The 1967 Stanley Cup final had Mike Walton and Larry Hillman of the Toronto Maple Leafs skating against Montreal's Dick Duff and Ralph Backstrom—all four, Kirkland Lakers. Two Cups later, local battlers Barclay, Bob and Bill Plager amassed two hours of playoff penalty minutes scuffling their way to the finals against the Duff-Backstrom Canadiens.

Still, it was a Millionaire's son who exemplified the brawling spirit of Sir Harry Oakes' kingdom. Oakes had helped to make Kirkland Lake's 1912 gold discovery, and then elbowed everybody out of the way, creating a $300 million fortune for himself. Legend has it that Oakes built his mansion within spying distance of the gold strike, felling and squaring 70 giant timbers in a single day to create an unobstructed view of the mine.

Sir Harry would have liked Robert Blake Theodore "Terrible Teddie" Lindsay. Son of Bert Lindsay of the Renfrew Millionaires, one of hockey's legendary early 20th-century pro teams (see page 173), Ted Lindsay moved to Kirkland Lake as a kid, and there at age 10, he would demonstrate the toughness that defined his career.

The temperature was 30 below in Kirkland Lake, one day in 1935. Still, Ted was out skating. The only concession he made to the cold was thrusting his mitts in his pockets. Thus handcuffed, he was fighting the wind when the ice cracked, catching a skate edge. Lindsay landed face first, breaking off two front teeth.

Returning home, Ted feared even greater punishment—maybe his mother wouldn't allow him to play hockey! Despite the pain, he concealed the injury, talking with his head turned and lowering his upper lip when smiling. Ted got away with the ruse for three hockey-playing weeks, but then his gums became infected and he was rushed to a dentist, who removed three teeth and installed a permanent plate.

A few years later, Lindsay led Holy Name School to two all-Ontario championships, where he was discovered and invited to play for St. Michael's renowned hockey team in Toronto. The Leafs somehow missed him, and at age 19, in 1944, he graduated to the Detroit Red Wings.

He was so good at being bad that he instantly won a nickname—Terrible Teddie. Lindsay played hockey as if everybody owed him money. He hit opposing players when they weren't looking and yelled at them when they were. Everyone in Detroit loved him. Elsewhere, except in Kirkland Lake, he was public enemy number 7 (his Red Wings number).

In the late 1940s, he joined with Gordie Howe and Sid Abel to form The Production Line. The unit came one-two-three in NHL scoring in 1949. Detroit finished first a record seven times in a row, winning four Stanley Cups. Lindsay and Howe were great friends, who lived and roomed together while ruling the hockey-playing world.

In 1956, the two linemates received death threats from Toronto fans before a playoff game. Lindsay retaliated by scoring the game's tying and winning goals. Leaving the ice, he placed the blade of his stick under his arm and pretended to fire a rifle at the crowd.

A year later, Lindsay took aim at the NHL, joining together with Doug Harvey and Jim Thomson to form the first players' association. The NHL broke the union, and all three players were traded within a few years.

Banished to the Chicago Blackhawks, Lindsay's glory days were over. But if he was angry or hurt, he didn't let anybody know. He still carried himself like an undefeated bantamweight champion. When he retired for the first time in 1960, Ted Lindsay left the game as the highest-scoring left winger and as the all-time penalty leader.

Hockey had become an obsession in Kirkland Lake long before Terrible Ted Lindsay's retirement, however. Interest in the sport exploded, spurred on by the heroics of this hometown hero and giving way to a tidal wave of talent from Kirkland Lake. "Good athletes were brought in to play hockey and fastball, and they worked in the mines and brought up families," said the town's next hockey star, Dickie Duff, in explaining how Kirkland Lake began shifting from importing hockey talent to exporting players. "The Legion, Kiwanis, Lions Club and a few others sponsored teams, which made for a very competitive league. Hockey gave the people a place to go and provided a topic of conversation during the long days underground in the mines." Soon, the town had new heroes—NHLers Duff, Backstrom, the Hillman brothers (Larry and Wayne) and Dick and Mickey Redmond, the latter of whom was a two-time 50-goal scorer for Detroit in the early '70s.

All of these subsequent players would acknowledge a debt of gratitude to the athlete who put Kirkland Lake on the hockey map, a player who until his last hockey breath remained the heir to Sir Harry Oakes. Ted Lindsay again showed his fighting spirit, when he was elected into the Hockey Hall of Fame in 1966. At the time, family members were not allowed to attend the event, and so the Hall refused to let Lindsay bring his family to the ceremonial banquet. "To hell with that," Lindsay responded. "If my wife and kids can't see the old man be honoured, what's the point? Thanks, but no thanks."

Terrible Ted raises his weapon of choice.

KITCHENER

FOUNDED

First settled by Benjamin Eby from Pennsylvania, other Mennonite families began to arrive in the area in 1806. In the 1830s, the settlement was named Berlin by a wave of crafts-men and working-class families who had emigrated from Germany. During World War I, the town was rechris-tened Kitchener, to honour Lord Kitchener of Khartoum, a British hero who had died at sea. The city's name may have been anglicized, but German influence runs deep to this day in Kitchener. Industrial families such as the Schneiders, Kaufmanns and Schlees founded companies that dom-inated the region's commerce for much of the 20th century, and the annual fall Oktoberfest festival is the largest of its kind in Canada.

NATIVE-BORN NHL PLAYERS

Don Awrey, Don Beaupre, Dick Behling, Mike Blake, Brian Bradley, Eric Calder, Dave Cressman, Gary Dornhoefer, Woody Dumart, Bill Goldsworthy, Lloyd Gross, Ott Heller, Art Herchenratter, Dutch Hiller, Larry Johnston, Bingo Kampman, John Keating, Kevin Klein, Jim Krulicki, Gary Kurt, Howard Mackie, Dave Maloney, Joe McDonnell, Howard Meeker, Harry Meeking, Kevin Miehm, Jim Mikol, Tom Miller, Adam Nittel, Kyle Quincey, Earl Reibel, Paul Reinhart, Steven Rice, Doug Risebrough, Jim Sandlak, Brad Schlegel, Milt Schmidt, Werner Schnarr, Steve Seftel, Earl Seibert, Oliver Seibert, Rob Shearer, Darryl Sittler, Nick Stajduhar, Ed Stankiewicz, Mike Stankiewicz, Mike Stevens, Scott Stevens, Cam Stewart, Dennis Wideman, Bennett Wolf, Jamie Wright

FAMOUS LOCAL TEAMS

Junior: Kitchener Dutchmen, Kitchener Greenshirts, Kitchener Jr. Rangers, Kitchener Rangers, Kitchener Redshirts, Kitchener-Guelph, Kitchener Union Jacks;
Senior-pro: Kitchener Army, Kitchener Dutchmen, Kitchener Greenshirts, Kitchener H/C, Kitchener Silverwoods, Kitchener Tigers, Kitchener Twin City, Kitchener-Waterloo Beavers, Kitchener-Waterloo Dutchmen, Kitchener-Waterloo Tigers

CURRENT POPULATION

204,000

The Kitchener-born Kraut Line of the Boston Bruins.

The Kraut Line

Kitchener-born Milt Schmidt returned home from Boston, in 1942, to say goodbye to his family before heading off to World War II. Leaving the house, he hugged his mother and sister, walked out the door, stopped, thought hard for a moment, dropped his pack and went back inside. "Mother, I'm going into a situation that, with a name like Schmidt, I don't know how well I'll be accepted over there," he said. "Do you mind if I change my name to Smith?"

"If you see fit to change it, go ahead," Mrs. Schmidt said, her face wet with tears.

On the way to join his company, Schmidt pondered his decision. "But then I thought that Mother and Dad had spent most of their time in Canada and they were Germans," he remembered. "So I just said, hey, it's been good enough for Dad and Mother. It's good enough for me."

Not everyone felt that way. Before 1916, Kitchener was known as Berlin—Canada's German capital. When World War I started, in 1914, being of German heritage in Canada was no longer a matter of easy pride. Even in Berlin, a bust

"Darryl, Darryl"

Darryl Sittler's great-great grandfather was a Mennonite farmer. The family would eventually become Lutheran, although St. Jacobs, the little town just outside Kitchener where Darryl grew up, remained Mennonite country. He and brother Ken earned 75 cents an hour sweeping King Street free of horse manure on Saturday mornings, when Mennonite farmers clip-clopped their buggies into town to market.

St. Jacobs was also Toronto Maple Leafs country, but Darryl (who played hockey in nearby Elmira) grew up a Jean Beliveau fan. And Sittler died a little when, in 1970, the Montreal Canadiens bypassed him twice in the draft (for Ray Martynuk and Chuck Lefley) before Toronto selected him with the eighth pick. For the next dozen years, Darryl Sittler repre-sented the hope of Leafs fans. A whirling dynamo with a wild mop of curls, number 27 recalled vintage Leafs heroes like Teeder Kennedy and Bill Barilko—kids who also had jumped from small Ontario towns into the Leafs' royal blue, eager to lead the province's team to glory.

And while Darryl never helped the Leafs to a Stanley Cup, he did provide glorious moments. While "drinking about the past," Leafs fans seldom make it to last call without remembering the playoff night that Sittler threw five in against the Philadelphia Flyers or, better still, the magical game against Boston in which he performed two weeks' work in a mere sixty minutes, tallying six goals and four assists against poor Dave Reece. Yet another Sittler highlight was the 1976 Canada Cup match where Darryl came down the left wing against Czech goalie, Vladimir Dzurilla, drawing him out by faking a slapshot, nudging the puck forward, waiting another stride, and then wristing a shot into the empty net to give Canada a tournament win.

Sittler would retire with most of the Leafs' scoring records and remains with the team as a goodwill ambassador. And wherever he goes on Leaf business, fans can't refrain from shouting out what was once the most famous cry in Maple Leaf Gardens, "Darryl, Darryl!"

of German emperor Kaiser Wilhelm was thrown into Victoria Lake. Given the public mood, a referendum on renaming Canada's Berlin was held in 1916—just two years prior to Milt Schmidt's birth.

None of the continuing, postwar anti-German sentiment mattered much to Schmidt while he was growing up at 130 Shanley Street, where his two favourite sports were hockey and hooky. "I was called into the principal's office [at King Edward Public School] for not doing my homework, because I was always on the ponds," he would later tell writer Kevin Shea. "The principal said, 'What ever is going to become of you?' I said, 'Mr. Bain, I'm going to be a professional hockey player.'"

In the early 1930s, at age 14, Schmidt took a step in that direction when he made the Kitchener Greenshirts, junior precursor to the legendary Kitchener Rangers. While playing for the Greenshirts, he quickly made friends with two local boys of German extraction—Bobby Bauer and Woodrow "Woody" Dumart. Bauer became a wing mate, while Dumart played defence.

In 1935, Dumart and Bauer joined the Boston Cubs, a Bruins farm team, and there they badgered manager Art Ross, suggesting their best friend Milt, still 17, belonged with them. Intrigued, Ross invited Schmidt to try out for the Bruins' International League team, the Providence Reds, the following season. The fall of 1936, the three boys all reported to Providence, Rhode Island, settled into a line, and created an immediate sensation, netting two or three goals a

A Kitchener Rangers puck.

game. "You fellas come from Kitchener-Waterloo," figured coach Al "Battleship" Leduc. "There's a lot of people of German descent from there. We gotta get a name for ya'—The Kraut Line!"

"We didn't mind," Schmidt said. Neither, at first, did fans throughout the National Hockey League, as The Kraut Line became the top offensive unit in hockey in the late '30s with the Boston Bruins. The Krauts helped the Bruins to the Stanley Cup in 1939 and 1941, and finished 1-2-3 in NHL scoring in 1940.

And then, the world exploded. Canada declared war on Germany in September 1939. On 11 December 1941, the Japanese attacked Pearl Harbour, bringing America into the world war.

With these events, Kraut became a pejorative once again. The Kitchener line for the Bruins couldn't be sure how to interpret the boos they were getting. The three felt as if everyone was looking at them, trying to decide something. The game of hockey, always a joy, a means of expressing their friendship and their pleasure in life, suddenly felt like a chore.

After prolonged soul-searching, staring into the dark from rattling train windows as they rocketed from NHL city to city, the three members of The Kraut Line enlisted, joining the Canadian air force. Having made the decision, they just wanted to leave their team, but the athletes had to play another game in Boston against Montreal.

They couldn't have expected what happened next. On 11 February 1942, The Kraut Line played the game of their lives, scoring 22 points in leading Boston to an 8–1 win over Montreal. The fans responded to the line's every move with passionate applause, shouting out the names of Schmidt, Dumart and Bauer. And when the game was over, both the Canadiens and Bruins players hoisted The Kraut Line on their shoulders, while the cheering, sobbing crowd sang "Auld Lang Syne."

The war deepened the linemates' friendship, maybe because some of their friends didn't come home. "Over there they had a saying," Schmidt remembered. "There used to be a beer called Burton beer. You'd ask, 'Where's Jack?' or 'Where's Joe?', and people would say, 'He went for a Burton.' In other words, they didn't know whether the pilot was shot down or a prisoner."

The Kraut Line reformed, in 1946, with the Bruins. The boys all got married—they would flip a coin over best man duties at each other's marriages. Schmidt eventually coached the Bruins, while Bauer returned home, taking the city's senior team, the Kitchener-Waterloo Dutchmen to Allan Cup championships in 1953 and 1955. Dumart retired in Boston and was official scorer at the Boston Gardens for years.

Hockey in Kitchener flourished. Native sons Darryl Sittler, Scott Stevens and Brian Bradley enjoyed storied careers when they reached the NHL in the 1970s. Still, the city's most inspirational hockey story would remain The Kraut Line—Bauer, Dumart and Schmidt. Indeed, the name still resonates in city rinks whenever the city's most famous atom team takes the ice. The club's name? The Kitchener Bauer-Krauts.

Bauer National Teams

Off the ice, Bobby Bauer was the toughest and most outspoken member of The Kraut Line. He sometimes represented most valuable player Milt Schmidt in salary negotiations and once famously threatened to withhold the services of all three Krauts until he secured a $500 raise for the linemates. After his National Hockey League career ended, Bauer went on to coach and manage the senior Kitchener-Waterloo Dutchmen, twice taking the Allan Cup-winning Dutchies to the Olympic Games—where the team first won a bronze medal in 1956 and then a silver medal in 1960. After that 1960 win, the Canadian Olympic team became a national program run by Bobby's brother, Father David Bauer.

LONDON

FOUNDED

The largest city in southwestern Ontario, London is situated on the Thames River. It was first settled in 1826, and was incorporated as a city in 1955. Called "The Forest City" due to surrounding parkland, London was an agricultural centre in its early years, but quickly developed a vast, diversified economy. The University of Western Ontario opened here in 1878.

NATIVE-BORN NHL PLAYERS

Bill Armstrong, Craig Billington, Mike J. Boland, Colin Campbell, Greg Campbell, Jeff Carter, Neal Coulter, Abbie Cox, Mike Craig, Rod Graham, Jeff Hackett, Ken Hammond, Dwayne Hay, Greg Hotham, Frank Howard, Dave Hutchison, Doug Jarrett, Seamus Kotyk, Brett Lindros, Eric Lindros, Don Luce, Craig MacTavish, Brad Marsh, Cody McCormick, Walt McKechnie, Murray McLachlan, Barrie Moore, Joe Murphy, Paul Nicholson, Jeff Paul, Goldie Prodgers, Craig Simpson, Andy Spruce, Charlie Stephens, Steve Stoyanovich, Joe Thornton, Scott Thornton, Mike Van Ryn, Jason Williams, Brian Wilsie

FAMOUS LOCAL TEAMS

Junior: London AAB, London Athletic Club, London Athletics, London Diamonds, London Knights, London Legionnaires, London Nationals, London Ontarios; **Senior-pro:** London AAA, London Mohawks, London Panthers, London Tecumsehs

CURRENT POPULATION

351,257

The London Knights celebrating their Memorial Cup win, 2005.

The Prodigy

London-born Eric Lindros could walk at eight months, skate at two years and ride a two-wheel bike by age three. At five, he was water-skiing. By age 13, in 1986, Eric was 5'11" and 160 pounds—and already a famous hockey player. His father sought the advice of Wayne Gretzky's and Bobby Orr's parents. The family converted their basement into a hockey shooting gallery for Eric and his younger brother Brett. A swimming pool was made into a winter rink. Lindros's parents also rented extra arena time for both the boys.

Eric was the first pick in the 1992 National Hockey League draft. He would win the league's most valuable player award in 1995 at the age of 22. Brett was a first round draft pick of the New York Islanders in 1994. Despite the best-laid plans, nothing is certain in hockey, however. Brett Lindros retired from the game at age 20, suffering from concussions. Head injuries would also seriously reduce Eric Lindros' effectiveness.

A Knight to Remember

Until the London Knights won the 2005 Memorial Cup by smothering forward sensation Sidney Crosby and the Rimouski Oceanic, 4–0, in a game played before a swooning hometown crowd, the city had suffered through a hockey championship drought that had gone on forever. The Knights had never come first in Ontario junior hockey or made the Memorial Cup finals in the team's 40-year history. Nor had any London team competed for the senior championship Allan Cup. Despite producing players the calibre of Eric Lindros, Joe Thornton, Craig Simpson, Joe Murphy and Goldie Prodgers, the last time that a local team won even a big provincial tournament was 16 January 1901, when the London Hockey Club knocked off a team from Stratford to win the Ontario intermediate title. And they had to give that trophy back!

What happened, in 1901, was that London recruited an unknown rookie, Campbell Lindsay, to play in the championship game. The Londoners mopped the rink with Stratford that evening, but a farmer at the game observed in a voice loud enough for Ontario Hockey Association officials to hear that the fella' racing around the rink that night was not the Campbell Lindsay he knew. An OHA gumshoe investigated and discovered that Lindsay had never left his farm the night of the big game. A $45 ringer, Frank Winn, had been brought in from Montreal instead. Oh, the ignominy, the shame—London was compelled to forfeit the trophy, and all the players on the team lost their amateur status.

Could the scandal have been a curse on London teams—the no-Winn jinx? For no London team would win a major championship until the exciting run of the 2005 Knights.

A Pro Turn

A star forward for the intermediate London Wingers in 1910, Goldie Prodgers was contacted by the Waterloo Colts of the old Ontario Provincial Hockey League about substituting for one of the team's injured players. Despite his nickname, Goldie wasn't interested in forfeiting his amateur status for a single game. We'll give you an assumed name, Waterloo assured him. So Prodgers agreed to suit up. Upon skating onto the Waterloo rink, he heard his real name called out and looked up to discover that the referee was Eddie Wettlaufer, a member of the Ontario Hockey Association exec-utive committee. "When in blue blazes did you turn pro?" the referee asked.

"Right now," Prodgers responded. The right choice, it turned out. Goldie would go on to a 12-year pro career, winning Stanley Cups for the Quebec Bulldogs (1912) and for the Montreal Canadiens (1916).

Ah, but what a way to break out of a slump! The hockey season of 2004–05 was the winter of our hockey discontent: With the National Hockey League in a protracted labour dispute, the game was suddenly played only by lawyers gathering cobwebs. Junior hockey, therefore, was king. And the Knights were the best teenage team in the country, from the beginning of the season, right up until the final week of May when the Knights put an exclamation point on a 79-win, nine-loss, two-tie run by concluding a convincing three-game sweep of the Memorial Cup before 8,905 fans in London's new John Labatt Centre.

Joining in was the largest television following ever for a Memorial Cup game, a peak audience of over one million Canadians. Many viewers, admittedly, tuned in to watch Oceanic centre Sidney Crosby and linemates Dany Roussin and Marc-Antoine Pouliot. Playing in tandem with defenceman Mario Scalzo and Patrick Coulombe, Rimouski's Big Five had dominated the semifinals against the Ottawa 67's, collecting 18 points in an impressive 7–4 win.

But Rimouski's Big Five were fatally discouraged in the Cup final by the piranha-like checking of London's best defensive unit—Trevor Kell, Brandon Prust and Dylan Hunter (coach Dale Hunter's boy). And as they had all year,

The game finished with a 4–0 victory for the Knights.

the Knights' two big offensive lines, led by tournament most valuable player Corey Perry and Memorial Cup all-star Danny Fritsche, took advantage of their opponent's every mental and physical lapse.

Early in the first period, two Oceanic forwards slapped London's Perry around as if they were trying to beat a confession out of him. Both were thrown off and on the ensuing power play Fritsche fired a bad angle shot under Rimouski goaltender Cedric Desjardins' blocker to make the score 1–0 for the home team. Later in the period, the Knights' indefatigable Robbie Schremp tested Desjardins with a low screamer that the Quebec goalie kicked back into play. Trailing Knights defenceman Bryan Rodney realized the mistake before anyone else and, racing hard, chipped the rebound into the yawning cage.

When Dave Boland got a goal in the second period to make the score 3–0, the London crowd filling the John Labatt Centre, every one of them dressed in Knights' green, broke into scattered shouts of "We want the Cup!" And in the bars along nearby Dundas Street, green-haired, green-painted University of Western Ontario fans really began to celebrate.

The third period offered more of the same, with the superbly balanced and efficient Knights team harassing Rimouski into exhaustion and London's green fans shouting themselves blue with pleasure, anticipating the city's 100-year-plus hockey championship drought was finally, mercifully, blessedly coming to an end. The game finished with a 4–0 victory for the Knights.

The ensuing celebration lasted for days. In the dressing room after the game, coach Dale Hunter—a farmboy from Petrolia, Ontario—advised Jim Kernaghan of the *London Free Press* that the Knights' great season would not have been complete without a championship. "In farming," he said, "the job isn't done until the crop is off. Our job [was] to win the Memorial Trophy."

And so, it could be said, 104 years after Campbell Lindsay failed to show up for work at a London rink, another Ontario farm hand finally lifted the championship curse.

NIAGARA FALLS

The Horseshoe Falls and Terrapin Tower viewed from Goat Island, painting by an unknown artist, c.1870.

FOUNDED

A European missionary made Niagara Falls one of North America's first tourist attractions, when he published a description of "a vast and prodigious cadence of water" in 1678. The first settlers didn't arrive until United Empire Loyalists sought sanctuary near North America's biggest waterfall, during the 1790s. After many name changes and municipal amalgamations, the city was officially named Niagara Falls in 1881. Initially, the mile-long avenue overlooking the falls was a gaudy showcase for hucksters and carnies, but in 1878 the government expropriated the land and turned it into parkland.

NATIVE-BORN NHL PLAYERS

John Arbour, Jim Bedard, Bill Cupolo, Kevin Dallman, Marty Dallman, Hank Damore, Nick Damore, Peter Fiorentino, Rick Foley, Orville Heximer, Max Kaminsky, Zenon Konopka, Larry Landon, Felix Mancuso, Bob Manno, George Massecar, Don McLean, Johnny Mowers, Terry O'Reilly, Frank Pietrangelo, Nick Ricci, Phil Roberto, Derek Sanderson, Jarrod Skalde, Frank Steele

FAMOUS LOCAL TEAMS
Junior: Niagara Falls Canucks, Niagara Falls Cataracts, Niagara Falls Flyers, Niagara Falls Thunder; **Senior-pro:** Niagara Falls Cataracts

CURRENT POPULATION
78,815

A Sixties Honeymoon

Derek "Turk" Sanderson, with the Niagara Falls Flyers.

"I had to leave Niagara Falls, see, 'cause the only good-looking chick in town hated me," Derek "Turk" Sanderson complained to Johnny Carson on NBC's *Tonight Show* on 15 December 1970.

Derek had an Export A dangling from his hand as he spoke, and he was sporting a classic '70s ensemble—Parker Brothers game-board checked pants, cowboy boots and an apache scarf. Carson got a kick out of Sanderson's dead-end street hipster act. In fact, everybody at the time was entertained by Derek, especially young hockey fans.

A combative, stylish centre, Sanderson won the Ontario Hockey Association scoring race while playing for the junior Niagara Falls Flyers in 1966–67, collecting 101 points. Then he jumped right into the lineup of the Boston Bruins, winning the NHL's rookie of the year award in the 1967–68 season. In 1970, six months prior to the Carson visit, during the playoff finals, Derek expertly swept a pass out from a corner scrum to Bruins teammate Bobby Orr, who then whipped the puck into the St. Louis Blues' net before taking off in the air to celebrate Boston's first Stanley Cup win in 29 years.

As far as Orr flew that famous, Cup-winning goal, Sanderson travelled a lot higher—and crashed a lot harder—during a honeymoon with fame that began in the late '60s.

Derek knew about honeymoons. Niagara Falls is the wedding capital of Canada. Not that Turk spent much time watching the *Maid of the Mist* tour boat lap the Horseshoe Falls. His machinist dad had fashioned a linoleum platform for the family's driveway, a launch pad that allowed Derek to fire pucks at a target, spring, summer and fall. Harold Sanderson also watched *Hockey Night in*

Derek Sanderson played
hard on and off the ice.

Falls Guys

The Niagara Falls Flyers, who
began to play in the city in 1960,
were perhaps the most successful Ontario junior team of
that decade, appearing in three
Memorial Cups and winning the
national championship titles
in 1965 and 1968. The '65 club,
which defeated the Edmonton
Oil Kings on the Kings' own rink,
was a legendary team, featuring
future National Hockey League
goalies Bernie Parent and Doug
Favell, along with skaters Gilles
Marotte, Rick Ley (15 at the time),
Don Marcotte, Jean Pronovost,
Derek Sanderson (who incited
a riot, popping Kings player Bob
Falkenberg when he was down),
Bill Goldsworthy, Jim Lorentz and
Rosaire Paiement. Dave Woodley
was the team captain.

   The Flyers won again in
1968, using three different uniforms to defeat the Estevan
Bruins. Both were farm teams for
the Boston Bruins and so played
in Bruins jerseys, creating great
confusion in the first game. After
that, the Flyers used Montreal
Jr. Canadiens and St. Catharines
Teepees uniforms.

Canada with his boy in the 1950s, pointing out to Derek how Teeder Kennedy
of the Leafs cheated when taking face-offs, moving his feet before the puck
dropped, to gain leverage on his opponent.

Derek liked getting an edge over the other guy. Playing Monopoly with sister,
Karen, he wet the underside of his forearms to lift orange 100-dollar bills off the
table. In hockey, he helped the junior Niagara Falls Flyers to the Memorial Cup
in 1965, an accomplishment that brought the Flyers and Boston's other Ontario
farm team, the Oshawa Generals, to the Boston Gardens for an exhibition match.

Frequently, by the late '70s, he was sleeping on park benches.

When Sanderson saw the attention that Generals defenceman Bobby Orr was
receiving, he cold-cocked his future teammate, starting a fight to ensure that the
crowd noticed him as well.

Soon, Sanderson was leading all other hockey players in getting noticed.
While with the Bruins, he grew his hair long, sprouted a moustache (the first in
the NHL since Garth Boesch's in the '40s), dated models, co-authored an autobiography, *I've Got to Be Me*, guested on Johnny Carson and on the *Merv Griffin
Show*, appeared in movies (*Jack the Ripper Goes West*), and invested in four
Boston nightclubs, places where he could comfortably entertain friends while
indulging in his beer-after–beer, two-packs-of-cigarettes–a-day habit.

Sanderson was making $75,000 for the Bruins in 1972, when the Philadelphia
Blazers of the World Hockey Association offered him $2,300,000 a season.
When his agent showed him the figure, Turk laughed, "It looks like a phone number." He signed for a better phone number, $2,650,000, becoming—in the fall
of 1973—the highest-paid athlete in the world.

The WHA didn't work out. Sanderson injured his back, accepted an $800,000
buyout and returned to Boston later that season, but somehow his game wasn't
the same. He went to the New York Rangers in 1974. But that stint didn't work out
either, although a local fan would name his son, now a star for the New York
Yankees, Derek Sanderson Jeter.

The St. Louis Blues, Vancouver Canucks and Pittsburgh Penguins all gave
Sanderson a chance, but he was mixing his friends with harder stuff now—vodka,
cocaine, pain killers. He lost all his money, an estimated $4 million. Frequently,
by the late '70s, he was sleeping on park benches. Once, he got into a fight with a
homeless man over a bottle. "Know who I am?" Sanderson asked.

"Sure, a drunk like me," the man grunted.

Somehow, in 1980, he found his way back home to Niagara Falls, to a field near
his parents' house on Stamford Street. Falling down on his knees in the long grass, he
asked God to be cured or killed. Sanderson says that he doesn't know what happened
next except that he ended up in the Hotel Dieu, a St. Catharines rehab centre, where
he finally ended a lifetime of addiction. (He had had his first beer at age seven.)

Miracles continued. Months later, his dad, the block off which Sanderson was
chipped, won $150,000 in a provincial lottery. And the hockey player moved back
to Boston, where his cautionary tale of '60s excess became a classic story of '80s
redemption. He soon (re)married, became a father (of two children) and found
work as a financial adviser, extolling the virtues of portfolio diversification to a client
base that would include a large number of celebrity athletes.

Fans will enjoy knowing that Sanderson occasionally plays golf with Bobby Orr
at a local country club. Both men have a three handicap, although they presumably score somewhat better if Turk, who may still have some Monopoly $100 bills
under his arm, is keeping score.

OSHAWA

FOUNDED

In 1876, Col. Robert Samuel McLaughlin transferred his carriage manufacturing company to Oshawa from Enniskillen, Ontario. In 1918, Chevrolet Motor Company of Canada and McLaughlin Carriage merged to create General Motors of Canada, Oshawa's largest employer.

NATIVE-BORN NHL PLAYERS

Scott Barney, Frank Bathe, Arnie Brown, Sean Brown, Les Colvin, Jeff Daniels, Dale DeGray, Dave Duerden, Craig Fisher, Dave Gorman, Brent Grieve, Larry Hopkins, Charlie Huddy, Jim Jackson, Ross Lowe, John McLean, Jeff Madill, Kevin McClelland, Shawn McCosh, Joe Nieuwendyk, Hank Nowak, Rob Pearson, Shawn Thornton, Pete Vipond, Sean Williams

FAMOUS LOCAL TEAMS

Junior: Oshawa Bees, Oshawa Blue Imps, Oshawa Chevvies, Oshawa Generals, Oshawa Legionnaires, Oshawa Majors; **Senior-pro:** Oshawa G-Men, Oshawa Patricians, Oshawa Sr. Generals, Oshawa Truckmen

CURRENT POPULATION

150,000

Three Generals

There was hockey in Oshawa before the Generals. In the 1920s, for instance, local junior teams battled for the Three O's championship, an annual competition involving clubs from Oshawa, Owen Sound and Orillia. But it wasn't until General Motors, for years the city's largest employer, began sponsoring a team, in the fall of 1937, that an Oshawa hockey club unified the city's hockey faithful. The junior Oshawa Generals were an instant local and national success during the World War II years, appearing in the Memorial Cup six of the team's first seven seasons and winning three national championships.

The team's unique playing style contributed to the Generals' mystique. The club was rich with characters and stars. Here's how Gordon Sinclair, *Toronto Star* reporter and beloved curmudgeon on the long-running *Front Page Challenge* TV

Oshawa, 1910.

The 1939 Memorial Cup-winning Oshawa Generals.

show, described the play of Oshawa-born netminder Bobby Forrester: "This [kid] has got so much showmanship he ought to be in the movies. He makes a flying tackle toward the puck, he dives, dances, sprawls, falls, crawls. He laughs, chatters, beefs and grunts. He stops pucks, all pucks. Whatever he's got, it's what he needs to be a great goalie."

The remainder of the team was mostly made up of Oshawa-area kids with stubby rink-rat names—Whip Shortt, Keith Krantz, Doc Dafoe, Scotty Reid, Max Yourth, Les Colvin, Don Daniels and Don McTavish. But the leading General was a Toronto recruit. A Christmas dinner away from 130 pounds when he arrived in Oshawa, in 1937, Billy Taylor might have resembled a Depression-era foundling, but the 18-year-old was a sensation on the ice—a lithe, quicksil-

An Oshawa Generals puck.

The Kid collected 28 points in nine Cup games, scoring nine goals in the first two games.

ver centre with more forward gears than any General Motors car. In 12 regular season games his first season, Billy the Kid, as he was known, scored 19 times, capturing the imagination of Oshawa Arena fans, who encouraged him with constant cries of "Go Bill-eeee!"

Like all great teams, the Generals were prone to unexpected drama. In the spring of 1938, the Toronto Marlboros and Oshawa Generals both refused to play the Ontario junior final in their opponent's rink. The championship match was moved to Galt, where an atmosphere of unending chaos prevailed. Three Toronto goals were called back. And the deciding goal in Oshawa's 2–1 victory was fired in after the final buzzer, according to the Marlies.

With the controversial win, the Generals were in the Memorial Cup, held at Toronto's Maple Leaf Gardens. The Generals were such a story now, that the final game in the best-of-five Cup final with the St. Boniface Seals was held before what was then the largest crowd in Canadian hockey history—15,617 spectators. In that deciding game, St. Boniface employed a historic, frequently copied defensive manoeuvre. The Seals designated Elmer Kreller to shadow Billy the Kid wherever he went. (Taylor called out to Kreller at one point, "I'm going in to take a leak. Ya' comin?")

The Generals lost that fifth game, 7–1, a score that left one young spectator who had ventured to the Gardens from Oshawa crying scalding tears. "As a kid, the Oshawa Generals were everything," remembered Wren Blair, who went on to become the general manager of the team in the '60s. "I sat there for about 25 minutes, I was crushed. I cried. They had beaten my Generals. But when I think of it now, I believe it was healthy—you have to learn to live with defeat."

And learn from it. The Generals, with Forrester and Billy the Kid returning, romped through the Memorial Cup the following season. The Kid collected 28 points in nine Cup games, scoring nine goals in the first two games against runner-up team, the Edmonton Athletic Club Roamers. By then, the Generals' star centre had devised a strategy to upset checkers. "I'd shadow one of their guys," he told sportswriter Trent Frayne, years later. "That way I was taking two of their guys out of the play."

The Generals would win the Memorial Cup again the next season (1940), finish as runner-up in both 1942 and 1943, and then reclaim the trophy in 1944. These Generals teams boasted many stars. The 1944 Memorial Cup champions included future NHL greats Ted Lindsay, Floyd Curry and Bill Ezinicki. Still, the Generals best-remembered player from the war years would

The greatest defenceman ever, Bobby Orr, captain of the Oshawa Generals.

YOU BET YOUR LIFE

In March 1948, American radio broadcaster legend Walter Winchell went to air with a breathless scoop: "Good evening, Mr. and Mrs. America and all the ships at sea! Let's go to press... A sports exclusive! Billy Taylor of the New York Rangers and Don Gallinger of the Boston Bruins are the players involved in hockey's gambling scandal!" With those words, the National Hockey League career of Billy The Kid Taylor, a former Oshawa Generals great, was over. The league had phone transcripts of Taylor placing bets on hockey games with a Detroit bookmaker. He was banned by NHL President Clarence Campbell for life. Devastated, Taylor moved to Florida for a while.

But he bounced back. Taylor had been through a lot. His father suffered lasting damage from poison gas in World War I and he, himself, had seen fighting with the Canadian infantry in World War II. In the 1950s, Taylor returned to southern Ontario, settling in Owen Sound where he coached intermediate and junior hockey. In 1970, the NHL lifted the ban on Taylor and Gallinger. Taylor worked as a scout for the Pittsburgh Penguins in the 1980s. To this day, he shares an NHL record with Wayne Gretzky—seven assists in single game.

never win a Memorial Cup. Playing alongside Curry and Ken Smith, Red Tilson led all Ontario juniors in scoring in 1942. The following year he volunteered for World War II and was soon killed in action. Since 1945, the Ontario Hockey League has honoured the Oshawa native's memory with the Red Tilson Award, given annually to league's most valuable player.

Oshawa had to wait until the 1960s for another player to lead them to the Memorial Cup. Ironically, when Oshawa first laid eyes on the city's second great General, he was no bigger than Billy "The Kid" Taylor. Of course, Bobby Orr was a Grade 8 student at the time. In fact, the 14-year-old still lived in Parry Sound and only travelled to Oshawa for games. "Imagine, the kid never made practice with the team and he made the second all-star team in the best junior league in Canada," general manager Wren Blair would later marvel.

Orr, who joined the Generals in 1962, changed the face of hockey in Oshawa, drawing so many spectators from in and around southern Ontario that, in 1964, the city built a new rink, the Civic Auditorium, to accommodate fan interest. With number 2 playing for the Generals, Oshawa became the third biggest hockey centre in Canada, after Montreal and Toronto. The defenceman with the brush cut made the cover of *Maclean's* magazine in 1966. And his scoring feats were daily sporting lore in newspapers across Canada—imagine a defenceman who led his team in goals! Indeed, Orr scored 38 goals for the Generals in 1965–66, contributing two more markers than Danny O'Shea, the team's leading forward.

Orr's team might have won the Memorial Cup in the spring of 1966, except that Orr badly aggravated a groin muscle in the second game of the seven-game final series against the Edmonton Oil Kings. With one good leg, he scored 28 points in 17 Cup games, defying his doctor's orders to compete in the last game, making the team's loss to the Oil Kings doubly painful for Orr. But then, how could a General not go down with his army?

Another 24 seasons would pass before Oshawa's most famous sports team would win another national junior championship. Again, a young superstar would lead the Generals, but this time, the star was a 17-year-old kid who had a half a foot and 100 pounds on the wartime General, Taylor. Eric Lindros was 6'3" and almost 230 pounds when he brought home a Memorial Cup to Oshawa in 1990, with a double-overtime championship win over the Kitchener Rangers.

Double Thrill

In 1990, the Oshawa Generals provided one of the great scenes in Memorial Cup history. Seconds after Oshawa defenceman Bill Armstrong's wobbling wrist shot evaded Kitchener Rangers goalie Mike Torchia to give the Generals a 4-3 double-overtime Memorial Cup win, Oshawa goalie Fred Braithwaite raced past celebrating teammates to console Torchia, a competitor Braithwaite had befriended in hockey tournaments growing up. The unlikely goal and stirring act of fellowship concluded a spectacular series run by the Generals, who had survived a 5–4 double-overtime semi-finals win, just to make it to the big game.

Seventeen-year-old Generals forward Eric Lindros contributed three assists in the win. And team captain Iain Fraser was named the Hamilton tournament most valuable player. Braithwaite, however, provided the play of the game, turning aside a shot from Rangers forward Jason Firth in a first overtime, close-in chance. "I can't believe it," Braithwaite said after the game. "I'm the only one on the team who slept last night, 'cause I didn't think I was going to play." Indeed, Braithwaite jumped into the Oshawa net after starting goalie Kevin Butt suffered a second-period leg injury.

OTTAWA

FOUNDED

French fur traders named the Ottawa River after the Outaouais First Nation in the middle of the 18th century. Between 1826 and 1832, Colonel John By oversaw the construction of the 125-mile-long Rideau Canal, which linked what became Bytown to Kingston. The city became incorporated as Ottawa on 1 January 1855. On 31 December 1857, the day before Ottawa's third birthday, Queen Victoria named the lumber town the capital of Canada. In the wintertime, a five-mile stretch of Ottawa's Rideau Canal becomes the world's longest skating rink.

NATIVE-BORN NHL PLAYERS

Derek Armstrong, Adrian Aucoin, Philippe Audet, Matthew Barnaby, Fred Barrett, John Barrett, Eric Beaudoin, Clinton Benedict, Bill Beveridge, Mike Bloom, Billy Boucher, Frank Boucher, George Boucher, Robert Boucher, Dan Boyle, Fred Brathwaite, Rod Brind'Amour, Harry Broadbent, Jeff Brown, Gordie Bruce, Mike Bullard, Leo Carbol, Bruce Cassidy, Andre Champagne, King Clancy, Terry Clancy, Bill Collins, Alex Connell, Harry Connor, David Cooper, Mike Corrigan, Chris Cruickshank, Barry Cullen, Brian Cullen, Ray Cullen, Harry Darragh, Jack Darragh, John Davidson, Dean Defazio, Frank Dunlop, Jerry Dupont, Ben Eager, Mike Eastwood, Stu Evans, Corey Foster, Art Gagne, Mike Gartner, Stewart Gavin, Edward Gerard, Billy Gilmour, Davie Gilmour, Suddie Gilmour, Ebbie Goodfellow, Kevin Grimes, Len Grosvenor, Milton Halliday, Sammy Hebert, Hal Hicks, Tim Higgins, Syd Howe, Rolly Huard, Kent Huskins, "Bouse" Hutton, Bill Inglis, Lloyd Jackson, Ryan Jardine, Aurel Joliat, Bobby Joliat, Pat Kavanagh, Kevin Kemp, Brian Kilrea, Ken Kilrea, Wally Kilrea, Ray Kinsella, Murray Kuntz, Jim Kyte, Rene Lafleur, Pete Laframboise, Mitch Lamoureax, Charles Larose, Gary Laskoski, Anthony Licari, Claude Loiselle, Kilby MacDonald, Reggie Mackey, Philip Maloney, Steve Maltais, Joseph Matte, Wally Maxwell, Gilles Mayer, Stan McCabe, Frank McGee, Jack McGill, Jim McKenny, Art Moore, Andrew McPherson, Bryan McSheffrey, Tyler Moss, John Newman, Sean O'Donnell, John Ogrodnick, Eddie Ouelette, Justin Papineau, Mark Paterson, Marc Potvin, John Quilty, Dan Quinn, Yip Radley, Brad Ralph, Luke Richardson, Rip Riopelle, Jamie Rivers, Shawn Rivers, Randy Robitaille, Harvey Rockburn, Derek Roy, Bud Saunders, David Saunders, Andre Savard, Marc Savard, Andy Schliebener, Allen Shields, Hamby Shore, Alf Smith, Brian Smith, Des Smith, Doug Smith, Gary Smith, Thomas Smith, Brad Smyth, Ted Snell, Harold Starr, Bruce Stuart, Hod Stuart, Chris Therien, Wayne Thomas, William Touhey, Rick Vaive, Robert Walton, Steve Washburn, Harry "Rat" Westwick, John Wilkinson, Doug Wilson, Hub Wilson, Murray Wilson, Stephane Yelle, Rod Zaine

FAMOUS LOCAL TEAMS

Junior: Nepean Raiders, Ottawa Aberdeens, Ottawa Canadiens, Ottawa Capitals, Ottawa Jr. Montagnards, Ottawa M&W Rangers, Ottawa Jr. New Edinburghs, Ottawa Jr. Rideaus, Ottawa Jr. Senators, Ottawa Jr. Shamrocks, St. Pats Juniors; **Senior-pro:** Ottawa Aberdeens, Ottawa Canadiens, Ottawa Capitals, Ottawa Civics, Ottawa Cliffsides, Ottawa Generals, Ottawa Montagnards, Ottawa Royal Canadiens, Ottawa Silver Seven, Ottawa Senators, Ottawa Shamrocks, Ottawa St. Pat's

CURRENT POPULATION

845,000

The Silver Streak

Lord Stanley of Preston, Canada's sixth governor general (1888–93), would leave behind two Ottawa landmarks and traditions—most obviously Preston Street, now the central avenue of a bustling Italian neighbourhood, but formerly a route that marked the outskirts of the city.

The second tradition was the pursuit of hockey excellence as symbolized by an award the governor general gave hockey—the Stanley Cup. Thanks, in large part, to Lord Stanley's enthusiastic patronage, that trophy would reside in Ottawa more than anywhere else between 1903 and 1927, a period in which a team known as both the Ottawa Silver Seven and the Ottawa Senators won hockey's grand prize 11 times.

British-born Lord Stanley first saw hockey in 1899, striding with his entourage into Montreal's Victoria Rink in the middle of a match between the Montreal Victorias and the city's Amateur Athletic Association team. After

A vintage postcard of the Parliament Buildings in Ottawa, c.1900.

Loblaws Superstar

Steve Yzerman's dad, Ron, a social worker, moved the family from Cranbrook, British Columbia, to Nepean, Ontario, just outside Ottawa, in 1975. Steve was 10 at the time and starved for hockey. He starred for the Nepean Raiders, the local junior B team, for a season, before moving on to the junior A Peterborough Petes and then, in 1983, to a mythic career with the National Hockey League's Detroit Red Wings.

But the official resumé of "Stevie Wonder," as he was nicknamed, fails to reveal a developmental period spent in the Loblaws parking lot at the corner of Baseline and Merivale Roads in Ottawa, where he played ball hockey every Sunday against best friend Darren Pang, a future NHL goalie. Ontario didn't allow Sunday shopping in the late '70s, which gave the friends a vast playing surface. The long runs to fetch errant balls helped further develop Stevie Wonder's incredible stamina. And trying to fire a tennis ball past quick-handed Pang into puny Canadian Tire nets would have sharpened his scoring eye. Pang, who would be best man at Yzerman's wedding, still visits him every summer on a lake north of Toronto, where his old buddy from Nepean has a cottage, a lodge once owned by former Toronto Maple Leafs owner Conn Smythe.

Playing hockey in front of Rideau Hall, 1900.

Battling for the 1905 Stanley Cup, "One-eyed" Frank McGee scored 14 goals in a single game against Dawson City.

acknowledging the crowd's applause and a thin, wavering rendition of "God Save the Queen" from a brass band labouring in the cold, the governor general found a seat and within minutes fell hook, line and pocket watch for Canada's winter pastime.

No wonder. For a man whose only recreation was politics—a sport slower than cricket and less civilized than boxing—how thrilling it was to be alongside genuinely happy citizens watching athletes perform feats of geometric daring on brightly lit ice! All those moving parts. The collisions. Frantic misses. Clear, obvious goals acknowledged by an impartial judge and a roaring crowd.

Like countless future Canadians, Lord Stanley celebrated his enthusiasm for hockey by building a backyard rink—ordering construction of an ice surface at his official Rideau Hall residence in Ottawa. His daughter played on a government house team. And Lord Stanley's private train transported the Rideau Rebels, a team his sons Arthur and Algernon played on, to out-of-town games. His Excellency himself spent a great deal of time in the royal box at Dey's Skating Rink, located at Gladstone and Bay, watching the Ottawa Generals, a senior team born in the city in 1884.

Three years after first encountering the sport, Lord Stanley gave lasting shape to his passion for hockey, commissioning the Dominion Challenge Trophy. News of the award was made public after a 12 March 1892 Rideau Club dinner. Lord Stanley couldn't attend, so an aide, Lord Kilcoursie, informed the club's cigar-puffing members of the trophy by reading a letter from the governor general:

> I have for some time been thinking if there were a challenge cup which could be held from year to year by the leading hockey club in Canada. There doesn't appear to be any outward or visible sign of the championship at present. Considering the interest that hockey matches now elicit and the importance of having the games played under generally recognized rule, I am willing to give a cup that shall be annually held by the winning club.

Later that year another of Lord Stanley's aides picked up the cherrywood-based silver trophy, at a cost of 10 guineas (equivalent to about $1,400 today) from a silversmith on Regent Street in London, England. Before long, what was now called the Stanley Cup would become, after the transcontinental railroad, Canada's second national dream. (Alas, Lord Stanley would never see a Stanley Cup game. He returned to England before the first competition, between the winning Montreal AAA team and his own Ottawa Generals in 1893.)

The second local team to compete for a national championship, the Ottawa Capitals, made a bid for the Stanley Cup in 1897 but were slapped aside, 15–2,

Governor general and big-time hockey enthusiast, Lord Stanley of Preston, June 1889.

The Rare Jewel

Ottawa's "King" Clancy could talk the ears off a field of corn. "He seemed in his ripe jauntiness to be everyone's benign uncle who shows up at reunions a little bombed," wrote Dick Beddoes. In his youth, King could do everything on a rink. Ordinarily a defenceman, he played all six positions for Ottawa in a 1923 Stanley Cup game against the Vancouver Maroons (taking the goalie's position when he was awarded a penalty). Clancy was the most popular man in Ottawa in the '20s and the last piece of the four-time Stanley Cup-winning team to be sold off during the Senators' Depression-era going out-of-business sale, raffled off to the Toronto Maple Leafs for $35,000 (money that Leafs owner Conn Smythe had won on a horse named Rare Jewel).

Among many legends regarding the King: He never took a drink and won but a single hockey fight. Surprisingly, the latter victory was over Eddie Shore. The Boston Bruins defender was already prone and on his knees, admittedly, when Clancy landed a KO punch on Shore's jaw. Staggering to his feet, the Bruins player shouted, "I'd like to see you do that again."

"Sure thing, Eddie," Clancy replied. "Get back down on your hands and knees."

SKATE, SKATE, SKATE

A five-mile ribbon of ice stretching from the Hartwell locks near Carleton University through Dow's Lake in the Glebe to the National Arts Centre on Wellington Street, the Rideau Canal skateway is famously the longest rink in the world. Stanley Cup winners Frank McGee and King Clancy learned to play hockey here. Frequently, they would have to do some snow shovelling first. Luckily for future skaters, crews have maintained the ice surface since the winter of 1970.

The Patriot

Frank McGee grew up on 185 Daley Avenue (now Auberge McGee's Inn) in Ottawa. He learned to skate on the Rideau Canal and before long he could get around town on the frozen waterway faster than by using the city's electric streetcars, which had been introduced the year he was born—1884. At 16, he lost the use of his left eye while playing hockey in an exhibition game to raise money for the Boer War. Undaunted, three years later, in 1903, he joined the Ottawa Senators. McGee scored 71 goals in 23 exhibition games during his career, but he saved his best play for the Stanley Cup, scoring 14 goals in a legendary 1905 victory against the Dawson City Nuggets. Later that spring, he broke his wrist and wasn't counted on in Ottawa's two-of-three series against Rat Portage, now Kenora. But when Ottawa lost the first game, McGee threw a heavy brace on his uninjured hand, providing the Rat Portage Thistles with a false target, and scored six goals in the remaining games, leading Ottawa to another Cup. "He was even better than they say," referee Frank Patrick reported. "He had everything—speed, stickhandling, scoring ability... He was strongly built, but beautifully proportioned, and he had an almost animal rhythm."

McGee retired to the civil service in 1906, but enlisted in World War I, finessing his blind left eye past doctors the way he had once outfoxed the Rat Portage Thistles. A machine gunner in the 21st Battalion, he was blown off the road by a bomb in December 1915. After a lengthy convalescence, McGee turned down a clerical position, instead returning to battle on Dominion Day, 1 July 1916. He disappeared at the Battle of Somme on 16 September 1916, and is presumably one of 220,000 soldiers buried in France in unmarked graves.

NO WAY TO TREAT A LORD

Lord Stanley's cup has been treated worse than a practice goalie. In 1905, the cup-winning Silver Seven were returning home victorious along the Rideau Canal, worse for an evening's celebration, when captain Harry Smith boasted he could drop kick the trophy across to the other side. He couldn't. Coach Alf Smith returned the next day to recover the dented prize. In 1927, Ottawa's King Clancy kept the trophy in his living room, where he filled it up with bills and cigar butts. The Cup, which continues to make the rounds of winning team members' hometowns during summer months, has suffered quite a few other indignities, including typos by engravers—who misspelled goalie Jacques Plante's name five times (Jocko, Jack, Plant, etc.) and referred to forward Alex Delvecchio as Belvecchio. The Cup was defiled yet again, when Krusty the Clown vomited into it in a 1998 episode of *The Simpsons*. And in 2004, Air Canada misplaced the three-foot-tall prize.

The Hall of Fame has kept the real trophy under glass since 1970. A replica is what we see being danced around the continent in the spring and summer.

by the Montreal Victorias and declined to participate in a second playoff game, mewling, "It would not be in the interest of hockey generally to continue the present contest."

A more vigorous crew, the Ottawa Senators (formerly the Generals), would attempt to wrest the Stanley Cup away from the Victorias in March of 1903. The Senators did indeed have a government connection. Blindingly fast rover Frank McGee, who had lost an eye in a 1900 exhibition match, was the nephew of Thomas D'Arcy McGee, a father of Confederation (and the 1868 victim of a Fenian assassin). The other six players were also from Ottawa, local boys who had learned to skate on the world's longest skating rink, a five-mile-long stretch of the Rideau Canal.

The first game in the two-game, total-goal series was held in Montreal during a Saturday ice storm. The weather was awful, and the night was eerie. A steamship, the *Montreal*, caught fire in the city's docks and flames from the exploding ship reflected off the wet mirror that was the iced-over harbour, drawing tens of thousands to the rooftops of nearby warehouses to watch. Straining under the weight of all the onlookers, one building collapsed into a twisted mass of broken beams and bodies, prompting the *Montreal Star* to describe the disaster as "one of the most dramatic occurrences in the city's history."

While the fire raged, a smaller drama was unfolding in the Victoria Rink. The Vics, playing out of their own building, knew they had to jump ahead of the Senators. But it was all Montreal could do to secure a tie that evening, as the game was called one-all a few seconds before midnight so as to ensure that the exhibition didn't desecrate the Sabbath.

Three nights later, on 10 March 1903, the teams resumed play in unseasonably warm weather on the spreading lake that was Ottawa's Dey Rink. A crowd

The Ottawa Silver Seven, 1905.

of 3,000 filled every corner of the arena, aisles included, with boys hanging from corner beams. The new governor general and his wife, Lord and Lady Minto, were also in attendance, assuming rail seats, where they were regularly splashed by passing players.

The couple didn't mind. Ottawa had waited for this evening since Lord Stanley first imagined the grand prize that now bore his name. At the four-minute mark, brothers Dave and Suddie Gilmour stormed the Vics' net, throwing off defenders. The Montreal goalie stopped Dave Gilmour's shot, but Suddie Gilmour banged in the rebound. "When Ottawa scored the first goal the din was deafening," the *Ottawa Citizen* reported. "And when they kept on scoring and it was obvious that the Stanley Cup was theirs, the crowd's enthusiasm was unparalleled in Ottawa's hockey history." Seven unanswered Senators goals later, three by Frank McGee, the gloating crowd began serenading the Montreal team by joining in the funeral dirge "Nearer My God to Thee"—the Edwardian sports fans' "version of the 'Na-Na Goodbye' song," in Ottawa hockey historian Paul Kitchen's words.

The Senators were Stanley Cup champions—the muddy lumber town of Ottawa had finally beaten big-city Montreal! Within days, the Senators went on to defend the Cup, defeating the Rat Portage Thistles, whereupon the Ottawa team was honoured with a banquet at Rideau Hall.

Except for McGee, whose father (John Joseph McGee) was clerk of the Privy Council, none of the players was accustomed to elegant dining. All those forks on the left sides of the plates were more intimidating than the swinging sticks they had encountered in the hands of the Montreal Vics. "Just do what I do," McGee advised teammates, knockabout fellows with names such as "Rat" Westwick and "Bouse" Hutton. Suppressing a smile, McGee began grabbing food and drinking from the finger bowl. Soon, all the Senators were gargling from their finger bowls. At the end of the celebration, the Senators were given silver pins, whereupon they earned a new nickname—the Ottawa Silver Seven.

The Silver Seven, as fans and newspaper writers now knew them, would become nationally famous over the next three seasons, defending the Stanley Cup 11 times from teams as far away as Dawson City in the Yukon Territory. The club eventually relinquished the Stanley Cup to the Montreal Wanderers in 1906, but remained a powerhouse contender, taking the Cup again in 1909 and 1910. McGee became a hockey legend.

Interest in hockey in the Ottawa Valley grew. In the decade between Lord Stanley's commissioning of the Stanley Cup and the Senators-Silver Seven's first Cup win, a new generation of players was born who would take the Senators to the team's second silver streak. Local goalies Clint Benedict and Alec "The Ottawa Fireman" Connell, as well as skaters Francis "King" Clancy and the Boucher brothers, George and Frank, were memorable players who helped Ottawa capture the Stanley Cup in 1920, 1921, 1923 and 1927.

The team would fold during the Depression, disappearing to St. Louis in 1933, only to return again in the form of the junior Ottawa 67's, who, beginning in 1967, would wear the Senators' familiar red-white-and-black barber pole sweaters. The Senators were reborn in 1992 as a National Hockey League team and began the city's new quest for the coveted trophy that Lord Stanley of Preston had given to the world.

Brian Kilrea, playing for the Springfield Indians.

Kilrea Was Here

The best Ottawa hockey story of the past 50 years belongs to Brian Kilrea. He was born here, into a hockey family. Uncles Hec, Ken and Wally all made their marks in the National Hockey League. Brian made the big leagues, too, performing in a handful of games for the Detroit Red Wings and the Los Angeles Kings. But "Killer," as old friends call him, played most of his 16-season career in the American Hockey League, where he displayed courage as the captain of the Springfield Indians in 1967, leading the team in a successful mutiny against Captain Queeg-like owner Eddie Shore.

During his playing days, Kilrea returned to Ottawa for summer work, variously running the Embassy Restaurant at Bank and Sparks Streets and the Townhouse Motel on Rideau Street, next to the old Nelson Theatre. In 1974, he found his true calling, coaching the Ottawa 67's, a junior team he led to Memorial Cups in 1984 and 1997. In 2003, he coached the 67's to his 1,000th victory, a Canadian Hockey League record that he continues to break every passing season.

PARRY SOUND

FOUNDED

Sheltered in a sound along the eastern shores of Georgian Bay, Parry Sound was first known as Wau-sak-au-sing, an Anishnabe (or Ojibway) word for "shining lake." In the 1820s, a British surveyor named the area Parry Sound after the Arctic explorer Sir William Edward Parry. Lumber, sawmills and regional shipbuilding fuelled the town's early growth, but most of its modern expansion has been sustained by the area's annual wave of summer cottagers and boaters.

NATIVE-BORN NHL PLAYERS

Neil Belland, Bobby Orr, Jerry Carson, Terry Crisp, Gary Sabourin

FAMOUS LOCAL TEAMS

Junior: Parry Sound, Parry Sound Pilots

CURRENT POPULATION

19,466

Bobby

Bobby Orr used every inch of Parry Sound's land and frozen waterways to make himself into a hockey player.

"We did most of our skating outdoors," he once said. "We had one rink. We had to wait our turn to go inside, but on Georgian Bay, on the Seguin River, the river that runs through town and the bay that the town is on, the school rink, parking lots, safe streets—we played everywhere. That's all we did."

All his old teammates, from the peewee Shamrocks to the guys who played with him on the Seguin, remember Bobby being bashful about his abilities; they also recall how he worked to include others in the magic of his game. But every now and then, the thrill of his talent overwhelmed him, and he would just take off like a paper scrap in the wind.

While still in kindergarten, Bobby was the youngest and best player in the Parry Sound Minor Squirt Hockey League. Soon, he was an underage bantam playing in a 1960 tournament in Gananoque, Ontario. He was a marvel. Some kids played forward; others, defence. Bobby played the entire rink, attacking the other team's end with the speed and fury of a downhill skier. If the goalie made a save, Bobby would suddenly rematerialize at his own blue line.

"See what I see?" Boston Bruins general manager Lynn Patrick asked the team's Oshawa junior affiliate coach, Hap Emms.

"I see what you see. Who is he?" Emms went to find out and returned minutes later. "Bobby Orr—nobody's sponsoring him," he said.

Still, he was so small. The summer he turned 13, Bobby got a job as a bellhop at Parry Sound's Belvedere Hotel. "I wasn't very strong," Orr remembered. "And people would come in with big bags, and I'd say, 'I gotta carry your bags.' But they wouldn't let me. And one time, my boss saw me leading [guests] who were carrying their own bags… I got in trouble."

So Bobby worked that summer on conditioning. Twice a day, he raced seagulls along the Parry Sound waterfront, running for miles. And he was always squeezing handgrips while walking around the Orr house on Great North Road.

In the fall of 1962, the grade eight student joined the Oshawa Generals. His dad, Doug Orr, would drive him to junior games that were sometimes in London, St. Catharines or Toronto. The next fall, Bobby moved to Oshawa, but

A young and determined Bobby Orr, on the ice for the Boston Bruins.

he phoned home every night. If his father or brothers answered, he was okay, but if his mother or one of his sisters, Pat or Penny, answered, Bobby would burst into tears.

Graduating to the National Hockey League at age 18 to play for the Boston Bruins, Orr continued to astonish. "First time I saw Orr, I was coming down the wing on him," remembered New York Rangers forward "Boom Boom" Geoffrion. "He was skating faster than me backward. I can see I can't get around him so I wind and shoot. He blocks the shot. I stop then turn to chase him. I look up, he's 20 yards the other way. I been playing hockey a long time, but I never saw a move like that."

For 11 seasons, Orr was the best player in the world. Twice he won scoring championships, the only defenceman to accomplish that feat. Twice he led the

Orr paid heavily for his daring style and determined scoring rushes.

Bruins to the Stanley Cup. Bruins teammate Gerry Cheevers swears Orr was so fast that he once deflected his own shot.

Author George Plimpton offered another classic Orr story, referring to a game between the Bruins and the Oakland Seals: "Orr lost his glove at mid-ice—it lay palm up like a [knight's gauntlet] discarded on the battlefield. Wheeling behind his own net, one bare hand on the stick, he came back up the ice with the puck, going at top speed, when suddenly, almost as an afterthought, he reached down and scooped his empty hand in the glove, never breaking stride...

"Then he went on through two defensemen. [Finally] goalie Gary Smith beat him. Best part of the story was that both benches groaned. The Oakland bench as well."

Orr paid heavily for his daring style and determined scoring rushes, however, undergoing 15 operations on his legs. He would wear out his body like a child ruins his clothes—knees first. At age 27, he could no longer be Bobby Orr and so he left the game, eventually becoming a hockey agent.

Orr would often return home to Parry Sound after his playing days were over. And his hockey memorabilia business is named after the street he grew up on—Great North Road.

In 2003, Bobby acquired a second Parry Sound address, when he opened the combined Bobby Orr Hall of Fame-Charles W. Stockey Centre for the Performing Arts. At the hall's opening ceremony, Orr's former coach Don Cherry introduced the local hero to a cheering crowd: "The clouds are coming in. Looks like a storm," Cherry said, then stole a glance at Orr. "Hold the clouds back, will ya?"

When Orr took the microphone, Parry Sound's favourite son was the same kid who phoned home from Oshawa to see how everybody back home was doing. "This is probably the most difficult thing I've ever had to do—to stand here and tell you how I feel," he said. "I've been a very lucky guy. I played on championship teams. I played for Canada. I've won some awards and I'm very proud of those accomplishments. But I don't think there's anything greater then to come home..."

Orr introduced his sisters, Pat and Penny, and his brothers, Ron and Doug. Fighting tears, he thanked his father, remembering all the car rides to games: "Thank you for the sacrifices you had to make so I could chase my dream." Then he spoke of his departed mother and grandmother: "I know they're watching."

After those words, Orr couldn't continue. He didn't have to, though. His hometown appreciated that he was speaking from the heart and filled his silence with grateful applause. Some things don't have to be said to family.

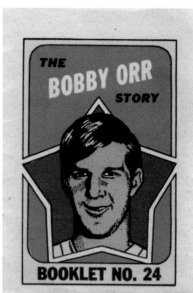

This novelty player card/comic is an example of the vast array of Bobby Orr memorabilia from the '60s.

PETERBOROUGH

Historic map of Peterborough, 1875.

FOUNDED

Peterborough was originally the site of a saw-and-grist mill that served pioneers scattered around the area. The small settlement, known as Scott's Mills, struggled until 1825 when the British government sought to alleviate poverty in Ireland by sponsoring 2,000 Irish emigrants to bolster the thin ranks of such "back townships" as Peterborough. In 1826, the site was named after its first government official, Peter Robinson, who established a "government house" in his log cabin. Lumber dominated the region's commerce until the 1890s, when U.S. inventor Thomas Edison chose Peterborough as the Canadian site of Edison Electric Co., the predecessor to General Electric.

NATIVE-BORN NHL PLAYERS

Zac Bierk, Hank Blade, Douglas Brennan, Norman Calladine, Rob Collins, Doug Crossman, Paul Curtis, John Druce, Doug Evans, Kevin Evans, Paul Evans, Mike Fisher, Larry Floyd, Mark Freer, Bob Gainey, Doug Gibson, Del Hall, Frank Heffernan, Kerry Huffman, Joey Johnston, Jeff Larmer, Steve Larmer, Jay Legault, Dean Morton, Cam Newton, Dennis Patterson, Corey Perry, Steve Peters, Herb Raglan, Ryan Ready, George Redding, Glen Seabrooke, Steve Self, Cory Stillman, Red Sullivan, Greg Theberge, Steve Webb, Brian Wesenberg

FAMOUS LOCAL TEAMS

Junior: Peterborough Canucks, Peterborough Jr. Bees, Peterborough Jr. Petes, Peterborough Juniors, Peterborough Lumber, Peterborough Petes, Peterborough Roadrunners; **Senior-pro:** Peterborough Petes, Peterborough Seniors

CURRENT POPULATION

74,600

Coaches' Corner

In 1974, Peterborough native Roger Neilson was coaching a local baseball team in a game against Kingston. The Peterborough players were in the field, nervously eyeing a Kingston runner dancing off third base. The pitcher wound and fired. His catcher received the ball, stood, and hurled a white sphere over the third baseman's head—at which point, the Kingston player trotted in to score.

But no, the catcher was at home plate with the ball in his glove! What he had thrown over the third basemen's head was a peeled apple.

The "hidden apple" trick was yet another ruse out of Roger Neilson's playbook. Coaching baseball was something Neilson did just for fun, mind you. Hockey was his full-time job and also the sport in which he created the most mischief.

Once, in the 1970s, when he was coaching the Peterborough Petes, the city's legendary junior hockey team, Neilson found his club ahead a goal with two men in the penalty box and a minute or so left in the game. A dire predicament, but Neilson figured that since no team could be down less than two men under existing rules, he would continue to throw out illegal players after faceoffs. Sure, he'd be penalized for too many men on the ice, but no additional players would actually have to serve a penalty. The ploy worked—the Petes managed to disrupt the opponent's power play with a series of stoppages and won the game. The rule was soon changed, so that any team attempting Neilson's trick would be punished with a penalty shot.

PETERBOROUGH MILLIONAIRE

Fred Whitcroft moved from Port Perry, Ontario, to Peterborough in 1891. In 1901, he scored eight goals to lead the junior Peterborough Colts to a 12–0 victory against a team from Stratford in the Ontario Hockey Association junior championship. He later played for the 1907 Stanley Cup-winning Kenora Thistles and then hired himself out to the Renfrew Creamery Kings (later called the Millionaires) of the National Hockey Association. After his playing days, Whitcroft coached the Edmonton Eskimos of the Alberta Professional Hockey league.

Scotty Bowman was given a new car by the Peterborough Petes for guiding the junior team to the Memorial Cup win in 1959.

It's ironic that a maverick such as Roger "Rulebook," as he became known, would receive his hockey break coaching in Peterborough, a town that is generally as straight as an accountant's ruler. In 1892, the Edison Company (now General Electric) started organized hockey in the city, sponsoring four hockey teams in a municipal league. The best of the clubs, wanting to make sure everyone knew exactly where they were from, called themselves the Peterborough Peterboroughs—or, as they would become known, the Petes.

In the 1950s, Canadian companies began to test market their wares in Peterborough, leading *Chatelaine* magazine to label the city the "ultra-average Canada town." One such "company" was the Montreal Canadiens, which

Inquisitive, eccentric and caring, Neilson touched everyone he coached. Every Petes player had a story about him.

moved its Kitchener junior farm team (the Greenshirts) to Peterborough in 1956. The transfer continues to be a resounding success. Since the team's inception, the Petes have only missed the playoffs twice, while making more Memorial Cup appearances (seven) than any other junior club in the country. The Petes have also produced more National Hockey League players (140) than any other Canadian junior team, including stars the calibre of Steve Yzerman and Chris Pronger.

Still, right from the beginning, when general manager Sam Pollock and coach Scotty Bowman moved in to create junior hockey in Peterborough, this city has always been the coaches' corner of Canada. Nineteen former Petes players or coaches eventually went on to coach in the NHL, including Bowman, Neilson, Mike Keenan, Gary Green, Jacques Martin and Colin Campbell. Indeed, even the city's most famous native-born hockey players, Hall of Famers Fred Whitcroft and Bob Gainey, would continue their careers by coaching and managing hockey teams.

Bowman, who went on from his coaching position with the Petes to win nine Stanley Cups with the Montreal Canadiens, Pittsburgh Penguins and Detroit Red Wings, helped create the model for what has always been the most fiscally responsible and mannerly (for a teenage hockey team, anyway) of junior hockey franchises. While coaching the Petes in the '50s, Bowman kept $10 of a player's $60-a-week allowance, investing the money in a savings account. If the player ran dry, he'd have to get William "Scotty" Bowman to co-sign a withdrawal at—where else?—the Bank of Montreal.

Scotty also conducted legendary bed checks, phoning at 11:00 p.m. to make sure players were in, then occasionally again at 11:30, to make sure they still were in. He would also cruise Water and Sherbrooke Streets in his car looking for wayward Petes. Players out on the town took to jumping into alleyways as soon as they saw a car approaching. One evening, Barclay Plager, a frequent carouser, was out with teammates when he saw headlights approaching. The players flinched, ready to fly, then noticed how widely set the lights were—a truck. With that bit of reassurance, they relaxed. Seconds later, Bowman pulled over in a borrowed truck and sent them all home with a $10 fine.

Bowman left the Petes in 1961, to eventually pursue his career as a celebrated NHL coach. In 1966, the Montreal Canadiens handed the Peterborough team to a private consortium in anticipation of the NHL expansion draft, which forced

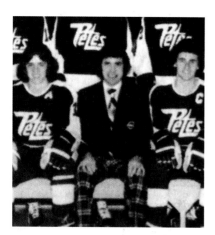

Coach Roger Neilson, with the Peterborough Petes in the 1970s.

The Best Player in the World

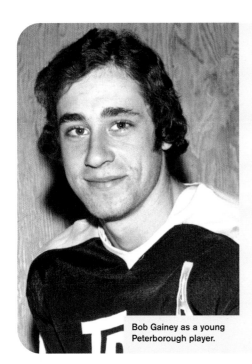

Bob Gainey as a young
Peterborough player.

"If you want a team game," Montreal Canadiens goalie and author Ken Dryden wrote in *The Game*, "where the goal is the team and the goal is to win, you need a player with an emotional and practical stake in a team game, a player to remind you of that game, to bring you back to it whenever you forget it, to be the playing conscience of the team. Like Bob Gainey." A defenceman growing up in Peterborough, where his dad worked at the Quaker Oats plant, Bob Gainey spent two years with the Peterborough Petes (1971–73) under Roger Neilson. There, he became a consummate defensive player, a big (6'2", 200 lbs) mobile forward who could skate another team's best scorer into an instant slump. Although he scored only 26 goals in junior, the Montreal Canadiens brain trust, general manager Sam Pollock and coach Scotty Bowman, themselves old Peterborough Petes hands, enlisted Gainey with the team's first draft pick in 1973. He produced instant dividends, providing defensive balance and quiet leadership to the showy Montreal scoring machine that won four Stanley Cups in a row from 1976 to 1979. The Soviet national team hockey coach called Gainey "the best player in the world." The defensive specialist would go on to captain the Canadiens. After winning a Stanley Cup as general manager of the Dallas Stars in 1999, he returned to Montreal to take over the Canadiens in 2003. Gainey maintains a home outside Peterborough.

clubs to give up their farm teams. That fall, Roger Neilson, previously a scout with the team, took over. With Neilson at the helm for the next decade, the Petes became a lab experiment in hockey. In his first season with the team, Neilson had a defenceman, Ron Stackhouse, replace the team's goalie in penalty shots, stopping six attempts, before the league changed the rules. The new coach also instructed goalies to leave their sticks in front of the crease before leaving the ice when, late in a game, netminders were removed for an extra attacker—an improvised tactic that resulted in yet another amendment to the rules.

Not all of Neilson's coaching moves would be frivolous, however. In the NHL, where he would instruct seven different teams, he authored the most important innovation in modern hockey, the neutral-zone trap manoeuvre, while coaching the Florida Panthers in 1991. The former high-school teacher was also a passionate advocate of player education, and during his regime with the Petes, he began the practice of rewarding players with education packages for service. Today, the team offers every player who doesn't make it into pro hockey $3,000 for college for every season played in Peterborough.

Inquisitive, eccentric and caring, Neilson touched everyone he coached. Every Petes player had a story about him. Future NHL player and coach Craig Ramsey liked to tell of the time he came into Neilson's office, head down, and began to confess his deep misgivings about hockey as a potential career. Afterward, he looked up to find Neilson feigning sleep, his way of telling Ramsey that his fears were groundless.

Neilson died in Peterborough in June of 2003. Honouring his lifelong commitment to education, the Ontario Hockey League, in 2005, created the Roger Neilson Memorial Award to be given to the top academic player attending university. And the Peterborough Petes, the most famous junior hockey coaching academy in Canada, acknowledged one of its most famous alumni by naming a street leading out of the team's Memorial Centre home after Coach Neilson: Roger Neilson Way.

POINT ANNE

FOUNDED
Point Anne was created in the early 1900s, to provide residences for Belleville Portland Cement and Lehigh Portland Cement factory workers. The building boom in the postwar years kept Point Anne alive until the late 1960s, but when the cement business shut down here in the early 1970s, the community became a virtual ghost town. Residents of Point Anne are now included in the Belleville census.

NATIVE-BORN NHL PLAYERS
Bobby Hull, Dennis Hull

FAMOUS LOCAL TEAMS
Not applicable

CURRENT POPULATION
Not available

THE STORY OF THE FARMER'S DAUGHTER

Five years younger, three Clairol shades darker, and a gear slower than his big "Golden Jet" brother, Dennis Hull endured lots of kidding while growing up. Particularly after an early '60s TV commercial that had Bobby elbowing his kid brother away from the bathroom mirror, admonishing his younger sibling to "lay off the greasy kid stuff" and go with Brylcreem ("a little dab'll do ya'").

Dennis, however, would get the last laugh. After a successful National Hockey League career spent mostly with the Chicago Blackhawks, the kid brother took to the road as hockey's most popular after-dinner speaker—the big attraction at golf tournaments and firefighters' conventions across Canada. Brother Bobby's trials and tribulations often figured into the younger Hull's monologues. One favourite story had Bobby and Dennis attending a public event in Prince Edward County, where they were confronted by a young woman who told Bobby, "My mother says you're my father."

To which Bobby responded, "Well, honey, say hello to your Uncle Dennis."

Golden Boy

The fourth of 11 children, Point Anne's Bobby Hull took to his life's work with the magical ease that distinguishes prodigies. The moment occurred on Christmas Day 1942. Santa had left a pair of skates that were only a little too big for Bobby. That afternoon his older sisters, Maxine and Laura, held the three-year-old still long enough to get extra socks on his feet, then chased after him outside.

"Remember now, no crying or the skates go back to Santa," Mrs. Hull called after him.

Bobby hit the nearby rink with an elaborate pratfall, like a duck surprised by November ice on a farmer's pond. But then he gathered himself up and soon managed a few chopping steps. His sisters had to guide him around, but not for long.

"I looked out the window a couple of hours later and I could hardly believe it," Mrs. Hull told sports writer Jim Hunt. For there was Bobby flying by, faster than a small-town rumour. "It was almost dark when I finally called him in for his Christmas dinner and by this time he could skate by himself without any help from his sisters."

Point Anne was a bustling cement town at the time, and Hull's dad was a plant foreman. But the surrounding country was devoted to agriculture. And so he grew up a Prince Edward County farmboy. "From the age of 10 on, I spent my entire summer holiday...haying, then thrashing [on a relative's farm]," Hull told author Charles Wilkins. "The older guys used to laugh, watching me stagger around trying to get those big sacks on my shoulders. They must have weighed 150 pounds each—and me just a pup. But I loved it anyway...and the meals! Oh, they were just heaven! See, the farmers along the road from about Shannonville to Marysville used to exchange help at thrashing time.... And the gals on these farms would always try to outdo each other at mealtime—they'd have anything from beef to pork to chicken to duck to lamb, and about 16 different pies and cakes. It was just fantastic the way those farm girls could cook. And I loved to eat—I needed it, I was working so hard. I was very ambitious as a kid, on the dogtrot all the time."

Hull excelled at hockey and left home for his sport at 14, playing for the amateur Woodstock Athletics, Galt Hawks and St. Catharines Teepees. Arriving in Chicago and the National Hockey League at the tender age of 18, he quickly

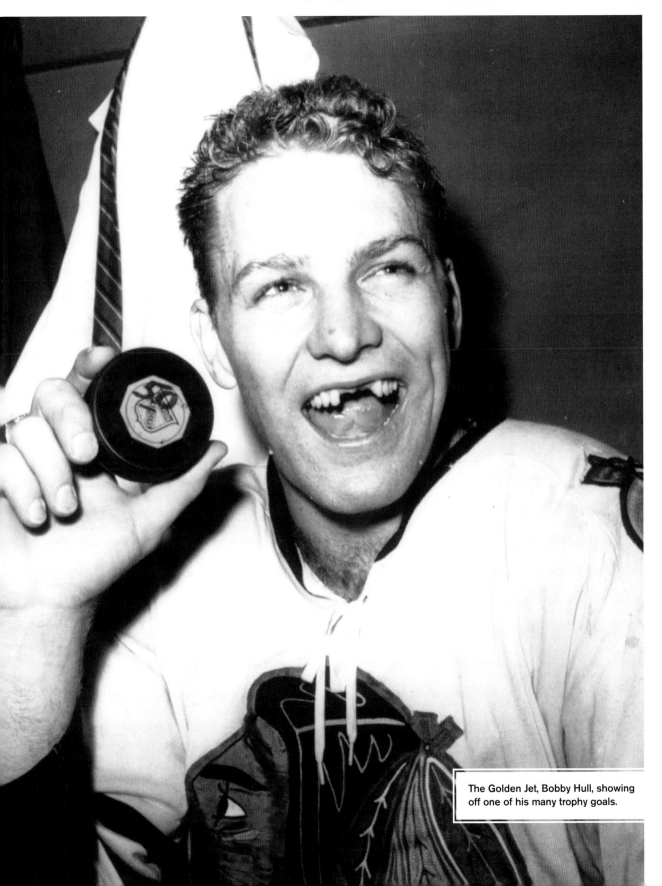

The Golden Jet, Bobby Hull, showing off one of his many trophy goals.

The Golden Brett

If Bobby Hull is the most famous player ever to come out of Point Anne, his son Brett is the best player born in nearby Belleville, Ontario. "The Golden Brett" scored 228 goals for the National Hockey League's St. Louis Blues in an astonishing three-season run (1990–92).

In addition to inheriting his father's deadly shot, Brett also has Uncle Dennis's wicked tongue. Brett Hull was driving through the midwest one summer with a friend, Tonto Toninato. Stopping the car to go stretch their legs, they were surprised by the sniffing of a big brown bear. "God, whatta' we do?" Toninato asked, his voice high with excitement. "We can't run, bear's faster than us."

Tonto turned to see Hull flying down the road. "Tonto," he shouted out, "it's not the bear I'm trying to out run."

brought the long-dreadful Blackhawks to the playoffs, helping his team win the Stanley Cup in 1961.

Everywhere he went, Hull was the player to see. And more than any Canadian athlete before him, he developed a talent for being watched. The fastest, strongest player in the game broke into a salesmen's grin when dealing with the public, yet still exhibited a shy graciousness that made his success, and mannequin good looks, compelling.

For a while, his story seemed to only get better. In 1962, Hull attained the glamorous 50-goal level; in 1966 he established a new record with 54 markers,

That Bobby Hull never disappointed—he would stand for hours outside bitterly cold arenas, smiling and signing autographs for fans.

and then followed with an astonishing 58 goals in 1969. Most valuable player trophies and endorsements were his inevitable due. Magazines featured him in photo spreads that showed him stripped to the waist, a blond Bond modelling bathing suits. On TV, he pitched hair cream, advising kid brother Dennis to "lay off the greasy kid's stuff."

Despite all the glamour, Hull was a creature of habit. He wore the same shoulder and shin pads his entire 23-year career, from Chicago to the World Hockey Association, where, in 1972, the "Golden Jet" received a million dollar signing bonus and as an added perk had a team named after him—the Winnipeg Jets.

Neither did he ever really leave southern Ontario. The remaining Point Anne cement factory closed down, but Prince Edward County remained home for Hull. In 1959, he purchased a ranch house with a view of the Bay of Quinte near Demorestville, a short boat ride away from his childhood home. And every summer, as soon as the weather got warm, he would come back, as if drawn by happy memories. "I loved those [long ago] summers," he told Wilkins. "That's where my love of agriculture and cattle comes from. And also from just driving through the country in the old 1930s Model A Ford, with my mom and dad and sisters and brothers. I'd see those old red-and-white Herefords out there on that green meadow...and I thought that if I was ever able to afford some, I'd buy 'em. And as soon as I could, I did." Indeed, the hockey star farmed at his country home, either by himself or with a partner, for decades.

His famous hockey-playing son, Brett, was born in nearby Belleville in 1964, during the late innings of an exhibition baseball game. (Dad reluctantly drove second wife, Joanne, to the hospital with his spikes still on.)

Fans now know that the Bobby Hull story was, in some ways, too good to be true. The Golden Jet occasionally crashed. There were failed, battle-scarred marriages and unfortunate public remarks. A few good jokes too, though. (Hull once commented on an NHL coach's abilities by saying, "He couldn't coach a dog in from a storm with a pork chop.")

Bobby wasn't the first hockey player to be better on than off the ice. And the best part of him, the exuberant farmboy who became hockey's brightest star in the 1960s, remains a valid memory. That Bobby Hull never disappointed—he would stand for hours outside bitterly cold arenas, smiling and signing autographs for fans. There were seldom any disappointments on the ice either, where he truly captured viewers' imaginations: circling the net, legs crossing over, ready to explode up the wing and unleash yet another fabulous slapshot.

RENFREW

FOUNDED
An Ottawa Valley lumber town founded in the early part of the 19th century, Renfrew boasted several sawmills by the 1850s. The county of Renfrew was formed on 8 June 1861.

NATIVE-BORN NHL PLAYERS
Lorne Anderson, Archie Briden, William Brydge, Alan Letang, Ted Lindsay, Jim Peplinski

FAMOUS LOCAL TEAMS
Junior: Renfrew Lions, Renfrew Timberwolves; **Senior-pro:** Renfrew Creamery Kings, Renfrew Millionaires, Renfrew Riversides, Renfrew Royals

CURRENT POPULATION
7,942

A League of Their Own

Fortunes could be made playing hockey for Ottawa Valley lumber barons in the early 20th century. Indeed, one lumber town had an entire hockey team of Millionaires.

Many Valley teams have acknowledged the woods and waterways that gave their cities life—for instance, the Pembroke Lumber Kings, the Smith's Falls Rideaumen and the Ottawa Cliffsides. But the real lumber king in the region came from Renfrew, not from up the line (as they say in the Valley) in Pembroke. M.J. O'Brien and his son Ambrose made a fortune moving lumber and building railroads. They also loved hockey and figured it would be grand if their Upper Ottawa Valley Hockey league team, the Creamery Kings, competed for the trophy everyone was making a fuss about—the Stanley Cup.

In 1909, the O'Briens' Kings challenged the Montreal Wanderers for the trophy emblematic of Canadian hockey supremacy. The bid was denied, however, by the Canadian Hockey Association, with the CHA declaring that only member teams were eligible for the Stanley Cup. That rule wasn't very Canadian, the O'Briens figured, so they took their marbles home, founding a new league, the National Hockey Association (NHA). The Montreal Canadiens were quickly in, as were the Montreal Maroons. The O'Briens also set up franchises in Cobalt and Haileybury. The Ottawa Senators would hop aboard for the 1910–11 season.

The Creamery Kings didn't quite capture the majesty of the O'Brien vision, so the Renfrew owners changed the team's name to the Millionaires. The O'Briens also scoured central Canada for talent, with money being no object, as the name of their team might suggest. From the Ottawa Senators, they paid Fred "Cyclone" Taylor $5,250 for a 12-game season, every penny of which was deposited in the bank before Taylor stepped onto the ice. (Baseball's biggest star, Ty Cobb, made $6,500 for a 154-game season that same year.) Montreal's Frank and Lester Patrick were also recruited, along with Cornwall's Newsy Lalonde. Bert Lindsay (Terrible Teddie's dad), in his trademark gleaming white pads, would play goal.

Becoming a Millionaire had its appeal. Hall of Famer Sprague Cleghorn, wearing only a topcoat, left a chorus girl in New York to arrive in the land of wind chill factor one December night. His brother and defence partner, Odie, was at the station, located outside Renfrew. Not a light could be seen for miles when Sprague stepped onto the platform. He could only recognize his brother, entombed in scarves and a hat, by his voice.

"Where in hell are we?" Sprague Cleghorn demanded. "What is this?"

REVERSE CYCLONE?

Sportsmen tossed money around as easily as kids threw snowballs in Renfrew, when M.J. O'Brien ruled local hockey in the early 1900s. The town's fans lost $5,000 to a Montreal group, betting that their Renfrew side could whip the Stanley Cup champion Maroons in a 1908 exhibition match. The champs prevailed, 3–1.

The most famous bet of the era, though, came when Renfrew Millionaires star Cyclone Taylor bet an *Ottawa Citizen* sportswriter $100 that he could score skating backwards on Ottawa Senators goalie Percy LeSueur. Taylor was widely reported at the time to have executed this very manoeuvre. Millionaires teammate Lester Patrick offered a dissenting opinion decades later, however: "On one of his rushes the Ottawa defence stopped Taylor cold and turned him around with his back to the Ottawa goal. He flipped the puck, backhanded. It nosed past the goaltender. I was on the ice and saw the whole thing.... But by the time the sportswriters had finished with it you'd have thought the Cyclone...repeated this performance about every night. The Cyclone didn't make the legend. The public did."

The 1907 Renfrew Millionaires.

"This is Renfrew," his brother laughed.

As it turned out, the brawling Cleghorns enjoyed Renfrew, and so did their fellow Millionaires. The players were received as town heroes by locals and fans who arrived by sled from the 'Prior (Armprior), Carp and Dunrobin. Four thousand fans crowded the Renfrew Arena for most games, some holding hot potatoes to keep warm; others resorting to more traditional winter comfort, rye whiskey. For out-of-town games in Ottawa, the Timberwolf Special, a jostling, smoke-filled train, took Renfrew fans back and forth.

For two glorious seasons, money and adventure on the Renfrew team flowed as fast as the rapids on the nearby Ottawa River. In addition to paying team members their regular salaries, O'Brien gave the team a bonus of $100 for every goal a Millionaire scored, then threw in an extra $50 to the individual scorer, which is perhaps why the Millionaires hit visiting towns like Vikings—one night, they sacked the Ottawa Senators, always a good team, 17–2.

For all their flair and panache, the Millionaires never won a Stanley Cup, for which they were now permitted to compete. The team vied for the Cup in 1910 and 1911, but they came in third place both times behind the Montreal Wanderers and the Ottawa Senators. By 1913, the team's owners quit hockey for more profitable pursuits. The O'Briens' Renfrew legacy includes the O'Brien movie theatre on Raglan Street. Their sporting legacy would be the National Hockey League, which grew out of the NHA in 1917. In fact, one of the franchises the O'Briens established in 1910 became the Toronto Blueshirts in 1912, renamed the Toronto Maple Leafs in 1927.

ST. CATHARINES

FOUNDED

Before white settlers arrived, St. Catharines was believed to be one of North America's most heavily populated Aboriginal encampments, with a burial ground that stretched for more than five acres. In the 1790s, this site became home to United Empire Loyalists fleeing the American Revolution. The expanding town was named St. Catharines in 1796, in honour of the deceased wife of the district's first representative to the Executive Council of Upper Canada. By the 1830s, after the completion of a wooden canal that connected the Welland and Niagara Rivers with Lake Erie, St. Catharines was a busy stopping point for trade ships on the Great Lakes. For much of the next century, the local economy was dominated by shipyards, which employed hundreds of workers to build ships.

NATIVE-BORN NHL PLAYERS

Roger Belanger, Brian Bellows, Bill Berg, Gerry Cheevers, Hank Ciesla, David Cullen, Rob Davison, Marv Edwards, Doug Favell, Bob Froese, John Gibson, Glenn Goldup, Jason Lafreniere, Garry Lariviere, Jack Martin, Bryan McCabe, Brian McKenzie, Mike Millar, Ellard O'Brien, Mark Plantery, Doug Robinson, Rob Robinson, Andy Rymsha, Ryan Savoia, Skeeter Teal, Rick Vasko

FAMOUS LOCAL TEAMS

Junior: St. Catharines Black Hawks, St. Catharines Falcons, St. Catharines Fincups, St. Catharines Teepees, St. Catharines Intermediates; **Senior-pro:** St. Catharines Chiefs, St. Catharines Pros, St. Catharines Saints

CURRENT POPULATION

129,170

DeePee

When Stanislav Gvoth was three, Nazi soldiers took him out into the backyard to play with guns—real guns. The year was 1943 and Hitler's army had invaded Czechoslovakia. German soldiers lived with the Gvoths in their two-room house.

After the war the Communists invaded Czechoslovakia, and life became worse. In 1948, Stanislav's aunt and uncle arrived from St. Catharines, Ontario, bringing candy for the two Gvoth boys. One night, Joe and Anna asked if they might take Stanislav, the younger son, back with them to Canada. Mrs. Gvoth said no. Just then, Stansilav burst into tears in the doorway. He was hungry and thought that his mother had turned down his mumbled request for toast. Mrs. Gvoth believed that the tears meant he wanted to leave home and so she consented to let her son go.

During his first weeks in Canada, the eight-year-old boy, who was now called Stan Mikita, watched kids playing hockey on the street from the window of his new home. The following week, he stood on the porch. Gaining courage, he finally moved to a perch on a snow bank. Sitting there, cupping his face in his hands, Stan studied the game as if pulling apart a mystery. "My first words of English were hockey words," Mikita later told sportswriter Dick Beddoes. "Puck, stick and goal."

Other, less desirable phrases followed. "The term for refugee back in the 1940s was 'displaced person,'" Mikita remembered. "That meant you were somebody who could be looked down upon. After years of teasing I was hostile. I had developed this feeling it was me against the world." Stan began collecting insults the way other boys saved hockey cards. The term DP—short for Displaced

Rudy

Winnipeg-born Rudy Pilous arrived in St. Catharines in 1938 to play for the local senior team, the Chiefs, and never left. Rudy started up the junior St. Catharines Falcons in 1943, coaching the team for three seasons before moving to lead teams in the American Hockey League. He returned to St. Catherines, in 1950, as general manager and coach of the junior team, renamed the Teepees, leading it to a Memorial Cup in 1954. And he owned the 1960 St. Catharines Teepees team, which also won the national championship. (The following season, he coached the National Hockey League's Chicago Blackhawks to the Stanley Cup, with a tent full of players from his Teepee days.)

More than anything, Rudy enjoyed talking about his junior coaching days. One favourite story involved getting the Teepees into the 1954 Memorial Cup. "We trailed Toronto St. Michael's by one goal late in a playoff. We pulled netminder Marv Edwards, even though the faceoff was in our own end. All of their players headed for the empty net." And the Teepees flew in the other direction with the puck. Hugh Barlow (part of the team's big line, with brothers Brian and Barry Cullen) scored on Toronto's Gerry McNamara with 28 seconds remaining. "We squeezed 4,200 people into the rink for that game, but I've met 40,000 who said they saw it," Pilous would often remark.

The Teepees went on to defeat the Edmonton Oil Kings for the 1954 Memorial Cup. In 1960, they won a second national championship, again against the Oil Kings. The Teepees became the St. Catharines Black Hawks in 1962, and, led by Marcel Dionne, lost to Quebec in the 1971 Memorial Cup semifinals (see page 84).

Stan Mikita, playing for the OHA
Junior "A" All-Stars.

Person—both infuriated and drove him. "[I felt that] the only way I could succeed was by being better than everybody else. I had to be the best at…hockey."

In St. Catharines, being the best meant playing for the Teepees, the junior team that played out of Garden City Arena (now Jack Gatecliff Arena) on Geneva Street. Mikita made the team in the fall of 1956, at age 16. Bobby Hull, Moose Vasko and Chico Maki were fellow teammates. In time these four players would all star on the 1961 Chicago Blackhawks team that won the Stanley Cup. For now, though, they comprised the most exciting team—with the most boisterous fans—in junior hockey.

"The Teepees were big," coach Rudy Pilous remembered. "We had 4,000 fans, regular. And, oh, they were noisy."

Mikita was a fan favourite, Pilous recollected. "He was from here. He was the smartest hockey player I ever saw, and he'd fight you if you looked crossways at him."

Stan was 5'8" and 152 pounds when he joined the Chicago Blackhawks in 1959. French fans called him "Le Petit Diable"—the little devil. Once in Montreal Stan got into a fight. Afterward, in the penalty box, the other player called him "a dirty DP." Stan flew at him with swinging fists. When fans booed, Mikita stood on the penalty bench and waved his arms as if he were conducting an orchestra.

After his rookie year in the National Hockey League, Mikita returned to Czechoslovakia. He didn't have a great visit. His first night home, his mom and

The hooked stick seemed to give his shot extra life.

dad took him aside and whispered, "Watch what you say, we don't know if your brother and sister are in the Communist Party."

Life was better back in Chicago and with the NHL. In some ways, Stan remained that little kid sitting on a snow bank, memorizing the best parts of everyone's hockey game. If a rival beat him with a trick move on a faceoff, Stan could duplicate the manoeuvre by the very next game. Once in Montreal, Mikita won 34 out of 35 faceoffs.

He also thought up tricks of his own. One practice, he cracked the blade of his stick and then angrily fired the puck away. But wait… Stan retrieved the puck and took a few more shots. The hooked stick seemed to give his shot extra life. Later, he hurried back to the dressing room and found another stick. After placing the heel under boiling water, he wedged the now pliable blade beneath a door until the stick felt ready to snap. The next morning he skated onto the rink for practice with a stick blade shaped like a capital C. Stan discovered that this banana blade put a real dance into his slapshot. The puck might drop a foot one time and take off like a spooked bird the next. With the help of this new trick, Mikita and teammate Bobby Hull came first and second, respectively, in the 1963-64 scoring season.

Stan took less pleasure in other statistics. Every year, he was a league leader in penalty minutes and body wounds. At age 27, he had close to 200 stitches on his face. He had also cracked his toes, broken a shoulder and heel, ripped muscles and had an ear sliced off so that it was hanging by a thread. After one game, he came home with red knuckles and a black eye.

"Daddy, I watched you play last night on TV," his two-year-old daughter Meg said.

"What did you think?"

"Oh, Daddy, you were so good, but sometimes the whistle blew and all the players went one way, you had to go all the way across the ice by yourself."

"I was going to the penalty box."

"But Daddy, you were away such a long time."

Stan looked at himself through his daughter's eyes and didn't like what he saw. What was he doing fighting and slashing all the time? From now on, I'm going to leave the stick work to carpenters and just play hockey, he told himself.

People couldn't believe it when Stan came back for the 1966-67 season. With his curved stick and straight-ahead attitude, he won the NHL's most valuable player award and established an all-time record for point-scoring. And, amazingly, Le Petit Diable also won the Lady Byng trophy for gentlemanly play. Where had the new Stan Mikita come from?

Actually, Stan would later admit, he'd been around the whole time—hiding behind Stanislav Gvoth.

SAULT STE. MARIE

FOUNDED

Called Bawating, meaning "rapid river," by the Anishnabe (or Ojibway), then, in 1668, renamed in French for St. Mary's Rapids by the Jesuits. Sault Ste. Marie was incorporated as a town in 1887, with the arrival of the Canadian Pacific Railroad. The Algoma Steel Company began producing steel here in 1902. And the Soo, as a city, was incorporated in 1912.

NATIVE-BORN NHL PLAYERS

Ken Belanger, Mike Buchanan, Billy Coutu, Paul DiPietro, Babe Donnelly, Arthur Duncan, Phil Esposito, Tony Esposito, Rico Fata, Brian Finley, Alvin Fisher, Ron Francis, Sean Gagnon, Don Grosso, Brian Helmer, Cole Jarrett, Joe Klukay, Jerry Korab, Bob LaForest, Chico Maki, Wayne Maki, James McBurney, Alexander McKinnon, Gerry Munro, Lou Nanne, Ted Nolan, Robb Palahnuk, Marty Pavelich, Fred Perlini, Didier Pitre, Matt Ravlich, Norm Schmidt, Chris Thorburn, Marty Turco, Gene Ubriaco, Dennis Vial, Jim Wiley, Mike Zuke

FAMOUS LOCAL TEAMS

Junior: Sault Ste. Marie Elks, Sault Ste. Marie Greyhounds, Sault Ste. Marie Indians, Sault Ste. Marie Legionaires, Sault Ste. Marie Marlboros, Sault Ste. Marie Nationals, Sault Ste. Marie Tagonas; **Senior-pro:** Sault Ste. Marie Greyhounds, Sault Ste. Marie Thunderbirds

CURRENT POPULATION

74,000

The Soo Greyhounds, 1924 Allan Cup winners.

Going to the Dogs

The senior Soo Greyhounds came into being in 1919. The name was a bit of canine one-upmanship on the Sudbury Wolves, the team's principal rivals. And as it turns out, the Greyhounds were indeed faster to seize the Allan Cup than Sudbury or any other team in northern Ontario, beating the Winnipeg Selkirks 6–4 in a two-game total-goal series held in Toronto in 1924. Bun Cook, later a star with the New York Rangers, would score two of those goals, thrilling the 500 Soo citizens who had paid the $23 return fare for a Canadian Pacific Railway sleeper to and from Toronto. Thousands of additional Soo fans greeted the team at home with a characteristic steel-town welcome—the victorious players were carted around town in a slag car, a house-sized vehicle used by Algoma Steel to transport molten metal.

The Soo Renaissance Period

Sault Ste. Marie—the Soo—has been a great hockey city ever since Cornwall centreman "Newsy" Lalonde skated off a train in 1905 ready to play for the Sault Ste. Marie Algonquins, the town's entry in hockey's first professional circuit, which was known as the International Hockey League. "During the second year of operation, the club had injuries," George Cowie, a team founder, wrote. "Lalonde was contracted and agreed to play. The train, with Newsy aboard, was three hours late and didn't arrive till game time. He stepped off dressed and ready to play, including skates. We put him on the ice in the second period and he scored three goals. He was paid the fabulous sum of $40 for four weeks."

A young Ted Nolan, playing for the Rochester Americans.

Migrating Bird Flies away with Cup

Ted Nolan grew up on one of the three Aboriginal reserves outside Sault Ste. Marie and trained to make the local junior Greyhounds by running up hills with an axe, chopping trees and then returning—sweat pouring off his back—to the reserve. He made the Greyhounds, playing alongside Wayne Gretzky in 1977–78, and eventually graduated to the National Hockey League with Detroit, where his career was cut short by back injuries. Returning to the Soo to coach, the man the Anishnabe called Migrating Bird, for his winter hockey pilgrimages, took the Greyhounds to three straight Memorial Cup finals in 1991, 1992 and 1993, finally winning the Cup on the third try in front of an ecstatic, cheering mob at the Sault Memorial Gardens. "The last 20 seconds there was a mist on the ice," Nolan told writer Chris Cuthbert of the team's 4–2 victory over the Peterborough Petes. "It was magical. The last 10 seconds I could see the players skating in slow motion."

9 BECOMES 99

The junior Soo Greyhounds arrived in the city in 1972. Five seasons later, their most illustrious player of all time arrived. Wayne Gretzky's hockey hero was number 9, Gordie Howe, so that's what Gretzky's number was all through minor hockey—until he got to the Greyhounds in the 1977–78 season, where Brian Gualazzi (now a Soo attorney) already owned the numeral. So 9 became 99. And 99 would soon become a teenage prodigy. Angelo Bumbacco, Greyhounds general manager at the time, remembers, "We knew he was a good player, but we didn't know he was that great. We'd score five goals and he'd get four goals and one assist. We'd score eight goals and he'd score seven and set up the other one. That's how dominant he was." Gretzky still holds the Greyhounds record for points in a season—70 goals and 110 assists for 182 points.

Lalonde would not be the only ringer imported to the Soo. Kingston's Bill and Bun Cook were stars on the storied Sault Ste. Marie Greyhounds senior team of the early 1920s, and Brantford's Wayne Gretzky became number 99 while playing for the junior Greyhounds in 1977–78. (The junior club later brought in Joe Thornton from London in the '90s.)

Lalonde, Gretzky and Thornton were imported centremen. Not that Sault Ste. Marie didn't homegrow famous pivotmen. Ron Francis graduated from the Greyhounds in 1981, to become a 1,798-point scorer in the National Hockey League. But it was another local playmaker, the focal point of the city's famous Italian hockey renaissance in the '60s, who would become the Soo's hockey centre of attraction.

Phil Esposito grew up in the Italian west end of the Soo, one of thousands of third-generation Italian-Canadians whose fathers worked for Algoma Steel and whose grandfathers had built the Trans-Canada Highway. As Chris Cuthbert points out in *The Rink*, the Soo's 1938 intermediate Northern Ontario Hockey Association championship team was as Italian as tiramisu, with names such as Naccarato, Vernelli, Sanzosti, Luzzi, Deluca and (future NHLer) Don Grosso. The next generation of Soo Italian players would be more impressive still—NHLers Phil and Tony Esposito, Lou Nanne, Matt Ravlich and Jerry Korab (the latter two athletes had Italian moms).

According to Phil Esposito's autobiography, *Thunder and Lightning*, the Espositos were an emotional bunch. And the air in the family home was thick with hurled oaths and kitchenware. "My dad had a temper," Esposito wrote. "I remember one time Tony was pushing his spaghetti away with his fork. He said, 'Aw, spaghetti again?' My old man was holding his fork, and he threw the fork at Tony and it stuck in his forehead."

Phil and Tony spent their emotions on hockey, with Tony becoming a fiercely combative Hall of Fame goalie, earning the nickname Tony "O" by recording 76 NHL shutouts. Phil was more complicated—a lazybones skater who would rather die than get off the ice or lose an important game. "When I was 10, I was playing hockey on my street when my appendix burst," he reported in his book. "But I wouldn't quit. I was hurting and throwing up all over the place, and finally I just collapsed. My mother threw me in the car, took me to Dr. Guardi five doors down. He told my mother to get me to the hospital immediately. They took my appendix out, and I remember when I came home...I had to sit by the window and watch my brother and other kids play."

Esposito hated being sidelined. Just as he hated not making the local bantam team, the Algoma Contractors, a club run by Angelo Bumbacco, future

No Canadian hockey player ever worked harder in an international series.

Greyhounds general manager. After the slight by the Contractors, Phil honed both his skating and yapping skills, playing and arguing all day and night with paesans at the outdoor rink at Queen and Andrew Streets (now Phil Esposito Park). Finally, he made the Algoma Contractors, and then, eventually, the NHL's Chicago Blackhawks, where he played alongside superstar Bobby Hull. A trade brought the Soo native to the Boston Bruins in 1967, where, working with hockey legend Bobby Orr, Phil became hockey's most prolific goal scorer.

Five years later, Esposito would make his most lasting contribution to Soo sporting lore, leading Team Canada (minus Bobby Orr, who was hurt, and Bobby Hull, who was with the World Hockey Association) to a dramatic, come-from-behind win against the Soviet Union in the 1972 Summit Series.

No Canadian hockey player ever worked harder or more effectively in an international series. Esposito was the best Canadian on the ice in all eight games, skating miles, checking, scoring and campaigning against official injustice with a virtuoso actor's flourishes. (First, came a martyred stare, followed by collapsed shoulders and arms flung wide in helplessness. How could Canada's Gary Bergman get a roughing penalty?)

Famously, Esposito stirred the country in the fourth series game in Vancouver (a 5–3 Soviet win), responding to boos with a TV lecture: "People across Canada, we tried, we gave it our best. For the people who boo us... Jesus, all of us guys are really disheartened," he told interviewer Johnny Esaw. "Every one of the 35 guys here that came out and played for Team Canada did it because we love our country."

The rebuke turned the series around, as Team Canada rode a cresting wave of popular support to defeat the Soviets in the final three games of the series. Esposito scored four goals and two assists in the last two games, with three points coming in the final 20 minutes of game eight, lifting Canada from a 4–2 deficit to a last-minute win on yet another Esposito-to-Paul Henderson goal. "I'd have killed to win that series. It scares me, but it's true," he said afterward.

After his playing days, Esposito would become a hockey executive and TV sports personality, moving with brash confidence from one American metropolis to another. But in a candid moment with writer Charles Wilkins, he admitted that he remained a Soo west ender wherever he roamed. "When I started going to the theatre in New York, I'm so big I'd always be worrying about whether or not the guy from behind could see. Here was this 40-year-old kid from the Soo slouched way down in his seat so as not to block the view."

Phil Esposito, playing for Team Canada in the 1972 Summit Series.

Grandfather Knows Best

Ron Francis grew up watching hockey at the Sault Memorial Gardens, but he almost didn't play junior at the arena. He had been thinking of accepting a scholarship to Cornell, but, eventually, he went with the Greyhounds' offer to play junior, with one condition: The junior team would pay for his university tuition if he didn't turn pro. The condition proved inconsequential, as Francis played but a single season for the Greyhounds before turning pro at 18 and going on to to a 24-year National Hockey League career that would see him help the Pittsburgh Penguins to the Stanley Cup in 1991 and 1992.

Francis enjoyed his season and a half (1980–82) performing in the Soo, although hometown fans could occasionally be rough. One night, after taking two foolish penalties, an older gentleman approached him in the penalty box and rapped him with his hat, ordering the player to "smarten up." Security grabbed the interloper immediately, but Ron told them to let him go. "It's OK, he's my grandfather," he explained.

STRATFORD

FOUNDED
Both the city of Stratford and the Avon River, which flows through it, were named in 1832 after Stratford-upon-Avon, England, the home of William Shakespeare. Stratford was a furniture manufacturing centre and railway junction when it was first settled, in the early 1830s. More recently, the Stratford Festival—an annual theatre event held every summer since 1953—has drawn hundreds of thousands of tourists to the city.

NATIVE-BORN NHL PLAYERS
Bill Chalmers, George Gee, Craig Hartsburg, Francis "Red" Kane, Nick Libett, Jud McAtee, Norm McAtee, Hank Monteith, Howie Morenz (born in Mitchell, ON), Allan Murray, Pat Murray, Rem Murray, Chris Taylor, Tim Taylor

FAMOUS LOCAL TEAMS
Junior: Stratford Braves, Stratford Cullitons, Stratford Kroehlers, Stratford Midgets; **Senior-pro:** Stratford Canadians, Stratford Combines, Stratford Cullitons, Stratford Indians, Stratford Majors, Stratford Nationals

CURRENT POPULATION
29,676

The Stratford Streak

In 1950, Canadian sportswriters were polled by Canadian Press to determine the most famous Canadian athlete in the first half of the 20th century. Four went with Maurice "The Rocket" Richard. Three chose Cyclone Taylor. Howie Morenz received the other 27 votes.

Morenz was born in 1902, in Mitchell, Ontario, and when 1920s sportswriters called him "The Stratford Streak" in response to the other great nicknames of the golden era of sports—"The Manassa Mauler" (Jack Dempsey) and "The Sultan of Swat" (Babe Ruth)—Morenz laughed and said, "No, boys, I grew up in Mitchell. It should be "The Mitchell Meteor"." Indeed, he played his first hockey in Mitchell, often a lone gladiator on the Thames, coaxing a chunk of coal along the ice with a homemade stick. He could skate for hours, outracing even the winter's cold.

Morenz's German-Canadian family moved to nearby Stratford when he was 14, where Howie decided to become a goalie, cramming wool stockings with Sunday supplements to serve as his goalie pads for his first organized game. Twenty-one pucks whistled by him that game. From then on, Howie played forward.

Soon he was the most famous person in Stratford, fashioning a new chapter in his legend with every game—scoring 11 goals for the senior Stratford Indians in Montreal one night, pouring in six for the junior Stratford Midgets in Kitchener the next. The first time sportswriter Elmer Ferguson saw the player, he had to shake his head; The Stratford Streak was skating so fast that everyone else on the ice appeared to be moving backward. And could he could shoot! Other players swept the puck. Morenz put all of himself into a shot, bowing the shaft of his stick before letting the puck fly.

The Montreal Canadiens and the Toronto St. Pats made Morenz offers after the Stratford sensation took the Midgets to the Memorial Cup in 1921, scoring six goals in a two-game, total-goal series that the Winnipeg Falcons won, 11–9.

Canadiens general manager Leo Dandurand, however, had the foresight to send an emissary bearing cash. Howie owed his tailor money, and he felt the weight of his other debts. The Habs covered them all. Morenz was now a Montreal Canadien.

Ontario was shocked that Morenz was allowed to go to Lower Canada—a term some understood to be more than a geographical designation. One minister wrote to a Toronto newspaper complaining that Dandurand was "luring an under-age boy to the wicked city of Montreal." In truth, Morenz took to Montreal like

"When he'd wind up behind the net he wasn't number 7, he was 777—just a blur."

a sailor to shore leave. He bought spats, wore three suits a day, played the ukulele at parties and drank in more than bright lights. The day before he was married, in 1926, he lost $1,500 on the horses.

Inside the arena, however, Morenz's lucky streak continued. During eight seasons with the Canadiens (1924–31), Morenz helped the team to three Stanley Cups, while he himself won two scoring championships and three most valuable player awards. But it was more than just numbers and trophies. Morenz captured the public's imagination, particularly francophone fans who happily accepted the story that number 7—"l'homme éclair" (lightning man)—was of French-Swiss origin.

Morenz perfected hockey's slalom run. "When he'd wind up behind the net he wasn't number 7, he was 777—just a blur," commented New York Americans former goalie and frequent opponent Roy Worters. King Clancy, who competed against The Stratford Streak when Clancy was a defenceman with the Ottawa Senators, once measured Morenz against other superstars: "I seen 'em all score goals," he told sportswriter Dick Beddoes. "Howe, wicked and deft, knocking everybody on their ass with his windshield-wiper elbows; Rocket Richard coming in mad, guys climbing all over him; Hull, booming a slapshot like a WWII cannon; Wayne Gretzky mesmerizing the defence as he waltzes across the blue line, then wafting a feathery pass to a fast-coming winger... But I never saw anybody—nobody—score a goal like Morenz on a furious charge down centre."

Morenz was loved in Montreal and hailed as a hero in his native Ontario as well—the most famous man in hockey. Streaks end by definition, however. A slump in 1933 turned into a drought in 1934. Dandurand couldn't stand to see the champion's decline, so he traded Morenz to Chicago. From there, the hockey player stumbled to New York. Six goals were all he had in him during the 1935-36 season.

The Canadiens rescued Morenz in 1936, bringing him back to Montreal and inserting him on a line once again with Aurel Joliat and Johnny "Black Cat" Gagnon. His play improved. The fans were happy. The remarriage seemed promising. Then the forward took an awkward spill into the boards while playing against the Chicago Blackhawks on 28 January 1937 at the Montreal Forum, breaking four bones in his ankle and leg.

Morenz knew his hockey career was over. When a player has reached the heights The Stratford Streak attained, crashing can be an awful business. While in hospital, Morenz drank to relieve pain and revive memories. One night he got up from the hospital bed. He wasn't supposed to. Maybe he thought he was back in Stratford, a kid again, hurrying to the game. Within a few steps, he fell. By the time he hit the floor, Howie Morenz, the greatest hockey player of his day, was dead.

Howie Morenz of the Montreal Canadiens.

SUDBURY

FOUNDED

Sudbury was originally a lumber camp called Ste-Anne-des-Pins (Saint Anne of the Pines). The town's fortunes changed forever during the construction of the Canadian Pacific Railway, in the 1870s. Blasting through rock to clear a path for the track, construction workers found glints of nickel copper ore. A mining town grew around the discovery. Sudbury was incorporated in 1883, its name coming from the CPR commissioner's wife, who had been born in Sudbury, England.

NATIVE-BORN NHL PLAYERS

Al Arbour, Larry Aurie, John Baby, Todd Bertuzzi, Frank Blum, Fred Boimistruck, Clarence Boucher, Andrew Brunette, Cummy Burton, Bryan Campbell, Wayne Carleton, Randy Carlyle, Marc Chorney, Bob Cook, Gary Croteau, Troy Crowder, Marc D'Amour, Gerry Desjardins, Ron Duguay, Craig Duncanson, Jack Egers, Bob Fitchner, John Flesch, Mike Foligno, Dave Fortier, Sean Gauthier, Aaron Gavey, Ed Giacomin, Mike Gillis, Redvers Green, Wilf "Shorty" Green, Dave Hannan, Shawn Heaphy, Jim Hofford, Shorty Horne, Yvon Labre, Marc Laforge, Kevin LaVallee, Dave Lowry, Bernie MacNeil, Troy Mallette, Derek McKenzie, Grant Mulvey, Paul Mulvey, Jim Pappin, Joel Prpic, Samuel Rothschild, Robert Sabourin, Mike Sands, Brian Savage, Rich Schulmistra, Al Secord, Daniel Seguin, Eddie Shack, Irv Spencer, Bob Sykes, Don Sylvestri, David Tataryn, Floyd Thomson, Jean-Guy Trudel, Kay Whitmore, Sean Whyte, Jim Wiemer, Robert Wilson, Roger Wilson

FAMOUS LOCAL TEAMS

Junior: Sudbury Cubs, Sudbury Jr. Wolves, Sudbury Cub Wolves, Sudbury Knights of Columbus, Sudbury Wolves; **Senior-pro:** Sudbury Creighton Mines, Sudbury Frood Miners, Sudbury Frood Tigers, Sudbury Industries, Sudbury Legionaires, Sudbury Mines, Sudbury Open Pit Miners, Sudbury Tigers, Sudbury Wolves

CURRENT POPULATION

155,219

Leader of the Pack

Local star Mike Foligno was one of the most successful and popular players in Sudbury Wolves' history, recording a franchise record of 150 points in the 1978–79 season with the junior team and delighting Wolves fans with a peculiar hop after every one of his goals, throwing his knees up to his chin. Foligno would perfect his trampoline-jump-in-a-basement celebration in the National Hockey League, recording 355 goals in a 14-year career with Detroit, Buffalo, Toronto and Florida.

In 2003, he returned to Sudbury, 23 years after he first left town, taking over as coach and general manager of the Wolves. Foligno also brought his son Nick with him, a forward who recorded 38 points in his 2004–05 rookie season—two more than his dad had recorded for the Wolves in his 1975–76 rookie year. Fans enjoyed having two Folignos to cheer for, and the Wolves established an attendance record in 2004–05, drawing an average of 4,270 fans a game.

The Old Lamplighter

It's fitting that a mining town such as Sudbury should produce, as its leading sports ambassador, a hockey legend with the nickname "The Old Lamplighter." That legend was Toe Blake—an inspirational leader who could beat teams wearing either skates or a fedora.

Toe, short for Hector (a name his kid sister never mastered), was born just outside Sudbury in Victoria Mines, which was a three-church community when he was born. But the mine that gave the town its name closed shortly after he was born, and consequently Blake grew into a hockey player in Sudbury.

By the time he was 19, everyone in the Big Nickel knew Toe Blake. He played for three local outfits in 1932—the junior Sudbury Cub Wolves, and two senior clubs, the Sudbury Wolves and the Sudbury Industries. Indeed, he secured a place in Sudbury sports history that season, leading the Cubs to a Memorial Cup over the Winnipeg Monarchs.

After that big win, Blake played senior for the Hamilton Tigers and declined a Toronto offer to turn pro. Most of Sudbury's best players would migrate south to play for the home-province Maple Leafs—Al Arbour, Eddie Shack, Jim Pappin and

The fabulous Punch Line, left to right: Maurice Richard, Elmer Lach and Hector "Toe" Blake.

Wayne "Swoop" Carleton in the 1960s, then later, Randy Carlyle, Al Secord and Mike Foligno. Blake moved to Montreal, however, instantly winning a Stanley Cup with the Maroons, in 1935, and then joining the Canadiens the following season. He led the National Hockey League in scoring in 1938–39, winning the nickname "The Old Lamplighter," as well as the league's most valuable player award.

Maurice Richard joined the Canadiens in 1942 and settled on a unit alongside Blake and Elmer Lach. They became the famous Punch Line. The Rocket could score; Lach could skate and pass; and Blake filled in everywhere, digging in corners, converting the Rocket's rebounds, setting up his own plays—doing whatever it took to win.

Perhaps Blake's greatest contribution was ensuring that the Rocket went off in the right direction. Blake had a big-brother air of confidence that made younger players comfortable. In Montreal's Stanley Cup-winning seasons of 1943–44 and 1945–46, captain Toe Blake was the obvious leader—the holler guy that players would follow into a fire. Still, for all his grit, he amassed only 12 minutes in penalties in both those seasons combined.

A leg injury ended his playing career, in 1948. He coached senior hockey in Valleyfield, Quebec, for a while. His old team, the Canadiens, meanwhile, couldn't seem to win the Stanley Cup, for all its talent, and fell apart again, in the spring of 1955, with the infamous Richard Riot over the star player's ejection from the team for the remainder of the season (see page 93). A new coach was needed. General Manager Frank Selke wanted Joe Primeau, a former Leafs star, but his assistant Kenny Reardon talked him into Blake, a bilingual leader with stature in Montreal, who might harness the Rocket.

Blake did not disappoint, leading the Canadiens to five straight Cups between 1956 and 1960. The Sudbury native was a tough coach. Dressing room lectures were sometimes conducted at a roaring jet engine decibel level. But he never embarrassed a player. When *Hockey Night in Canada* cameras were introduced to the Montreal Forum, Blake began yelling at the clock when dressing players down, ensuring that TV viewers couldn't determine the object of his scorn.

Blake was proud of where he came from and he made sure that Montreal scheduled preseason games with his old team, the Sudbury Wolves. During one famous meeting between the clubs, Blake was reminded of how the Sudbury team had got its last name.

The Canadiens were winning handily that night. Still, Blake worked his chewing gum, pushing his fedora back whenever the Canadiens repelled a Wolves attack. Near the game's end, Sudbury finally scored. The old Sudbury

As a coach, "The Old Lamplighter" Toe Blake would take the Montreal Canadiens to eight Stanley Cups wins in 13 seasons (1956–68).

Toronto Maple Leaf coach, Punch Imlach (right) keeps Eddie Shack after practice for a little chalk talk.

The Love Shack

The last week of February 1966 was a great moment in pop music history, with Nancy Sinatra's "These Boots Are Made for Walkin'"; the Bobby Fuller Four's "I Fought the Law"; the Beatles' "Nowhere Man"; and the Stones' "19th Nervous Breakdown", all vying for the number one spot,. But none of these classics could dislodge Douglas Rankine and the Secrets' jingle "Clear the Track, Here Comes Shack", from the top spot in Canada AM's top 40 that week.

The Shack in question was Sudbury's Eddie Shack, who played the game with all the abandon of a big puppy let loose in a wide field. As the success of "Clear the Track" demonstrated, fans loved Eddie, one of the great characters in the sport.

Shack could neither read nor write. He had started working in a Sudbury farmers' market at the age of eight and had stuck with the job, explaining, "Nobody ever paid you for being in Grade 3." On the road, he bugged other players to read him the sports section, saying, "I only got Grade 4, eh?"

Finally, an exasperated teammate put down the paper and said, "Tell me Eddie, how'd you ever get out of Grade 3?"

"Easy," he said, winking. "Used to lend the teacher my car."

auditorium exploded. Out from behind a curtain at one end of the building, the effigy of a wolf sprang forth, racing a guy wire that lapped the building high above the fans. With that, the sound of real wolves broke through auditorium loudspeakers. Then fans joined in, shouting, "Ow-ow-a-oooo, ow-ow-a-ooooo!"

Blake fumed at the bench. He hated being embarrassed. Yelping fans had barely settled in their seats when the puck returned to the Montreal zone. Captain Doug Harvey had both the puck and the trace of a smile on his face. Instead of clearing the puck behind the net, he fired it past startled teammate and goalie Jacques Plante. The barely winded Roadrunner burst through the curtain again, whizzing around the auditorium. Harvey returned to the bench, biting his lip. "Are you nuts?" Blake screamed.

"Sorry, Toe," Harvey responded. "It was worth it, just to see that wolf again."

Blake would tell that story decades later at a Sudbury hockey banquet, bringing down the house. A master of communications long before such a degree was available in school, Blake knew the value of humour—when to loosen up the guys with an offbeat story.

In 1967, journalist Red Fisher captured one of Blake's best routines for *Montreal Star* readers. The Canadiens were in a slump at the time. Blake came

"Whatever happens tonight, give the fans a show."

into the dressing room after a hard practice. He paced the room, staring at the floor. Players nudged each other. Conversations died. Now everyone stared at the coach. "Ralph," Blake finally called out to number 6, Ralph Backstrom, "I've got something to say to you."

Players braced themselves. Backstrom was in a slump. Blake always yelled at players he knew could take it—Backstrom, John Ferguson, Jean-Guy Talbot. But Ralph was down. Who knew how he'd react today?

"You know, about a month ago, we decided to have our door painted at home," Blake continued, pacing. "So the painter carefully removed the 2 and the 0 and the 6 from the front door. He did a pretty good job. Everything looked nice, except for one thing: The painter forgot to put back our address.

"You know weeks went by, and the mailman was going past our door and nobody could blame him because how was he supposed to know that our number was 206, if the numbers weren't there? The delivery men would come up our street, but they couldn't deliver the parcels and our groceries because the numbers weren't there. So for weeks we were missing mail and deliveries and, hell, how long was this going to go on?

"Finally, I got hold of the painter and I said to him, 'Listen, Dugal, when am I going to get back the numbers?'

"'Well, I'll tell you,' he said, 'I've got the 2 and I've got the 0, but I can't find the 6. No sir, I can't find it.'

"'It's funny you mention that, Dugal,' I told him, 'because we've got a 6 on our club, and I haven't been able to find him for the last two months either.'"

Backstrom and the Canadiens burst out laughing. Back-up goalie Charlie Hodge got a particular kick out of the story. "What are you laughing at, Charlie?" Toe snapped. "I could say the same thing about all the numbers between 1 and 30."

Now the players were really whooping it up, reacting with a single voice—a team, again! Blake ended by saying, "Whatever happens tonight, give the fans a show. Give them some entertainment. It's the least they deserve."

The Canadiens won that night, of course. They almost always did when Blake was behind the bench.

THUNDER BAY

FOUNDED

In 1678, the French had a fur-trading outpost at the junction of Lake Superior and the Kaministiquia River. The Northwest Company took over the trading post in 1803. Though a community known as Fort William already existed here, a Colonel Wolseley, arriving in the area in 1870 on his way to the Riel Rebellion, renamed a shipping depot Prince Arthur's Landing in honour of Queen Victoria's third son. For the next century, Fort William and Prince Arthur would wrangle over amalgamation, an event that finally came to pass in 1970, when the twin cities merged and took on the name of a local body of water, Thunder Bay. Thunder Bay is often referred to as the Lakehead, because it is situated at the top of the Great Lakes system.

NATIVE NHL PLAYERS
(FORT WILLIAM)

Jack Adams, Pete Backor, Steve Black, Gus Bodnar, Barton Bradley, Ron Busniuk, Larry Cahan, Tom Cook, Alex Delvecchio, Lee Fogolin, David Gatherum, Pete Goegan, Bud Jarvis, Ed Kachur, J. Bob Kelly, Danny Lewicki, Murdo MacKay, Louis Marcon, Rudolph Migay, Bud Poile, Donald Poile, Charlie Sands, Wayne Stephenson, Gaye Stewart, Ralph Stewart, Joe Szura, Ted Tucker, Gary Veneruzzo,

James Ward, Aubrey Webster, Benny Woit, Stephen Wojciechowski

NATIVE NHL PLAYERS
(PORT ARTHUR)

John Adams, Stanley Baluik, Ken Brown, Ray Ceresino, Dave Creighton, Franklin Daley, Bruce Gamble, James Haggarty, Steve Hrymnak, Connie Madigan, Jim McLeod, Stu McNeill, Nelson Pyatt, John Schella, Kenneth Stewart, Gord Wilson

NATIVE NHL PLAYERS AFTER
1970 MERGER (THUNDER BAY)

Jeremy Adduono, Rick Adduono, Peter Bakovic, John Bednarski, Robert Bodak, Rick Bragnalo, David Bruce, Mike Busniuk, Danny Gruen, Jeff Heerema, Mike Hordy, Bill Houlder, Tony Hrkac, Jason Jaspers, Trevor Johansen, Greg Johnson, Ryan Johnson, Scott King, David Latta, Trevor Letowski, Norm Maciver, Jeff McDill, Lou Nistico, Steve Passmore, Walt Poddubny, Taylor Pyatt, Steve Rucchin, Patrick Sharp, Eric Staal, Vern Stenlund, Ron Talakoski, Mike Tomlak, Vic Venasky, Rob Whistle, Murray Wing, Colin Zulianello

FAMOUS LOCAL TEAMS
(PORT ARTHUR)

Junior: Port Arthur Bruins, Port Arthur Flyers, Port Arthur Juniors, Port Arthur Lake City, Port Arthur Marrs, Port Arthur North Stars, Port Arthur

Ports, Port Arthur West End Bruins; **Senior-pro:** Port Arthur Bearcats, Port Arthur Columbus Club, Port Arthur Indians, Port Arthur Pascoes, Port Arthur Ports, Port Arthur Shipbuilders, Port Arthur Shuniahs, Port Arthur Thunder Bays

FAMOUS LOCAL TEAMS
(FORT WILLIAM)

Junior: Fort William Beavers, Fort William Canadians, Fort William Cubs, Fort William Dominoes, Fort William Forts, Fort William Hurricanes, Fort William Hurricane Rangers, Fort William Kams, Fort William Maroons, Fort William Rangers; **Senior-pro:** Fort William Canada Car, Fort William Forts, Fort William Hurricanes, Fort William Legion, Fort William Maple Leafs, Fort William Thundering Herd, Fort William Wanderers

FAMOUS LOCAL TEAMS AFTER 1970
MERGER (THUNDER BAY)

Junior: Thunder Bay Beavers, Thunder Bay Hurricanes, Thunder Bay Twins, Thunder Bay Vulcans; **Senior-pro:** Thunder Bay Beavers, Thunder Bay Flyers, Thunder Bay Twins

CURRENT POPULATION
109,016

The Flying Forts

One of the most famous planes in World War II was the 74-foot long, 104-foot wide, $276,000 Flying Fortress—between 1935 and 1945, the fastest and most expensive long-range bomber of its day.

Three famous bombers also came out of northern Ontario during the war years. In fact, these young men came from the same town and would play on the same line for the Toronto Maple Leafs. The Lakehead cities have indeed produced a treasure trove of hockey silverware—nine Allan Cup championships and two Memorial Cup wins, not to mention 88 National Hockey League players. Still, any conversation about Lakehead hockey always starts with the story of three Fort William hockey players: Gaye Stewart, Gus Bodnar and Bud Poile, or as Canada knew them during the war years, the Flying Forts.

Linemates on the Toronto Maple Leafs during WWII, the Flying Forts all hailed from Fort William (now Thunder Bay); left to right Bud Poile, Gaye Stewart and Gus Bodnar.

Maybe the trio captured fans' imaginations because the players made their marks so young. Eighteen-year-old Gaye Stewart joined the Maple Leafs for the 1942 playoffs, won a Stanley Cup, then raced home to finish his high school year. Stewart would win the NHL rookie award the next season playing alongside another teenager from Fort William, Bud Poile. And in 1943–44, 17-year-old Gus Bodnar arrived in Toronto, scoring a goal for the Leafs 15 seconds into his first game. He, too, would win the NHL rookie award.

Poile (army) and Stewart (navy) joined the war effort in the fall of 1944, but the Flying Forts were all together again in 1947 for Toronto's spring championship drive. At least one of the Flying Forts participated in three of the Maple Leafs' Stanley Cup-winning seasons (1942, 1945, 1947), playing before tens of thousands in Maple Leaf Gardens.

Years later, however, Bodnar would tell hockey writer Bill Boyd that some of his happiest hockey memories were from playing on wind-blasted outdoor Fort William rinks in front of fans reluctant to cheer for fear of freezing their tonsils. "[Hockey] was all outdoors," Bodnar remembered. "Firemen would flood vacant lots. Then we'd have to look after them. And there was river skating. It was great when the wind would clear off a big space. The ice was so hard you had to have really sharp skates. Most of the time we sharpened our skates with a file.

"It was so darned cold. I'm talking 20, 30 below. We didn't mind, but we didn't get many people watching us. I remember the butcher's meat came in brown wax paper, so I'd put on a thin sock, wrap the paper around [my foot], then put on a wool sock. That helped a bit."

Bodnar first met Poile when the two of them made the junior Fort William Hurricane Rangers in 1940 ("Hurricane" was presumably an acknowledgment of the winds that roared off Lake Superior). Gaye Stewart was on the cross-city rival team, the Port Arthur West End Bruins. Competition between the teams was fierce but stimulating. "I look back and think those were some of my best days in hockey," Bodnar recalled.

The Lakehead cities' winning streak in hockey would continue after The

Flying Forts. Port Arthur's Edgar Laprade would win the NHL rookie award in 1946, making him the third Fort William or Port Arthur player to capture the prize within four straight years. And in 1948, the Port Arthur West End Bruins won the Memorial Cup. In addition, while in the NHL, Fort William's Jack Adams, general manager of the Detroit Red Wings, put together a team that would win seven league championships in a row and four Stanley Cups between 1948 and 1955. One of his star Red Wings players would be Fort William's Alex Delvecchio, who starred for Detroit for 24 seasons.

Fort William hockey players even had luck dabbling in other sports. Ben Woit, a key member of the city's 1948 Memorial Cup team, told Bill Boyd about the first day he and Indianapolis Colts (American Hockey League)

"I look back and think those were some of my best days in hockey," Bodnar recalled.

teammate Terry Sawchuk had at the track in the late '40s. (Both players would jump to the Detroit Red Wings in the early 1950s.)

"We asked a guy what we were supposed to do and he said, you bet. So we started betting, a dollar each. We win the first six games in a row… We go to the window for the seventh race, and suddenly there's a crowd around. The word is out that we're winning, and they all want to know what we're betting. We say we don't know. Then, a waiter comes over and says there's someone wants to see us upstairs in the restaurant.

"We go up there. [Then superstar singer] Frankie Laine's sitting at a table. What do you know, if we don't win the seventh, too. He buys us dinner and he asks who we're betting on, and we said we don't know. Anyway, we won that one, too, eight or nine in a row."

Nine would appear to be Thunder Bay's lucky number. In the spring of 2005, Derek Levanen of the Thunder Bay Bombers scored in overtime against the Montmagny Sentinelles, to give the Thunder Bay senior team a 4-3 win and the 2005 Allan Cup. The Bombers first had to dispense with Theoren Fleury's Horse Lake Thunder before reaching the finals. With the win over the Sentinelles, Thunder Bay celebrated a record ninth Canadian senior championship.

BEST SENIOR HOME IN CANADA

The national playoff for senior hockey supremacy in Canada, the **Allan Cup**, was valued almost as highly as the Stanley Cup in the first 55 years of the 20th century. This senior hockey championship was valued so highly, in fact, that most competitive senior teams sprinkled their roster with, shall we say, semi-pro players. In the mid-1950s, however, after television made the **Toronto Maple Leafs** and the **Montreal Canadiens** available across the country, senior hockey lost much of its allure and truly became the province of passionate, committed amateurs. Whatever the era, Thunder Bay teams dominated the sport. The **Port Arthur Bearcats** won the Allan Cup in 1925, 1926, 1929 and 1939, while the **Thunder Bay Twins** took the trophy in 1975, 1984, 1985 and 1989. The **Thunder Bay Bombers** won the award in 2005.

Unhappy Jack

A force of nature to rival Lake Superior, "Jolly" Jack Adams is the only hockey player to have his name on the Stanley Cup as a player, manager and coach. Adams represented Fort William as a junior with the Fort William Maple Leafs in the old Northern Michigan Hockey League in 1914–15, and later won Stanley Cups as a centre with the Toronto Arenas (1918) and the Ottawa Senators (1927). He is most famous, however, for assembling the great Detroit Red Wings team of the late '40s, then tearing the club apart in a vengeful fury, in 1956, after players voted to form a union. A scene in the CBC movie *Net Worth*, in which Adams (played by Al Waxman) shows up at the rink, on the first day of training camp, to upbraid the team after a Cup loss to the Canadiens the previous spring and singling out even Ted Lindsay ("Terrible Ted, my ass"), is one of the great moments in sports movies. Actor Waxman later offered a thoughtful assessment of his character to journalist Gare Joyce:

Adams had a happy marriage but no children. So he made the team his family. The players were his boys. He stood beside Lindsay when he took his U.S. citizenship. He was godfather to his players' kids. He went to their weddings, approved their marriages, but resented their mates… He called Howe "The Big Fellah" but wouldn't let him get married until he was 25. This man had immense love, but with love came a proprietorial. The players were children and chattel. Adams put together one of the great teams of all time, the Wings teams of the '50s. When they lost to Montreal, he didn't just look at it as a disappointment. He looked at it as betrayal by his children. When Lindsay put together a players' association, he took it as the ultimate betrayal.

TIMMINS

FOUNDED

Trading posts existed in the Timmins area in the early 18th century, but Timmins remained largely unsettled until 1909, when prospector Harry Preston lost his footing on a rocky knoll and stripped clean a blanket of moss to reveal a vein of gold. In 1911, Noah Timmins created a town to house the workers at the nearby Hollinger Mine.

NATIVE-BORN NHL PLAYERS

Bill Barilko, Baz Bastien, William Cameron, Real Chevrefils, Armand Delmonte, Shean Donovan, Tony Grabowski, Pat Hannigan, Paul Harrison, Ron Hudson, Al LeBrun, Rick Lessard, Frank Mahovlich, Pete Mahovlich, Hector Marini, Hill Menard, Howie Menard, Raymond Powell, Dale Rolfe, Allan Stanley, Steve Sullivan, Eric Vail

FAMOUS LOCAL TEAMS:
Junior: Timmins, Timmins Combines, Timmins Golden Bears; **Senior-pro:** Timmins Buffalo Ankerites, Timmins Canadians, Timmins Flyers, Timmins Majors, Timmins Allied Steelers, Timmins Seniors

CURRENT POPULATION
50,000

NASHVILLE CATS

Like so many native Timmins National Hockey League stars before him, Steve "Sully" Sullivan played for the Toronto Maple Leafs. But he would star for the Chicago Blackhawks, where he was their best player in 2001 and 2002, before joining Timmins native Shania Twain's lead and going country, travelling to Nashville to play for the NHL's Predators. In 2004, Sullivan would meet Twain backstage at Shania Twain Day in Timmins.

The Big T

The famous Toronto hockey team that won four Stanley Cups in the '60s might have been properly called the Northern Ontario Maple Leafs, as more than half the team came from the province's northern mining towns. Dick Duff, Larry Hillman and Mike Walton hailed from Kirkland Lake. Tim Horton came from Cochrane. Eddie Shack and Jim Pappin were Sudbury natives, while George Armstrong was raised in Falconbridge, just outside the Big Nickel.

Perhaps most important of all, were the Timmins contingent: dependable-as-a-Swiss-clock defender Allan Stanley, and occasional Superman—"The Big M"—Frank Mahovlich. Other natives from the Big T might have made it to the Leafs lineup that decade, except that two of the city's most famous players, Les Costello and Bill Barilko, had been called away—Costello, to the priesthood, and Barilko, by God himself.

Three of these local legends were once together in a Timmins rink. The year was 1949. Frank Mahovlich, then just 11, was in the stands watching, while the city's reigning hockey heroes were both on the ice. The players' ice time was short-lived, though, for barging Barilko lined up Costello and banged him high into the crowd. Mahovlich was mesmerized. "I'd never seen anything like it," he would later say.

Mahovlich would find his access blocked to Timmins' main employer. The player's father, Peter Mahovlich, a Croatian immigrant who had settled in Schumacher, now part of Timmins, went to every one of the city's gold, silver, copper and zinc mines and told the foremen, "My sons, Frank and Peter, don't work here—ever!—understand?" Working underground was a hard life, especially in the '40s and '50s. Big Pete, a miner himself, walked with a limp, the result of a work-related fall. He wanted another kind of life for his sons—something better than climbing into stiff-with-sweat, vinegar-smelling mining gear for shifts so long that you never saw the sun in winter.

Frank Mahovlich would learn that professional hockey had some gruelling

The Big M Frank Mahovlich crashes the net for the Maple Leafs.

shifts, as well. A good Catholic boy, he arrived in Toronto in 1953 at age 15 to play hockey for the Leafs' (Catholic) junior team, St. Mike's.

His first day in town, he got off the train at Toronto's Union Station, grabbed a streetcar on Bay Street, and headed for St. Michael's school at Bathurst and St. Clair. Frank's hometown of Schumacher was five minutes by foot every which way, so the teenager grew apprehensive after the streetcar motored for 10 minutes without any sign of his school. He ran to the front of the car. "Have we passed St. Michael's yet?" he asked the driver.

Apparently not. The car travelled several miles and a dozen stops.

"We pass St. Michael's?" he asked again.

No, he was told.

An eternity ticked by. Were they still even in Toronto? Sick with worry, Frank made another pilgrimage to the front of the streetcar. "Are you sure we haven't missed St. Michael's?"

"Sit down and shut up, and I will tell you when we pass St. Mike's!" the driver told him.

Frank's early hockey days in Toronto were filled with great moments. He was the best junior player in the province. Bobby Hull, then with the St. Catharines Black Hawks, once recalled how Mahovlich went through teams "like a dose of salts traveled through a widow's body." Frank soon became The Big M, on account of the M on his St. Mike's jersey, but also because Leafs executive King Clancy took to calling him Moses. Besides, no sportswriter wanted to tangle with spelling Mahovlich 10 times a story, when on deadline.

The Big M won the National Hockey League rookie-of-the-year award with the Leafs in 1957–58, and scored 47 goals for Toronto in the first 56 games of the 1960–61 season. He seemed on the verge of becoming the new Howe, Beliveau or Richard—the next Canadian standard bearer of hockey excellence.

As it turned out, Frank never reached the Everest summit of 50 goals—not that season or ever. Mahovlich was a sensitive, finely tuned athlete who would spend his hockey prime toiling for a coach and general manager every bit as abrasive as the streetcar driver he'd met that first day in Toronto.

Punch Imlach believed in defensive play; Frank was a creative playmaker. Imlach was The Big I—"I won this...I won that." And just as I precedes M in the alphabet, so general manager-coaches came ahead of stars in the NHL, during the 1960s. Imlach deliberately maimed his big star's name ("Mahalovich") and mocked him in the papers ("Hockey is mainly a streetcar named desire, and sometimes Frank misses the train"). Worse, he punished the team with marathon skating sessions—sometimes hours at a time the morning after a bad game, just circling the rink until the players experienced the copper taste of exhaustion on their tongues.

Frank helped the Leafs win four Stanley Cups in Toronto (1962–64, 1967), but he was frequently unhappy. Some fans at Maple Leaf Gardens booed him. Twice, he had to leave the team in the middle of the season, suffering from nervous exhaustion. Ironically, like his mining dad in Timmins long before, Frank's job prevented him from seeing much sun in the wintertime.

At long last, in 1968, he was traded to Detroit. "I feel like somebody lifted a piano off my back," he said at the time. Finally he was The Big M again, scoring 49 goals on a line with Gordie Howe. In 1971, Mahovlich was traded to Montreal, where he would enjoy the happiest days of his career, playing with younger brother, Pete, helping the Canadiens win Stanley Cups in 1971 and 1973. Watching the re-energized Big M play became a joy again—seeing how he grabbed the puck in open ice, then tore off, chest high, arms swinging from side to side, conquering the rink with ever-increasing strides.

After Bill Barilko and Frank Mahovlich, Timmins' legacy of whirlwind skaters would be reconfirmed in the 1990s with the arrival of forward cylone Steve Sullivan.

The Ballad of Bill Barilko

The most frequently requested photograph from the Hockey Hall of Fame is the 1951 shot of Bill Barilko suspended in mid-air, watching the puck sail past Montreal goalie Gerry McNeil's outstretched blocker. The son of Russian immigrants, Bashin' Bill Barilko was a wild-as-grass kid who played on Timmins' top junior team, the Holman Pluggers, in 1942. Bill skated like someone falling out of a tree, but, oh, could he hit. His first stop after Timmins was Los Angeles and the Hollywood Wolves (Western Hockey League), where he impressed not only hockey scouts with his checks, but also a legion of female fans, some of whom proposed marriage on fancy stationery. In 1947, at age 20, Bill arrived with the Toronto Maple Leafs during a blizzard, startling veterans with the cheery salute, "Boys, the sun is really shining." Shortly before his famous 1951 goal, Leafs coach Joe Primeau threatened to get a big hook to yank Bill off the ice when he skated out of position. After leaving his post to win the Stanley Cup, Barilko grabbed Primeau and laughed, "Bet you're glad you didn't use the hook this time?" The goal won Toronto the Stanley Cup, making Bill famous right across Canada. A few months later, back in Timmins, he begged a local sportsman, Dr. Ernie Hudson, to take him up north in his plane to go fishing in James Bay. Barilko's mother didn't want him to go. She had a premonition. The plane never returned, occasioning the largest manhunt in Canadian history. The searchers didn't find the plane. The Leafs stopped winning the Stanley Cup. Some called the losing streak "The Curse of Bill Barilko." The rumours and curse continued. Then, in 1962, Toronto finally won again. Timmins native Frank Mahovlich was climbing into a convertible for the '62 Stanley Cup parade when a fellow player approached with news: "They found Billy's body," he said.

TORONTO

FOUNDED

Like many other Canadian settlements, Toronto's early history was shaped by hostilities between France and Britain. In 1750, the French built Fort Toronto on the east bank of the Humber River. After defeating France in 1760, in the Seven Years War, the British took control of Toronto. In 1812, Toronto was once again buffeted by international tensions when the United States declared war against Britain. Toronto was raided twice and, in 1813, briefly taken by U.S. forces. Peace was declared the following year, and the town's rapid expansion continued with the arrival of waves of immigrants from Britain and elsewhere in Europe. Upon Confederation, in 1867, Toronto was named the capital of the new province of Ontario.

NATIVE NHL PLAYERS

Doug Acomb, Douglas Adam, Jeff Ambrosio, Peter Ambroziak, Mike Amodeo, John Anderson, Lou Angotti, Syl Apps Jr., Anthony Aquino, Bob Armstrong, Tim Armstrong, Frederick Arthur, Steve Atkinson, Vern Ayers, Reid Bailey, Earl Balfour, Steve Bancroft, Darren Banks, Norm Barnes, Dave Barr, Bruce Bell, Frank Bennett, Drake Berehowsky, Nick Beverley, Hugh Bolton, Bruce Boudreau, Rick Bourbonnais, Bill Bowler, Carl Brewer, Ken Broderick, Len Broderick, Ross Brooks, Gord Brydson, Bruce Bullock, Edward Burke, Marty Burke, Dave Burrows, Mike Byers, Terry Caffery, Bret Callighen, Patsy Callighen, Scott Campbell, Steve Cardwell, Billy Carroll, Anson Carter, Gino Cavallini, Paul Cavallini, Rob Cimetta, Jason Cirone, Dan Clark, Wally Clune, Gary Coalter, Steve Coates, Carlo Colaiacovo, Tom Colley, Gary Collins, Brian Conacher, Charles Conacher, Lionel Conacher, Pete Conacher, Roy Conacher, Edward Convey, Michael Corbett, Norm Corcoran, Rob Cowie, Dale Craigwell, Bart Crashley, Brian Curran, Trevor Daley, Bob Davidson, Robert DeCourcy, Valentine Delory, Gerry Denoird, Kevin Devine, Gary Dillon, Wayne Dillon,

Chuck Dinsmore, Peter Douris, Bruce Draper, Kris Draper, Bruce Driver, John Drummond, Rick Dudley, Ken Duggan, Steve Durbano, William Durnan, Jeff Eatough, Tim Ecclestone, Tom Edur, Gary Edwards, John English, Bob Essensa, Chris Evans, Daryl Evans, Paul Evans, Randy Exelby, Norman Farr, Walt Farrant, Glen Featherstone, Tony Featherstone, Mark Fitzpatrick, Paul Flache, Patrick Flatley, Adam Foote, Vernon Forbes, Dwight Foster, Jimmy Fowler, Bob Frampton, Lou Franceschetti, Bob Fryday, Lawrence Fullan, Jody Gage, Percy Galbraith, Troy Gamble, Bill Gardner, Dave Gardner, Ray Gariepy, Dudley Garrett, Steve Gatzos, Jack Gelineau, Mario Giallonardo, Paul Gillis, Kenny Girard, Brian Glennie, Fred Glover, Howie Glover, Warren Godfrey, Larry Goodenough, Chris Govedaris, David Goverde, Pat Graham, Adam Graves, Jeff Greenlaw, John Grisdale, David Haas, George Hainsworth, Bob Halkidis, Doug Halward, Red Hamill, Reg Hamilton, Ron Handy, Jeff Harding, David Harlock, Bill Harris, Billy Harris, Dale Hawerchuk, Darren Haydar, John Henderson, Murray Henderson, Adam Henrich, Red Heron, Greg Hickey, Andre Hidi, Randy Hillier, Dan Hinton, Lionel Hitchman, Todd Hlusko, Paul Hoganson, Albert Holway, Scott Howson, Allan Huggins, Bob Hurlburt, Ron Hurst, Brent Imlach, Peter Ing, Johnny Ingoldsby, Ron Ingram, Gary Inness, Robbie Irons, Richard Jackman, Art Jackson, Harvey Jackson, John Jakopin, Gary Jarrett, Wes Jarvis, Bill Jennings, Bernie Johnston, Ed Kastelic, Mike Keating, Donald Keenan, Chris Kelly, Mike Kennedy, David Kerr, Rick Kessell, Frank King, Hobie Kitchen, Bill Knibbs, Paul Knox, Mike Knuble, Chris Kontos, Joe Kowal, Alan Kuntz, Ken Kuzyk, Nick Kypreos, Neil Labatte, Ron Lalonde, Steve Langdon, Craig Laughlin, Danny Lawson, Gary Leeman, Manny Legace, Ken Lockett, Bob Lorimer, Darren Lowe, Steve

Ludzik, Chuck Luksa, Dave Lumley, Jack Lynch, Steve Lyon, Calum MacKay, Barry MacKenzie, Kevin Maguire, Mark Major, Nevin Markwart, Gary Marsh, Paul Marshall, Tom Martin, Dennis Maruk, Jamie Masters, Bead May, Jamal Mayers, Clifford McBride, Sandy McCarthy, Tom McCarthy, Tom "Jug" McCarthy Brian McCutcheon, Brian McDonald, Robert McDonald, Donald McGregor, Mike McKee, Steve McKenna, Sidney McNabney, Gerry Meehan, Brent Meeke, Greg Meredith, Scott Metcalfe, Glen Metropolit, Rick Middleton, Greg Millen, Norm Milley, Craig Mills, William Mitchell, Alfie Moore, Angelo Moretto, Marc Moro, Elwyn Morris, Dave Morrison, George Morrison, Jim Moxey, Craig Muni, Dunc Munro, Brian Murphy, Mike Murphy, Ken Murray, Rob Murray, Jason Muzzatti, Mark Napier, David Nemirovsky, Lance Nethery, Michael Neville, Mike Nykoluk, John O'Flaherty, Keith Osborne, Mark Osborne, Danny O'Shea, Kevin O'Shea, Mike Palmateer, Brad Park, George Parson, Joe Paterson, Doug Patey, Larry Patey, Steve Payne, Mike Peca, Mike Pelyk, Jim Pettie, Charles Phillips, Harry Pidhirny, Alex Pirus, Thomas Polanic, Tom Price, Keith Primeau, Mike Prokopec, Harvey Pulford, John Purves, Bill Quackenbush, Maxwell Quackenbush, George Ranieri, Greg Redquest, Dave Reid, David Reid, Jim Roberts, Jimmy Roberts, Eddie Rodden, Paul Ronty, Bill Root, Mike Rosati, Rolly Roulston, Ronnie Rowe, Kent Ruhnke, John Salovaara, David Salvian, Peter Sarno, Ganton Scott, Howard Scruton, Luke Sellars, George Servinis, Sean Shanahan, Steve Shields, Jack Shill, William Shill, Steve Shutt, Michael Siltala, Todd Simon, Cliff Simpson, Al Sims, Donald Smillie, Al Smith, Arthur Smith, Hooley Smith, Norman Smith, Sidney Smith, Stuart Smith, Rod Smylie, Christopher Speyer, George Standing, Fred Stanfield, Jack Stanfield, Jim Stanfield, Phillip Stein, Bill Stewart, John Stewart,

Toronto, looking toward the Post Office, c. 1890.

Steve Stone, Mike Stothers, Ken Strong, Frank Sullivan, Peter Sullivan, Pee Wee Summerhill, Rick Tabaracci, Tony Tanti, Ralph Taylor, Bill Terry, Rhys Thomson, Morris Titanic, Daniel Tkachuk, Kirk Tomlinson, Mike Torchia, Raffi Torres, Mike Veisor, Steve Vickers, Jeff Ware, Chick Webster, Donald Webster, Kevin Weekes, Stephen Weiss, Bill White, Barry Wilkins, Behn Wilson, Dunc Wilson, Lefty Wilson, Ron Wilson, James Witherspoon, Jason Woolley, Roy Worters, John Wright, Howard Young, Warren Young, Ron Zanussi, Peter Zezel

FAMOUS LOCAL TEAMS

Junior: Toronto Aura Lee, Toronto Bowles Rangers, Toronto British Consoles, Toronto Canoe Club, Toronto Cubs, Toronto Danforths, Toronto Eurekas, Toronto Granites, Toronto Lions, Toronto Marlboros, Toronto Moose, Toronto Nationals, Toronto Native Sons, Toronto St. Andrews, Toronto St. Michael's Majors, Toronto Victorias, Toronto Young Rangers;

Senior-pro: Toronto 228th, Toronto AAC, Toronto AC Maroons, Toronto Arenas, Toronto Argonauts, Toronto Army Daggers, Toronto Army Shamrocks, Toronto Aura Lee, Toronto Blueshirts, Toronto British Consols, Toronto Canoe Club, Toronto Crescents, Toronto Dominions, Toronto Dukes, Toronto Falcons, Toronto Goodyears, Toronto Granites, Toronto Lyndhursts, Toronto Maple Leafs, Toronto Millionaires, Toronto Nationals, Toronto Navy, Toronto Ontarios, Toronto Pros, Toronto Riversides, Toronto Shamrocks, Toronto St. Pats

CURRENT POPULATION

4,682,897

Opening night at Maple Leaf Gardens, 12 November 1931.

The Maple Leafs Are Coming

British soldiers in the War of 1812 were the first to earn the most famous name in Canadian sports. The scarlet tunics of the Brits made them easy bull's eyes for American snipers, so the soldiers began stripping maple trees, tucking leaves into their uniforms for camouflage. Soon the Yanks began calling their British enemies "Maple Leafs."

More than 100 years later, in 1926, another soldier, a decorated World War I hero, lifted the design from a maple leaf badge of service, applying the crest to the jersey of a sports team that would conquer English-speaking Canada. The war hero was Constantine Falkland Cary Smythe, and his hockey team, the Toronto Maple Leafs.

The self-made millionaire was born a few blocks from Maple Leaf Gardens, the rink he built during the cold heart of the Depression. But before making his money and building the Gardens, Conn Smythe made himself into a flinty, fearless operator in France, on the killing fields of World War I. He won the Military Cross in 1916, completing a daring rescue near enemy lines, and later transferred to the Royal Flying Corps, where the Protestant reconnaissance pilot argued continuously with his Irish Catholic co-pilot observer over the path to salvation. One day, their plane was hit. As the vessel whistled earthward, spitting flames, Smythe shouted to his mate, "In about a minute we're going to find out which one of us is right."

He walked away from that crash and a subsequent argument with a German captor, who promptly shot Smythe—the bullet pierced the prisoner's flight jacket without touching any of his 120 pounds. Surviving prison camp, Smythe returned to Toronto, where, proceeding on the assumption that his luck was endless, he amassed a fortune in construction while coaching the successful University of Toronto hockey team, a feat that won him employment, in 1926, with the National Hockey League's newborn New York Rangers. A few months into the general manager's job, however, he was fired and he took his $10,000 settlement to Montreal, riding every penny on his old alma mater in a hockey game against McGill University. U of T won. Smythe then staked his swelling bankroll on the underdog NHL team, the Toronto St. Pats, in a match against the Ottawa Senators, scoring big again. Next, he made the biggest gamble of his life, purchasing the last place, friendless St. Pats for $160,000 with gambling winnings.

Much of Smythe's success up until then had been the result of luck and daring, but he soon proved how well he understood business, hockey, Toronto—indeed, the whole Dominion of Canada. At the time, the St. Patricks were a failed franchise, playing out of a small rink—the Mutual Street Arena—to a working-class Irish fan base. And pro hockey was viewed skeptically, with players and teams across the country steadfastly holding onto their amateur status. Many who knew the game believed that senior hockey represented the true Canadian sporting ideal.

Smythe moved quickly to elevate the status of his new enterprise. He said that he got the idea for his team's new name and logo from one of his old war medals, but the maple leaf was already a universal Canadian symbol, replicated on pennies, nickels, dimes and quarters. By changing the team's name from the St. Patricks to the Maple Leafs, adding a veined leaf crest and changing the sweater colours from Irish green to Great Lakes blue, the Toronto owner began to transform a private club into a national institution.

Opening night speeches at the Gardens, with a young Foster Hewitt on the left.

Opening Night Jitters

On 6 February 1922, Foster Hewitt was kibitzing with *Toronto Star* deskmate, Gordon Sinclair, when his boss shouted, "Foster, c'mere a minute. Got a job for you." The job was a junior hockey game between the Toronto Argonauts and the city's Parkdale club.

When Foster arrived at the Mutual Street Arena, he discovered the *Star* had removed three seats next to the penalty bench, replacing them with a phone booth and stool. Foster sat there munching on a five-cent hot dog and figured out how to deliver a hockey broadcast. The assignment wasn't easy. The *Star* had forgotten to put air holes in the booth. And instead of talking into a microphone, Hewitt had to use a telephone. After every few minutes, the operator would ask for change.

Didn't matter. Foster got caught up in the game, talking nonstop for three hours. Along the way, he developed the excited style that made him famous. His trademark cry "He shoots, he scores!" just came to him.

Nobody at the *Star* thought about the broadcast until letters poured in. The game had been a sensation. Foster Hewitt was now Canada's first sportscaster and soon began broadcasting National Hockey League St. Pats games.

By 1931, the St. Pats had become the Maple Leafs. Owner Conn Smythe asked Hewitt where he wanted to be stationed in the team's new building, Maple Leaf Gardens. Hewitt coveted an aerial view, so he visited a store on Bay Street, marching up and down stairs in search of an ideal perspective. The fifth floor, 56 feet from the sidewalk, seemed perfect. At that distance, he could see everyone, yet he could pick out individuals. "I want my booth 56 feet above the ice," he told Smythe.

The opening of Maple Leaf Gardens was a gala affair. The crowd wore tuxedos and fancy dresses. Hewitt was all dressed up and eager to visit his broadcast perch. But when he got to the top of the Gardens, his blood turned colder than the ice below. The catwalk to his booth was no wider than his hips. And there were no guardrails! He started crossing over the rink like a high-wire walker, flapping his arms. Then, he made the mistake of looking down. The ice, five stories below, was a magnet pulling at his chest. Foster Hewitt fell to his knees and crawled the rest of his way with his eyes closed.

In time guardrails were installed, and two local stations grew into a national network. By the late 1930s, no one needed a radio to hear Foster Hewitt. He was in the air. Political pundit Dalton Camp remembered encountering Hewitt's voice while on leave from the army:

> I recall walking an empty street in a cold Canadian town on a Saturday night, in the sharp, biting cold, smoke rising from chimneys of huddled, shuttered houses, inside lights dimmed by drawn curtains, and then hearing the voice of Foster Hewitt… Hearing the unseen but familiar rhythms of the game, the urgent voice, and the sound of the crowd rising and falling as a chorus as practiced as any church choir. It was an epiphanous moment and, I have since thought, there has been nothing like it, nothing so unique, in all the entertainment arts in the national memory.

The 1967 Leafs celebrate their
Stanley Cup win.

Crucially, he promoted the Maple Leafs as virtuous action heroes. Players
had to wear a suit and tie on the road. And no card game stronger than rummy
was allowed on train rides. Trent Frayne, in a marvelous essay on the Leafs
owner, noted that Smythe twice introduced a team captain to national broadcast
audiences as, "Syl Apps, our captain, who does not smoke or drink."

The owner's boldest course of action was to build a grand new stage for
hockey during the most nerve-racking years of the Depression. Designed by
Ross & Macdonald, an elite Montreal architectural firm that had also designed
Toronto's Royal York Hotel, College Park and Union Station, Maple Leaf
Gardens was completed in five fast months, during 1931, for $1.5 million dollars.
Not just a hockey rink, the Gardens was an antidote to the Depression, a dream
refuge from the grim realities of the day. "We want a place to go, where people
can go with evening clothes, if they want to come there from a dinner or party,"
is how Smythe imagined the Gardens in a conversation with Greg Clark of the
Toronto Star. "We need...everything new and clean, a place that people can be
proud to take their wives or girlfriends to."

Smythe understood and knew how to play the media. His father had been
a reporter for the old *Toronto World*. And he would give Maple Leafs radio broadcaster Foster Hewitt full access to the new Gardens, allowing him to choose
the location of his workspace. Smythe also insisted on staging Hewitt's work on

Saturday, the social night of the week. By the end of the 1930s, Hewitt's tense, vivid renditions of games in Smythe's "evening gown" arena reached one in five Canadians—two million rapt listeners every Saturday night. Smythe had turned a floundering franchise into Canada's team in less than a decade.

Of course, winning helped. And Smythe deserves enormous credit for fashioning a team that appeared in 13 Stanley Cups between 1931 and 1951, winning seven times. The old reconnaissance pilot had Leafs contests documented, and he would study game film, looking for weaknesses in his team. He also personally kept a strict accounting of who was on ice for goals, who scored in meaningful games and who padded their resumés with pile-on counters against already defeated teams. Other teams wouldn't be using film or statistical plus/minus breakdowns for another 30 or 40 years.

In the '40s, Smythe oversaw Frank Selke's retooling of the Leafs farm system, which gave the Leafs two feeder teams—St. Michael's and the Marlboros—playing under Smythe's eagle eye at Maple Leaf Gardens. That the teams should be built on religious grounds was Conn Smythe's idea. "Put the dogans in the Micks' school and put the Protestants in with the Marlboros," is how he put it. Playing off religious affiliations of the day was a master stroke. And it was often said that the Leafs enjoyed an unfair advantage over other NHL teams because of St. Mike's, a famous Catholic institution that left the Leafs with a scout in every parish across Ontario (See page 196).

Smythe drove his franchise hard. In the early days, he ran around the boards on a ramp outside the rink, berating officials and his own players with a rasp of

Conn Smythe gets a turn with the Cup.

The Buccaneer

Harold Ballard's father owned a Toronto skate-manufacturing business, and Ballard became a speed skater who turned to managing local hockey teams. In 1932, he first came to public attention, taking the senior Toronto National Sea Fleas to the Allan Cup, but losing with the same team unexpectedly to the United States in the world championships. Ballard would see more losses than wins in the future.

Managing the Toronto Marlboros junior and senior teams in the '50s led Ballard to joint ownership of the Maple Leafs with Stafford Smythe and John Bassett in 1961. Subsequent to a bitter split with Bassett, and after that, Smythe's death, Ballard took over the team in 1971. After spending a year in jail for fraud, Ballard eased into happy control of the Gardens, generally comporting himself like a wrestling villain thumbing his nose at the crowd. Tearing out a portrait of Queen Elizabeth from the arena for more seats, he snarled, "What position does she play?" He also pulped Foster Hewitt's historic broadcast booth and once shut off the taps and turned up the heat in the Gardens at a Beatles show to boost refreshment sales. After a few bright years in the 1970s, Ballard's Leafs remained pretty well locked in the National Hockey League basement through the '80s. Conn Smythe once commented on his successor: "I wouldn't give him a job at 10 cents a week because I don't like his way of doing business... To me he's like one of those old pirates who would go to sea and battle and board each other and take whatever was there. If they had to walk the gangplank they didn't holler. That's his way of living."

a voice that could have peeled a potato. The following morning, he would appear for work before anyone else, meeting secretary Madeleine McDonald, to whom he would dictate notes on the previous night's game over coffee. (Once, he became so preoccupied with his musings that he failed to look up and notice that a waiter had spilled scalding coffee on McDonald's lap.)

Another morning-after Smythe ritual was inspecting the Gardens. A *Globe and Mail* reporter once commented that the "Taj Ma-hockey," as the arena was sometimes then called, "was a model of cleanliness. It was swept and cleaned with antiseptic tenderness after every attraction and woe betide the man responsible, if the master of the mansion chanced to spot a peanut shell on the floor the day after a big event."

Smythe's relentless drive and imperious management style made enemies and drove friends away. In Smythe's world, sentiment was for Christmas cards. He traded Hap Day, his most loyal player in the '30s, when the time came, then later pushed Day the executive, a man who as a coach brought the team three

If Smythe was hurt by Selke's defection, he never let on.

Stanley Cups in a row (1947–49), out of the Leafs administration in a reorganization move. And when Frank Selke, a man who had mortgaged his house to finance the building of the Gardens and who had made an invaluable contribution to the team's on-ice success, failed to be at his post one day when Smythe walked by, the owner left a strongly worded reprimand on the executive's desk. Selke quit, leaving his own note: "Lincoln freed the slaves." Selke's departure would be a blow, for he would move to the Montreal Canadiens, where he would build the team's 1950s empire.

If Smythe was hurt by Selke's defection, he never let on. He went his own way, playing hunches, presuming he was smarter than everyone else. He bought King Clancy from the Ottawa Senators with the proceeds of a big horse-racing payoff, betting on a horse that had been encouraged by a flask of brandy. Yet, he would turn away from ex-Leaf Billy "The Kid" Taylor when the hockey player was excommunicated from the NHL for gambling on hockey.

Smythe wouldn't see his own actions as hypocritical. Others gambled because they were weak. He did so because he knew he was going to win. The Leafs owner also reflected many of the prejudices of the day and would routinely begin speeches at sports banquets with the phrase, "Gentlemen and Frenchmen." Still, the Maple Leafs, under Smythe's leadership, were often a manifestation of their owner's best qualities—valiant heroes who once, down three games to nothing against the Detroit Red Wings in the 1942 Stanley Cup finals, responded to coach Hap Day's impassioned reading from the letter of a 14-year-old girl, who prayed "please, please" for a Leafs comeback, by storming out and winning four straight games and the Stanley Cup.

Smythe could also be credited for making good choices of character in the players he handpicked. Many of the Leafs were upstanding "Boys' Own Adventure" hero types. The Leafs' first captain, Hap Day (1927–37), only ever sampled liquor by dipping a finger first in his champagne glass and then in his mouth, after the team won a Stanley Cup. "Gentleman Joe" Primeau, the brains on the famous 1930s Kid Line, was as courteous as his nickname might suggest. Syl Apps, who joined the Leafs in 1936, after competing for Canada in the pole vault competition in the Berlin Olympics, once offered to give back his salary to Smythe after breaking his leg in a game. (Apps' strongest on-ice

Getting Religion

The two top junior teams for the Leafs, during the club's glory years, were the Toronto Marlboros and the Toronto St. Michael's Majors. Leafs owner Conn Smythe called them his Dogan and Protestant teams. Between the Marlies and the St. Mike's, the two teams won 11 Memorial Cups and sent hundreds of players on to the National Hockey League. Some of the great Marlboros to make the Leafs are Ron Ellis, Bob Pulford, George Armstrong, Carl Brewer, Bob Baun, Red Horner, Pete Stemkowski, Jim McKenny, Billy Harris, Jim Pappin and Harry Neale. Famous St. Mike's grads to jump to the NHL varsity club include Red Kelly, Dick Duff, Frank Mahovlich, Jim Thomson, Tim Horton, Dave Keon, Tod Sloan, Billy Taylor, Ed Chadwick and Gus Mortson.

Joe Primeau.

KIDDING AROUND

The Toronto Maple Leaf's Kid Line—Joe Primeau, Busher Jackson, and Charlie Conacher—were all grads of the Toronto Marlboros farm team, and Jackson and Conacher were local boys as well. The trio were also 1-2-4 in National Hockey League scoring in 1931–32, the season the Gardens opened and the Leafs first won the Stanley Cup.

Toronto fans loved the three players, particularly taking to Conacher and Jackson, who took kidding around to an extreme. "Busher" Jackson earned his nickname as a rookie. Trainer Tim Daly asked him for help carrying sticks. "Carry them yourself," Jackson responded.

"Well I'll be a son-of-a-bitch if you ain't one smart busher," Daly replied. The name stuck.

Conacher went by "The Big Bomber" and was less likely to entertain unwelcome comments or requests. Legend has it that the forward was out for a skate one practice and Smythe bellowed out a critique of his play. The player drifted to the boards. "One more crack like that," he promised Smythe, "and I'll whack your f—— head off." Smythe liked players with sand in them, as long as they produced.

expression of displeasure was "By hum!") Ted "Teeder" Kennedy, Leafs hero of the '40s, was also a player of enormous integrity. Kennedy was a plodding skater but a determined goal-scorer who picked up his play when John Arnott, a leather-lunged fan high in the Gardens, belted out a yell, "C'mon, Teeeeederrr!" In a gesture that characterized the bond between the Toronto team and its fans, Kennedy would—decades later—serve as a pallbearer at Arnott's funeral.

Forever the fighter, Smythe formed his own "Sportsman Battalion" in World War II and was badly wounded by a bomb in Caen, France, in 1942. He would walk with a cane after that, and in the '50s began to withdraw from the running of the Leafs. He sold his interest in the team to his son Stafford and to Harold Ballard in 1961, although he would bail the two men out of trouble the following year when, one drunken night at the Royal York Hotel, Ballard sold star player Frank Mahovlich to the Chicago Blackhawks for $1 million dollars. The elder Smythe cancelled the deal, with no authority except the force of his personality, telling the Maple Leafs board of directors, "The sale is not in hockey's best interests. The money is going back."

Good thing, too, for Frank Mahovlich would help the Leafs to their last hurrah. Coach-general manager Punch Imlach's Toronto club would win three Stanley Cups in a row from 1962 to 1964, then a fourth championship in 1967.

The old man with a cane was there to enjoy the wins and to bask in his considerable accomplishments. As Trent Frayne put it, Conn Smythe "adjusted the style and social patterns of the country to his own tastes and [dressed] the roughneck game of hockey in black tie and mink and for a time reshaped the Saturday-night habits of millions of people from one coast to another." Smythe, more than anyone else, is responsible for creating what is now called the Leaf Nation. In his time, he made the maple leaf so popular that in 1965 the symbol became the chief component of the Canadian flag.

Suprisingly, Smythe was not pleased by that last development. Prime Minister Lester Pearson, during his term in office, ran into the Leafs' founder once at a social gathering (the two men had been University of Toronto classmates) and kidded Smythe about his anti-flag rhetoric. "What are you complaining for, Conn? Our new flag has a maple leaf!" Pearson said.

"But it's in the Detroit Red Wing colours!" Smythe rasped.

Punch Imlach.

Punchlines

Toronto-born coach and general manager of the Maple Leafs team that won the Stanley Cup four times in the 1960s, Punch Imlach had a tongue that was as sharp as a filed skate. In his second coming with the Leafs (1979–81), Imlach commented on defenceman Borje Salming's contract demands by saying, "Borje has Rosedale tastes and Mississauga talent." The *Globe and Mail*'s Rex McLeod had the best-ever counter-Punch. When Imlach had been released from the hospital after having his gallbladder removed, the journalist suggested that "the doctors had removed Punch's bladder but left the gall."

WHITBY

FOUNDED

A Lake Ontario harbour town, Whitby was incorporated in 1855. Whitby grew from a population of 1,000 to more than 3,000 in its first decade and was, for a time, the second biggest Canadian port on Lake Ontario after Toronto. During World War II, the city was the location for Camp X, the secret spy school founded by Sir William Stephenson, the Canadian-born master intelligence agent who is the subject of the book, *A Man Called Intrepid*.

NATIVE-BORN NHL PLAYERS:
Joe Nieuwendyk (born in Oshawa, ON), Gary Roberts

FAMOUS LOCAL TEAMS:
Junior: Whitby Dunlops, Whitby Flyers, Whitby Knob Hill Farms, Whitby Lawmen, Whitby Mohawks, Whitby Warriors; **Senior-pro:** Whitby Dunlops, Whitby Warriors

CURRENT POPULATION
13,594

Go Dunnies, Go!: The Whitby World Beaters

For two glorious seasons, Wren Blair's Whitby Dunlops were the most famous and popular hockey team in Canada outside the Maple Leafs and the Canadiens.

Blair was a hustling dreamer—a milkman who ran a senior B hockey team, the Oshawa Truckmen, out of an office in his basement. His 1953–54 club was competitive. And the Oshawa rink was packed. Then came disaster. Fire ravaged the Truckers' home, reducing the players' equipment to ashes.

Blair raised $5,000 to keep the team going, won the 1954 Ontario senior B championship over Simcoe (on the road) and then set up in nearby Whitby, where the general manager-coach began an immediate search for sponsors. The Dunlop Rubber Company had just opened a plant in the city. Whitby's mayor interceded on Blair's behalf, suggesting that the English-based firm might be interested in generating corporate goodwill. A Mr. Anderson sent Blair a cheque for $100 along with the company's fondest regards. Blair returned the money attached to a letter he later showed author Scott Young:

Dear Mr. Anderson,

I'm sure that a cheap bunch of Englishmen like the Dunlop Rubber Company need this $100 more than we do. Keep your goddamn money and I'll buy Goodyear.

The Dunlop people were intrigued. Twenty senior officers, most of them Brits, visited the Whitby arena for a game, which happened to be against a team sponsored by their corporate rivals, the Kingston Goodyears. All it took was one period, for the English visitors to become desperate fans. A Dunlop representative, with $200 stuffed in his fist, found the Whitby dressing room during the second intermission. "Give these to your boys, and tell them it's a great show," the executive advised Blair, reminding him of the two-all score. "We've got to win!"

The 1957 world champion Whitby Dunlops celebrate with coach Wren Blair.

That they did, and the Whitby Dunlops were born. The Dunnies would take the 1956 senior B championship. Blair then tried to enter the senior A division, which would allow Whitby to compete for the Allan Cup. The team was refused, so Blair set up his own A league to compete for the cup, convincing Pembroke, Cornwall, Brockville, Kingston and Belleville to join the confederacy.

Whitby played even better in 1956–57. With the Dunlop Rubber Company bankrolling expenses, Blair paid his guys $20 and $25 a match, five more

"This is one of the best games we've seen in a while," broadcaster Foster Hewitt enthused. Significantly, he kept calling the Dunnies "the Canadians."

dollars than other teams offered. And players liked working for a coach who worked hard for them. After games, Blair raced to his typewriter to poke out enthusiastic accounts of the team's play for the local newspaper.

Whitby took to the Dunlops like tire rubber to the road. Most of the boys, including high scorers Bob Attersley and George Samolenski, along with Gordie Myles, Fred Etcher, Don McBeth and Tom and Ted O'Connor, came from Oshawa. Each of them had played for the Oshawa junior Generals, as had captain Harry Sinden, who had grown up just 30 miles down Highway 401 in Toronto.

The Dunnies defeated Kitchener in the spring of 1957, winning Whitby the rights to play the North Bay Trappers for the Ontario Hockey Association senior crown. By now, local interest in the Dunlops was so great that playoff games were held in Toronto's Maple Leaf Gardens. Whitby edged the Trappers in seven games, and then routed the Spokane Comets to win the Allan Cup.

With the national championship, the Dunlops won the honour of representing Canada in a 1957 match against the Russian National Team during the height of the Cold War. Whitby faced the Russians, the reigning Olympic champions, in a November game at Maple Leaf Gardens that occasioned a Friday CBC-TV edition of *Hockey Night in Canada.*

Before that game, Blair nervously approached Maple Leafs general manager Conn Smythe about recruiting recently retired Leafs great Sid Smith for the Dunlops. Smythe, a famous curmudgeon, eventually grunted his approval. The words "For how much?" somehow escaped Blair's mouth.

"What do you mean, for how much?" Smythe thundered. "For nothing! You think you're the only goddamn Canadian?"

In front of a packed house, 200 reporters and a national TV audience, the Russians scored two early goals before Blair pitched a fit and ordered Dunlop Alf Treen to "cream a couple" of Soviets. He did. The Russian team was suddenly a champion racehorse that lost its stride. The Dunnies kept hitting, and then they started scoring.

"This is one of the best games we've seen in a while," broadcaster Foster Hewitt enthused. Significantly, he kept calling the Dunnies "the Canadians."

The Dunlops surprised Russia that night, 7–2. They were certified as Canada's team then, travelling by boat to Oslo, Norway, to represent their country in the 1958 World Hockey tournament. (Blair was unafraid of everything except flying.)

While in Norway, the team was flooded with letters, telegrams and good luck charms from across Canada. The charms worked. The team went into the third period of the gold medal game tied with Russia, two all. Then, with

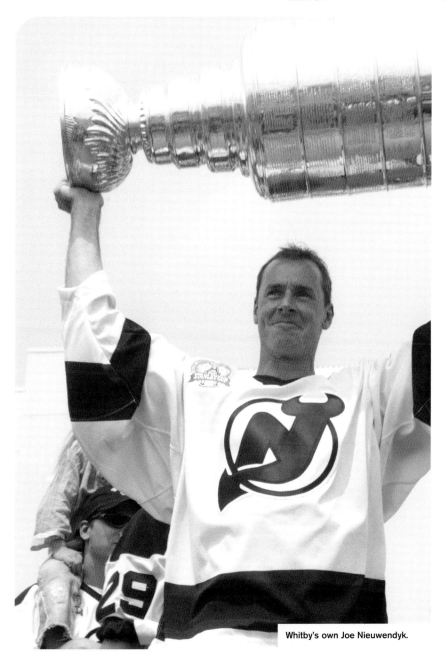

Whitby's own Joe Nieuwendyk.

Whitby Puppies

Best friends in grade school, Joe Nieuwendyk and Gary Roberts snuck down from Whitby to an arena on the outskirts of Toronto during their summer holidays in the mid '70s to watch one of *Hockey Night in Canada*'s famous "Showdown" all-star shootouts. After watching the celebrity contest, the kids quickly headed outside the arena, where, Lord Almighty, they came across one of Lanny McDonald's broken sticks. According to Nieuwendyk, he could barely lift it. The stick was like Excalibur.

A dozen years later, both Niuewendyk and Roberts were Stanley Cup winners, alongside veteran McDonald, as second-year players on the Calgary Flames. And the Whitby boys never stopped kidding McDonald about how strong he used to be. Lanny didn't mind. In fact, he and fellow old-timer Joey Mullen used to take the two Whitby puppies out for exercise on the road. "There were always the four of us, hanging around together," McDonald told Eric Duhatschek of the *Globe and Mail*. "It was Joey Mullen and me, plus the two kids. We'd go on the road and it was like the two odd couples, the kids and the old men. We used to have so much fun together, going for dinner, playing golf. They kept Joey Mullen and I young with their youth and enthusiasm and craziness."

three minutes to go, the Russians' best forward danced in alone on Whitby goalie Roy Edwards. "I can't watch! I turn my head away," Blair later recounted to author Scott Young. "All of a sudden I hear our guys yelling. I know somehow they haven't scored. I said, 'What the hell happened?' and someone said, 'He pulled Roy right out flat on his ass and hit the top of the crossbar.' The puck bounced free and Bobby Attersley took off down the ice, right down the rink and scored, to make it 3–2."

The final game score was 4–2. Days later, stuffed with seafood and German beer, the world beaters returned home on a slow boat to Whitby, the Dunlops' reputation forever secure as Canada's most famous ever senior hockey team.

WINDSOR

FOUNDED
Located across the Detroit River from Detroit, Windsor was originally a Jesuit settlement and remained under French control until 1797. The city has grown in tandem with its American neighbour, Detroit, throughout the years. In 1904, the Ford Motor Company set up a base in Windsor.

NATIVE-BORN NHL PLAYERS
Pat Boutette, Bob Boughner, Sean Burke, Keith Crowder, Ken Daneyko, Tie Domi, Clarence Drouillard, Ken Hodge, John Jackson, Ed Jovanovski, Rick Kehoe, Tim Kerr, Ed Mio, Steve Moore, Bob Probert, Joel Quenneville, Brad Smith, Ray Timgren, Ron Wilson

FAMOUS LOCAL TEAMS
Junior: Windsor Blues, Windsor Bantam Bulldogs, Windsor Royals Windsor Compuware Spitfires, Windsor Spitfires, Windsor Jr. Spitfires; **Senior-pro:** Windsor Alpines, Windsor Army, Windsor Bulldogs, Windsor Chryslers, Windsor Colonial Tools, Windsor Ford, Windsor Gotfredson, Windsor Mills, Windsor Royals, Windsor Ryancretes, Windsor Spitfires

CURRENT POPULATION
208,402

HARD MEDICINE

Windsor's junior Spitfires— the Spits—have been a civic institution since 1969. Local star "Motor City Smitty" Brad Smith, played and coached for the team. Defenceman Ed Jovanovski, who helped Canada to a gold medal at the 2002 Olympics, is also a former Spitfire. Other alumni include Joel Quenneville, Corey Stillman and Jason Spezza.

The best edition of the Spits was probably the 1987–88 club. Led by Kelly Cain (66 goals) and character players Adam Graves and Glen Featherstone, the team never lost a regular season game after Christmas. In the Memorial Cup, held in Chicoutimi, Quebec, the Spitfires again went undefeated in the opening round and were up 3–0 to the Medicine Hat Tigers early on in the finals, before having the spit taken out of them by a late Tiger rally, losing 7–6.

Heavyweight Championship of Windsor

Staring hard across the river at Detroit and wedged below parts of Michigan and Ohio, Windsor is Canada's southernmost city. Because of its proximity to "Motor City" Detroit, Windsor has also developed as a car-manufacturing centre, a union town.

In keeping with its blue-collar roots, the Canadian city's local hockey teams have names that might be tattooed onto the arms of biker gang members: the Bulldogs, the Spits, the Hornets. As for Windsor hockey players, they're like Ford trucks—built tough. Once, Tie Domi was playing here in junior when a fight broke out in the Windsor Arena. Tie looked up and spotted his dad trading haymakers with a fan, shrugged, then turned back to the game. "[My dad] escaped from Albania dodging machine-gun bullets, he could handle that guy," is how he later explained his seeming lack of concern.

Domi would become one of Windsor's two National Hockey League heavyweight champs. The other was troubled rebel, Bob Probert, who retired from the game undefeated, but not unharmed. Probert's father, Al, was a Windsor police detective who let his boys drink at home when they were underage. The gesture didn't improve a difficult relationship with Bob. Al Probert died of a stroke at 52, a week before his boy left in 1982 to play junior hockey in Brantford. Bob was 17. He'd been an alcoholic for about a year.

Probert was also a sweet kid who craved acceptance. The simultaneous urge to rebel and the desire to please was an ongoing inner conflict. As he progressed through junior to the Detroit Red Wings, where he was regarded as a hometown hero, the 6'3" winger was either in trouble or making amends. "He couldn't stand

Tahir "Tie" Domi with the Toronto Maple Leafs.

for you to be mad at him," Detroit coach Jacques Demers told the *New York Times*. "One night a young girl had given him a dozen roses, and he gave them to me for my wife. Another fan gave him a teddy bear, and he gave it to me for my daughter. In 17 years of coaching, I haven't had all angels. I thought I'd seen it all, but I hadn't seen anyone like him. He's the one who, sentimentally, hit me the hardest... You see him, even when he's just gotten in trouble and he has that look that says, 'I'm sorry, help me.'"

Then again, there was the time Demers tried to get Probert to quit smoking. They were in the Red Wings dressing room. Probert just nodded and fished out a smoke, lighting up with the blowtorch players use to tailor their stick blades.

On the ice, maybe the player's demons helped. Probert went into corners like he was looking for the guy who stole his car. He created room on the ice for himself and teammates, scoring his share of goals. And if he got into trouble, well, that was a two-minute infraction, five minutes, tops. Penalties off ice weren't so easy to manage, however. In March 1989, he was arrested for possession of cocaine at the Detroit-Windsor Tunnel and spent 90 days at the Federal Medical Center in Rochester, Minnesota.

Windsor's other prized fighter, Tie Domi, made the NHL in the 1989–90 season, three years after figuring out his life in a Peterborough bus station. He had been a star athlete in Windsor before moving to nearby Belle River, where the community slogan is "Everybody loves everybody." After playing for the Windsor Bulldogs (junior B), he left home at 17 for the elite junior Peterborough Petes.

Tie didn't love Peterborough at first. He wasn't getting much ice time, couldn't get untracked. So he left. Domi was at the bus station when he realized he couldn't

Chevy's Last Ride

The best young player of his era, Real Chevrefils scored 52 goals for the junior Barrie Flyers in 1950–51. In 1956–57 he counted 31 goals in the National Hockey League for the Boston Bruins.

Sadly, Chevrefils' appetite for hockey was often overcome by a thirst for alcohol. In 1959, by the age of 27, he had worn out his welcome in the NHL. His last great hockey moment came with the Windsor Bulldogs, a senior team that he led to the Allan Cup in 1963, chipping in 11 points in the team's nine-game ride to the senior hockey championship. "Chevy" was through with hockey the following season and retired in Windsor, spending his last days living above a tavern called the Lincoln House. He was dead at age 49.

go through with leaving. How could he explain quitting to his dad? Before coming to Windsor, John Domi braved gun fire while escaping from Albania into Greece, never even stopping for the bullet that entered his skull above the right eye.

Armed with new resolution, Domi went back to the Petes. Soon after his return the Petes were playing the Kingston Canadiens and notably Marc Laforge, the league's number-one tough guy. In the dressing room, the Peterborough players were discussing Laforge when Domi piped up, "Don't worry, I'll take care of him." His teammates looked around. Domi was 5'9"; Laforge, 6'3". But they had never

Tie threw off his gloves. Probert landed the first punch, though, a chopping overhand left.

seen Tie fight. Halfway into the game, Domi was thrown on the ice with Laforge and went right after him. The two traded punches. Timber! Laforge went down.

Hearing the fans cheer and his teammates rapping their sticks against the boards as he skated to the bench, Domi finished the plan he had devised in the Peterborough bus terminal. He would be as tough as his old man. Everyone would notice him, regardless of his size. He'd be David, taking on every team's Goliath.

Tie fought his way to the NHL. At the same time, he did charity work, helping in the community, always getting along with people while off the ice. He knew who he was and what he had to do. Once a fan hurled a banana at Tie, calling him a gorilla. Domi skated over and picked up the fruit, peeling and eating it on the spot.

The inevitable fight between Windsor's David and Goliath occurred on 2 December 1992, at Madison Square Garden in New York. Domi was a New York Ranger; Probert, a Detroit Red Wing. Seconds into the game, the crowd jumped up with a thrilled howl as Probert and Domi came together for a faceoff, glaring at each other like heavyweights before the bell. Probert moved first, testing Domi with two cross-checks. Domi responded with a sneer. He'd enjoy whatever happened next.

Probert hit him harder. Tie threw off his gloves. Probert landed the first punch though, a chopping overhand left. Domi grabbed Probert's jersey at the left shoulder to restrict his leverage. Probert switched to his right hand and landed a series of uncontested blows, driving Domi to the ice. But Tie wouldn't stay down. Up on his skates again, he thrust his head into a furious windmill of right hands.

When referees pulled him away, Domi was laughing. He skated away, arms high in triumph. Others could beat you, but you could only defeat yourself. That was a lesson his dad taught him.

Seeing him grinning, the hometown crowd exploded into cheers. (Domi would always get this same reception. Moving to the Toronto Maple Leafs in 1994, he perfected his Little Big Man persona, playing effective hockey while amassing more fights and penalties than anyone who had ever played the game.)

Probert, meanwhile, drifted to the penalty box, listless, hands still balled into fists, looking like a sleepwalking killer in a 1940s film noir thriller. He had won the fight against Domi. In fact, he won all his hockey fights. Unfortunately, Probert experienced more than a few losses getting to and from the rink. Moving from Detroit to the Chicago Blackhawks in 1994, he was suspended for the entire season for violating the league's substance abuse policy.

After 2002, Probert retired, returning home to Windsor, where the hockey star continues to experience the same struggle that the guy down the road working at General Motors faces—raising a family properly and making it through every day in one piece.

Bob Probert.

The new MTS (Manitoba Telecom Services) Centre in Winnipeg, currently the thrashing ground of the American Hockey League's Manitoba Moose, is a splendid modern facility, a building so thoroughly automated that forward-thinking fans, pecking away on a computer, can order what they want on their hot dog along with an appropriate beverage hours before game time. Hours later, when they arrive at their seats, customers are greeted by a smiling hostess bearing their order. All that's left for a fan to do is cheer.

Although the 21st-century Moose are kings of local hockey, there was a time when local Monarchs ruled not only Manitoba but also the entire Canadian junior hockey dominion. The Winnipeg Monarchs won the Memorial Cup three times (1935, 1937, 1943) in what was Manitoba's junior jamboree, a 29-year period between 1931 and 1959 when provincial teams appeared in national championships 15 times, winning 10 Memorial Cups.

Today, Manitoba has only one major junior hockey team, the Brandon Wheat Kings, but in the 1930s, 10 junior clubs, including the Kenora Thistles from the western edge of Ontario, fought mightily for the right to represent the province in the national junior championships. All that competition is what Brandon-born sportswriter Trent Frayne figures was the obvious cause of the Manitoba junior hockey renaissance. At the time, Winnipeg was the capital of western Canadian hockey and the fourth largest city in the country, after Montreal, Toronto and Vancouver. Today the city ranks ninth in population among Canadian cities.

Winnipeg also enjoyed a great senior hockey tradition—the Winnipeg Victorias won the Stanley Cup in 1896, 1901 and 1902, and local senior teams had won the senior championship Allan Cup seven times up to 1931. Bred amid this competitive spirit, a new generation of Manitoba players would emerge to dominate Canadian hockey.

"Just look at all the junior teams you had playing in and coming through Winnipeg [in the '30s]," recalls Frayne, a sports columnist for the *Winnipeg Tribune* before he relocated to Toronto in the '40s. "Teams were playing hockey all over the city. First of all you had two rinks, the Winnipeg Amphitheatre,

Opening Spread: Manitoba star Bobby Clarke, on the ice for the Philadelphia Flyers in the 1980s.

Johnny on the spot: Johnny McCreedy won both the Memorial Cup (Winnipeg Monarchs, 1937) and Allan Cup (Trail Smoke Eaters, 1938, and Kirkland Lake Blue Devils,1940) early in his career. The Winnipeg forward also won a World Championship gold medal with Trail in 1939. And in 1942, Johnny set up fellow childhood pal, Pete Langelle, with the game seven-winning goal over Detroit that gave Toronto Maple Leafs the Stanley Cup.

Indoor Hockey, circa 1900

Born in Limestone Ridge, Ontario, in 1892, Dick Irvin grew up in Winnipeg and played for senior teams in Winnipeg and in Regina before going on to a distinguished National Hockey League coaching career, winning the Stanley Cup for the Toronto Maple Leafs in 1932 and for the Montreal Canadiens in 1944, 1946 and 1953. His son, Dick Irvin Jr., is a long-time contributor to *Hockey Night in Canada*. Dick Irvin Sr. provided the following account of his first-ever childhood trip to play hockey indoors to Bill Roche, author of *The Hockey Book*:

Kids in our neighbourhood in Winnipeg had a pickup hockey team that played on outdoor ice... We arranged a game with another gang of youngsters in Dauphin, Manitoba, about 14 miles east. The big attraction for us was the fact that the little community of Dauphin had an indoor rink, and none of us had played in one of those wonderful things.... [Dad] bundled the hockey team into a bobsleigh, hitched a team of horses, and away we went in below-zero weather... What we found was something pretty wonderful. The goalposts were poplar trees, extending from the ice to the roof... A lantern hung on each goalpost above the goalies' heads. There were no boards around the playing surface. Oil lamps provided dim light and splattered big shadows across the ice... The natural ice was fast, and smoother than outdoor rinks...there was no wind to blow a kid off his skates. It was just a fairyland to me, that's all. Then came the return home...a blizzard had come up...and the roads were full of drifting snow. We rode...huddling at the bottom of the sleigh and gasping as the blizzard swirled past, stinging snow in our faces.

Duke McDonald   Cliff Workman   Gordie MacKenzie   Boyd Johnson   Spunk Duncanson   Earl Adams (manager)

Team poster of the Elmwood
Millionaires, 1941.

the "Amph," and the Olympia Rink. And the Amph had five teams that played
in what was called Manitoba's South Division—the Winnipeg Monarchs and
Winnipeg Rangers would be hosting the Kenora Thistles, Flin Flon Bombers
and Portage la Prairie Terriers. Those were the South Division teams.

"Then there were the North Division teams that played out of the big
Olympia Rink. The Elmwood Millionaires, they were another Winnipeg junior
team. And you had the St. Boniface Seals, from St. Boniface, which is [now
part of] Winnipeg. And coming through to play these teams you had the St. James
Canadians and the Brandon Native Sons and...who else? The Selkirk Fishermen.
Well, that was a lot of hockey teams, and they would try and knock the hell out
of each other to win the provincial championship. After which, if memory
serves, all there was left was the Regina Pats. And if the Manitoba team beat
the Pats they were in the Memorial Cup, playing a team from the big bad
East. There was tremendous competition at the time, great players, and that
made for exceptional teams. Every year, some Manitoba city had the team
to beat, some new star on the horizon."

The champion Memorial Cup Winnipeg Monarchs team of 1937, for
example, had two great teenage lines, reflecting the ethnic diversity of the
Red River Valley. The first unit was a National Hockey League-bound trio

Junior hockey kings: the 1937 Memorial
Cup-winning Winnipeg Monarchs.
Top row (left-right): Weber, Aitcheson,
Field, assistant trainer, Kowacinak,
Dent, Vandaele, Neil; bottom row
(left-right): Martel, Robinson, Clement,
Pike, Langelle, McCreedy, Reault.

Rocket launcher: Dick Irvin was Maurice Richard's first coach with the Montreal Canadiens. Here, Irvin congratulates Richard, Henri Richard, and Toe Blake.

of Ukrainian-Scottish-English origin: Dick Kowcinak, Johnny McCreedy and Alf Pike. The second unit was advertised as The Flying French Manitobans—Lucien Martel, Paul Rheault and Pete Langelle. (Langelle, in fact, was born Peter Landiak and was Ukrainian in background, but the Monarchs persuaded him to change his name in a bid to attract French fans from Winnipeg and St. Boniface.)

The Monarchs weren't the only junior championship team to come from Manitoba. Wally "The Whirling Dervish" Stanowksi led the St. Boniface Seals to the Memorial Cup in 1938. The Winnipeg Rangers took the national trophy in 1941 and 1943. In 1942, the Portage La Prairie Terriers had their turn. And the Flin Flon Bombers, with fiercely determined Paddy Ginnell, Ted Hampson and Orland Kurtenbach, upset the Ottawa-Hull Canadiens, to win the Memorial Cup in 1957.

All these teams played in rinks that could not compare to the MTS Centre. In Winnipeg, the Amph was a drafty barn, with wooden pews that left departing fans with wounded backsides. And the bigger Olympia facility had sections of rink that visiting players complained were as dark as a closet. Still, the old rinks were heaven, and the stars who performed there, gods, as far as local fans were concerned.

"Turk Broda, with the Brandon Native Sons, and the Whirling Dervish, Wally Stanowski, were schoolboy heroes in Manitoba," recalls Frayne. "And teams like the Elmwood Millionaires and the Winnipeg Monarchs and Winnipeg Rangers, the Flin Flon Bombers, they were the next best thing to the NHL as far as we were concerned, only they were right in your own city... It was a great era to be a hockey fan in the province."

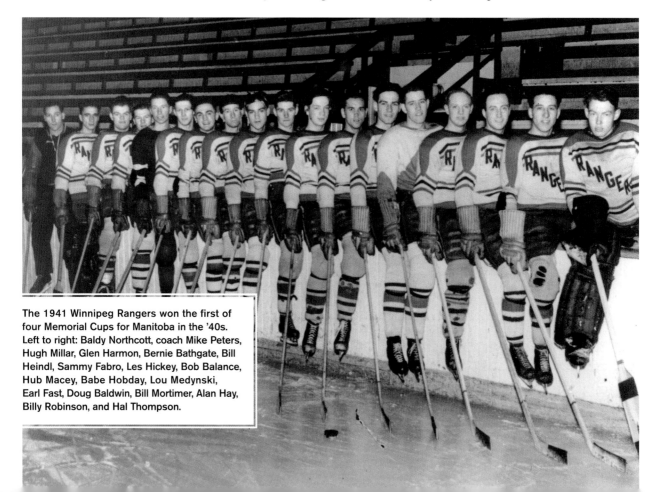

The 1941 Winnipeg Rangers won the first of four Memorial Cups for Manitoba in the '40s. Left to right: Baldy Northcott, coach Mike Peters, Hugh Millar, Glen Harmon, Bernie Bathgate, Bill Heindl, Sammy Fabro, Les Hickey, Bob Balance, Hub Macey, Babe Hobday, Lou Medynski, Earl Fast, Doug Baldwin, Bill Mortimer, Alan Hay, Billy Robinson, and Hal Thompson.

BRANDON

FOUNDED
In early 1881, General Thomas Rosser chose the site for what is now Brandon, Manitoba, as a Canadian Pacific Railroad settlement. The name Brandon goes far back in the region's history. The explorer Capt. Thomas James moored his ship in James Bay near Brandon Hill in 1631, and the Hudson's Bay Company had a trading post named Brandon House. Brandon was incorporated as a city on 30 May 1882, and quickly became the centre of a growing farm community. The second largest city in Manitoba is also known as the Wheat City, and the surrounding area is frequently referred to as Westman.

NATIVE-BORN NHL PLAYERS
Dan Bonar, Jack Borotsik, Walter "Turk" Broda, Harold Brown, Larry Brown, Lude Check, Ronald Chipperfield, Jimmy Creighton, Kimbi Daniels, Bill Fairbairn, Glen Hanlon, Ron Hextall (born in Poplar Point, MB), Jamie Hodson, Eddie Johnstone, Gord Lane, Dwight Mathiasen, Brad Maxwell, Rob McVicar, Chris Oddleifson, John Paddock, Cam Plante, Bill Ranford, Bryce Salvador, Chuck Scherza, Alex Smart, Ted Taylor, Ken Wregget

FAMOUS LOCAL TEAMS
Junior: Brandon Bobcats, Brandon Elks, Brandon Bees, Brandon Maple Leafs, Brandon Native Sons, Brandon Rangers, Brandon Travellers, Brandon Wheat Kings; **Senior-pro:** Brandon Hockey Club, Brandon Olympics, Brandon Regals, Brandon Wheat Kings

CURRENT POPULATION
42,000

Brandon's Native Son

The second best story about Turk Broda has the goalie joining a band of National Hockey League all-stars in the early 1940s, for a Hollywood exhibition series against the Montreal Canadiens. After one game, the pride of Brandon, Manitoba, fell into the company of a barhopping soldier. Military police were dispatched to look for them. The GI they found at dawn, stoned as a statue, passed out in front of a nightclub. Broda was inside, still very much awake, working out a duet on the piano with jazz legend Hoagy Carmichael. Later that afternoon, playing on memory and coffee, the goalie shut out the Canadiens, 1–0.

Walter Egan Broda would receive two nicknames in his life. The first, "Turkey Face" or "Turk," came courtesy of neighbourhood pals who counted more freckles on his face than there were on a turkey egg. Later, playing hockey for the NHL's Toronto Maple Leafs, he earned a sobriquet more in keeping with his character and stature: "The Fabulous Fat Man."

"I remember one summer I was with friends in Brandon's Stanley Park and the great Turk Broda wandered by, wearing a Detroit Olympics jacket," remembers sportswriter Trent Frayne. "This was right before Toronto Maple Leafs owner Conn Smythe bought him from the Detroit Red Wings' farm team for $8,000. Of course we all knew him, because he played for the Brandon Native Sons. He almost took the team to the Memorial Cup [in 1933]. Anyway, this particular day Turk sat down on the park bench and regaled us all with stories of big league hockey.

"Well, that was pretty heady stuff for a couple of boys from Brandon. He was

A sketch of grain elevators in Brandon, circa 1888, by Melton Prior.

Lorne Chabot.

Those Bus Rides

Brandon's slogan, "City of wheat, never knows defeat," pays tribute to the region's economic base. But the Manitoba city is also renowned for producing goaltenders. Local National Hockey League netminders include Turk Broda, Glen Hanlon, Bill Ranford, Ken Wregget and Ron Hextall (born in nearby Poplar Point). In addition, big-league netminders "Sugar" Jim Henry, Ron Low and Lorne Chabot began their hockey careers playing for junior or senior teams in Brandon.

Hextall, who backstopped the junior Brandon Wheat Kings from 1981 to 1984, offered one explanation for why city teams have graduated so many goalies. The reason could be "those bus rides," he once told sportswriter Trent Frayne. In Hextall's day, the Wheat Kings travelled by bus from Brandon to Seattle or Portland and back—3,500 miles of staring out windows, looking for bits of movement and colour in snowy flatlands. In time, Brandon goalies developed the eyesight of prairie falcons. "I spent three years riding those buses," Hextall told Frayne. "Once we went 30 hours straight from Kelowna to Brandon."

a hero in Manitoba. Turk was a roly-poly, upbeat guy, big smile, very outgoing. Bad games never bothered him. He had the ability to forget hard times and move on. He seemed imperturbable. Conn Smythe used to say, 'When the going got rough in the playoffs, Broda's emotions rose to normal.'"

An ability to shrug off adversity was much admired at the time. When Frayne is asked what people in Brandon did for a living the summer he met Broda, he answers quickly, "A lot did nothing. This was the Depression. Farms closed, people rode trains. Plenty of men were hopping trains, looking for a chance somewhere else."

If fans appreciated Broda's sunny optimism, they also related to his shambling, regular-guy demeanor. Sportswriter Dick Beddoes observed that Broda "resembled a pound of butter left out of the fridge overnight." Perhaps because Broda made being a hockey star seem as much fun as fans hoped it would be, the 5'9", 200-pound netminder became something of a 1940s folk hero. In Brandon, goaltending became a matter of civic pride. And local-born future NHL goalies would include Glen Hanlon, Ron Hextall, Bill Ranford and Ken Wregget. Elsewhere, Broda's story became an enjoyable annual saga, as every spring the netminder would show up at playoff time seemingly just a little bit fatter and a little more fabulous.

Broda led the Leafs to five Stanley Cups between 1942 and 1951, despite spending 1944 and 1945 in the navy. And his goals-against average for 13 playoff NHL seasons was a microscopic 1.98. At a time when scoring dynamo Maurice "Rocket" Richard could solve every other goalie, the player was forced to admit, "I cannot beat Turk Broda."

Only once, toward the end of his career, did The Fabulous Fat Man's weight prompt any real controversy. And that brings us to the best story about Broda. In November 1949, with the Maple Leafs on a six-game winless streak and the Grey Cup about to invade Toronto and eat up a week of sports coverage, Leafs owner Conn Smythe decided that Broda was too fat and ordered him to lose nine pounds, telling the goalie that he had to slim down to 190 pounds by the following Saturday or he wouldn't play.

Ron Hextall makes another save.

Toronto Maple Leafs goalie
Turk Broda, working on his diet.

Wheat Kings' Elusive Crown

One of the most storied franchises in western junior hockey, the Brandon Wheat Kings, twice came agonizingly close to Memorial Cup crowns. In 1949, the Kings were down three games to one to the Montreal Royals, with another matched tied, and then came back winning two games at home, 2–1 and 5–1, behind the scintillating goaltending of Ray Frederick. With the series tied, the Canadian Amateur Hockey Association ordered an eighth game at a neutral site— Winnipeg. National interest in the series was so great that CBC radio summoned legendary hockey broadcaster Foster Hewitt to broadcast the decisive contest. The Kings were ahead, 4–2, in the third period, but the Royals—led by the great Dickie Moore—piled in four straight goals, thereby taking the Memorial Cup back to Quebec.

Thirty years later, the Wheat Kings came even closer to winning, as a club anchored by defenceman Brad McCrimmon and a potent top line of Brian Propp, Laurie Boschman and Ray Allison, took the team to the finals against the Peterborough Petes, where Brandon lost, 2–1, in overtime on a goal by the Petes' Bob Attwell.

The media ran with the story like a hooked marlin. The day after Smythe's edict, Toronto papers had front-page photos of Turk at home staring glumly at a plate decorated with wilted lettuce. The next day, North American media picked up the "Battle of the Bulge." Papers across Canada showed a staged shot of Broda at practice, squatting in the net with a pagoda of pancakes in front of him. The CBC radio show *The Happy Gang* featured periodic updates on the goalie's condition. An American newsreel company did a feature on Broda's weight battle, and soon theatregoers across the continent saw a pre-movie short dramatizing the goalie's efforts to slim down.

Broda made the 190-pound target in time for the Saturday night game, shutting out the New York Rangers, 1–0, and earning a rousing ovation as he left the ice, as a band broke into "She's Too Fat for Me" for the umpteenth time that night. "It was incredible when you think of it, a front-page national story about some boss telling an employee to lose weight," Trent Frayne laughs. "But Turk Broda was a guy people really enjoyed. He was a colourful figure who came along at the right time, I guess. People loved him."

Bobby Clarke, 1966.

Flinty II

Famed American cartoonist Al Capp, creator of L'il Abner, was so intrigued by the legend of Flintabbatey Flonatin, the eccentric science-fiction character who inspired the Flin Flon town name, that he designed the highway statue of "Flinty," who greets visitors driving into Flin Flon. The city also has a travelling ambassador who might equally be named Flinty. One of the most prolific scorers in the history of western junior hockey, Bobby Clarke totalled 488 points in three seasons for the Flin Flon Bombers (1966–69). Despite a lifelong battle with diabetes, he went on to captain the notorious Broad Street Bullies edition of the Philadelphia Flyers, and after Phil Esposito and Paul Henderson, Clarke was the most important member of the 1972 Team Canada, which defeated the Soviet Union in the Summit Series. Scrawny, fresh-faced, with a gap-toothed smile and a wild flounce of blond curls, Bobby might have looked like a toddler stretched by a funhouse mirror, but he came from the Ted Lindsay school of "do-what-it-takes-to-win" hockey. And he was as adept at drawing blood as he was at winning faceoffs. In the words of hockey writer Andrew Podnieks, Clarke had "the heart of a pack of lions."

FLIN FLON

FOUNDED
Flin Flon is a northern mining town straddling the Manitoba-Saskatchewan border. Copper was discovered here, in 1915, by prospector Tom Creighton. Mining firms would arrive the next decade. The town continued to grow in the 1930s, as prairie farmers abandoned their land during the Great Depression to find work in the mines. Flin Flon remains a mining town, and because of the nearby lakes it has also become a tourist destination.

NATIVE-BORN NHL PLAYERS
Ken Baird, Ken Baumgartner, Bobby Clarke, Matt Davidson, Kim Davis, Dean Evason, Al Hamilton, Gerry Hart, Ronald Hutchinson, George Konik, Ray Maluta, Dunc McCallum, Eric Nesterenko, Mel Pearson, Reid Simpson, Ernie Wakely

FAMOUS LOCAL TEAMS
Junior: Flin Flon Midget Bombs, Flin Flon Midget Bombers, Flin Flon Bombers; **Senior-pro:** Flin Flon Bombers

CURRENT POPULATION
7,243

Bombertown

It is somehow fitting that the greatest moment in Flin Flon hockey history, the Bombers' 1957 Memorial Cup final against the Ottawa-Hull Canadiens, has been captured in a musical, for Flin Flon itself is something of an artistic discovery.

In 1915, six prospectors were combing northern Manitoba, 540 miles or so northwest of Winnipeg. On the second month of what had been an unrewarding journey, one miner—Tom Creighton—stooped to find a weathered copy of science-fiction writer J.E. Preston-Muddock's *The Sunless City* on rocky ground. That night, Creighton picked through the tattered volume and learned the story of Josiah Flintabbatey Flonatin, an eccentric grocer who piloted a submarine through a bottomless lake, threading a golden hoop into another world. The next day, Creighton and his friends came to the shoreline of a lake strewn with bright rock containing traces of copper, zinc and gold. Right then and there, the dancing men decided to name their mine Flin Flon, after the nickname of the wild dreamer in *The Sunless City*.

Arts and entertainment would continue to play a role in the development of the Manitoba-Saskatchewan border town. In the '50s, the general manager of what locals call The Company (the Hudson Bay Mining and Smelting Company) also directed the Flin Flon glee club. "Do you sing?" was a question that came with any interview for a mining job. "If you sang, you had an in to a job," Flin Flon solicitor Mark Kolt would later tell Kevin Prokosh of the *Winnipeg Free Press*. "If you sang tenor you were hired on the spot. This led to an unnaturally good singing group."

Hockey was the city's true passion, however. A senior edition of the Flin Flon Bombers, starring future Detroit Red Wings great Sid Abel, arrived in 1936. (The name was the result of a name-the-team competition. A miner, Joe Pieper, came up with the winner.) But it would be the junior Bombers, who began playing in 1948, who made the city famous.

Mostly local boys, the sons of prairie farmers blown here by the Depression in search of work, the Flin Flon Bombers played a style of hockey that was as

A Letter Home

A portion of an open letter from Gerry Hart, a defenceman who would enjoy a 15-year National Hockey League career, to his old junior team, the Flin Flon Bombers:

I was born January 1, 1948 at the Flin Flon General Hospital, a New Year's Baby! My mother Dorothy was a nurse, and my father Frank worked for the Hudson Bay Mining and Smelting Company in the "tankhouse." My sister Naomi was born a year and a half later. At the time we lived on South Hudson, in a small one and a half story wood frame house with no water works and a wonderful garden that my father was very proud of.

My hockey career began as it did for most youngsters in Flin Flon: outdoor rinks, frozen lakes and Saturday mornings with Pinkie Davie's community club program.

There were many people at that time who gave a lot of themselves to promote the youth hockey programs. I am forever thankful to my dad for the hours he spent coaching and driving me to the rink, and to gentlemen like Roy Jarvis, Gordon Mitchell and Gordie Grindle for their dedication to the sport, as well as to many others. I am also thankful to "Frenchy" Pelletier for letting me sneak into the old arena through the curling rink to watch the Bombers play!

Playing for the Flin Flon Bombers was certainly my goal at a very early age. When my turn came, Paddy Ginnell entered the scene and left an indelible impression on all of us. Paddy brought a new sense of pride, enthusiasm and toughness to the team. With Paddy's leadership the winning tradition of the team continued and his positive outlook was the springboard for many of us to continue to pursue hockey beyond the Bombers. Paddy taught the meaning of the word "character" and what it meant to a hockey team. Role players like Craig Reichmouth contributed as much but in different ways as did the talented Bobby Clarke and Reggie Leach. The tradition was set for many years to come. To this day, Flin Flon is known in every hockey city in North America for its "Bombers."

I left Flin Flon in 1968 and went to play professional hockey for 15 years. I had short stints with the Detroit Red Wings, Quebec Nordiques and St. Louis Blues, but my best years were with the New York Islanders. Some of the most memorable moments in New York were games against the Philadelphia Flyers and my old teammates Bobby and Reggie. I finished my hockey career in St. Louis in 1983. I have recently come to the realization that I have actually lived in New York longer than any other place. However, I still think of Flin Flon as my home. My summers in Flin Flon with my family and my sister Naomi's family are truly some of the most memorable activities that we do as a family.

Thanks, Flin Flon! It was you who gave me the opportunities for success, and it was you who taught me the values that would carry me through life. To you, Flin Flon, my sincere gratitude and appreciation, for you are always there every summer when I come home.

May God bless all of you.

Sincerely,
Gerry Hart

intimidating as the team's name might suggest. Competing in the Saskatchewan Junior Hockey League, Flin Flon won six provincial titles in a row (1952–57), saving the best for last. In the spring of 1957, the Bombers made the finals of the Memorial Cup, playing at home against the farm team of the Montreal Canadiens, an Ottawa-Hull club managed and coached, respectively, by Hall of Fame legends Sam Pollock and Scotty Bowman.

Fans weren't sure what the Flin Flon players would find more daunting, the challenge of being in the Memorial Cup or taking on a team wearing the fabled *bleu-blanc-rouge*. After all, the parent Canadiens, with Richard, Beliveau, Geoffrion, Moore, Harvey and Plante, were considered the best hockey team ever made. Saturday nights on *Hockey Night in Canada*, the Canadiens toyed with other National Hockey League teams like a kitten swatting about a ball of string. And now, right here in Flin Flon, wearing the same famous uniforms, Montreal's junior team was taking to Community Arena ice to challenge the Bombers.

The junior Canadiens even had a member of hockey's royal family, the diminutive younger brother of both Maurice "Rocket" Richard and Henri "The Pocket Rocket" Richard. His name: Claude "Vest-Pocket Rocket" Richard. Other junior

Main Street in Flin Flon, 1929.

The underdog Flin Flon Bombers whoop it up after dispensing with Sam Pollock and Scotty Bowman's Montreal Jr. Canadiens, moments after winning the 1957 Memorial Cup.

Habs included future NHLers Ralph Backstrom, Murray Balfour and Bobby Rousseau, along with J.C. and Gilles Tremblay.

The Canadiens won two out of three matches played in Flin Flon, encouraging locals to believe that the Bombers were indeed tilting at windmills. But when the series shifted to Regina's Exhibition Stadium for the final four games, Flin Flon began to show the mining town grit that had made the team six-time provincial champions.

The stars of the team were local. Ted Hampson won the Saskatchewan scoring race that year and linemate George Konik was named the league's most valuable player. But maybe the heart of the team was Paddy Ginnell, a forward from Dauphin, Manitoba.

"As a player Paddy was just as tough as an old boot," remembered John Ferguson, the Montreal Canadiens' legendary enforcer, who played against Ginnell while a member of the Melville Millionaires, another Saskatchewan junior team. "Those were great teams that we had in the '50s in Melville and Flin Flon. Players would go right from there into the NHL."

With Ginnell arriving in corners with the force of a rock slide, and Hampson and Konik chipping in the occasional goal, the Bombers won games four and five in Regina by identical 3–1 scores. The Canadiens took the next game six, 4–2, setting the stage for the decisive seventh contest.

The series was winning headlines across Canada now, as Canadiens general manager Sam Pollock slyly attempted to intimidate his hosts by threatening to return east unless his team received better accommodation and refereeing—an obvious attempt to stress the superior breeding of the Canadiens team. The insult riled fans from both Regina and Flin Flon. Now all of Saskatchewan and Manitoba wanted the Bombers to kick the Flintabbatey Flonatin out of their visitors.

Ottawa and Flin Flon were locked in a two-all tie midway into the third period of the seventh game, when Ted Hampson banged home the biggest goal of his life—giving Manitoba a 3–2 lead. With Orland Kurtenbach, a late addition from Saskatchewan's Prince Albert Mintos, checking Canadiens star Ralph

"That was a charmed time, everything came together for this place."

Backstrom into exhaustion and Ginnell (who scored Flin Flon's second goal) banging every Canadiens player in sight, the Bombers managed to hang on and win the city's only national championship.

Forty-two years later, Flin Flon natives were still singing out in celebration over the Bombers' win. In 1999, the city's 100-voice choir, under the direction of the city solicitor (and leading composer) Mark Kolt, put on *Bombertown*, a multimedia theatrical production that used the Bombers' 1957 Memorial Cup win as the backdrop for a musical romance. "That was a charmed time, where everything came together for this place," Kolt told the *Winnipeg Free Press*. "It was a Cinderella team that proved to the world they could play with the best. People have a heartfelt feeling for that team, much more than those great Bobby Clarke-Reggie Leach Bomber teams, because there were no superstars and there was a much larger proportion of local players."

Members of the 1999 Flin Flon Bombers appeared on film in the production. "We got the Bombers out on a Sunday in late January and filmed them for five hours re-enacting highlights of that classic 1957 series," says Kolt. The images were used as background images in the play.

Almost 200 people were lined up on Flin Flon's Main Street before 9, the morning tickets went on sale for *Bombertown*. The musical would prove to be the biggest hit in Flin Flon since Paddy Ginnell left town. Over 3,000 people, almost half the town's population, would see the theatrical homage.

Flin Flon Bombers star, George Konik, playing later for the Minnesota Saints of the WHA.

Flin Flon Flu

After playing pro hockey in the Western Hockey League from 1956 to 1966, Paddy Ginnell returned to Flin Flon in the late 1960s to coach the junior Bombers, recreating the team in his own image. Bomber stars of the era included Flin Flon locals Bobby Clarke and Gerry Hart, along with "The Riverton Rifle," Reggie Leach, all of whom contributed to the Philadelphia Flyers Stanley Cup clubs in 1974 and 1975. Under Ginnell, the Bombers won provincial and league championships in 1967 (Manitoba Junior Hockey League), 1969 and 1970 (Western Canada Hockey League). The team also led western hockey in splints and bandages during this era, as the Bombers finished their checks into the second and third row of the Whitney Forum. One visiting coach put a red cross on his team's bus as it left town. Before long, players on other teams began developing a sudden illness when they came to play in Flin Flon, an affliction known as the Flin Flon flu.

View of St. Boniface, July 1872.

ST. BONIFACE

FOUNDED

A Roman Catholic mission built, in 1818, on the banks of the Red and the Seine Rivers, St. Boniface quickly became the primary French-Canadian settlement in western Canada. Louis Riel was born here in 1844 and would spearhead efforts to have the French and Metis cultures of the Red River area given official recognition as a condition for Manitoba entering into Confederation in 1870. Riel headed a short-lived rebellion in 1885 and was executed in Regina, Saskatchewan, later that year. In 1883, St. Boniface was incorporated as a town. It became absorbed by the city of Winnipeg in 1972 and is now commonly referred to as the French District.

NATIVE-BORN NHL PLAYERS

Gary Blaine, Gerry Brisson, Ed Bruneteau, Mud Bruneteau, Rosario "Lolo" Couture, Marcel "Ching" Dheere, Butch Goring, Howie Hughes, Gord Labossiere, Dan Lambert, Derek Laxdal, Bob Leiter, Ray Manson, Ray Neufeld, Dave Richardson, Dave Richter, Wilf Starr

FAMOUS LOCAL TEAMS

Junior: St. Boniface Braves, St. Boniface Canadians, St. Boniface Riels, St. Boniface Saints, St. Boniface Seals; **Senior-pro:** St. Boniface Mohawks

CURRENT POPULATION

108,000

Manitoba Mud

Hockey's oldest fans understand that while highlights of today's games are digitally archived and can be replayed in perpetuity with no loss of picture resolution, matches from the sport's Palaeozoic era—hockey's radio days—sometimes provided more lasting memories. How else to explain the legend of Mud Bruneteau, a player who became famous for scoring a goal that no more than 10,000 fans saw but that everyone remembers?

The feat in question, which occurred on 25 March 1936, decided a two-day, six-hour, nine-period Stanley Cup playoff encounter between the Detroit Red Wings and the Montreal Maroons—a contest that at times resembled a Depression-era dance marathon more than a sporting event. Hockey's longest-ever game began at 8:34 p.m. and ended at 2:25 the next morning. But if fans were surprised by the length of the match, they were even more shocked to learn the author of the historic goal. When listeners who stayed up half the night to follow the game told friends who had scored the deciding goal, the response was typically, "Who on earth is Mud Bruneteau?"

Modere Fernand Bruneteau was born in St. Boniface, Manitoba, the birthplace of Metis and French-Canadian firebrand Louis Riel. St. Boniface remained resolutely French at the time of Bruneteau's birth, in 1914. Young Modere received a French-Catholic education at DeAndreis High School, where one of the brothers had trouble with his name and began calling Bruneteau Mud.

The student didn't mind, and the singular name seemed to mark Bruneteau as an individual who would go his own way. Young men from his neighbourhood customarily went on to work in St. Boniface's livestock and meat-packing district, the biggest in Canada in the 1930s. And local hockey players hoped to join the popular hometown St. Boniface Seals, winners of the Memorial Cup

Working overtime: Modere "Mud" Bruneteau, Detroit Red Wings.

Hero of the 1938 Memorial Cup with the St. Boniface Seals, rushing defenceman Wally "The Whirling Dervish" Stanowski went on to pilot the Toronto Maple Leafs to four Stanley Cups in the 1940s.

Spring Break, 1938

One of the more famous and certainly most playful junior hockey teams to come out of Manitoba between the war years was the St. Boniface Seals club that defeated the Oshawa Generals in the 1938 Memorial Cup. Led by captain Billy Reay and rushing defenceman Wally "The Whirling Dervish" Stanowski, who were both Winnipeg boys, the Seals turned the April Memorial Cup into both a hockey triumph and an epic spring-break comic misadventure. After winning the Memorial Cup at Toronto's Maple Leaf Gardens in front of 15,617 fans, the largest crowd ever to witness a hockey game in Canada at that time, the boys were scheduled to attend a civic luncheon in their honour the next day. Deciding that such a ceremony would be altogether too dull for the team's tastes, one of the Seals phoned the hotel hosting the affair and advised the maître d' that the festivities were being advanced from one o'clock to noon. The whole team then hurried to the hotel, gobbled their meals and left nothing but a few breadsticks for the dignitaries who arrived at the proper hour. The fun would continue on the train ride back to St. Boniface, when the Seals locked team coach Mike Kryschuk in a ladies' washroom.

in 1938, while extravagant dreamers imagined playing someday for the French-Canadian Montreal Canadiens.

Mud Bruneteau, on the other hand, played hockey in nearby Winnipeg for the Winnipeg Junior Knights of Columbus. And instead of working for Union Stockyards, the biggest employer in St. Boniface, he took a job at the Norris Grain Factory in Winnipeg, where in the summer of 1934, he walked into his boss's office and spotted a calendar of the National Hockey League's Detroit Red Wings on the wall. "I want to play for the Red Wings," he advised grain executive C.E. Babbitt.

Two seasons later, Bruneteau was indeed a member of the Stanley Cup-bound Detroit team. Not that anyone noticed. He was 21 at the time, a quiet rookie who had managed two goals in 24 games. Mostly, he sat on the end of the bench, waiting to spell fatigued teammates.

On 24 March 1936, Bruneteau would be in luck, for by the third period of the still scoreless Cup playoff game between the Red Wings and the Maroons, every one of his teammates was beyond tired. The Montreal Forum that night was unseasonably warm. And no Zamboni ice-making tractors existed at the time. The rink was flooded by hand. Warm temperatures and a frantic crowd breathing cigarette exhaust overcame the capabilities of the Forum's cooling system. The rink was a shallow lake by the first overtime.

The game had also been a particularly hard-hitting affair. In a hockey storyline that could have only come out of the Depression, a Detroit fan offered to pay Bucko McDonald $5 for every Maroon he belted to the ice, and from the first period onward, the Red Wing defenceman went out of his way to pile up his reward money. "We had agreed on a limit of $200," he later told Jim Proudfoot of the *Toronto Star*. "I knocked down 37 Maroons before it was over. He paid me $185, which was a lot of money in the 1930s."

Bruneteau began to see more ice time after the calendar changed to March 25, and at the end of the eighth period found himself in need of one of the brandy-and-orange-juice pick-me-ups that players were allowed between periods.

It was 2:25 a.m. The crowd gasped, and then some began to cheer.

Minutes later, with an alcohol glow still spreading through his system, Bruneteau hopped over the boards with linemate Hec Kilrea. The St. Boniface native would say he remembered what happened next as if it had all been a dream. Kilrea rushed down the ice with the puck. Bruneteau drove to the net. Seconds later, a pass came right to him, soft and perfect, like someone dealing an ace right into his hands. Without thinking, the rookie instinctively lifted the puck over a sliding, splashing Montreal goalie, Lorne Chabot, and into the open net.

Nothing happened at first. "It was the funniest thing," Bruneteau recalled. "The puck just stuck there in the twine and didn't fall to the ice." The red light signalled a goal, however. It was 2:25 a.m. The crowd gasped, and then some began to cheer.

Leaving the ice with victorious Red Wings teammates, Bruneteau received another surprise. "[Montreal fans] were handing him money as he came off the ice," son Ray Bruneteau remembers his father telling him. "Five dollars, 10 dollars, whatever. He put the money on a table in the dressing room and all the players split it up." Why Montreal fans would pay tribute to an enemy hero is an enduring mystery. Although it should be remembered that in dance marathon contests in the '20s and '30s, winners always received cash prizes.

After scoring the most famous overtime goal in hockey history, Bruneteau's career proceeded in an orderly fashion. Detroit won the Stanley Cup that spring, its first ever, rolling over Montreal and Toronto. And Bruneteau would play 10 more seasons for the Red Wings, serving as co-captain for a while. From there, he wound down his career playing with brother Eddie for the Omaha Knights of the United States Hockey League in the late '40s. He coached Omaha for a year, and then later opened a popular local bar in the Nebraska city, where new customers inevitably asked, "Mud Bruneteau, why do I know that name?"

He never minded telling them.

Every spring that an NHL playoff game creeps into a second overtime, Modere Fernand Bruneteau's story is told again. To this day, his name resonates with Canadian hockey fans around the world. Once, his nephew Richard, a plastic surgeon, was operating in San Francisco when a nurse addressed him: "Mr. Bruneteau." The attending anaesthesiologist, a Canadian, snapped his head around and asked, "Are you the son of Mud or Eddie?"

Best Dressed

William "Tulip Billy" Reay graduated from the junior St. Boniface Seals to a successful 10-year career in the National Hockey League, playing a regular shift with the Montreal Canadiens from 1945 to 1953. Later, he coached the Toronto Maple Leafs (1957–58) and the Chicago Blackhawks (1963–77). It was as a coach, dressed in three-piece suit, starched white shirt, French cuffs and a fedora picked out by his wife Clare, that the reason for the "Tulip" in Reay's name became evident. *Hockey Night in Canada* play-by-play man Danny Gallivan invariably referred to the St. Boniface coach as "dapper Billy Reay."

SELKIRK

FOUNDED

In 1812, Scottish nobleman Thomas Douglas, the fifth Earl of Selkirk, purchased 160,000 square miles of Red River property from the Hudson Bay Company. He hoped to create a better life for poor Scottish and Irish peasants. The first migrants, who were from Glasgow, arrived there in 1813. Selkirk's grand experiment would leave him impoverished at his death in 1820. But Selkirk grew to be a modestly successful farming and lumbering settlement. The town of 400 was incorporated in 1882. By then, Selkirk was known as a fishing port.

NATIVE-BORN NHL PLAYERS

Terry Ball, Richard Chernomaz, Paul Goodman, Alfie Michaud, John Morrison, Harry Oliver, "Bullet" Joe Simpson, Neil Wilkinson

FAMOUS LOCAL TEAMS
Junior: Selkirk Fishermen, Selkirk Steelers; **Senior-pro:** Selkirk Steelers

CURRENT POPULATION
9,752

Thomas Douglas, Earl of Selkirk, 1812.

Skates of a Fisherman

While playing in the 1920s for the New York Americans—Prohibition bootlegger "Big Bill" Dwyer's National Hockey League team—"Bullet" Joe Simpson bid goodbye to one season by sharing a bottle of his owner's premium hooch with teammates in the dressing room. The player then proceeded to the Madison Square Garden exits, where he was surprised by the arrival of the arena's new tenants, Ringling Brothers and Barnum & Bailey Circus. A number of caged lions and bears, spotting Simpson, turned and let out a wind-tunnel roar. The hockey player turned on his heels and returned to the dressing room, advising teammates, "That must have been a bottle of bad booze, boys. I thought I saw a bunch of wild animals out there in the hall."

Ferocious animals and bootleggers are only a small part of the epic adventure that was Bullet Joe's life. Born in 1893, Simpson learned to skate on a frozen slough just down the road from his house and earned his reputation speeding down the rink in hockey civil wars involving the best young players in Selkirk. "Manitoba Avenue ran east-west in the middle of Selkirk," he remembered. "The boys living in the north end were the north team and those south of Manitoba Avenue made up the south team."

As a teenager Simpson graduated to the town's most famous team, the junior Selkirk Fishermen. (Selkirk opened Manitoba's first hatchery the year Simpson was born; an early tugboat that worked out of Selkirk on the Red River was called *The Fisherman*.) Upon turning 21 in 1914, he played senior hockey with the Winnipeg Victorias, enlisting to serve in World War I the following year. Before going overseas, however, the rushing defenceman led the Winnipeg 61st Battalion team to the 1916 senior Allan Cup, accumulating six points in four games against teams from Fort William, Ontario, and Regina, Saskatchewan.

While overseas with the 43rd Cameron Highlanders, the hockey player's nickname took on a more solemn meaning. Fighting alongside a battalion commanded by Major Winston Churchill, the young infantryman was wounded at the Battle of the Somme (1916), then later at the Battle of Amiens (1918).

"Bullet" Joe Simpson, playing for the New York Americans in the 1930s.

"Bullet" Joe Simpson, a war hero just back from France, with the Edmonton Eskimos, in 1920.

Arriving home with the Medal of Honour, Lieutenant Simpson joined the senior Selkirk Fishermen, where he became a star in the senior Manitoba Hockey League, firing 19 goals in 10 games during the 1919–20 season.

Simpson was playing pool in Winnipeg that summer, when Kenny Mackenzie, a representative of the Edmonton Eskimos, a team in Alberta's Big-Four league, offered him $3,000 to turn professional. Chalking up his pool cue, Simpson told Mackenzie that if the scout could sell the deal to his father, the Eskimos had themselves a defenceman. Mackenzie somehow convinced Mr. Simpson that pro hockey was not an iced road to gambling and depredation, as many believed at the time, and in the fall of 1920, Simpson arrived in Edmonton, playing alongside another Selkirk native, John Morrison. Three years later, in 1923, Simpson led the Eskimos to the Stanley Cup finals, where the team was swept in two games by the powerful Ottawa Senators.

In 1925, Simpson's father's worst fears were realized when Joe was sold, along with Morrison and Roy Rickey, to bootlegger Big Bill Dwyer and the New York Americans. After the Selkirk native arrived in the Big Apple, Dwyer's press agents provided Bullet Joe with a new, geographically inaccurate nickname, "The Blue Streak from Saskatoon."

Simpson played five seasons for the "Amerks" (1925–31) and then coached the club from 1932 to 1935, accumulating more tall tales and real-life adventures. The Americans' headquarters were in the Forrest Hotel, a mob hangout half a block from Madison Square Garden. Mobsters "Dutch" Schultz and "Legs" Diamond lived there, as did Broadway storyteller Damon Runyon. The Americans used to make fun of Runyon, whom they encountered in the lobby taking his young girlfriend's pooch out for nightly strolls. The ridicule might have had something to do with Runyon's lifelong disdain for hockey. "The business left me palled," Runyon wrote of a game involving the Americans. "Neither team scored while I was in the building, largely because of the agility of the two goaltenders, who were padded like stuffed sausages."

After his hockey career, Bullet Joe Simpson allowed his nickname to lapse, opting for the slower-paced life of running a hardware store in Coral Gables, Florida, owned by retired Winnipeg hockey player Art Coulter. In 1962, Simpson was inducted into the Hockey Hall of Fame. Selkirk would remember the most famous graduate of the Selkirk Fishermen in 1994, when the city's Marine Museum of Manitoba restored an old flat-bottomed freighter, renaming the vessel, *Joe Simpson*.

Crutchy

John "Crutchy" Morrison learned to skate on the Red River, and his father Dave was an early coach of the Selkirk Fishermen, the town's famous junior team. A lifelong friend of hockey star "Bullet" Joe Simpson, Morrison followed an almost identical career trajectory, playing alongside Simpson on the junior Selkirk Fishermen, Winnipeg 61st Battalion, senior Selkirk Fishermen, Edmonton Eskimos and New York Americans (1925–26). Upon retiring from hockey, Morrison returned to Selkirk where, like Simpson, he opened a hardware store, J.W. Morrison Hardware. The origin of the player's nickname, Crutchy, remains a mystery.

WINNIPEG

FOUNDED

From 1869 to 1870, Winnipeg was the scene of the Red River Rebellion, a struggle between local Metis—led by Louis Riel—and settlers from eastern Canada. Though the rebellion was crushed, negotiations stemming from the conflict paved the way for Manitoba to become the fifth province in 1870. The city of Winnipeg was incorporated in 1873. The name Winnipeg is a combination of Cree words: *win*, meaning "muddy," and *nipee*, meaning "water." Winnipeg was the fourth largest city in Canada before World War II. Today, it ranks ninth.

NATIVE-BORN NHL PLAYERS

Reg Abbott, Clint Albright, Bill Allum, John Arundel, Doug Baldwin, Cam Barker, Andy Bathgate, Frank Bathgate, Paul Baxter, Bill Benson, Frank Bialowas, Andy Blair, Lonny Bohonos, Larry Bolonchuk, Ryan Bonni, Dan Bourbonnais, Ralph Bowman, Jack Bownass, Darren Boyko, Andy Brannigan, George Brown, Al Buchanan, Bill Burega, Red Carr, Art Chapman, Brad Chartrand, Bob Chrystal, Cam Connor, Joe Cooper, Riley Cote, Art Coulter, Joe Crozier, Joe Daley, Ernie Dickens, Jim Dobson, Jordy Douglas, Keith Duncan, Bruce Eakin, Gary Emmons, Brian Engblom, Bill Ezinicki, Wilf Field, Tom Fowler, Frank Frederickson, Karl Friesen, Owen Fussey, Herb Gardiner, Paul Gauthier, Bill Gooden, Jackie Gordon, Lee Goren, Slim Halderson, Jim Hargreaves, Ted Harris, Andy Hebenton, Jim Henry, Phillip Hergesheimer, Wally Hergesheimer, Bryan Hextall, Dennis Hextall, Ike Hildebrand, Kevin Hodson, Cecil Hoekstra, Ed Hoekstra, Dave Hrechkosy, Lex Hudson, Ted Irvine, Douglas Jackson, Paul Jerrard, Ching Johnson, Jim Johnson, Bill Juzda, Mike Keane, Duncan Keith, Scott Kellman, William Kendall, Julian Klymkiw, Neil Komadoski, Brent Krahn, Joseph Krol, Adolph Kukulowicz, Arnie Kullman, Eddie Kullman, Justin Kurtz, Max Labovitch, Pete Langelle, Ted Lanyon, Jamie Leach, Mike Leclerc, Grant Ledyard, Chuck Lefley, Barry Legge, Doug Lewis, Brian Loney, Ron Loustel, Norm Lowe, Bill MacKenzie, George Maneluk, Mike Maneluk, Jack Mann, Bill Masterton, Frank Mathers, Fred Maxwell, Eddie Mazur, Kevin McCarthy, John McCready, Ab McDonald, Jack McLean, Nick Mickoski, Al Millar, Craig Millar, Perry Miller, Amby Moran, William Mosienko, Bryan Muir, Rick Newell, James Patrick, Steve Patrick, John Peirson, Cliff Pennington, Greg Phillips, Alf Pike, Nels Podolsky, Geoffrey Powis, Ken Reardon, Terence Reardon, William Reay, Craig Reichert, Edmond Reigle, Mike Ridley, Gus Rivers, George Robertson, Russ Romaniuk, Tom Roulston, Church Russell, Jack Ruttan, Terry Sawchuk, Dave Semenko, Joe Shack, Fred Shero, Alex Shibicky, Ron Shudra, Al Simmons, Alex Singbush, Warren Skorodenski, Edward Slowinski, Vern Smith, Arthur Somers, Lorne Stamler, Darryl Stanley, Wally Stanowski, Alexander Steen, Pete Stemkowski, Blair Stewart, Art Stratton, Billy Taylor, Luc Theoret, Jimmy Thomson, Joseph Thorsteinson, Kevin Todd, Marcel Tremblay, Brad Turner, Lindsay Vallis, Nicholas Wasnie, Duvie Westcott, Len Wharton, Carey Wilson, Cully Wilson, Stephen Witiuk, Bob Woytowich

FAMOUS LOCAL TEAMS

Junior: Winnipeg Argonauts, Winnipeg Assiniboia, Winnipeg Barons, Winnipeg Black Hawks, Winnipeg Braves, Winnipeg Canadians, Winnipeg Columbus Club, Winnipeg Elmwoods, Winnipeg Esquires, Winnipeg Falcon Rangers, Winnipeg Falcons, Winnipeg Jets, Winnipeg Jr. Monarchs, Winnipeg Monarchs, Winnipeg Pilgrims, Winnipeg Saints, Winnipeg St. Johns, Winnipeg St. James, Winnipeg South Blues, Winnipeg Strathconas, Winnipeg Victorias, Winnipeg Winnipegs; **Senior-pro:** Manitoba Moose, Winnipeg All Stars, Winnipeg 223rd Battalion, Winnipeg 61st Battalion, Winnipeg Argonauts, Winnipeg Army, Winnipeg Buffaloes, Winnipeg CNR, Winnipeg CPR Railway, Winnipeg Eaton's, Winnipeg Falcons, Winnipeg Flyers, Winnipeg Hudson's Bay, Winnipeg Jets, Winnipeg Kings, Winnipeg Lombards, Winnipeg Maple Leafs, Winnipeg Maroons, Winnipeg Monarchs, Winnipeg Nationals, Winnipeg Native Sons, Winnipeg Navy, Winnipeg Packers, Winnipeg RCAF, Winnipeg Shamrocks, Winnipeg St. John's, Winnipeg Strathconas, Winnipeg Tammany Tigers, Winnipeg Victorias, Winnipeg Winnipegs, Winnipeg Ypres

CURRENT POPULATION

671,000

Hurrah for the West!

(*MANITOBA FREE PRESS* HEADLINE, 1901, AFTER WINNIPEG VICTORIAS WON THE STANLEY CUP)

The first western Canadian hockey team to take on central Canada, the Winnipeg All Stars took to Ontario and Quebec ice as if on a three-week power play. The senior Victoria Hockey Club and the Winnipeg Winnipegs were created in late 1890. Less than three years later, city sportsmen merged the town's first senior clubs into the Winnipeg All Stars, sending the team rattling east on a Canadian Pacific Railroad train in quest of glory. Arriving in Toronto on 8 February 1893, the All Stars whipped the Toronto Victorias, 8–2, and then powdered an Osgoode Hall team, 11–5. Led by the Winnipeg Wonder, speed-skating champion Jack McCulloch, the Winnipeggers went on to win eight of 11 contests against the best clubs from Toronto, Kingston, Ottawa and Montreal, outscoring opponents 63 to 40.

The response from their hosts was equal parts surprise and resentment. One *Kingston Daily British Whig* reporter sniffed, "What would you expect from fellows who have ice to practice upon the whole year?"

Eastern trash talk and the All Stars' success excited a surge in Winnipeg hockey patriotism. By 1896, an estimated 30 clubs were in action at local rinks. Interest in winning the three-year-old Stanley Cup (and beating the East!) was high. And in February of that year, the city's best team, the Winnipeg Victorias, travelled to Montreal to challenge the Montreal Victorias for the hockey championship of the Dominion.

On Valentine's Day 1896, the Winnipeg Vics hopped onto Montreal's famed Victoria Rink in crimson jerseys decorated with yellow bison crests.

"Montreal to-night is clothed in sack-cloth and ashes..."

The arena was crammed with 2,000 Montreal fans, along with a Winnipeg booster club—25 high rollers who, hours before game time, slapped down $2,000 in bets on the bar at Montreal's Windsor Hotel. Back home, many more Vics fans crowded into Winnipeg hotel foyers stained blue with cigar and cigarette smoke to hear CPR telegraph readers shout out reports on the unfolding game. "Superintendant Jenkins and Mr. Thos. Masters of the C.P. Telegraphs manipulated the keyboard," according to the *Manitoba Free Press*, "while Manager Tait, in clarion tones, but with a distinct Scotch accent, sang out the bulletins."

With every missive, the Winnipeg sportsmen began slapping each other on the back a little harder. In Montreal, Winnipeg Vics manager and captain Jack Armytage, accepted a pass in the slot at the 10-minute mark and relayed the puck "fairly between the posts," according to the *Free Press*. Then, early in the "second game" (second half), Attie Howard, called "the truest shot in the Dominion," managed to entice the disc past the Montreal goalkeeper." With a two-goal lead, the Winnipeg team went into a 19th-century version of the neutral-zone trap, bringing their forwards back and inviting Montreal Victorias attackers to wander, in purposeless circles, at the rink's equator. When a Montreal player managed to penetrate the Winnipeg zone, he was discouraged from scoring by the attentions of Fred "The Remarkably Steady" Higginbotham at "cover," and goalie Cecil "Whitey" Merritt, standing ready between the posts, his white cricket pads gleaming.

At the conclusion of the 2–0 game, the Winnipeg Victorias became the first team outside Montreal to win the Stanley Cup. The next day, the *Manitoba Free Press* offered a front-page account of the game so patriotic that it might have come with war bonds. Below the upper-case headline, A FAMOUS VICTORY, the game report began:

> Montreal, Feb. 14—There is joy in the ranks of the Winnipeg touring hockey contingent to-night. The magnificent Stanley Cup, emblematic of the championship of the Dominion, is theirs. They presented it to the Queen City of the west, as a

A splendid cyclist, oarsman, and figure skater, Jack McCulloch won the world speed-skating championship in 1897. Four winters earlier, "The Winnipeg Wonder" helped a city all-star hockey team to a successful exhibition tour of Ontario.

valentine won as it was on February 14th. Well and worthy was the victory; long and determined the battle, and for the first time in the history of the hockey champions of the effete east they had to submit to a complete whitewash.

The blizzards from the land of the setting sun, which trouped into Montreal on Wednesday evening, created no little stir in the breasts of Montrealers... Alas for the frailty of human hopes, Montreal to-night is clothed in sack-cloth and ashes, and the sports have gone to sleepless beds with empty pocketbooks. The "Peg" contingent on the other hand have enough money to start a private bank. No less than two thousand cold plunkers were passed over the Windsor Hotel counter after the match to-night, and went down into the jeans of Winnipeg supporters.

The Winnipeg Victorias' first Stanley Cup win marked the beginning of the city's five-decade reign as the capital of western Canadian hockey (the Vics would beat the Montreal Victorias for the Stanley Cup again in 1901). Indeed, a case could be made that Winnipeg was the most successful amateur hockey city in Canada for the first half of the 20th century, for a Winnipeg team would reach the final of the senior Allan Cup every year between 1911 and 1920, winning in 1911, 1912, 1913, 1915, 1916 and 1920. In junior hockey, Winnipeg teams appeared in the Memorial Cup finals eight times between 1929 and 1946, taking the championship in 1931, 1935, 1937, 1941, 1943 and 1946.

Dale Hawerchuck was the first star of the Winnipeg Jets, averaging 42 goals a season in his years with the club (1981–90).

The Winnipeg Victorias, in 1895, a year before they became the first team outside Quebec to win the Stanley Cup. Moustachioed goalie "Whitey" Merrit, front left, is holding an early goalie stick, slightly built up on one side above the blade.

A Falcons' view of Europe: members of the 1920 Winnipeg Falcons sightseeing overseas prior to their gold medal win in Antwerp, Belgium.

Winning teams inevitably reflected the multicultural nature of the city, a rich stew of English, French, Aboriginal, German and Ukrainian cultures, along with Protestant, Catholic, Mennonite and Jewish faiths. One Icelandic-Manitoban team, the Winnipeg Falcons, won both the Allan Cup and a gold medal at the Antwerp Winter Games in 1920. And a Winnipeg working-class neighbourhood like East Kildonan, which was made up of Ukrainian, Irish, English and German populations, produced a hockey line with Alf Pike, Dick Kowcinak and Johnny McCreedy that won the Memorial Cup for the junior Winnipeg Monarchs in 1937. Another Ukrainian player from the city's East Kildonan area, Terry "Uke" Sawchuk, would become the finest National Hockey League goalie of his generation.

But perhaps the classic tale of Winnipeg hockey multiculturalism is the story of Peter Landiak, a Polish-Ukrainian from East Kildonan, who grew up on the same block as hockey's famous Whirling Dervish, Wally Stanowski. Indeed, the best friends graduated to the Toronto Maple Leafs, where Landiak scored the game-seven 1942 Stanley Cup-winning goal over the Detroit Red Wings—except that the hockey player was no longer Peter Landiak at the time. Years earlier, when Landiak and Stanowski tried out for the junior Seals, the junior team in what was then Winnipeg's French twin city, St. Boniface, the Seals' management persuaded Landiak to change his name to Pete Langelle in order to attract French fans.

Winnipeg writer Scott Young captured the pluralistic ideal of local hockey in his best-selling adolescent fiction hockey series, which began with *Scrubs on Skates*. In that book, the story of a fictitious Winnipeg team at Northwest High, Young has local sports reporter Lee Vincent comment:

> Lee loved lineups, because to him lineups always told the true story of a sport. He read the names now... Paul Brabant and Junior Paterson in goal. The defence names he had were Bill Spunska, Adam Lawrence, Gordon Jamieson, Groucy DeGruchy and Rosario Duplessis. The forwards were Pete Gordon, Stretch Buchanan, Henry Bell, Alec Mitchell, Hurry Berton, Horatio Big Canoe (there was one for you, the tall lanky Indian boy who stick handled as if the puck was

NORTHWEST COMPANY

A generation of Canadians grew up on Scott Young's stories of hockey-playing kids Pete Gordon and Bill Spunska, from Northwest High in Winnipeg. Young's first book, *Scrubs on Skates*, came out in 1952. The sequel, *Boy on Defence*, appeared the following year. The third book in the series, *A Boy at the Leafs' Camp*, arrived in 1963. All of these teen fiction novels were profoundly moral tales characterized by vivid characters and authentic hockey action. Many boys dreamed of playing defence alongside Bill Spunska and of maybe getting to know his easy-smiling, fair-haired sister Sarah.

The Winnipeg Jets scouted talent from Sweden in the 1970s, including Anders Hedberg.

Bobby Hull with the Winnipeg Jets.

taped to the end of his stick), Pincher Martin, Winston Kryshuk, Benny Wong.
He didn't know how many races were represented there, but now they were on
one team, all trying... Forever after this season these boys...would remember the
names on this team and know that people of all races could get along when they
had something in common.

Winnipeg entered another golden era in its hockey history on 27 June 1972,
when the 33-year-old "Golden Jet," Bobby Hull, landed in town. He brought
downtown traffic to a halt by holding a joyous, shouting press conference at the
corner of Portage and Main during weekday rush hour, to announce that he was
signing with the World Hockey Association's (WHA) Winnipeg Jets. The arrival of
Hull, among the biggest stars ever to play the game of hockey (see page 232), lent
credibility to the new team and league, intended to rival the NHL, and led to three
WHA Avco Cup championships for the Winnipeg Jets, in 1976, 1978 and 1979.

Jean Beliveau called Terry Sawchuk
"the best goalie I ever played against."

Uke

Winnipeg-born Terry "Uke" Sawchuk inherited goalie pads from an adored older brother, Mike, who died of a heart attack at the age of 17. Sawchuk would make himself the most famous goalie of his generation with this haunted equipment, without ever managing to make the accompanying curse disappear.

Sawchuk was the leading scorer on his minor league teams, when he wasn't in nets. And writer Scott Young remembers seeing him play baseball for the Elmwood Giants of the senior-pro Man-Dak league as a teenager, hitting "booming home runs in community parks on warm prairie evenings." Sawchuk would bring with him that athleticism, along with an almost frightening level of concentration to goaltending, first with the Winnipeg Rangers, a local junior team, then later, most famously, with the Detroit Red Wings in the 1950s. The goalie invented the crouched style, dipping his unmasked face low to his knees to get a better read on the puck. And he would hold himself rigid in what became a classic pose, coiled and waiting for a shot or deflection. When he was playing his best, he was a magician so good that he could make the net behind him disappear. In the spring of 1952, he gave up only five goals in eight Stanley Cup playoff games with the Detroit Red Wings. He also recorded more shutouts, 103, than any other goalie in the history of the game.

Still, trouble, injury and sickness were lifelong companions. Sawchuk's face was marked with over 400 stitches from errant pucks and sticks. An opposition forward once skated across his left hand, severing the tendons. He had also punctured a lung in a car crash. And his right arm was two inches longer than his left, as the result of various operations.

Sawchuk died at the age of 40, from internal injuries that resulted from an awkward fall after an argument with a teammate in a New York bar. "He was the greatest goalie I ever saw, and the most troubled athlete I ever knew," commented *Detroit Free Press* sportswriter Joe Falls.

Perhaps not surprisingly, given the multicultural hockey tradition of the city, the Jets employed an enlightened immigration policy, as the team became the first North American hockey club to extensively scout Europe, emptying Sweden of hockey talent in the mid-1970s with the signing of Ulf Nilsson, Anders Hedberg, Kent "Magic" Nilsson, Lars-Erik Sjoberg and Willy "The Wisp" Lindstrom. That the forward line of Hull-[Ulf] Nilsson-Hedberg was arguably the best line in hockey at the time became evident on 5 January 1978, when the Jets defeated the Soviet national team, 5–3, in maybe the best game a local team ever played in Winnipeg. Hull had three goals that night; Nilsson, two. And

Who needs the NHL, when the Moose is on the loose?

Hedberg provided the exclamation point for the win, jumping up in the dressing room after the game to exclaim, "Guys, do you know what we've accomplished? We were the first club team to ever beat the Soviet national team in a game. Ever! That was an unbelievable accomplishment."

Four WHA teams, including the Winnipeg Jets, were incorporated into the NHL in 1979, but at a cruel price. WHA teams were stripped of all but two skaters—the championship Jets were grounded. Two seasons later (1980–81), the team finished dead last, at one point going without a win for 30 games. The Jets would improve immediately, securing a first overall draft pick by virtue of their miserable season, using it to take Dale Hawerchuk, a Toronto-born

JET TRAILS

When Bobby Hull first arrived with the Winnipeg Jets in 1972–73, he played on The Luxury Line, with Christian Bordeleau and Normie Beaudin. Two years later, stylish forwards Anders Hedberg and Ulf Nilsson moved in alongside Hull, and the fast-moving unit, which changed lanes like Ferraris on the Autobahn, and dazzled the World Hockey Association for four seasons (1974–78), collecting 573 goals.

The Team Nobody Wanted

Eight Winnipeg teams competed in the Allan Cup senior finals between 1911 and 1920, winning six national championships, but no local senior club flew so high as the Winnipeg Falcons who, in 1920, went from taking the Allan Cup to winning Canada's first-ever Olympic hockey gold medal. However, before beating the world in Antwerp, Belgium, the Falcons first had to defeat local prejudice.

In the early 1900s, Winnipeg wasn't yet the melting pot it would eventually become. "Help wanted" signs in local businesses sometimes came with the catch, "Icelanders need not apply." Similarly, the Falcons, a team comprised of Icelandic Canadians, were refused entry into the Winnipeg City League, and so became known as "The Team Nobody Wanted." Four of the Falcons, Konnie Johanneson, Frank Fredrickson, Bobbie Benson and Wally Byron, served together in the same unit in World War I and then returned home determined to form their own league.

The Falcons went on to defeat all civic competition before travelling to Toronto to sweep the University of Toronto, 3–2 and 8–3, thereby capturing the Allan Cup. Having secured the title as the best senior club in Canada, the eight-member Winnipeg squad later set sail aboard the RMS *Grampian* for the Antwerp Olympics. Canada was losing the gold medal game, 2–1, to the United States with a minute left, when the team amassed a furious assault, tying the game on a goal by Romeo Rivers with 33 seconds remaining. (Canada would win the gold medal on the basis of an earlier 2–1 overtime win over the Americans.)

The once-shunned Falcons returned home to a mile-long parade down Main Street and Portage Avenue. They would receive an additional tribute in 2005, when the Canadian national hockey team honoured the Falcons by donning the team's gold-and-black uniforms in a World Cup of Hockey match against the United States. Canada won that game, 2–1.

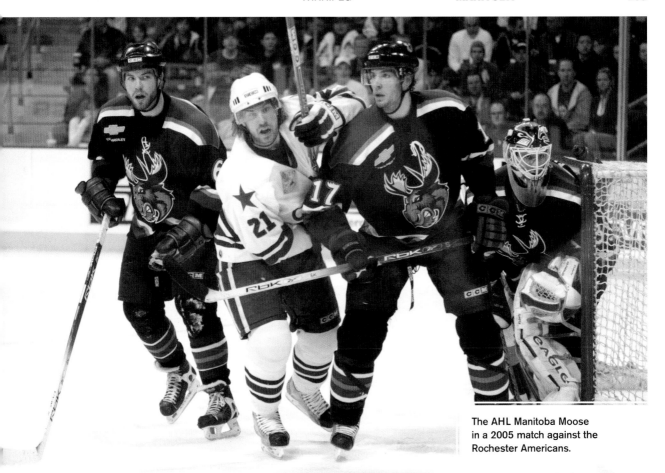

The AHL Manitoba Moose in a 2005 match against the Rochester Americans.

Ukrainian kid who led the feisty, young "Scrubs on Skates" '80s edition of the Jets to respectability. Alas, the Jets were stuck in the NHL's Western Conference, which included the powerhouse Calgary Flames and Edmonton Oilers, and hence never graduated beyond their division in the playoffs.

By the mid-1990s, escalating salaries and the limitations of playing in the Winnipeg Arena, a lovely old building that resisted a series of makeovers, made NHL hockey economically unviable in Winnipeg. After a series of painfully unsuccessful financial rescue missions, the Jets left the city, bound for Phoenix, Arizona, in 1996. The team's last game in Winnipeg, an April 28th playoff "whiteout" against the Detroit Red Wings, for which fans dressed entirely in white to show support of the team, bidding the Jets goodbye with rousing, prolonged cheers, left some departing players in tears.

Hockey itself did not leave the city, of course. The Manitoba Moose, a farm team for the NHL's Vancouver Canucks, would soon become the most financially successful team in the American Hockey League. And as a February 2005 *New York Times* report on the Moose noted, "with the National Hockey League season all but extinguished [because of a protracted labour dispute], Winnipeg's American Hockey League team, the high-scoring Manitoba Moose, has emerged as the hottest box-office draw of any professional hockey team in Canada." Or, as the story's headline put it, "Who needs the NHL, when the Moose is on the loose?"

Fans honour the Winnipeg Jets on the team's final game, 28 April 1996.

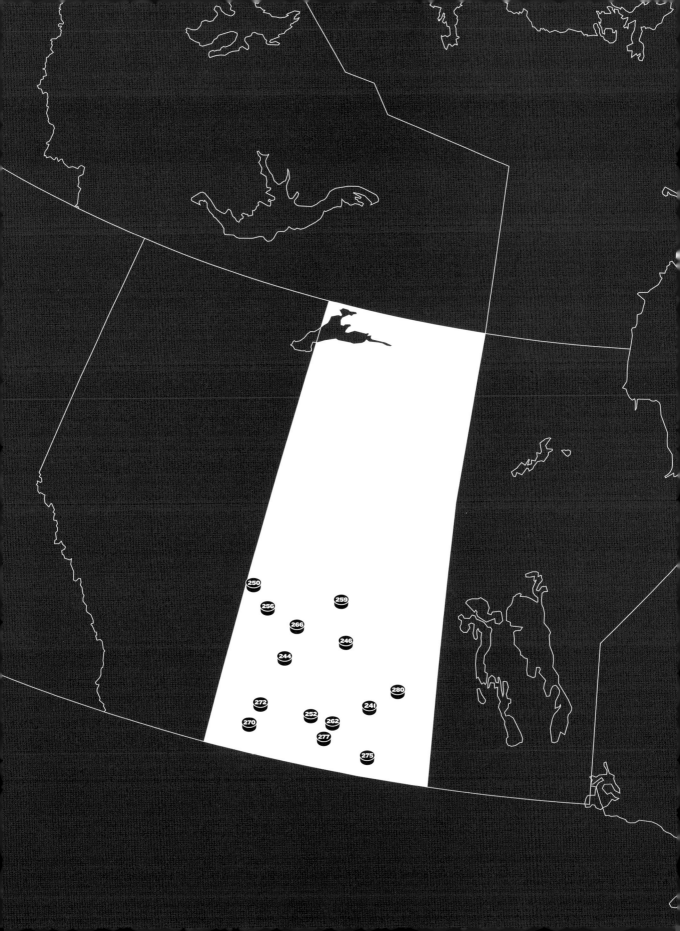

Opening Spread:
Hayley Wickenheiser
in action against Russia
at the 2006 Olympics.
The women's team
would go on to win
the gold medal.

Workers gather for the harvest
at a Saskatchewan farm.

Canadians are always pleased to note that Gordie Howe was born in the tiny town of Floral, Saskatchewan. Perhaps, it somehow flatters the country to think that the sport's most illustrious performer came to greatness playing on untended frozen sloughs and rivers in the heart of the Dominion.

Saskatchewan produces almost 50 percent of Canada's wheat. And during the months when farms and cattle ranches are burdened with snow, the province instead manufactures hockey heroes, who seem to grow naturally in small towns made famous by the exploits of their players. Before Gordie Howe, Saskatchewan produced Max, Doug and Reg Bentley, the famous Dipsy Doodle Dandy Brothers from the farm community of Delisle. Among hockey's greatest stars at the time of World War II, Max and Doug Bentley learned the moves that would earn them so many bright adjectives while darting around piles of animal slop on a farm rink. Prior to the Bentleys, the province boasted four-time National Hockey League most valuable player Eddie Shore, born in Fort Qu'Appelle and raised in Cupar, Saskatchewan, both towns of less than 500 people. Eddie Shore's rancher father financed the building of the town's arena to help keep his boys out of trouble.

A census of small-town Saskatchewan reveals a star player at every stop, it seems. Fern Flaman, a six-time NHL all-star, came from Dysart. Goalies Charlie Rayner (Sutherland), Glenn Hall (Humboldt), Johnny Bower (Prince Albert) and Emile "The Cat" Francis (North Battleford) all made the Hockey Hall of Fame. So did Sid Abel, a forward from Melville who played with Gordie Howe on the Detroit Red Wings' great Production Line in the 1950s. Another contemporary of Howe's and fellow Hall of Famer, Bert Olmstead (from Sceptre, Saskatchewan), was maybe the most underappreciated performer on the great Montreal Canadiens teams that same decade. And a quarter-century later, Bryan Trottier (Val Marie), Bernie Federko (Foam Lake), Theoren Fleury (Oxbow) and Wendel Clark (Kelvington) would all emerge from small prairie towns to attain hockey greatness in the NHL.

The Moccasin Goalie

No one else has captured the blazing skies and sun-brightened colours of the prairie winter with the evident passion of artist and children's book author William Roy Brownridge. Born in 1932, in Rosetown, Saskatchewan, Brownridge—the youngest of five children—overcame physical affliction (spina bifida and club feet) to play goalie for his town's intermediate team, a story he would retell in the inspirational and now-classic children's tale, *The Moccasin Goalie*.

"My inspiration to paint comes from three sources," Brownridge once wrote. "Perhaps most significantly, as a child I suffered from a physical condition that greatly hindered my ability to walk and run. As a child of the prairies, it was only natural that my eye would focus on things such as galloping horses and the grace and power of an outdoor hockey game.... I grew up loving the wintertime, both its shining beauty and its starkness. It was within this environment of action and arctic weather that my brothers—Bob and Don—emerged as my role models, my heroes. I was mesmerized, watching as they cut down the ice, swooped in on the puck like a bird of prey, banked away sharply, then glided like a great eagle on an updraft."

The great Gordie Howe celebrates an early milestone, his 1,000th point.

A February 2004 broadcast of *Hockey Night in Canada*'s annual "Hockey Day in Canada," held in Shaunavon, Saskatchewan, a town of 1,800 tucked into the southwest corner of the province, offered conclusive proof that the prairie province was a "cold house" hockey factory. According to the program, Saskatchewan, with a population that has remained around one million for more than 25 years, has produced more NHL players per capita—some 422 in all—than any other province, American state or northern European country. "I think geography has something to do with [Saskatchewan's] success," Mark Odnokon, a Saskatchewan-based NHL scout and former junior with the Prince Albert Raiders, told a CBC reporter. "There are no major cities in the province, like Toronto, Vancouver or Montreal. I teach in a small town [Shellbrook] and the central focus is the hockey rink. My guys practice once or twice a week, play a game outdoors, and play shinny inside after school. In a big city, midgets will have one practice a week."

Ice time and per capita statistics are only so helpful in explaining why so many Saskatchewan youngsters have achieved greatness in world hockey arenas, however. Saskatchewan natives have a consuming passion for the sport that can perhaps best be explained by telling a story involving Shaunavon's Hayley Wickenheiser.

Saskatchewan's Sid Abel (centre) and Gordie Howe (right) were two-thirds of Detroit's Production Line. Ted Lindsay is on the left.

Ted Hargreaves, c. 1973.

Saskatchewan Goes for Gold at '68 Olympics

The 1968 Canadian Olympic hockey team had an unmistakable Saskatchewan flavour, as the coach, Hazlet's Jackie McLeod, trainer Scotty Clark (from Saskatoon) and seven skaters on the team were all from the prairie province. Players included Ted Hargreaves (Foam Lake), Gary Begg (Moosomin), Fran Huck (Regina), Morris Mott (Creelman), Marshall Johnston (Birch Hills) and Herb and Gerry Pinder (Saskatoon). The 1968 Canadian amateurs travelled to Prague in hope of a medal and they didn't disappoint, defeating teams from the United States, Czechoslovakia and Sweden. Canadian downhill skier Nancy Greene sat on the team's bench wearing a recently won gold medal, during the team's 3–0 win over Sweden. McLeod's team played the powerful Soviet Union for the gold medal, losing 5–1. The Saskatchewan players would return home with bronze medals.

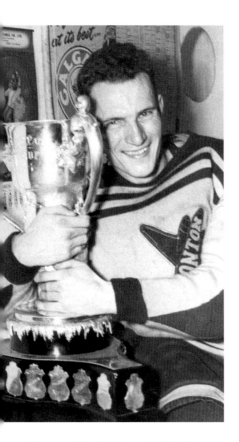

Vanguard, Saskatchewan's Al Rollins, here celebrating a win with the Edmonton Flyers, would later win the NHL's 1953–54 NHL's Most Valuable Player Award with the last place Chicago Blackhawks.

Hayley's father, Tom Wickenheiser, was fast asleep one night and woke up with a start (see page 270). He could hear something happening outside the house. But that was impossible: It was in the middle of a bitter-cold winter evening. He had seen all of his kids to bed. Padding downstairs, he checked for burglars, and then was drawn to the kitchen window by a familiar scratching sound. Staring out into the inky darkness, he saw the form of his daughter Hayley, then aged seven, flying around a neighbour's rink, trying to sneak in an extra hour of work. The practice paid off, for in the 1990s Hayley Wickenheiser would become known as the best women's hockey player in the world, furthering Saskatchewan's reputation as the home of small-town hockey superstars.

CUPAR

FOUNDED

Located 46 miles northwest of Regina and within a 20-minute drive of the Qu'Appelle Valley, the town of Cupar is situated on the plains of Saskatchewan's finest grain-growing region. Like many other prairie communities, Cupar sprang to life in 1905 with the arrival of the Canadian Pacific Railroad. In fact, a Scottish CPR official named the settlement after the town of Cupar in Fifeshire, Scotland.

NATIVE-BORN NHL PLAYERS

Eddie Shore (born in Fort Qu'Appelle, SK), Rob Tudor

FAMOUS LOCAL TEAMS

Senior-pro: Cupar Canucks, Cupar Cubs

CURRENT POPULATION

591

The Far Shore

Eddie Shore's father, T.J. Shore, financed the first indoor rink in Cupar, Saskatchewan, a small town across the Qu'Appelle Valley from Regina. Eddie and his older brother, Aubrey, were born in nearby Fort Qu'Appelle, but they grew up outside Cupar. The boys didn't play much hockey as children, and Eddie Shore more likely developed his sporting instincts breaking in stallions on his father's ranch.

Life on the Cupar family spread was probably also the source of Eddie's driving need to succeed, for after his father lost the family fortune in an unadvised business venture, he eventually committed suicide. And Eddie's older brother was a merciless tease. When Aubrey Shore made the hockey team at the Manitoba Agricultural College in Winnipeg, Eddie wondered if anybody interested could join the club.

"Anybody but you," Aubrey sneered.

Eddie would still enjoy telling the "anybody but you" story to reporters over 50 years later.

Perhaps T.J. Shore had a rink built in Cupar to divert his quarrelsome boys. Whatever the case, by 1921, the Shore brothers had made the senior Cupar Cubs the talk of Saskatchewan hockey. Out-of-town games were winter jamborees, and almost everyone in Cupar crowded into Canadian Pacific Railroad cars to support the Cubs on raucous train rides to Regina, Saskatoon and Moose Jaw.

Cupar frequently won these contests, and Aubrey Shore became a hero, the best hockey player in town. Eddie Shore was good, too, and determined to get better. While his older brother abandoned the sport, Eddie signed with the senior Melville Millionaires in 1923–24, and then began jumping the pro hockey ladder two rungs at a time, joining the Regina Caps of the Western Canadian Hockey League in 1924–25 and the Edmonton Eskimos of the Western Hockey League the following season. In the fall of 1926, Shore made the National Hockey League's Boston Bruins just short of his 24th birthday.

Along with Lester and Frank Patrick (see page 330), Shore was one of the earliest prototypes of the rushing defenceman, scoring more than 10 goals a year his first five NHL seasons, an unheard of feat. At 5'11" and 190 pounds, he was often the biggest, always the strongest, and frequently the meanest, man on the

EDDIE'S FIRST TEAM

A senior hockey team has played out of Cupar, Saskatchewan, since 1907. Eddie and Aubrey Shore played for the senior Cupar Cubs in the early 1920s, taking the team to the provincial championship in 1922, where they lost to the Melville Millionaires. Today, the Cupar Canucks, as the team has been known since 1990, play out of the Cuplex and have dedicated a nearby park, the Shore Recreational Park, to the Shore family.

Eddie Shore has a rare smile for NHL president Frank Calder in 1939. Shore was the first defenceman to win the league's MVP trophy (1932–33). He would win the award four times.

ice. In late 1933, playing against the Toronto Maple Leafs in the Boston Gardens, he grew furious watching Ace Bailey foil a Bruins power play with an elaborate solo dash around the rink. Regaining the puck, Shore made for the Leafs net, but was chopped down by King Clancy. When the Bruins defenceman lifted himself up, he found Bailey with his back turned. Accelerating hard, Shore dipped his shoulder and caught Bailey in the kidneys, sending him pinwheeling over his shoulder. According to a reporter covering the game, the sound of Bailey's head hitting the ice was "like a pumpkin being cracked by a baseball bat."

In the dressing room afterward, a doctor stood over the shaking Bailey and declared, "If this boy is Roman Catholic, we should call a priest." Minutes later Shore arrived to apologize, but he couldn't find the words. "It's OK, Eddie," Bailey told him. "I guess it's part of the game." Then, he fell into a coma.

Bailey's father bought a gun and travelled to Boston, looking for Shore, but he was intercepted by police. Newspaper editorialists across Canada called for something beyond the 16-game suspension that the NHL handed down. Bailey recovered, after two operations, but he never played again.

As it happened, Shore gladly accepted the part of hockey's leading villain, showing up for pregame skates wearing a black cape that would be whisked away by a pretend valet before the puck was dropped. (Perhaps if he was going to be disliked, Shore wanted it to seem like his idea.) Writing in *Collier's* magazine, Kyle Crichton suggested that Shore was the biggest draw in hockey, in the 1930s. "What makes him that," Crichton elaborated, "is the hope, entertained in all cities but Boston, that he will some night be severely killed."

Shore's bad guy pose masked an iron determination to succeed and to get what he wanted done, whatever the cost. Bruins coach Art Ross told hockey writer Bill Roche about the time his star defenceman missed a train for Montreal because of a traffic accident. Shore tried to charter a plane, but a snowstorm had closed the Quebec airports. A wealthy friend offered him a limousine and chauffeur, and at eight o'clock that evening, Shore was on the road with a road map and a less-than-willing driver, 400 miles from Montreal.

Hard, slanting snow soon made the road disappear, and the driver slowed to a speed beyond Shore's endurance. Well, what did a fancy Boston chauffeur know about driving in snow? The Saskatchewan rancher's son took over behind the wheel, pulled into a filling station, strapped chains across the back tires and headed back onto the road. The windshield wiper surrendered next. Shore opened up the top section of the window and stared into a razor blizzard of sleet, reading the road through narrowed eyes. Four times, while travelling through the Appalachians in the middle of the night, Shore lost his bearings and flew off the road. Four times, he climbed out of the car and shouldered the big sedan back onto the highway, with the chauffeur momentarily at the wheel.

In the morning, Shore stopped for fuel and coffee at a New Hampshire gas station/diner. A few hours later, in Quebec now, the car slipped off the road again, this time sliding into a deep gulley. Shore walked to a farmhouse and, depending largely on hand gestures, offered an explanation of his predicament to a French farmer. The man nodded and, eight dollars later, returned to the scene of the accident with Shore and a team of horses, pulling the car out of trouble.

Eighteen hours after taking to the road, Shore startled teammates by pulling into Montreal's Windsor Hotel at 6 p.m. He had a steak and then staggered onto the team bus, walking on legs drunk with fatigue. As soon as he put on his skates though, he knew he was going to be fine. He played a regular shift, leading the Bruins to a 1–0 win over the Montreal Maroons. Eddie Shore scored the game's only goal.

Eddie Shore hockey card, 1933–34.

Eddie's Last Team

Eddie Shore's father lost the family fortune in a business venture, so Eddie wasn't about to let anyone take his money when he bought the Springfield Indians of the American Hockey League in 1940. Running the team until 1976, he carried a gun while transporting the team payroll. And the one-time ranch hand, who had learned to compete by training stallions, finished his sporting days breaking in younger athletes to the ways of Eddie Shore-style hockey.

Shore believed that goalies shouldn't go down on the ice, so he sometimes had his netminders practice with nooses, hung from crossbars, strung around their necks. All this in a rink as dark as a closet, since arena lights were turned off during practice to save money.

Sometimes Shore got his goalie alone in a dark rink and drilled him for hours. Without a puck. The goalie crouched in the net, rope around his neck, pretending to make kick and glove saves. Shore sat up in the stands, watching. Silent, mostly. But every now and then, when the goalie succumbed to fatigue, Shore would call out slowly, "You missed that one, Mister."

The Indians were a great business success and won the American Hockey League championship Calder Trophy on five occasions.

DELISLE

DELISLE SKATING RINK

Season Ticket 1920-21

NAME *Miss J. Bentley*

Children — 6 to 10 yrs.
Children — 10 to 14 yrs. — 4.00.
Ladies' — 4.00.
Gentlemen — 6.00.

J C Coop
MANAGER

Jane Bentley's 1920–21 skating pass
to a Delisle rink.

FOUNDED

Located 25 miles southwest of
Saskatoon, Delisle grew alongside the
Goose Lake Railway Line, built in
1907–08. The town was incorporated
in 1913. Delisle has always been an
agricultural community, but two
potash mines also provide employment for local citizens.

NATIVE-BORN NHL PLAYERS
Doug Bentley, Max Bentley, Reginald
Bentley, Dick Butler, Jack Miller

FAMOUS LOCAL TEAMS
Senior-pro: Delisle Tigers

CURRENT POPULATION
884

Dipsy Doodle Dandies

A tiny agricultural community 20 minutes down Highway 7 from Saskatoon,
Delisle was named after, and made famous by, two sets of brothers. The Goose
Lake Railway Line ran through land owned by Amos, Eugene, Eddie and Fred
Delisle. When a town sprang up alongside the train station in 1908, locals took
to referring to the new settlement as Delisle.

But if the small Saskatchewan community received its name from the
Delisle family, the town's fame would be derived from the celebrated Bentley
brothers. One of the farms outside Delisle was owned by William Bentley, a
one-time speed skater who, in addition to cultivating crops and cows, raised two
hockey teams. There were 13 Bentley children, and every one of those kids
learned to skate by grabbing needed items from a heap of equipment by the back
door, then dashing off to play hockey on nearby ice made hazardous by wandering cattle. "We took in all the ice we could," one of the children, Scoop Bentley,
told the Canadian online history website, Our Roots. "Mostly we played on the
road, which was smoothed over by horses and sleighs. We shot on goal all day
long, and every once in a while we'd break a window on the veranda. But the
real reason we were so agile was because we had to skate around slop piles in
the yard."

The seven Bentley daughters formed a family outfit and were said to have
gone undefeated in exhibition matches with prairie rivals. The younger sons,
however, caused the bigger stir. Five Bentley boys, Reg, Roy, Scoop, Doug and
Max, played for the Drumheller Miners in the rough-as-sandpaper Alberta
Senior Hockey League, between 1937 and 1939.

Max was 17 years old, his first season, and so skinny that he was said to have
resembled three sleeves when he was wearing a suit. His waiflike appearance was
deceiving, though. Players a decade older and 100 pounds heavier tried to clobber
him back to Delisle. No one managed, however, for all those miles manoeuvring
around frozen farm waste had left a permanent wrinkle in the 135-pound centre's
skating style.

The only player who always seemed to know where Max Bentley was going,
was his brother and linemate Doug. In 1938–39, the two Bentley boys tied for
the lead in scoring in the Canadian Amateur Hockey Association, with 53 points
each in 32 games.

National Hockey League teams were intrigued. Max was invited to try out
for both the Boston Bruins and the Montreal Canadiens, but he failed to pass

The five Bentley brothers, Doug, Max,
Reg, Roy and Scoop, scored 93
of the Alberta Senior Hockey League
Drumheller Miners' 120 goals in
the 1938–39 season.

the physical inspection. The lifelong hypochondriac was too short, too skinny, too nervous-looking. Consequently, the Canadiens' club physician wrongly determined that Max had a heart condition. NHL hockey, the doctor suggested, would kill him within a year.

Doug Bentley managed to make it to the Chicago Blackhawks, in the fall of 1939. He did well and begged management to give his brother Max a chance. "He can skate me into the ground," Doug told Blackhawks owner Bill Tobin.

"Max is too small, Doug. I'm sorry," the owner replied.

Doug slammed the door so hard, exiting the office, that Tobin was persuaded to change his mind. Max made the club that year. Two seasons later, in 1942–43, Doug

The Bentleys were now among the most famous hockey players in Canada.

Bentley edged Rocket Richard for the NHL scoring race, with 73 points. Max, his centreman, counted 70 points. Older brother Reg even joined them on the same line for 11 games that season, before returning to a lengthy minor league career.

Every kid who ever read Ron McAllister's 1940s collection, *Hockey Heroes*, knows how the Bentleys developed their fabulous wrist shots. "Milking cows," the boys' father, William Bentley, told McAllister, who hosted a popular CBC sports radio show on Sunday afternoons. "There's nothing like milking cows to build hockey players with steel in their wrists. My boys have milked enough cows to stretch from [Delisle] to the Rocky Mountains, standing tail to tail."

The Bentleys were now among the most famous hockey players in Canada. Fans were particularly attracted to Max, whose improbable darting turns inspired the most evocative hockey nickname of the war years—Max "The Dipsy Doodle Dandy from Delisle" Bentley.

Max would become an even bigger story in 1947, when Toronto Maple Leafs owner Conn Smythe pulled off one of the biggest trades in NHL history, sending five starting players, Gus Bodnar, Bud Poile, Gaye Stewart, Bob Goldham and Ernie Dickens, to Chicago for the Chicago centre. Bentley played six seasons for the Leafs (1947-53), helping the team to three Stanley Cups. Although he retired before the television era fully arrived, making a player's style and character instantly evident, a generation of hockey fans had already memorized Max Bentley's habits and habitat.

Decades later, it is still difficult for old-time hockey fans to speak of Dipsy Doodling Max Bentley without mentioning Delisle, Saskatchewan.

Doug and Max Bentley, c. 1930.

A Real Chicago Shootout

In addition to playing on the same line for the Chicago Blackhawks, Max, Doug and Reg Bentley all married Saskatchewan girls named Betty. Their wives became Betty-Max, Betty-Reg and Betty-Doug. Betty-Doug liked to tell stories about how intimidating Chicago seemed, in comparison to Delisle. She explained that the first time Doug Bentley saw the Chicago Stadium, he shook his head and said, "Boy, this place sure could hold a lot of hay."

"Doug and I were two country bumpkins in a city of that size, with the reputation it had," Betty-Doug told Our Roots. "Once Doug, Bill Mosienko and John Mariucci were coming out of the [Chicago] stadium after a practice. Shots were being fired everywhere. The boys were scared to death and hid behind a car. It was only a regular Chicago robbery, but the boys thought they were being shot at for losing the game the night before."

BENTLEY GIRLS "BEAT BLISTERS" OFF BOYS

In addition to taking on local girls' teams, the Bentley girls, Billie, Mary, Pearl, Ruth, Tannis, Grace and Jane, regularly took on the six mostly younger Bentley boys in backyard games that were refereed by their father. Who won? "My girls' teams," the senior Bentley reported to sportswriter Stan Fischler, "could beat the blisters off the boys nine times out of 10."

HUMBOLDT

FOUNDED

In the mid-19th century, Humboldt was a resting place on the Red River Cart Trail, which connected Red River and Edmonton. A combination telegraph station and stagecoach depot was built here in 1876. The settlement was named Humboldt after German explorer and scientist Baron Friedrich Heinrich Alexander von Humboldt. The Canadian Northern Railroad reached the settlement in September 1904. German Benedictine monks of St. Peter's Colony were among the first inhabitants, and more German settlers followed. The town of Humboldt, which is located 70 miles of Saskatoon and 143 miles north of Regina, continues to celebrate Oktoberfest and Sommerfest with annual festivals.

NATIVE-BORN NHL PLAYERS

Jerry Engele, Glenn Hall, Ralph Klassen, Brad Lauer, Tony Leswick, Ross Lonsberry, Kyle McLaren, Brendan Witt

FAMOUS LOCAL TEAMS

Junior: Humboldt Broncos, Humboldt Indians;
Senior-pro: Humboldt Indians, Humboldt Sunocos

CURRENT POPULATION

5,161

Humboldt, date unknown.

Mr. Goalie

Born in Humboldt, Saskatchewan, in 1931, the hockey player who earned the nickname "Mr. Goalie" began his career as a dipsy-doodling forward, explaining his elaborate stickhandling dashes during pond hockey games to biographer Tom Adrahtas by saying, "There weren't more than two pucks in town, and if you had one of them, boy, you did a trick to keep it."

If Glenn Hall's hometown was short of pucks during the Depression, it didn't have any goaltenders. Hall and his friends played on a frozen slough transformed into a roughly framed rink with connecting planks jammed hard into snowbanks. Some days the weather got so cold that the planks split with a resounding crack. No player wanted to stand around in nets to see what might happen to him.

When Hall joined a Humboldt peewee team, he was recognized as the best player and named captain. Because the club had no coach, the challenge of creating a lineup fell to Hall. He asked every member of the team if they would be goalie, but no one wanted the job. By default, then, Glenn Hall became a goalie at age 10. The youngster soon came to enjoy the challenge of netminding, constantly moving to keep warm, inventing new bits of choreography with every deflection or screen shot. Sometimes, the excitement was so great that Hall found he couldn't sleep the night before a game.

Two events changed his life as he entered his teenage years. The first turning point occurred when the goalie for his town's junior team, the Humboldt Indians, quit. Though underage for junior hockey, Hall took his place, performed well and was invited to a tryout camp in Saskatoon, Saskatchewan, by the National Hockey League's Detroit Red Wings. All of the province's best young players were there, including future superstar Gordie Howe. One scrimmage, a bulky catching glove Hall had been supplied with fell off just as a wave of attackers approached. Someone took a hard high shot. Hall snatched the puck with

Baby-faced Glenn Hall, with the
Edmonton Flyers. Hall would graduate
to the Detroit Red Wings in 1955.
Incredibly, he wouldn't miss a game
in nets until 1963.

a bare hand, as if picking an apple off a tree. With that save, the 14-year-old instantly became an NHL prospect.

The other important development came while the youngster was visiting his grandparents' farm outside Humboldt. Hall wasn't a farm boy: His father was a Canadian National Railroad engineer. Still, he'd been to his grandparents' place before. But now that he was a goaltending prodigy—a player everyone tested their own game against—he found he had a new appreciation for the solitude of farm life.

And so the shape of Glenn Hall's life was defined. Winters, he tested his jangling nerves against the best young hockey players in Canada; and summers, he would return to the prairies, where he worked a second job, sometimes flipping burgers at a restaurant, saving to buy a farm.

Hall played goal for Red Wings farm teams in Windsor, Indianapolis and Edmonton, before finally making the NHL club in 1955. Two seasons later, Detroit sent him to Chicago, where he came into his own as the best goalie in hockey with the Chicago Blackhawks, stealing a Stanley Cup for the team in 1961 (with playoff triumphs over Montreal and Detroit) and winning Vezina trophies as the league's best goalie in 1963 and 1967. He would finish out his career

Tony "Mighty Mouse" Leswick, with the Edmonton Flyers.

Mighty Lucky Mouse

Though only 5'6", Humboldt, Saskatchewan's Tony "Mighty Mouse" Leswick once bodychecked Maurice Richard so hard that the Montreal Canadiens forward brought down the protective shield above the boards in a hail of broken glass. Leswick, who played with the National Hockey League's New York Rangers and Detroit Red Wings from 1946 to 1958, was a nemesis of the Canadiens. In the seventh game of the 1954 Stanley Cup finals, the Detroit forward sent all of Montreal into mourning. "It was early in overtime, I don't know, maybe four or five minutes in," Leswick would later tell *Hockey Digest*. "We were trying to change our forwards. I had the puck around center ice or so and I just wanted to do the smart thing and throw it in… So I flipped it, nice and high, and turned to get off the ice. The next thing, everyone's celebrating. It had gone in. I said, 'You've got to be kidding. Get out of here!' What had happened was, Doug Harvey went to glove the puck and put it down on the ice, but instead, he had accidentally deflected it past goalie Gerry McNeil… It was just one of those things. But that goal gave us the Cup."

with the St. Louis Blues, winning another Vezina together with Jacques Plante in 1969, before retiring in 1971.

At one point, the unmasked goalie played a record 502 games in a row, performing in every minute of regular season and playoff games between 1955 and 1963 despite numerous facial wounds from hockey and a famously nervous stomach that had him vomiting before every game, sometimes between periods—a habit that discouraged his wife, Pauline, a native of Kelvington, Saskatchewan, from spending much time in the kitchen. ("How would you like to cook for a guy who is going to throw up what you just made in a matter of hours?" she asked her husband's biographer.)

Inevitably, it became harder for Hall to leave the land he loved for the hard game in which he took such pride.

What made Hall's 502 game record even more extraordinary, is that he played the game with a tumbling acrobatic style requiring twice the number of moving parts other goalies had. Unlike Terry Sawchuk and Jacques Plante, Glenn was a reflex goalie, who hung back in the crease, legs spread, head down, collapsing to the ice on low shots and springing nearly out of his skates to bat away high drives.

Hall lasted despite provoking NHL general managers, a group accustomed to getting its own way, with a tongue that was as sharp and pointed as a skate blade. After leading the NHL with 12 shutouts his rookie year, the 24-year-old fought Detroit owner Jack Adams for a $500 raise, to bring his salary to $8,000. After a bitter dispute, Adams relented, advising his young goalie not to tell any of his teammates about his new salary. "Don't worry, Mr. Adams," Hall replied. "I'm ashamed of it, too."

In 1965, Hall finally bought his dream property, a small grain farm near Stony Plain, a small town 20 miles west of Edmonton, Alberta. For the next six seasons, he continued to play hockey, often enjoying the games, the competition and the camaraderie, but all the while growing tired of the sport: Practice, the grind of travel, nagging injuries and annual contract disputes.

In the 1965–66 season, rookie goalie for the Chicago Blackhawks Dave Dryden roomed with Hall. "Sometimes after a game Billy Hay [a teammate from Lumsden, Saskatchewan], who was a good friend of Glenn's, would come up to the room, too. They'd sit and maybe have a beer, and just talk about the West. Sometimes they'd call a friend out [there] and just ask him to describe the plains."

Inevitably, it became harder for Hall to leave the land he loved for the hard game in which he took such pride. Late every summer, perhaps not coincidentally at contract time, the Blackhawks would phone, wondering where Hall was. Training camp had started. He was still at home on the farm, and he had a standard excuse when they phoned. He was busy painting the barn. After hearing the same excuse for several seasons in a row, Blackhawks manager Billy Reay complained, "Glenn must have the biggest barn in Canada."

Perhaps not surprisingly, upon retiring to his farm, Hall couldn't give up hockey entirely. He became a goalie coach for the St. Louis Blues and the Calgary Flames, and he seemed to take undisguised pleasure in passing on trade secrets to grateful youngsters. Occasionally, the acerbic humour that goalies resort to as a second level of protection would evidence itself. Hall made a point of attending Calgary Flames star forward Lanny McDonald's tearful retirement press conference. After the emotional ceremony, Hall approached McDonald, smiling. "You never saw a goalie cry when he retired," he observed.

Dead Letter Department

Mr. Goalie, Glenn Hall, once told a Toronto *Globe and Mail* reporter that playing professional hockey sometimes drove him so mad that, "All I want to do is stand out in a corner of that 160 acres I've got near Edmonton and holler, 'Screw you! Screw you! Screw you!' until I'm good and hoarse and hear the 'You!' You! You!' echo back across the field." One of those occasions would have been the summer of 1960, when he got a letter from the owner of the National Hockey League's Chicago Blackhawks, Tommy Ivan, turning down the goalie's request for a raise. Both of Hall's names were misspelled in the piece of correspondence, which read:

> Mr. Glen Howell
> 15806 94-A Ave.
> Edmonton, Alberta, Canada
>
> Dear Glen:
>
> In answer to your letter with your request for your basic salary…
> No. 1. Your request is too high.
> No. 2. I have been reviewing your previous contracts since you joined the Chicago hockey club and I find that regardless of the results, attendance, etc. of the Chicago hockey club, you have had a raise in your salary every year.
> I think we have been more than fair in our dealings, and as training camp is rapidly approaching, I would like to hear from you as soon as possible.
>
> Very truly yours,
> Thomas N. Ivan

LLOYDMINSTER

FOUNDED

When the provinces of Alberta and Saskatchewan were created in 1905, the border was created through the heart of what was then the two-year-old town of Brittania Settlement. Eventually, local citizens changed the name of the town to Lloydminster, in honour of Reverend George Exton Lloyd. In Middle English, minster means "mother church." Reverend Lloyd held that alcohol was the world's leading poison, so liquor was forbidden in the town through the first decades of the 20th century. Technically, Lloydminster remained two towns, with separate municipal administrations, until 1930. In its early years, most of its citizens actually lived in Saskatchewan, but the majority of recent growth has taken place in Alberta. Municipal offices were relocated to the Alberta side of the border in 2000. Oil and farming are the dominant local industries.

NATIVE-BORN NHL PLAYERS

Lloydminster, AB: Cory Cross, Lance Ward; **Lloydminster, SK:** Colby Armstrong, Garnet Bailey, Lyle Bradley, Blair Chapman, Barry Gibbs, Bob Hassard, Larry Leach, Justin Mapletoft, Wade Redden, Spence Tatchell

FAMOUS LOCAL TEAMS

Junior: Lloydminster Blazers; **Senior-pro:** Lloydminster Border Kings

CURRENT POPULATION

21,000

The two-province town of Lloydminster in its infancy, 1906.

Wheatfield Soul

Straddling the Alberta-Saskatchewan border, Lloydminster is officially an Alberta city, though the 8,000 citizens who live on the Saskatchewan side of the 50th Avenue border are exempt from paying provincial sales tax, an Alberta perquisite. Still, for hockey purposes, the city can be placed in Saskatchewan simply because of Wade Redden, a brilliant contemporary defenceman who—like so many stars from the prairie province—skated out of a small farming community into pro hockey fame.

The descendant of Metis settlers, Redden has a story that is comparable to that of Saskatchewan's first great rearguard, Eddie Shore.

In Redden's case, his grandfather, Jim Redden, helped build a rink in Hillmond, Saskatchewan, where a small cluster of homes fan out into a patchwork quilt of farms, a 20-minute drive from Lloydminster.

Fifty people were living in Hillmond in 1963 when seven locals, including the elder Redden, constructed what became known as the "Silverdome," an aluminum-topped hockey Thermos that still manages to leave the rink, along with its players and fans, cold from November through March. In 1982, Jim's grandsons, Wade and Bart Redden, first took to Silverdome ice, a surface made smooth by a tractor with a makeshift flooding device attached to the back. The kids, ages five and six, were the best players on the local peewee team, the Hillmond Tom Thumbs. While Pat and Gord Redden felt an inner glow watching their two boys play, pride wasn't enough to keep spectators warm most winter days, so the couple took the precaution of wearing snowmobile outfits and heavy toques.

Granddad Jim and the rink's co-builders relied on a more primitive form of insulation. "At one end of [the rink], there's a concession stand with a balcony up over top of it," Gord Redden advised hockey writer Bob McKenzie. "Most

The Lloydminster
Border Kings, 2000–01
Allan Cup champions.

Border Kings of Canada

Lloydminster's senior hockey team, the Lloydminster Border Kings, won the Canadian senior championship Allan Cup in 2001, defeating the Petrolia Squires, 7–2, in a game played at the Squires' home rink in Sarnia, Ontario. Wade Redden's brother, Bart, was a forward on the team. Border Kings goalie Jason Clague was the tournament's most valuable player. The Allan Cup all-star team included Border Kings defenceman Merv Mann and Border Kings forwards Scott Hood, Greg Brown and Ian Munro.

nights, there'd be five or six of the older guys, my dad included, and they'd always sit up there together in the balcony watching the kids below. Two of them would bring a mickey and the others would go get the coffee. They would mix the whiskey into the coffee. That kept 'em warm."

Wade and Bart Redden benefited from professional instruction at the Silverdome, provided by none other than their dad. Prior to settling on his 1,400 acre farm and cattle ranch, Gord Redden had suited up for the junior Regina St. Pat's team that lost in the 1969 Memorial Cup finals to the Montreal Junior Canadiens. Wade Redden once called his father the best coach he ever had. The younger Redden has also given credit to his hometown Silverdome. "I don't think I would have been the same player without that rink," the defenceman once said. "We could skate as much as we liked, almost any time we liked."

Skating as much as Wade liked, meant skating all the time. And here maybe we can identify a characteristic of Saskatchewan's best players, from Eddie Shore to Gordie Howe to Bryan Trottier—an appetite for physical labour that is second nature to those who grow up working the land. Like the Saskatchewan stars who came before him, Wade Redden became a player teams could count on to play every shift, all night, season after season.

Wade, who was born in Lloydminster, went to high school there and made the junior Lloydminster Blazers at age 15. From the Blazers, he progressed to the Western Hockey League's Brandon Wheat Kings, where he became the best teenage defenceman in the country, leading the Canadian junior team to world championships in 1995 and 1996. The second pick in the 1995 National Hockey League draft turned pro with the NHL's Ottawa Senators the following season. By 2005, he was among the team's most respected players, greatly admired by the city's hockey fans, and also by teenaged female bloggers, who have been known to fire his photograph around the Internet with the alacrity of a smoothly executed power play.

A frequent visitor home, Redden bought satellite TV and a backyard swimming pool, which he helped install, for his parents' farm in Hillmond with one of his first NHL pay cheques. His parents had an opportunity to use the TV one night in the fall of 1996, during an epic sports vigil that pretty much defines local interest in hockey.

Gord and Pat Redden first drove down Highway 16 from Lloydminster to North Battleford to see their son Bart play a hockey game, then climbed back into their car and raced back to Hillmond to watch a taped Radio-Canada replay of Wade's professional debut, an Ottawa Senators-Montreal Canadiens contest. Arriving home to a quiet farmhouse to watch French-language coverage of one of their sons performing thousands of miles away in front of 20,000 fans was a surreal, wrenching experience...and rewarding, too, for the 19-year-old scored a goal on his first NHL shot. "I just bawled," Pat Redden told *Ottawa Sun* journalist Kathleen Harris. "I couldn't believe it."

Wade Redden led the Canadian junior team in the mid 1990s.

Chief Thunder Stick

Born on Christmas Day 1933, Fred Saskamoose came from the Sandy Lake Reserve in Saskatchewan and grew up in a fire-heated 20-by-20-foot log house, living primarily on a diet of rabbit and fish. At age eight, he was taken from his family and sent to St. Michael's, a French missionary school in Duck Lake. There, he learned to love hockey, sacrificing his weekly allotment of dessert to a senior student for another hour of ice time.

A hockey sensation, Saskamoose was signed by the National Hockey League's Chicago Blackhawks in 1950, at age 16, for a $100 bonus and began play with the junior Moose Jaw Canucks. He became the Canucks' captain, centring a multicultural line that included a black teammate and an Asian player. Saskamoose honoured his linemates by lacing his skates with black and yellow laces. After his last game with the Canucks, in 1954, he joined the Chicago Blackhawks for 11 games.

Being the first full-blooded First Nations player to join the NHL was frequently a trial. NHL radio interviewers often introduced themselves with the solemn greeting, "How!" The player took to raising his hand and replying, "Howe, Gordie Howe." After a short stint in the NHL, Saskamoose played senior hockey throughout western Canada, where fellow Aboriginal Canadians flocked to see him play, hailing him with various nicknames, including "Chief Thunder Stick" and "Chief Running Deer."

MOOSE JAW

FOUNDED

The first white settlers to the Moose Jaw area arrived in 1881. When the CPR arrived in July 1882, the settlement consisted of five tents. By 1883 the town had swelled to include six stores, five saloons and 40 houses. Moose Jaw was incorporated in late 1903. In 1985, a truck fell through a downtown street, revealing a system of tunnels that local historians believe served as passageways between saloons and brothels during the 1920s. It has long been rumoured that Al Capone, said to be an occasional visitor to Moose Jaw during American prohibition, smuggled booze from the prairie city to Minneapolis and Chicago.

NATIVE-BORN NHL PLAYERS

Frank Ashworth, David Bararuk, Mike Blaisdell, Brent Gilchrist, Clark Gillies, Norman Johnson, Norm Larson, Bill Lecaine, Bill Lesuk, Reed Low, Butch McDonald, Larry McIntyre, John Miner, Chico Resch, Don Saleski, Doug Smail, Kenneth Smith, Glen Sonmor, Ed Staniowski, George Swarbrick, Jim Wiste, Martin Zoborosky

FAMOUS LOCAL TEAMS

Junior: Moose Jaw Canucks, Moose Jaw CPR, Moose Jaw Crescents, Moose Jaw Cubs, Moose Jaw Hardware, Moose Jaw Monarchs, Moose Jaw Warriors; **Senior-pro:** Moose Jaw, Moose Jaw Canucks, Moose Jaw Falcons, Moose Jaw Lions, Moose Jaw Maroons, Moose Jaw Millers, Moose Jaw Millionaires, Moose Jaw Pla-Mors, Moose Jaw Tigers, Moose Jaw Victorias

CURRENT POPULATION

32,131

Moose Jaw Warriors

For hundreds of years, what is now Moose Jaw was a winter encampment for the Cree and Assiniboine nations. Every fall the two would nestle in the valley of the Missouri Couteau, a range of hills climbing 500 feet above the Saskatchewan prairie. The Cree called their winter shelter Moosegaw, meaning "warm breezes."

Approximate pronunciation led to the settlement eventually being called Moose Jaw, and over the decades, to endless bad jokes. The city's most famous athlete, Clark Gillies, delighted in beating inquisitive Americans to the punch line when asked about his hometown. "You're from what?" strangers would call out, laughing. "Where's Moose Jaw?"

"Six feet from a moose's ass," Gillies always replied.

Gillies missed playing for Moose Jaw's most famous hockey team. The Moose Jaw Canucks started up in the 1934–35 season, and represented the city for five decades. The most famous edition was the best junior team in western Canada in the late '40s, winning five Saskatchewan titles in a row (1945–49) and twice progressing to the national championship Memorial Cup (1945, 1947), with a roster that included future National Hockey Leaguers Bert Olmstead, Metro Prystai and Emile Francis. The Canucks continued to compete in major provincial junior hockey until 1970, when the club dropped to Tier II status for 14 seasons before passing into extinction, giving way, in 1984, to the Western Hockey League's elite junior Moose Jaw Warriors. (The Warriors' first star was Theoren Fleury of Oxford, Saskatchewan.) Since then, Moose Jaw has been Warriors hockey country.

Clark Gillies, playing for the
New York Islanders.

Born in 1954, Clark Gillies was too young to join the Canucks when the team was still playing major junior hockey, so he travelled an hour west down Highway 1 to the Queen City, joining the Canucks' old arch rivals, the Regina Pats. After helping the junior team to a Memorial Cup win in 1974, the mountainous forward (6'3", 220 pounds) joined the NHL's New York Islanders, where he was named "sheriff" of an expansion team (class of '72) that had been pushed around like so many mops by division rival, the Philadelphia Flyers, the two previous seasons.

Gillies was ambivalent about being an enforcer. He was a schoolboy legend in Moose Jaw—quarterback of the high school football team, and in summer a farmhand in the Major League Baseball Houston Astros organization, signed at 16 by Pat Gillick (later of the Toronto Blue Jays) to play minor league ball in Covington, Virginia.

Gillies called baseball "a good summer job," but his heart was in hockey. His father, Don, a talented amateur, had imparted to him a purist's passion for the game. Clark was not allowed to grip a hockey stick until he had proven he could skate without falling. And his' ideal of what hockey should be was formed as a kid, when he and his older brother would lace up their skates on the front stoop and then glide two blocks down the frozen street to the neighbourhood rink for day-long games of pickup hockey, where Clark imitated Bobby Hull, his hero, flying around the ice, free of care and gravity.

Once in New York, though, Gillies was expected to drive through people, fight and intimidate. Veteran teammate Bob Nystrom told him, "Freight trains don't drive like Volkswagens." Gillies was big, with a five o'clock shadow that turned into a beard by second period. And he came from Moose Jaw. The team wanted him to be tough—all the time. He wasn't. Gillies scored more than 30 goals six times in his 12-year career, but he never collected more than 100 minutes in penalties in a season.

Gillies understood, however, that there were times to stand forward. The year prior to his arrival, the Islanders had been embarrassed by Philadelphia's

The 1944–45 Memorial Cup finalists, Moose Jaw Canucks. Star Bert Olmstead is seated in the bottom row, second from the end, far right.

Dave "The Hammer" Schultz, a big tough guy from Waldheim, Saskatchewan, who once skated by the New York bench and double dared the team—anybody, everybody—to take him on. No one did.

In Gillies' first season, New York came up against Philadelphia in the 1975 spring playoffs. The Islanders were winning one game with half a minute left, when Shultz was sent onto the ice. He knew what to do, fixing the 20-year-old rookie Islander with the jailhouse stare that heavyweight champs use to intimidate young contenders. The Philadelphia crowd jumped to its feet, screaming. Gillies stopped, shook off his gloves, and then poured all of his weight into a punch that momentarily flattened Shultz's face, draining his arms and legs of energy. Two blows later, the big Flyers forward fell to the ice. "Don't let him hit me anymore," Shultz pleaded, when the referee jumped in to stop the fight.

Many New York fans believe that the expansion Islanders became a contending team that night, and that they became champions five springs later when Gillies again turned gladiator. Prior to the second duel, Gillies and his teammate Nystrom were watching television when a local sportscaster suggested that the Boston Bruins would take the Islanders in the playoffs in five games. The bigger, badder Bruins, he said, would intimidate New York.

The TV announcer was, indeed, correct in anticipating what the Islanders would be up against. Gillies scored the overtime winner in the first game of the 1980 series with the Bruins, but he knew that Boston, with a trio of tough wingers, Terry O'Reilly, John Wensink and Stan Jonathan, would be back. Sure enough, Wensink took on Nystrom early into that second game and O'Reilly found Gillies in a scrum, calling out to the Islander, "You're mine." The two staged an epic battle, which Gillies won convincingly. His hands were scarred red after the game.

Still, he knew the fight wasn't over. O'Reilly was a player of enormous fortitude; not a bully who would turn coward, as Schultz had done. Indeed, O'Reilly fought Gillies every game that series. Gillies won his battles but had to repair to the washroom immediately prior to heading out onto the ice. "I was so tense and uptight," he told Steve Jacobson of New York's *Newsday*. "It made me sick to my

Detroit "Doc" Costs Canucks Cup

The Moose Jaw Canucks were so good in the 1940s that the Regina Pats were reformed in an effort to restore the city's junior hockey honour. The Pats originally folded during World War II, and no local team had emerged to replace them.

Scotty Melville of the Regina *Leader-Post* wrote, in 1946, that he "was sick and tired of watching Moose Jaw clobber us at every turn." He suggested that the Queen City's remaining top junior teams, the Abbots and the Commandos, merge to become the Pats. The rebirth took place, but the Canucks beat the revived Pats, anyway, on their way to the 1947 Memorial Cup, where the Moose Jaw team was trimmed four straight by the Toronto St. Michael's Majors.

The Canucks' best chance for a national championship had, in fact, come in 1945, when a team coached by Roy Bentley, starring his brother Bev Bentley, along with Bert Olmstead and Metro Prystai, had also lost to the Majors, four games to one. At that time, however, the Canucks' best player, Gerry Couture, wasn't in the lineup for any of the games, having supposedly remained home to write medical exams at the University of Saskatchewan. What a surprise the Canucks had when they arrived in Toronto for the Memorial Cup playoffs, to find that Couture, their much-needed player, was there, too!

The absent forward had been called up by the National Hockey League's Detroit Red Wings to play in the Stanley Cup finals against the Toronto Maple Leafs. And just as the Majors won the Memorial Cup, the Maple Leafs won the Stanley Cup that spring.

Gerry Couture, playing for the Montreal Canadiens.

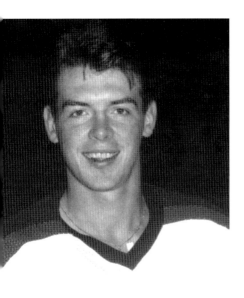

Small Wonder

A Metis descendant, Theoren Fleury was born in Oxbow, Saskatchewan, but grew up in Brandon, Manitoba, a farm community near the Saskatchewan border. His mother, Donna, named him Theoren after a character in the children's classic, *Old Yeller*. Fleury's father, Wally, a former senior hockey player, drove the icemaker at the town rink, and as a child Theo accompanied him to games, staying on to fly around fresh ice in the Zamboni's wake. His parents were considered eccentrics by the town: Donna developed an addiction to Valium; and Wally drank, hitting taverns during his son's game and then showing up afterward, barging into the dressing room to sing his son's praises.

Though a great player, Theo had to prove his worth to skeptics every game. He was small, 5'5" and 130 pounds, when at age 16 he joined the junior Western Hockey Association's Moose Jaw Warriors in the 1984–85 season. Fans loved him. He played every shift as if his team was behind a goal in the final minute of play. Fleury scored more than 60 goals twice for the Warriors, yet he wasn't taken until the eighth round of the 1987 National Hockey League draft—a slight that only caused to him to redouble his efforts. He helped the NHL's Calgary Flames win the Stanley Cup his first season in the league (1988–89), and scored 51 goals two years later.

Fleury would eventually fall prey to the disease that damaged his parents, checking himself into the NHL's substance abuse program three times between 2001 and 2003. He last played in the NHL with the Chicago Blackhawks in 2003. Whatever his problems, his hockey legacy remains: Theoren Fleury was a five-time all-star, an Olympic gold medal winner (2002), and an inspiration to all athletes who have been told that they weren't big enough or good enough to realize their dreams.

Theo Fleury, with the
Moose Jaw Warriors.

stomach before a game, to think of having to do that—tonight I'm going to have a fight. I'm not going to get beat up, so much as I'm going to be hurting someone tonight."

The Islanders went from eliminating the Bruins to taking the 1980 Stanley Cup; they proceeded to win the trophy three years in a row after that. Gillies formed part of the team's top line during the championship reign, playing on the right side of Bryan Trottier, a centreman from Val Marie, Saskatchewan. Montreal-born sniper Mike Bossy patrolled the left wing.

Like all successful sheriffs, Gillies didn't have to show how tough he was after he'd developed a reputation for being able to look after his team. Once, Chicago forward Jerry "King Kong" Korab showed up in the corner looking for the Islanders' top scorer. "Where's Bossy?" he shouted.

"Behind me," Gillies replied, ending the search.

Gillies was glad to let opposition players off with warnings. His most enjoyable times on the ice came during pregame sessions that reminded him of playing hockey with his brother back in Moose Jaw, flying around the neighbourhood rink. "Fighting bothered me," he told Jacobson. "I used to love practice, the free-wheeling and making plays. Fights were a distraction."

Gillies' best moment in hockey came long after his 1988 retirement, when, in 2002, he was flying back to Moose Jaw with his wife, Pam, and his daughters, Jocelyn, Brooke and Briana, to visit his mother, Dot, on her 80th birthday. During a Toronto layover, he received an emergency cell phone call at the airport. His family looked on, watching as Gillies broke down.

"What's wrong?" his wife demanded.

"Nothing—these are happy tears," the reluctant warrior of Moose Jaw replied. "That was the NHL. I've made it to the Hall of Fame."

NORTH BATTLEFORD

FOUNDED

For generations, the Cree and Blackfoot fought along the shores of the North Saskatchewan and Battle Rivers. Eventually, they called the second tributary "Fighting Water," which is where the later names Battle River and Battleford were born. A fort was built between the rivers, so that trappers could bring furs to sell. The fort became a town in 1874; and two years later, a contingent of North West Mounted Police arrived. A railroad was built on the north side of the river, attracting settlers to the town that would later become known as North Battleford.

NATIVE-BORN NHL PLAYERS

Ron Delorme, Bobby Francis, Emile Francis, Bruce Hoffort, Dale Hoganson, Skip Krake, Merlin Malinowski, Corey Schwab, Greg Sheppard, Morris Stefaniw, Al Tuer

FAMOUS LOCAL TEAMS

Junior: North Battleford Beavers, North Battleford North Stars;
Senior-pro: North Battleford, North Battleford Beavers

CURRENT POPULATION

13,692

EMILE FRANCIS'S STORY:

A Chicken Every Sunday

Hockey Hall of Famer Emile Francis left North Battleford as a teenager and played parts of six seasons as a goalie in the National Hockey League with the Chicago Blackhawks and the New York Rangers (1946–52). He would later turn to coaching, leading the New York Rangers and the St. Louis Blues, between 1965 and 1983. Francis returns to Saskatchewan every summer, to visit family and friends.

I was born in North Battleford in 1926 and grew up at 1421 Arthur Street, north of town. My father was born in Wales, and my mother, Bordeaux, France. She could speak French, though I only ever understood enough to know when a French hockey player was mad at me. Anyway, my father died when I was six. And my uncle Ab Bidard looked after me, showed me how to play sports and everything. I owed him a lot.

When I was a kid, senior hockey was it—North Battleford Beavers against Battleford Millers. Those games were wars. The Beavers were my team. They used to practise in a slough, north end of town. Outdoors, if you can believe it. I'd go and watch 'em whenever I could. Them and the Toronto Maple Leafs on the radio Saturday nights was hockey in those days.

First Beavers game I saw, I was eight. There's a story there. It was Beavers against the Flin Flon Bombers—senior hockey. Sid Abel was the star of the Bombers. Now games at the North Battleford Arena were 75 cents, 25 cents for kids. I didn't have a penny in my pocket, but I was going to see that game. Visiting teams used to dress at Miller's Hotel, then walk—with their overcoats on—a block to the arena. I showed up outside the hotel two hours before the

Emile "The Cat" Francis shows his form for the Chicago Blackhawks in 1947.

game. When the Bombers come out, I walked up to the biggest player, Butch Stahan, and said, "Mister, I sure would like to see you play, but I don't have money for a ticket." Butch stuck me under his overcoat and took me inside. Once I got my foot in the door, I was off like a shot.

I saw that game, people cheering, the bright lights on the ice, and oh, boy, I knew what I wanted to be, a hockey player. North Battleford had a great team—Vic Myles, George Allen and Squee Allen, all future NHLers. They went on to the Allan Cup in 1937, lost to Sudbury and folded. They just went broke trying to win, I guess. When I started playing junior for North Battleford in 1941 at age 15, we were the Beavers, too. Everything was Beavers in North Battleford— senior, junior, intermediate hockey. In fact, I wore Ken Davis's—the old senior Beavers goalie's—pads. The old wool uniforms just got passed on and on.

People ask how come so many great players come out of Saskatchewan. All I can say is that if you were any good, you got all the ice time in the world. Cripes, when I went to separate school, there was no coach. I was 10, the nuns asked me to manage the hockey team. I used to play forward first period, score a goal, then throw the pads on and go back in nets, figuring I could hold them from there. My Uncle Ab, he came back on leave from the war, he said to me, 'Emile, you want to go anywhere in hockey, pick a position.' I figured, well, goalie's on 60 minutes, forward 25—right then and there, I became a goalie.

On top of playing junior for the Beavers, I was in the New Battleford Commercial League, too. The RCMP had a team there. Commercial Cleaners was another team. One day a guy from Metropole, a town outside North Battleford, came up to me and said, "I want you to play goal for us. I can't pay you," he said, "but every game you show up, I'll give you a chicken and a dozen eggs." Tell you what, my brother Pat, mother and I sure ate a lot of chicken that winter.

Another time, I was playing for the Beavers in Saskatoon, a guy came up to me after the game and said, "I'm with the Detroit Red Wings. We own your rights." He wanted me to sign.

I said, "For what?"

"I played in Philadelphia and Washington, Detroit's farm teams for two seasons, and then I turned 18 and came home to enlist. It was my time."

He said, "Come with me," took me to his car, opened the trunk, and showed me a trunk full of red gabardine hockey jackets with Red Wings crests on 'em. "Pick one," he says.

I said, "I want a new pair of goalie skates, too."

He closed the trunk and said, "Sorry, we'll sign someone else." Month later, I came back to Saskatoon, played a pretty good game, he was outside the dressing room again. First thing he says is, "What size do you take?"

And that's how I became a professional. This is during the war, eh? Lot of players were overseas. Detroit camp in 1943, I was one of two goalies. Harry Lumley was 18, and I just turned 17. I played in Philadelphia and Washington, Detroit's farm teams for two seasons, and then I turned 18 and came home to enlist. It was my time. This was 1945. I was on my way overseas, when the war in Europe ended. So they sent me to Vernon, B.C., for the battle in the Pacific. Then the Pacific war ended. There I was doing nothing, waiting for a discharge. Who knew how long that was going to take?

Then, I hear the brigadier wants to talk to me. He tells me the only way I can get out fast is by going to school. He looks at me and says, "I hear you're a goalie. How would you like to go to school in Medicine Hat?" Turns out he was connected to the junior team there. Couple of days later, I was sent to Regina. When I got there, a car was running outside the camp waiting to take me to Medicine Hat.

I played junior there with the Moose Jaw Canucks, great team with Bert Olmstead and Metro Prystai. Moose Jaw was affiliated with the Chicago Blackhawks, so next year I was playing in Chicago with Max and Doug Bentley. I've seen a lot of hockey, but the most exciting line I ever saw was Max and Doug Bentley with Billy Mosienko. Oh, could they skate and pass the puck. I became friends with the Bentleys and started playing on their baseball team in the summer. I was shortstop. Roy, Max, Doug, Reggie and Roy's boy, Bev Bentley, were the rest of the infield. I remember once we were in Saskatoon playing, a fan shouted out, "Hey Francis, how'd you get in the lineup—marry one of the Bentley girls?"

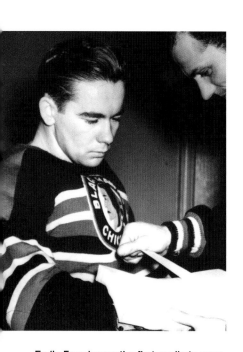

Emile Francis was the first goalie to wear a baseball-style trapper's glove. "It was a George McQuinn model," Francis says. "He was a first baseman for the New York Yankees in the late '40s. Bought it at a sporting goods store and had a sleeve put on special."

PRINCE ALBERT

FOUNDED

In 1776, explorer Peter Pond helped establish a fur-trading post on the north side of the North Saskatchewan River in what would later be known as Prince Albert. Settlers led by Reverend James Nisbet put down roots on the opposite shore in 1866, building a Presbyterian mission. The community was named after Prince Albert, in honour of Queen Victoria's husband. Three prime ministers have served the Prince Albert riding: Sir Wilfred Laurier (1896), William Lyon Mackenzie King (1926) and John George Diefenbaker (1953). Prince Albert's primary industries are mining, forestry and agriculture.

NATIVE-BORN NHL PLAYERS

Mike Bales, Todd Bergen, Johnny Bower, Angus "Scotty" Cameron, Scott Daniels, Tavis Hansen, Dale Henry, Dave Manson, Ryan McGill, Jerome Mrazek, Jeff Nelson, Todd Nelson, Denis Pederson, Terry Ruskowski, Joey Tetarenko, Rick Wilson

FAMOUS LOCAL TEAMS

Junior: Prince Albert Blackhawks, Prince Albert Hawks, Prince Albert Raiders; **Senior-pro:** Prince Albert Mintos

CURRENT POPULATION

34,291

Parade for Prime Minister Wilfrid Laurier in Prince Albert. Laurier represented Prince Albert in 1896.

Horseplay

When Johnny Bower was a kid, he brushed his teeth three times a day: first thing in the morning; before going to bed at night; plus another time after hockey. Why the third time? Well, that had something to do with how kids played hockey back in Prince Albert, Saskatchewan, during the Depression.

Bower became a goaltender because his family didn't have money for skates. What with Johnny and eight sisters to feed, his parents couldn't even afford hockey sticks. Lucky for John, his dad, a railroad employee, was working up north one day and spotted a tree with an L-shaped limb. There's something my boy can use, he figured, whittling the branch into a heavy goalie stick.

Pads were easier. Johnny carved up an abandoned mattress to make springy pontoons, and then bound them to his legs with rubber bands.

He still didn't have a puck, but that didn't matter. Boys in Prince Albert could pick those up any time. What they did was follow behind a farmer's wagon on its way into town. When the horse shivered, dropping a steaming loaf of manure on the hard white road, Johnny and his friends let out a gleeful howl. "Better a vacancy than a poor tenant," a farmer would comment, smiling.

The boys were on the droppings quickly, before the manure froze, trimming the piles into appropriately shaped discs, then patting them even with their stick blades. Before long, they had more than enough for a game on nearby frozen sloughs, no matter how many pucks disappeared into the snow banks.

A few years later, Johnny finally received proper foot gear and learned to skate in prairie gales so fierce that other players' voices could only be heard downwind. And with his big stick, which he wielded like a broadsword, he acquired a knack for diving out flat on the ice and poking the puck away from wingers.

Just as important, maybe, Johnny developed a sense of humour that would preserve him through 40 hockey winters. Whenever he was asked what it was

P.A. Wins Memorial Cup

Prince Albert goes by two other names. Locals often refer to the city as P.A., and in winter, when the junior Raiders are doing well, it is also known as Hockey Town North.

Junior hockey really began here in 1972, when Terry Simpson, a coach from nearby Shellbrook, took over a Tier II junior Raiders team that had won only three games in 11 matches, and then proceeded to go on what was essentially a 13-year winning streak. Under Simpson, the Raiders won four Tier II national titles (Centennial Cups) before entering the premiere junior division Western Hockey League in 1981–82. Three seasons later, in 1984–85, the team was in the Memorial Cup finals. Simpson's big line that season consisted of Dan Hodgson, Dave Pasin and Tony Grenier. In the championship game, held in Drummondville, Quebec, Hodgson set up five goals in a 6–1 Prince Albert win. The team returned home to an ecstatic motorcade down Central Avenue. Simpson also coached the Canadian national junior team to a world title in 1986, before going on to a long National Hockey League coaching career.

In 2005, the Raiders' old arena, the Communiplex, was given a $1 million facelift and renamed the Art Hauser Centre. The Raiders average 3,300 fans most seasons, more than their home rink's advertised seating capacity. Additional fans stand. In P.A., it is often said, there are two seasons: hockey season and waiting-for-hockey season.

like playing hockey with prairie road apples, he said, "Oh, not bad, as long as you brush your teeth afterward."

Exaggerating his age to get into World War II, the 15-year-old joined the Queen's Own Cameron Highlanders in 1940, but he returned home in time to lead the junior Prince Albert Black Hawks to a Saskatchewan junior championship and a preliminary round Memorial Cup playoff loss to the Moose Jaw Canucks during the 1944–45 campaign. He also landed a local railroad job and the promise of a secure future, but when the Cleveland Barons of the American Hockey League called offering a $50 bonus, Bower couldn't resist. He spent the next eight seasons in Ohio (1946–53), where the unmasked goalie lost most of the teeth he had so carefully polished after his early road apple games. He also picked up more than 200 stitches on his face, from errant sticks and pucks.

The stitches, Bower never minded. "We had an insurance deal where we got five dollars a stitch," Johnny told Bob Dolgan, a Cleveland *Plain Dealer* reporter. "If the doctor only needed two stitches, I'd tell them to give me a couple more so I could get another ten bucks."

Shortly after he joined the National Hockey League's Toronto Maple Leafs, in 1958 and at age 34, Johnny began wearing dentures, which he kept in his locker during games. After one contest, he came back to the dressing room, grabbed a towel from his locker and then headed to the shower. Upon his return, he inserted his teeth. Only they didn't fit. Looking around, he noticed teammates laughing into towels. "Yaach!" Bower shouted, figuring team clown Eddie Shack had switched his teeth. Finally, Leafs captain George Armstrong admitted he'd taken them. "Where'd you get the other ones," Bower asked after fitting in the proper dentures. "A dentist or something?"

"No, an undertaker," Armstrong replied.

Bower and the Leafs enjoyed more than laughs in the 1960s, winning the Stanley Cup in the spring of 1962, 1963, 1964 and 1967. In most of those playoffs, Bower did something to ruin the hopes of the Montreal Canadiens. In the spring of 1963, he shut out the Canadiens twice, allowing a mere six goals in five games. Montreal star Jean Beliveau said of Bower, "For me, I don't know, he was the toughest goalie I ever faced. One time, I had the puck in front of a wide open net. I shot, lifting my arms, sure I had scored, and somehow he kicked a leg out making the save. To this day, I still can't believe he made that stop."

By the mid-1960s, Bower had become one of Canada's most beloved characters. The Depression-era road apples story was now hockey lore, and the question of

Johnny Bower.

Johnny Bower, hero of song and story: Bower helped the Toronto Maple Leafs to four Stanley Cups in the 1960s.

Honk If You Like Christmas

In the fall of 1965, musician Chris Young visited Toronto's Maple Leaf Gardens looking for hockey players to sing on a Christmas song he hoped to produce for charity. "When Chris came into the room and asked if anyone would be interested in helping out, most of the guys dashed for the showers," Leafs goalie Johnny Bower told hockey writer Chris Loman. The obliging goalie agreed to lend his foggy tenor to the song, and soon found himself in a CBC Toronto studio with a children's choir that included his son, John Jr.

The resulting single, "Honky the Christmas Goose" (flip side, "Banjo the Mule"), reached number 29 on the Canadian charts in the last week of December 1965. The song told the story of an overweight, soundless goose who saved Christmas Eve for Santa by finally learning how to blow his nose, thereby breaking up congested air space over cities with a penetrating trumpet cry. The chorus of the song went, "Honky, Honky the Christmas goose/ Got so fat that he was no use./ 'Til he learned how to blow his nose/ Honk! The way a goose nose blows."

his age had also turned into an annual comedy routine. Bower had served in the war, but come every training camp he still claimed to be 39.

Prince Albert's Old Man Winter played a crucial part in the Leafs' Stanley Cup upset of the favoured Canadiens in 1967 and then he played his final game two seasons later, at age 45. He continued in the Leafs organization for another 20 years, scouting and coaching goaltenders. And he made countless public appearances across the country, winning smiles and enthusistic applause wherever he went—even in Quebec, where he had made Montreal Canadiens hockey fans miserable for more than a decade.

One Canadiens fan, however, never quite forgave Bower, which led to a practical joke that provided the old goalie with one of his best hockey laughs. Johnny was 77 at the time, and scheduled for a serious medical operation—a triple heart bypass. The surgeon who performed the surgery was a transplanted Quebecer living in Toronto, Daniel Bonneau. The operation went well, but when Johnny woke up from one of his sleeps a few days later, he had to take a long gulp. There, standing smiling in front of him, stood the man he had trusted with his life—wearing a Montreal Canadiens sweater!

Inauguration Day decorations,
South Railway Street, Regina, 1905.

REGINA

FOUNDED

The site of present-day Regina was first identified as "Pile of Bones" by First Nations people who hunted the area's treeless plains, stacking evidence of bison kills into triangular columns of sun-bleached bones. The city came about with the arrival of the railroad in 1882. That year, Regina became the headquarters of the North West Mounted Police, as well as the seat of government for the Northwest Territories. When Saskatchewan was declared a province in 1905, Regina was named its capital.

NATIVE-BORN NHL PLAYERS

Dale Anderson, Chris Armstrong, Murray Balfour, Sandy Beadle, Harry Bell, Curt Bennett, Gordon "Red" Berenson, Dwight Bialowas, James Black, Glen Burdon, Garth Butcher, Gord Buttrey, Drew Callander, Jock Callander, Joe Carveth, Barry Cummins, Kevin Dahl, Lorne Davis, Don Deacon, Robert Dirk, Rocky Dundas, Duke Dukowski, Mark Ferner, Dunc Fisher, Dan Focht, Bill Folk, Scott Garland, Ryan Getzlaf, Dirk Graham, Taylor Hall, Terry Harper, Scott Hartnell, Jamie Heward, Bill Hicke, Ernie Hicke, Brian Hill, Terry Hollinger, Fran Huck, Kim Issel, Gerry James, Lou Jankowski, David Karpa, Bob Kirkpatrick, Mark Kirton, Terry Kleisinger, Chris Kunitz, Robbie Laird, Jack Lancien, Kim MacDougall, Paul Masnick, Walter McCartney, Jim McGeough, Jackie McLeod, Joby Messier, Earl Miller, Gerry Minor, Bernard Morris, Murray Garth, Dana Murzyn, Bill Orban, Garry Peters, Eric Pettinger, Gord Pettinger, Rich Preston, Alan Rittinger, Nick Schultz, Darrell Scoville, Mike Sillinger, Donald Smith, Chris Snell, Ron Snell, Al Staley, Doug Stevenson, Arthur Strobel, Bill Sutherland, Bob Turner, Norman Tustin, Gord Wappel, Billy Warwick, Knobby Warwick, Doug Wickenheiser, Larry Wright

FAMOUS LOCAL TEAMS

Junior: Regina Abbotts, Regina Aces, Regina Blues, Regina Boat Club, Regina Caps, Regina Commandos, Regina Crescents, Regina Falcons, Regina Generals, Regina Jr. Aces, Regina Maple Leafs, Regina Monarchs, Regina Pat Blues, Regina Pats, Regina Rangers, Regina Victorias, Regina Wares; **Senior-pro:** Regina 77th Battery, Regina Abbotts, Regina Aces, Regina Army Caps, Regina Braves, Regina Capitals, Regina Caps, Regina Commandos, Regina Pats, Regina Rangers, Regina Shamrocks, Regina Victorias, Regina-Vancouver Maroons

CURRENT POPULATION

178,225

The 1920–21 Regina Victorias.

Hockey Royalty

Even before the Patricias, or "Pats," a team named after Queen Victoria's granddaughter, arrived in Regina in 1917, hockey in Saskatchewan's capital city seemed like a royal idea.

One of Saskatchewan's first hockey matches, an 1894 affair between Moose Jaw and Regina, was marked by song, speeches and a grand oyster supper. Like most hockey games in Saskatchewan at the time, the contest was but one component in a winter carnival that also featured costume balls, uproarious barrel-jumping events, one-mile races and "fancy skating" exhibitions.

Not that there was any question as to the main attraction. On 25 January

The Regina Rocket

Bill Hicke began going to Regina Pats games in 1945, when he was seven years old, with his older brother John. "Mom gave us 10 cents each to take the streetcar, but we'd grab the backs of cars and get a bumper ride all the way down Elphinstone Street and Dewdney Avenue to old Exhibition Stadium, with our big mitts on our hands and mukluks on our feet," he told writer John Chaput. "We'd stop at Murray Balfour's place near the Grey Nuns [now Pasqua] Hospital. Mrs. Balfour always invited us in. We'd get warm, and then walk the last four or five blocks."

Ten years later, Hicke himself would be a member of the Regina Pats, playing on a line with friend Murray Balfour. A superb skater with a bewildering repertoire of moves, Hicke led the Pats to runner-up appearances in the 1955, 1957 and 1958 Memorial Cups finals and was considered among the two or three best junior prospects of the decade. "Your principal job, you will understand, is to take Maurice Richard's place if and when he retires," Frank Selke, general manager of the National Hockey League's Montreal Canadiens advised Hicke in a letter before the right winger arrived at training camp in 1959.

Bad health and the weight of great expectations prevented Hicke from ever reaching his promise. In the fall of 1967, given a chance to play full-time with the NHL expansion Oakland Seals, the Regina forward rediscovered his great talent, collecting five goals and seven assists in his first seven games, but then collapsed in practice with a profound allergic reaction. Rushed to the hospital, he spent two weeks in a coma.

Retiring from hockey because of ill health, he returned to Regina in 1973, purchasing a local sporting goods store from former NHLers Bill and Gus Kyle. Hicke would return to the junior Pats as part owner and general manager in the 1980s, and in 1993 he coached the team he had once starred for. After his death from cancer in the summer of 2005, his old junior team honoured the Regina Rocket by having players wear number 17 patches (Hicke's retired number) on their uniforms for the duration of the 2005–06 season.

1894, the Regina *Leader* confirmed that "hockey is fast becoming the great winter sport in Regina." Less than a month later, a sextet from Moose Jaw arrived in Regina eager to compete for a silver trophy emblematic of intercity hockey supremacy. While the host team won, 8–2, the star of the evening was silver-tongued, silver trophy bearer Nicholas Flood Davin, the Irish-born owner of the Regina *Leader* and a local Tory member of parliament.

"Mr. Davin, MP, said it was a great pleasure to him to hand the prize to the winners, not because Regina had won, but because a more manly game of any kind he had never witnessed," his paper reported. "Mr. Davin had often regretted the limited character of his attainments. In ballrooms he regretted he could not dance, and witnessing a polo match he could not play polo, but never [had his deficiencies been more evident than in watching a game of hockey]…Mr. Davin said—and he meant nothing political—the process shown here that evening by boys and lads, by young gentlemen and young ladies (who participated in the skating races), showed that throughout the future in all contingencies the North West would be able in brain and sinew to hold her own…. The rival hockey teams [later] adjourned to Mr. J. England's where an oyster supper was served…. An hour or two was spent in singing songs, reciting and speeches."

The member of parliament's stirring words anticipated the arrival of the

The Happy Motoring Man

Regina's Murray Westgate was the commercial host of *Hockey Night in Canada* TV broadcasts from 1952 to 1968. Here is his account of how he came to become the most famous service station dealer in Canada:

I was born in Regina in 1918. When I graduated from high school, we were in the Depression. No jobs. So I went back to art school, did some amateur theatre. After I was discharged from the service in World War II, I went back to Regina where I did more amateur drama—I really had the bug—for a group called Little Theatre. After that I moved to Vancouver, but if you want to grow strawberries, you have to go where they grow them, so in 1940 I got on a bus for Toronto. One day I got a job to do an Imperial Oil promotion film. I played a smiling, nicely dressed man, a gas station dealer on one side of the street. And another fellow played the bad dealer across the way. He was a slob with no customers. They'd show this film to gas station dealers at conventions. Then TV came along, and, as I understand it, they were having trouble finding a fellow to play an Imperial Oil dealer on *Hockey Night in Canada*. Finally, someone at Imperial Oil said, "Well, why don't you use this bird we've been using in our films?" And that's how I got the job. At first, when we did commercials live, I'd rehearse two or three hours for my parts, which would be two or three commercials. And I'd introduce the Hot Stove League first intermission. My sign off was, "Always look to Imperial for the best." A lot of people didn't know I was an actor. I can't tell you how many times someone stopped me on the street and asked me to look at their car.

The 1924–25 Regina Patricias, in front of an arena in Toronto, after winning the first game of the Dominion Championship.

Regina Patricias, the west's first hockey dynasty and a lasting symbol of the pro-monarchist sympathies that ruled much of the Dominion at the time. Princess Patricia of Connaught was the daughter of His Royal Highness, Prince Arthur, Duke of Connaught, Canada's governor general from 1911 to 1916.

When a 12-team junior league began in Saskatchewan in the fall of 1917, the three local teams adopted names that offered further proof of Queen City's royal affiliations: the Regina Monarchs; the Regina Victorias, or "Vics"; and the Regina Patricias. Named after the popular princess, the Patricias were a powerhouse from the beginning, taking eight successive Saskatchewan junior championships (1918–25) and representing the west in the first Memorial Cup in 1919, eventually bowing to the University of Toronto. The team lost a second national championship to Fort William in 1922, before winning national titles in 1925 and 1930 and finally reigning supreme over Canadian junior hockey.

Of course, the team's first star was a Duke. Defenceman Landis "Duke" Dukowski led the team to its 1919 Memorial Cup try (and later went on to captain the National Hockey League's Chicago Blackhawks). Subsequent stars had less regal nicknames: Eric "Cowboy" Pettinger was the leader of the 1922 Pats, while forward "Cagie" Kenny Doraty and goalie Jack "The Elongated Custodian" Cunning took the team to its first junior championship, beating the Toronto Aura Lees in an epic 1925 battle.

Police intervention, required in that deciding game of 1925 (which was won by the Pats, 5–2), contributed to the drama of the win. Doraty became involved in a wild swinging match with Toronto's Alex "Shrimp" McPherson. The players' fight became upgraded from a donnybrook to an all-out brouhaha when both benches cleared and slipping-sliding police rushed out on ice, turning the game into an improbable Keystone Cops misadventure. The comic aspect of the scene was not lost on Doraty and McPherson, who were spotted in the penalty box afterward, laughing into their sleeves.

Despite this success, the Pats and another local junior team, the Falcons, folded in the 1927–28 season, merging with the Regina Monarchs to form an all-star club that stormed through Toronto to beat the Ottawa Gunners in the 1928 Memorial Cup final, thanks to the scoring of Harold "Mush" March (seven goals in three games). But the wholly reconstituted Patricias were back in the Memorial Cup two years later, thanks to the efforts of another star forward with a striking nickname, left winger Frank "Buzz" Boll, who led the Regina Pats to a 1930 Cup win over West Toronto.

The oldest junior hockey club in the world would add to its legacy in subsequent decades. After disbanding once more during World War II, the Pats re-emerged as the best in the west in the 1950s, appearing in the Memorial Cup five times that decade, with a lineup featuring some of the most famous names in Saskatchewan hockey: Neudorf's Eddie Litzenberger; a kid from Lumsden with the best-ever name for a prairie hockey player, Red Hay; and then there were all the Pats' Regina-born stars—Red Berenson, Terry Harper, Fran Huck and the biggest western junior star of the 1950s, Billy Hicke. In 1974, the Pats would win a fourth Memorial Cup for the Queen City, thanks largely to the work of goalie Ed Staniowski and forward Dennis Sobchuck.

While Staniowski was the most successful Regina Pats goalie, winning the Canadian major junior player of the year award in 1975, another would-be Pats netminder went on to a more memorable professional career. Larry Walker, of Maple Ridge, British Columbia, struck out in 1982 and 1983 efforts to make the Regina hockey team and then decided to give his other sport, baseball, a try. He turned pro with the Montreal Expos in 1989 and became king of baseball in 1997, winning the National League's most valuable player award while a member of the Colorado Rockies.

RIGHT ON THE MONEY

One of Canada's favourite royals, Princess Patricia, was Queen Victoria's grand-daughter and the third child of Canada's fourth governor general, the Duke of Connaught. The Regina Patricias, or Pats, are named after her, as are the four current Edmonton- and Winnipeg-based divisions of Princess Patricia's Canadian Light Infantry. Princess Pat was particularly popular in Canada during World War I. In addition to her ceremonial role as colonel-in-chief of Princess Patricia's Canadian Light Infantry, the princess knit thousands of socks for Canadian soldiers. In 1915, she sent a box of maple sugar and a card to every Canadian serving overseas. Princess Patricia's image was later used on 1917 Canadian one dollar bills.

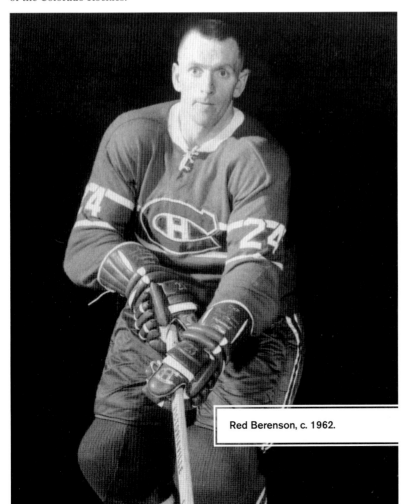

Red Berenson, c. 1962.

SASKATOON

FOUNDED
Prime Minister John A. Macdonald was looking to develop the prairies, when Toronto's Methodist community banded together in the early 1880s to form the Temperance Colonization Society. In June 1882, minister John Lake led society members to a site on the South Saskatchewan River. In 1883, the earliest streets and avenues of Saskatoon were surveyed. The name of the city is a derivation of mis-sask-quah-toomina, the Cree name for a local berry. Saskatoon became a city in 1906, with a population of 4,500. Today, Saskatoon is the largest city in Saskatchewan.

NATIVE-BORN NHL PLAYERS
Chad Allan, Keith Allen, Ralph "Red" Almas, Mel Angelstad, Brent Ashton, Ryan Bayda, Wade Belak, Ron Boehm, Derek Boogaard, Russ Brayshaw, Cam Brown, Dave Brown, Kim Clackson, Gerry Couture, Hugh Currie, Roberts Dawes, Dan Ellis, Shane Endicott, Todd Ewan, Perry Ganchar, Wilbert Gardiner, Michael Garnett, Chris Hajt, John Harms, Billy Hay, Jim Hay, Chad Hinz, Gordie Howe (born in Floral, SK), Vic Howe, Lloyd Klein, Dieter Kochan, Don Kozak, Moe Lemay, Jack Leswick, Peter Leswick, Pat Lundy, Vic Lynn, Keith Magnuson, Chris McAllister, Larry Melnyk, Donald Morrison, Roderick Morrison, Jack Norris, Rod Norrish, Dave Parro, George Pesut, Rick Pilon, Gerry Pinder, Gary Rissling, Larry Sacharuk, Cory Sarich, Bob Schmautz, Cliff Schmautz, Jeff Scissons, Scott Scissons, George Senick, Randy Smith, Bob Stephenson, Billy Thompson, Darren Van Impe, Ed Van Impe, Darren Veitch, Mick Vukota, Jess Wallin, Harry Watson, Fred Williams, Gordie Williams, Bus Wycherley

FAMOUS LOCAL TEAMS
Junior: Saskatoon Blades, Saskatoon Blazers, Saskatoon Chiefs, Saskatoon Dodgers, Saskatoon Falcons, Saskatoon Hilltops, Saskatoon Jr. Chiefs, Saskatoon Jr. Quakers, Saskatoon Jr. Wesleys, Saskatoon Legionaires, Saskatoon Lions, Saskatoon Mercurys, Saskatoon Nutana, Saskatoon Olympics, Saskatoon Pats, Saskatoon Quakers, Saskatoon Rovers, Saskatoon Royals, Saskatoon Wesleys; **Senior-pro:** Saskatoon Blazers, Saskatoon Civics, Saskatoon Crescents, Saskatoon Elites, Saskatoon Elks, Saskatoon Empires, Saskatoon Falcons, Saskatoon HMCS Unicorn, Saskatoon Hoo-Hoos, Saskatoon Hudson's Bay, Saskatoon Nationals, Saskatoon Navy, Saskatoon Pilgrims, Saskatoon Quakers, Saskatoon RCAF, Saskatoon Real Estate, Saskatoon Sheiks, Saskatoon Strathconas, Saskatoon Tigers, Saskatoon Westerns, Saskatoon Wholesalers, Saskatoon Brandon, Saskatoon-St. Paul Regals

CURRENT POPULATION
196,811

The Saskatoon Quakers, 1933.

A Western Hero

The story of Saskatoon hockey, if recounted chronologically, should probably begin with the Saskatoon Quakers, who won a world championship for Canada in Milan in 1934. That same year, the Quakers' hometown was chilled by the murder by drowning of Jack Leswick, one of the three local Leswick brothers who made it to the National Hockey League. But in Saskatoon hockey lore, even Mussolini and murder mysteries will have to yield to the story of Saskatoon's—and Canada's—greatest hockey player: Gordie Howe.

"Mr. Hockey" was born in Floral, Saskatchewan, in 1928. The Howes weren't rich. Their home, when the hockey player was born, was a three-walled shack. The fourth side of the house was a hill. But Howe's parents soon moved from Floral to a modest home in nearby Saskatoon, where they raised five daughters and four sons. Both Floral and Saskatoon can claim Howe as their own, then, although it is probably more true to say simply that Gordie Howe is a product of Saskatchewan—a potent symbol of the same prairie populism that brought Tommy Douglas and the Co-operative Commonwealth Federation (CCF) to provincial power in the '40s.

One winter during the '30s, a woman appeared at the Howe door with a gunny sack over her shoulder. It was the Depression: She was broke, and her

The ice-covered Saskatchewan River, which the wind polished free of snow, offered seemingly endless hockey adventure.

family was hungry. Gordie's parents had nine mouths to feed, but this woman needed help. Mrs. Howe offered the stranger the family milk money. The woman smiled and emptied her bag. Gordie and his sister Edna grew excited when skates bounced to the floor. Not wanting to pick favourites, Mrs. Howe gave them a boot each. Jumping into their coats, the squealing kids hurried to the back garden—a patch of black corduroy with ice in every furrow.

And that's how Gordie Howe learned to skate, pushing hard on one foot, like he was running a skateboard, and then gliding off between rows of decaying vegetables on a single blade. "We did this every day until one day Edna got cold and went inside," Howe remembered in his autobiography, *And Howe.* "I followed her and when she took the skate off, I put it on and she never saw it again."

Skating made winter magic, Gordie discovered. The wrinkled, fast-frozen plains surrounding Saskatoon became up-and-down carnival rides. The ice-covered Saskatchewan River, which the wind polished free of snow, offered seemingly endless hockey adventure. "You could skate all the way to the next city," he later remembered. Most days, he and his friends raced on their skates down to the piers at the Grand Trunk Bridge, where they enjoyed the use of three sets of boards. That way, no one had to chase a puck to Moose Jaw if he missed a hard pass. Some games went all day, the player recalled. "Imagine a 12-hour game. You'd go home and eat, come back and say, 'Who's winning?'"

Life in Saskatoon moulded Gordie Howe into a great athlete. Every day, he carried splashing pails of water from a community well, to top up a 45-gallon drum on the family porch. One summer, he helped his dad in construction. By late August, he could drag five bags of cement at the same time. Hunting and fishing for spending money, meanwhile, gave Howe the vision and sporting habits of a prairie falcon. Summer mornings, he fished the Saskatchewan River for pike and walleye, which he sold to a local Chinese restaurant: a nickel a regular-size fish, ten cents a lunker. After the harvest season, he was flat on his stomach in farmers' fields, staring down a slingshot, waiting for groundhogs to peep from their holes. Farmers paid crisp one dollar bills for 100 gopher tails.

Although he was strong and well coordinated, Howe didn't play organized hockey at first. No money for equipment. Then, one fall day, he was out looking for a game with a pal, Frank Sheddon. Ice hadn't formed on the river, so the boys were in the fields outside the Westmount School District field, skating on the slough ponds that were always first to freeze. The ice there was young, transparent almost like a window. Gordie was halfway across one pond when he

Quakers Win World on $400

The Saskatoon Quakers were the city's most famous senior team in the '30s and '40s. Saskatoon lost the Allan Cup finals to the Moncton Hawks in 1933, but when the New Brunswick team declined an invitation to the 1934 world championship in Italy, citing economic hardship, the Quakers went instead. Team manager Johnny Walker, a former Canadian Pacific Railway employee, told a writer from Our Roots, a Canadian historical website, "Quaker Oats gave us $400, and we wore their little men on our shirts. To pay our expenses, we started in Prince Albert and played games all across Canada, travelling on CPR sleepers. I paid the CPR from the gates and they had a bill against me for the whole trip."

The team travelled by CP steamship to Liverpool and played teams in nine European countries, every one of which was gripped by the political intrigues that would soon lead to World War II. "They were watching for spies, so I carried all the passports," Walker explained. "I couldn't take money out of Berlin, but luckily the CPR had offices in all those places. They banked money…and credited me with sterling in London."

The Quakers won or tied 48 games in their 51-match European tour, performing in front of 353,000 fans in Norway, Sweden, Germany, Czechoslovakia, Austria, Switzerland, Italy and France. The team took the World Championship with a 2–1 win over the United States. The Saskatoon team showed up at the awards banquet in pressed tuxedos. The Americans, a group from Boston, showed up in casual clothes and soon began pelting the Canadians with dinner rolls. "Immediately, Mussolini's boys chased the Americans out and threatened them."

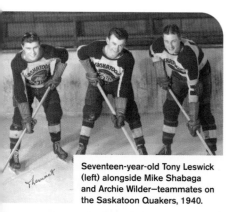

Seventeen-year-old Tony Leswick (left) alongside Mike Shabaga and Archie Wilder—teammates on the Saskatoon Quakers, 1940.

Bad News

Three Saskatoon Leswick boys—Tony, Pete and Jack—made it to the National Hockey League. A former star for the senior Saskatoon Quakers, Tony Leswick played with Gordie Howe on the great Detroit Red Wings teams of the early '50s, earning the nickname "Mighty Mouse" for his frequent run-ins with Rocket Richard. Pete Leswick was a career minor leaguer who enjoyed brief NHL stays with the New York Americans (1936–37) and the Boston Bruins (1945–46).

Maybe the most talented player in the family was the eldest brother, Jack "Newsy" Leswick, who led the American Hockey Association in scoring in 1932–33 before being called up by the NHL's Chicago Blackhawks, where the 22-year-old centre had his named engraved on the 1934 Stanley Cup. Jack Leswick was called Newsy because friends said he was always bursting with stories. Before leaving Chicago, Leswick signed a new contract with the Blackhawks and then raced to Winnipeg for a holiday with Pete, anxious to tell his younger brother all about life in the NHL. One evening he left their rented cottage, saying he was going for a walk. His lifeless body was pulled from the Assiniboine River a week later. His gold Blackhawk pocket watch was missing, and no one could find his Chevrolet. Newsy Leswick's body was returned to Saskatoon and was buried in Millbrook Cemetery. To this day, his death remains a mystery.

heard what sounded like the snapping of a branch. Turning, he found himself alone. Then he noticed Frank reaching out of the ice.

Gordie walked his shuddering friend home. The day was so cold that Frank's frozen clothes cracked when he moved. Next day Gordie called on his best friend, who was now sick with pneumonia. There would be no hockey for Frank that winter. Mr. Sheddon asked the young visitor if he was going out for the Red Wing peewee team that season.

"Can't," Gordie said, looking down.

"Why not?"

"No equipment."

When he was ready to leave, Frank's dad was waiting at the door with his son's hockey equipment. "May as well use these," he told him. Soon Gordie was playing three different positions—goalie, defence and forward—on five teams. He was surprised when people noticed he could shoot from both the left and right sides. Couldn't everybody?

Gordie was clearly a natural. At 14, he represented Saskatoon in an exhibition match against provincial NHL all-stars, including the dipsy-doodle-dandy Bentley brothers, Max, Doug and Reg, from Delisle, Saskatchewan. He scored a goal and was the strongest player on the ice. Then Doug Bentley speared him in the stomach when the referee wasn't looking. Gordie collapsed. "Slow down, son!" Max Bentley laughed, skating past.

Bentley might as well have saved his breath, for Gordie Howe wouldn't be slowing down for another 40 years. After flubbing an audition with the New York Rangers at age 15 because of homesickness, Howe attracted the attention of Jack Adams of the Detroit Red Wings in the fall of 1944. The Red Wings had him privately tutored on their farm team in Galt, Ontario, for a season (see page 132) by ex-NHLer Al Murray, then sent him to play for the Omaha Red Wings in 1945–46, where the still painfully shy 17-year-old once hid from an ardent female fan by exiting the rink through the washroom window.

The young player became number 9 that hockey year, with a typical lack of fuss. The Omaha trainer advised the Saskatoon athlete that the team had traded its number 9; did Howe want the prestigious number?

"No," Gordie replied. He was doing all right with 17.

Gordie Howe in action against the Boston Bruins.

"It will get you a lower berth on the train," the trainer said.

"I'll take it," Howe responded.

The following season, 1946–47, Howe made the NHL's Detroit Red Wings. Motor City fans instantly took to the quiet, mop-haired kid with zoot-suit shoulders. And the youngster seemed to improve, getting stronger and more confident with every shift. His first season in the league, he handled Rocket Richard in a fight. The goals started to come three years later, at age 21, when he was put on a line with Ted Lindsay and Sid Abel.

Detroit's Production Line became the class of the league in the 1949-50

He was surprised when people noticed he could shoot from both the left and right sides. Couldn't everybody?

season. Sid Abel, of Melville, Saskatchewan, was the playmaker. Ted Lindsay provided grit and passion. But it was Howe who made the trio the best in hockey.

The kid who had toppled groundhogs with a slingshot at 25 yards could now lay a pass through a tangle of legs onto the stick of a breaking linemate. And rival defencemen found him harder to budge than a stalled car. One move seemed to illustrate all his talents. Skating down his wing, the right-handed forward warded off checkers with his left forearm, controlling the puck with his right hand on the stick. Swinging behind the goal, Howe would then pull out in front on the opposite side of the net, switching hands on his stick mid-pirouette, and snap off a bullet drive as a left-handed shot.

Howe added one more element to his game in the fall of 1950. The previous spring, he had tumbled into the boards in a mix-up with Toronto Maple Leafs' Teeder Kennedy, fracturing his skull. Howe's mother rushed from Saskatoon to be by his side as doctors performed a 90-minute operation credited with saving his life. From then on, Howe marked his territory with casual acts of violence, using his shoulder, elbow and stick to discourage the attention of opponents.

The extra elbow room helped Detroit's number 9 become the NHL's top scorer. And the rough acts of frontier justice, in combination with his laconic manner, earned Howe the reputation of being an authentic western hero. Big Gordie won six NHL most valuable player trophies, in 1952, 1953, 1957, 1958, 1960 and 1963. He scored 103 points for Detroit at age 41.

Howe retired from hockey two years later, but returned to play with his sons, Mark and Marty, in the World Hockey Association in 1973–74, winning the MVP of that league. Back in the NHL with the New England Whalers in 1979–80, the 52-year-old appeared in an all-star game played in Detroit, collecting an assist and an ovation every time he stepped on the ice.

Some hockey writers have said that Gordie Howe played hockey with such economy of movement that only connoisseurs of the game could discern his great talent. But that's not true at all. Once, during the 1950s, basketball legend Bob Cousy went to his very first hockey game, played at the Boston Gardens. Detroit was in town to take on the Boston Bruins. Cousy knew nothing about hockey except that some fellow named Gordie Howe, an athlete he had never seen, was supposed to be its best player. He watched less than a minute of action before turning to a friend. "That must be Gordie Howe," he said, pointing to Detroit's number 9.

Saskatoon Blade

A brilliant hockey player and skater, Saskatoon-born Norman Faulkner volunteered for World War I and fought at Vimy Ridge, where he was wounded in 1917, eventually causing him the loss of one of his legs. Convalescing in France, Faulkner horrified nurses by insisting on skating on a nearby frozen pond. A year later, he was back in Canada and skating regularly on a single leg. He soon turned professional and began skating in exhibitions throughout the west. A contemporary of Faulkner's, John Booker, provided the following account of a 1919 Calgary performance: "For the first minute of [Faulkner's] exhibition there was no applause, but then he fell end-over-end, removing all doubt that there was any gimmick or any invisible wires. The subsequent applause was deafening."

SHAUNAVON

FOUNDED
Located in the southwest corner of
Saskatchewan, 30 miles from the
American border, Shaunavon sprang
from a village to a town in 1913,
with the arrival of the Canadian Pacific
Railway. The town has long been
a service centre of the surrounding
agricultural community. Oil was
discovered near here in 1952.

NATIVE-BORN NHL PLAYERS
Gary Aldcorn, J.J. Hunter, Rhett
Warrener

FAMOUS LOCAL TEAMS
Not applicable

CURRENT POPULATION
1,775

Shaunavon, 1906.

Hayley's Midnight Run

Hayley Wickenheiser's parents presented her with glistening white figure
skates when she was three, in 1981. The child didn't even pretend to be happy.
She wanted brown hockey skates! Maybe hockey was in her Saskatchewan
blood. After all, her cousin Doug Wickenheiser had been picked number one in
the National Hockey League draft by the Montreal Canadiens a year earlier.

Every winter, as soon as the first good cold snap hit in Shaunavon,
Hayley's dad, Tom, a schoolteacher, would bundle up and hurry into the backyard. Shaunavon is a farm town an hour's drive from Swift Current. Winter
nights are long and clear. The only sound in the world is your next footstep in
the snow. Before getting down to business, Tom Wickenheiser would check
the sky. Some nights, the stars were bright as Christmas lights. Then he'd open
the hose.

The rink would be ready after a few such evening-long sessions. Out
Hayley would race, in her 99 hockey jersey, attempting to duplicate some bit
of magic that her favourite player, Wayne Gretzky, had performed on *Hockey
Night in Canada*.

Hayley discovered right away that she loved hockey. At five, she began
playing locally in a boy's league. Every time she stepped on the ice, she felt the
same tug of excitement in her stomach that comes from flying a kite too high
in the sky.

One cold winter night before Christmas in 1985, Tom Wickenheiser
rolled over in his sleep and heard something. It was past midnight. He sat up.

The kids, Hayley, Ross and baby Jane, had to be in bed. Marilyn, his wife,
was asleep beside him. Padding downstairs, Wickenheiser made sure it wasn't
a burglar and then moved to the kitchen for a glass of water and heard the
scratching sound again. Leaning close to the window, Tom picked up the outline
of a small figure floating across his neighbour's backyard. That's when he
figured out the noise—someone was ragging a puck.

Hayley! It was 20 below and his seven-year-old had snuck out of bed and
jumped into her equipment to play hockey on a neighbour's backyard rink.

The extra practice paid off. Before long, Hayley was the best young hockey
player, boy or girl, in Shaunavon. At 15, she made the Canadian women's
Olympic hockey team. After that, her life seemed to pick up speed, like a close
game at the end of the third period. Soon, Hayley Wickenheiser and Cassie

Hayley Wickenheiser celebrates her goal in the first period of the Women's Ice Hockey semi-final game against Finland at the 2002 Olympics in Salt Lake City.

Campbell were leading the Canadian national team to a decade of glory. Every time her team needed a big goal, Hayley was there, it seemed. Blowing past American defenders to set up Nancy Drolet for the overtime winner in the Women's 1997 World Championships in Kitchener...firing the winning goal in Canada's 3–2 gold medal Olympic win in Salt Lake City in 2002...collecting the insurance goal in the team's 2-0 2004 Women's World Championship win in Halifax...helping the women's team to a second gold at the 2006 Olympics.

Before the 2004 championship, Wickenheiser took a sabbatical from woman's hockey, joining the Kirkkonummi Salamat, a men's team in Finland, and becoming the first woman to collect a point in a men's professional league. She played 23 games for Salamat in the 2003–04 season, scoring two goals and adding 10 assists.

Wickenheiser received some criticism for playing in Finland. Why would she want to play in a men's league? It didn't make sense. Then again, neither did sneaking out of the house as a child to play hockey on a dark rink all by herself after everyone else had gone to bed.

The impulse for both actions was the same: Hayley Wickenheiser wanted to be the best hockey player she could be. And the only way she could do that was by exploring the outer limits of her talent.

SWIFT CURRENT

An early photo of Swift Current.

FOUNDED

Centuries ago, First Nations people began camping on the site of what is present-day Swift Current, calling the intersection of the fast-running creek that runs into the North Saskatchewan River *kisikaciwan*, meaning "it flows swiftly." When French fur traders stopped in the same place they were moved to a similar observation, naming the body of water Rivière au Courant, or Swift Current. Canadian Pacific Railroad surveyors followed the fur traders' path. Swift Current became a city in 1914, as European settlers began to take possession of farms and ranches outside the city core.

NATIVE-BORN NHL PLAYERS

Shane Belter, Jeff Buchanen, Jack Forsey, Marc Habscheid, Bill Hogaboam, Boyd Kane, Trent McCleary, Travis Moen, Darcy Regier, Jeff Toms

FAMOUS LOCAL TEAMS

Junior: Swift Current Broncos, Swift Current Indians, Swift Current-Estevan

CURRENT POPULATION

14,821

Changing Currents

Both Swift Current and its prodigal hockey team, the Broncos, had reason to be happy on 30 December 1986, as the team bus pulled onto the highway for a 90-minute ride to the Queen City to take on the rival Regina Pats. The Swift Current Broncos were an original member of the junior Western Hockey League, formed in 1966. Although the Broncos were perennial favourites, the city had let the team slip away to Lethbridge, Alberta, in 1974. Now, in 1986, the smallest town in Canada to sponsor a major junior team was thrilled to have the Broncos back, thanks to a syndicate of local businessmen who had repurchased the team from Lethbridge months earlier. The Broncos were getting better, too, and after a slow start, coach Graham James's team was contending for a playoff berth.

Skies were gun-barrel grey and a northwest wind pulled curtains of snow from nearby fields onto the Trans-Canada as the bus pulled out at 3:30 that afternoon. Still, inside the bus, the mood was holiday cheerful. Joe Sakic and Sheldon Kennedy were up front, chatting. Trent Kresse and Scott Kruger, two top scorers, began playing cards with Chris Mantyka and the highly regarded rookie Brent Ruff. Teammate Bob Wilkie turned to a Stephen King novel.

Five minutes into the trip, bus driver Dave Archibald steered the coach onto a railway overpass. The roads were good. The temperature had been above freezing that afternoon. What Archibald didn't know was that a wind tunnel had formed under the railway overpass, chilling the pavement overhead into a ramp of black ice. As the bus lost its grip on the road, the driver shouted "Hold on!" The vehicle missed a turn, tearing off highway signs as it sailed off the overpass, landing back end first on its right side, then sliding 218 yards along a farmers' side road.

The four card-playing Broncos at the back, Kresse, Kruger, Ruff and Mantyka,

The 1986 Swift Current Broncos.

were dead before the bus ended its awful skid. Everyone else scrambled the length of the crumpled vehicle through broken glass, leaping through the empty front window into the cold. Brian Costello, a reporter who travelled with the team for the Swift Current *Sun*, encountered goalie, Trevor Kruger, Scott Kruger's younger brother, wandering around calling for his dead sibling. "Sorry, Trevor," was all the journalist could to say to him.

Swift Current residents couldn't believe what had happened until newspaper headlines the following day confirmed that the nightmare was real. Four thousand people, a quarter of the city, attended a memorial service at the Swift Current Civic Centre six days later. Coach James stirred the emotions both of the community and of every player in his club when he insisted that future teams treat the Broncos with the respect the team deserved. "Play hard," he demanded. "We don't want any hollow victories."

In Prince Albert, Regina, and everywhere they played, the Broncos were greeted with standing ovations in the next weeks. Joe Sakic and Sheldon Kennedy reached inside themselves to become great players, leading the Broncos into the playoffs, where the team bowed out to the Prince Albert Raiders. The Swift Current juniors were even better the following year, as Sakic led the Western Hockey League in scoring. By the 1988–89 season, the Broncos were virtually unbeatable, winning 33 out of 36 games at home. Sakic was gone, joining the National Hockey League's Quebec Nordiques at age 18, but Kennedy continued to lead the team, along with defenceman Bob Wilkie and goalie Trevor Kruger.

Every Saturday night game that season was a sellout at home as fans from nearby Shaunavon, Gull Lake, East End, Climax and Cadillac arrived in winter caravans to share in the greatest Canadian junior hockey story of the year. The Broncos stormed to the Memorial Cup with the best junior record in the country that season, meeting the Saskatoon Blades at the Saskatchewan Place Arena for the Cup final—the only time the national junior championship final has involved two Saskatchewan teams.

Kennedy scored for the Broncos early in the game, and Swift Current held a 2–0 lead going into the second period. The Blades came back, however, taking the lead with three goals. The game was tied 3–3 going into overtime. Saskatoon jumped to the offensive and appeared ready to pull off an upset, firing five consecutive shots at Broncos goalie Trevor Kruger, the kid who two years earlier had lost his brother to a patch of black ice outside Swift Current. Trevor turned away every shot. After Saskatoon's fifth try, a third member of the Kruger clan, younger brother, Darren, took Swift Current's only shot of the overtime, a drive from the blue line that teammate Tim Tisdale, standing close to the net, deflected

The Sheldon Kennedy Story

Inside the Swift Current Civic Centre, there is a plaque that reads, "What we keep in our memory is ours unchanged forever," in tribute to the four junior Swift Current Broncos who died in a tragic bus accident on 30 December 1986. This sentiment also describes the life of Sheldon Kennedy, a brilliant forward for the Broncos who led the team to a Memorial Cup win in 1989. He also endured five years of physical, emotional and sexual abuse at the hands of his Swift Current coach, Graham James.

Kennedy broke down in the National Hockey League, as his tortured past made the game of hockey impossible. He played with the Detroit Red Wings, Calgary Flames and Boston Bruins between 1989 and 1997, but was prone to unexplained depression and bouts of alcoholism. While a member of the Boston Bruins, Kennedy stepped forward to testify against James, a brave act that was rewarded by league-wide support from sympathetic NHLers. Kennedy, the one-time farm boy from Elkhorn, Manitoba, is now retired from the sport.

After serving a three-and-a-half year sentence in jail, James left Canada and is currently coaching hockey in Spain.

through Saskatoon goalie Mike Greenlay's pads, to give Swift Current the 1989 Memorial Cup championship. Even Saskatoon fans responded to the goal with cheers, for after the tragedy of 30 December 1986, the Swift Current Broncos were very much Saskatchewan's home team.

Coach Graham James was *Inside Hockey* magazine's Man of the Year in 1989. He would lead the Broncos to four more winning seasons before leaving the city to coach the WHL's Calgary Hitmen in 1994, telling reporter Ashley Prest of the *Winnipeg Free Press*, "I don't think you can ever prepare yourself for what happened here [in Swift Current]. I feel like King Lear—I've experienced both ends of the spectrum. You can never get higher than winning a Memorial Cup and never get lower than when four of your players are killed."

Two years later, other tragedies that had befallen James's team came to light. Sheldon Kennedy, a Broncos player who had gone on to play for the National Hockey League's Calgary Flames, missed a team meeting. When Flames coach Pierre Page found Kennedy in his darkened hotel room, the player was suicidal. His old coach, Graham James, had sexually assaulted him every week from the time he was 14 until he was 19, Kennedy explained, shaking. He still hadn't got over it. He never would. A year later, James was charged with sexual assault in a separate case. Kennedy bravely stepped forward, helping to put his tormentor in jail for more than three years.

Swift Current rallied following the ugly James debacle, as it had from the fateful bus accident, and the Broncos continued. One tragedy the townspeople try to remember, as the memory serves a noble purpose; the other they try to forget because, as every prairie farmer knows, some crops are simply too difficult to harvest.

Frenchman River Valley Bronco

The Swift Current Broncos' first star, Bryan Trottier, grew up in Val Marie, a town of 160 residents about an hour's drive south of Swift Current. His Metis great-great-grandfather, Patrice, was Canada's last registered buffalo hunter and worked in the same Frenchman River Valley that Chief Sitting Bull brought his people to after the 1876 Battle of the Little Big Horn. Bryan's father and sister formed a country-and-western band that played bars in Saskatchewan, southern Alberta and northern Montana. Bryan played guitar, too, but he was better at hockey, a game he learned on the frozen stretches behind his father's farm. His most faithful teammate was a border collie named Rowdy, who played one-on-one with Bryan on the coldest days of the year, jumping high to snatch the puck in his teeth.

After a season with the Humboldt Broncos in the Saskatchewan Junior Hockey League, Trottier graduated to the Western Hockey League's Swift Current Broncos in 1972, at age 16, where he played with Dave "Tiger" Williams and Terry Ruskowski. He was drafted in the second round by the National Hockey League's New York Islanders in 1974, but would remain for another year with the Broncos, who were then transferred from Swift Current to Lethbridge. Bryan's father was furious, figuring that his son belonged in the NHL. The Islanders placated the elder Trottier by buying him a tractor—a worthy investment for the league, it turned out. Bryan Trottier joined the Islanders in 1975–76, winning the rookie of the year award. He was the most valuable forward on the Islanders team that won four Stanley Cups in a row between 1980 and 1983 and was named the NHL's most valuable player in 1980.

WEYBURN

FOUNDED

Like many prairie towns, the south Saskatchewan town of Weyburn sprang to life with the arrival of a railroad. In 1898, the Soo Line was built, connecting Moose Jaw, Saskatchewan, with Minneapolis, Minnesota. Weyburn grew up around a railway station house and a freight shed. W.O. Mitchell, author of *Who Has Seen the Wind*, was born in Weyburn in 1914. Tommy Douglas, the future premier of Saskatchewan, also served here as a Baptist minister in the 1930s. Many of the companies that support the southeast Saskatchewan oil reserves are now located in Weyburn. Farming also remains an important economic activity today.

NATIVE-BORN NHL PLAYERS

Rene Chapdelaine, Larry Giroux, Gizzy Hart, William Holmes, Walt Ledingham, Brian Marchinko, Jim McTaggart, Rick Shinske, Dave Williams

FAMOUS LOCAL TEAMS
Junior: Weyburn Elks, Weyburn Red Wings, Weyburn Wanderers; **Senior-pro:** Weyburn Beavers, Weyburn Wanderers

CURRENT POPULATION
9,534

Weyburn grain elevators c. 1928.

Prairie Tiger

Weyburn received its name from a 19th century Scottish explorer who, after wading across the Souris River to the present site of the city on a mercilessly hot summer day, remarked that he'd suffered a "wee burn." A century later, hundreds of hockey players would offer up the same complaint after tangling with Weyburn, Saskatchewan's most famous hockey export, "Tiger" Williams.

David Williams was first called Tiger at the age of five by a Weyburn hockey coach. The name stuck. Tough as a prairie winter and determined to make good, Tiger was working as a $1,000-a-week roughneck in the Alberta oil fields even as he was rough-riding the left wing for the junior Swift Current Broncos, where he collected 108 goals and 954 penalty minutes in three eventful seasons (1971–74).

Williams joined the National Hockey League's Toronto Maple Leafs in 1975 and became an immediate fan favourite, playing alongside Lanny McDonald and Darryl Sittler throughout the late '70s. Sittler once described Tiger's unique strategy for getting into game shape during practice: "Tiger would take those long strides and turn on the speed—down to the end of the rink with no indication that he was going to turn and follow the boards behind the net. He didn't turn, he just jumped and hit the glass as hard as he could. [Then] down to the other end of the ice he went, same thing, Bam!" Tiger's features certainly told the story of how he played the game. A writer once observed that Williams's face was so flat that he could bite a wall.

Tiger could score, too. He fired in 241 goals during his 14-year career. After most goals, the one-time Weyburn farm boy would celebrate with an elaborate western pantomime, bending way down to ride his hockey stick while pretending to twirl a lasso with his free right hand. If any onlookers were bothered by the extravagant display, they never mentioned it to him.

Williams played with equal gusto off the ice. Former Toronto Maple Leafs president Don Giffin was, like Williams, an avid gun collector, and he once invited the Leafs out for a pheasant hunt. Afterward, they repaired to Giffin's Mississauga mansion to reflect on the day's shooting over drinks. Giffin was showing Williams the pride of his collection, a weapon that Tiger took to be an elephant gun. "Got any shells for these?" Williams asked. Giffin produced a fist-sized bullet from a drawer. Tiger loaded up, walked onto the front porch, breathed in the magnificent lilac calm of the evening, then blew the head off the nearest streetlamp.

Williams was traded from Toronto to the Vancouver Canucks in 1980, where he laboured hard and fruitfully for another four seasons, enjoying a career-best 35 goals in 1980–81. Williams would also play for the Los Angeles Kings (1985–88) and for the Hartford Whalers (1987–88). He retired in 1988 with 3,966 penalty minutes, an NHL record since broken by Tie Domi.

The many hours that Tiger spent in the penalty box made him something of an expert in conflict resolution. In 2005, the winter of hockey's discontent, with a labour disagreement keeping the NHL arenas that once came alive with Tiger safaris now glum and quiet, Weyburn's most famous hockey citizen told the *Globe and Mail*'s Eric Duhatschek how he would resolve hockey's economic troubles:

> All you've got to do is drive an hour north of Calgary and turn right and at the first farm on the left, you pick up Joe Alberta Farmer. Then I'll go to Regina and drive an hour south and at the first farm to the right, I'll pick up Joe Saskatchewan Farmer. Then we'll get somebody to do that in Manitoba, too, and we'll take all three to Toronto and I guarantee you, in a matter of four hours, they'd have the whole thing solved.

The Mayor of Weyburn

Running a prairie junior hockey team has been likened to being mayor six months a year: The coach is responsible to everyone in town during the season. If this comparison is true, then coach Dwight McMillan has been running Weyburn for most of the last 35 years. McMillan has served three terms with the Weyburn Red Wings: 1972–76, 1982–86, and from 1989 on. During that time, he has won close to 1,000 games, more than any other coach in Canadian junior hockey history except for Ottawa 67's coach Brian Kilrea. And McMillan has taken the Red Wings to two Tier II, Junior A championships—in 1984 (over the Orillia Travelways) and in 2005 (defeating the Camrose Kodiaks).

McMillan's history with the team goes beyond coaching. He was an original Red Wing, there in the fall of 1961 when Tommy Douglas dropped the ceremonial first puck for the junior franchise's inaugural game at the Weyburn Colosseum.

McMillan grew up on a farm in Lashburn, Saskatchewan. In addition to playing for and coaching the Red Wings, he has worked for close to 40 years at the oil and gas company now know as EnCana. When it was suggested that his coaching win total made him a Canadian junior hockey legend, McMillan's response was characteristically modest. "Oh, I wouldn't say that," he replied. "I'm just a farm boy workin' at an oil company and coaching a hockey club."

Dave "Tiger" Williams, here playing for the Los Angeles Kings, earned his stripes with the junior Swift Current Broncos. He scored 52 goals (and collected 310 penalty minutes) in the 1973–74 season.

WILCOX

FOUNDED

A small farming community south of Regina, Wilcox is home to the Paterson, Pioneer and Saskatchewan Pool grain elevators. The community is famous for farming, the major economic activity here for over 100 years, and for the Athol Murray College, home — since the 1930s — of the famous Notre Dame Hounds. Liberal finance minister Ralph Goodale was born on a farm outside Wilcox.

NATIVE-BORN NHL PLAYERS
Garth Boesch, Dick Metz, Don Metz

FAMOUS LOCAL TEAMS
Junior: Notre Dame Hounds

CURRENT POPULATION
250

"God of the Notre Dame clan, grant that the mother who bore me suffered to suckle a man! So help me God, no mistakes, let's go!"

Wilcox, Saskatchewan, is a three-grain-elevator farming town located 27 miles southwest of Regina. Hockey commentator Chris Cuthbert once noted that Wilcox (population 250) is so small that the only red lights in town are located behind the nets in the town's hockey rink, workplace of the junior Notre Dame Hounds.

The Athol Murray College of Notre Dame was founded by Monsignor Athol Murray, grandnephew of Sir John A. Macdonald and scion of a wealthy Toronto family. After dabbling in journalism and the law, Murray entered seminary and was eventually sent to Saskatchewan, becoming parish priest of Wilcox in 1927. He quickly expanded the local Catholic grade school into a high school and college, forging an affiliate relationship with Ottawa University during the Depression. Students without financial resources were not turned away. Some farmers paid for their sons' enrolment with livestock or crops.

Murray insisted that Notre Dame students were taught the classics, which he took to mean Latin, Greek and hockey. He himself coached the hockey team, employing a boisterous style that belied his religious training. Once during the 1940s, his team was ravaged by measles. Down 9–0 to Regina, a fuming Murray entered the dressing room and exclaimed, "Goddamit, guys, if you can't beat them, at least give them measles."

A hard-drinking charmer, Père Murray built Notre Dame into a prairie institution, fighting through occasional hard times with prayer and canny networking. During one rough stretch, when the school was running short of food, he asked the students to ask God for a miracle. The next day, a shipment of Spam arrived at the college, courtesy of Prime Minister John Diefenbaker.

Shortly after Murray's death in 1975, Notre Dame reverted from college to high school. In 1980, the school's bantam team, coached by Barry MacKenzie and featuring future National Hockey Leaguers James Patrick, Gord Kluzak, Gary Leeman and Gord Sherven, won the 1980 Air Canada midget championship. Seven years later, Notre Dame entered a team in the Saskatchewan Junior

Athol Murray, coach of the College of Notre Dame hockey team, fires up his team prior to a 1947 game.

League and made it to the Western Canadian junior championships against the Calgary Canucks.

During those 1988 finals, the Canucks jumped to a three-game lead in the best-of-seven series, but the Hounds refused to quit, gathering around goalie Curtis Joseph before the fourth game to chant the team's pregame rallying cry: "God of the Notre Dame clan, grant that the mother who bore me suffered to suckle a man! So help me God, no mistakes, let's go!" The Hounds won that game, then two after that, thanks to Joseph's efforts as well as the scoring prowess of the team's top forward, Rob Brind'Amour, like Joseph, a future NHL all-star.

With the series tied at three wins apiece, the Notre Dame team travelled to Calgary. So did the entire school, some 350 students who bussed to Calgary, painting their faces the team colours (red and white) and filling an entire end of the Canucks' rink.

The Hounds were up 3–2 with a few minutes left when Calgary was awarded |a penalty shot. As Joseph prepared for the Canuck shooter, Notre Dame students called upon the spirit of Athol Murray to help them in his team's hour of need, chanting, "Père be there, Père be there." Sure enough Joseph turned aside the breakaway and Notre Dame won, going on to take the Tier II junior championship Centennial Cup over the Halifax Lions the following week.

Notre Dame continues to be recognized as one of Canada's top hockey schools. The illustrious high school typically has boys playing in the Saskatchewan Junior Hockey League and in the South Saskatchewan Junior B League, as well as girls playing in the midget South Central Hockey League and in the Regina Hockey League. Boys play in three different bantam leagues, as well. Over 100 Notre Dame Hounds have been drafted or signed by NHL teams. Famous Hounds include Garth Boesch, Rob Brind'Amour, Wendel Clark, Russ Courtnall, Pat Elynuik, Gord Kluzak, Bill Kyle, Gus Kyle, Vincent Lecavalier, Gary Leeman, Curtis Joseph, Dick Metz, Don Metz, James Patrick and Brad Richards.

The Hound Line

The National Hockey League's Toronto Maple Leafs featured a trio of Notre Dame alumni on the same line in the mid-'80s. Christened "The Hound Line," the unit of Gary Leeman, Wendel Clark and Russ Courtnall led the Leafs to the NHL semifinals in 1985–86.

Clark, from Kelvington, Saskatchewan, remains a cult hero in Toronto. He has often credited his days at Notre Dame with his later success. A great skater, Clark particularly enjoyed playing in Notre Dame's Olympic-sized rink, which is wider than junior and NHL-standard rinks. The fact that the rink was heated was also nice. Prior to arriving at Notre Dame in grade nine, Clark played on outdoor rinks all across the province. The rink in Invermay, Saskatchewan, was the coldest, he told author Chris Cuthbert. "We changed lines from the dressing room. It was −40 outside, −40 or colder in the rink. We were too young to sit on the bench, so every two minutes they would blow a whistle so we could change. Five in and five out of the dressing room. It was just too cold to sit out there."

Yorkton, 1909.

YORKTON

FOUNDED
Located near the Manitoba border, approximately halfway between Winnipeg and Saskatoon, Yorkton was founded in 1882. The promise of land brought pioneers from the Ukraine, beginning in 1891. Perhaps the city's most famous immigrants were Harry and Abe Bronfman, who arrived from Russia in 1905 and purchased the Balmoral Hotel on Livingstone Street. During Prohibition, the brothers began selling "medicinal liquor" from a drugstore located next to "The Bal," creating what became the Seagram liquor empire. Ironically, the largest liquor store in Saskatchewan currently stands where the Bal, the former stomping ground of bootleggers, once operated.

NATIVE-BORN NHL PLAYERS
Mike Chernoff, Brent Fedyk, Leslie Kozak, Mervin Kuryluk, Clayton Pachal, Lawrence Popein, Metro Prystai

FAMOUS LOCAL TEAMS
Junior: Yorkton Terriers; **Senior-pro:** Yorkton Flyers, Yorkton Legionnaires, Yorkton Terriers

CURRENT POPULATION
15,107

Sons of the Soil

Metro Prystai, the best-known hockey player to hail from Yorkton, Saskatchewan, was four years old in 1933 when he learned to skate. Twin brothers, Bill and Harry, were off at school when Metro slipped a pair of his brothers' skates on over his shoes, bundled up for the cold, then wobbled out to the frozen road outside his house, delighting in the sudden easy freedom of movement as he carved his way around the frozen streets of his neighbourhood.

If the little boy had bumped into anyone during his travels, he might have chirped "*Dobryy ranok*," Ukrainian for "good morning," for Metro only learned English when he started grade school. Chances are a neighbour would have understood. Yorkton was founded in 1882 by 200 homesteaders from York County, Ontario, but in subsequent decades, many early settlers came here in response to offers of free land that the Canadian government placed in leaflets distributed throughout the Ukraine. With wheat prices soaring and the prairies largely unoccupied, Clifford Sifton, Prime Minister Laurier's minister of the interior from 1896 to 1905, called for the Canadian west to open its doors to the "stalwart peasant in a sheepskin coat, born on the soil, whose forefathers have been farmers for ten generations, with a stout wife and a half-dozen children." Between 1891 and 1914, approximately 170,000 Ukrainians settled in Canada, many in western provinces.

Prystai's father tried farming, but eventually became a railroad section man, working the tracks. Metro knew early on that he wanted to take neither of these directions. Sports became his life—baseball in the summer and playing hockey and watching the famed senior Yorkton Terriers in the winter. "If I didn't have a nickel to get in to watch [the Terriers], I'd try to get in by carrying a player's skates. Sometimes I'd have to wait until the third period, when I could get in for nothing," Prystai told author Bill Boyd in the book *Hockey Towns*.

"The Terriers were the biggest thing in Yorkton in winter," Stan Obodiac, a Yorkton native and former Terriers player, once recalled. The team represented the sporting ideal of every kid in town, he explained. "If you couldn't make the NHL

STAN THE MAN

Yorkton native Stan Obodiac played on the senior Lethbridge Maple Leafs team that won the World Hockey Tournament in Paris in 1951. In France, Obodiac established a World Tournament record that will never be broken, scoring 12 goals and 12 assists in six games. In the 1950s, he covered baseball as a reporter for his hometown newspaper, the Yorkton *Enterprise*, while playing on the city's top ball team, the Yorkton Cardinals. Getting good publicity for his team would prove harder in his next job: Obodiac later served as the public relations director for the National Hockey League's Toronto Maple Leafs during the hectic, frequently miserable Harold Ballard years, working for the team from 1958 to 1984.

like Metro Prystai...you dreamed of playing for the Terriers. When the Melville Millionaires came to play, that was what you talked about all week. Nobody had money—this was the Depression. So kids would wait outside until the ticket window closed and the fellow who looked after security went inside. Then you could go in free... Oh, your feet were cold by then, you may have been outside for hours, waiting. And it wasn't much [warmer inside]. Indoor rinks weren't heated then."

Because Yorkton had no junior team, Prystai skated for the Moose Jaw Canucks as a teenager, playing on a line with future National Hockey League great Bert Olmstead in two Memorial Cup finals (1945 and 1947). Prystai made the

"The Terriers were the biggest thing in Yorkton in winter"

The Yorkton Terriers, 1937.

NHL's Chicago Blackhawks in the fall of 1947, spending three seasons in Chicago before being traded to the Detroit Red Wings, where he occasionally worked on a line with Gordie Howe and won championships in 1952 and 1954.

Metro's parents visited him once in Detroit, taking in a game at the Red Wings' rink, the Olympia. "[Dad] didn't know about heated arenas," Prystai later told Bill Boyd. "So he's dressed for a prairie winter. My seats were beside Alex Delvecchio's and Benny Woit's, so Julie Woit gets to talking with him. All the time my dad's getting hotter and hotter in his big wool coat, sweating like hell. Suddenly he says in his heavy accent, 'Hey, somebody musta turned up the sshh-team.'"

Metro himself was a little naïve about big city life his first winters outside the prairies. When he first arrived in Chicago, he gravitated to the Mid-West Athletic Club, where he befriended a seemingly concerned sports fan who wanted to know everything about the Chicago Blackhawks, how everyone was feeling, whether anyone on the team had been hurt; at one point, the affable stranger even offered Prystai a job.

"What do I have to do?" the hockey player wondered.

"Carry a gun," famed gangster Al Capone's kid brother, Maddy Capone, replied.

Prystai quickly eased away from the relationship and was glad to be traded to Detroit. "He seemed nice, and I'm a kid from Yorkton—what the hell do I know?" is how he explained his unwitting friendship with a vice-president of Murder Incorporated. The crew-cut Prystai soon became a fixture with the Red Wings, scoring two goals and an assist in the Red Wings' 4–0 Stanley Cup clinching victory over the Montreal Canadiens in 1952.

That same summer, Prystai returned home to play third base for the Yorkton Cardinals in the Manitoba-Saskatchewan baseball league. Because Yorkton had no pro hockey team, the city's best players sometimes could only represent their city in baseball. In 1952, the Cardinals' top pitcher was Vern Pachal, a 50-goal scorer the previous winter for the Eastern Hockey League's Springfield Indians. The shortstop was Stan Obodiac, a former Terriers forward who had led the senior Lethbridge Maple Leafs to the Paris World Hockey Championship in 1951. Metro Prystai played third, while his brothers, Bill and Harry, patrolled the outfield.

The only baseball team in the league not to use American imports that summer, the entirely Yorkton-born Cardinals made the 1952 playoffs, with a lineup that would have made former minister of the interior Clifford Sifton proud. In the course of a double play, the ball might have gone, for example, from infielder Prystai to Obodiac to Yaholnitsky. The team's top pitchers, Pachal and Ernie Koruluk, almost always won, although the city's newspaper, the Yorkton *Enterprise*, notes that the Cardinals lost a close match to Saskatchewan's Kamsack Cyclones in the summer of 1952, to Cyclone pitchers Steve Stavrianoudakis and Mike Berezowksi.

Metro Prystai, c. 1951.

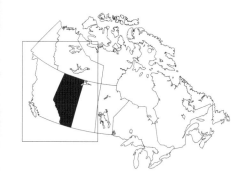

Opening Spread:
Edmonton-born
Calgary Flames player
Jarome Iginla and
Andrew Ference
celebrate a 2004
playoff goal.

In the 1980s, the Crown and Anchor pub in Red Deer, Alberta, a city equidistant between Calgary and Edmonton, became the site of such intense hockey rivalry that management was forced to paint a stripe down the middle of the bar to separate Edmonton Oilers and Calgary Flames fans. Because Edmonton is north of Red Deer and Calgary is south, Edmonton supporters congregated north of the stripe. To ensure that washrooms remained neutral, Antler Van Hellemond, a deer head dressed in referee Andy Van Hellemond's jersey, stood guard above the fireplace.

The bar was crowded during the regular season, but come National Hockey League playoffs, Crown and Anchor manager Eamon McCann had to throw a chain outside the door two hours before the opening faceoff to turn away the overflow of fans. Once the game started, the bar came alive with mischief. If the Oilers' Wayne Gretzky complained to referees on TV, a Calgary fan might traipse into enemy territory with one of the bar's hockey cocktails, Wayne's Whine-on-Ice. Losing a bet at the Crown and Anchor could lead to hospital care. For instance, after one playoff defeat, an Oilers fan was obliged to dress up in a Calgary jersey and allow himself to be tied to a nearby lamppost. Flames supporters then bought up all the cream pies in Red Deer, and proceeded to make a mess of his face. Afterward, the pie victim discovered he couldn't hear—until puzzled doctors cleared a pint of meringue from his ears.

If the 1980s hockey rivalry between the National Hockey League's Flames and Oilers converted Red Deer into a pie-throwing war zone, it also turned the principal cities into participants in the most uncivil war in Canadian hockey history. Civic hockey feuds are rampant across Canada. Ongoing battles between Sydney and Glace Bay on Cape Breton Island, not to mention between Sudbury and Sault Ste. Marie in northern Ontario, are intense. And for 40 winters, until the NHL expanded from six to 12 teams in 1967, the Toronto Maple Leafs and Montreal Canadiens offered the defining national sports drama. But even the Toronto-Montreal hockey feud was never as intense and personal as the Calgary-Edmonton conflict, a rivalry that once prompted a betrayed Flames supporter to show up at the home rink with the following sign: "I'd rather have a sister in a brothel, than a brother who's an Oilers fan."

Calgary and Edmonton are located 160 miles apart, an afternoon drive along Highway 2. The cities share a common background: Both were once military trading posts, Fort Calgary and Fort Edmonton. And Alberta's two largest cities share partnership in the province's lucrative oil industry. As with many blood feuds, however, familial similarities only serve to make the siblings' differences more apparent. In addition to serving as home to the oil industry's research and service sector, Edmonton is the provincial capital and location of the University of Alberta. Being a government-university town, Edmonton is more sedate and more given to ceremony than its southern counterpart. The city also prides itself on being cosmopolitan, hosting annual international jazz, folk and alternative theatre festivals.

Located in the heart of Alberta's "oil patch," Calgary is where the oil action is, home to the head offices of Petro-Canada, Shell Canada and EnCana. The city also hosts "the greatest outdoor show on earth," the Calgary Stampede. And while Calgary has grown well beyond the clichés that once defined

The Great One: Wayne Gretzky with
the Edmonton Oilers.

The Battle of Alberta: The Flames
versus Oilers rivalry, which came
to a head in the 1980s, continues
in the 2005–06 season.

Cow Town (it now boasts, for example, a vital independent film scene), the city
continues to embrace the maverick spirit.

Civic differences between the provincial rivals are particularly manifest in
hockey. Historically, Edmonton has been an eager participant in national and
international hockey tournaments. In junior hockey, Edmonton teams have
made the finals of the Canadian championship Memorial Cup a dozen times;
Calgary, on the other hand, has appeared in the national championship only
once since the Roaring Twenties. Edmonton teams have also represented Canada
in international competitions. The Edmonton Mercurys won the World Hockey
championships in London, England, and an Olympic gold medal for Canada at
the 1952 Olympics held in Oslo, Norway. More iconoclastic by nature, Calgary
declined an invitation to participate in the original North American World Hockey
Association, formed in 1972.

Perhaps the definitive Calgary hockey figure is Mervyn "Red" Dutton, who
served overseas with Princess Patricia's Canadian Light Infantry in World War I,
receiving shrapnel wounds to the leg. Doctors wanted to amputate, but Dutton
told them off and returned to Canada, skating every day through two winters to

strengthen his leg. Evidently recovered, the defenceman went on to star for the Calgary Tigers in the old Western Canadian Hockey League from 1920 to 1926. When the WCHL folded, he played and coached in the National Hockey League for another 15 seasons, mostly with the New York Americans, and then returned to Calgary, in 1940, to make a fortune building the Standard Gravel and Surfacing Company. The NHL made him president of the league in 1943, promising to eventually allow him to revive the "Amerks" franchise, but in 1946, when Dutton

"It doesn't matter how well you do," the stranger told Fletcher, "as long as you beat Edmonton."

Alberta royal wedding: Wayne Gretzky and Janet Jones, 16 July 1988.

understood that this was an unlikely possibility, he resigned, vowing that he would never again set foot in an NHL rink. The NHL was full of liars, and the game, he believed, simply wasn't any good anymore. Eventually, the NHL came crawling back to Dutton. When the Atlanta Flames were transferred to Calgary on 9 October 1980, Dutton agreed to drop the ceremonial first puck.

If Edmontonians are often exasperated by the bluster of their southern neighbours, Calgarians are equally unaccepting of what they perceive to be Edmonton's imperial pretensions. By the 1980s, these tensions were all too much. The Edmonton Eskimos won the Canadian Football League's Grey Cup in 1975, 1978, 1979, 1980, 1981, 1982 and 1987, while the National Hockey League's Oilers won the Stanley Cup in 1984, 1985, 1987, 1988 and 1990—all that glory compared to the Flames' sole 1989 Stanley Cup. And, oh, did Edmonton rub in their victories. Halfway through the '80s, the description, City of Champions, began showing up on Edmonton's letterhead and highway signs.

The worst moment for Calgary came when Wayne Gretzky and his sweetheart, Hollywood actress Janet Jones, married in Edmonton in the summer of 1988, shortly after the Oilers won their fourth Stanley Cup of the decade. Dubbed "Canada's royal wedding," the event was covered live on television. The Edmonton Symphony Orchestra played in the background, prior to the wedding ceremony. Thousands of Edmontonians lined the streets outside the church. Jones had a train on her gown that might have gone from the net to the blue line. Calgarians were dumbfounded. Edmonton was already home to the premier of the province; did it really need a king and queen, as well?

When general manager Cliff Fletcher took the Atlanta Flames to Calgary in 1980, he got his marching orders from a fan on the street his first day on the job. "It doesn't matter how well you do," the stranger told Fletcher, "as long as you beat Edmonton." A tall order, it turned out, for the Oilers, with Gretzky, Mark Messier, Grant Fuhr, Glenn Anderson, Jari Kurri and Paul Coffey in the lineup, plus Glen Sather behind the bench, became the best and most charismatic hockey team of the decade. Incredibly, Fletcher and company would build a club that was at times even better than the Oilers. Twice, in fact, the Flames went to the Stanley Cup (1986 and 1989) in a decade that saw Canadian professional hockey interest shift from central Canada to Alberta.

In Alberta, itself, the Edmonton-Calgary sports war always split the province as evenly as the proprietors of the Anchor and Crown had carved up their Red Deer pub. And the evolution of the Calgary Flames into the territory's second legion of hockey superheroes, with the arrival of stars Lanny McDonald, Al MacInnis, Joe Nieuwendyk, Doug Gilmour, Gary Roberts and Theo Fleury, turned an idiosyncratic family feud into what was the most thrilling Canadian hockey story of the decade.

CALGARY

FOUNDED

Calgary was settled in 1875, by the North West Mounted Police. When the Canadian Pacific Railway arrived in 1883, the fort became a thriving town. Agriculture dominated the town's economy until oil was discovered in the region in 1914. When Imperial Oil struck a geyser in the Leduc field near Edmonton in 1947, Calgary's convenient central location made the city the logical base for the foreign and domestic oil, gas and service companies that rushed in. Calgary's fate as the oil and gas capital of Canada was sealed.

NATIVE-BORN NHL PLAYERS

John Adams, Stewart Adams, Peter Allen, Mark Astley, Jared Aulin, Scott Bailey, Bob Bassen, Hank Bassen, Nolan Baumgartner, George Boothman, Mike Brodeur, Murray Brumwell, Don Cairns, Brian Carlin, Todd Charlesworth, Dean Chynoweth, Braydon Coburn, Rob Conn, Al Conroy, Cory Ross, Greg Crozier, Les Cunningham, Rob DiMaio, Micki DuPont, Murray Eaves, Brad Ference, Bill Gadsby, Normand Gainor, Harrison Gray, Dany Heatley, Mike Heidt, Tony Hemmerling, Archie Henderson, Fred Hergerts, Alex Hicks, Matt Higgins, Josh Holden, Pat Hughes, Tim Hunter, William Hutton, Connor James, Terry Johnson, Greg Joly, Ben Knopp, Joey Kocur, Krystofer Kolanos, Darryl Laplante, Craig Levie, Herbie Lewis, Bob Liddington, Evan Lindsay, Darcy Loewen, Roland Martin, Wayne McBean, Frank McCool, Lyle Moffat, Mike Moller, Glenn Mulvenna, Troy Murray, Mike Needham, Steve Nemeth, Robert Nilsson, Baldy Northcott, Lawrence Nycholat, Myles O'Connor, Darryl Olsen, George Pargeter, Brent Peterson, Chris Phillips, Domenic Pittis, Stacy Roest, Mike Rogers, Tony Savage, Kevin Schamehorn, Sweeney Schriner, Sean Selmser, Brandy Semchuk, Warren Sharples, Trevor Sim, Jason Smith, Brent Sopel, Ron Stewart, David Struch, Jeff Tambellini, Bobby Taylor, Brent Thompson, Paul Thompson, Rocky Thompson, Ryan Tobler, Garry Unger, Shaun Van Allen, Mike Vernon, Wes Walz, Kyle Wanvig, Edward Wares, Greg Watson, Chris Wells, Jason Widmer, Bob Wilke

FAMOUS LOCAL TEAMS

Junior: Calgary Beavers, Calgary Buffaloes, Calgary Canadians, Calgary Canucks, Calgary Centennials, Calgary Chinooks, Calgary Grills, Calgary Hitmen, Calgary Hustlers, Calgary Jimmies, Calgary Monarchs, Calgary Ramblers, Calgary Royals, Calgary Shamrocks, Calgary Wranglers;
Senior-pro: Calgary 78th Battery, Calgary Alberta Grain, Calgary Arenas, Calgary Army, Calgary Bronks, Calgary Buffaloes, Calgary Canucks, Calgary Combines, Calgary Cowboys, Calgary Flames, Calgary Imperials, Calgary Mustangs, Calgary Navy, Calgary Rangers, Calgary RCAF, Calgary RCAF Mustangs, Calgary Rotarians, Calgary Spurs, Calgary St. Mary's, Calgary Stampeders, Calgary Tigers, Calgary Trojans, Calgary Victorias, Calgary Wanderers

CURRENT POPULATION

886,000

The Wild West

In 1891, the population of what is now Alberta stood at 25,000, and Calgary and Edmonton were frontier towns with populations of less than 1,000 apiece. Montreal teams were already vying for the Stanley Cup on the elegant, indoor Victoria Skating Rink when Alberta's first hockey game, a 4 January 1893 match held in Calgary between the Town Boys and the Tailors on the outdoor Star Skating Rink, took place. The Boys won, 4–1, but their civic hockey dynasty would be short-lived. Two weeks later, a North West Mounted Police team defeated the Boys, 4–0, in a contest played on a frozen stretch of the Bow River.

The first Alberta hockey teams were social clubs made up of the province's British-Albertan business elite. Newspapers of the day record that a Brewster, of Brewster Bus Lines (then wagon trains), played on a Banff hockey team in 1898. That same winter, Clarence Lougheed, son of Senator James Lougheed and uncle of Alberta's future premier, Peter Lougheed, was the goaltender for the Calgary College team in an 8–4 loss to Calgary Public School.

Despite the blueblood pedigrees, Calgary hockey was frontier wild from the start, as confirmed by a lyrical first-person report in the *Calgary Herald* on 3 January 1896:

View of Fort Calgary, by William Winder, 1877.

Canadian Gothic: Joseph Kneeshaw and his family in Calgary, 1905 or 1906.

When I come home,
If I come home,
Escaped from all the "flies"
You may behold a broken nose
Likewise two sweet eyes
Good night, Good night,
I go to strive for glory and for gore,
To chop the fellows till
I can't chop anymore,
And if I fall upon the ice,
Then you shall share the pain,
Of him who lost his youthful life,
But won the hockey game.
—A.B. Ankler

Calgary's formative hockey years were as lawless as they were rough. In 1902, the city began to sponsor a junior championship, the Jackson Cup Challenge. Calgary beat Banff, 5–2, that first year. Two years later, an Edmonton club travelled south in a bid to capture the Cup. Calgary defeated the visitors on the ice, but Edmonton won all the post-game arguments. Calgary, it seems, had employed three seniors. Edmonton further charged that Calgary had hogged all the best practice times. Calgary's response was along the lines of, what, you want to talk or play hockey? Edmonton took the next train home. The skate would be on the other foot later that winter, however, when the same Calgary team travelled to Medicine Hat and was smoked, 6–0, by a Hat squad that employed the services of four seniors.

The story that best illustrates the Wild West days of early Alberta hockey involves Calgary and nearby Bassano. In 1910, the Canadian Pacific Railway built a dam in Bassano. Alberta entrepreneur Sam Whiting quickly bought up land in the district, offering lots to settlers with the sales pitch, "Bassano—best in the West by a dam site!" After establishing a town, Whiting recruited an all-star hockey team from senior teams in British Columbia, and set out to conquer Alberta hockey—starting with an invitation to Bassano's boisterous neighbours.

The Calgary team arrived with an entourage of gamblers, and before the contest, more money was laid down on bets than on booze at the Bassano Hotel. As reported by Jim Coleman in Bill Roche's *The Hockey Book*, the high-stakes

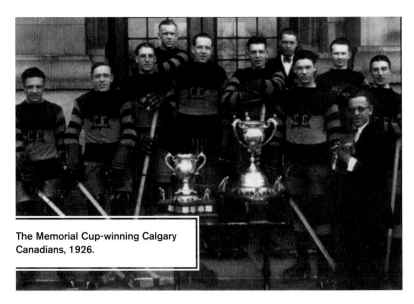

The Memorial Cup-winning Calgary Canadians, 1926.

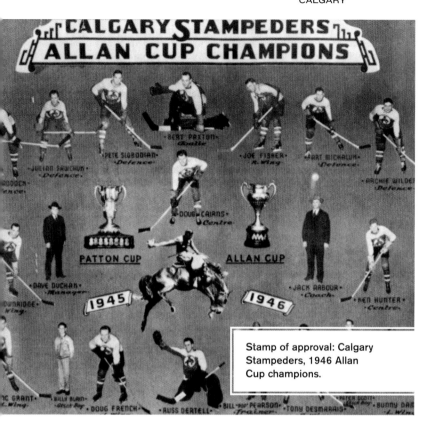

Stamp of approval: Calgary Stampeders, 1946 Allan Cup champions.

game was tied at the end of 60 minutes. The teams agreed to an overtime session. Two minutes into the extra frame, the Bassano rink exploded with happy shouts when the home side scored. Before the cheers died, however, a gambler pulled out a knife and severed a belt that controlled the lights. A split second later, the arena was black as sin. Sensing a con, Calgary players refused to leave the ice, and the two teams argued in the dark while a repair crew—presumably Calgary supporters—risked electrocution to rewire the rink. Before too long the lights popped back on, to a mixture of groans and cheers.

And so the overtime continued, with Calgary scoring two more goals, thereby winning the game. "But that wasn't the end of it!" Coleman writes. "The Calgary celebrants were quaffing great flagons of spirits in the Bassano Hotel when, to their amazement, the referee of the game was shoved into the bar, followed by a posse of grim-faced Bassano citizens. The referee climbed atop the bar and in a quavering voice, announced that all bets and debts were cancelled because the game hadn't been completed within a stipulated time limit. Those were the days when the referee's decision was final in sports-gambling matters. There is no record of what happened to the referee. However, knowing the Albertan temper, we would suggest he lies in an unmarked grave somewhere on the Western plains."

Alberta became a province in 1905. And Alberta hockey became better organized soon after that, although the sports history, *Alberta on Ice*, acknowledges that "it would be over 50 years before any concentrated effort was made to train referees." Despite a native aversion to regulators, the Alberta Amateur Hockey Association was created on 29 November 1907 in Red Deer. The Alberta Professional Hockey League debuted that fall. Three years later, two Alberta newspapers, the *Calgary Herald* and the *Edmonton Journal*, joined together

Saddle up: An aerial view of Calgary's Saddledome. Two years in construction, the Flames' home rink was officially opened on 15 October 1983.

Calgary Flames cheer as the game with Montreal ends giving them the Stanley Cup victory, 25 May 1989. From left are Dana Murzyn, Joe Nieuwendyk, Lanny McDonald and Gary Roberts.

to sponsor the Alberta Amateur Hockey Championship, which was first won by the Calgary St. Mary's in the 1910–11 season.

Calgary would have some outstanding junior teams, particularly in the mid-1920s, when the Calgary Junior Hockey League's Calgary Canadians dominated the provincial scene, defeating the Kingston Juniors to win the Memorial Cup in March 1926. In the 1970s, coach Scotty Munro directed the Calgary Centennials of the Western Canadian Hockey League to three division championships. And the Calgary Hitmen have represented the city in elite junior hockey since 1978. Still, the Hitmen, who lost, 7–6, to the Ottawa 67's in the 1999 junior championships, are the only city team to make it to the Memorial Cup after the Canadians, tangible proof that Calgary has been a senior-pro hockey town for the last 100 years, with three teams, the Calgary Tigers, the Calgary Stampeders and the Calgary Flames, taking turns dominating local hockey.

The Western Canadian Professional Hockey League's Calgary Tigers would become the first local club to compete for the Stanley Cup, losing to the Montreal Maroons in the Quebec team's hometown in 1924, while the Stampeders—the beloved Stamps!—represented the city in nine different leagues, winning the senior Allan Cup in 1946 as members of the Alberta British Columbia Hockey League. No local team, however, would dazzle and torment Calgary hockey fans in the manner of the National Hockey League's Calgary Flames, owners of the city's hockey heart since 1980.

Calgary's major pro team was born in Georgia. The name Flames refers not to burning fires on Alberta oil fields but to General Sherman's torching of Atlanta during the American Civil War. The Flames flickered in the capital of Georgia from 1972 until 1979, drawing middling crowds and exiting without a struggle in the preliminary playoff round almost every season. When owner Tom Cousins offered the team for sale, the only prominent citizen to rally behind the Atlanta franchise was Winnipeg-born actor Glenn Ford.

The Flames were purchased, in 1980, by Vancouver entrepreneur Nelson Skalbania, who promptly flipped the club, selling it 18 months later to six Calgary businessmen. The move north invigorated the franchise. The Flames made the playoff semifinals their first season in Calgary, playing out of the old Stampede Corral (capacity 7,242) while, across the street, the Olympic Saddledome, with its distinctive cowboy-seat top, was under construction.

The Flames fell naturally into a rivalry with the NHL's Edmonton Oilers. And at first, the '80s looked like another long decade for Calgary sports fans. They had just endured legendary quarterback Warren Moon's Edmonton Eskimos football dynasty—five Canadian Football League Grey Cups in a row, from 1978 to 1982—and then along came the Oilers. God Himself seemed to be whispering in the ear of Edmonton management between the 1979–81 seasons, as the team secured the services of future Hall of Famers Wayne Gretzky, Mark Messier, Paul Coffey, Grant Fuhr, Glenn Anderson, Jari Kurri and Kevin Lowe, instantly producing the greatest show on ice.

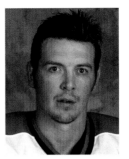

Theoren Fleury with the Calgary Flames.

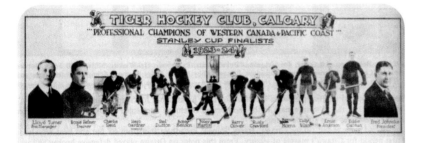

Tigers Marooned

From 1921 to 1925, the Calgary Tigers played in the old Western Canada Professional Hockey League along with the Edmonton Eskimos, Regina Capitals, Saskatoon Crescents and Calgary Tigers. In the 1923–24 season, the Tigers beat the Capitals, 2–0, earning the right to play the champions of the Pacific Coast Hockey League, the Vancouver Maroons. The Tigers won the series fair and square, two games to one, winning at home, in front of 5,000 fans, before taking the decisive third game, held in Winnipeg. After the game, the jubilant Tigers hopped on a train to Montreal to meet the Canadiens for the Stanley Cup. Minutes later, the Tigers were shocked to see the Maroons climb aboard for the eastern journey, as well. "We were amazed that Vancouver was to be included in [a Stanley Cup final tournament] after we beat them," forward Red Dutton claimed in *Alberta on Ice*. The Tigers beat the Maroons again in Montreal, but bowed to the Canadiens two straight (6–1, 3–0) in the Stanley Cup finals. Prime Minister Arthur Meighen dropped the ceremonial puck in the first game.

Calgary-born Mike Vernon was a member of the 1989 Stanley Cup-winning Flames team.

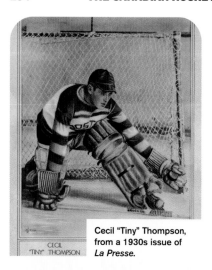

CECIL
"TINY" THOMPSON

Cecil "Tiny" Thompson, from a 1930s issue of *La Presse*.

$50 a Week and All the Smokes You Want

The first two Calgary players to make it big in the National Hockey League were brothers, Cecil "Tiny" Thompson and Paul Thompson. The former played for the Calgary Monarchs in junior before jumping to the Boston Bruins in the 1928–29 season. The talented goalie helped the Bruins to a Stanley Cup his rookie year, allowing three goals in five games. His nickname "Tiny" was, in fact, a reference to the netminder's minuscule goals against average (0.60), as opposed to his height (5'10"). The Hall of Famer won the Vezina Trophy as the league's best goalie in 1930, 1933, 1936 and 1938, finishing his 12-year career with an astonishing 97 shutouts.

Paul Thompson, Tiny's brother, would take the junior Calgary Canadians to the Memorial Cup in 1927. He then played for the NHL's New York Rangers and Chicago Blackhawks. Both brothers were first team members on the 1938 all-star team. Paul Thompson also appeared in Cameo cigarette ads during the Depression, earning $50 a week and all the smokes he wanted.

Incredibly, Flames general manager Cliff Fletcher would build an arguably more talented club within six seasons, scouring the hockey world for talent. He drafted star defenceman Al MacInnis, pride of Port Hood, Nova Scotia, in 1981; traded for the most famous moustache in hockey, Hanna, Alberta's Lanny McDonald, in 1982; and plucked Hakan Loob out of Sweden, in 1983. Two seasons later, in 1985, Fletcher selected an American collegian, defenceman Gary Suter (Madison, Wisconsin); traded for Joey Mullen, a sniper from Hell's Kitchen, New York; and promoted Calgary-born netminder Mike Vernon. In the following months, working with low draft picks, by virtue of the team's success, he somehow managed to obtain Joe Nieuwendyk and Gary Roberts, best friends from Whitby, Ontario, along with Russell, Manitoba's Theoren Fleury, while trading for defenceman Brad McCrimmon (Dodsland, Saskatchewan) and Doug Gilmour (Kingston, Ontario).

"It was the most exhilarating experience in my hockey career."

By the middle of the 1980s, the two Alberta clubs were the two best teams in hockey. Flames-Oilers games were alternately beautiful and savage affairs, filled with moments of artistry and power—Gretzky or Loob evading an approaching checker with a sideways swoop; Anderson cutting full speed at the net, heedless of defenders; the Flames setting up a power play, pinballing the puck around the left side of the rink as they eased right point man MacInnis into the clear for an unseen blast that would yank the meshing behind a goalie back with a violent snap.

There were fights, too. Wild West brawls. One game, Calgary's Doug Risebrough threw himself at Edmonton's Marty McSorley. The two were finally pulled apart by referees and Risebrough found himself in the penalty box. Looking down, he noticed he had McSorley's sweater in his trembling hands, so threw it to the floor, stomping on the blue and orange jersey with his razor-sharp skates. When the tantrum was over, he threw what looked like a handful of used-car-lot ribbons back out on the ice.

Yet for all their evident talent and passion, the Flames died out in the playoffs, except, as every Calgary fan remembers, in the springs of 1986 and 1989. In that first year, the Flames and Oilers were locked in a division final, game seven, third period tie. And then came one of those unusual breaks that, in the past, had usually gone to the other team in Calgary hockey games. Way back in 1896, for example—14 years before a Calgary team was sabotaged by a wire-cutting Bassano gambler—a local team had lost a civic challenge match to Medicine Hat when, according to *Alberta on Ice*, "the Calgary goalkeeper turned around and had his back to the puck. A reporter suggested he was...asking a boy [in the crowd] how much time was left," when an alert Medicine Hat shooter fired in the winning goal.

The deciding marker in the 1986 playoff game held in Edmonton was even more unlikely. The Oilers' Steve Smith, ordinarily the steadiest of defenders, circled behind his net, relaxed, looking for a breaking winger, and then fired a clearing pass that bounced off the back of his own goalie's leg; when Grant Fuhr, the Edmonton netminder, snapped his head around, even his goal mask looked surprised to find the puck and game-winning goal in his net. "It was the most exhilarating experience in my hockey career," general manager Fletcher would say of the Flames' elimination of the Oilers that night.

Calgary Flames' star Jarome Iginla doffs his Stetson to the team's fans at a public rally during the team's 2004 playoff run.

Calgary Flames' fans during the 2004 playoff run. An area west of the Saddledome known as "The Red Mile" saw gatherings of 100,000 red-clad fans after games in the 2004 playoffs. Although crowds were rowdy, only one arrest was made.

Arriving back home in the Calgary airport after a 30-minute flight, the team was mobbed by an estimated 25,000 fans, the same number of people who had lived in all of Alberta 100 years earlier. "It was quite a scene," Fletcher commented. "We felt a sense of accomplishment. In the minds of southern Albertans it was probably better than winning the Stanley Cup."

The '86 team would lose to the Montreal Canadiens the next series, but they returned to the Stanley Cup finals three seasons later, more determined and better equipped, to face Montreal yet again. Coached by Terry Crisp, the best-ever Calgary team featured a murderously efficient power play, with poised playmakers MacInnis and Suter on the points and ever-digging Doug "Killer" Gilmour flanked by darting marksmen Mullen and Loob up front. Rookies Nieuwendyk and Roberts, along with the veteran McDonald, were on the second power play line. Little Theo Fleury was a fourth line scene-stealer, racing from the pack and throwing himself belly first onto the ice, like a kid on a water slide, when he scored. And when the Flames built a lead, strong-as-oak forwards Joel Otto, Jim Peplinski and Tim Hunter would finish teams off with rugged physical play.

The '89 team won the Cup in convincing style. After losing a heartbreaking game three in Montreal—allowing a tying goal in the last half-minute of regulation play, then letting in an overtime marker, thereby going down in the series two games to one—the Flames rallied, winning three straight, two in Montreal. With the teams tied one-all, entering the third period of game six, the Flames scored three goals—a go-ahead marker from McDonald and two more from Gilmour. With the 4–2 win, Calgary became the only visiting team ever to win a Stanley Cup on Montreal Forum ice. Calgary celebrated the Flames win the way Theo Fleury responded to a big goal, going on a wild tear, as an estimated 50,000 fans crowded into downtown bars to paint the town Flames orange.

The team would engineer one more miracle run. In the spring of 2004, after 15 years of frustration, a coach from Viking, Alberta, Darryl Sutter, along with a superstar from Edmonton, Jarome Iginla, and a big Finnish goalie, Miika Kiprusoff, led the team to an improbable playoff march, as the team captured first the city's, then the province's, and finally, the country's heart by

Gads and Ulcers

The two most famous Calgary hockey players to enter the National Hockey League in the 1940s, Frank McCool and Bill Gadsby, had dramatically different dispositions and careers. "Ulcers" McCool played for the junior Calgary Canadians (1937–38) before attending college at Gonzaga State in Spokane, Washington. Entering the armed forces in World War II, he was soon discharged because of an ulcerous stomach—all of which made his next career move unlikely, for McCool left the army to tend goal for taskmaster Conn Smythe's National Hockey League Toronto Maple Leafs. McCool played little more than a season with the Leafs, winning the Calder Trophy in 1944–45 and helping the Leafs to a Stanley Cup, with four shutouts in eight games. During the finals against the Detroit Red Wings, he occasionally tore from the net to down a glass of milk in the dressing room, in order to calm his tortured stomach. He would quit the Leafs the following season, at age 27, retiring from hockey but not from taxing work. Returning home, he joined the Calgary *Albertan*, eventually becoming publisher of the paper in 1977.

Bill Gadsby, on the other hand, skated unperturbed through a 20-year NHL career. In 1939, as a child, he and his family travelled to England. War in Britain was declared upon their arrival. The Gadsbys attempted to return home, but their boat—the *Athenia*—was torpedoed by German subs. The family spent long hours bobbing in a crowded lifeboat on the Irish Sea. After that life-threatening incident, hockey seemed little more than a lark, and "Gads" was cool as a glass of milk in his long career as a defenceman with the Chicago Blackhawks, New York Rangers and Detroit Red Wings (1946–66). He never even minded all the cuts he took to his face, which reputedly required more than 600 stitches, perhaps because the defenceman took out an insurance policy that awarded him $5 a stitch.

Ironically, despite being named to seven all-star teams in the course of his distinguished, two-decade career, the Great Gadsby never won a Stanley Cup, whereas McCool managed to collect a Cup in an NHL career that lasted only 20 months.

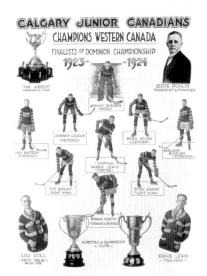

Calgary Wins Memorial Cup

A group of Calgary sportsman, Musty McGill, Lloyd Turner, Eddie Poulin and Jimmy Condon (owner of the Palace of Eats on 8th Avenue and 1st Street West) put together a highly competitive Calgary Junior Hockey League in the 1922–23 season. Three junior teams represented the city in the '20s—the Calgary Hustlers, the Calgary Maple Leafs (starring Stu Peppard, uncle of actor George Peppard) and the Calgary Canadians. The Canadians, run by manager and president Eddie Poulin, were the team that would make a lasting mark on Calgary hockey, however. The 1923–24 team made the Memorial Cup finals, losing to Cooney Weiland's Owen Sound Greys. Two seasons later, the Canadians were back, with a team that consisted entirely of local boys, including future National Hockey League all-star Paul Thompson. The finals, held in the Winnipeg Amphitheatre, were a best-of-three-games affair, with the Kingston Tigers winning the first game, 4–2. The Canadians rallied, however, winning the next two games, 3–2. Thompson scored two goals in the final game, to give Calgary its only Memorial Cup win. More than 9,000 whooping fans greeted the Canadians on the team's return home to Calgary four days later. A grand turnout, considering the fact that the population of Calgary was 65,000 at the time. The players all received gold watches.

muscling past Vancouver, heavily favoured Detroit and San Jose in the preliminary rounds of the playoffs. All of the series were, in their own ways, extraordinary. The Flames' Martin Gelinas scored the clinching goal in every round. The team played six deliciously tense overtime games. Kiprusoff finished Detroit off with consecutive 1–0 shutouts. Iginla scored a few "Gordie Howe hat tricks" (a goal, an assist and a fight) along the way. And defenceman Mike Commodore had his hair styled into a great orange afro.

Once again, Calgary went Wild West over a hockey team. The Saddledome hosted beard-growing contests. And during and after every playoff game, tens of thousands of young fans, dressed (and sometimes undressed) in Flames colours, took to the Red Mile, a downtown corridor, for impromptu, beer-fuelled, Mardi Gras-style parades.

In the Stanley Cup finals, the Flames took on the Tampa Bay Lightning. The Flames were winning three games to two by the sixth game, played at the Saddledome. The score was tied, two-all, in overtime. If Calgary were to score, the team would win the Stanley Cup. Craig Conroy of the Flames whacked at a puck in the Tampa Bay goal crease. The puck just crossed the line—a goal! Calgary wins!—when goalie Nikolai Khabibulin kicked it back out with a flick of his right goal pad. A replay on the U.S. ABC TV feed showed that Calgary had, in fact, scored and won. If a Bassano gambler had cut the lights at that point, maybe officials would have seen the error of their ways.

In fairness to on-ice referees, the goal was evident only to the slow-motion camera eye. But as it was, the winning goal went unnoticed. Tampa Bay won the game the next period and then captured the Stanley Cup, the following game, in Florida.

With the loss, Flames fans sunk lower than the Bow Valley. In the late summer of 2005, the team received good news, however. A new collective bargaining agreement, passed after a season-long work stoppage, imposed a salary cap on all NHL teams, giving small-market teams such as Calgary and Edmonton, who had lost their Hall of Fame players in the early '90s to big-spending American teams, an equal chance at the Stanley Cup. Given the infectious passion of Calgary fans, it seems probable that the team from southern Alberta will soon rise again.

Orange you glad you're in Calgary? Flames defender, Mike Commodore would tint his hair Halloween orange during the team's 2004 playoff run.

EDMONTON

FOUNDED

In 1795, the Hudson's Bay Company built a trading post in central Alberta known as Edmonton House. A small town of 700 during the early 1890s, Edmonton swelled in 1898, when gold was discovered in the Klondike. In 1904, Edmonton was incorporated as a city, and in 1905, it became the capital of the new province of Alberta. A black gold rush further enriched the city after 1947, when drillers discovered oil in nearby Leduc.

NATIVE-BORN NHL PLAYERS

Jonathan Aitken, Doug Anderson, Dave Babych, Wayne Babych, Doug Barrie, Shawn Belle, Brian Benning, Jim Benning, Perry Berezan, Mike Berger, Fred Berry, Blair Betts, Larry Bignell, Tom Bladon, Jason Botterill, Jay Bouwmeester, B.J. Boxma, Johnny Boychuck, Gary Bromley, Gerry Brown, Gilbert Brule, John Bucyk, Randy Bucyk, Al Cameron, Craig Cameron, Gene Carrigan, Bill Carse, Jason Chimera, Chris Chisolm, Erik Christensen, Dave Chyzowski, Dean Clark, Mac Colville, Neil Colville, Mike Comrie, Paul Comrie, Pat Conacher, Don Cutts, Bunny Dame, Billy Dea, Gerald Diduck, Chris Dingman, Hnat Domenichelli, Dave Donnelly, Steven Dykstra, Jim Ennis, Andrew Ference, Vernon Fidler, Brian Ford, Kyle Frearich, Jamie Gallimore, Bob Geale, Dave Goertz, Randy Gregg, Kevan Guy, Len Haley, Greg Hawgood, Paul Healey, Jay Henderson, Chuck Holmes, Dave Hoyda, Kelly Hrudey, Cale Hulse, Jarome Iginla, Brad Isbister, Rick Jodzio, Eddie Joyal, Mark Kachowski, Matt Keith, John Kelly, Dean Kolstad, Russ Kopak, Dan Kordic, John Kordic, Dave Kryskow, Stu Kulak, Daymond Langkow, Scott Langkow, Brian Lavender, Dale Lewis, Warren Luhning, Jamie Lundmark, Dave Marcinyshyn, Gord Mark, Richard Matvichuk, Kevin Maxwell, Darrell May, Tubby McAuley, Ross McKay, Jamie McLennan, William McNeil, Gerry Melnyk, Glenn Merkosky, Mark Messier, Hugh Millar, Brad Millar, Jason Miller, Roy Mitchell, John Mokosak, Derek Morris, Richard Mulhern, Hap Myers, Brantt Myhres, Tyson Nash, Scott Nichol, Scott Niedermeyer, Bill Oleschuk, Josh Olson, Dave Orleski, Greg Parks, Dave Pasin, Allen Pederson, Pete Peeters, Perry Pelenski, Matt Pettinger, Dion Phaneuf, Fernando Pisani, Ray Podloski, Steve Reinprecht, Kyle Rossiter, Paul Runge, Phil Russell, Philip Samis, Terran Sandwith, Andy Schneider, Wally Schreiber, Jim Shires, Gary Shuchuk, Geoff Smith, Jarrett Smith, Mark Smith, Nathan Smith, Harold Snepts, Doug Soetart, Lee Sorochan, Gordon Strate, Jason Strudwick, Brian Sutherby, Andy Sutton, Ken Sutton, Darrel Sydor, Rob Tallas, Dave Thomlinson, Jim Thomson, Tim Tookay, Garry Valk, Darren Van Oene, Mickey Volcan, Ed Ward, Shane Willis, Jerry Wilson, Gary Yaremchuk, Ken Yaremchuk, Zarley Zalapski

FAMOUS LOCAL TEAMS

Junior: Edmonton Athletic Club, Edmonton Athletics, Edmonton Bruins, Edmonton Canadians, Edmonton Caps, Edmonton Crusaders, Edmonton Enarcos, Edmonton Eskimos, Edmonton Ice, Edmonton Imperials, Edmonton Maple Leafs, Edmonton Mets, Edmonton Movers, Edmonton Oil Kings, Edmonton Poolers, Edmonton RCAF, Edmonton Red Wings, Edmonton Southsides, Edmonton Strathconas, Edmonton Victorias, Edmonton Yeoman; **Senior-pro:** Edmonton Albertas, Edmonton Deacons, Edmonton Dominions, Edmonton Elks, Edmonton Eskimos, Edmonton Flyers, Edmonton Hockey Team, Edmonton Hustlers, Edmonton Maritimers, Edmonton Monarchs, Edmonton New Method, Edmonton Oilers, Edmonton Oil Kings, Edmonton Shamrocks, Edmonton Superiors, Edmonton Thistles, Edmonton Vics

CURRENT POPULATION

648,000

A speed photograph of Edmonton hockey players, taken by MacLennan and McGowan, January 1927.

The World in Their Pocket

Fortune arrives in unexpected and spectacular ways in Edmonton. The central Alberta community was a sleepy trading post of less than 1,000 residents when gold was discovered to the north, in the Klondike, in 1898. Soon a fat, snaking queue of prospectors poured through the "back door" to the Yukon, buying up equipment and merchandise. Edmonton doubled in population, business and excitement within two years.

In 1890, in a nearby village, close to what is now Edmonton International Airport, a telegraph office was built. "We shall name it after the first person who comes in," Mr. McKinley, the operator decreed. Soon after that, Father Hippolyte Leduc, the future vicar general of Edmonton, swung through the door. Fifty-seven years later, Imperial Oil was drilling outside what was now the town of Leduc. The company had spent $12 million on 130 unrewarding forays into the soil when, on 13 February 1947, tool pusher Vern "Dry Hole" Hunter changed Edmonton's fortunes and his own nickname by ordering a discouraged crew to drill another five feet at the end of a long shift, tapping into a vast reservoir of oil. The strike excited another boom, as Edmonton's population grew sixfold in the next 40 years.

Edmonton's most famous hockey teams would be subject to the same sometimes unexpected, thrilling bonanzas that prompted the growth of Alberta's capital city. Edmonton officially became mad for the sport of ice hockey in 1902, building the grandest indoor arena in the Northwest Territories, the Thistle Roller and Ice Rink, at the corner of 102 Street and 102 Avenue. With a $13,000 nine-trestled miracle structure—no pillars!—to play in, city sportsmen formed an all-star senior hockey club, the Edmonton Hockey Team. Three thousand fans, a third of the town, showed up on Christmas Day 1907, to watch a game between Edmonton and Strathcona (now South Edmonton).

The home side won, 9–7, exciting civic fantasies of a Stanley Cup win. And in 1908, the Edmonton Hockey Team, champion of the Alberta Hockey League, stacked with imports the calibre of Lester Patrick and Didier Pitre, both from Montreal, and Bert Lindsay, from Renfrew, Ontario, ventured to Quebec to challenge the Montreal Wanderers (unsuccessfully) for the Cup. Two seasons later, the Edmonton team—informally, the Eskimos—again travelled east, this time bowing to the Ottawa Silver Seven.

The Eskimos went broke trying to win a national championship, and as early as 1909 the team's management promoted the idea of a western pro league that might compete with the National Hockey Association. Calgary killed the plan, however, by refusing to build a modern arena. Prominent Calgary player and cigar store owner Dan McLeod bristled at the notion of professionalism. "I never received a cent playing hockey and I never intend to," he said. "I am only a professional when it comes to selling cigars."

Edmonton and Calgary formed their own four-team senior circuit in 1919, but the Big 4 (Calgary Canadians, Calgary Tigers, Edmonton Eskimos, Edmonton Dominions) fell prey to internecine quarrelling and dissolved in 1921 when the Canadians and Tigers protested the Eskimos' acquisition of Bill Tobin. The goalie wasn't a true resident of Alberta, Calgary teams claimed.

Edmonton would always be more open to the outside hockey world than its south city rival. A local businessman, meat-packing mogul Cliff Gainer, sponsored the Edmonton Superiors, a local senior team, on a 38-game tour of

Edmonton's Thistle Roller Rink, 1902.

An Edmonton hockey team, c. 1904.

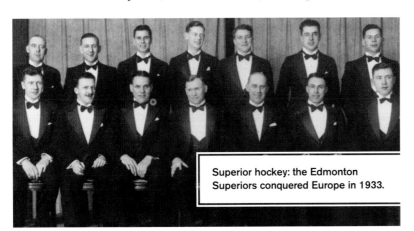

Superior hockey: the Edmonton Superiors conquered Europe in 1933.

Edmonton's 1949 championship "Mercs."

Europe in 1933. Seventeen years later, the Edmonton Waterloo Mercurys, bankrolled by James Christiansen of Waterloo Motors, again toured the European continent, winning the world hockey championships in London, England. In the 1952 Oslo Olympics, the "Mercs" became the last Canadian hockey team to win a first-place medal until the Canadian women's and men's teams struck gold in 2002.

During the early '50s, local junior and pro teams also entered into a fruitful affiliation with the National Hockey League's Detroit Red Wings, an arrangement that would help make Edmonton the pre-eminent hockey city in western Canada for close to two decades. From 1950 to 1966, city clubs won two world championships (the Mercs, in 1950, 1952), captured three Western Hockey League crowns (Edmonton Flyers, in 1953, 1955, 1962), and appeared in eight junior Memorial Cup championships, winning two national titles (Edmonton Oil Kings, in 1963, 1966).

When the World Hockey Association, a rival of the National Hockey League, was created in 1972, Edmonton became a charter member—as did Quebec City, Winnipeg and, so everyone thought, Calgary. But a week before a league meeting, at which teams were slated to receive financial bonding, Calgary dropped out. "I have made up my mind that I'm personally not interested in world hockey," announced the club's chief executive, Scotty Munro. "I've worked for many years to get a major junior hockey league in the west, and for it to be a development league for professional players." And so, the Edmonton Oilers would be Alberta's lone WHA representative for most of the seven years (1972–79) the association was in operation.

Although capsule histories of the Oilers inevitably begin with teenage sensation Wayne Gretzky arriving in November 1978, instantly turning the team into a WHA championship contender and, three seasons later, into the most exciting team in the NHL, the Edmonton Oilers' Stanley Cup gusher—five thrilling championships between 1984 and 1990—was preceded by seven hard years of dry drilling.

"Wild" Bill Hunter in the mid 1970s.

The Oilers were brought to life by Wild Bill Hunter, a Saskatoon hockey sales-man with a line of patter as long as his white sideburns. Hunter grew to believe in hockey miracles while playing for Father Murray's junior Notre Dame Hounds during the 1930s. After running several Saskatchewan franchises (the senior Melville Millionaires, the junior Regina Pats), he moved to Edmonton, quickly taking the junior Oil Kings to the Memorial Cup in 1966. Bringing pro hockey to Edmonton, however, would be his enduring sales triumph. Here's Hunter at a 1972 Edmonton press conference, a few short months before the Oilers took to

The Oilers were brought to life by Wild Bill Hunter.

the ice, skating around the fact that he didn't yet have a sales team in place for a nonexistent hockey club that would play in an entirely too small rink:

> I find finance the dullest subject in the world. The game is the important thing. Does anybody ask about NHL finances? You can ask any question, and I'm not afraid of answering them. But don't ask any foolish questions because I don't answer foolish questions... People are buying our season tickets like hot cakes, and we aren't out making calls yet. Just this morning somebody phoned the office for ten. We won't sell more than 20 to one individual or organization, because we only have 4,500 season tickets available... Gentlemen, tell your companies to buy their season tickets now, because with only 5,200 seats in the building, there will be no free tickets. Even Bill Hunter will have to pay to get in.

The WHA was a nomadic, grandfather-and-son league of marquee players approaching retirement—ex-NHL stars Bobby Hull, Gordie Howe, Frank Mahovlich, Dave Keon and Norm Ullman—and teenagers still eligible for junior hockey who wanted to turn professional before reaching 20, as required by the NHL. Team collapses and transfers were common. The WHA began with 12 and ended with six teams, although with all the moving around, 35 differ-ent owners would hold teams over the years. (The Calgary Cowboys, for example, showed up in 1975–76 and disappeared the following season.)

Few hockey fans can remember all the WHA franchise shifts, but certain memories endure. The New Jersey Knights played in the Cherry Hill Arena, a rink with no showers in the visiting team's dressing room. Player benches were mini-grandstands, three short pews providing room for 15 skaters. The coach was forced to sit in the first row with paying customers, where angry fans shout-ed for him to "Siddown!" if he jumped up to shout instructions to his team.

Perhaps the story that best illustrates the circus atmosphere that charac-terized the WHA involved the league's first championship team, Gordie Howe's Avco Cup-winning Houston Aeros. Apparently, the team rented ele-phants for players and coaches to ride on during a civic parade. At one point, Aeros coach Bill Dineen saw the great beast in front of him seize up and drop five pounds of used straw on the pavement. Good thing these babies can't fly, Dineen told himself, chuckling. Just then, the elephant he was riding scooped the spreading pile up in its trunk, tossing it overhead into the coach's lap.

Colourful tales and Wild Bill Hunter's showmanship kept fans curious for the first few winters. Newspaper photographers were invited to witness the Oilers' first big acquisition, Jim Harrison of Provost, Alberta, wheel a shopping cart full of one dollar bills out of the team's offices to celebrate his $75,000-a-year contract. Hunter later signed Normie Ullman, a local boy and former NHL great with Toronto and Detroit, along with the storied Jacques Plante for the team's 1973–74 campaign. But Ullman and Plante were over 40. And the Oilers,

The Great Gretzky celebrates on the ice during the 1986–87 season.

The 1926 Edmonton Eskimos, which featured Eddie Shore.

Mess

Mark Messier's great-uncle Howard Dea was a star for the 1922–23 Edmonton Eskimos team that lost to the Ottawa Senators in the Stanley Cup. Mark's father, Doug Messier, was a regular on the Edmonton Flyers team that won the Western Hockey League title in 1962, shortly after Mark turned one. It came as no surprise, then, that the Edmonton-born youngster would take to skating and hockey easily. He was strong enough to earn the nickname "Moose" as a teenager and enjoyed shooting and throwing his husky body around as a Tier II junior player for the Spruce Grove Mets and for the Saint Albert Saints of the Alberta Junior Hockey League.

Instead of graduating to elite junior, Mark jumped right into the World Hockey Association as a 17-year-old forward with the Cincinnati Stingers, scoring a single goal, but also a 12-punch knockout of big Edmonton Oilers centre Dennis Sobchuck over the course of 55 games. The fight impressed Sather, who was behind the Edmonton bench at the time. And Oilers scout Barry Fraser loved the way the kid skated, with fluid, determined strides, always in a hurry to get there before everyone else. Then there were his bloodlines. The young player was still a project, but the Oilers had time and so took him with their second pick in the 1979 draft.

Like the other teenage Oilers the team drafted in its first years, Messier was a speed reader when it came to learning hockey. At age 20, he was a 50-goal National Hockey League centreman. And if Gretzky, Paul Coffey and Jari Kurri gave the Oilers their matchless flair, Messier provided the buccaneer spirit that allowed a bunch of kids to presume they could conquer the hockey world.

Messier wasn't intimidated by anyone. Once, in the early '80s, Gretzky, Messier and Kevin Lowe were invited to Hugh Hefner's Playboy mansion. They were supposed to take a limo, but grabbed a cab in their haste and then got out at the front gate, figuring they would walk the rest of the way. How far could it be from the gate to the mansion? Far, apparently, and the twisting road was all uphill. Messier lost his patience for the endless maze of leafy hedges and shouted out in exasperation, "If Hugh Hefner comes walking by in his pyjamas and that pipe, I'm going to sucker him!"

Mark Messier with the NHL playoff Conn Smythe Trophy, 1984.

Edmonton Expresses

Hockey legend Eddie Shore (see page 243) played for the professional Western Hockey League's Edmonton Eskimos for a single season (1925-26), taking with him to the National Hockey League's Boston Bruins both a lasting nickname, "The Edmonton Express," and a wife, Doris, star pitcher for an Edmonton woman's softball team. The city would have another NHL-bound Edmonton express in the 1950s, a junior and minor league sponsorship deal with the NHL's Detroit Red Wings that allowed local players a chance to jump from the junior Edmonton Oil Kings to the Western Hockey League's Edmonton Flyers before graduating to Detroit. Local stars Norm Ullman and Johnny Bucyk made just such a journey in the early '50s, playing on the Oil Kings team that appeared in the 1954 Memorial Cup and on the 1955 WHL championship Flyers edition (with goalie Glenn Hall). Ullman, Bucyk and Hall, all future Hockey Hall of Famers, joined the Red Wings in the fall of 1956.

The Oil Kings, meanwhile, continued their successes, appearing in a record seven Memorial Cups in a row from 1960 to 1966, winning national championships in 1963 and 1966. The '66 team was coached by Wild Bill Hunter and featured Jim Harrison and Al Hamilton. All three men would be part of the World Hockey Association's Edmonton Oilers in the club's debut season (1972–73).

under Hunter's reign, drifted from contention. He and his partner, Dr. Charles Allard, eventually sold out to Vancouver real estate dealer Nelson Skalbania, who brought in local businessman Peter Pocklington.

The team improved in the 1976–77 season, under new management, signing left winger Glen Sather, a former Edmonton Oil King, off the roster of the NHL's Minnesota North Stars. Sather quickly became player-coach of the Oilers, taking the team to the playoffs in the spring of 1977.

That summer, in an act that defined the WHA's slippery-as-ice financing, Skalbania purchased 51 percent of the WHA's Indianapolis Racers for $1 (while retaining 50-percent ownership of the Oilers) and then signed Sudbury Greyhounds 17-year-old junior phenom Wayne Gretzky to a four-year $1 million personal-services contract, joking, "If he can't play hockey, he's going to be the most expensive handball partner I've ever had." Gretzky played well in Indianapolis, but less than 5,000 fans showed up at Racers games. Skalbania bailed, selling Gretzky, forward Peter Driscoll and goalie Eddie Mio, along with his option to purchase back the Oilers to Pocklington for $825,000. In November 1978, Wayne Gretzky became an Edmonton Oiler.

Gretzky's Oilers finished first in the WHA's last season, 1978–79, losing to the Winnipeg Jets, the league's best-run franchise, in the finals. The following season, the NHL and WHA merged, with Edmonton, Winnipeg, the Quebec Nordiques and the Hartford Whalers joining the NHL. (The WHA's Birmingham Bulls and Cincinnati Stingers were given cash settlements and folded.)

The cost of entry to the NHL was steep: Already cash-starved teams would both have to pay a $6 million entry fee and dismantle their teams, protecting only two goalies and two skaters. WHA teams would also be picking last in the 1979 junior draft.

Still, the Oilers had several advantages. Oil-rich Edmonton was an economic boom town. With both Gretzky and the NHL to market, the Oilers sold 14,200 season tickets to the five-year-old Northland's Coliseum in a four-day period after the merger. The team also had a general manager-coach, Glen Sather, and

Kevin Lowe with the Edmonton Oilers. Lowe would later become general manager of the Oilers.

Without a big budget to compete with other NHL teams for Swedish and Czech hockey talent, Oilers scouts concentrated on Finland in the early 1980s. The decision paid big dividends right away with the signing of Jari Kurri in 1980.

a chief scout, Barry Fraser, who had an idea of what kind of team might succeed in the 1980s.

The WHA's Winnipeg Jets, Sather and Fraser figured, was the way to go. The Oilers would play a furiously up-tempo, offensive game. The team would look for skaters, skill players, following the Jets' lead of scouring Europe for talent. Because the team had a limited scouting staff and Sweden had already been picked clean, the Oilers would concentrate on still untapped Finland. The Oilers went into the 1979 NHL draft with the last choice in the first round and no second round pick. Yet, the team left the session dramatically improved, selecting a first line defenceman, Kevin Lowe, with the 21st overall pick, and then, in the third round (48th overall), taking Mark Messier, an unbroken stallion who would become, after Gretzky, the best player in the game through the '80s. Glenn Anderson, a right winger as fast and reckless as Messier, was taken with the 69th overall pick.

At age 19, Gretzky tied Marcel Dionne for the NHL scoring title, with 137 points in the 1979–80 season. The following draft, the Oilers became exponentially better again, taking Paul Coffey, the most exciting defenceman since Bobby Orr, with the team's first pick, and then—much later—choosing an unheralded Finnish winger with scoring promise, Jari Kurri (69th pick) and a bouncing little netminder with ice water in his veins, Andy Moog (130th overall).

Although "Team Teenager" showed flashes of talent, the club wouldn't show its true character until the spring of 1981, when it went up against the Lafleur-Robinson-Gainey edition of the Montreal Canadiens, a 103-point club just two seasons removed from the last of four Stanley Cup wins in a row (1976–79). The Oilers had finished under 500 that season, gaining 74 points in 80 games. Canadiens goalie Richard Sevigny predicted that "Lafleur would put Gretzky in his back pocket in the series."

Hockey Night in Canada colour man Gary Dornhoeffer went down to the dressing rooms a few hours prior to the Canadiens-Oilers game in Montreal and was astonished to find the Edmonton team playing ball hockey with a roll of tape in the dressing room, just like peewees might do until their dads came in and shouted at them to settle down. To Dornhoeffer's and the hockey establishment's surprise, the boisterous, young Oilers went out and shocked

Iggy's Best Hockey Lesson

Jarome Iginla's early life confirms the old African proverb that it takes an entire village to raise a single child. Jarome's dad, Adekunle Iginla, grew up in Nigeria, on the west coast of Africa. His mom, Susan Schuchard, was born in the United States. Jarome made his nationality clear from the beginning, however, as he was born in Edmonton on Canada Day, 1 July 1977. Jarome's parents divorced when he was small, so it really did take a lot of people to look after him. His mom worked two jobs. Dad was at medical school. Jarome frequently stayed with his grandparents. His mom also enrolled him in community programs: basketball, bowling, tennis, public speaking, music, art, you name it. And Jarome's grandfather signed the youngster up for hockey.

The little boy learned to skate on an outdoor rink near his home in St. Albert, a suburb of Edmonton. But "Iggy" once said that his best hockey lesson came on a day he wasn't even allowed outside. That memorable moment occurred on an Alberta-cold winter morning. Not a speck of red was showing in thermometers. Jarome's grandparents gave him a book and ordered him to stay inside. All day! Luckily, the book was about something Jarome had recently started to play—hockey. Or rather, the book was about a single player: Maurice "The Rocket" Richard! Iginla loved reading about Richard's tenacity, and took the book to heart.

In time, Jarome would become a great goal scorer himself, leading the Western Hockey League's junior Kamloops Blazers to consecutive Memorial Cup wins in 1994 and 1995 before joining the National Hockey League's Calgary Flames. In 2003 and 2004, Jarome Iginla led the National Hockey League in scoring, winning the Rocket Richard Trophy as the league's top scorer. He gave credit to the memory of Richard in winning the reward, acknowledging how the Rocket's life story had made him a better hockey player. In the spring of 2004, Iggy took the Flames to the Stanley Cup finals, inspiring hockey fans everywhere and proving that sometimes a single child can raise an entire country.

Mark Messier.

the Canadiens that night, winning easily, 6–3. Gretzky collected a goal and five assists, while teammate Dave Hunter checked Lafleur into exhaustion. The following game, goaltender Moog was steady as a spring rain, taking care of a 2–1 win.

As the team arrived at the Montreal airport the following morning, the young Oilers gathered around a fat pile of La Presse newspapers with a bold headline:

"GRETZKY MET TOUS LES CANADIENS DANS SA POCHE."

The players turned to Kevin Lowe, whose family ran a dairy in Lachute, Quebec. "It means," Lowe said, smiling, "that Gretzky put all the Canadiens in his pocket." Making good on the newspaper's claim, the next game, in Edmonton, Gretzky finished off the former Stanley Cup champions in the best of five series with three goals in a 6–2 win.

In the next round, a very close, six-game, quarter-final loss to the (eventually Stanley Cup-winning) New York Islanders, the team spontaneously broke into song on the bench during games, singing out, "Here we go, Oilers, here we go."

And go they did, albeit with a few stumbles at first. The team picked up Grant Fuhr, the best goalie of the '80s, in the 1981 summer draft, but blundered two straight playoffs, suffering an unlikely first-round upset to the Los Angeles Kings in the spring of 1982—including an embarrassing 6–5 loss in a game in which they were up 5–0 going into the third period—and a four-game sweep in the finals, to the rigorously professional New York Islanders in 1983. After that, however, the Oilers pretty much had the hockey world in their pockets for the rest of the decade, finally conquering the Islanders in the 1984 finals and beating past two-championship calibre teams, first the Islanders and then the Calgary Flames, to become the dominant team of the era. The powerhouse Oilers ultimately won five Stanley Cups in seven seasons.

In addition to all their success, the Oilers played thrilling hockey. Gretzky and Kurri developed a telepathic bond, executing gorgeous give-and-go plays inside the enemy blue line. Gretzky, the famed number 99, averaged over 207 points a season between 1981 and 1986, while Kurri scored 71 and 68 goals in the 1984–85 and 1985–86 campaigns. Streaking comets Messier and Anderson

Even the role players on these Oilers teams had panache.

had a provocative guest star on left wing every season it seemed, including Ken "The Rat" Linesman, Kent "Magic Man" Nilsson, and the ever-antagonistic Esa Tikkanen ("The Grate One"). Defenceman Paul Coffey was the league's fastest skater and best power play point man.

Even the role players on these Oilers teams had panache. Gretzky bodyguard Dave Semenko was the rare NHL intimidator who could wound a foe with irony. Once Jack "Killer" Carlson, a rival tough, brushed against Semenko, looking for trouble. The Oilers forward dispatched his opponent with a derisive sneer: "How'd you get your nickname, Killer—did you shoot your dog?"

The Oilers also had Glen "Slats" Sather, a fourth-line penalty killer from Wainright, Alberta, who earned a master's degree in hockey psychology while seated at the end of the bench during his nine-year NHL career (1967–76). With head scout Barry Fraser's help, Coach Sather drafted a team full of players he wanted to be: fast, fluid scorers. And he let them loose all the time, setting a coaching precedent by using his best forwards as penalty killers to take advantage of open ice. Sather was also a master motivator, who could breathe confidence into his own team while putting other coaches' teams off their game plan. An expert with the needle, Slats could get under the skin of a turtle with his behind-the-bench barbs and insults.

A spirited, supremely well-coordinated team, with any number of working-class heroes, including a quietly dependable defence corps anchored by Kevin Lowe and unsung free agents Charley Huddy and Randy Gregg, the Edmonton Oilers became Canada's hockey team in the 1980s. Like the great Montreal Canadiens teams of the 1950s and 1970s, the Oilers made hockey a better sport. And they left behind a crowded highlight reel of memories: 20-year-old Grant Fuhr, born just outside Edmonton in Spruce Grove, Alberta, destroying the New York Islanders' championship mystique with a heroic 1–0 stand in the first game of the 1984 Stanley Cup finals; Glenn Anderson finally putting away the Philadelphia Flyers, in the 1987 Cup finals, by blowing a long slapshot between goalie Ron Hextall's pads late in the seventh game to give the Oilers a comfortable 3–1 lead; Gretzky, in a 1988 playoff match in Calgary, breaking down the left side during a tie overtime game, drilling a high one over goalie Mike Vernon's shoulder; and Mark Messier, with Gretzky and Coffey traded, taking the team on his broad shoulders throughout the 1990 playoffs, giving the team its fifth Stanley Cup.

It could easily be said that the Oilers haven't been as good ever since. Then again, neither has any other hockey team.

Spruce Grove, Alberta, goalie Grant Fuhr had maybe the fastest glove hand in hockey history.

HANNA

FOUNDED

By the late 19th century, cattlemen began settling in Alberta's southern heartland, drawn to this area by the cropped grass that grew on the rolling countryside. In 1909, homesteaders from as far away as Scotland, Germany and Russia migrated to the area that became known as the Hand Hills or short grass country. A town was established when the Great Northern Railway built a station in 1912 to service a track between Calgary and Saskatoon, known as the Goose Lake Line. The settlement was named after D.B. Hanna, then president of the railway. The town's first settlers were so devoted to hockey that every winter two dressing rooms on skids were hauled onto a nearby frozen lake.

NATIVE-BORN NHL PLAYERS
Lanny McDonald

FAMOUS LOCAL TEAMS
Senior-pro: Hanna Hills Hornets

CURRENT POPULATION
3,000

McDonald's Farm

Lanny McDonald's early life would make a hardened cynic believe in the little house on the prairie. McDonald was born—and played hockey—in Hanna, Alberta, but grew up on a farm outside nearby Craigmyle, a village so small that Toronto hockey writer Frank Orr once joked the streetlights dimmed when someone turned on a toaster.

"Shows how much those big city guys know," McDonald responded in his autobiography, *Lanny*. "Craigmyle didn't have streetlights!"

McDonald went to a three-room schoolhouse. His mom was the teacher, and his father, Lorne, a defenceman on the local senior hockey team, the Hanna Hills Hornets. The four McDonald children, two boys and as many girls, helped with farm chores. Lanny held the bucket while his dad milked the farm's five cows, all of whom had names. And at night the family played games of cards—whist or crib—while looking out a window that afforded a generous view of velvet grasslands tumbling down to Hand Hills Lake.

The lake was where Lanny learned to skate, at age five, in the winter of 1958. He took to the activity right away and soon found a way to get everywhere on blades, skating along a frozen creek outside his house the three miles to school some mornings. At recess and lunch, he was back on the ice, for the three-room schoolhouse had an adjoining rink, cobbled together one summer by fathers in the district.

Life was a team sport in Craigmyle and Hanna. Everyone got together for brandings, butchering rings and Alberta's oldest rodeo event, the Hand Hills Stampede. Neighbours also pitched in during hard times. One year, the McDonald combine broke down during harvesting, a potential disaster. The next day, Lanny ran outside the farmhouse to see neighbours riding a noisy caravan of combines up the drive, looking to help. The fields were cleared within hours.

Being neighbourly extended beyond the harvest season in Alberta's heartland. Summer Sundays, after church, most of the congregation idled in the parking lot, chatting, and then headed to the park in a long line of cars for enormous picnics followed by a lazy afternoon game of baseball.

A teenaged Lanny McDonald, playing for the Medicine Hat Tigers in 1969.

But hockey was always the McDonalds' sport. Two or three times a week in winter, Lanny joined his father on the 18 mile drive to Hanna. Lorne McDonald played on the city's senior team in the No. 9 League, named so because all of the towns in the league—from Sherness to Endiang—were located on Highway 9. Lanny was the stick boy. And at age six, he, too, began playing organized hockey, progressing from mighty mite to midget in Hanna. League hockey, along with all the skating he did around Hand Hills Lake, not to mention ceaseless chores and hours of snapping pucks against the basement wall, left the teenager with iron wrists and an enthusiastic, barrelling skating style.

Soon, Lanny was the best player on the Hanna Bantam Elks, on the verge of taking the team to a provincial championship. But then a blinding winter storm buried the Hand Hills under a fat quilt of snow before a big playoff game. Lanny's father had no way of getting his son into Hanna for the important game. Just as the situation looked impossible, the phone rang. It was a neighbour calling to say that if Mr. McDonald could get Lanny to his farm, he'd run him into town in his

Even the Montreal crowd applauded, happy for the Calgary hockey player.

truck. "My dad got out the tractor, and we crossed the fields to the Moench farm," McDonald remembered in his autobiography. "Mr. Moench got his three-ton truck going and we ploughed through the three- and four-foot drifts to the bus. We won, 17–3, and went on to [win the provincial] championships. Thank god for neighbours."

Lanny McDonald left the Hand Hills at age 16, a small-town kid prepared to think the best of everyone. His talent and optimism were rewarded everywhere he went. Playing elite junior hockey for the Medicine Hat Tigers, he jumped to the team's top line with Tom Lysiak and Wayne Anderson and scored goals in bunches, becoming a fan favourite (his number 8 is retired in the Hat). He was taken fourth overall in the 1973 National Hockey League draft, by the Toronto Maple Leafs, and would become a western icon in Toronto, of all places, growing a droopy moustache that made him look like a cowboy hero's sidekick. He played on a famous line with great friend Darryl Sittler. The two were as popular in Toronto as Lysiak and McDonald had been in Medicine Hat. In 1976, playing for Canada in the international Canada Cup, McDonald set Sittler up for a memorable overtime goal against Czechoslovakia that gave Canada the tournament win.

McDonald was one of the most popular hockey players in the mid-1970s and showed up regularly on television, smiling through his broom handle moustache, selling Canadians everything from mufflers to Carnation milk. A momentary reversal had him traded to the Colorado Rockies in 1980, but he persevered and in 1982 was back in Canada again, captain of the great Calgary Flames team that heroically battled the Edmonton Oilers throughout the '80s.

Lanny scored 66 goals for the Flames in the 1982–83 season. And in 1989, he finished his career in the most satisfying fashion. In the third period, game six of the 1989 Stanley Cup finals, with Calgary and the Montreal Canadiens locked in a tie, McDonald bolted from the penalty box to take a feathered pass from Joe Nieuwendyk, skated in past the blue line and snapped a wrist shot over goalie Patrick Roy's shoulder to give Calgary a lead that it would never relinquish.

McDonald's last act as a professional hockey player was skating around the Montreal Forum with the Stanley Cup held high over his head. His teammates were behind him, cheering. Even the Montreal crowd applauded, happy for the Calgary hockey player. But then, Lanny McDonald's life and career had always been filled with good cheer. Somehow, he had managed to bring the fellowship of the Hand Hills of Alberta with him everywhere he travelled.

ME AND MY SHADOW

After his first season with the National Hockey League's Toronto Maple Leafs (1973–74), Lanny McDonald didn't bother with a razor on the car ride from Toronto back to Alberta. By Saskatchewan, he had a red beard. At the end of the summer, the hockey player trimmed his facial hair back to a tidy accountant's moustache—a look he stayed with until 1977, when he saw Albert "Sparky" Lyle, an ace lefthanded relief pitcher, take baseball's New York Yankees to the World Series sporting a moustache that looked like something that belonged on a 19th century prospector. McDonald was entranced and let his own lip hair down. "I never dreamed of what was to come," he wrote in his autobiography, *Lanny.* "My moustache has become part of me... I've been offered money by various companies to shave it off during a commercial, my father has tried to bribe me into getting rid of it and my uncle Jack has threatened to take the sheep shears to me. But my moustache, to me, is me."

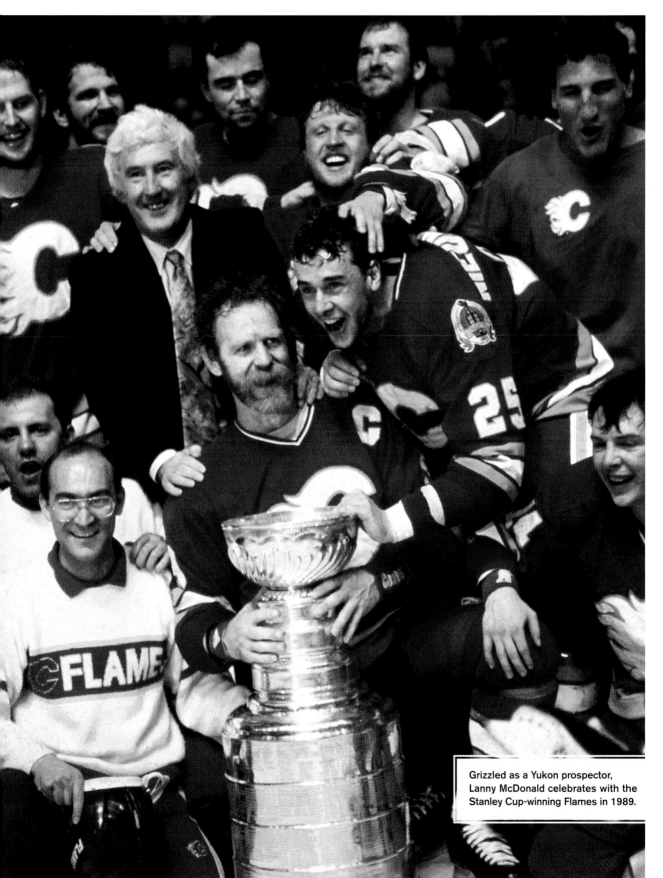

Grizzled as a Yukon prospector, Lanny McDonald celebrates with the Stanley Cup-winning Flames in 1989.

LETHBRIDGE

FOUNDED

First Nations people lived in this area in virtual isolation until the 1860s when American traders arrived, establishing an illicit whisky trade. Montana businessmen built a post, called Fort Whoop-Up, out of which they sold a potent liquor brewed from river water, chewing tobacco and lye. The concoction devastated the First Nations community and Prime Minister Sir John A. Macdonald formed the North West Mounted Police in 1874 to restore peace in the area. A more sober economic base emerged after 1874, with the discovery of rich coal deposits. The town was named Lethbridge after William Lethbridge, the first president of the North Western Coal company, in 1882.

NATIVE-BORN NHL PLAYERS

Doug Barkley, Allan Egeland, Aut Erickson, Adrian Foster, Len Frig, Earl Ingarfield, John MacMillan, Harvie Pocza, Victor Stasiuk, Robert Wood

FAMOUS LOCAL TEAMS

Junior: Lethbridge Broncos, Lethbridge Hurricanes, Lethbridge Maple Leafs, Lethbridge Native Sons, Lethbridge Silver Kings; **Senior-pro:** Lethbridge Bombers, Lethbridge Hockey Club, Lethbridge Lumber, Lethbridge Maple Leafs, Lethbridge Vets, Lethbridge Y's Men, Lethbridge YMCA

CURRENT POPULATION

68,712

Prairie farmhouse, Lethbridge, 1908.

Payment in Adventure

The Lethbridge team that defeated all challengers at the world amateur hockey championships in Paris, 1951, learned the game in the open-air rinks of Lethbridge's north side, where, to compete, players learned to scrape and shovel as well as to skate and score.

Located south of Calgary, Lethbridge is the rare Canadian city where the weather might be too bad and too good to play outdoor hockey on consecutive days. Blizzards brewed high in the nearby Rocky Mountains can ambush the city without warning. Twenty-four hours later, a warming chinook may tumble down from the same mountains, replacing January with May.

The city's first hockey team was known as the Lethbridge Hockey Club, a senior outfit, formed in 1908, that played in a league with Fort Macleod, Pincher Creek and Coleman. Lethbridge won its first game, 9–3, over Coleman, in a match that lasted one period. Snaking rains came after that, turning the rink into a vat of slush.

Neither the weather nor Lethbridge hockey had changed much when Nap Milroy, Hector Negrello, Billy Gibson and Karl Sorokoski grew up in the 1930s, teammates from peewee through to senior. Lethbridge skaters were all-weather players. Their adaptability would become useful on the Lethbridge Maple Leafs' 1951 tour of Europe, a four-month expedition that would take them through outdoor rinks and a wide variety of bad weather.

"I started playing on the outdoor rinks, like all kids in those days, in wind, snow and cold," Milroy explained to Dylan Purcell of the *Lethbridge Herald*. "When we went overseas, we played outdoors a lot of the time, in sleet and snow, and we even played in the rain. One game we not only cleaned the ice between periods, but stopped every few minutes to clean the snow off the ice during the game. But that didn't bother us—we'd done that all our lives."

The Lethbridge Leafs, 1949–50.

Although considered amateurs, the Leafs received a hockey salary during the regular season. The team secured favourable outside jobs for the players, as well. Star Billy Gibson worked for Sicks' Lethbridge Brewery. (He was a beer taster, teammates joked.) Ken Branch, Lou Siray and Bert Knibbs were employed by the Shaughnessy Coal Mine.

The Maple Leafs were charter members of the senior Western Hockey League in the '40s. When the WHL collapsed, the team joined the Western Canadian Intermediate League, securing the Alberta provincial title in the 1949–50 season, then defeating Trail (British Columbia) and Melville (Saskatchewan) to win the western Canada championship. Weeks later, the Canadian Amateur Hockey Association declared that Lethbridge would represent Canada in the 1951 Paris world championship.

Being Canada's team was a great honour, but it was also a financial burden to the players. Their families would have to survive on a reduced income while the athletes were away. And the four-month expedition itself was not prefinanced. The Maple Leafs would live from hand to mouth, on gate receipts from exhibition games played abroad. Nevertheless, the Leafs left Lethbridge on 17 December 1950 in high spirits, off to conquer the world.

That mood changed swiftly, however. The team's Canadian Pacific Railroad train knifed through a farmer's truck at a prairie intersection days later. The Leafs had little time to grieve, for there was always hockey business to attend to on this trip. The Lethbridge team's first payday was against the Melville Millionaires. The Millionaires' owner, Bill Hunter (see page 301), had set up an exhibition match, and his team was eager to prove that the wrong team was representing Canada overseas. "We waxed them 7–1," Lethbridge's Billy Gibson would remember with a satisfied laugh.

Hours after stretching their legs in the Melville Arena, the Leafs were snug in their CPR sleepers, hurtling eastward. Five days later, the team arrived in Halifax and boarded the *Scythia*. The team spent Christmas of 1950 on rough seas, with many of the players locked in their cabins. These were prairie boys,

The Uke Line

A one-time member of the junior Lethbridge Maple Leafs (1946–47), Vic Stasiuk left home at age 18, embarking on a momentous professional career that was highlighted by a 14-year stay in the National Hockey League (1949–63). In the early 1950s, he was an energetic part-time contributor to the Detroit Red Wings championship teams, showing signs of blossoming talent in the spring of 1955 by chipping in five goals toward the Wings' Stanley Cup championship playoff run. The following season, Stasiuk was traded to the Boston Bruins, where he would soon be united with Edmonton-born Johnny Bucyk and Bronco Horvath of Port Colborne, Ontario, forming what became known as The Uke Line. (The trio were all Ukrainian-Canadians.) In the 1957–58 season, the trio became the first three players on the same line in NHL history to score more than 20 goals in a season. Stasiuk also played in the 1960 all-star game. Throughout his NHL career, he came home summers and played semipro baseball in Lethbridge.

flatlanders. After riding ocean swells for a week, the team wobbled off the ship in London and caught a bus to Nottingham, England. The next night, still green from their ocean crossing, the team lost to Nottingham, 8–6. In fact, Lethbridge lost its first five games in England. The CAHA flew into a panic, dispatching reinforcements Billy Flick, Dennis Flanagan and Mickey Roth, from Ontario's senior Stratford Indians.

By then, however, the Maple Leafs had found their skating legs. Soon the team was locked in a 44-game European winning streak. The schedule was ridiculous, really. To finance the trip, the team played 62 games in 14 European countries, sometimes a game in a different city every night for a week. In 10 weeks, the team covered 31,000 miles by trains, planes and buses, before arriving in Paris. "We played 13 games in 14 nights in Switzerland," Billy

"There we were in the Palais des Sports, ready to face the world."

Gibson told the *Lethbridge Herald*. "We traveled every day and never slept in the same bed twice." Added Ken Branch, laughing, "You never would get time to see your underwear fully dried before you were leaving a hotel."

Although they never had two nickels to rub together, the Maple Leafs were paid in full with adventure. "We put our uniforms on in churches and in hospitals, and I remember playing outdoors at racetracks where they'd have horse racing after the hockey game," Gibson recalled. In Lausanne, Switzerland, the team performed in a soccer stadium in front of 21,000 fans—more spectators than the number of people living in Lethbridge at the time. Gibson looked up at one point during the game and saw boys high in swaying fir trees above the stadium, trying to watch the game for free. Being the visiting team, the Leafs had few supporters, except in Munich, Germany, where a small, vocal group cheered the team's every move. Afterward, the fans approached the players and explained that they had been prisoners of war incarcerated in Lethbridge during World War II.

Being true sons of Lethbridge, the Maple Leafs enjoyed playing in all weather conditions. One outdoor game, the rain was so bad that the referee put thumbtacks on the puck to help it glide over the watery ice. The Leafs were impressed. Here was an official who could have found work in Lethbridge any winter.

By March 1951, the Maple Leafs finally reached Paris. The team couldn't have known what to expect. They hadn't played the Americans and they were understandably fearful of the British team, which was made up almost entirely of Canadian ex-pats. Besides, international hockey was always fraught with intrigue. In 1951, the Czechoslovakian team didn't make the trip; the entire squad had been rounded up and imprisoned by the Russian KGB, when it was discovered that several players had been planning to defect in Paris.

The Leafs started off strongly in the Paris games, routing Finland, 11–1, and Norway, 8–0, within the first two days of the tournament. After a badly needed day off, the team faced its first major test: Great Britain. The Brits jumped to an early 1–0 first period lead, but after chewing each other out in the dressing room during the intermission, the Canadian players lost their colonial inhibitions and scored 17 unanswered goals. Lethbridge was almost as good the next day, defeating the Americans, a club team from Lewiston, Maine, 16–2.

The only remaining contenders were Switzerland and Sweden. The Swiss were strong skaters, but they couldn't shoot. "If ever I was condemned to stand before a firing squad, my last wish would be that the Swiss side fired the salvo, because in that case I'd be sure to make it out alive," a French sports journalist wrote of the Swiss during this tournament. The Leafs would surrender a single goal to the Swiss, winning 5–1. With that victory, Lethbridge made the finals.

Exactly three months after the team left Alberta, on 17 March 1951, the Maple Leafs faced off against Sweden for the world championship. More than 17,000 fans crowded into the Paris arena that evening. The Lethbridge team had also received a number of telegrams from Canada that morning, including a special message from Alberta. ("We expect confidently you to retain championship for Canada," wrote the Edmonton Mercurys, 1950 world champions.)

Billy Gibson recalls being overcome by emotion several times before the opening faceoff. Looking down the blue line at his teammates, he remembered how the team had got to this point: the playoff wins against Trail and Melville; all those games in Europe, from Munich to Milan; the time Tom Wood missed a train, because he'd become engrossed in a biography of Franklin Roosevelt, and was lost for a day; Hector Negrello meeting his aunt and uncle for the first time in Italy; Stan Obodiac, the team's high scorer, up late every night, writing dispatches of the team's progress for the *Lethbridge Herald*. What would Obodiac be writing, telling all their friends and families back home, after this evening's game? Gibson already knew the answer to that question.

"There we were in the Palais des Sports, ready to face the world," he would recall. "There were tears in my eyes, my flesh was covered with goose bumps. I couldn't have been prouder of that team...I just knew we were going to win."

The Leafs did all of Canada proud that evening, defeating Sweden, 5–1. Stan Obodiac's summary of the deciding game would read as follows: "All of a sudden the game was over... This was our 40th straight game without a defeat. Then they played 'Oh Canada,' and raised our flag for the victory. We all faced it as it rose to the top. Bill Gibson said there was a tear in his eye. Tommy Wood said it was the happiest day in his life... One of the [telegrams] from home said that the Lethbridge radio station was announcing, 'CJOC Lethbridge, the home of the world champions.' We like that."

The Lethbridge Vets, with Frank Boucher, 1920.

Frankie Do-Right

The North West Mounted Police were sent to Lethbridge in 1874 and soon transformed Fort Whoop-Up into orderly, civilized Lethbridge. Growing up in Ottawa, Frank Boucher was thrilled by the stories of how the Mounties had tamed the west. At age 19, in 1920, he joined the Mounties and was stationed in Lethbridge, where he reported to duty, certain he would soon be putting down a range war. "The detachment commander gave Frankie a curry comb, a pitchfork and a small wheelbarrow, and escorted him to a building behind the office. In the building there were 12 horses which nickered affectionately at Boucher," sportswriter Jim Coleman once reported. "A year later, Boucher of the Mounted still hadn't fired a single shot, but he had learned all about the duties of a personal maid to 12 horses." During that year, Boucher played for the Lethbrige Vets of the Alberta Senior Hockey League. But after coming to the conclusion that the west had already been won, he bought his way out of the NWMP for $50 and returned home to play pro hockey for the National Hockey League's Ottawa Senators.

View of Medicine Hat.

MEDICINE HAT

FOUNDED

Many legends exist to explain Medicine Hat's curious name, but the most widely accepted explanation is a Cree tale about a medicine man who lost his *saamis*, or warbonnet, in the South Saskatchewan River while fleeing a Blackfoot assault. Settlers arrived in 1883 and the subsequent discovery of natural gas reserves and clay deposits spurred an increase in the town's size. By 1910 some of the town's less imaginative residents lobbied to rename the community Gasburg or Smithville. The outcry over the potential loss of one of North America's most unique town names was so great that even writer Rudyard Kipling waded into the debate, to successfully convince residents to hold on to their, well, hat.

NATIVE-BORN NHL PLAYERS

Warren Babe, Murray Craven, Eddie Dorohoy, Joe Fisher, Hector Highton, Corey Hirsch, Rick Hodgson, Blaine Lacher, Jamie Linden, Trevor Linden, Neil Little, Al McLeod, Paxton Schafer, Douglas Young

FAMOUS LOCAL TEAMS

Junior: Medicine Hat Elks, Medicine Hat Scoundrels, Medicine Hat Tigers; **Senior-pro:** Medicine Hat Blades, Medicine Hat Monarchs, Medicine Hat Tigers

CURRENT POPULATION

51,249

Two in a Row

While playing for the hometown junior Medicine Hat Tigers in 1986–87 and 1987–88, Trevor Linden remained in the "Hat" in the summer to help on the family ranch. He was there when Brian Burke, assistant general manager of the National Hockey League's Vancouver Canucks, phoned to see if the teenager could travel to Vancouver to take a psychological test. The Canucks had the second overall pick in the 1988 NHL amateur draft and were thinking of taking the strapping 6'4", 220-pound forward. But first they wanted to see if the rancher's son had the proper makeup: Would he be tough enough mentally to handle the pressure of do-or-die professional playoff hockey?

"I'm sorry sir, I can't make the test," Linden reluctantly told the Canucks executive. "I have to help my father with the cattle that day. It's kind of important."

"What is it exactly that you'll be doing?" Burke wondered.

"Well, as the cattle come into the pen, I'm the one who grabs them and throws them down and pins them while they brand and castrate them," the 18-year-old said.

Linden's explanation prompted a momentary silence, after which Burke decided, "OK, you can skip the test."

The Medicine Hat forward would go on to star with the Canucks, becoming captain of the team at age 20, in 1991, then leading the Canucks, three seasons later, to the Stanley Cup finals against the New York Rangers. He scored 12 goals and 25 points in the memorable spring '94 NHL playoffs, including the team's only two goals during game seven of the finals in a crushing 3–2 loss to Mark Messier's Rangers. Linden's stature only improved in subsequent years, as he gracefully ceded the Canucks' captaincy to Messier when the legendary forward arrived in Vancouver, in 1996. He later won two Canadian humanitarian awards, the King Clancy Trophy and the Gillette World Champion Award, and was elected by his peers as president of the NHL Players Association in 1998.

Trevor Linden with the Vancouver Canucks.

Memorial Cup champions,
Medicine Hat Tigers, 1988.

There is talk of Linden as a potential political candidate in British Columbia. But even if he were to reach public office on the west coast, it is unlikely that he could attain the same public stature he once enjoyed in his native city. Forget about member of parliament or mayor; the people of Medicine Hat were prepared to name Linden king of the city after he took the local junior team, the Tigers, to two Memorial Cup championships in the springs of 1987 and 1988.

People in the Hat love junior hockey and have ever since 1970 when an ownership team that included George Maser, Rod Carry and Joe Fisher, a Hat native and one-time forward for the National Hockey League's Detroit Red Wings (1940–44), purchased the team. As of 2005, the waiting list for Medicine Hat Tigers season tickets was almost a thousand subscribers long. And the team routinely sells out the 4,000-seat Medicine Hat Arena.

A city of 53,000 located 180 miles south of Calgary, Medicine Hat leads the rest of Canada in sunny skies, with 2,512 hours of sunshine and 265 dry days a year. And perhaps it's all the good weather that makes the city's hockey fans optimistic and youthfully inclined. For their part, the junior Tigers have rewarded their fans' hopefulness from the beginning. The 1972–73 team reached the Memorial Cup semifinals with a club that boasted Alberta hockey legends Tom Lysiak (High River) and Lanny McDonald (Hanna), along with three sturdy enforcers, Bob, Brad and Ken Gassoff, all brothers, who were born to play for a petroleum-producing town. Goalies Kelly Hrudy, currently a *Hockey Night in Canada* commentator, and eventual NHL all-stars Pete Peeters and Chris Osgoode also played for the Tigers. More recently, defenceman Jay Bouwmeester jumped from the Tigers to the NHL's Florida Panthers at age 18, in 2003.

Still, Medicine Hat has had only one Tiger like Trevor Linden, a clean-scrubbed, serious kid who showed the forcefulness of his personality at age 11 in his first summer job, gathering stray golf balls in a Santa Claus-sized bag at a driving range at the Connaught Golf Course outside town. He had done the same job the summer before, at age 10. Now, he was a year taller and further from the ground; he figured he deserved a raise. "It was the hardest thing I've ever had to do," Linden later reflected. "I got 25 cents a shag bag and thought I should get more. My boss gave me 30 cents a bag, instead of 25."

Six years later, Linden brought that same resilience with him to the Medicine Hat Tigers. He was 16 at the beginning of the 1986–87 season, a gangly youngster who sometimes took a few strides to get his feet, elbows and shoulders aligned. But he was beyond determined and had a habit of scoring big goals. "Trevor Linden was a knock-kneed kid when he started here," remembers Bob Ridley, who at age 25, in the team's first season, began driving the Tigers team bus and delivering radio play-by-plays of Medicine Hat games. "But Trevor was a

PLEASE DON'T EAT THE CHANDELIERS

The Medicine Hat Tigers had an element of beginners' luck working for them. The junior team was created in 1970 from players left unprotected in a Western Hockey League relocation draft. Two picks, John Sinkfield and Henry Van Drunen, refused to report, so the Tigers had to make do with forwards Tom Lysiak and Lanny McDonald, skinny 17-year-olds who filled out sufficiently to have outstanding Western Hockey League and National Hockey League careers.

The linemates also led Medicine Hat to the 1973 Memorial Cup tourney, where they bowed out in the semifinals to the Quebec Remparts. Five hundred Medicine Hat fans made the trip, a deeply unsettling experience for Medicine Hat travel coordinator Pat Cooke. "[One night, Montreal] hotel security asked me to come and get a man who was hanging off the chandelier and eating the light bulbs," Cooke told former Medicine Hat sportswriter Ed Willes. "[After the games] we were waiting for the buses to the airport and our fans were out on the streets directing traffic with Styrofoam hats on their head... We finally got them out of there. After they all left, I poured myself a stiff drink and went and spent a quiet week with my mother."

winner—you could see that by the [first] Memorial Cup. He had started to fill out. Teams had trouble moving him in front of the net... He became the team leader, the guy everyone looked to to score the big goal."

Linden would score the two biggest goals in Medicine Hat Tigers' history in 1987. The team made the Memorial Cup that spring the hard way, facing elimination four times in seven-game series with the Saskatoon Blades and the Portland Winter Hawks, before travelling east to play in the Memorial Cup round-robin tourney against the Oshawa Generals and the Longueuil Chevaliers. In the Cup playoffs, the Tigers reached the finals with 6–0 and 3–1 wins over Longueuil.

The championship game was held in Oshawa, and the heavily favoured hometown Generals were well rested, having dispatched Longueuil and Medicine Hat early in the tournament. A minute and a half into the game, Linden's first shift on the ice, the big Medicine Hat forward silenced the Oshawa crowd by hurtling down the right wing and snapping a hard shot over Generals goalie Jeff Hackett's shoulder to make the score 1–0 for the Tigers. Ten minutes later, Linden banged through two defencemen, as if making his way through saloon doors, scoring again to give the team a 3–1 lead going into the second period. The Tigers then coasted to a convincing 6–2 win, giving Medicine Hat its first national championship.

The win sparked a year-long celebration in the Hat. The following season, Linden and linemate Rob DiMaio, as well as Scott McCrady, Mark Pederson and Wayne McBean, were all recruited by the Canadian junior team that won the 1988 world championship in Moscow (Linden also made the World junior all-star team), and in May that year, the Tigers repeated their success as Memorial Cup champions, coming back from a 3–0 deficit to win the national crown, 7–6, on a late goal by Mark Pederson. "Three rings in one year, it's unbelievable," Linden said in the dressing room afterward, referring to two Memorial Cups and a world junior title. "Everyone back in the Hat must be going crazy."

They were. Twenty thousand fans showed up at the Tigers' victory parade. "I think that junior hockey is bigger in western Canada than anywhere else in the country," Tigers bus driver and play-by-play man, Bob Ridley, would later tell a CBC-TV journalist. "In Medicine Hat or Red Deer, the team is a matter of civic pride. The Tigers are the big story here every winter. And it's the same throughout the west... You can tell who we are by watching our hockey teams."

The Great Gaboo

Medicine Hat's Eddie "The Great Gaboo" Dorohoy was the rare hockey player whose shots were feared by both goalies and general managers. Dorohoy played for the Lethbridge Native Sons after World War II and led the Alberta Junior Hockey League in points in 1946–47, collecting 64 assists in 33 games. Impressed by the player's evident talent, the National Hockey League's Montreal Canadiens signed Dorohoy the following season.

While in Montreal, the fearless centreman first displayed his talent for upsetting hockey executives. The Canadiens were in the midst of a slump, when coach Frank Selke brought a hockey net into the dressing room and scolded every player for his inability to score. Coming to the 20-year-old Medicine Hat native, Selke observed, "Eddie Dorohoy, you've got no goals and no assists, how do you explain that?"

"I've been trying to score from too sharp an angle—the end of the bench," was the rookie's rejoinder. He was banished from the NHL, the following day.

Dorohoy went on to enjoy a successful 16-year career in the minor leagues, scoring 109 points in 1958–59 for the Calgary Stampeders of the pro Western Hockey League. But the player never lost his antagonism for hockey bosses. Dorohoy once complained about the WHL's Vancouver Canucks by saying, "[General manager] Coley Hall is so cheap he wouldn't give you the sleeves off his vest."

RED DEER

FOUNDED

The Waskasioo, or Elk River, was named by the Cree after the animals that gathered there to feed. Scottish homesteaders confused migrating herds of elk with the rust-coloured deer of their homeland and so called their new settlement Red Deer. Fort Normandeau was built in 1885 to defend against a possible expansion of the Riel Rebellion. Red Deer remained a small farming town until oil and gas fields were discovered after World War II and it is now Alberta's third biggest city, after Calgary and Edmonton.

NATIVE-BORN NHL PLAYERS

Ronald Anderson, Oscar Asmundson, Glenn Hicks, Trent Hunter, Brad Leeb, Greg Leeb, Paul Manning, Chris Mason, Randy Moller, David Rochefort, Ray Schultz, Mark Tinordi, Mike Toal, Russ Walker, Blake Wesley, Glen Wesley

FAMOUS LOCAL TEAMS

Junior: Red Deer Ramblers, Red Deer Rebels, Red Deer Rustlers;
Senior-pro: Red Deer Army, Red Deer Buffaloes, Red Deer Imperials, Red Deer Rangers, Red Deer Rebels, Red Deer Wheelers, Red Deer Wranglers

CURRENT POPULATION

75,923

Red Deer, 1904.

The Red Deer Rebellion

No city reflects Alberta's meteoric growth over the past 60 years better than Red Deer. Before World War II, the community was an agricultural resource centre with a population hovering around 5,000. Oil and gas discoveries turned Red Deer into a '50s boom town. But even when the Sutter brothers hailing from Viking, Alberta—Brian, Darryl, Duane, Brent, Rich, and Ron—skated through the city in the 1970s, playing on the Tier II junior Red Deer Rustlers (see page 322), the city numbered less than 30,000. Then in the '90s, Red Deer experienced another growth spurt, doubling in size while attracting an elite junior hockey team in 1992, the Red Deer Rebels, and three years later, a hopeful cattle farmer and one-time Red Deer hockey player named Brent Sutter.

Sutter built a 3,200-square-foot ranch house with his own hands on a 1,000-acre farm outside the city and was raising cattle, Red Angus and Simmental crosses. While the Sutter farm flourished, in town, the Rebels languished in the lower rungs of the Western Hockey League. Perhaps because he had a farmer's aversion to seeing machinery run improperly, Sutter decided to buy the team. The cost was a reflection of Alberta's soaring fortunes. In 1995, the Calgary Hitmen, another WHL team, sold for $750,000. The price tag for the Rebels, put on the market four years later, was $3.2 million.

And so, in the summer of 1999, at age 36, without a day of executive or coaching experience, Brent Sutter took over as owner, president, general manager and coach of a mediocre, though certainly modern, junior hockey team. When he acquired the team, the Rebels' bus had been customized to serve teenage hockey players' needs, with Internet access at every seat and satellite television. Sutter, who had won two Stanley Cups with the National Hockey League's New York Islanders in 1983 and 1984, didn't mind the Radio Shack accoutrements;

The most famous junior coach in Canada, the Red Deer Rebels' Brent Sutter. Sutter coached the Canadian juniors to world championships in 2005 and 2006.

he just didn't like the work ethic of the players who were lounging in the well-upholstered seats. The new owner also sensed the clubhouse atmosphere in the Rebels' managerial suite. A season later, the front office had been completely turned over, and only four Rebels were left from the team Sutter had inherited.

Indeed, the owner-coach had made the team over in his family's image. "The Sutters grew up scared, not knowing whether the crops were going to come in," NHL coach Mike Keenan once observed. The brothers played the game the way a farmer goes about his job, as if the welfare of his family depended on that day's work, Keenan said. Hockey, to the Sutters, was a means of survival and a measure of character.

Brent Sutter's 2000–01 Rebels team was hand selected. Most players were in Red Deer via trades. Kyle Wanvig, a Calgary-born forward, was brought in on 24 October 1999, in an exchange with the Kootenay Ice. A month later, after the

Sticking with the Rebels

After taking over as owner-coach of the junior Red Deer Rebels, Brent Sutter happened to be reading a story in the Red Deer *Advocate* about Mikel McIver, a teenager with Down's syndrome who said that his dream was to become the stickboy for the Rebels. Sutter took the newspaper to trainer Dave Horning and said, "Let's get on this." McIver has been the stickboy for the Rebels ever since. "I have a nephew that has Down's syndrome," Sutter told Randy Turner of the *Winnipeg Free Press*. "And he's the most lovable and caring kid there is, and Mikie's no different. I don't look at it as being Down's syndrome. I look at it as being up syndrome."

The 2005-06 Red Deer Rebels celebrate a goal.

Rebels lost eight of nine games, Sutter shipped four players to the Prince Albert Raiders for an 18-year-old Edmonton defenceman, Ross Lupaschuk.

The team had a hard set of regulations: short hair, mandatory schoolwork, early curfews. Bars and the Red Deer Casino were see-you-later offences. Sutter backed the old-fashioned rules to the hilt. And he never allowed the team to cheat itself.

The coach's tirades became the stuff of legend. Once, the Rebels played a lacklustre game in Prince George, British Columbia, and Sutter banished half the team to the dressing room by the third period. The Rebels finished with five players on the bench. When the thoroughly modern bus arrived back home the next morning, the Rebels were told to get into their wet underwear and hit the stationary bicycles. Players also had their composite graphite sticks taken away. They would have to use old-fashioned wooden sticks until more effort was shown.

The team went on a record 18-game winning streak late in the year.

To remind them of that commitment, Sutter had players tape their wood sticks with white tape upon which a single word was printed: Work.

Sutter later advised *Winnipeg Free Press* writer Randy Turner of what he had told the Rebels in the dressing room after the Prince George game. "You're not holding yourself accountable to Red Deer and central Alberta," Sutter said. "We expect commitment. We expect work."

The Red Deer Rebels began the 2000–01 season working hard, winning their first seven games. Before Christmas, the team went on another tear. A 5–0 shutout of the Saskatoon Blades, in early January, put them in first place in the WHL, a distinction they enjoyed for the rest of the schedule. They kept on winning, 11 in a row at one point, climbing to number one in the national Canadian Hockey League rankings by the end of January.

The city of Red Deer responded. The team's rink, the Enmax Centrium, with a seating capacity of 5,700 fans, averaged 5,900 fans in the second half of the 2000-01 season. Some nights, the team's beaming proprietor, Brent Sutter, stood out in front of the rink on 19th Street, handing out standing-room tickets to fans.

And the dream season just seemed to get better and better. The team went on a record 18-game winning streak late in the year. Star forward Justin Mapletoft won the scoring award. Goalies Shane Bendera and Michael Garnett established a CHL record with 11 regular season shutouts. In the WHL playoffs, the Rebels disposed of the Lethbridge Hurricanes in the opening round, four games to one. Next came a series with the Calgary Hitmen. The Rebels took the series four games to two, winning the deciding match 4–0 in Calgary's Saddledome, in front of 13,101 disappointed Calgary fans. The Rebels then rolled over the Swift Current Broncos and Portland Winter Hawks in subsequent playoffs, earning the right to represent the west in the Memorial Cup, held in 2001 in Regina.

Now came the hard part. After a 70-game season and four playoff rounds, the Rebels had to compete in a round-robin tournament with three teams: the host Regina Pats; Ontario champion, the Ottawa 67's; and the Val d'Or Foreurs of the Quebec Major Junior Hockey League.

As is always the case in the Memorial Cup, the Red Deer players found themselves contending with a different kind of pressure. Teams vying for the Cup haven't played each other before. And there are no counterattacks like in seven-game playoffs. Teams get one chance at each other in the preliminaries. Drillmasters can't game plan, unlike in lengthy playoff series. In short, the Memorial Cup is made for players, not for coaches.

Kris Versteeg, 2005–06.

The 2001 Memorial Cup-winning Red Deer Rebels, pose for a celebratory photo op.

But Sutter's work had already been done with these Rebels, none of whom any longer needed the word "work" written on his stick blade to understand what made a successful team. Jeff Smith, a towering, 6'6" Regina-born forward, hammered in an overtime goal, to give Red Deer a 5–4 opening game win against Val d'Or. The Rebels then beat Ottawa, 4–2, before suffering a setback to Regina, 5–2. By virtue of their first two wins, however, the Red Deer team was awarded a berth in the finals.

The Memorial Cup final, a rematch between Red Deer and Val d'Or, was a wild, somersaulting affair. The Rebels looked poised in the first period, scoring on their two chances, with Lupaschuk and Wanvig, two of Sutter's earliest franchise acquisitions, taking part in both goals. Then, in the second 20 minutes, Red Deer was given a lesson in Quebec-style fire-wagon hockey, as Val d'Or piled up five goals, gaining a 5–3 lead. Maintaining his cool, Lupaschuk responded by setting up Joel Stepp for a goal, with only a second remaining in the second period. In the third frame, Wanvig converted a smart Lupaschuk pass to tie the game. The thrilling, back-and-forth championship match went into an edge-of-your-seat overtime.

Coach Sutter's voice was a hoarse grumble by the end. "Get the puck on the net!" he called out to defenceman Doug Lynch, playing up at the Val d'Or blue line late in overtime. Lynch couldn't have heard him. Didn't matter. The Rebels understood what Sutter wanted by now. The defenceman reached the loose puck, firing a desperate shot. Forward Jeff Smith, moving in front of the net, waved at the puck, altering its wobbling flight past a startled Val d'Or goalie. Brent Sutter's Red Deer Rebellion, a return to basic hockey values—hard work, teamwork—was over. Eighteen months after Sutter had taken over the floundering franchise, the Red Deer Rebels were Memorial Cup champions.

For the following week, the streets and bars were alive in Red Deer, from the biker hangouts in the old hotels at Ross Street and Gaetz to Wild Bill's Sports
Bar at the North Hill Inn, where the logo is, "As much fun as you can have without taking your boots off." The Rebels, too, would be celebrating. Forward Kyle Wanvig, tournament most valuable player, shouted, "I got a thousand bucks [prize] and I'll be spending it on the boys!" in the dressing room after the win.

The owner-coach of the Rebels wouldn't have much time to celebrate, however. Once he got back to Red Deer, he'd point his built-for-winter 2500 Dodge Ram Turbo diesel pickup northeast of the city toward home. February is calving season. He'd want to check on the three-month-old calves and tend to a thousand other things on the ranch. A Sutter's work is never done.

Hockey Night in Canada host Ron MacLean laces up for his weekly game of pick-up hockey in 2002.

A Born Referee

Red Deer's Ron MacLean grew up, an only child, in a family divided by hockey and politics. His air force father was a Conservative and Montreal Canadiens' fan, while his mom supported the Liberals and the Toronto Maple Leafs. And so Ron received the referee's calling at birth, stepping between his parents during hockey playoffs and elections.

Although a promising player, MacLean's childhood aversion to confrontations prevented him from going far in Alberta hockey. "I wasn't a fighter," he says. "And I was playing midget Triple A in Red Deer. This was 1975, and the western hockey was the roughest in Canada. One game I'd just hurt my thumb playing football, but that probably didn't matter. I got into an altercation with another player. He dropped his gloves. I just skated away. I later got cut from the team."

MacLean turned to refereeing, a hobby that he would enjoy for more than 20 years while he pursued his other passion: broadcasting. As a teenager, he had a late-night show on a local radio station, CKRD, and would put on the longest songs in the record library after 11:30 p.m. so that he could race home to watch *The Tonight Show with Johnny Carson*, on NBC TV.

At the same time, he followed the Red Deer Rustlers, and he remembers Brent Sutter helping the Tier II junior team win the national Centennial Cup in 1980 on a bad knee. The following season, MacLean took over as the Rustlers' radio play-by-plan man. Four years later, he was hosting Calgary Flames broadcasts on CKPD. In 1986, MacLean was hired to do the same job on *Hockey Night in Canada*, where all of his officiating skills, along with the glib assurance he had picked up studying Johnny Carson, came into play during his first-period intermission spot with Don Cherry, "Coach's Corner."

The unscripted segments have become the most popular segments of the ongoing HNIC broadcasts. The ever-erupting "Coach," Cherry, is obviously the star of the show, but his eternally fair-minded partner, MacLean, is at least as responsible for keeping the nation's longest-running TV comedy-drama on the air. The born referee works at keeping Cherry away from costly misconduct penalties. In his own way, MacLean is as much a Canadian type as his more celebrated co-star. He is a natural conciliator and a staunch advocate of a pluralistic Canada. "We're not here to see through each other," MacLean tells audiences in speaking engagements across the country. "We're here to see each other through."

Hockey in Viking, 1912.

VIKING

FOUNDED

Norwegian settlers moved to this central Alberta region in the early 1900s, to take advantage of Canada's homesteading program, and named the town's first post office Viking. In 1909, the small hamlet moved when the Grand Trunk Pacific Railway built a station outside the town. Moving proved easier than naming the new community. Grand Trunk engineers favoured naming the station Meighen, after future prime minister Arthur Meighen. Residents thought Meighen sounded too much like "mean," and a vote was called to settle the debate. In the end, history prevailed, and a small farming town called Viking slowly grew on the Alberta prairie, to serve the area's surrounding farms.

NATIVE-BORN NHL PLAYERS

Brent Sutter, Brian Sutter, Darryl Sutter, Duane Sutter, Rich Sutter, Ron Sutter

FAMOUS LOCAL TEAMS

Not applicable

CURRENT POPULATION

1,081

A Viking Odyssey

Maybe none of the six Sutter brothers from Viking, Alberta, would have made it to the National Hockey League had it not been for that day in 1971 when Brian, the second oldest and the most talented hockey player in the family, was cut by the junior Tier II Red Deer Rustlers.

Brian didn't know what to do. His life until then had been farming and hockey. Farming was a career he hoped to pursue when he was older and more settled. First though, he wanted to play hockey, as far as he could go. And here a Red Deer coach, Cec Swanson, had just told him that as far as Brian could go was age 15. The teenager wandered around Red Deer all day, feeling nearly as faded as his jeans, trying to find the words to tell his parents what had happened.

That night, he finally got on the phone. If he was expecting sympathy, he didn't get it from his father, Louis, a tough Alberta farmer who chewed wheat instead of gum and liked it that there were gophers on his 1,400-acre farm because he could blast them with his .22. "Dad asked me if I wanted to be a hockey player, or whether I wanted to come home," Brian Sutter would tell writer Chris Cuthbert. "He said if I wanted to play, I better get my ass back in there and talk to somebody. So I went back in. I guess they weren't used to a kid saying I'm not leaving, so they sent me to the Junior Bs. I stayed with them for two or three weeks, and then I was back to the Rustlers to stay."

And there you have the story of Sutters—six hockey-playing brothers who wouldn't quit, even if they were fired.

Louis and Grace Sutter raised seven children, all boys. The eldest, Gary, decided not to pursue hockey professionally, although like his siblings, he loved playing the game once chores were done on the family farm, 14 kilometres outside Viking. Every one of the Sutter boys could operate a tractor at age 10. Hockey, they learned before that. The seven Sutters, Gary, Brian, Darryl, Duane, Brent and the twins, Rich and Ron, played together on a slough at the back of the farm, wearing secondhand skates purchased at Marshall Wells Hardware in town. When spring arrived and the ice grew thin, the boys brought

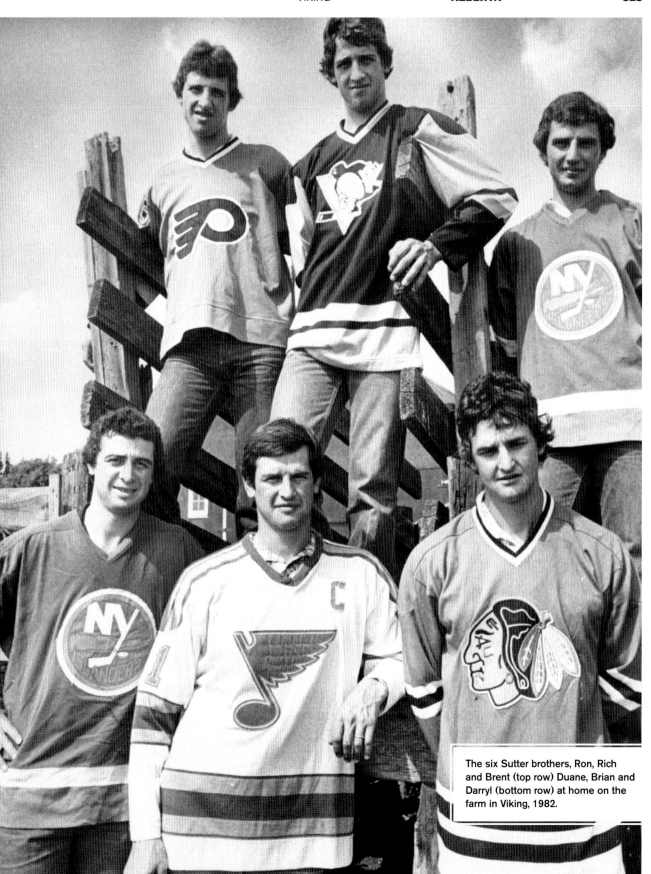

The six Sutter brothers, Ron, Rich and Brent (top row) Duane, Brian and Darryl (bottom row) at home on the farm in Viking, 1982.

the game into a 30-by-50-foot barn hayloft ribbed with hockey sticks stacked against the wall.

The brothers played there all summer, climbing a worn staircase in the broiling heat, to engage in three-on-three ball hockey contests that escalated into civil wars with a high stick or elbow. The games were impossible, really: Sutters couldn't accept defeat, and in family matches, at least three Sutters were bound to lose. "Cripes, did we take it seriously," middle Sutter, Duane, once remarked. "The losers wouldn't speak to the winners for days. I can remember a few times when things got so hot in the barn games that our dad would take the tennis balls away for a few days until it cooled off."

For all their fighting, the brothers remained steady teammates on the farm. They had hours of chores to do every day. And they accepted the direction of their father, a former amateur boxer, without question.

Brian Sutter, in particular, illustrated the difference between natural hockey players and natural team players. Brian was the latter. When Cec Swanson took Sutter back to the Red Deer Rustlers after the teenager had been cut from the team, the coach was amazed that for all the boy's spirit and fight, he responded to the challenge of team play with energetic commitment. Brian was a forward who worked hard in the areas of the rink that don't attract highlight film cameras. He was a relentless checker in the corners and an unquestioning patriot on the bench and in the dressing room. Of course, when a goal was needed, he could do that, too. Or die trying. Off the ice, he remained clearheaded, eternally responsible to the team—in other words, a coach's dream.

Free Cars!

A small town roughly 80 miles southeast of Edmonton, Viking, Alberta, did not have a proper hockey arena until the early 1950s. The town couldn't get public financing. Then in 1951, a local Canadian National Railroads employee and sportsman, Laurie Rasmussen, came up with a bold entrepreneurial plan: a car raffle. What the town would do was give away free cars. Well, not exactly free. Contestants would have to spend $5, a ticket, to enter Viking's Car of the Month Club, which would give them a chance to win one of 12 new, boat-sized 1952 Plymouth Deluxe sedans. And when the money poured in, the town could build an arena.

Somehow, Rasmussen convinced town council to go with what at first looked like an unlikely plan. If everybody in Viking, a town of 700 people, bought five tickets, they'd still only have $3,500, barely enough to cover the cost of one car. Rasmussen had that one covered, though. He figured that they could advertise on an Edmonton radio station, CFRN, and get all of western Canada to help build the arena.

In fact, the CNR employee underestimated the appeal of the city's Free Car! derby. The first car giveaway attracted $53,000 in ticket sales. With the profit from the first year's Car of the Month Club, Viking opened its new public rink, called the "Carena," on 9 July 1952. That day, the town of Viking more than quadrupled in size, as the Car of the Month Club had a special, two-free-cars-an-hour giveaway that attracted 5,000 ticket holders from across western Canada along with American tourists from Wisconsin and California.

Hockey broadcast legend Foster Hewitt was brought in from Toronto to open the arena, which was located on 51st and 53rd Streets. One of the 5,000 in attendance, that summer day, was Louis Sutter, father of the six Sutter boys who would all play minor hockey in the Carena. (Future National League Hockey player and coach Glen Sather, whose mother owned a dress shop in Viking for two years, also played minor hockey in the Carena.) The rink served Viking faithfully until 2005, when fire damaged much of the building.

Brian played two seasons for the Rustlers, graduated to the elite junior Lethbridge Broncos, then jumped almost immediately into the 1976–77 lineup of the NHL's St. Louis Blues, where he became a faultless two-way player. Secure in the knowledge that a Sutter could indeed make it in hockey, Darryl and Duane Sutter were the first of Brian's siblings to trace his career path, similarly moving from the hayloft to the Red Deer Rustlers, then the Lethbridge Broncos, and the NHL. Duane landed with the New York Islanders, where he helped the team to four straight Stanley Cups (1980–83), and Darryl, meanwhile, scored 40 goals his first season with the Chicago Blackhawks (1980–81). Brent was the next to make

Of course, when a goal was needed, he could do that, too.

the pros, when in the fall of 1981, he joined Duane on the Islanders' Stanley Cup spree. The twins, Rich and Ron, then made the NHL, in the 1983–84 season, and were both playing for the Islanders' rival, the Philadelphia Flyers, the following season. (Like their older brothers, Brent, Rich and Duane all played for Red Deer and for Lethbridge in junior.)

Six Sutters were playing in the NHL, during the 1984–85 season. When the Flyers played the Islanders, four Sutters were sometimes on the ice at the same time, a situation that led to the same kind of yapping and shoving that had characterized the family hayloft ball hockey games back on the farm in Viking. Referee Ron Wicks intruded on one four-Sutter corner pileup, tried to sort out the haggling, and then simply shook his head, commenting, "I really feel sorry for your mother."

Between 1976 and 2001, the six hockey-playing sons of Louis and Grace Sutter played a combined total of 4,994 NHL games, scoring 1,320 goals and collecting 2,935 total points. But perhaps the true measure of the brothers' impact on hockey is that they became a part of the sport's language—an adjective, in fact. Today, when scouts talk about a player's talents, they describe a tenacious two-way forward as having Sutter-like skills.

And the Viking odyssey very much continues in Alberta. Darryl coached the NHL's Calgary Flames to the 2004 Stanley Cup finals, while Brent is coach and general manager of the elite junior Red Deer Rebels. In both 2005 and 2006, he presided over the Canadian junior world championship team.

In 2005, the boys all returned to Viking to bury their dad. Darryl had driven in from Calgary, after Stanley Cup games the previous summer, to visit with him, even if only for a few hours, when Louis was sick with cancer. Despite being busy, Darryl had made the long return trips because he was the closest of the brothers to home; it was his duty to represent the others.

Darryl's brother Brent once said that doing what was needed without being asked twice was how the Sutter farm worked. It was also, he said, what made the boys successful hockey players. "The discipline Mom and Dad instilled in us [was invaluable]," he told Jim LeFebvre of the *Calgary Herald*. "By discipline, I mean getting off the school bus and knowing there were chores that had to be done around the farm. Not thinking of a way to get out of them or finding an excuse to put them off or whining about how unfair it was. Just doing them, whether it meant getting on the tractor out in the fields, feeding the cattle or the pigs, mending a fence…whatever. If one of us wasn't around, someone else took his work. And with so many of us in the family, well, we got used to a team atmosphere very quickly. You had to trust the brother next to you, the same way you had to trust the teammate next to you."

THE FIRST SUTTER GOLD RUSH

Before the six Sutter brothers, Brian, Darryl, Duane, Brent and the twins, Rich and Ron, made their fortunes in the National Hockey League, during the 1970s and 1980s, there was another Sutter family bonanza. On 24 January 1848, the boys' great-great uncle, Gen. Johann Augustus Sutter, a wealthy California farmer, commissioned a carpenter, John Marshall, to build a sawmill on his Sacramento River estate. Arriving at the stream, the builder was astonished to find a spray of glistening gold nuggets. The California Gold Rush of 1849 would begin a year later on the fast-flowing border of General Sutter's farm.

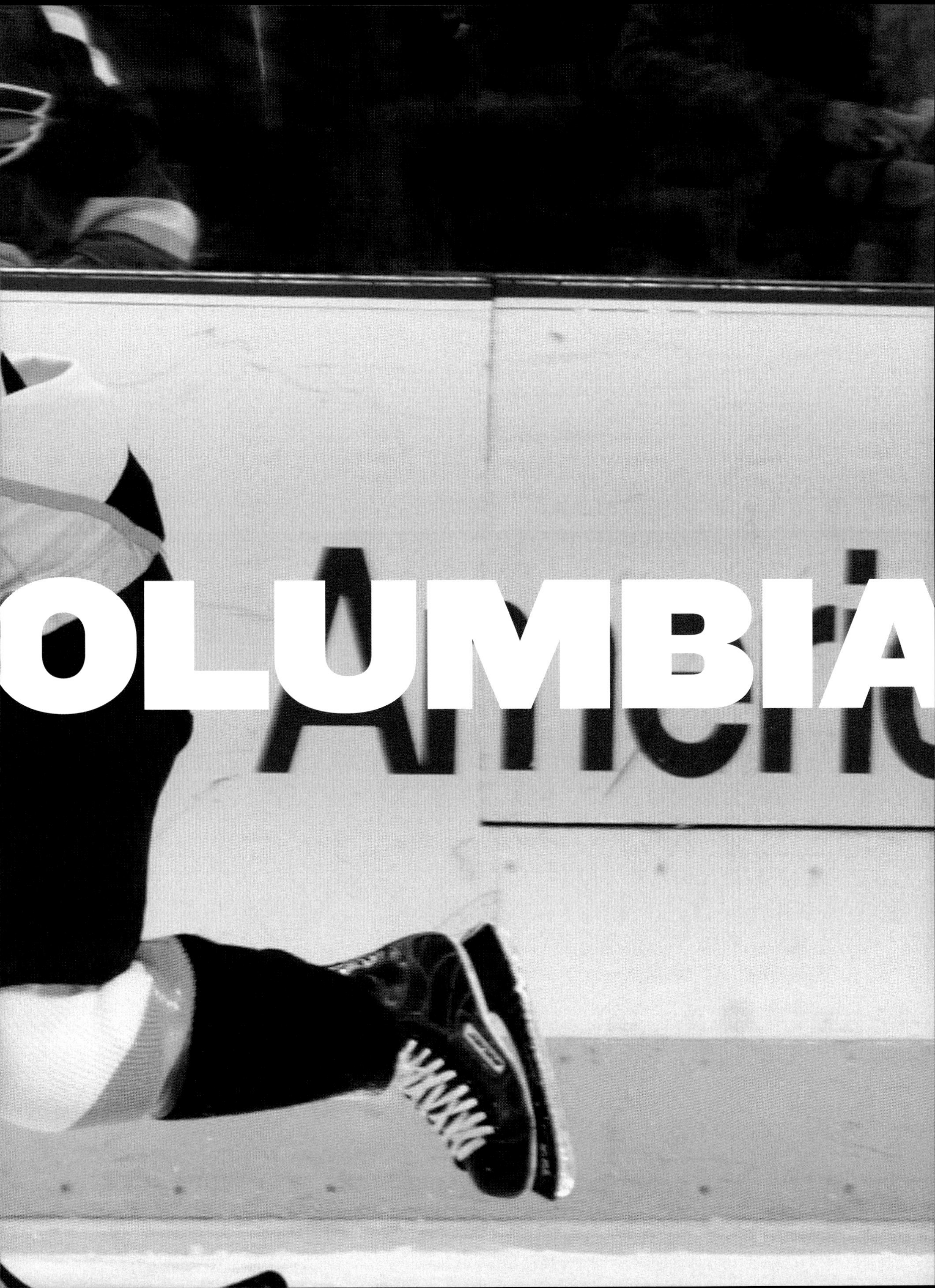
OLUMBIA

P

ro hockey wilted after the high-flying (and scoring!) Edmonton Oilers–Calgary Flames rivalry expired in the early 1990s. The National Hockey League grew too expensive for Winnipeg and Quebec City and moved, en masse, into American college football country—Florida, Georgia, Arizona and Ohio—opening up so many new franchises that for a while it seemed as if the league might have to consult the Hubble Telescope to find unexplored hockey territory.

Between 1991 and 2003, the NHL jumped from 21 to 30 teams. With relentless expansion, came an emphasis on keeping the puck out of the net. Defence, it became apparent, can be taught by coaches, while the imagination and skill required to spirit a puck past armed guards are granted by a higher authority. Hockey needed a new messiah, fans cried during the 2004–05 NHL lockout season. Someone who could re-imagine the game, who could make hockey faster and more of a crowd pleaser.

Someone like Frank and Lester Patrick. The Quebec-born Patrick brothers established hockey in British Columbia in 1912, building Canada's first artificial rinks and creating three franchises—the Vancouver Millionaires, the Victoria Senators and the New Westminster Royals—in the Pacific Coast Hockey Association. In bringing hockey to Vancouver Island and to British Columbia, the brothers did more than simply give life to a new league: The Patricks reinterpreted hockey itself, introducing a variety of rule changes and innovations that made for a radically new and improved game.

Before the Patricks and the PCHA, hockey had no forward passes or blue lines. Goalies weren't allowed to fall to stop a puck. Teams didn't change lines on the fly. There were no playoffs. Although the PCHA (later the Western Canadian Hockey Association) would only survive 14 seasons (1912–25), West Coast–style hockey would last forever, as the eastern National Hockey League adopted every one of the Patricks' innovations. Frank and Lester also sold their franchises and players to the new American entries in what became the expanded NHL of the mid-'20s. Lester's Victoria team evolved into the Detroit Red Wings. He himself was named the first general manager and coach of the New York Rangers. Another WCHA club, the Portland Rosebuds, became the Chicago Blackhawks.

Opening Spread: Paul Kariya, with the Nashville Predators, heads for the net in March 2006.

The Silver Fox, Lester Patrick.

The Vancouver Millionaires, Stanley Cup winners, 1914–15.

Scott Niedermayer.

The Patricks were among the most famous migrants to come to what was Canada's fastest growing province in the 20th century. Those who followed introduced their children, as a matter of course, to the sport the Patricks had popularized. To date, the most famous hockey players that B.C. has produced are second- and third-generation immigrants, who took to Canada's sport with the passion of the converted: Paul Kariya, a Japanese-Scot from Vancouver; Cranbrook's Steve Yzerman, a descendant of Dutch-Czechoslovakian ancestors; and Joe Sakic, who grew up speaking Croatian in Burnaby.

Recently, B.C. has made its mark on Canadian hockey by becoming a "cold bed" of elite junior hockey, with more franchises in the Western Hockey League (six) than Alberta (four), Saskatchewan (five) or Manitoba (one). One of those teams, the Kamloops Blazers, was the most successful junior team in Canada between 1984 and 1996, accumulating six Western Hockey League titles and three Memorial Cups. So outstanding was the Kamloops team that in the 2004 World Cup final (formerly the Canada Cup), held in Toronto, five members from the famed Blazers—Shane Doan, Jarome Iginla, Scott Niedermayer, Robyn Regher and coach Ken Hitchcock—were part of the Canadian team. Niedermayer and Doan scored the second and third goals, in a 3–2 win. No other Canadian junior team had more than one member on the squad. From their perspective in heaven, which many B.C. citizens hold to be close to Vancouver Island, Frank and Lester Patrick must have been pleased.

BURNABY

FOUNDED
Burnaby sprang to life in the late 1880s, after a new trolley line between New Westminster and Vancouver drew land speculators, tradesmen and settlers to the heavily wooded region between the two towns. In 1892, the settlement was named after Robert Burnaby, a merchant, businessman and local politician who had explored and helped to develop the region. Logging was the town's major industry in its early years, but it has since evolved into a suburban arm of Vancouver and a transportation hub for a variety of nearby communities.

NATIVE-BORN NHL PLAYERS
Derek Bekar, Ken Berry, Chris Joseph, Jason Labarbera, Dwayne Lowdermilk, Brian Lundberg, Michael MacWilliam, Darren McCarty, Byron Ritchie, Cliff Ronning, Joe Sakic, Claudio Scremin, Greg Zanon

FAMOUS LOCAL TEAMS
Junior: Burnaby Bluehawks, Burnaby Bulldogs, Burnaby Hawks

CURRENT POPULATION
205,000

Burnaby in the 1950s.

Immigrant's Dream Come True

Joe Sakic recorded two goals in Canada's 5–2 gold medal win over the United States in the 2002 Olympics. In scoring Canada's fifth goal, Sakic collected a pass at centre and exploded up the ice, as linemate Brendan Shanahan withdrew to fuss with an enemy defender. Once inside the American line, Sakic found goaltender Mike Richter. Both shooter and stopper froze momentarily. The Canadian forward then jerked sideways, dipping a shoulder and shooting. Richter sprawled, too late. The puck was behind him.

With the goal, Canada secured its first men's hockey gold medal since 1952. The Canadian bench emptied, to congratulate Sakic—who would soon be named the world tournament's best player. Amidst the jubilation, the goal scorer found Shanahan. "Why didn't you join me? I was going to pass it to you," he said.

"That's why I didn't join you," Shanahan deadpanned.

Joe Sakic, the best shooter in hockey, is notoriously shy of the spotlight. Known as "Burnaby Joe" in his native British Columbia, number 19 goes, instead, by the nickname "Quoteless Joe" in Denver, where he performs with supreme effectiveness and scant publicity for the National Hockey League's Colorado Avalanche. Which is fine with Sakic, who—as a kid growing up in Vancouver, B.C.—figured out how to skate before he learned English.

Joe's father, Marijan Sakic, was born in communist Yugoslavia. The son of a stonemason, Marijan worked 14-hour days hefting boulders in his youth. One night at the age of 15, without a word to his family, he slipped across the border into Austria. "I was not scared," the elder Sakic told journalist Woody Paige. "I didn't believe [the guards] would kill a boy."

Marijan Sakic soon immigrated to Canada. "They want new people," he understood. On the boat ride over, he also heard that it was warm in B.C., so upon landing in Quebec City, he caught a train all the way west to Vancouver, where he worked as a bus driver and a longshoreman before finding carpentry work in construction. Soon after, he met a lively girl, Slavica, at a Croatian community dance. The two married six months later, and within four years had three children, Rosemarie, Joey and Brian.

After work, the family man sometimes went with his mates to social clubs. A television was always on. At night, hockey filled the screen. One winter day in 1973, the weather was too cold to pour concrete. Marijan was sent home. He collected his children, taking them to the rink. His family was Canadian, and it was time the kids learned to skate.

Joey was four. He had never been on ice and he didn't understand English. The Sakics spoke Croatian at home. Still, the little boy displayed telltale ambition. "In no time he was out there playing [hockey] with older boys," Marijan remembered. "He didn't want to play with boys his own age."

The next winter, Rosemarie declared she was going to be a figure skater. Marijan and Slavica took a deep breath and borrowed $300 for the kids to take lessons at Vancouver's North Shore Winter Club. Marijan was determined to see his investment through. The kids had to work at their chosen sports the way he did his job—hard. Rosemarie was soon the best young skater at the club.

Burnaby Joe Sakic scores against the United States in the 2002 Olympic gold medal game.

Around that time, a coach at the club saw Joey spinning around the ice and asked if wanted to play hockey. Joey was shy, still learning English at school, trying to fit in. Next year, he said. He took power skating lessons in the meantime. The following season, the seven-year-old played organized hockey and was the best player in the league the moment he stepped on the ice.

Seeing how important winter sports were to their children, Marijan and Slavica moved the family to the Vancouver suburb of Burnaby and to a house down the road from 4-Rinks (now 8-Rinks), a multi-arena complex. Marijan also built a plywood rink in the backyard, where Joey and Brian refined their shooting skills.

Soon, Joey was at 4-Rinks all the time, paying a dollar for early morning open-hockey sessions, and then hanging around, hoping to catch on in pickup games. One spring day, his mother caught him crying. "Hockey is over," Joey explained. Don't be crazy, she replied. This is Canada. Winter will be here soon enough.

The Sakic children were good at winter, indeed. In 1984, Rosemarie was the Canadian junior figure-skating champion. Joey said he wanted to play in the NHL. He was only a kid, but Marijan, for whom work was a religion, was impressed at how his eldest boy respected his tools. "Most boys," he told Woody Paige, "come home and throw their wet and dirty skates in the closet. Joe would clean his skates, dry them out, sharpen the blades and put them up. He always respect the game."

At age 16, Joey collected 83 goals for the midget Burnaby BC Selects. The next summer, he moved to Swift Current, Saskatchewan, to play junior hockey. In Swift Current, he attended Comprehensive High School. He had never been on a date, but soon he was going steady with a sophomore named Debbie. Joey was also progressing in hockey, scoring 60 goals for the Broncos. The NHL's Quebec Nordiques made him their second first-round pick in the 1987 draft. Joey shocked the team by saying he wasn't ready to turn pro yet. Next year, he promised.

Instead, Joey returned to Swift Current to complete high school. Brian Sakic, Joey's brother, was also with the Broncos now. (He would later play minor league hockey, until a knee injury ended his playing career.) The team was doing well, and Joey continued to see his girlfriend.

Then, after Christmas 1987, Joey became an adult, became Joe Sakic in a single afternoon. The bus the team was taking for an away game flew off an overpass

Burnaby J. Fox

Actor Michael J. Fox's great ambition as a youngster was to make it in the National Hockey League, but the closest he came to the NHL was playing ball hockey on the street with Glenn Anderson, a fellow Burnabyite who starred for the Edmonton Oilers in the 1980s. Fox left Burnaby for Hollywood at about the same time, and was soon starring as Alex Keaton on *Family Ties*, the definitive Reagan-era American TV sitcom. He would befriend NHLer Cam Neely, another product of the suburbs of Vancouver (Maple Ridge). While in Hollywood, Fox bought a satellite dish, in order to follow Neely's Boston Bruins games.

In 1994, the actor was working in New York, when the Vancouver Canucks played against the New York Rangers in the Stanley Cup finals. Fox flew his mom to New York for a Stanley Cup game, on the condition that she would restrain her enthusiasm for the Canucks. "She's got to understand what Madison Square Garden fans are like," he told the *Vancouver Sun*. Fox advised his mother that "if you get up and scream every time [Canucks player] Pavel Bure touches the puck, you may end up with a .357 Magnum popped against your head."

and crashed. The Broncos players scrambled through a hole where the front window had been. Except for teammates Trent Kresse, Scott Kruger, Brent Ruff and Chris Mantyka, who had been crushed—killed instantly—under the back of the bus (see page 272.) "Clearly, you grow up in a hurry after something like that," Sakic told *The Sporting News*. "It changes your whole outlook on life and makes you appreciate what you have."

Sakic lifted his game after the tragedy and was named the Canadian junior player of the year in 1988. The following season, he enjoyed a solid rookie campaign with the Nordiques, scoring 23 goals. He was invited to play on the

"You have the talent to lead this team from the bottom to the top."

Canadian team in the world championships that spring, but he wasn't sure he wanted to go. Teammate Peter Stastny convinced him otherwise. A defector from Czechoslovakia, Stastny recognized himself in his young teammate. Both shared an old-world gravity. "At the end of your career you don't remember the 82 games in the regular season," Stastny told Sakic. "You remember the game where you play for your country against the best in the world."

Sakic played for Canada, and although no medal was won that year, he returned for his second NHL year as a dramatically improved player. Nevertheless, the Nordiques struggled for wins that season, and at the end of the campaign veteran Stastny was traded. Before departing, he told Nordiques management that 20-year-old Sakic should be named captain. Then, he sought out Joe to say goodbye. "You have phenomenal ability," he told him. "You have the talent to lead this team from the bottom to the top. That puts you into a position to achieve a level of satisfaction few people ever experience. This is your team now."

Sakic had always wanted to be a professional hockey player, but the immigrant's son, who had first played hockey on rented skates, was a reluctant star. It had been his dream to make a team, not to lead it. "He could score as many goals as he wanted," his father said, reflecting on Joe's Burnaby hockey days. "But he liked to pass and make his teammates score."

Sakic was never one for speeches, either. "I was taught you don't talk about yourself," he once said. "It sounds too much like bragging."

What Sakic brought to his role, instead, as team captain, was something he had learned from his father's long days of hard work in construction: Being a leader isn't about making speeches; it's about showing up at work every day ready to do your job, and it's about being responsible to co-workers and family.

"I work hard, my kids work hard," Marijan once told Woody Paige. "I just want them to have it better than I did." Joe Sakic's life would be a Canadian immigrant's dream come true. He married his high school sweetheart, Debbie, and became the father of three children. And he went on to have a fabulous career, making millions of dollars every year playing hockey. Eventually, he built a retirement home for his parents in White Rock, B.C., installing satellite TV so that Marijan could watch all his son's games. (After every contest, the father still phones his eldest boy to tell him how he can improve, just as back in the days when Joe was Joey.)

The Quebec Nordiques team that Sakic inherited from Peter Stastny moved to Colorado—becoming the Avalanche—and won Stanley Cups in 1996 and 2001. The following year, Sakic helped Canada win an Olympic gold medal. Sakic was assistant captain on the Olympic team and captain of the Stanley Cup-winning Colorado Avalanche teams, proving to himself and to everyone else that he didn't have to be Joe Superstar to lead a team to greatness. Burnaby Joe would do.

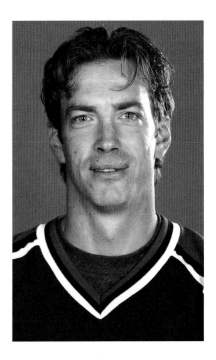

Way to go Joe: Joe Sakic with the Colorado Avalanche.

CRANBROOK

FOUNDED

Cranbrook is located in the south-east corner of British Columbia, in the heart of the Kootenay Rockies. Although Aboriginal peoples, fur traders and explorers frequently passed through this scenic region, no settlers arrived until the Canadian Pacific Railway, in 1898, made the site a divisional branch for its newly built Crowsnest Pass railway line through the southern Rockies. The town, which was founded in 1905, was named in honour of an early settler, a British colonel whose ancestral home was located in Cranbrook, England.

NATIVE-BORN NHL PLAYERS

Ray Allison, Greg Andrusak, Glen Cochrane, Ryan Huska, Jon Klemm, Brad Lukowich, Jason Marshall, Ted McAneely, Bob Murdoch, Don Murdoch, Randy Petruk, Corey Spring, Frank Spring, Steve Yzerman (Brothers Rob and Scott Niedermayer grew up and live in Cranbrook, but were born, respectively, in Cassiar, BC, and Edmonton, AB.)

FAMOUS LOCAL TEAMS

Junior: Cranbrook Colts, Kootenay Ice; **Senior-pro:** Cranbrook Royals

CURRENT POPULATION

18,476

Hockey Moms and Dads

The Yzerman family didn't skate until they moved to Cranbrook, British Columbia. Father, Ron, who worked as a social worker, was a second-generation Canadian. His own father had arrived in British Columbia from Holland early in the 20th century, finding work as a lumber camp cook. The family of Ron's wife, Jean, came from Czechoslovakia. The couple met and married in Vancouver, and were transferred to Cranbrook in the early 1960s because of Ron's job.

At first, the Yzermans found it hard to believe that Vancouver and Cranbrook were in the same province. Although both cities were situated just north of the U.S. border, Vancouver enjoyed green Christmases, while Cranbrook, further east, perched in a wrinkle of the Kootenay Rockies, remained snow-covered most winters.

Ron never played hockey as a kid, but as his boys grew older, he sensed that not playing Canada's national sport wouldn't do in the Kootenays. "When Stephen and Michael were five and six, Cranbrook was probably the same as all little towns in Canada," he told Ed Arnold in *Hockey Town*. "There was a minor hockey association in the East Kootenay area that needed volunteers. Winters were long and cold. There was plenty of natural ice around.

"Nine of the 10 youth hockey teams were run by RCMP members. We had a sergeant in our area with kids on the team [and he] wanted to know if our kids wanted to play... He had an ulterior motive. If my kids wanted to play, even though they had more than a one-year age difference, they could play on the same team—if I would coach."

Soon, Ron found himself driving his boys to a nearby arena every Saturday. For tykes, the rink was divided by temporary boards at the red and blue lines. Three games would be going simultaneously, with more than 25 small children skittering about the arena, while parents sat in the stands, jerking further awake with every sip of coffee.

Ron Yzerman enjoyed coaching, although he considered himself more of a recreation director. And he couldn't get over how much his kids loved hockey. Saturday nights, the boys watched *Hockey Night in Canada* as if hypnotized. By their second season in minor hockey, Michael and Steve were getting good—real good. If he put both of his sons in a game, Ron found that the other team never got the puck. So he took turns playing one in net. Typically, his team would win, 6–0, with one of his kids getting a shutout and the other, six goals.

The following year, 1973, Ron was transferred to Kamloops, British Columbia, a city of 50,000—more than five times bigger than Cranbrook. With the move, he retired from coaching, but not from being a hockey parent. In Kamloops, his boys made the Moose Lodge Pups, an elite team that practised at five in the morning. "We had to get up, and get the boys up for 4:30," Jean Yzerman reported to Arnold. "They would still be sleeping, and we'd dress them, put on their skates, take them to practice, bring them home, feed them and get them ready for school."

The next year, the Yzermans moved to Nepean, Ontario, a satellite community outside Ottawa. Ron and Jean discovered that hockey now ruled their lives. They had to save and sacrifice for the boys to play, paying not only for skates, sticks and equipment, but also for rink practice time, tournament travel and team jackets. They also had to contend with the soap opera histrionics of other hockey parents. Every new city, they would have to skate around parents who were angry because their surefire National Hockey Leaguer had been relegated to a checking line by the Yzerman kids. Sometimes, the Yzermans wondered if it was all too much.

In Nepean, their elder boy, Michael, decided that it was. Elite junior or a college hockey scholarship was beyond his abilities, he discovered. That was hard. And who knew about Steve? In 1985, he had already taken Nepean teams to tournament championships in Quebec City, Montreal and Oshawa. At the same time, however, the 16-year-old was only 5'9" and 150 pounds; too small, perhaps, to go all the way.

That summer, Steve Yzerman was drafted by the Peterborough Petes, maybe the best franchise in Ontario's elite junior league. Every Thursday and Saturday for two years, Ron and Jean Yzerman would drive to Peterborough and back to watch Steve play. Friday mornings, the couple would arrive back home at three

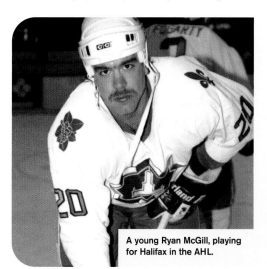

A young Ryan McGill, playing for Halifax in the AHL.

Cranbrook Ices Memorial Cup

The Edmonton Ice junior hockey team transferred to Cranbrook in 1998, and played in the Memorial Cup two seasons later, losing three straight games in the Halifax 2000 tournament. Coach Ryan McGill figured that his small-town team was blinded by the national media spotlight and vowed that if he ever got the team to the Memorial Cup again, he would attempt to normalize the players' schedule. When the Ice made the Memorial Cup finals in Guelph, Ontario, in 2002, McGill took the team on long bus drives between games, just like in Cranbrook. Only instead of journeying to play hockey, McGill took the boys sightseeing. Cranbrook's tour of southern Ontario was evidently successful, as the team, which was led by captain Jarret Stoll, high-scoring forward Colin Sinclair and goalie B. J. Boxma, defeated the Victoriaville Tigres, 6–3, to take the 2002 Memorial Cup. The team also presumably enjoyed seeing Niagara Falls and taking in a Toronto Blue Jays baseball game.

Eye on the prize: A young Steve
Yzerman with the Detroit Red Wings.
He would later captain the team
to the Stanley Cup in 2002.

in the morning, shut their eyes for four hours, and then jump for the morning
alarm to go to work.

Just as Ron and Jean Yzerman were returning home from their jobs later
that afternoon, four provinces west, back in Cranbrook, B.C., Carol Niedermayer
was picking her boys up from school for lunch. Carol had grown up as a skating
champion in Saskatchewan. And she wanted her boys, Scott and Rob, to experience the joy that came with skimming across a frozen slough under a dying
mid-afternoon sun.

At lunch, she took the boys out for a quick sandwich and for 45 minutes
of purposeful skating at a nearby rink. After school, the trio headed out once
again, blades over their shoulders, for one of the many frozen ponds that deco-
rate Cranbrook. Winter weekends were best of all, as the Niedermayers and
two other neighbourhood families packed up cars with provisions and headed
out to glittering, firmly frozen lakes outside the city, where adults built camp-
fires by the shore and scraped the ice free of snow, as their kids climbed excitedly
into their skates, not wanting to waste a second of skating.

Carol Niedermayer's tutoring yielded immediate dividends. Rob and Scott were the two best hockey players to come out of the Kootenays since Steve Yzerman. The two boys won a provincial minor league title for Cranbrook in 1986, as Rob scored four goals in a win over Prince George.

Several years later, junior hockey took the Niedermayer boys away from home. Scott played for the Memorial Cup-winning Kamloops Blazers (1992), while Rob, a year younger, ventured to Manitoba to skate with the Medicine Hat Tigers (1990–93).

Carol taught many other local kids how to skate while working with her sons. And at one time, Cranbrook's recreation department asked if she wanted some kind of remuneration for efforts. She said no, that she simply enjoyed teaching the kids. That satisfaction was reward enough, as it is for tens of thousands of mom and dad hockey coaches like Ron Yzerman and Carol Niedermayer across the country.

As it turned out, Ron and Carol were among the few dedicated hockey parents to have their efforts rewarded with glory. Steve Yzerman would become, along with Wayne Gretzky and Mario Lemieux, the greatest hockey player of his generation, taking the National Hockey League's Detroit Red Wings to three Stanley Cups (1997, 1998, 2002). The best skater in the NHL, Scott Niedermayer won as many Cups with the New Jersey Devils (1995, 2000, 2003.) Rob Niedermayer, too, would achieve NHL success, playing for the Florida Panthers, the Calgary Flames and the Anaheim Mighty Ducks. In 2002, both of Cranbrook's most illustrious hockey-playing sons, Steve Yzerman and Scott Niedermayer, played on Canada's gold medal-winning Olympic hockey team. (That same spring, the Kootenay Ice, Cranbrook's elite junior hockey team, won the Memorial Cup.)

With these successes, it seemed unlikely that hockey could get any higher in the Kootenays. Then, in 2003, Scott's New Jersey Devils played Rob's Anaheim Mighty Ducks for the Stanley Cup. Scott and the Devils won. Arriving back in Cranbrook after the series, the Niedermayer brothers chartered two helicopters and flew the Stanley Cup up to the top of Mount Fisher—the highest point in the southern Rocky Mountains—so that Scott could have his photo taken with the Cup at the very top of the world.

A STRAIGHT SHOOTER

Decades after teaching her boys how to skate, Carol Niedermayer, the mother of National Hockey League stars Scott and Rob, decided to conquer the empty nest syndrome by filling enemy nets—joining a 12-team recreational hockey league in Cranbrook in 1999. Carol plays for the Cranbrook Shooters alongside Tara Klemm, sister of Jon Klemm, a member of the NHL's Chicago Blackhawks. "[Carol] can skate circles around most of us half her age," team captain Shannon Fisher says of the former skating instructor. "She's a phenomenal skater, our oldest player and best skater."

Brothers Rob and Scott Niedermayer display the trophy after Team Canada's win of the gold medal in Prague, 2004.

A vintage 1950s postcard of Kamloops.

KAMLOOPS

FOUNDED

Kamloops is located at the meeting point of the North and South Thomson Rivers in central British Columbia. Its name is drawn from the First Nations word *kahm-a-loops*, which means "meeting of the waters." The first Aboriginal settlers in the region were the Shuswap tribe of the Interior Salish Nation. The first Europeans to arrive in the area were fur traders, who came in the early 1800s. In 1811, a trading post was established. The establishment was bought and sold several times and was finally taken over by the Hudson's Bay Company in 1821. The town grew, as mining discoveries, lumbermen and ranchers arrived to tap the area's rich resource base. Today, forestry, tourism and mining are the town's primary industries.

NATIVE-BORN NHL PLAYERS

Don Ashby, Ajay Baines, Rick Boh, Craig Endean, Stu Grimson, Darrell Hay, Doug Lister, Bert Marshall, Tom Martin, Rudy Poeschek, Mark Recchi, Tim Watters

FAMOUS LOCAL TEAMS:

Junior: Kamloops Blazers, Kamloops Braves, Kamloops Buckaroos, Kamloops Chiefs, Kamloops Junior Oilers, Kamloops Rockets; **Senior-pro:** Kamloops Chiefs, Kamloops Cowboys, Kamloops Elks

CURRENT POPULATION

81,699

A Blaze of Glory

The junior Kamloops Blazers host an alumni weekend every year, inviting ex-players back to central British Columbia for 48 hours of golf, an exhibition hockey game and maybe a little fishing (the Kamloops trout is regarded as one of North America's most beautiful and combative game fish). In 2004, the franchise held two reunions: The first, as always, in Kamloops during the summer; and a second, more exclusive, affair later that autumn in Toronto, where a former Blazers' coach and four players led Team Canada to an amazing win at the World Cup.

Few hockey followers would be surprised that Kamloops had more players on the national squad than any other Canadian junior club, for the Blazers were the most successful junior team in Canada between 1984 and 1996, accumulating three Memorial Cups, six Western Hockey League titles and 10 WHL West Division first-place finishes in a 12-year "blaze" of glory.

The Toronto game was a particularly satisfying Blazers reunion, as "Team Kamloops," defeated Finland, 3–2, in the World Cup title match. Ex-Blazer Scott Niedermayer fired in Canada's second goal, and another Kamloops grad, Shane Doan, counted the winner, sneaking into the crease to delicately putt in a clearing pass from behind the net. Former Blazers Jarome Iginla and Robyn Regehr also contributed to Canada's World Cup victory. And Ken Hitchcock, a one-time Blazers bench boss, served as an assistant on the coaching staff.

The Blazers' hockey dynasty and the team's hold on "the Loops" are all the more astonishing given that the junior franchise only arrived in Kamloops in the fall of 1981, when the New Westminster Bruins (formerly the Estevan Bruins) were purchased by the National Hockey League's Edmonton Oilers, setting up business in the creaky old galleon on Victoria Street known as Memorial Arena. The Kamloops Junior Oilers lasted for three seasons before

Mark Recchi in action with
the Philadelphia Flyers.

Edmonton sold its junior franchise to local businessmen. At this point, the franchise became known as the Blazers, and under new coach Ken Hitchcock, the team finished first four out of five subsequent seasons, travelling as far as the Memorial Cup playoffs in 1986 and 1990.

Hitchcock is widely credited with starting Kamloops' hockey Blaze. Weighing in at close to 300 pounds, and mean as a toothache when his team didn't play up to expectations, Hitchcock was a memorable figure behind the Blazers' bench. And he had a sure understanding of what kind of hockey would succeed in blue-collar Kamloops. Hitchcock looked for grit and talent, finding two local contributors with those characteristics in assistant Don Hay, a firefighter who played Tier II junior hockey for the Kamloops Rockets of the British Columbia Junior Hockey League, and the team's first star, Mark Recchi, a two-way forward with a lunch-pail work ethic that made him a favourite in Memorial Arena.

The Blazers also effectively recruited the province immediately to the east, drafting Shane Doan and Darcy Tucker from Halkirk and Endiang, Alberta, and lucking out in 1992 on a 5'4" 15-year-old bantam forward from Edmonton. Blazers' then-director of scouting, Stu MacGregor, saw the kid in two tournaments and loved his temperament and skating ability, so he drafted the youngster in spite of his size. That fall, the Blazers were delighted to find that Jarome Iginla had grown six inches and packed on an action figure torso over the spring and summer months.

Hitchcock assistant Tom Renney had taken over the team by the 1991–92 season when the Blazers, led by Scott Niedermayer and Mike Mathers, won the team's first Memorial Cup, as Zac Boyer scored on a breakaway with 14 seconds left, to defeat the Sault Ste. Marie Greyhounds, 5–4. The Blazers' storied run would get even better.

The following season (1992–93), the team moved from the well-loved, if musty, Memorial Arena to the ultra-modern, 5,500-seat Riverside Coliseum (now the Sport Mart Place), with long-time assistant, Don Hay, the Kamloops

Mean as a toothache when his team didn't play up to expectations, Hitchcock was a memorable figure.

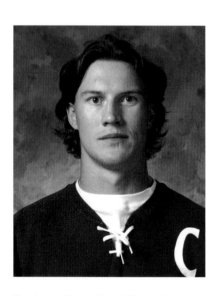

Kamloops Blazers' grad Shane Doan, with the Phoenix Coyotes.

firefighter, taking over as the Blazers coach. Every game was now a sellout, with all of Kamloops fighting to get into the new rink to see a team full of young stars, who would soon include Jarome Iginla, Hnat Domenichelli, Nolan Baumgartner and Shane Doan.

With a roster loaded with 16- and 17-year-olds, the 1993–94 Blazers started slowly, playing under .500 for the first 16 games, but the team came together at mid-season, going on a giddy 29-game home-ice winning streak to finish the season. The playoffs were more of the same, as the team once again won the Memorial Cup—this time, four and out in Laval, Quebec.

The Blazers were even better the following season, when Kamloops hosted the Memorial Cup. The 1994–95 team was ranked number one in the country all season. And every regular season home game was thrilling foreplay to fans who expected the team to win everything in the home building in the spring of 1995. Doan and Iginla emerged as stars. The Riverside Coliseum was standing room only every night, with fans, usually dressed in white, clapping along wildly after every Blazers goal to the team's theme song, Bachman-Turner Overdrive's "Takin' Care of Business." The Blazers would indeed "take care of business" in the Memorial Cup, clobbering the Detroit Jr. Red Wings, 8–2, becoming the only team to win three Memorial Cups within a four-year period.

With the team's success, the Blazers became Kamloops' most famous and highly regarded citizens. Regardless of how successful players become in the National Hockey League, when Blazers return during alumni weekends, they are immediately reclaimed as hometown heroes. World Cup winner Shane Doan told Ian MacIntyre of CanWest News about what happened to him the last time he returned to Kamloops:

"I remember when you played with the Blazers," a waitress called to him, when he sat down in a local restaurant. "What are you doing now?"

"I'm still playing," he said.

"Oh yeah, where?" the waitress chirped. She had no idea about Doan's subsequent success representing Canada in international games or his rewarding years with the NHL's Phoenix Coyotes.

"The Blazers are everything to that town," Doan said. "They're the be all and end all."

KELOWNA

FOUNDED

Kelowna is located in the heart of the Okanagan Valley, in the interior of southern British Columbia. Fur traders travelled through the area on the Brigade Trail in the early 1800s, but not until Oblate Missionaries arrived, in 1859, did the area overlooking Lake Okanagan have its first settlers. *Kelowna* is an Aboriginal word for "grizzly bear," and legend has it that the settlement earned its name after local First Nations people spied a heavily bearded settler emerging from his underground sod house. The shaggy settler was not the only curiosity witnessed by local indigenous peoples. Aboriginal tales about a water demon called Ogopogo, in Okanagan Lake, were so convincing, that in the 1920s the provincial government installed devices on a government-operated ferry to repel, as one local

newspaper described it, "the attacks of Mr. Ogopogo and his family." Kelowna's first settlers sustained themselves with grain farms and ranching, but irrigation advances enabled farmers to plant lush apple, peach, plum, cherry and apricot orchards, as well as vineyards, all of which dominate local commerce to this day. Currently, there are more than 40 vineyards outside the city.

NATIVE-BORN NHL PLAYERS

Steve Bozek, Josh Gorges, Ryan Jorde, Jason Ruff, Mitch Wilson

FAMOUS LOCAL TEAMS

Junior: Kelowna Blazers, Kelowna Buckaroos, Kelowna Rockets, Kelowna Spartans, Kelowna Wings; **Senior-pro:** Kelowna Penticton-Combines

CURRENT POPULATION

105,691

Ogopogo Logo

For hundreds of years, First Nations tribes that canoed across Lake Okanagan offered up a toll to *N'ha-a-tik* ("snake in the lake"), tossing an animal overboard before journeying across the 80-mile-long, 590-feet-deep lake. European settlers began seeing the serpent in the 1860s. Sightings have continued until this day and are consistent. The tubular creature is long as a station wagon, undulating, with an oversized goat head topped off with bulging, Marty Feldman eyes. In 1926, Roy W. Brown, editor of the *Vancouver Sun*, gave credibility to rumours of the creature by writing, "Too many reputable people have seen [the monster] to ignore the seriousness of actual facts." The serpent's name, Ogopogo, comes from music hall ditties that were popular in the Okanagan Valley in the 1920s. In 1924, a Bill Brimblecomb, of Vernon, B.C., amused a Rotary Club luncheon with, "I'm looking for the Ogopogo/His mother was a mutton/His father was a whale/I'm going to put a little bit of salt on his tail." Alas, or perhaps luckily, no one has come close enough to Ogopogo to resort to seasonings. And a $2-million reward to prove the existence of what some experts consider to be a primitive whale has gone uncollected. The Western Hockey League's Kelowna Rockets adopted Ogopogo as their logo when the team was created in 1995.

Rocketing to Success

There are more than 5,500 acres of vineyards surrounding the central British Columbia city of Kelowna. Located in the Okanagan Valley, between the Cascades and the Rockies, Kelowna's climate is warm and dry. Less than six inches of rain fall annually in the southern tip of the valley, the only patch of land in Canada that is classified as desert.

No big-name hockey player has ever come from "Summer City," the name that travel brochures often use for Kelowna. Local kids didn't grow up playing hockey for five months of the year on rivers and sloughs. Nearby Lake Okanagan has, however, produced a $2-million monster forward who, in 2004, dominated the Canadian junior Memorial Cup.

The monster is Ogopogo, ill-tempered Canadian cousin of the Loch Ness monster and also the logo for the junior Kelowna Rockets, one of the great success stories in the Western Hockey League's recent penetration of the B.C. interior. (The $2 million price tag associated with the monster is local reward money for anyone who can capture the melon-eyed, goat-headed serpent, who has, for centuries, startled local boaters and bathers.)

Kelowna took over the Tacoma Rockets franchise in 1995. In 1998, Cranbrook, further east in the Kootenays, was also granted a WHL team. Both clubs were quick to enjoy local and national acclaim, with the (Cranbrook) Kootenay Ice taking the Memorial Cup in 2002 and Kelowna winning the national junior championship two years later, at home, in front of a jubilant, T-shirted crowd that spread like a halo outside Prospera Place arena.

The Rockets celebrate their
2004 Memorial Cup championship
at home in Kelowna.

The Kelowna Rockets
logo—featuring their
Ogopogo mascot.

Kelowna had been a good hockey town prior to the arrival of the Rockets. In 1961, the Kelowna Buckaroos became a charter member of the British Columbia Junior Hockey League, the province's first Tier II junior loop. And the Kelowna Spartans, another BCJHL team, would win the national Tier II Centennial Cup.

Still, Kelowna had never had a hockey hit like the Rockets, a team that arrived just as the city entered a period of unprecedented growth. The Rockets' home address, as of 1999, the swish, ultramodern, 6,800-seat Prospera Place Arena, is one manifestation of the city's growing prosperity. As of 2005, the city was the fifth most expensive housing market in Canada, behind Toronto, Montreal, Vancouver and Victoria.

Like the growing tourist centre the team represents, the Kelowna Rockets are well marketed. Choosing merchandise-friendly Ogopogo as the team logo was a brilliant stroke. And the team again displayed public-relations savvy when hosting the 2004 Memorial Cup. Every game in the tournament was sold out. During the tournament, the team erected a massive tent outside the arena and broadcast the game on large screens, so that locals without tickets could share in the excitement of the Rockets' championship game with the Gatineau Olympiques.

The swelling crowd was rewarded when late in the third period of a 1–1 game, Kelowna forward Justin Keller cut in on the Gatineau net, ramming the puck between Gatineau goalie David Tremblay's legs to give the Rockets the Memorial Cup. Kelowna goalie Kelly Guard, who gave up three goals in four games, was named the tournament's most valuable player.

After the game, the city toasted the Rockets' success well into the night. There were no aquatic reports of Ogopogo sightings the entire day.

Kelowna Rockets' Justin Keller
in action, 2005.

New Westminster, c.1950.

NEW WESTMINSTER

FOUNDED

Located on the north bank of the Fraser River, southeast of Vancouver, New Westminster is western Canada's oldest city. Settlers were first drawn to the region in the 1850s, after gold was discovered in the Thompson River in British Columbia's Kamloops region. The influx of thousands of miners and speculators to British Columbia prompted the newly formed colonial government to seek military assistance from England. Colonel R.C. Moody and the Columbia Detachment of Royal Engineers were dispatched to the frontier town to maintain law and order and to survey the largely unexplored region. The settlement was named after Queen Victoria's favourite London neighborhood, Westminster, in 1860, and Canada's first city west of the Great Lakes was incorporated. New Westminster served as the capital of B.C. between 1858 and 1866, but when the gold rush evaporated, the province's capital shifted to Victoria. The city was devastated again, in 1898, when a fire virtually destroyed the entire downtown area, devastation that took a full decade to rebuild. Today, New Westminster serves as a small suburb of sprawling Greater Vancouver.

NATIVE-BORN NHL PLAYERS

Doug Berry, Colin Forbes, Brent Hughes, Nathan LaFayette, Mark Lofthouse, Tom McMurchy, Ken Quinney, Jordan Sigalet, Ryan Walter, Barry Wilcox, Terry Yake

FAMOUS LOCAL TEAMS

Junior: New Westminster Bruins, New Westminster Cubs, New Westminster Royals; **Senior-pro:** New Westminster Canadian Pacific Airmen Lodestars, New Westminster Fraser Mills, New Westminster Royals, New Westminster Spitfires

CURRENT POPULATION

54,207

Always a smile on his face: Walter "Babe" Pratt, with the Toronto Maple Leafs in 1944.

Babe in the City

Walter "Babe" Pratt was a 1920s Winnipeg schoolyard legend who smacked baseballs, Babe Ruth style, out of city ballparks. A decade later, the strapping, 6'3", 200-pound athlete was an eager star on the National Hockey League's New York Rangers. In Manhattan, The Babe again proved worthy of his nickname, carousing at both the Cotton Club and Latin Quarter, nightclubs that the great Bambino, long-time star with the New York Yankees, once frequented.

Sometimes, Pratt combined socializing and work. Once, Pratt and forward Neil Colville noticed Lana Turner, Hollywood's "Sweater Girl," in the front row at Madison Square Garden with bulldog-faced movie-star bad guy, Edward G. Robinson. "Babe, how about giving me a chance to introduce myself to that Turner doll?" Colville asked. "Next time we go by, give me a little bump over the boards into her lap." Pratt obliged, and met Colville at the bench.

How did it go? he asked.

"Fine, if you happened to be crazy about Edward G. Robinson," Colville complained.

On the ice, in 1940, Babe helped the Rangers win a Stanley Cup in Toronto, a feat he celebrated, according to legend, by attempting to hijack a streetcar to

New York. Two seasons later, an exasperated Rangers general manager, Lester Patrick, traded the supremely talented but seemingly incorrigible defenceman to the Toronto Maple Leafs, where owner Conn Smythe had Babe room with coach, Hap Day, a teetotaller. In Toronto, Pratt scored 17 goals, and in 1943–44 he won the league's most valuable player award.

Still, Babe eventually tried Smythe's patience. The Leafs owner thought of himself as an inspirational speaker, and was prone to "Gentlemen, life is a horse race!" parables.

"You guys remind me of two racehorses I once used to own," Smythe once rasped at his players before a big game. "Sir Marlboro was fast out of the gate, like this hockey

Incredibly, the Royals scored four straight goals, one by The Babe himself.

club. He was a front-runner, good until they turned for home. But in the stretch, Sir Marlboro faded, forced back with the also-ran bums!" Smythe glared at his players.

"But Shoeless Joe, my second horse, he'd start slow and then come on and on, and when it counted, he'd lunge and stick his nose in front to win! Gentlemen, that second horse was my kind of hockey club."

The embarrassed players remained quiet, studying the floor. Then Babe called out to teammate Bob Davidson, who was beside him, "Which end of the f—— horse are you?"

In 1946, Pratt was suspended by the NHL for gambling. The 16-game sentence might have been worse, except that Babe hadn't bet against the Leafs. Smythe was, himself, an inveterate gambler. (Shoeless Joe was named after a baseball player accused of throwing the 1919 World Series.) Nevertheless, Smythe got rid of Pratt after he returned from his suspension, trading him to the Boston Bruins, where the player quarrelled with general manager Art Ross.

Which is how, at age 32, in the summer of 1948, Babe Pratt found himself playing golf in a rubber suit at the Mayfair Lakes Golf Club in Richmond, B.C., with hockey legend Cyclone Taylor. Pratt had come west to rescue his career, joining both the minor league New Westminster Royals of the Pacific Coast Hockey League, as player-coach, and Alcoholics Anonymous. After slimming down to his playing weight (hence the rubber suit), Babe would pass both tests, winning consecutive most valuable player awards in the PCHL and remaining as sober as Hap Day from that time onward.

On the West Coast, living in a port town that welcomed rogue adventurers, Pratt finally found home. He was also happy to resume an old rivalry with Lester Patrick, who had recently been fired by the New York Rangers and had returned to his home, Victoria, to manage the PCHL's Victoria Cougars. Cougars-Royals games became turbulent affairs, with the best action sometimes coming after the game, when a sportswriter might ask Babe about his old boss. "Lester Patrick is so cheap, he wouldn't give a worm to a blind robin," Pratt once commented. Another time, he said of his rival, "Lester isn't close or tight, he's goddamned adjacent."

In 1950, Pratt offered New Westminster fans memorable proof of the headstrong optimism that ruled his nature when, with 14 minutes left in a game that the Royals were losing, 6–2, he decided—what the hell?—to pull his goalie and go on the attack. Incredibly, the Royals scored four straight goals, one by The Babe himself, to tie the game, 6–6.

After coaching, Pratt worked for a while in the lumber industry, but returned to Vancouver in 1970, to become the colour man on Vancouver Canucks games when the team joined the NHL. He was sitting in Vancouver's Pacific Coliseum

Royals Never Win at Home

The New Westminster Royals were the first team in Canada to win a hockey game on artificial ice, beating the Victoria Senators, 8–3, on 3 January 1912, at a game played in the Victoria Arena. The Royals, Senators (later the Aristocrats) and Vancouver Millionaires were original members of the Pacific Coast Hockey Association (see page 360), British Columbia's first professional hockey league, founded by Frank and Lester Patrick. The Patrick brothers had hoped to build an arena in New Westminster, but they never completed financing for a local rink. Instead, the Royals played all their games in nearby Vancouver. The Royals won the first Pacific Coast Hockey Association championship, with a team that included Hockey Hall of Famers Hughie Lehman, Harry Hyland and Moose Johnson. Without its own rink to play in, the Royals lost money, and after the 1913–14 season they ceased operation, relocating to Oregon in the United States, where Moose Johnson, strange to say, became a Portland Rosebud.

that year, entertaining a group of reporters with old war stories from the NHL, when Cyclone Taylor, then 90 years old, appeared on the ice for a workout, which he did several times a week.

"How many goals would Cyclone Taylor score in the NHL today?" Pratt was asked.

"Oh, 19 or 20 a season," Pratt responded, staring out at his old golf partner.

"But Babe, he was one of the greatest players in the history of the game," the reporter persisted.

"Yeah, but he's 90 years old," Babe replied.

After his broadcasting days were through, Pratt remained with the Vancouver Canucks in a community-relations capacity. He won his last hockey bet in 1988. Reporters covering the Canucks kicked in some money to a pool, and then placed a bet on the attendance that night. Pratt guessed the winning number, 14,858, but never collected his prize. He suffered a heart attack before the game and died on his way to the hospital. Reporters went to a bar and used his winnings to toast one of hockey's most original and invigorating characters. "Babe was 72," Archie McDonald wrote in the *Vancouver Sun*, "going on 27."

Stan Smyl, playing for the Vancouver Canucks.

Punch and Steamer

The Estevan Bruins transferred to New Westminster in 1971 and soon went on an extraordinary run, which saw the junior team make it to the Memorial Cup championships four consecutive springs—winning the Canadian national championship in 1977 and 1978. The Bruins coach was the aptly named Ernie "Punch" McLean, a Western Hockey League legend who once ripped a toupée off a passing linesman, explaining, "I reached out to tap [Harv Hildebrandt] on the head and my hand caught in his hair. He was wearing a toupee, which came off in my hand. So I just dropped it to the ice."

The Bruins had many star performers on the team that won the 1977 Memorial Cup at home in New Westminster, defeating the Ottawa 67's, 6–5. The top defencemen, Barry "Bubba" Beck and Brad Maxwell, were both top-10 draft picks in the National Hockey League 1977 draft. And John Ogrodnick scored 59 regular season goals on the team that downed the Peterborough Petes, 7–4, in the 1978 final. But the key player on the Bruins' championship run was Stan "The Steamer" Smyl, a workaholic right winger who became one of the most popular hockey players ever to perform in Vancouver. From New Westminster (a Vancouver suburb), Smyl went straight to the NHL's Vancouver Canucks, where he scored more than 20 goals per season for eight straight seasons. The Canucks retired Smyl's number 12 when he retired in 2000, having played hockey a quarter of a century in the Vancouver area.

PENTICTON

The Penticton Vees, 1955.

FOUNDED

Penticton is a city in south-central British Columbia, between Okanagan Lake and Skaha Lake. The name Penticton is derived from the local Salish First Nation language and can be roughly translated to mean "a place to stay forever." Penticton's primary economic strengths are tied to tourism, wine production and fruit orchards. The city annually hosts the Ironman Canada Triathlon, along with the Okanagan Wine Festivals and the Pentastic Hot Jazz Festival.

Penticton also is the home of some of the province's best recreational skiing opportunities.

NATIVE-BORN NHL PLAYERS

Ross Fitzpatrick, David McLelland, Andy Moog

FAMOUS LOCAL TEAMS

Junior: Penticton Broncos, Penticton Knights, Penticton Panthers, Penticton Vees;
Senior-pro: Penticton Vees

CURRENT POPULATION

30,095

Penticton Steals World Cup

Penticton wasn't supposed to win the world hockey championship in 1955. In the 1954 tournament, a Toronto senior squad, the East York Lyndhursts, fell easy victim to the Russian national team, 7–2. How could the Penticton Vees, a senior club representing a small town in the balmy, fruit-growing Okanagan Valley, match up against a national team from the Empress of Winter, Mother Russia?

Concerned nationalists, Conn Smythe, owner of the National Hockey League's Toronto Maple Leafs, and Dick Irvin, coach of the Montreal Canadiens, proposed that the six NHL teams lend Penticton one player each for the 1955 tournament, to be held in Krefeld, West Germany. At least let us send you a proven goaltender, Smythe pleaded with Penticton player-coach Grant "Nobby" Warwick.

But Warwick, a scrappy forward who had spent nine seasons in the NHL, most of them with the New York Rangers, was just as patriotic as Smythe. And the Regina-born player-coach felt that he couldn't betray teammates who had fought hard to win the Allan Cup, in a furiously tense seven-game series with the Sudbury Wolves. As is true of all senior national Allen Cup winners, the team had earned the right and demonstrated its ability to play in the world championship. Besides, Warwick's Penticton team had two good goalies, Ivan McLelland and Don Moog. The Vees would win it on their own as a team, the coach resolved, or they wouldn't go to Germany. It was that simple.

But nothing was ever easy in international hockey, where rough play isn't tolerated on the ice, but all crime short of murder is common in committee meetings. When the Vees arrived in Germany, the team was told that 10 players were ineligible. Their passports identified them as hockey players. Professionals! Manager Clem Bird assured frowning bureaucrats that the athletes had been reinstated as amateurs. Paperwork was introduced. After much grumbling, Penticton was allowed to compete.

Penticton hero of '55, Grant Warwick with the New York Rangers.

Competing was exactly what Warwick, who formed the team's top line, alongside his brothers Bill and Dick, intended to do. In the previous year's international tournament, East York had eschewed physical play to stay out of the penalty box. Against the high-scoring Russians, the Canadian team had received the majority of infractions anyway. And the Big Red Machine had taken full advantage of power play opportunities and Canada's uncharacteristically passive play to roll to an easy win. Not this time. We have to play our game, Warwick told players. Fighting in the corners and banging along the boards. Penalties will come. But if we're going to be shot, better to be shot as a lion than as a lamb.

The Vees played hard in Germany, from the dropping of the puck, with defencemen George McAvoy and Kevin "Crusher" Conway throwing their weight around and Vees forwards forechecking tenaciously. And if an opposition

Representing Canada, let alone the "Free World," is an enormous burden.

skater managed to get past Penticton's defence, that player had to contend with Vees goalie Ivan McLelland, a 22-year-old from South Porcupine, Ontario, who had developed lightning reflexes as a kid, fighting 13 brothers and sisters for toast at breakfast.

The Vees won their first seven games in the tournament by a combined score of 61–6. McLelland was outstanding, and the feisty Warwick boys, all of whom stood under 5'7", scored goals in fat clusters, with Bill collecting six markers in a 12–1 win over the U.S. and then scoring two more in a nerve-racking 5–3 victory against Czechoslovakia.

The team's play made them sudden heroes in Canada. Broadcast legend Foster Hewitt relayed games back home (and to armed forces bases in Europe) on the radio. In the championship final against Russia, 4,000 Canadian army and air force personnel showed up to support the Vees. Despite being played on a Sunday morning, Canadian time, the game delivered the biggest radio audience ever recorded for a Canadian sporting event. In churches, smiling clergymen delivered updates of the game. Penticton was up one...two.

With every goal and thumping body check, the Vees' military supporters in Krefeld crept closer to delirium. Smelling Goliath's blood, broadcaster Hewitt grew more impassioned. Maybe the only Canadians involved in the unfolding spectacle who remained calm were the Vees, who retreated into a defensive shell upon capturing a lead.

"We won, 5–0, and really we had a much tougher time against Czechoslovakia and Sweden," McLelland later told the *Vancouver Sun*. "Those days you didn't play the trap, but after we got up a couple of goals, we [clogged the defensive zone] and I think I only faced 15 or 16 shots."

When the game ended, many Vees broke down with the playing of the national anthem. The team had been under pressure for months. Before even setting sail for Europe, coach Warwick had received a note from a fellow Saskatchewan hockey enthusiast. "Just a last shout of good luck," wrote Father Athol Murray of Notre Dame College in Wilcox, Saskatchewan. "Your little gang is setting out as the Knights Errant of Western Freedom. The whole Free World is pulling for you."

Representing Canada, let alone the "Free World," is an enormous burden. And perhaps the players hadn't allowed themselves to contemplate the enormity of their burden until after they'd won. Some of them couldn't stop shaking and sobbing. Goalie McLelland was struck dumb, when brought to meet Hewitt for an interview. "Mr. Hewitt, I'm so nervous," he stuttered.

Andy Moog with the Edmonton Oilers in 1983.

Vee-chips off the Old Block

Before going off to Krefeld, West Germany, to take on the world, coach Nobby Warwick of the 1955 world champion Penticton Vees declined the offers of a proven National Hockey League netminder. His goalies, Ivan McLelland and backup Doug Moog, would be good enough. Ironically, both McLelland and Moog would have children who played net in the NHL. Penticton-born Andy Moog led the Edmonton Oilers to their first playoff triumph—the 1981 upset of the Montreal Canadiens. And Dave McLelland, another Penticton native, played for the Vancouver Canucks in the 1972–73 season.

Kevin Conway (right) in action against the Soviet Union in the 1955 World Championship final in West Germany. Everyone listened to Foster Hewitt's radio broadcast back in Canada.

"Ivan, you just shut out the Russians, you shouldn't be nervous talking to me," Hewitt replied.

When the Vees received the World Championship cup, however, their trembling euphoria soon gave way to a darker mood. "Now that trophy..." Billy Warwick later told sportswriter Allen Abel. "When we got it, it was in three pieces. The Russians must have been mad about losing it, and heaved it and smashed the thing... I was so mad, I said, 'They'll never see this thing again.' And they haven't. When we came home, I had a restaurant in Penticton, where we had the trophy on display. There was this jeweller friend of mine, and I asked him, 'Do you think you could get a trophy just like this made up?' Some guy in Vancouver finally made it for us, and he only charged 60 bucks."

The $60 trophy returned to Europe, where it would be borne aloft by subsequent Russian teams. The original solid silver trophy, valued at $7,500, remained for years in the window of Warwick's restaurant, in balmy, beautiful Penticton, British Columbia.

Trail, 1896.

TRAIL

FOUNDED

Tucked away in the southeastern corner of British Columbia, Trail was little more than a rest stop on the Dewdney Trail, a path that served as a trade route from the coast to the interior in the mid-1800s. Trail's fortunes changed in 1890, when a rich gold and copper ore discovery in a nearby mountain drew waves of prospectors and mining companies. Unlike most boom towns on the coast, Trail's gold rush laid the foundation for a strong mining industry, which dominates the local economy to this day. After the gold ran out, exploration crews found copper, lead and zinc deposits that were rich enough to sustain local smelters and a fertilizer plant that still operate to this day.

NATIVE-BORN NHL PLAYERS

Ed Cristofoli, Adam Deadmarsh, Butch Deadmarsh, Gary Donaldson, Dallas Drake, Ray Ferraro, Shawn Horcoff, Barret Jackman, Rich Kromm, Tim Lenardon, Cesare Maniago, Mike Matteucci, Steve McCarthy, Don McLeod, Garth Rizzuto, Steve Tambellini, Mike Zanier

FAMOUS LOCAL TEAMS

Junior: Trail Smoke Eaters, Trail Selects, Trail Smokies; **Senior-pro:** Trail Canucks, Trail Smoke Eaters

CURRENT POPULATION

7,575

Trail versus Trail

The first Trail Smoke Eaters team to win a world championship played almost flawless defensive hockey, defeating opponents by a goal count of 42–1, over the course of eight games, in the 1939 Switzerland world hockey championships. The Smokies' only real trial came in the second round, against Czechoslovakia, a team that seemed to know its Canadian opponents' every move, probably because the Czech coach, Mike Buckna, was, himself, from Trail and grew up with many of the players on the Smoke Eaters' team. Buckna, who would build the Czechoslovakian national team into an Olympic contender, held the Smoke Eaters to a 2–1 win. According to the book *Trail on Ice*, by Murray Greig, the Smoke Eaters protected the puck throughout the tournament with crisp, short "checkerboard passes." Smoke Eaters stars included goalies Duke Scodellaro and Buck Buchanan, who piled up 21 shutouts on the team's 63-game European tour. Johnny McCreedy, who contributed to the National Hockey League's 1941 Stanley Cup-winning Toronto Maple Leafs team, was the Smoke Eaters' most potent offensive weapon.

The '61-ers

One of the largest lead-zinc refineries in the world, Teck Cominco, is the primary industry in the West Kootenays. Trail, British Columbia, is a Cominco company town, with smelter smokestacks dominating its skyline. Indeed, the Smoke Eaters, the city's famous hockey team, have frequently had an image of chimneys on their blast furnace orange jerseys.

But the Trail Smoke Eaters didn't get their title from Cominco. The name was inspired by the behaviour of Carroll Kendall, star of Trail's 1929 senior team. In the playoffs that year, Trail faced Vancouver. The locals took a bad penalty, and disgruntled fans littered the ice with refuse, including a still fuming pipe. Kendall sorted through the rubbish and found what he wanted, taking a long, satisfying draw on the pipe as he skated off. The following day, a cartoon of him and his teammates, their heads floating on a wreath of tobacco smoke, appeared in the Vancouver Province. An accompanying story referred to Trail players as "SMOKE EATERS."

After that incident, Trail hockey teams have almost always been Smoke Eaters. A current edition plays Tier II junior hockey out of the Trail Memorial Centre. The Cominco Arena, located inside, is festooned with memories of Smoke Eaters glory, with banners honouring the 1938–39 senior team that won the Allan Cup and then sauntered through the world tournament, allowing one goal. Another ribbon acknowledges the 1961 senior team. Not that anyone in Trail needs a banner to remember the club that gave the city its slogan, Home of Champions. Many of the players from that 1961 edition still live in Trail. And a case could be made that "the '61-ers" have owned their native city ever since they returned as champions.

Maybe it was the way they won, that made them Trail's team. For in beating the world in Switzerland, the Smoke Eaters exhibited the elbows-out swagger that characterizes the best Canadian mining hockey teams.

The 1961 Smoke Eaters warred with playing coach Bobby Kromm, known as "The German General," and openly disliked their Canadian Amateur Hockey Association bosses. Kromm didn't like the CAHA, either, and resisted demands to replace Seth Martin, a lanky netminder from nearby Rossland, B.C., who worked as a fireman at Cominco. The CAHA figured Martin was a journeyman. "In the end, Bobby told the CAHA to go to hell," forward Norm Lenardon advised Scott Russell, for the book, *The Rink*.

Kromm did, however, agree to accept a backup goalie, Claude Cyr, Jacques Plante's understudy with the National Hockey League's Montreal Canadiens. The Smoke Eaters showed their support for Martin, their long-time co-worker and teammate, when Cyr joined the team on a prairie tour. "We decided to test [Cyr], so we gave him to the team from Yorkton for an exhibition game," former Smoke Eater Cal Hockley told Russell. "We scored 14 goals on him, and after that he had a little more respect for us."

Cyr had more trouble with coach Kromm's practices, which involved two hours of relentless skating. In the grinding, five-week, 18-game European exhibition tour that preceded the March World Cup tournament, the team would play a game, collapse exhausted in dingy hotels or drive all night in buses to the next city, where instead of eating, they would face more skating drills. "Jacques Plante didn't have to skate in Canadiens' practices," Cyr complained to Kromm.

"You ain't Jacques Plante," was the coach's withering response.

Even if the grinding drills had not been an issue, the Smoke Eaters' tour did not get off to a good start. Trail lost an exhibition game to Sweden, 4–0, and two

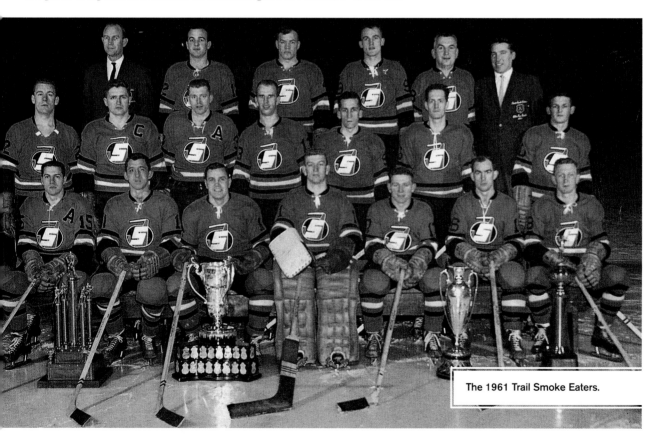

The 1961 Trail Smoke Eaters.

out of three games to Russian teams. The team's ineffective play led to a rumour that their tour might be cancelled. Soon, they were feuding with their CAHA representatives, a middle-aged couple who presumed to act as chaperones for grown men with families at home. Halfway into the tour, the team even deserted its German general. "There was one time in Finland when we said, 'Piss on you, Kromm! You practice, and we're going out for dinner,'" is how Hockley explained the mutiny. "He stood at the door and screamed, but we went out for dinner." A few days later, playing coach Kromm, who'd broken his nose in an exhibition match in Norway, hung up his Smoke Eaters jersey. He would coach, but he wouldn't play with the team in the Swiss world championships.

The 35-day exhibition series ended on a dismal note. The CAHA representatives fled the team for a hotel suite in Lausanne and the Smoke Eaters went on to Italy on their own, racing from a game in Cortina, without showering, for a bus to Austria, where they caught a train in the middle of the night for Switzerland. "It was a cattle car," forward Addie Tambellini told Russell. "We were all wrapped up in our Hudson's Bay coats, trying to keep warm, going to a world tournament."

Further indignities awaited the team, before its first game. When the bus dumped the players off at the arena, there were no baggage handlers, and the players had been dropped at the wrong end of the rink. The Smoke Eaters were breathing fire, when they finally got onto the ice. "When the gate opened, we came out of there like a stick of dynamite," is the way Hockley has described it.

Jim Proudfoot, who covered the tournament for the *Toronto Star*, later suggested that the Smoke Eaters' hellish European tour was the making of the team. "It was the classic motivation of a hockey team," he told Russell. "That siege mentality of us against everybody else."

The first team that got in their way, but only for a while, was the Swedes. A month earlier, this European team had outshot Trail, 56–27, winning easily. But Trail didn't give away anything to Sweden the second time around, outhustling and banging their opponents from the start. By the third period, the Swedes were as shy as wallflowers at a dance, and the Smoke Eaters waltzed to a 6–1 win.

The world champion Trail Smoke Eaters in Geneva, 1939. The twin stacks are still smoking on their jerseys.

An Anti-Smoking Campaign

Teck Cominco, Trail's largest employer, helped build the Trail Memorial Centre, which was conveniently located at the foot of the Cominco refineries so as to allow the hockey-playing Smoke Eaters, most of whom worked at the plant, to hurry to the rink after a shift. For decades, the Smoke Eaters' hockey crest, twin smokestacks, reflected Cominco's involvement with the team. In 2000, the city decided to promote a more environmentally friendly image, by modifying the junior Smoke Eaters' logo, scrubbing out the plumes of smoke to create smokeless stacks. Former Smoke Eaters goalie Seth Martin was appalled, telling the *National Post*, "It's a crime to change it. It's terrible." Martin was on holidays in 2000, wearing his old (still smoking) team jacket in Disneyland, when a fan stopped him and asked about all the players on the world championship 1961 Trail Smoke Eaters team. "Every time you go somewhere, people see that logo and say, 'Oh, you're a Trail Smoke Eater. How's the old team doing?'" Martin told the newspaper.

The 1930–31 Trail Smoke Eaters.

Seth Martin.

After that, the Smoke Eaters drubbed West Germany, 9–1, with Dave Rusnell, a former Yorkton Terrier who had settled in Trail, scoring three goals. Next, the United States and East Germany fell by scores of 7–4 and 5–2. Then, Trail played Czechoslovakia, in a game that marked the beginning of goalie Seth Martin's European legend.

The Czechs outplayed Trail for much of the game, but Martin, the first masked netminder that the Europeans had encountered, confounded opposition forwards by reading their every offensive move. The Czechs managed one goal in the dying seconds of the first period, but the masked goal robber held them off after that. Smoke Eaters forward "Pinoke" McIntyre, who grew up with Martin in Rossland, B.C., chipped home the equalizer and the game ended, 1–1.

Trail then blew past Finland, 12–1, to set up the deciding match, a game against Russia that Canada would have to win by two goals in order to beat the Czechs for the gold medal. Trail would only manage 12 shots on the Russian net in the game. Incredibly, more than half of the team's first six shots found the back of the net, and the club went into the third period with a 4–0 lead. At the other end, Martin was a nightmare for Russian shooters. Every time they looked to shoot, a masked man was in front of them.

"He knew what Jacques Plante knew," Jim Proudfoot suggested, referring to a game in 1965, when Plante had come out of retirement to play for the Montreal Junior Canadiens and defeated the Russian national team, 2–1. "The Russians based their offensive patterns on soccer. Instead of banging away, they wanted to have an open shot. Knowing that, Seth always knew where the shot was coming from."

The Russians managed a goal in the third period, but with two minutes remaining, Trail forward Lenardon stole the puck in the Russian end and fought past a defender, firing the clinching goal while falling to the ice. The Trail Smoke Eaters were once again on top of the hockey world.

"We had a group that would walk through fire for any one of the other guys," Cal Hockley would say many years later, of the '61-ers, teammates who became brothers, fighting for their country in Europe. "I still think we have the best hockey team that's ever been put together."

Seeth! Seeth!

Until Paul Henderson and Phil Esposito led Canada to a win over the Soviet Union in the Summit Series of 1972, Seth Martin was the most famous Canadian hockey player in Europe. The Trail Smoke Eaters goalie helped his team to a gold medal in 1961, and was again in nets when the Trail Smoke Eaters represented Canada in the 1963 world championship, held in Stockholm. Although the 1963 team finished fourth, Martin was again named goaltender of the tournament. He repeated that feat in the 1964 and 1966 world championships, playing goal for a Canadian amateur national team before returning to Trail and to the Smoke Eaters.

Born in Rossland, British Columbia, six miles outside of Trail, Martin was a fireman at the Cominco refinery. He made his first goal mask in the plastics shop of Trail's largest employer. Martin played one season for the National Hockey League's St. Louis Blues (1967–68). He remained with Cominco throughout his hockey-playing career, although he took advantage of his local popularity to also open a sporting goods store in Trail. Martin was just as famous in European hockey circles, where autograph hounds followed him out of arenas with shouts of "Seeth! Seeth!"

VANCOUVER

FOUNDED

Before European settlers arrived, the Coast Salish people used Vancouver's natural harbour as a place to gather food and trade. European explorers "discovered" the Vancouver region in the late 1700s. Spanish captain Jose Maria Narvaez arrived in 1791, and was followed a year later by British naval captain George Vancouver. In 1827, the Hudson's Bay Company built the area's first permanent non-Aboriginal settlement. Initially, the area was called Granville, but it was renamed after Captain Vancouver, in 1886, when the city was formally incorporated. Today Vancouver serves as a flourishing port of trade between Canada, the United States and Asia.

NATIVE-BORN NHL PLAYERS

Glenn Anderson, Nathan Barrett, Barry Beck, Sebastien Bordeleau, Tim Bothwell, Doug Buhr, Jim Camazzola, Tony Camazzola, Steve Clippingdale, John Craighead, Brad Dalgarno, John Ferguson, Norm Foster, Link Gaetz, Joaquin Gage, Gord Hampson, Dick Healey, Randy Heath, Dave Hindmarch, Chris Holt, Tony Horacek, Paul Houck, Paul Kariya, Steve Kariya, Steve Kelly, Dan Kesa, Sasha Lakovic, George Lyle, Doug Lynch, Dean Malkoc, Sean McMorrow, Peter McNab, Steve Montador, Doug Morrison, Shaone Morrisonn, Steve Parsons, Ken Priestlay, Larry Romanchych, Darcy Rota, Todd Simpson, Larry Skinner, Mark Taylor, Greg Tebbutt, Alex Tidey, Dave Tomlinson, Steve Tuttle, Wayne Van Dorp, Phil Von Stefenelli, Simon Wheeldon

FAMOUS LOCAL TEAMS

Junior: Vancouver Centennials, Vancouver Giants, Vancouver King George, Vancouver Nats, Vancouver Villas; **Senior-pro:** Vancouver Blazers, Vancouver Canucks, Vancouver Lions, Vancouver Maple Leafs, Vancouver Maroons, Vancouver Millionaires, Vancouver Norvans, Vancouver RCAF, Vancouver St. Regis, Vancouver Vanguards

CURRENT POPULATION

582,045

Posing on felled trees on Georgia Street, Vancouver, c. 1886.

Frank's Dream

Nova Scotia transfer student James Creighton brought the Halifax Rules of hockey to McGill University and Montreal, in 1875, allowing fresh eyes to reimagine a sport that would continue to spread west with the railroads. The Halifax-Montreal game remained unchanged for another 30 years, until 1907, when two sons of Quebec, Frank and Lester Patrick, moved to British Columbia. There, with a new climate, an untapped audience to conquer and few resident experts to stifle creative thinking, the brothers reinterpreted and improved the game of hockey once again. In bringing hockey to the westernmost province of Canada, Frank and Lester Patrick created British Columbia's first hockey outfit, the Pacific Coast Hockey Association, won a Stanley Cup for Vancouver and Victoria and shared enough adventure to stock a hundred dime-store novels.

The Patrick family had its roots in rural Quebec. Joseph Patrick, an ambitious Irish Methodist farmboy, left home for Drummondville in 1881, taking a job as a store clerk and marrying a local schoolmarm, Grace Nelson. The general store was a success and Joe soon established a mill in Daveluyville, near Quebec City. The Patrick family, which grew to include eight children, led a largely idyllic life, darkened by an accident that marked the second and third children. After a snowstorm, seven-year-old Frank and his younger brother, Ted, took to the woods with a sled. Frank was pushing Ted, when their board found a grooved logging trail and took off like a spooked animal. The sled overturned just as horses pulling a load of timber appeared. Frank watched as his brother was pulled under the hurtling express. Everyone told Frank that it wasn't his fault, but he assumed that it was. His brother survived, but lost his right leg in the accident.

In 1893, the Patricks moved to Montreal. That winter, the Montreal Amateur Athletic Association won the first Stanley Cup. Frank and Lester were consumed by the hockey craze that was sweeping the city of 250,000. With the St. Lawrence River frozen, the brothers skated to Nun's Island, shopping from tree to tree for hooked branches to knock around tin cans in daylong games of river shinny. Eventually, Lester became a collegiate hockey champion, but then he abandoned McGill for money-making enterprises, including scalping hockey tickets with pal Art Ross. After seeing western star Tom Mix at a rodeo, Lester ventured to Calgary to become a cowboy, only to discover that he cared neither for horses nor 12-hour workdays. Attempting to return home, the 17-year-old ran out of money in Manitoba, and so he joined the Brandon Wheat Kings, creating a sensation by leading the Wheaties to an unsuccessful 1904 Stanley Cup challenge of the Ottawa Silver Seven. Afterward, the defenceman trooped the rest of the way home to Montreal, eventually serving as captain of the local Wanderers team, which took the Stanley Cup away from Ottawa in 1906.

Meanwhile, Frank Patrick completed his studies at McGill, where he too was a celebrated rearguard. Off the ice, he was different from his famous older brother, however. Frank was deliberate, watchful, a bit of a dreamer, perhaps. Significantly, he began his senior career as a referee, where he was free to indulge his clinical fascination with the game of hockey.

As for the head of the family, Joe Patrick's Montreal-based timber company was a roaring success. Still, he was a businessman in need of fresh challenges. And he had heard of the redwoods of British Columbia—trees as wide as a house! Also, there was a city there called Nelson, which was his wife's maiden name. A great sign, surely. In 1907, the family business moved west.

Canada's most popular weather front in the early 20th century: Fred "Cyclone" Taylor.

A Cyclone in Vancouver

Before donating the Grey Cup to the Canadian Football League in 1909, Governor General Earl Grey gave Fred "Cyclone" Taylor, hockey's first superstar, his enduring nickname. Born in Tara, a small town in Ontario's Bruce County, Taylor began playing hockey and lacrosse in 1889 in nearby Listowel, at the age of six. In his early twenties, he was a star for Portage-la-Prairie in the Manitoba Hockey League and for the Houghton (Michigan) Portage Lakers of the International Hockey League, where his athletic, rink-long dashes earned him the sobriquet, "The Listowel Pistol." In 1907, he began working for the civil service in Canada's capital, while moonlighting as a defenceman for the Ottawa Senators. His first hour on the latter job attracted 7,100 fans, including Governor General Grey and a curious McGill University student named Frank Patrick. That night, Taylor scored four goals with a virtuoso flair that inspired the governor general to remark, "Number four, Taylor... He's a cyclone, if I ever saw one." A local reporter overheard the comment, and from then on the hockey player was Cyclone Taylor.

Taylor first played in Vancouver's Denman Arena as part of a touring National Hockey Association all-star team in 1912. The tour was a three-game series, but Taylor injured his hand prior to the games and couldn't shoot. He performed a few ceremonial twirls in the first two games, but in the third contest he was let loose in the third period of a tied game and exploded off the bench like a horse from a burning stable. Breaking up a play, he raced the length of the ice, hurtled past two defenders and then sent a perfect blind pass to Art Ross for the go-ahead goal. The applause for that move had barely died when Taylor again tore down the ice, speeding through an entire team before feathering a pass to Jack Darragh for another score. The Vancouver fans jumped to their feet, cheering. And really, they wouldn't stop for a decade.

The following season he was star rover on the Pacific Coast Hockey Association's Vancouver Millionaires, where he continued to thrill fans for the remainder of his storied career (1912–22). He was an active member of the Vancouver community after his hockey retirement, eventually serving as commissioner of immigration, for British Columbia and the Yukon Territories.

Situated on the southern tip of Lake Kootenay and surrounded by lush stands of forest stretching to the white-topped Valhalla, Monashee and Selkirk mountains, Nelson was everything Joe Patrick had hoped for. And the entire family, except for Ted, fell in love with B.C.

While Lester and Frank may have taken to their new environs, keeping them at home was another matter. The Edmonton Eskimos enlisted Lester in their unsuccessful 1908 Stanley Cup challenge of the Montreal Wanderers.

Frank proposed blue lines that would divide the ice into thirds.

The following season, the Wanderers, Ottawa Senators and Renfrew Millionaires wired Lester, all on the same day, offering contracts for the 12-game National Hockey Association season. The eldest Patrick boy advised Montreal he would play for $1,200. Ottawa was told he would need $1,500. As for Renfrew, well, Lester didn't want to go there, at all, so asked the Millionaires for $3,000, plus expenses. To his astonishment, Renfrew said yes. Lester stalled, saying he would only go if Frank could tag along, at $2,000. Terrific, Renfrew replied. And so, with reluctance, the Patrick boys became Millionaires.

The brothers' behaviour during their stay with the Ottawa Valley team defined their developing partnership. Charismatic Lester entertained civic leaders with after-dinner speeches and enjoyed a romance with the boss's daughter. M.J. O'Brien, lumber baron owner of the Millionaires, even lent Lester his horse and buggy to escort Stella O'Brien around town. Frank, meanwhile, palled around with teammates, forging lasting friendships with Cyclone Taylor and Newsy Lalonde.

The highlight of the Patricks' Renfrew sojourn was a trip to New York, where the Millionaires stayed at the Waldorf-Astoria, a posh hotel that might hold half of Renfrew. The purpose of their visit was an exhibition series against NHA all-stars. (The Millionaires won, three straight.) Most competitors in the 1910 series spent their off-hours in Times Square taverns, gargling spirits. Not Frank, though. For reasons that would soon become apparent, the young defenceman gravitated, sketchbook in hand, to Madison Square Garden, the largest indoor emporium in the world.

At the end of their season with the Millionaires, the Patrick boys returned home to B.C. determined to help their father with his lumber empire. Frank, however, also had a new idea altogether for a family business. Joe Patrick's second son felt he had something to prove: Ted Patrick was spending his idle hours, which multiplied daily, at one of Nelson's 32 taverns. Frank blamed himself; the sledding accident had left Ted bitter, Frank believed. Frank also felt responsible for a more recent calamity. He had hired "Gimpy" Jack, a troubled hockey player, as a lumber camp night watchman. Jack fell into the bottle one evening, and subsequently the camp burned down.

These misfortunes, for which Frank faulted himself, left him insecure about his place in the family. Years later, he told a reporter about how, when an eight-day rain had washed 10 million feet of Patrick lumber down the Columbia River, Joe and his sons had raced to reclaim their treasure, with Frank and Lester defiantly hopping to the front of an acres-wide raft of logs, only to have bandits chew up the timber at their feet with a spray of bullets. As he remembered hearing the urgency in Joe's call to back away, Frank wistfully noted, "My father was afraid of losing Lester."

Now, Frank had a plan to win his father's respect and to reinvent the family business. Meeting with Lester and Joe, at home during the winter of 1911, Frank shared his dream for creating a western hockey league. Never mind that B.C.

Opening Night, 1970

Elite professional hockey returned to Vancouver when the National Hockey League's Vancouver Canucks began to play in Pacific Coliseum on Saturday, 9 October 1970. Eighty-three-year-old Cyclone Taylor, Canada's first hockey star, and a Vancouver Millionaire from 1912 to 1922, received one last hurrah from locals when he dropped the ceremonial first puck. Early Canucks games were notable for their Saturday night starting time, five o'clock, locally, so as to be in sync with *Hockey Night in Canada* contests, three time zones away in Toronto and Montreal. The team's first uniform was also unique, with a dropped hockey stick across the chest for a logo and a blue-green colour scheme that flagrantly defied every Canadian mom's fashion edict: Blue and green should never be seen, not even in a washing machine. Oh, well, it was the 1970s, a decade that recognized plaid as a primary colour. Stern, hard-working Orland Kurtenbach (number 25) was the Canucks' first captain, and oversized Saint Paddy's Day parade float Pat Quinn protected little Charlie Hodge in net. Barry Wilkins scored the first-ever Canucks goal in that first Saturday night game, which was played against the Los Angeles Kings. The Canucks' first team of TV broadcasters included Bill Good, Jim Robson and the immortal Babe Pratt.

Todd Bertuzzi and captain Marcus Naslund watch intently from the Vancouver Canucks bench.

winters weren't conducive to natural ice; the Patricks would build artificial rinks, like the ones in New York and Boston. The lifelong student of hockey also had a million ideas for how to improve the game. At the time, no forward passing was permitted in hockey, which led to frequent offsides. To address the problem, Frank proposed blue lines that would divide the ice into thirds. Forward passes would be permitted in centre ice (and eventually, everywhere). In addition, in the Patricks' league, goalies would finally be allowed to fall to stop a puck. And Frank would also introduce penalty shots; permission to change lines on the fly; and a playoff system that would reward contending teams that failed to finish first, a lucrative innovation that would be adopted by all professional leagues.

Frank also dreamed of a multiplex showcase in B.C.'s largest city, Vancouver. The arena would be bigger than Madison Square Garden, with room for 10,500 fans. The rink would also contain a commercial ice-making plant and a swimming pool, along with four curling surfaces that could be summoned like various blades on a Swiss Army knife. And the best rink in the world would be home to the best hockey players in Canada. Just look what Renfrew, a town with a fan base of 3,500, had done with the Millionaires, Frank suggested. There were 101,000 people in Vancouver alone. And a good team, a club starring Cyclone Taylor and Newsy Lalonde, say, would attract fans from nearby Burnaby and Richmond.

Joe Patrick, who had just sold his lumber company for $440,000, was thrilled by Frank's plan. Lester had reservations, though. What if Edmonton or Calgary did not want to join; could a B.C. league compete with the NHA for eastern players? And was it possible to assemble a new league, while building a set of artificial rinks—all in the space of a year? Lester voted against the proposal, but when Joe gave his blessing to Frank's dream, the eldest son became an enthusiastic backer of the Pacific Coast Hockey Association. He even bowed to Frank's desire to run the premier franchise in Vancouver. Lester would look after the Victoria club.

In the months ahead, many of Lester's fears were realized. The PCHA was a subject of ridicule in the east. The warm, wet coast just wasn't hockey country, or at least that was the prevailing wisdom. "[Old man Patrick] and the two kids must be suffering from very high fever," commented the *Montreal Star*. Fearing catastrophe, Calgary and Edmonton dropped out. The Vancouver Millionaires,

If Vancouver's new rink was not multidimensional, its owner was.

Victoria Senators and New Westminster Royals, therefore, were forced to go it alone. And only enough time and resources were available to build two artificial rinks, one in Victoria and one in Vancouver. (New Westminster would play home games at the Vancouver rink.)

Frank was so busy with his recruiting efforts, in the east, that he couldn't oversee the construction of the $270,000 Denman Arena, located near the entrance to Stanley Park—a park named after the donor of the Stanley Cup. As a result, the sports complex was not quite the architectural wonder that he had envisioned. Denman Arena contained no swimming pools or curling rinks. It was, however, a grand hockey rink, everyone agreed. And on 5 January 1912, the Vancouver team played its first game in the red brick fortress, defeating New Westminster, 8–3.

If Vancouver's new rink was not multidimensional, its 26-year-old owner was. Frank Patrick was the president of the PCHA, as well as owner-coach-star player of the Millionaires. In a 23 January 1912 game, with one eye nearly swollen shut from a whack to the head, he scored six goals, the most ever by a professional defenceman, in a 10–4 win over New Westminster. Less than 5,000 people were in attendance for the feat, however. The Victoria and Vancouver rinks were half-filled most nights, despite a roster of stars that included Newsy Lalonde and former Kenora Thistles players Tom Phillips and Si Griffis (Vancouver); the great goalie, Hughie Lehman, and Moose Johnson (New Westminster); and Bert Lindsay, Lester Patrick and Walter Smaill (Victoria).

Determined to increase audience numbers, Frank decided to play the one remaining card at his disposal. Shortly after the season began, he sent a telegram to an old friend: "Dear Fred, Having a wonderful time. Wish you were here. Frank." That off-season, Frank travelled to Ottawa to meet with Fred "Cyclone" Taylor. Taylor initially agreed to the terms Frank proposed for joining the Vancouver team, but the National Hockey Association pulled some strings on Parliament Hill, and for a while, it looked as though hockey's most exciting weather front would be staying in Ottawa. Frank then called on B.C. Premier Richard McBride, who leaned on fellow Conservative, Prime Minister Robert Borden. The following winter, the most famous player in hockey had become a Vancouver Millionaire.

With Taylor in the lineup, the Millionaires sold out their second game in the 1912–13 season, attracting close to 11,000 fans, more spectators than had ever watched a hockey game in Canada. Over the next seasons, the PCHA routinely defeated NHA clubs in challenge matches. And in 1914, Lester's Victoria Aristocrats (the renamed Senators) travelled to Toronto to take on the Blueshirts, a team that would later become the Toronto Maple Leafs, for the Stanley Cup.

Upon arrival, the Aristocrats were told that Cup trustees had not received Victoria's Stanley Cup paperwork. The games would merely be exhibition

Phil the Net

In 1945, the Vancouver Canucks received a franchise in the Pacific Coast Hockey League, winning the league championship the following season with a team that included goalie Al Rollins, a former National Hockey League most valuable player and Vezina Trophy winner. In 1952, the PCHL merged with the Western Hockey League to form a new professional loop, the Western Hockey League. The Canucks were a successful franchise for close to two decades. Johnny Bower, Andy Bathgate and Tony Esposito all played for the Canucks at one time. But, far and away, the most beloved of the WHL's Canucks was Phil Maloney, a playmaking centreman who won the league's most valuable player designation in 1956, 1962 and 1963. "The Fox," as he was known locally, enjoyed a second career as a Vancouver Canuck, coaching and managing the NHL's Vancouver Canucks in the mid-1970s.

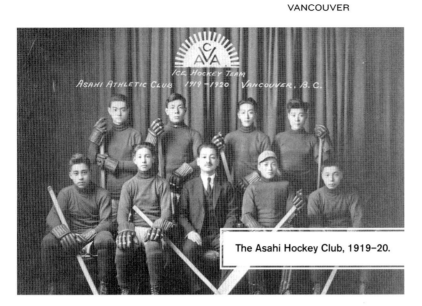

The Asahi Hockey Club, 1919–20.

ASAHI ATHLETIC CLUB

Vancouver's Asahi Athletic Club was an integral part of the city's Little Tokyo neighbourhood, and an inspiration for athletically inclined Japanese-Canadian kids throughout the Lower Mainland. The club sponsored teams in both hockey and baseball. The baseball team forged a dynasty in the Vancouver Senior City League, winning championships from 1937 to 1941. The club came to a tragic end, however, when, after Japan's 1941 bombing of Pearl Harbour, the ballplayers were among the 23,000 innocent Japanese-Canadians sent to internment camps in the interior of British Columbia and Alberta.

matches. The visitors were furious, but they played anyway. When the Blueshirts emerged victorious, however, the win was declared a Stanley Cup victory by the NHA. This after-the-fact decision infuriated the Victoria players, who figured that they had been set up to play a Stanley Cup series that they could only lose.

The Patrick brothers persevered, determined to make their league more competitive and to ensure that underhanded bureaucracy would not get in the way of a championship win. Despite being under 30, Frank had been around a hockey rink a few times, and before the 1914–15 season, he and his older brother engaged in some hockey insider trading, swapping some of the best players from the Portland Rosebuds (the replacement for the relocated New Westminster team) to the Millionaires. The PCHA's best goalie, Hugh Lehman, as well as star forward Ken Mallen and defenceman Jimmy Seaborn, became valuable Vancouver property. Frank also recruited "The Wee Scot," Duncan MacKay, a diminutive speedball from Chesley, Ontario, who could keep up with Cyclone Taylor. With these additions and the necessary Stanley Cup paperwork notarized and filed, the Millionaires were ready to welcome the NHA champion Ottawa Senators to Denman Arena for the first championship ever played in B.C.

Prior to the best-of-five series, news of the Stanley Cup finals and of the "Great War" dominated Vancouver's seven newspapers: the *Saturday Sunset*, *News Advertiser*, *Sun*, *Daily News*, *Daily Province*, *World* and the New Westminster *Columbian*. "The stage is set for what should prove one of the greatest series of hockey games ever played in Canada," the *Sun* advised readers.

The Ottawa team arrived in Vancouver on the Grand National Railway, out of Chicago, with a party of local dignitaries, led by Frank Patrick, welcoming them at the Columbia Avenue depot. In addition to all his other duties, Frank chaperoned the Senators on an automobile tour of Vancouver, taking the boys along Marine Drive, the scenic route that threads through the coast and the mountains of West Vancouver. He also made sure that the visitors had their picture taken beside the "Big Tree" in Stanley Park.

For the series opener, Vancouver furnished extra tram cars to ferry what amounted to 10 percent of local citizens to the game. Jitneys (taxicabs) and horse-drawn carriages also did a brisk business in the hour prior to the 8:30 p.m. start, dropping off spectators with prepaid $1.50, $1 and 75-cent tickets by the mob pressing toward the Player's cigarettes window for 50-cent rush seats.

Paul Kariya with the Anaheim Mighty Ducks in 2003 action.

Comeback Stories

Paul Kariya's grandparents, Isamu and Fumiko, were taken by military police from their Vancouver home in June 1942 and brought to an internment camp in Greenwood, a depleted mining town 180 miles east of Vancouver. Paul's father, Tetsuhiko, or T.K., was born there in 1943. The Kariyas (along with 10 other families) lived in what had been an abandoned Greenwood hotel for six years. Isamu worked on a road crew, earning 25 cents an hour alongside Caucasians who received 60 cents for similar work. The Kariyas didn't dwell on the "enemy alien" days of their unjust internment. And T.K. went on to play rugby for the University of British Columbia and for Canada's national team.

T.K.'s son Paul Tetsuhiko Kariya, born in 1974, was a hockey prodigy, playing at age nine against 14-year-olds, a circumstance that invited comparisons between him and his childhood hero, Wayne Gretzky. Paul even tried to skate like Gretzky, racing down the ice bent at the waist, as if playing hockey in a low-ceilinged room. At age 19, Paul joined the University of Maine Black Bears, helping the team to its first national championship and—in 1993, during his freshman year—winning the Hobey Baker Award as the best college player. Two years later, he scored 50 goals for the National Hockey League's Anaheim Mighty Ducks. A fluid skater, with an extra forward gear he could resort to inside the enemy blue line, Kariya also possessed superior rink vision; like Gretzky, he could imagine and respond to unfolding plays in a manner that eluded mortal players.

After helping Canada to a world championship in the 2002 Olympics—with a goal in the gold medal game—Paul displayed the perseverance that defined the Kariya family in a 2003 Stanley Cup final game against the New Jersey Devils. Kariya had been battling concussions for five seasons, and when Devils defenceman Scott Stevens caught him with his head down in this game, he hit the ice like a felled tree. A half-minute later, Kariya twitched awake. Still, as teammates carried him off the ice, the forward's legs weren't working. That was it for the rest of the series, spectators figured. They didn't know the Kariyas. Incredibly, Paul returned minutes later to a great ovation from home fans, and on his second shift, he found the puck and room up the left boards. Once inside the Devils' blue line, he fell into a slapshot, his stick coming down like a scythe, propelling the blurred slapshot over goalie Martin Brodeur's outstretched glove for a heroic, game-winning goal.

Paul's brothers Steve and Martin also went on to play professional hockey, with Martin's hockey adventures offering a satisfying late chapter to the Kariya family story. Isamu and Fumiko Kariya were almost deported to Japan from Canada in 1949. Decades later, their grandson Martin Tetsuya Kariya would be taken there by hockey, when in 2005, he signed a contract with Japan's HC Nikko Icebucks.

When Millionaires forward Barney Stanley scored on Ottawa's Clint Benedict halfway through the first period of game one, the Vancouver News Advertiser reported, "The crowd rose en masse. Cheer after cheer went up and the players responded with ever greater effort, and during the remainder of the session they traveled at terrific speed, with play first at one end and then at the other."

The Senators couldn't keep up for long. In creating the PCHA, Frank and Lester Patrick fashioned a fast, unceasing brand of hockey, and the unstinting pressure would catch up with the Senators late in all of the Denman Arena

It was, however, a grand hockey rink, everyone agreed.

encounters. In game one, Cyclone Taylor breezed through Ottawa's defence for two goals, while Frank Patrick also tallied. The Wee Scot, Duncan MacKay, completed the scoring in the third period, "threading through the entire Ottawa team," in the words of the *Vancouver Province*, to make the final score Vancouver 6, Ottawa 2. In the next contest, Ottawa forged an early 2–0 lead, but again, the team crumbled late in the game, as Cyclone Taylor thrilled fans with three goals in an 8–3 Millionaires win. The third and deciding game was more than PCHA architect-president-owner-coach-player Frank Patrick might have dreamed of, back in Nelson, B.C., when he had talked his family into a new western hockey league: With much of Vancouver and his family present (except for long-lost brother Ted), the Vancouver Millionaires trounced the Senators, 12–3, winning the 1915 Stanley Cup in three straight games by a margin of 26 to five goals.

Frank was higher than nearby Mount Garibaldi, after bringing Vancouver and British Columbia their first Stanley Cup.

The National Hockey League moved into the big northeast cities of the United States, ushering in an era of unprecedented prosperity for the eastern league, and the PCHA could not keep up. The Patricks wisely sold players to recoup much of their investment. The Portland Rosebuds became the NHL's Chicago Blackhawks, while the Victoria Cougars (formerly the Aristocrats) evolved into the NHL's Detroit Red Wings.

Lester Patrick would successfully manage the NHL's New York Rangers for more than two decades, earning the nickname "The Silver Fox" while winning the Stanley Cup in 1928, 1933 and 1940. Sadly, however, Frank Patrick's hockey dreams stopped coming true after the PCHA. He coached the NHL's Boston Bruins, but couldn't get along with general manager Art Ross, who formerly had been a good friend from way back in Montreal. A management job with the league's Montreal Canadiens didn't work out, either. Frank started drinking late in life: The sledding accident that had forever damaged the life of his younger brother Ted seemed to take an even greater hold of Frank in his final decades.

Not that the great hockey man ever stopped hatching plans for new empires. Frank lost a fortune, looking for oil both in B.C.'s Cariboo Country and in northern Alberta's Peace River region. (Ironically, oil would later be discovered in both locations.) He also tried, prematurely, to interest the Canadian government in a scheme for postal codes that would modernize letter delivery. Then, there were the plans for outdoor domed stadiums—designs that littered his desk decades before the Houston Astrodome opened in 1966.

Frank Patrick died broke. If accomplishments are counted as riches, however, the man who established hockey in British Columbia remains forever a Vancouver Millionaire.

Hockey's greatest innovator, Frank Patrick, with the Vancouver Millionaires in 1911.

The World's Tallest Totem Pole, Victoria, 1950s.

VICTORIA

FOUNDED

Victoria was first settled in 1843 as a trading post by the Hudson's Bay Company. In 1858, the young port town was transformed into a booming gateway to British Columbia, when thousands of speculators arrived by steamers on their way to gold discovered on the mainland. When B.C. became the sixth province of the Dominion of Canada in 1871, Victoria was named the province's capital. Today, Victoria is primarily a government, retirement and tourism centre.

NATIVE-BORN NHL PLAYERS

Don Barber, Jeff Batters, David Brumby, Bruce Cowick, Jesse Fibiger, Ron Grahame, Mike Green, Richard Hajdu, Rick Lapointe, Darryl Maggs, Lynn Patrick, Muzz Patrick, Joe Reekie, Geordie Robertson, Torrie Robertson, Mike Stutzel

FAMOUS LOCAL TEAMS

Junior: Victoria Cougars, Victoria Salsa; **Senior-pro:** Victoria Aristocrats, Victoria Army, Victoria Cougars, Victoria Cubs, Victoria Maple Leafs, Victoria RCAF Seahawks, Victoria Salmon Kings, Victoria Senators, Victoria Navy

CURRENT POPULATION

335,000

Christmas Skating Party

Buffered by Pacific Ocean waters that hover eternally at 50°F, Victoria enjoys relatively mild winters that occasionally refuse to dip below freezing. In the first decade of the 20th century, citizens of the province's capital city could be found golfing or sailing over the Christmas season. Hockey existed only in the muscle memory of transplanted Easterners.

Elsewhere in B.C., the sport was played intermittently by raw though enthusiastic recruits. When Lester Patrick, former star defenceman of the National Hockey Association's Montreal Wanderers, arrived in Nelson, B.C., in 1907, to help his Quebec family establish a lumber business in the province's interior, he was approached by a senior team in the Kootenay League. That December, Patrick suited up for the Nelson Victorias in a match against the rival Nelson Thistles. Playing in front of a boisterous crowd of 500 spectators, jammed together on the sagging wooden stands of an outdoor rink, the Victorias won, 5–0. Patrick, just coasting, scored all five goals.

Four years later, the Patricks turned from lumber to the hockey business (see page 356). In a summit meeting that took place in the family home on Edgewood Avenue in Victoria, Frank Patrick, Lester's hockey-playing brother, talked their father, Joe, a born adventurer, into turning most of the $440,000 that had come from the sale of the Patrick Lumber Company into a West Coast professional hockey league. Canada's westernmost province was ready for hockey, Frank insisted. All that was needed was ice—artificial ice. The plan had the Patricks building two artificial arenas—one in Vancouver, the other in Victoria—for three provincial city teams: the Victoria Senators, the Vancouver Millionaires and the New Westminster Royals (New Westminster would play on the nearby Vancouver rink).

The obvious problem with the plan was that the Patricks didn't know how to make artificial ice. No one in Canada did. In 1911, there were perhaps a dozen warm weather ice-skating rinks in the world, all outside Canada: Six in the United States, and the remainder in London, Paris, Melbourne, Nice and Vienna. Making matters more difficult, the Patricks hoped to have the rinks built in a mere nine months, in time to open the Pacific Coast Hockey Association in early 1912.

As it happened, Lester was married on the afternoon of 9 March 1911 to Grace Linn, of Nanaimo, B.C. The eldest brother decreed that he would have to take a break from the Patricks' hockey empire, to provide his bride with a proper honeymoon. Not necessarily, Frank countered, offering his brother and sister-in-law a round-trip honeymoon vacation from Victoria to Boston, Detroit, Cleveland and Pittsburgh. When Grace discovered that these cities all had recently constructed artificial rinks, she put her foot down. Boston would be lovely, but she wasn't about to spend her honeymoon on an engineer's tour of refrigeration units.

And so, the newlyweds travelled to Boston shortly after their wedding, to celebrate their nuptials—and to inspect the Boston Arena. Upon arriving in New England, Lester was tickled to learn that some of his old friends from the Montreal Wanderers and Ottawa Senators would be playing an exhibition series in the arena days later. What is more, promoters hadn't recruited an official for the game. Ever the entrepreneur, Lester offered his services for $50 a game (which was more than what players were receiving). The promoters were furious, but entirely out of options.

It is hoped that Mrs. Patrick didn't travel with Lester into the bowels of the Boston Arena, for artificial rinks at the time were refined models of the 1876 London Glacarium, the world's first warm-weather ice rink. And inspecting the Glacarium's cooling system would be as much fun as visiting a tannery. The rink's floor was six inches of concrete covered with four inches of dry earth and a half-foot of packed cow hair. On top of this base, builders then packed thick timber planks, lathered with tarred animal hair, with a network of copper pipes laid on top of the gooey fur. In a nearby machine room, a pounding steam engine turned sulphuric acid into a condensed liquid, fuelling a vast refrigeration

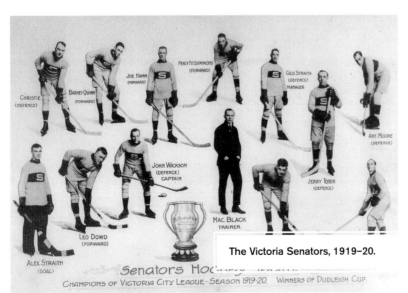

The Victoria Senators, 1919–20.

Cougars Out-Fly Frenchmen

Frank and Lester Patrick made hockey better by making it faster. The brothers' first league, the Pacific Coast Hockey Association (1912–21), introduced the forward pass. Lester's Western Canadian Hockey League Cougars (1921–25) were the first team to change on the go, with fresh troops hopping the boards as spent teammates returned to the bench through the player's gate. When the National Hockey Association's Montreal Canadiens travelled west to take on the Cougars for the Stanley Cup in the spring of 1925, even The Flying Frenchmen couldn't keep up with Victoria. Like all eastern teams, the Canadiens waited for an official break to change lines. Players sometimes endured seven-minute shifts. The Cougars might have twice changed lines by then. Montreal skaters were reported to have resembled gaffed salmon by the third period of a 5–2 first-game loss to Victoria. The Canadiens were again outplayed in game two of the best-of-five series, as Victoria skated to a 3–1 win. The Canadiens threw themselves into the next encounter, with Howie Morenz scoring three goals in a 4–2 victory, but the Quebec team had nothing left for the following match, losing 6–1. Stars of the last B.C. team to win the Stanley Cup included Hall of Fame goalie Harry "Hap" Holmes and two Icelandic-Canadians from Winnipeg, Frank Frederickson, the WCHL's top goal scorer, and "Slim" Halderson. Both Frederickson and Halderson performed on the senior Winnipeg Falcons team that won the World Hockey championship in 1920 (see page 232).

unit, which in turn cooled a chemical solution that flew through the pipes in the rink floor.

With his tour of the arena complete, Lester Patrick refereed the exhibition games and enjoyed a splendid meal—along with his wife—at the invitation of his old teammate Cyclone Taylor, before returning by train to Victoria. He had plenty of work to do. The Victoria franchise was Lester's, and he would now have to oversee the hurried construction of an arena to be built on six lots, purchased for $10,000, at the corner of Cadboro Bay Road and Epworth Street in Oak Bay, a suburb of Victoria. Lester considered the price outrageous. But then, Victoria was in the midst of a land boom. Subdivisions in Fairfield and Quadra were opening up, and nearby Esquimalt was expanding its naval base. Published reports suggested that the city's population might jump from 25,000 to 125,000 in three years' time. Properties bought for $4,000 on a Saturday were being flipped for $5,500 by the following Monday.

The 3,500-seat Willows Arena, which jumped to life on schedule and in record time, packed cow hair and all, cost the Patricks $110,000, a fortune in those days. But Canada's first artificial rink was ready for its grand public opening on Christmas Day 1911. The day itself was a glorious advertisement for Victoria—a warm Tuesday in late December, with the surrounding Pacific a royal blue that mirrored the high, cloudless sky. Curious citizens dressed in fine church clothes arrived at the arena on the Willows streetcar, while wealthier citizens arrived by horse-drawn carriage. More than 800 skaters arrived at the Willows Arena that afternoon; more citizens, including Lt. Gov. Thomas William Paterson, showed up just to watch and listen. A brass band from the Canadian navy base at Esquimalt was on hand to provide waltz music, although little of what transpired on the ice could be described as dancing.

"The great majority of those attending had never even worn skates, a fact that caused a record run on the city's sporting goods shops and, later, the household medicine cabinets," Eric Whitehead reported in his book, *The Patricks: Hockey's Royal Family.* "The big crowds watching from the seats

General manager Lester Patrick famously stepped out of the executive suite to successfully tend goal for the New York Rangers in the 1928 Stanley Cup finals.

probably had more fun than those on the ice, where skaters engaged in a hilarious melee, with bodies all over the ice and strewn around in piles. Some of the smarter ones wobbled their uncertain way around the ice surface clutching the boards while the band played on. As one local newspaperman described the scene, 'You could tell who the Easterners were. They were the ones standing up.'"

Lester and Frank Patrick's West Coast hockey empire remained standing for a dozen years (1912–25). And Lester Patrick became Victoria's most celebrated hockey citizen, winning a Stanley Cup for the city, in 1925, as coach of the Western Canadian Hockey League's Victoria Cougars, and raising two children, Muzz and Lynn Patrick, who themselves would play in the National Hockey League. Muzz and Lynn would, in fact, play for their father, the first coach and general manager of the NHL's New York Rangers. Lester Patrick

"If you hope to have hockey next season, you will accept these intangibles as contracts and pay me my money."

joined the NHL in the fall of 1926, after he and brother Frank folded their league, selling five teams (Victoria, Vancouver, Calgary, Edmonton and Saskatoon) to emerging American franchises in the National Hockey League for close to $400,000 U.S.

Just how Lester pulled off the going-out-of-business sale to the NHL offers some insight into the man whose name would become synonymous with Victoria hockey. The Patricks didn't own the players in the Western Canadian Hockey League. The league had no reserve clause. Players would be free agents when teams folded. But like the eminently proper city he represented, Lester Patrick was a distinguished, respectable figure. When, in a Montreal boardroom, lawyers for the Detroit club asked to see contracts proving that the Patricks owned the rights to the players they hoped to sell to the Detroit, Chicago, Boston and New York franchises, Lester Patrick smoothed his trousers and stood up from the table. "Gentlemen, I have no papers," author Eric Whitehead quotes him as saying. "All I have is my word and, hopefully, your good will. Now, if you hope to have hockey…next season, you will accept these intangibles as contracts and pay me my money. If not, I will forget the entire arrangement and withdraw my players."

A half-hour later, Lester Patrick strolled from the Montreal meeting with a quarter-million dollars. The Victoria Cougars would become the NHL's Detroit Cougars (and, eventually, the Detroit Red Wings). Patrick, himself, joined the New York Rangers in the 1925–26 season—for the astronomical sum of $18,000. He would stay with the team for two decades and three Stanley Cups before returning to retire, like so many other Canadians, in Victoria. Hockey was in his blood, however. And upon returning for good to his home city, he became the owner (until 1954) of the Pacific Coast Western Hockey League's Victoria Cougars.

Since 1966, the NHL has honoured significant contributors to hockey in the U.S. with the Lester Patrick Award. In Canada, his legacy includes the artificial arenas that allow hockey to be played year-round in more than just British Columbia. A recent study by the Canadian Electricity Association suggests that there are now 2,327 ice arenas and 1,322 curling rinks in Canada that take advantage of the artificial ice technology brought to this country by honeymooner Lester Patrick.

"Harry, I'm going in goal!"

A theatrical figure who was often compared to John Barrymore, the great actor and unapologetic ham, Lester Patrick liked to invite reporters into his office, where he offered grand soliloquies on epic hockey moments, throwing himself about the room to illustrate his tales.

Patrick himself made hockey history in the 1928 Stanley Cup finals. Lorne Chabot, goalie for the Rangers, was felled by a shot from Montreal Maroons forward Nels Stewart. The Rangers didn't carry a spare goalie, and the NHL refused to allow the team to use Ottawa Senators netminder Alec Connell, who was in attendance at the Montreal Forum. The Rangers were given 10 minutes either to come up with a substitute or forfeit the game, at which point Patrick announced to New York's trainer Harry Westerby, "Harry, I'm going in goal!" The 44-year-old manager-coach then donned unfamiliar goalie equipment (as well as a toque) and skated out between the pipes in what was a scoreless game. He was brilliant and, of course, very dramatic—shouting and gesturing to teammates between kick saves. Patrick allowed only a single goal in two periods. To make the story better, the game went into overtime, with a Frank Boucher goal giving the Rangers a win. The tale of Patrick's unexpected heroics instantly entered into hockey folklore. His performance also helped the New York Rangers to their first Stanley Cup.

THE TER

Opening Spread: Jordin
Tootoo of the Nashville
Predators, 2004.

Sir John Franklin, 1830.

The first recorded hockey game in northern Canada took place near Deline (formerly Fort Franklin) on the western shore of Great Bear Lake when, in 1825, members of Sir John Franklin's expedition took time to strap on skates and knock around the plug from a rum barrel (see page 377). Franklin's report of this game was filed in a letter to a colleague in Britain. "Until the day before yesterday, 20th October, we had comparatively little snow," Franklin wrote to Victorian geologist Roderick Murchison. "We endeavour to keep ourselves in good humour, health and spirits by an agreeable variety of useful occupation and amusement. Till the snow fell, the game of hockey, played on the ice, was the morning's sport."

Despite sure proof that there was a hockey "morning" in Fort Franklin early in the 19th century, *Hockey Night in Canada* did not arrive in the North until 1967, Canada's centennial year. The game did not arrive on Saturday night, however, as it did in the rest of the country. Instead, the CBC sent a "frontier package"—four hours of highlight coverage—northward every day. The packages sometimes took a week to circulate throughout the region. And as one viewer put it, in a complaint to the CBC, "There's nothing like a week-old [National Hockey League] hockey game...to make you feel a part of the nation."

Frontier packages ended in 1973, when the Anik satellite was launched, bringing full network coverage to Canada's North—Nunavut, the Northwest Territories and the Yukon. (Today, CBC North broadcasts in four different time zones and 10 languages—English, French, Inuktitut, North and South Slavey, Dogrib, Chipewyan, Inuvialuktun, Gwich'in and Cree.) *Hockey Night in Canada* travelled to Nunavut in 2002, at which time the show's stars, Don Cherry and Ron MacLean, visited Iqaluit.

Hockey is now played across Canada's North, and tournament play with southern teams is increasingly common. Team Kivalliq and Team Baffin annually compete for the right to compete at the Maritime-Northern Canadian Junior C Championship. And many other northern tournaments are held, including the Arctic Circle Cup and the Avataq Cup.

According to Hockey Canada, close to 1,000 young hockey players are enrolled in amateur hockey in the North. These kids can watch *Hockey Night in Canada* at the same time as everyone else in the country. Perhaps the best proof of the growth of hockey in the North comes in the inspirational presence of Rankin Inlet's Jordin Tootoo, the first Inuk to make the NHL—hockey's first true Northern Light.

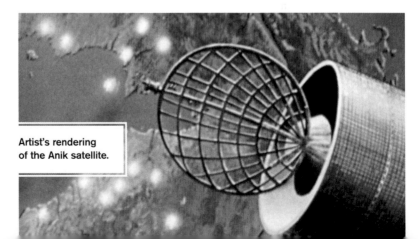

Artist's rendering
of the Anik satellite.

DAWSON CITY

FOUNDED

Named after George M. Dawson, who explored the Yukon for the Canadian government in 1887, Dawson City, at the juncture of the Yukon and Klondike Rivers, was a First Nations fishing camp until gold was discovered nearby in 1886. A decade later, Dawson City was the largest city in Canada west of Winnipeg, with a population of 40,000. The First Nations people in the region immediately moved downriver to Moosehide, when outsiders began to arrive in droves. The gold rush brought dance halls, telephone service (eventually) and fancy hotels with steam heat.

Industrialist-philanthropist Andrew Carnegie donated $25,000 toward the building of a library. The rush ended in the summer of 1899, when 8,000 prospectors departed the Yukon for adventure elsewhere. By then, large mining operations had taken over the Klondike gold beds. Today, gold mining and tourism are the city's main industries.

NATIVE-BORN NHL PLAYERS
Not applicable

FAMOUS LOCAL TEAMS
Junior: none; **Senior-pro:** Dawson City Klondikers

CURRENT POPULATION
1,251

Front Street, Dawson City, Yukon Territory.

The Klondikers

Much has been made of the arduous trek the all-star Dawson City Klondikers undertook in travelling to Ottawa to challenge for the 1905 Stanley Cup, a 23-day journey that began with a 10-day walk to Whitehorse. But the Klondikers probably weren't as put out by the journey as one might expect, for the trip to Ottawa wasn't as difficult as the players' race to join the Yukon gold rush had been six or seven years earlier.

In the summer of 1897, 68 tired but very rich men climbed off a boat in San Francisco, their knapsacks heavy with precious stones gathered near Dawson City. "Gold! Gold! Gold! Gold!" shouted a newspaper headline the next day. Golden nuggets studded the banks of the Yukon and Klondike Rivers like raisins in a pudding, the paper reported. Soon, prospectors from around the world poured north to the Yukon in search of fortune.

One of those searchers was Albert Forrest, future goalie for the Klondikers. Albert was 11 when his father sold everything in Trois-Rivières, Quebec, securing passage for his family on the Canadian Pacific Railway to British Columbia, where the Forrests fought their way through the Rocky Mountains on foot, joining thousands of dreamers in a slow-moving column up the Chilkoot Pass.

Most of the trekkers would have disputed the accuracy of the term "pass" upon arriving at the summit, a near perpendicular 12-storey block of ice. Hundreds turned back. Some tumbled to their death. But many more rode the bottom of their trousers down the other side, picking themselves up in a forest beside a lake. There they camped in a tent city, hacking down trees that were quickly lashed into timber rafts. Then, the race really began: 550 miles along the brawling Yukon River to stake a claim in the Klondike gold fields.

In Dawson City, there were 50,000 people, many of them as wild as the rapids that carried them into town. There was "Diamond Tooth" Gertie, a dance-hall girl with a gem in her tooth, and "Swiftwater" Bill Gates, who bought up

Albert Forrest in camp, ca. 1920. This photo was taken during a boat trip from Milk River, via the Missouri and the Mississippi, to the Gulf of Mexico.

Dawson Creek challenged for the Stanley Cup in 1904, making an epic trek across the continent to lose to the Ottawa Silver Seven. Top row (left-right) Hector Smith, George Kennedy, Lorne Hannay, Jim Johnstone, Norm Watt. Bottom row (left-right) Albert Forrest, Joe Boyle and Randy McLellan.

Joe Boyle (left) and Swiftwater Bill Gates on their way to Dawson City, date unknown.

every chicken in town when his sweetie (who liked eggs for breakfast) announced they had split up. Bill and thousands of other Stampeders worked the narrow tributaries off the Yukon and Klondike, streams with tantalizing names such as Bonanza Creek, El Dorado Creek and Too Much Gold Creek.

A year later, in 1899, the gold rush was pretty much over. The best sites were being worked by established mining outfits, and 8,000 prospectors left the Yukon that summer. Dawson City became more civilized, as evidenced by the participants in a four-team civic hockey league that sprang up in 1901. One club consisted of members of the Royal Canadian Mounted Police; another was made up of civil service employees. A third team was known as the Dawson Amateur Athletic Association. Lastly, there were the Eagles.

The league played its first season on natural rinks carved out of the fast-frozen Yukon River, even though unholy winds kept interest down in January and February. The following winter, in 1902, the DAAA constructed the first enclosed rink west of Manitoba. Here, players and fans soon began talking about the Stanley Cup, and in 1903, sheriff Jack Eilbeck, president of the Civil Service Athletic Club, issued a challenge to the national champions, the Ottawa Silver Seven.

Dawson City had some reason to think it belonged on the same ice as the famed Ottawa side. Weldy Young, a former star on the Silver Seven, was working a claim on Lower Dominion Creek just outside town. And Lionel Bennett of the Civil Service team had been a star in Nova Scotia senior hockey. Dr. Randy McLennan, another Civil Service star, had played for the Stanley Cup as a member of the Queen's University team.

In September of 1904, the Stanley Cup trustees accepted Eilbeck's proposal. Unfortunately for Sheriff Jack, he was no longer running the Civil Service Athletic Club. He had been fired for trying to steal the local baseball championships—offering civil service jobs to candidates whose only qualifications for clerical work was an ability to smack a baseball halfway to Whitehorse.

Joe Boyle, self-proclaimed King of the Klondike, took over managing the team. That November Boyle began to select an all-star team, with Weldy Young overseeing workouts. In addition to Young, Bennett and McLennan, hotheaded Norman Watt (formerly of Aylmer, Quebec), George "Old Sureshot" Kennedy and Hector Smith of Selkirk, Manitoba, eventually made the team, now called the Dawson City Klondikers. In goal, Young turned to 18-year-old Albert Forrest, who had never played the position but had won most of the skating races at the 1903 Dawson City Winter Carnival.

The team left Dawson City on 19 December 1904, to cheering crowds. A few hours later, the trouble started.

North West Mounted Police, some in costume, playing hockey in Dawson City, c. 1890s.

The play of the Klondikers impressed everyone in the city. And a dozen players who hadn't made the team organized a second all-star club to challenge the Klondikers when they returned to Dawson City with the Stanley Cup.

Unfortunately, days before the Klondikers were to leave for Ottawa, the team received a double dose of bad news when it was discovered that its best players—Young and Bennett—couldn't make the trip. Young had a job conflict, and Bennett feared for the health of his wife, who had been dragged half a block by a runaway sleigh the previous winter. Lorne Hannay, who was playing senior hockey in Brandon, Manitoba, and a reserve, Archie Martin, were chosen in their place.

The Klondikers' travel itinerary had been carefully coordinated. The team was to dogsled the new overland route to Whitehorse; catch a train to Skagway, Alaska; then board a boat for Vancouver, British Columbia, where a Pullman coach would carry the players across the country to Ottawa. The team left Dawson City on 19 December 1904, to cheering crowds. A few hours later, the trouble started.

There was no snow on the pass to Whitehorse and dogsleds were useless. The Klondikers had to walk. The *Ottawa Journal* reported, "The first day the Klondikers covered 46 miles, the second 41. The third day saw some of them struggling to cover 36 miles, some suffering with blistered feet. To proceed, these had to remove their boots. It may give an idea of the hardship they faced when it is recorded that the temperature went down to 20 degrees below zero [towards the end of their march]."

Ten days after leaving Dawson City, the team arrived in Whitehorse to discover that a violent snowstorm had caused an avalanche outside the city. The team missed its steamship at Skagway and so dawdled for three days in the Alaskan harbour (drinking heavily, it was rumoured) before catching a second steamship that became lost in heavy seas and fog, travelling past Vancouver to Seattle and forcing another delay. Eventually, the Klondikers found their Pullman coach and whistled across the country, picking up substitute Lorne Hannay in Winnipeg, before pulling into Ottawa 11 days late and 48 hours before their best two-out-of-three Stanley Cup series was scheduled to begin.

Newspapers across North America and as far away as Europe were full of stories of the Klondikers' 23-day travel nightmare, whipping up interest in the championship series. According to the *Ottawa Journal*, crowds cramming Dey Rink on Gladstone Avenue were "hysterical." And Governor General Earl Grey was among the sellout crowd who saw the barber pole-striped Silver Seven take on a Klondike team dressed in black sweaters trimmed with Yukon gold.

Games, at the time, consisted of two 30-minute periods, and the Klondikers were down only 3-1 after the first half, thanks largely to the nimble work of Albert Forrest. But in the second half, the Klondikers "faded away like a snowball beneath a June sun," as the *Toronto Telegram* put it, losing 9–2.

Dawson City was unbowed in defeat. The team's Norman Watt had clubbed Ottawa's Alf Smith late in the game. And manager Joe Boyle complained about bad refereeing in a dispatch to the *Dawson Daily News*. "We'll be ready next game," he assured readers back home.

Echoing this confident tone, Watt, loitering at a local saloon, was overheard by a reporter to say of Silver Seven superstar Frank McGee, "Who the hell's McGee? He don't look like much."

McGee—nursing a broken wrist—had coasted that first game, scoring a single goal. To do more, given Ottawa's overwhelming advantage, seemed risky and ungallant, he must have figured. Having heard Watt's curt dismissal, however, McGee became more industrious, scoring 14 goals in a 23–2 drubbing of Dawson City. At one point, the legendary Ottawa forward (see page 162) counted eight goals in as many minutes, four of them in 140 seconds, racing around the Klondikers as if they were so many pylons in a skating drill. The *Ottawa Citizen* summed up the Klondikers' predicament the following day. In facing a truly inspired Frank McGee, "Dawson had the chance of a bun in the hands of a hungry small boy."

Having lost the Stanley Cup, the Klondikers continued on their eastern tour, travelling to the Maritimes before doubling back to Quebec, venturing down into Pennsylvania, up through Ontario and on into Manitoba. At one point, they played 12 games in as many nights. The team won as often as it lost—thanks in part to Weldy Young, who had joined the team in Montreal. Overall, Dawson City won 11 games and lost 13 on its eastern tour.

When the 24-game expedition was over, the team retraced its journey and went home. On 5 April 1905, five players arrived in Whitehorse and decided to walk the remaining 400 miles back to Dawson City. Albert Forrest was the first to arrive, receiving a hero's welcome home.

The Klondikers' trip, an epic tale of enterprise and bravado, was widely covered by the press of the day. At one point, the media reported that the King of the Klondike, Joe Boyle, had made a fortune on the expedition. If so, the players never saw any of the loot. The Yukon team did, however, make hockey history. The Ottawa Silver Seven-Dawson series is among the most famous Stanley Cups ever played. And Dawson City's gruelling journey through avalanche and storms will forever be part of Canadian hockey lore.

BOYLE TELLS HOW KLONDIKERS LOST

Newspaper headline of "Klondikers" story, *Dawson Daily News*, 17 January 1905.

The King of the Klondike's Queen

Joe Boyle, the manager of the Dawson City team that challenged for the 1905 Stanley Cup, was variously known as the "King of the Klondike" and "Captain Boyle". Born in Toronto, Boyle was a lifelong adventurer. While in the Yukon, the "captain" navigated prospectors along the wild, frothing Whitehorse River. A decade later, he financed his own machine-gun company in World War I. He claimed to have attempted a rescue of the Romanovs, the Russian royal family, from the Bolsheviks in 1917. A year later, he had an affair with Queen Marie of Romania, who wrote in her diary, "Boyle's relentless energy and almost hypnotic power over others—I never saw such a man, such willpower…" In his time, Boyle would receive the Distinguished Service Order and the Order of the Star of Romania. Alas, the Stanley Cup eluded him.

DELINE

Winter view of Fort Franklin (1825), from a watercolour painting by George Back.

FOUNDED

Located just south of the Arctic Circle on the western shore of Great Bear Lake, in the Northwest Territories, Deline (pronounced De-le-na) is the home of the Sahtu Dene people. The town's name means "where the water flows," in the Slavey language. Deline was formally adopted as the community name in 1993. Before that time, Canadians called the town Fort Franklin, after Sir John Franklin, the famed British explorer who crossed Great Bear Lake in 1825. During World War II, the Canadian government took over the Eldorado Mine at nearby Port Radium and began producing uranium for a secret American nuclear bomb project. Dene villagers were employed to carry radioactive material—as a result of which, many of them would die of cancer several decades later. The first school was built in Deline in 1952. Winters in the town begin in October and last until May; in summer, temperatures can rise to 30°C.

Great Bear Lake is among the most highly regarded fishing destinations in North America. In 2001, one angler landed a 74-pound lake trout.

NATIVE-BORN NHL PLAYERS
None

FAMOUS LOCAL TEAMS
Junior: Deline Little Chiefs

CURRENT POPULATION
625

A Useful Occupation and Amusement

Depiction of Franklin's expedition on Great Slave Lake, 1821, artist unknown.

In the late summer of 1825, legendary British explorer Sir John Franklin led a crew of British seamen, French-Canadian voyageurs and a handful of Aboriginal hunters, along with assorted wives and children, to an embankment on the west shore of Great Bear Lake, just south of the Arctic Circle. Upon raising a silk Union Jack, Franklin proposed that the new settlement be called Fort Reliance. His entourage, which numbered close to 50, vehemently opposed the suggestion. The only proper name for the camp, they insisted, was Fort Franklin.

The explorer was overcome, not simply because of the affectionate tribute from his command: His ailing wife had sewn the flag that now stiffened in the breeze, presenting it to him just before he'd left Liverpool, England, that spring; weeks later, Franklin received word that she had died.

Self-reliance was an attribute that Franklin valued highly. In his accounts of the 1825 expedition, the explorer expounded on the value of physical activity in battling the ennui that came with winter isolation. He urged his men "to play any game they might choose; and on these occasions they were invariably joined by the officers… By thus participating in their amusements the men became more attached to us, at the same time that we contributed to their health and cheerfulness. The hearts and feelings of the whole party were united in one common desire to make the time pass as agreeably as possible to each other, until the return of spring should enable them to resume the great object of the Expedition."

At Fort Franklin, many of the group's activities took place on what Franklin referred to as "the little lake," later to be called Grey Goose Lake—a lagoon

The Deline Little Chiefs.

The Sahtu Cup

Every November when Great Bear Lake freezes, the ice is cleared for the citizens of Deline to begin playing hockey. The best local peewee team, the Deline Little Chiefs, won the Sahtu Cup for the third year in a row, in 2004. *Sahtu* **is the word used by the local Aboriginal people, the Sahtu Dene, to refer to Great Bear Lake. The Deline Little Chiefs compete with other teams in the Northwest Territories, working with local senior and old-timers' hockey teams to raise funds for weekend-long trips to Norman Wells and Hay River.**

connected by a canal to the wide and sprawling Great Bear Lake. Located 300 yards beyond the fort and infinitely better behaved than the unpredictable Great Bear waterway, Little Lake was where Franklin's "Esquimaux" fished for salmon, trout and northern pike, and where the company's four Chipewyan hunters tracked migrating caribou late in the summer. After the lake froze in mid-October, Franklin's party was once startled to see a white wolf tear off across the ice and take down a slip-sliding fox.

When the ice was thick enough to walk on, Franklin's men, women and children took to Little Lake wearing skates strapped to their boots. Historians have surmised that the blades either were fashioned by the fort's blacksmith, or made from moose bone, perhaps even from animal antlers.

"Until the 20th October, we had comparatively little snow," Franklin wrote to a friend in the fall of 1825. "We endeavour to keep in good humour, health and spirits by and agreeable variety of useful occupation and amusement. Till the snow fell, the game of hockey, played on the ice, was the morning's sport." The coupling of the words "ice" and "hockey" in Franklin's letter is one of the earliest references to Canada's national sport on record. The Little Lake game, which was played by Europeans, Aboriginal peoples, French-Canadian voyageurs, perhaps even women and children, doesn't weaken the contention that hockey first became a collective pastime in Nova Scotia and a formal sport in Montreal. But this early record of a rustic form of hockey does suggest that the urge to escape winter's confinement by flying across the ice on winged blades, whipping clubs in hand, one team against another, proved irresistible to almost everyone who came to explore Canada.

RANKIN INLET

FOUNDED

Despite its sparse population, the territory of Nunavut has been inhabited continuously for 4,000 years by the Inuit. *Nunavut* means "our land" in Inuktitut, the language of the Inuit. The first recorded visit by Europeans to Nunavut came in 1576: British explorer Martin Frobisher thought he'd discovered gold at Iqaluit while searching for the illusory Northwest Passage to India. After Iqaluit (formerly Frobisher Bay), Rankin Inlet is the largest city in Nunavut. Located on the western shore of Hudson Bay, Rankin Inlet was originally a mining town. Between 1957 and 1962, nickel and copper were mined here by the Inuit. The community began to flourish in the 1970s, when the government of the Northwest Territories moved its regional headquarters here. In 1999, when the Canadian territory of Nunavut was created, Rankin Inlet became recognized as a Nunavut community. Seventy-nine percent of the citizens of Rankin Inlet are Inuit.

NATIVE-BORN NHL PLAYERS

Jordin Tootoo (born in Churchill, MB)

FAMOUS LOCAL TEAMS

Senior-pro: Team Killavaq

CURRENT POPULATION

2,058

Exploring Rankin Inlet, 1893.

Two Two

When most kids in Canada want a snack, they can walk or bike to the corner store for chips. In Rankin Inlet, 155 miles south of the Arctic Circle, hungry Inuit kids basically do as they have done for 5,000 years.

As hungry and energetic kids, Terence and Jordin Tootoo bundled up, racing each other outside their house into the bright sun, laughing. After crunching through hard snow for a mile or so, Terence would shush his younger brother as they came upon an ice field of caribou. When one animal drifted from the herd, the boys inched forward, lifting their rifles...

K-rack! K-rack!

The rolling echo of the shots created a stampede, leaving only the shocked straggler, staggering sideways, collapsing to the ground. Pulling out a knife, Terence would open the caribou at the stomach, reaching for its still warm kidney. After a few bites, he'd give the rest to Jordin.

Imported food is expensive in Rankin Inlet. A gallon of milk costs $14, and the Inuk hunt to eat. At young ages, Terence and Jordin were out with their dad, learning to track animals. Jordin shot his first wolf when he was 12. Hunting wasn't a game for them—it was survival. For sport, the two boys played hockey on nearby ponds, learning the game in the tradition of Gordie Howe and Rocket Richard.

There were no referees. Darkness lasts for 20 hours a day in Rankin Inlet in winter—a ref couldn't see much, anyway. Neither could players, sometimes. Maybe that's why the Tootoos played such a bashing, straight-ahead style of hockey.

And the two brothers never stopped. No matter how cold it got in January, Terence and Jordin could not be kept off the ice. They would still be out there well after supper. It would be dark, blowing snow—didn't matter. "Just a half

Brothers Jordin, on the left, and Terence played together for the Opaskwayak Cree Nation Blizzard in 1998.

hour more," one brother would shout when his mom called them in for bedtime.

"Yeah, half an hour," the other one echoed.

Whether playing hockey or hunting in endlessly bright Arctic summers, Terence and Jordin pushed each other further and faster. When they began playing organized hockey, no one could stop them. Their Rankin Inlet team beat more experienced teams from down south. Though still young, the boys were suddenly leaders of the Inuk community—famous beyond their years.

At 16, Terence left home for Thompson, then The Pas, Manitoba. Jordin, 13, went off to play in Spruce Grove, Alberta. For a while, they played together for the Cree Nation Blizzard of the Manitoba Junior Hockey League.

Upon returning to Rankin Inlet, they were heroes. Adults called them by their full names. "We're happy for you Terence Tootoo. Keep making us proud."

But they were still kids. In Manitoba, the family sponsoring the boys had made up beds in different rooms. Terence said no thanks. He and his brother wanted to sleep together, like when they were small.

Terence became the first Inuk to play professional hockey, starring for an American minor league team, the Roanoke Express. His first season, he won the team's rookie award. He missed his family though, especially Jordin. And he worried. Once after a game, a teammate asked why he seemed depressed.

"I shouldn't have taken that penalty," Terence said, shaking his head.

"Relax, no one's perfect," his teammate said.

"I felt like I let the team down."

Though younger, Jordin was bigger and stronger than Terence. He could fire a slapshot close to 100 miles an hour. And his body checks shook the paint off prairie rinks. Perhaps he was destined to be a hitter: His Inuit name, Kudluk, means "thunder."

Before long Jordin was a star in the junior Western Hockey League with the Brandon Wheat Kings (1999–2003). In 2000, he was drafted by the Nashville Predators of the National Hockey League. Everybody said he was a cinch to make the Canadian junior hockey team. Terence didn't have to look after his younger brother anymore.

One night, in the summer of 2002, the boys were out drinking with friends in Brandon, Manitoba. Terence dropped his brother off, then drove home. Police stopped him. Terence had too much alcohol in his blood, and he was arrested.

He left Jordin a goodbye note: "Jor, go all the way."

With this penalty, Terence felt he had really let the team down—his brother, his family, Rankin Inlet. When the police returned him to his Brandon residence, he found a rifle and disappeared into the woods, as an ailing animal might drift from the herd. He left Jordin a goodbye note: "Jor, go all the way. Take care of the family. You're the man. Ter."

Many wondered if Jordin would be able to accept his brother's death. The two boys were as close as the numerals—22—that both wore on their jerseys. Jordin had always looked up to Terence. Funny thing was, in some ways, nothing changed after Terence was gone. Jordin still looked up to his big brother; only now he had to lift his head a little higher.

"Thunder" went on to star for the Canadian junior hockey team in 2003. The following fall, he made the Nashville Predators and became the first Inuk to score an NHL goal. Jordin would later give an assist on the goal to his brother on the family's website. "To my late brother," he wrote, "I know you're looking down on me, keeping me strong and using every day to make both of us better people."

Jordin Tootoo's life offers evidence of the dramatic changes in the Inuk community. His grandmother was born in an igloo, whereas the young player has his own Internet website. In a single week, he might fly from Nashville to Los Angeles and Vancouver, playing hockey in palaces, in front of tens of thousands. Millions more watch him at home on TV.

Still, for all these developments, Jordin Tootoo's life is not completely different from that of his ancestors. For one thing, he still eats many of the typical foods of his people. Every month that he is away, his mom sends him a package from home—caribou, seal and whale skin.

And Jordin returns every summer to Rankin Inlet, where he trains for the coming hockey season. Only instead of working in a gym, as other NHL players do, he races the ragged 100-foot hills around his parents' home, leaping from perch to perch with a small cousin on his back. To help build up his arms, he will also make the same journey carrying five-gallon jugs in his hands.

Wherever he goes children follow Jordin, shyly wishing him well. Even by himself, though, on the vibrant Arctic tundra where he grew up with his brother, he is never alone.

Once, he was entertaining a TV camera crew from down south. "Jordin, why don't you take them to see the caribou?" his father suggested. Jordin took the crew with him, up over a hill. There, they saw a herd of 20,000 caribou, maybe

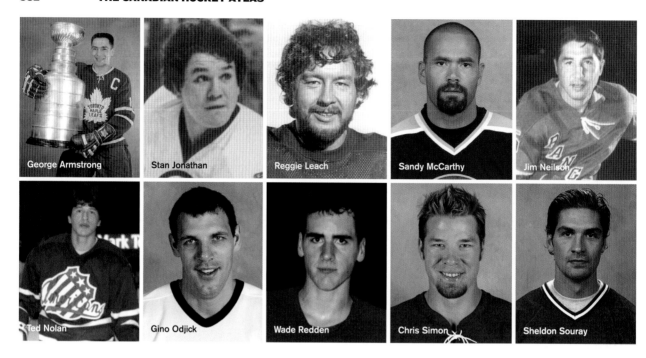

George Armstrong

Stan Jonathan

Reggie Leach

Sandy McCarthy

Jim Neilson

Ted Nolan

Gino Odjick

Wade Redden

Chris Simon

Sheldon Souray

Aboriginal Hockey

According to Old Joe Cope, an elder of the Maritime Mi'kmaq, his people were playing ball hockey on the frozen rivers and lakes of Nova Scotia and New Brunswick hundreds of years ago. And Mi'kmaq carvers perfected the first hockey sticks (see page 44). In addition to Jordin Tootoo (see previous story), some of the other more prominent Aboriginal people in Canada to play in the National Hockey League are listed below:

George Armstrong (Mohawk) Skead, Ontario. Nicknamed "Chief" Armstrong, he was long-time captain of the Toronto Maple Leafs team that won four Stanley Cups in the 1960s.

Jonathan Cheechoo (Cree) Moose Factory, Ontario. Cheechoo is a talented goal scorer, who currently plays with the San Jose Sharks.

Stan Jonathan (Mohawk) Ohsweken, Ontario. Jonathan was an overachieving forward on the Boston Bruins in the 1970s, where he played for mightily appreciative coach Don Cherry.

Reggie Leach (Metis) Riverton, Manitoba. "The Riverton Rifle" played on the right side of Bobby Clarke on both the junior Flin Flon Bombers and the Philadelphia Flyers. During the 1970s he was widely considered to have one of the best shots in hockey.

Sandy McCarthy (Mi'kmaq) Toronto, Ontario. This scrappy winger began his NHL career with the Calgary Flames in 1993. He went on to play for a number of other NHL teams.

Jim Neilson (Cree) Big River, Saskatchewan. Neilson grew up in a Saskatchewan orphanage after his Danish mink-rancher father and Cree mother divorced. Between 1962 and 1974, he was a rock-steady defenceman for the New York Rangers.

Ted Nolan (Anishnabe, or Ojibway) Sault Ste. Marie, Ontario. In the 1980s, Nolan played briefly for the Detroit Red Wings and the Pittsburgh Penguins, before a back injury ended his career. Turning to coaching, he took the junior Sault Ste. Marie Greyhounds to a Memorial Cup win in 1993. Currently, he is coach and director of hockey operations for the Moncton Wildcats of the Quebec Major Junior Hockey League (see page 178).

Gino Odjick (Algonquin) Maniwaki, Quebec. Odjick was an enforcer for the Vancouver Canucks, where he served as Pavel Bure's bodyguard. Odjick went on to play for a variety of other NHL teams in the 1990s and beyond. His childhood idol was Stan Jonathan.

Wade Redden (Metis) Lloydminster, Saskatchewan. Redden is an all-star defenceman who currently plays for the Ottawa Senators (see page 250).

Fred Saskamoose (Sandy Lake Cree) Ahtakakoop First Nation, Saskatchewan. Saskamoose became the first full-blooded Aboriginal to play in the NHL, joining the Chicago Blackhawks for 11 games in 1954 (see page 252).

Chris Simon (Anishnabe, or Ojibway) Wawa, Ontario. For years, Simon was one of the most imposing figures in the NHL; a powerful forward (6'4"). He scored as many as 29 goals with the Washington Capitals in 1999–2000.

Sheldon Souray (Metis) Elk Point, Alberta. As of 2005, Souray was considered one of the top defenders on the Montreal Canadiens. He recently divorced Anjelica Bridges of the TV series *Baywatch*.

Bryan Trottier (Metis) Val Marie, Saskatchewan. Trottier was the heart of the New York Islanders team that won four Stanley Cups in a row (1980–83). He was voted most valuable player of the NHL, in the 1979–80 season.

more. It was a warm day. A halo of bugs followed every animal. After a while, one animal reacted to the attention, triggering a stampede.

A cameraman gasped, "Oh, God."

Now the animals were racing toward them. The impact of the caribous' thundering hooves vibrated up from the ground. Jordin remembered how Terence used to calm him down when they neared a herd of caribou. The younger brother now marched toward the galloping animals.

The lead caribou in the herd saw Jordin Tootoo approaching. Perhaps he seemed more than just one person somehow. One by one, a hundred, then a thousand, the caribou stopped 30 feet short of him. They stared for a while, snorting, and then turned away slowly and went about their business.

Sometimes pretending to be calm and actually being calm amount to the same thing.

Northern star: Jordin Tootoo with the NHL Nashville Predators.

Appendix: Naming names

Listed below are the names of NHL players who were born in towns and cities not included within the main text of *The Canadian Hockey Atlas*.

As in the main chapter text, where a player was raised in one town, or is particularly associated with one town, but born in another, the player's place of birth is noted in parentheses.

NEWFOUNDLAND AND LABRADOR

Baie Verte
Brad Brown

Carbonear
Daniel Cleary

Come-by-Chance
Bob Gladney

Grand Falls
Don Howse
Dave Pichette
Tony White

Labrador City
Chad Penney

Mount Pearl
Darryl Williams

PRINCE EDWARD ISLAND

(All players are listed in the chapter)

NOVA SCOTIA

Amherst
Craig Martin
Bill Riley
Red Stuart
Sherman White

Bedford
Shawn MacKenzie

Berwick
Craig Hillier
Wallace Wilson

Glace Bay
David Amadio
Doug Doull
Sandy Snow
Doug Sulliman

Guysborough
John McKinnon

Kentsville
Jerry Byers

Lockeport
Mal Davis

Middleton
Bob Hess

New Waterford
Trevor Fahey

North Sydney
Paul Andrea
Flash Hollett
Bobby Smith

Oxford
Claude Bourque

Parrsboro
Stan Jackson

Port Hawkesbury
Aaron Johnson

Sydney Mines
Tony Currie

Wolfville
Ted Stackhouse

Yarmouth
Jody Shelley

NEW BRUNSWICK

Bayfield
George Allen
Viv Allen
James Riley

Big Cove
Everett Sanipass

Campbellton
William Dickie
Cory Larose
John LeBlanc
Bill Miller
John Stevens

Cape Tormentine
Sherman White

Causapscal
John-Guy Morrisette

Chatham
Rick Knickle
Jim Malone

Dalhousie
Gordie Dwyer

Dorchester
Forbes Kennedy

Edmundston
Roland Rossignol

Grand Falls
Gerry Ouellette

Newcastle
Eddie Wiseman

Port Elgin
Bob Copp

Quispamsis
Randy Jones

Shediac
Scott Pellerin

St. Steven
Don Sweeney

Sussex
Mike Eagles
Joe Lamb

Woodstock
Sid Veysey

QUEBEC

Acadie
Bruno Gervais

Acton Valley
Frank Breault

Allomette
Leo Lafrance

Alma
Mario Tremblay

Amos
Guillaume Lefebvre

Amqui
Sebastien Caron

Ancienne Lorette
Patrice Bergeron
Mario Marois

Ange-Gardien
Michel Bolduc

Anjou
Martin Brochu
Eric Fichaud
Felix Potvin

Arthabaska
Philippe DeRouville

Arvida
Bill Dineen
Sam St Laurent

Asbestos
Gilles Hamel
Jean Hamel
Don Marcotte
Sean McKenna

Aylmer
Leo Gravelle

Bagotville
J.C. Tremblay

Baie-Comeau
Yves Belanger
Dave "Moose" Morrisette

Beauceville
Stephane Veilleux

Beauport
Maxime Ouellet
Michel Ouellet
Michel Picard
Christian Tanguay

Bellefeuille
Francis Belanger

Beloeil
Olivier Michaud

Blainville
Pierre Dagenais

Boucherville
Gilbert DeLorme
Stephane Quintal

Bout de L'Isle
Bucky Buchanan

Bristol
Bill Cowley

Brownsburg
Pierre Giroux
Gilles Lupien

Buckingham
Robert "Spiff" Campbell
Bill Clement
Claude Lemieux
Rod Lorrain

Cap-de-la-Madeleine
Pierre Aubry
Alain Daigle
Jean-Guy Talbot
Leon Rochefort

Cap-Rouge
Frederic Henry

Caughnawaga
Bobby Simpson

Chambly
Denis Herron

Chambly Basin
Tony Demeres
Fern Perreault

Chandler
Mathieu Garon

Charlemagne
Daniel Gauthier

Charlesbourg
Marc Chouinard
Jean-Philippe Cote

Charles Bel'Chas
Guy Labrie

Coaticook
Christian Proulx

Cowansville
Stephane Beauregard
Bob Richer

Delson
Marcel Cousineau

Dolbeau
Alain Caron

Donnacona
Eddy Godin
Gaetan Royer
Remi Royer

Duparquet
Elmer Vasko

East Broughton
Mario Lessard

Ferme-Neuve
Jose Charbonneau
Daniel Dore

Gaspé
Pascal Trepanier

Gaspesie
Fern LeBlanc

Gatineau
Daniel Briere
Francois Guay
Eric Landry
Steve Martins
Christian Soucy

Granby
Michel Dion
Marc Tardif
Fred Thurier

Grand-Mere
Russ Blinco
Benjamin Carpentier
Fred Corriveau
Fern Rivard

Greenfield Park
Sylvain Couturier

Harve'-St-Pierre
J.F Jomphe

Hauterive
J.C. Bergeron

Hebertville-Station
Frederic Chabot

Ile-Bizard
Vincent Lecavalier

Ile-Perrot
Rich Leduc

Joliette
Lucien DeBlois
Andre Faust
Jonathan Girard

Jonquiere
Denis Dupere

Kenogami
Joe Hardy
Pierre Pilote

Kirkland
Brandon Reid

Knowlton
Nels Crutchfield

L'Abord-a-Plouffe
Jean-Guy Lagace

L'Annonciation
Roger Leger

La Serre
Bob Mongrain

Labelle
Bobby Guindon

Lac-a-la-Tortue
Marcel Pronovost

Lac-St-Charles
Martin Biron
Mathieu Biron

Lac-St-Jean
Armand Gaudreault
Jean Ratelle

Lachute
David Campbell
Denis Hamel
Kevin Lowe

Lafontaine
Yann Danis

Lasalle
Jeff Chychrun
Patrick Cote
Gilles Gratton
Norm Gratton
Danny Groulx
Daniel Guerard
Jacques Lemaire
Mike O'Neill
Marc Reaume
Anthony Stewart

Laurent
Mathieu Darche

Lauzon
Andre Lacroix

Laverlochere
Bob Ritchie

Lemoyne
Maxime Talbot

Les Saules
Alexandre Picard

Levis
David Gosselin

Longueuil
Daniel Berthiaume
Pierre Bouchard
Richard Brodeur
Claude Evans
Luc Gauthier
Bruno Gervais
Francois Groleau

Lotbiniere
Charles Langlois

Magog
Al Langlois

Malartic
Yves Bergeron
Michel Briere
Lucien Grenier
Jim Watson

Maniwaki
Marc Labelle
Gino Odjick

Masham
Jocelyn Gauvreau

Mason
Herbert Rheaume

Massawippi
Bruce Cline

Matane
Alain Cote
Jacques Lemieux
Yves Racine

Mayo
Hazen McAndrew

Mont-Laurier
Dan Cloutier
Sylvain Cloutier
Jocelyn Lemieux
Alexandre Rouleau

Mont-Louis
Jude Drouin

Montmagny
Alain Cote

Montmorency
Gilles Tremblay

Notre-Dame-de-la-Salette
Richard David

Nouvelle
Louis Sleigher

Outremont
Tom Draper

Padoue
Serge Bernier

Palmarolle
Rogie Vachon

Papineau
Louis Berlinquette

Peribonka
Michel Goulet

Pierrefonds
Normand Lacombe
Peter Worrell

Pierreville
Matthieu Descoteaux

Plattsville
Albert Siebert

Pointe-aux-Trembles
Yves Beaudoin
Jacques Locas
Yannick Tremblay

Pointe-Claire
Marc Boileau
Alex Burrows
Jeff Williams

Pointe-Gatineau
Denis Savard

Pont-Rouge
Joe Juneau

Port Alfred
Jean Gilbert

Repentigny
Benoit Hogue
Pascal Leclaire
Alexandre Mathieu
Richard Nantais

Richmond
Sylvain Lefebvre

Rimouski
Alain Raymond

Ripon
Stephane Richer

Riviere-du-Loup
J.F. Soucy

Robertsville
Dan Poulin

Rosemere
Jean-Yves Roy

St-Agapit
Antoine Vermette

St-Alexis-des-Monts
Jean-Francois Damphousse

St-Anicet
Leo Quenneville

St-Apollinaire
Philippe Boucher

St-Bonaventure
Patrick Lalime

St-Charles
Christian Laflamme

St-Charles-Bellechasse
Guy Labrie

St-Clec
Mathieu Benoit

St-Emile
Real Cloutier

St-Ephrem
Eric Bertrand

St-Esprit
Gilles Gilbert

St-Etienne
Edmond Bouchard

St-Francis-d'Assisi
Mike Labadie

St-Gabriel-de-Brandon
Dick Sarrazin

St-Georges-de-Beauce
Jesse Belanger

St-Hilaire
Bob Champoux

St-Hyacinthe
Michel Archambault
Ossie Aubuchon
Denis Dejordy
Jean Gladu
Vincent Riendeau

St-Janvier
Alain Belanger

St-Jean
Art Alexandre

Claude Larose
J.F. Quintin

St-Jean-Richelieu
Jeff Deslauriers

St-Jerome
Tod Campeau
Patrick Lebeau
Stephan Lebeau
Marc-Andre Thinel

St-Joseph-de-Beauce
Junior Lessard

St-Lambert
P.C. Drouin

St-Laurent
Mathieu Darche

St-Leonard
Normand Aubin
Maxim Lapierre

St-Louis-de-France
Marc-Andre Bergeron

St-Malo
Michel Petit

St-Maurice
Eric Laplante

St-Odilon
Simon Nolet

St-Prime
Gilles Bilodeau

St-Raymond
Jean-Marc Richard

St-Remi-de-Tingwick
Conrad "Connie" Dion

Ste-Adele
Stephane Charbonneau
Francois Leroux

Ste-Agathe
Ronnie Stern

Ste-Anne-de-Bellevue
Benoit Brunet
Hec Lepine
Pit Lepine
Phil Myre

Ste-Anne-de-la-Parade
Benoit Dusablon

Ste-Anne-des-Plaines
Jonathan Delisle

Ste-Elizabeth
Stephane Guerard

Ste-Foy
Claude Boivin
Simon Gagne
Steve Penny
Patrick Roy
Stephane Roy

Ste-Genevieve
Bob Sauve
Jean-Francois Sauve

Ste-Justine
Alex Tanguay

Ste-Marie-de-Beauces
Jonathan Ferland

Ste-Rose
Martin Desjardins

Sept-Iles
Guy Carbonneau
Steve Duchesne
Karl Dykhuis
Rob Zettler

Shawinigan
Martin Gelinas
Jacques Mailhot

Shawnigan Falls
Gerard Desaulniers
Jean Lamirande
Marcel Paille
Jacques Plante
Andre Pronovost
Claude Pronovost
Jean Pronovost
Gino Rozzini

Shawville
Murph Chamberlain
Edward Finnigan
Frank Finnigan
Terry Murray
Marc Rodgers

South Durham
Jean-Paul Leblanc

Taschereau
Pierre Larouche

Temiscamingue
Gaston Gingras
Rich Lemieux
Jack Rathwell
Andre Savard

Terrebonne
Alain Heroux
Yves Heroux

Thetford Mines
Michel Dumas
Bob Fillion
Marcel Fillion
Mario Gosselin
Daniel Poudrier
Patrice Tardif

Val d'Or
Serge Aubin
Daniel Bouchard
Dany Sabourin

Valleyfield
Pierre-Luc Emond
Mario Faubert
Martin Gendron
Rosario Joanette
Albert Leduc
Pierre Plante
Yves Sarault

Vanier
Patrick Poulin

Verdun
Normand Baron
Jim Bartlett
Eric Charron
Guy Charron

Ed Courtenay
Jean Cusson
Denis Cyr
Polly Drouin
Ron Harris
Gord Hollingworth
Claude Legris
Fern Majeau
Don Marshall
Rick Martin
Jim Peters
Les Ramsay
Jean Savard
Dollard St Laurent
Dan Vincelette
Wally Weir
Moe White

Ville St. Pierre
Martin Lapointe

Ville-de-Vanier
Rene Leclerc

Vinton
Tod Sloan

Windsor
Rejean Cloutier

Yamaska
Armand Mondou

ONTARIO

Agincourt
Bob Babcock

Ajax
Jeff Beukeboom
Brent Burns

Alexandria
Joel Trottier

Alliston
Larry Gould

Arnprior
Dan Fridgen
Randy Pierce

Atikokan
Gary Sampson

Aurora
Norm Dennis
Harold Holmes
Karl Stewart

Ayr
Buddy Maracle

Bancroft
Rod Schutt
Bryan Watson

Barriefield
Mickey Blake

Barry's Bay
Larry Trader

Beamsville
Ryan Christie
Paul Laus

Beaverton
Basil McRae

Beeton
John Gould
Warren Holmes
Jim Rutherford

Belle River
Mike Natyshak

Belleville
Dan Bain
Drew Bannister
Dickie Boon
Bill Boyd
Dale Clarke
Matt Cooke
Bob Crawford
Lou Crawford
Marc Crawford
Bob Dillabough
Red Doran
Gerry Goyer
Rick Green
Brett Hull
Jack Laviolette
Eric Manlow
Norm Maracle
Rick Meagher
Andrew Raycroft
Brad Richardson
Chris Valentine
Eddie Westfall

Belmont
Larry Courville

Blackburn
Hec Kilrea

Blenheim
Todd Warriner

Blind River
Tom Cassidy
Claude Julien

Bolton
Lorne Duguid

Bothwell
Brett MacDonald

Bourget
Joseph Matte
Roland Matte

Bowmanville
Ken Davies
Brent Hughes

Bracebridge
Irvine Bailey
Bill Carson
Frank Carson
Roger Crozier
Kris King

Bradford
Dodger Collings

Braeside
Lucas Lawson

Bramalea
Andrew Cassels
Chris Felix
Mike Weaver

Brampton
Mike Danton
Mike Dwyer
Todd Elik
Mike Forbes
Mike Jefferson
Randy Johnston
Sheldon Keefe
Tom Laidlaw
Rick Nash
Kris Newbury
Jamie Storr
Mike Wilson

Brockville
Brian Chapman
Herb Foster
Randy Ladouceur
Hank Lammens
Alyn McCauley
Michael McMahon
Noel Price
Cully Simon
Thain Simon

Brucefield
Aaron Lobb

Brussels
Jack McIntyre

Burke's Falls
Dave Downie

Burlington
Jeff Christian
Adam Creighton
Dan Currie
Mark Lawrence
Scott McKay
Scott McLellan
Adam Munro
Bob Murra
Mark Reeds
Michael Schutte
Ron Sedlbauer
Mark Visheau
Chad Wiseman

Byron
Rob Ramage

Cache Bay
Carl Smith
Nakina Smith

Callander
Bill Barber

Campbellford
Charles Shannon
Gerry Shannon

Capreol
Joffre Desilets
Jim Mayer
Doug Mohns

Cardinal
Rusty Crawford
Todd Gill

Carleton Place
Bill "Bat" Phillips

Carlisle
Jeff Daw

Carp
Kurtis Foster

Cayuga
Ray Emery
Frank Martin

Cedar Springs
Hal Jackson

Chapleau
Floyd Curry
Adie Lafrance
Ron Schock
Jason Ward

Charletone
Lorrain Thibeault

Chatham
Chris Allen
Rick Chinnick
Dave Gagner
Lee Giffin
Bob Gryp
Jeff Jackson
Dave Kelly
Dennis McCord
Randy Murray
Donald Willson
Brian Wiseman

Chelsey
Mickey MacKay

Chesley
Paul MacDermid

Chesterville
John Sorrell

Cobalt
Max Bennett
Kent Douglas
Joseph Levandoski

Cobourg
Dean Hopkins
Randy MacGregor
Paul Terbenche
Marty Wilford
Justin Williams

Cochenour
Mark Vermette

Cochrane
Tim Horton

Collingwood
Claire Alexander
Jason Arnott
Bernard Brophy
Roy Burmeister
Eddie Bush
James Herberts
Albert Hughes
Lindsay Middlebrook
Reg Noble
Randy Osburn
Paul Shakes
Darryl Sly

Coniston
Andy Barbe
Randy Boyd
Jimmy Fox

Cooksville
Barry John Salovaara

Copper Cliff
Sylvio Bettio
John Sleaver
Jerry Toppazzini
Zellio Toppazzini

Corunna
Paul Ysebaert

Creighton Mines
William Regan
Brian Smith

Delhi
Barry Boughner

Deloro
Wayne Brown

Deseronto
Windy O'Neill

Douro
Jack Coughlin

Downeyville
David Lucas

Dresden
Ken Houston

Dryden
John Muloin
Dennis Owchar
Chris Pronger
Sean Pronger

Dublin
Jack Crawford

Dunnville
Ryan Barnes
David Fenyves
Ernie Parkes

Durham
Jeff MacMillan

Eardley
Hib Milks

Earlton
Rosaire Paiement
Wilf Paiement

East York
Ralph Intranuovo

Eganville
Gord Byers
Shawn Heins
Dale McTavish

Elgin
Vic Ripley

Elliot Lake
Alex Henry

Elmira
Ric Seiling
Rod Seiling
Daniel Snyder

Elmwood
Puss Traub

Embrun
Martin Pierre

Espanola
Arthur Gauthier
Tim Jacobs
Bob Jones
Jim Jones
Leo Lamoureux

Essex
Bruce Crowder
Rick Heinz

Etobicoke
Randy Cunneyworth
Manny Fernandez
Steve Halko
Steve Valiquette

Exeter
Paul Pooley

Falconbridge
Dale McCourt

Farran's Point
Cy Denneny

Fergus
Edwin Chadwick
Wilfred McDonald
Doug Rombough

Ferris
Ken Wharram

Finch
Ken McRae

Forest
Bill Lochead

Forks of the Credit
Aldo Guidolin

Fort Erie
John Brenneman
Randy Burridge
Mike Cirillo
Paul Gardner
Tom Reid
Brian Stapleton

Fort Frances
Dave Allison
Mike Allison
Murray Bannerman
Raymond Frederick
Earl Johnson
Ed Kryznowski
Chris Lindberg
Tim Sheehy

Fort Perry
John Roach

Gananoque
Tim Keyes

Garafraxa County
Bert Lindsay

Georgetown
Adam Bennett
Bob Goldham
Brian Hayward

Geraldton
Bo Elik
Mark McMahon

Gloucester
Michael Blunden
Steve Guenette

Goderich
Al Dewsbury
Gary Doak
Larry Jeffrey
Jack Price

Gore Bay
Bobby Burns

Gravenhurst
Mickey McGuire

Grimsby
Kevin Bieksa
Bob Warner
Cy Wentworth

Hagersville
Brian Watts

Haileybury
Jim Culhane
Leo Labine
Gord Spence

Haliburton
Bernie Nicholls
Ron Stackhouse

Hawkesbury
Lionel Bouvrette
Yvan Joly
Rich LaFerriere
Denis Larocque

Ralph MacSweyn
Dan McGillis

Hearst
Claude Larose

Heathcote
Robert Rowe

Hespeler
Paul Woods

Hewsbury
Lionel Bouvrette

Highland Creek
Brock Treadway

Holland Landing
Darrin Madeley

Hornepayne
Mike McEwen

Humber Summit
Ron Attwell

Humberstone
Ted Kennedy

Huntsville
Jack Bionda
Ethan Moreau
Norman Shay

Iroquois Falls
Paul Gagne
Roger Lemelin
Gerry Rioux

Kanata
Adam Dewan
Travis Scott
Todd White

Kapuskasing
Mitch Babin
Curt Brackenbury
Ted McCaskill
David Pulkkinen

Kemptville
Des Roche

Kerr Lake
Harry Frost

Keswick
Ernie Godden
Curtis Joseph

Kincardine
Paul Henderson
Denis Riggin
Pat Riggin
Jordan Willis
John Wilson
Larry Wilson

King City
Rick Hampton

Lakewood
Moe Mantha

Lambeth
Reggie Thomas

LaSalle
Andy Delmore
Derek Wilkinson

Leamington
Kirk Bowman
Tim Hrynewich
Kris Manery

Randy Manery
Pat Ribble
Brad Selwood

Levack
Frank St Marseille
Dave Taylor
Limestone Ridge
Dick Irvin

Lindsay
Jamie Allison
Ron Ellis
Joseph Junkin
Rick MacLeish
Don Maloney
Joe Primeau
Dave Roche
Bill Speer
Tom Thornbury

Listowel
Jeff Bloemberg
George Hay
Larry Huras
Bert Hughes
Darwin McCutcheon
Paul McIntosh
Fred "Cyclone"
  Taylor, (Hockey
  Hall of Fame;
  never played
  in NHL)

Little Current
Danny Cox

Lucknow
Murray Murdoch

Lynden
Lloyd Cook
Red Horner

Manitouwadge
Mike Moher

Markdale
Chris Neil
Brad Tiley

Markham
Mike Gellard

Marmora
Greg Terrion

Massey
Pete Horeck

Matheson
Bob McCord

Meaford
Herbert Mitchell
Darren Pang
George Smith
Sparky Vail

Midland
Herb Drury
Wayne King
Alex McKendry
Mike Robitaille

Millbank
Jim Nahrgang

Millgrove
Danny Syvret

Milton
Mike Kaszycki
Peter McDuffe
Enio Sclisizzi

Mimico
Fran Harrison
Brendan Shanahan

Mine Center
Edgar Laprade

Minesing
Frank Foyston

Mississauga
Don Biggs
Brad Boyes
Greg Gardner
Greg Gilbert
Tom Kostopoulos
Mike Lenarduzzi
Manny Malhotra
Grant Marshall
Jeff Maund
Bill McDougall
Geoff Platt
Dave Poulin
Allan Rourke
Jeff Shevalier
Jason Spezza
Matthew Stajan

Mitchell
Dan Gloor

Moose Factory
Jonathan Cheechoo

Morrisburg
Mike Casselman
Joseph Miller

Mount Albert
Gordon Reid

Mt. Dennis
Donald Head

Nanticoke
Harold Cotton

Naughton
Arthur Ross

Nepean
Jamie Baker
Dan Ratushny
Jason York

New Hamburg
Jeff Kalbfleish

New Liskeard
Hal Cooper
Marc Lamothe
Lonnie Loach
Gus Mortson
Rod Willard

New Toronto
Ed Sandford

Newmarket
Herbert Cain
Jim Cain
Aubrey Clapper
Mike Kitchen
Randy Legge
Jamie Macoun
Chris McRae
Geoff Sarjeant
Shayne Stevenson
Bill Thoms
Keith Wright

Newton Robinson
Bob Pulford

Nilestown
Charlie Stephens

Nobleton
Nick Boynton

North Bay
Stanley Brown
Ab DeMarco
Bob Dupuis
Pierre Gagne
Ray Giroux
Bob Gracie
Ron Hoover
Gord Kannegiesser
Sheldon
  Kannegiesser
Larry Keenan
Pep Kelly
Hec Lalande
Howie Lockhart
Bryan Maxwell
Graeme Nicolson
Peter Palangio
Anthony Poeta
Larry Regan
Tyler Rennette
Ken Richardson
Craig Rivet
Brent Tremblay

North York
Jason Allison
Sean Avery
Chris Campoli
Jason Dawe
Mike Fountain
Paul Ranger
Gary Roberts
Brian Wilks
Michael Zigomanis

Norwood
Frederick Doherty

Oakville
Eric Cairns
Bruce Dowie
Matt Foy
Vic Hadfield
Bob Kelly
Greg Smyth
Rob Zamuner

Ohsweken
Stan Jonathan

Orangeville
Bert Wilson

Orillia
Rick Ley
Richard Scott

Osgoode
Todd Flichel

Owen Sound
Norm Armstrong
Leslie Binkley
Clarence "Hap" Day
Ted Graham
Ben Grant
Gordon Henry
Buck Jones
Melville Keeling
Norm Locking
Stanley Long
Harry Lumley
Pat McCreavy
Steve McLaren

Mike Minard
Nathan Perrott
Gerald Reid
Curtis Sanford

Paisley
Barney Stanley

Palmerston
Lorne Ferguson

Paris
Syl Apps Sr.
Ken Ellacott
Jay Wells

Pembroke
James Anderson
Hubie Anslow
Harry Cameron
Gord Fraser
Gus Giesebrecht
Randy Holt
Doug Keans
Hugh Lehman
Dutch Nighbor
Clarence Raglan
Leo Reise
Ray Sheppard
Bobby Trapp
David Trottier

Penetanguishene
Andy Bellemer
Bert Corbeau
Patrick DesRochers
George McNamara
Brian McReynolds
Don Tannahill

Perth
Les Douglas
Carl Liscombe
Billy Smith
Floyd Smith
Gord Smith

Petawawa
Warren Mohns

Petersburg
Glen Cressman

Petrolia
Todd Bidner
Brian Dobbin
Bobby Gould
Terry Holbrook
Jody Hull
Dale Hunter
Dave Hunter
Mark Hunter
Michael Leighton
John Van Boxmeer

Pickering
Glenn Healy

Plattsville
Albert "Babe"
  Siebert

Port Colborne
Harry Dick
Don Gallinger
Scott Gruhl
Bronco Horvath
Daniel Olesevich
Donald Simmons

Port Credit
Bert Peer

Port Dalhousie
Red Mitchell

Port Hope
Dennis O'Brien
Shane O'Brien
Ron Smith
Paul Terbenche

Port Perry
Fred Whitcroft

Portsmouth
Edward Nicholson

Prescott
Leo Boivin
Kevin MacDonald
Earl Roche

Preston
Vern Kaiser
Barry Sullivan
Bob Wren

Puslinch
John Cullen

Randolph
Howard McNamara

Ravenswood
John McIntyre

Red Lake
Mitch Molloy

Rexdale
Colin Patterson

Richmond Hill
Luciano Borsato
Michael Cammalleri
Frank Nigro
Jeff O'Neill
Keith Redmond
Bob Wall

Ridgeway
Skip Teal

Rockland
Sammy Godin
Evariste Payer
Serge Payer

Ruthven
Floyd Hillman

St. George
Adam Munro

St. Lambert
Phil Stevens

St. Mary's
William "Riley" Hern
(Hockey Hall of
Fame; never
played in NHL)
Dan McCarthy

St. Paul
Mark Bell

St. Thomas
Dave Hudson
Kent Hulst
Bill McKenzie
David Shaw
Joe Thornton
Jack Valiquette

Sarnia
Tim Bernhardt
Shawn Burr

Jerry Butler
Dino Ciccarelli
Mike Crombeen
Michael Dark
Lloyd Haddon
Duke Harris
George Harris
Steve Hazlett
Jamie Hislop
Gary Holt
Henri Lehvonen
John McCahill
Ian McKegney
Wayne Merrick
Robbie Moore
Bob Neely
Kraig Nienhuis
Rob Palmer
Jason Simon
Mike Stapleton
Pat Stapleton
Pat Verbeek
Don Ward
Joe Ward

Scarborough
Brad Aitken
Chris Berti
Mark Botell
Jeff Cowan
Thomas Cowan
Wayne Cowley
Doug Dadswell
Iain Fraser
Stephen Guolla
Mike Johnson
Greg Koehler
Steve Konroyd
Chris Kotsopoulos
Paul Lawless
Bryan Marchment
Mike Marson
Andrew McBain
Gavin Morgan
Larry Murphy
Wayne Primeau
Jamie Ram
Mike Ricci
Mike Richard
Ken Sabourin
Derrick Smith
Brad Tapper
Rick Tocchet
Ron Tugnutt
Terry Virtue
Steve Weeks
Tim Young
Rob Zepp

Schomberg
Darryl Bootland
Bill Kitchen

Schumacher
Norman Defelice
Gord Hannigan
Raymond Hannigan
Jim Mair
Dean Prentice
Eric Prentice

Seaforth
Boyd Devereaux
Charlie Mason
Dave McLlwain

Reginald Reid
Mike Watt
Ralph Weiland

Seneca Township
Roy Edwards

Sharon
Matt Ryan

Shelburne
Aaron Downey

Silver Mountain
Jack Walker

Simcoe
Rob Blake
Jassen Cullimore
Leonard Kelly
Geordie Kinnear
Dwayne Roloson
Ryan VandenBussche
Rick Walmsley

Sioux Lookout
Jimmy Roy

Skeed
George Armstrong

Smiths Falls
Terry Carkner
Rob Dopson
Gary McAdam
Donald McKenney

**Smooth Rock
Falls**
Grant Martin
Dick Mattiussi
Jean-Paul Parise

South Porcupine
Danny Belisle
George Blair
Les Costello
Murray Costello
Red Doran
Don Lever
John McLellan
Bob Nevin
Bud Stefanski

South River
Laurie Scott

Stirling
Rob Ray

Stittsville
Matt Bradley
Kenneth Doraty

Stoney Creek
Tyrone Garner
Mark Popovic
Leo Reise
Jack Stoddard

Stouffville
Keith Acton

Strathroy
Brian Campbell
Darryl Edestrand
Andy McDonald
Steve McKichan

Stratton
Gord Davidson

Sturgeon Falls
Leo Bourgeault
Dan Frawley

Shep Mayer
Gerald McNamara

Sundridge
Greg de Vries
Bill McCreary
Keith McCreary

Swansea
Glenn Brydson

Sydenham
George Abbott

Tecumseh
Warren Rychel

Terrace Bay
Daniel Schock
Charlie Simmer

Thamesford
Tommy Filmore

Thessalon
Jack Markle
Merlyn Phillips

Thornhill
Michael Henrich
Dominic Moore

Thorold
Armand "Bep"
Guidolin
Fred Speck

Tillsonburg
Bill Anderson
Lloyd Andrews
Russell Oatman

Tinturn
Stephen Kraftcheck

Trenton
Mel Bridgman
Gord Brooks
George Ferguson
John Garrett
Steve Graves
Jack Hamilton
Steve Smith
Tom Tilley

Trout Creek
Gerry Odrowski

Unionville
Bob Beckett

Vankleek
Andrew Allen

Vankleek Hill
Connie Brown

Varney
Edward McCalmon

Victoria Harbour
Amos Arbour

Victoria Mines
Hector "Toe" Blake

Walkerton
Doug Brindley

Wallaceburg
Doug Shedden

Waterloo
Bobby Bauer
Jim Lorentz
Clare Martin

Waubaushene
Jack Arbour
Ty Arbour
Jack Portland

Wawa
Denny Lambert
Chris Simon

Webbwood
Rusty Hughes

Welland
Paul Bissonnette
Ken Breitenbach
Yvon Corriveau
Bob Cunningham
Wayne Groulx
Nathan Horton
Bill Huard
Matt Johnson
Mark LaForest
Daniel Paille
Gary Swain

West Sutton
Laurence Molyneaux

Weston
Barry Ashbee
Paul Coffey
Iain Duncan
Rob Garner
Mike Liut
Adam Oates
Craig Ramsay

Wheatley
Glen Skov

White River
Trevor Halverson

Williamstown
Kent McDonnell

Willowdale
Kirk McLean
Gord Murphy

Winchester
Matt Carkner
Ken McRae
Larry Robinson
Moe Robinson

Wingham
Dave Farrish

Woodbridge
Steve Eminger
Jimmy Jones

Woodstock
Doug Shelton
Jeff Zehr

Woodsville
Billy McGimsie
(Hockey Hall of
Fame; never
played in NHL.)

York
Glen Sharpley
Michael Ware

MANITOBA

Baldur
Tom Johnson

Basswood
Stu Smith

Beausejour
Bob Davie

Birtle
Rick Berry
Bill Derlago
Ron Low

Carman
Ed Belfour

Carroll
Clem Loughlin
Wilfred Loughlin

Cowan
Walter Boyer

Dauphin
Chuck Arnason
Don Caley
Brad Church
Mike Korney
Peter Slobodzian

Deloraine
Don Dietrich
Don Gibson
Marty Murray

Dugald
Trevor Kidd

Elkhorn
Sheldon Kennedy

Eriksdale
Ted Green
John Stewart

Foxwarren
Pat Falloon
Mark Wotton

Gilbert Plains
Blaine Stoughton

Gimli
Helge Bostrom
Greg Carroll

Glenboro
Mel "Sudden
Death" Hill

Gretna
Hal Winkler

Grosse Isle
Bryan Lefley

Grunthal
Ken Block

Hamiota
Bing Juckes
John Marks
Wayne Ramsey
Dallas Smith

Hartney
Jim Agnew
Hugh "Red" Conn
Spunk Sparrow

Holland
Glen Harmon

Lac du Bonnet
Kyle Kettles

Letellier
Dick Bouchard

Manitou
Ron Huston

Mariapolis
Rene Trudell

McCreay
Kirby Law

Melita
Gary Hall

Minnedosa
Peter Leboutillier
Curt Ridley
Frank Stahan

Neepawa
Shawn Byram
Shane Hnidy
Mark Kolesar
Bill Mikkelson

**Notre Dame de
Lourdes**
Jean-Pierre Vigier

Oak Lake
Ted Taylor

Oakville
Moose Sherritt

Pilot Mound
Lyle Phair
Jack Stewart

Pine Falls
Bill Watson

Poplar Point
Dennis Hextall

Portage la Prairie
Arron Asham
Gordon Bell
Joe Bell
Rick Blight
Gordon Fashoway
Peaches Lyons
Leo Murray

Riverton
Reggie Leach

Russell
Christian Chartier
Mervyn "Red" Dutton
Theoren Fleury (born
in Oxbow, SK)

St. Charles
George Johnston

St. James
Cecil Browne
Harry Taylor

St. Lazare
Dave Chartier

Ste. Rose
Burke Henry

St. Vital
Pete Kelly

Sherridon
Steve Andrascik

Snowflake
George McFarland

Souris
Archie Fraser
Jay More
Andy Murray
(NHL coach)
Arthur Townsend

Steinbach
Dale Krentz
Sean Tallaire

Stony Mountain
Bill "Smiley"
  Meronek
Hugh Millar
Babe Pratt

Swan River
John McDonald

The Pas
Murray Anderson
Curt Giles
Hub Macey (born in
  Big River, SK)

Thompson
Curtis Leschyshyn
Cameron Mann
Keith McCambridge

Transcona
Cal Gardner

Treheme
Florent Robidoux

Virden
Jim Murray

Winkler
Eric Fehr
Dustin Penner

Winnipegosis
Danny Johnson

SASKATCHEWAN

Admiral
James Bedard

Allan
Willie Brossart

Aneroid
Patrick Marleau

Asquith
Hal Picketts

Assiniboia
Doug MacDonald
Clint Smith

Aylsham
Greg Classen

Balcarres
Doug Trapp

Big River
Jim Neilson
Barry Pederson

Bengough
Earl Robertson

Birch Hills
Marshall Johnston

Blaine Lake
Hughie Coflin

Borden
Bill Hajt

Canora
Cliff Koroll
Cam Severson
Tyler Wright

Carlyle
Brenden Morrow

Central Butte
Clarke Wilm

Churchbridge
Lionel Heinrich
Kevin Kaminski

Climax
Gord Kluzak
Rocky Trottier

Craik
Jim Archibald
Garnet Exelby
Jeremy Reich

Craven
Frank Ingrim

Creelman
Morris Mott

Cudworth
Gerry Ehman
Orland Kurtenbach
Paul Shmyr

Dinsmore
Jim Leavins

Divide
Les Colwill

Dodsland
Don Gillen
Bob Hoffmeyer
Brad McCrimmon

Drake
Robin Bartel

Dunblane
Stephen Buzinski

Dysart
Fernie Flaman
Bill Kyle
Gus Kyle

Edington
Harvey Bennett

Esterhazy
Chris Herperger
Frank Mario

Estevan
Blair Atcheynum
Al Nicholson
Trent Whitfield

Eston
Ronald "Max"
  Sutherland

Fairlight
Vic Myles

Falkirk
Alec Woods

Fielding
Neil Hawryliw

Fillmore
Buzz Boll

Fleming
Frederick Gordon

Foam Lake
Pat Elynuik
Bernie Federko
Dennis Polonich

Fort Qu'Appelle
Frank Waite

Frobisher
Thomas Dewar

Gainsborough
Lew Morrison
Ralph Nattrass

Goodsoil
Ron Greschner

Gravelbourg
Larry Hornung

Grenfell
Bryan Hextall
Max Sutherland

Gull Lake
Jim McKenzie

Hafford
Jason Herter
Roger Kortko

Herbert
Henry Dyck

Hudson Bay
Grant Jennings
Larry Lozinski
Trent Yawney

Indian Head
Jeff Lank

Jansen
Ken Schinkel

Kamsack
Jack Church
Darcy Hordichuk
Harold Phillipoff
Wayne Smith

Kelvington
Wendel Clark
Barry Melrose

Kerrobert
Curtis Murphy

Kindersley
Bob Bourne
Lorry Gloeckner
Joel Kwiatkowski
Dave Lewis
Jim Mathieson
Dick Meissner
Greg Paslawski

Kinistino
Gordie Nelson
Gordon Redahl

Lac La Ronge
Glenn Johannesen

Lac Pelletier
Lloyd Ailsby

Landis
Tony Hemmerling
Edward Zeniuk

Lang
Dennis Sobchuk
Eugene Sobchuk

Langenburg
Kelly Buchberger

Lanigan
Bob Baun
Wade Brookbank
Brian Propp
Todd Strueby

Lashburn
Dwight Carruthers

Loon Lake
Ed Cooper

Lucky Lake
Darin Kimble
Glen Smith

Lumsden
Beattie Ramsay

MacNutt
Duane Rupp

Major
Laurie Boschman

Mankota
Gord Sherven

Manor
Murray Armstrong

Maple Creek
Barry Dean
Gordon Poirer

Maryfield
Lynn Powis

Meadow Lake
Len Esau
Jeff Friesen
D.J. King
Mike Siklenka

Melfort
Lorne Henning
Lane Lambert
Pat MacLeod

Melville
Sid Abel
Phil Besler
Tim Cheveldae
Jim Franks
Todd McLellan
Alex Motter
Jarrett Stoll
Archibald Wilder

Milestone
Garth Boesch

Montmartre
Norm Beaudin

Moosomin
Dennis Abgrall
Charlie Corrigan
David Dunn
Dave Tippett

Naicam
Lynn Loyns

Neudorf
Ed Litzenberger

Nipiawin
Lyndon Byers

Nokomis
Doug Horbul
Elmer Lach

Norquay
Lloyd Gronsdahl
Edwin Panagabko

Odessa
Jackie Schmidt
Joseph Schmidt

Oxbow
Lindsay Carson
Reg Kerr
Aren Miller

Paddockwood
Shayne Toporowski

Paradise Hills
John Rogers

Pierceland
Grant Erickso

Ponteix
Mark Lamb

Porcupine Plain
Kelly Chase

Prelate
Mark Pederson

Punnichy
Nolan Yonkman

Quill Lake
Lyle Odelein
Selmar Odelein
Ed Vokes

Radville
Darcy Verot

Rama
Barry Nieckar

Redvers
Dean Kennedy

Rosetown
Randy Ireland

Rosthern
Jim Hrycuik
Richie Regehr
Robyn Regehr
Arthur Wiebe

**Sandy Lake
Reserve**
Fred Saskamoose

Scepter
Bert Olmstead

Semans
Peggy O'Neill

Shellbrook
Craig Valette

Silton
Harold "Mush"
  March

Smiley
Blake Evans

Speers
Morris Lukowich

Spy Hill
Jeff Odgers

Star City
Robert Solinger

Stoughton
Lorne Carr

Strasbourg
Greg Hubick

Sutherland
Hal Laycoe
Chuck Rayner

Togo
Ted Hampson

Torquay
Joel Stepp

Tubrose
Fred Hucul

Unity
Curtis Brown
Boyd Gordon
Barrie Meissner

Val Marie
Bryan Trottier

Vanguard
Al Rollins

Vonda
Lulu Denis

Wakaw
Dave Balon
James Latos
Dave Michayluk

Waldheim
Dave "Tiger" Schultz

Wapella
Brett Clark

Warman
Edwind Dyck

Watrous
Regan Kelly
Paul Meger

Watson
Max McNab

Wawota
Brooks Laich

Wetaskawin
Rod Buskas
Martin Sonnenberg

White City
Chris Szysky

Wilkie
Ralph Keller

Wynard
Wade Skolney
Richard Zemlak

Yellow Grass
Nolan Schaefer
Peter Schaefer

ALBERTA

Banff
Kevin Smyth
Ryan Smyth

Bankhead
Frank Jerwa
Joe Jerwa

Bashaw
Brad Berry
Dave Reierson

Bassano
Brian Maloney
Mark Marquess

Beaumont
Marc Magnan

Beaverlodge
Jerry Holland
Chris Schmidt
Matt Walker

Bentley
Clayton Beddoes
Perry Turnbull
Randy Turnbull

Blackie
Jeremy Colliton
Pat Egan

Blairmore
Doug Houda

Bonnyville
Jim Harrison

Bow Island
Troy Loney

Cadomin
Milan Marcetta

Calahoo
Frank Banham
Craig Berube

Camrose
Tyler Bouck
Scott Ferguson
Steve Gotaas
Josh Green
Percy Jackson
Alex Kaleta
Arthur Michaluk
John Michaluk

Caroline
Jim Vandermeer

Carstairs
Tony Stiles

Castor
Darcy Tucker

Coleman
Rick Rypien

Cold Lake
Alexander Auld
Doug Hicks
Kevin Krook
Dave Shand

Coronation
Travis Brigley
Justin Hocking
Brett Scheffelmaier
Dwayne Zinger

Daysland
Matthew Spiller

Drayton Valley
Greg Pankewicz

Drumheller
Don Campbell

Duchess
Jeff Shantz

Edson
Mike Buzak

Elk Point
Sheldon Souray

Enterprise
Audley Tuten

Fairview
Ryan Shmyr

Fort McMurray
Harlan Pratt
Nolan Pratt
Scottie Upshall

Fort Saskatchewan
Mike Commodore
Joffrey Lupul
Kiel McLeod
Carl Mokosak
Ray Whitney

Fort Vermillion
Dan Hodgson

Glendon
Stan Smyl

Grand Cache
Dean McAmmond
Travis Roche
Howard Walker

Grand Center
Garry Howatt

Grand Prairie
Galen Head
Clint Malarchuk

Grossfield
Donald McFadyen

Halkirk
Shane Doan

Hardisty
Darrel Anholt

High Prairie
Tom Lysiak
Kelly Pratt

High River
Bruce Greig
Mark Greig
John McKenzie

Hines Creek
Bradley Zavisha

Hinton
Dave Scatchard

Hobbema
Ted Hodgson

Hythe
Ken Solheim

Innisfall
Gary Bauman
Dallas Gaume

Jasper
Ian Herbers
John Hilworth
Brian Young

Lac La Biche
Rene Bourque
Darren Reid

Lacombe
Larry Mickey
Darin Sceviour
Bryce Wandler
Randy Wyrozub

Lamont
Gene Achtymichuk

Leduc
Dixon Ward

Legal
Shawn Legault

Mannville
Kyle Calder
Mike Rathje
Miles Zaharko

Milo
Bob Stumpf

Morinville
Jason Holland

Myrnam
Rocky Saganiuk

Nanton
Philip Crowe
Orest Kindrachuk

Olds
Kevin McDonald

Onoway
Paxton Schulte

Peace River
Wade Campbell
Kelly Kisio
Ken Lovsin
Chris Osgood
Alex Ritson
Brian Skrudland

Pincher Creek
Ray Cote
Leigh Verstraete
Darcy Wakaluk

Ponoka
Gregg Boddy
Jim McCrimmon
Greg Smith
Stan Weir
Harry York

Provost
John Chad
Norm Ullman

Redwater
Todd Fedoruk

Rimbey
Dylan Gyori

Rocky Mountain House
Dean Magee
Butch Paul
Brad Stuart
Nick Tarnasky

St. Albert
Joe Benoit
Emanuel Viveiros

St. Paul
Kyle Brodziak

Sexsmith
Garry Edmundson

Sherwood Park
Ryan Bach
Jeff Ewasko
Tony Twist
Dave Van Drunen
Cam Ward

Slave Lake
Gord Kruppke

Spruce Grove
Stu Barnes
Ryan Bast
Nathan Dempsey
Grant Fuhr
Grant Stevenson

Stettler
Bob Falkenberg
Justin Hocking
Brian Ogilvie

Stony Plain
Steven Goertzen

Swalwell
Brian Tutt

Swan Hills
Alan May

Trochu
Kevin Haller

Two Hills
Brad Werenka

Vegreville
Edward Diachuk
Zenith Komarniski
Brent Severyn

Vermillion
Bill "Cowboy" Flett
Ron Jones
Eddie Kenny
Grant McNeill
Jeff Woywitka

Wainwright
Doug Lecuyer
Glen Sather (born in High River, AB)

Warburg
Lindy Ruff

Wetaskawin
Rod Buskas
Val Fonteyne
Gus Marker
Martin Sonnenberg

Westlock
Roland Boutin
Greg Polis

Willingdon
Cody Rudkowsky

Youngstown
Norm Burns

BRITISH COLUMBIA

100 Mile House
Sandy Moger
Scott Robinson

Abbotsford
Ryan Craig
Brad Moran

Campbell River
Daryl Andrews
Len Lunde
Matt Underhill

Castlegar
Travis Green
Dane Jackson
Steve Junker
Doug Kostynski
Darcy Martini
Gord Walker

Chemainus
Robin Bawa
Doug Bodger

Chetwynd
Dody Wood

Chilliwack
Dave Archibald

Christina Lake
Kevin Sawyer

Coal Creek
Stan Smith

Comox
Brett Mclean
Cam Neely

Coquitlam
Garrett Burnett
Brent Henley
Terry McDonald

Courtenay
Jason Bowen

Creston
Jamie Huscroft
Darren Jensen
Randy Rota

Dawson Creek
Dan Brennan
Craig Redmond
Phil Sykes

Delta
Mark Morrison
Ed Patterson

Duncan
Greg Adams
Geoff Courtnall
Russ Courtnall
Matt Ellison
Brad Palmer

Fernie
Shane Churla
Frank Hughes
Jason Krog
David Leneveu
Dan Smith

Fort St. James
Bryan Adams
Jim Playfair
Larry Playfair
Brian Spencer

Fort St. John
Mark Hartigan
Chris Jensen
Al Stewart

Golden
Doug Barrault

Grand Forks
Ronald Areshenkoff

Hazelton
Ron Homenuke
Alan Kerr
Brandon Smith

Hope
Jeff Hoggan
Kyle Kos

Houston
Ryan Stewart

Kimberley
Len Barrie
Don Martineau
Mike McBain
Jason Wiemer

Kitimat
Don Nachbaur
Jeff Staples

Lac La Hache
Al Karlander

Ladysmith
Tony Feltrin

Langley
Chris Heid
Jordan Krestanovich
David Morisset

Maple Ridge
Andrew Ladd

Merritt
Eddie Beers
Ron Fischer
Paul Kruse

Miskel
Gordon Turlick

Murrayville
Robb Gordon
Danny Lorenz

Nakusp
Brad Larsen

Nanaimo
Wayne Bianchin
Gene Carr
Al Hill
Trent Kaese
Mark Rycroft

Nelson
Greg Adams
Danny Gare
Mike Laughton
Pat Price

Osoyoos
Neil Eisenhut
Mitch Fritz
Chuck Kobasew

Pitt Meadows
Brendan Morrison

Port Alberni
Ron Andruff
Paul Cyr
Jim Hiller
John Newberry
Davis Payne

Port Hardy
Chris Murray

Port McNeil
Greg Fox
Willie Mitchell
Rob Skrlac

Port Moody
Jeff McLean

Powell River
Micah Aivazoff
Brad Bombardir
Danny Lucas
Gary Lupul
Terry Richardson
Richard Seeley

Prince George
Murray Baron
Kerry Ketter
Greg Kuznik
Stewart Malgunas

White Rock
Jeff Bandura

Mark Morrison
Daryl Reaugh
Turner Stevenson

Princeton
Stephen Peat

Quesnel
Rod Dallman
Bob Gassoff
Brad Gassoff
Errol Rausse

Revelstoke
Bruce Holloway

Richmond
Scott Hannan
Dave Mackey
Brent Seabrook
Mike Valley

Rossland
Seth Martin
Derek Mayer
Joe Zanussi

Salmon Arm
Bruce Affleck
Kris Beech

Sandon
Cecil "Tiny" Thompson

Sechelt
David Oliver

Shuswap
Rocco Reinikka

Sicamous
Rob Flockhart
Shea Weber

Smithers
Ron Flockhart
Dan Hamhuis
Rob Millar
Jimmy Watson
Joe Watson

Summerland
Larry Hale

Surrey
Greg Black
Marc Brown
Mike Brown
Colin Hemingway
Mark Janssens
Bill Muckalt
Gary Nylund
Bob Rouse
Joel Savage
Barry Smith

Terrace
Wade Flaherty
Dale Kushner
Jeff Sharples

Vernon
Eric Brewer
Jarrett Deuling
Eric Godard
Ken Holland
King Kwong
Bruce Major
Jason Podollan
Jerred Smithson

YUKON

Faro
Gerard Dicaire

Whitehorse
Bobby House
Bryon Baltimore
Peter Sturgeon

NORTHWEST TERRITORIES

Hay River
Rob Mcvicar
Geoff Sanderson

Inuvik
Zac Boyer

Yellowknife
Vic Mercredi
Greg Vaydik

Index

Note: Page references in **bold** type indicate photographs.

Picture Credits

Every effort has been made to correctly attribute all material reproduced in this book. If errors have unwittingly occurred, we will be happy to correct them in future editions.

FRONT COVER Photo by See Spot Run Inc.

BACK COVER (clockwise from top left) Photo by Nick Laham/Getty Images; Hockey Online; Hockey Online; Photo by Graig Abel/Getty Images; Hockey Online; Hockey Online

2 © Château Ramezay Museum collection, Montreal

5 Courtesy of Sher-Wood Corp.

8 www.istockimages.com

10-11 Photo by Charles Laberge/Getty Images

14 Courtesy of the Memorial University Student Union

17 Hockey Online

18 Vancouver Canucks

19 (left) SANL 1.26.01.155 Courtesy of the Sports Archives of Newfoundland Labrador; (right) Corner Brook Royals

20 Photo by Bruce Bennett Studios/Getty Images

21 www.Fredspucks.com

23 Toronto Maple Leafs

24-25 Photo by Jim McIsaac/Getty Images

28 Taken from *A Prince Edward Island Album: Glimpses of the Way we Were* (Willowdale: Hounslow Press, 1987).

29 (both) Photo reproduced courtesy of Charlie Ballem

30 (right) Photo reproduced courtesy of Charlie Ballem

31 Reproduced courtesy of Black Islanders, Jim Hornby, Institute of Island Studies, 1990

33 Hockey Online

34-35 Images courtesy of My Father's House Bed & Breakfast, Murray Harbour www.myfathershouse.ca

36 PAPEI I 2320-93-10

37 Florida Panthers

38-39 Photo by Mitchell Layton/Getty Images

43 Library and Archives Canada nlc-5764

44 (left) Nova Scotia Sport Hall of Fame; (right) Garth Vaughan Collection

45 (left) Taken from *Antigonish Town and County*, (Halifax: Nimbus Publishing, 2004), p. 212; (top right) Nova Scotia Sport Hall of Fame; (bottom right) Winnipeg Jets

47 Photo by Hulton Archive/Getty Images

48 Garth Vaughan Collection

49 Photo by Andre Ringuette/Getty Images

50 Collection of Ernie Fitzsimmons

51 Photo by Elsa/Getty Images/NHLI

53 Kitchener Rangers

54 (top) © www.canadianheritage.ca id #10207; (bottom) New York Rangers

55-56 Nova Scotia Sport Hall of Fame

57 (left) Courtesy of the Truro Bearcats. Image provided by Specialized Printers; (right) Garth Vaughan Collection

59 Garth Vaughan Collection

60-61 Photo by Bruce Bennet Studios/Getty Images

64 Heritage Resources #7762, Saint John

65 (left) www.Hockeymemorabilia.com; (right) Garth Vaughan Collection

66 (left) Heritage Resources #7526, Saint John; (right) © Brian Smith–February 2005

67 New Brunswick Sports Hall of Fame PHF 85.2-7

68 Hockey Online

69 Image provided by New Brunswick Sports Hall of Fame PHF 2003.3-11a

71 (left) New Brunswick Sports Hall of Fame PHF 70.1-23; (right) Montreal Canadiens

72 P82-150

73 PANB P11-214

74 Photo supplied by www.StompinTom.com under authorization by Stompin' Tom Limited

75 New Brunswick Sports Hall of Fame PHF 73.1-18

76-77 Photo by Bruce Bennett Studios/Getty Images

80 (both) Hockey Online

82 Hockey Online

83 (left) Hockey Online; (right) Coll. Société historique de Saguenay (Fonds V.-Tremblay) No. 10090

84 Detroit Red Wings

85 Montreal Canadiens

86 Montreal Junior Canadiens

87 (left) Quebec Aces; (right) Hockey Online

88 Library and Archives Canada

89 Ottawa '67s

90 Laval Voisins

91 Reproduced courtesy of Melenny Productions Inc. Photo: Pierre Dury

93 (top) McCord Museum, Montreal MP–0000.25.1030; (bottom) Taken from *Historic Montreal Past and Present*, (Montreal: Henry Morgan & Co., Ltd., no date), p 71.

94 Château Ramezay Museum collection, Montreal

95 Library and Archives Canada nlc-6599

96 Star Weekly

97 Hockey Online

98 Hockey Online

99 Taken from *The Montreal Canadiens*, (Toronto: Van Nostrand Reinhold, 1980), p. 154.

100 (left) McCord Museum, Montreal M2001.43.1; (right) Hockey Online

101 Montreal Canadiens

102-104 Hockey Online

106 Hartford Whalers

107 (right) Hockey Online; (left) Montreal Canadiens

108 Montreal Junior Canadiens

109 Sher-Wood Corp.

110 Courtesy of InGlasCo Corp. Ltd.

111 Sorel Eperviers

112-116 Hockey Online

117 Classic Cards

118 Image reproduced courtesy of les Tigres de Victoriaville

119 Montreal Junior Canadiens

120-121 Photo by Rick Stewart/Getty Images

124 Hockey Online

125 Library and Archives Canada PA-111399

126 Peterborough Examiner

127 Hockey Online

129 Hockey Online

130 Library and Archives Canada C-008355

132 Hockey Online

133 (both) Cambridge Sports Hall of Fame

134 (top) Hockey Online; (bottom) Photo courtesy of Hugh A. Campbell

135-136 Hockey Online

137 (left) Guelph Biltmores; (right) Toronto Star

138 Hamilton Tigers

141 (left) Lake of the Woods Museum; (right) Vancouver Millionaires

142 Whig-Standard/Michael Lea

143 (both) Taken from *Hockey's Captains, Colonels & Kings*, (Erin: Boston Mills Press, 1986) endpage; p. 55.

144 (left) Library and Archives Canada PA-127274; (right) Hockey Online

145 (both) Hockey Online

146-148 Hockey Online

149 Toronto Maple Leafs

150 Courtesy of InGlasCo Corp. Ltd.

151 (top) CP (Nathan Denette); (bottom) Photograph Ernie Fitzsimmons

152 Collection of Ernie Fitzsimmons

153 (top) Taken from *Niagara*, (Toronto: University of Toronto Press, 1969), p. 19; (bottom) Niagara Falls Flyers

154 Hockey Online

155 (left) Ontario Hockey Association Archives; (right) Toronto Public Library

156 Courtesy of InGlasCo Corp. Ltd.

157 Oshawa Generals

159 Taken from *From Ottawa with Love: Glimpses of Canada's Capital through Early Picture Postcards*, (Ottawa: National Capital Commission, 1979).

160 (top) Library and Archives Canada nlc005953-v5; (bottom) Collection of Ernie Fitzsimmons

161 (left) Collection of Ernie Fitzsimmons; (right) Library and Archives Canada PA-026737

163 Library and Archives Canada PA-091046

164 Springfield Indians

165 Hockey Online

166 From the collection of Stephen Cole

167 Taken from *A Centennial Volume published by the City and County of Peterborough*, (Toronto: University of Toronto Press, 1967).

168 (top) The Peterborough Examiner; (bottom) Taken from *Hockey Town: Life Before the Pros*, (Toronto: McClelland and Stewart, 2004), p. 114.

169 The Peterborough Petes

171 Photo by Bruce Bennett Studios/Getty Images

172 Photograph Ernie Fitzsimmons

174 Library and Archives Canada PA-055158

176 OHA Junior "A" All-Stars

177 © Courtesy of the Sault Ste. Marie Museum. Photo taken by M. A. Coulson, Photographer, Sault Ste. Marie, Ontario

178 Rochester Americans

179 Team Canada

181 Collection of Ernie Fitzsimmons

183 (left) Hockey Online; (right) Collection of Ernie Fitzsimmons

184 Michael Burns

186 (left) Toronto Maple Leafs; (middle and right) Collection of Ernie Fitzsimmons

189 Hockey Online

190 Toronto Maple Leafs

192 (top) Taken from *Toronto Illustrated, 1893*, (Toronto: Consolidated Illustrating Co., 1893), p. 14; (bottom) Hockey Online

193 Library and Archives Canada C-29556

194 Hockey Online

195 Alexandra Studio

197 Toronto Maple Leafs

198 Taken from *The Inside Story of Conn Smythe's Hockey Dynasty— A Fascinating History of the Toronto Maple Leafs Hockey Club*, (Toronto: Pagurian Press, 1969)

199 Wayne Kewin/Whitby Dunlops Sr. A. Hockey Club

201 Ernie Fitzsimmons

203 Photo By Dave Sandford/ Getty Images

204 Hockey Online

205 Chicago Blackhawks

206-207 Photo by Bruce Bennett Studios/Getty Images

210-211 Manitoba Sports Hall of Fame

212 (top) Hockey Online; (bottom) Manitoba Sports Hall of Fame

213 Glenbow Archives NA-978-3

214 (left) Library and Archives Canada nlc-6320. Reproduced with the permission of Topps Cards; (right) Photo by Bruce Bennett Studios/Getty Images

215 Hockey Online

216 Flin Flon Bombers

217 (left) Detroit Red Wings; (right) Bill Kirkwood

218 H. McCraig

219 Minnesota Saints

220 (top) Library and Archives Canada 58703-v6; (bottom) Detroit Red Wings

221 Collection of Ernie Fitzsimmons

222 Montreal Canadiens

223 (top) Library and Archives Canada C-001346; (bottom) New York Americans

224 (both) Hockey Online

226 Manitoba Sports Hall of Fame

227 (top) Winnipeg Jets; (bottom) Library and Archives Canada C-079305

228 © Brian Johannesson

229 (left) © University of Manitoba Archives & Special Collections, Winnipeg Tribune Collection; (right) From the collection of Stephen Cole

230 Winnipeg Jets

231 Joe Scherschel

233 (top) Courtesy of the Manitoba Moose, Photo by Rusty Barton, Manitoba Moose; (bottom) CP (Dave Buston)

234-235 Photo by Al Bello/ Getty Images

238 (left) Saskatchewan Archives Board RD 773 (2); (right) Reproduced with permission of Orca Book Publishers

239 (both) Hockey Online

240 (left) Edmonton Flyers; (right) Winnipeg Jets

242 Hockey Online

243 Library and Archives Canada nlc-6313, Reproduced with the permission of Topps Cards

244-245 Taken from *Hockey Heritage: 88 Years of Puck Chasing in Saskatchewan*, Courtesy of the Saskatchewan Sports Hall of Fame and Museum

246 University of Saskatchewan SPC MssC565/2/11.28

247 Collection of Ernie Fitzsimmons

248 Edmonton Flyers

250 University of Saskatchewan SPC Pamphlets 1xx-20

251 (left) Doug Mathieson; (right) Photograph Ernie Fitzsimmons

252 Chicago Blackhawks

253 (left) New York Islanders; (right) Taken from *Hockey Heritage: 88 Years of Puck Chasing in Saskatchewan*, Courtesy of the Saskatchewan Sports Hall of Fame and Museum

254 Montreal Canadiens

255 Moose Jaw Warriors

257-258 Hockey Online

259 University of Saskatchewan SPC Pamphlets, 1xx-12

260 Hockey Online

261 Toronto Maple Leafs

262 (top) E.C. Rossie, Saskatchewan Archives Board, RB 930; (bottom) Regina Victorias

263 Edmonton Oilers

264 Glenbow Archives NA-2565-15

265 (left) Montreal Canadiens; (right) National Currency Collection, Currency Museum, Bank of Canada

266 Saskatoon Public Library LH 4138

268 (left) Saskatoon Archives; (right) Hockey Online

269 University of Toronto Skating Archive

270 University of Saskatchewan SPC Pamphlets, 1xx-1298

271 ROBERT SULLIVAN/AFP/ Getty Images

272 University of Saskatchewan SPC Pamphlets, 1xx-1501

273 Photo courtesy of the Swift Current Broncos

274 Hockey Online

275 University of Saskatchewan SPC Pamphlets, 1xx-1645

276 Hockey Online

278 Notre Dame College Archives

279 Hockey Online

280 University of Saskatchewan SPC Pamphlets, 1xx-324

281 (top) Taken from *Hockey Heritage: 88 Years of Puck Chasing in Saskatchewan*, Courtesy of the Saskatchewan Sports Hall of Fame and Museum; (bottom) Detroit Red Wings

282-283 Photo by Jeff Vinnick/ Getty Images

286 Hockey Online

287 Edmonton Oilers

288 CP

289 Glenbow Archives NA-98-10

290 (left) Glenbow Archives NA-4100-2; (right) Manitoba Archives, Foote Collection, 1107

291 (left) E. W. Cadman, Oliver Studio; (right) Glenbow Archives NA-5654-58

292 CP (Hans Deryk)

293 (left) Glenbow Archives NA-4717-1; (right, both) Calgary Flames

294 Hockey Online

295 CP (Jeff McIntosh)

296 Photograph by Corey Hallisey

297 (left) Glenbow Archives NB-16-500; (right) Calgary Flames

298 Glenbow Archives NC-6-11932b

299 (left) City of Edmonton Archives EA-544-3; (right, top) Taken from *Alberta on Ice*, (Edmonton: GMS Ventures, 1985), p. 7. (bottom) City of Edmonton Archives EA-10-2217

300 (left) Alberta Provincial Archives; (right) Alberta Provincial Archives

301 (top) Edmonton Oilers; (bottom) Glenbow Archives ND-3-3106a

302 CP (Dave Buston)

303 Edmonton Oilers

304 Photograph Ernie Fitzsimmons

305 Edmonton Oilers

307 Morley L. Fach, Lapp Collection

309 Photo by B. Bennett/Bruce Bennett Studios/Getty Images

310 City of Lethbridge Archives and Records

311 Sir Alexander Galt Museum

313 Alberta Provincial Archives

314 (bottom) Vancouver Canucks

315 Richard Lapp Collection

317 (top) Red Deer District Archives p. 234-68; (bottom) Courtesy of the Red Deer Rebels

318-319 Courtesy of the Red Deer Rebels

320-321 CP (Adrian Wyld); (Rick Madonik)

322 Glenbow Archives NA-1758-17

323 CP

326-327 Photo by Elsa/Getty Images

330 (both) BC Sports Hall of Fame & Museum

331 Photo by Donald Miralle/ Getty Images

332 Grant-Mann Lithographers Ltd. of Vancouver (S-1224)

333 LAURENCE COUSTAL/AFP/Getty Images

334 CP/Everett Collection

335 Colorado Avalanche

337 Team Halifax

338 Hockey Online

339 Photo by Sean Gallup/ Getty Images

340 Grant-Mann Lithographers Ltd. of Vancouver

341 Philadelphia Flyers

342 Phoenix Coyotes

343 Wachlin Photo

344 (left) Courtesy of the Kelowna Rockets; (right) Kelowna Rockets/Cindy Rogers

345 Kelowna Rockets/Swanky Photographic

346 (top) Grant-Mann Lithographers Ltd. of Vancouver (S-1139); (bottom) Toronto Maple Leafs

348 Vancouver Canucks

349 (top) BC Sports Hall of Fame & Museum; (bottom) Hockey Online

350-351 BC Sports Hall of Fame & Museum

352 Trail Historical Society

353 BC Sports Hall of Fame & Museum

354 (both) Trail Historical Society

355 BC Sports Hall of Fame & Museum

356 Taken from *Vancouver Recalled*, (Saanichton: Hancock House Publisher, 1974), p. 71.

357 BC Sports Hall of Fame & Museum

359 Photo by Jeff Vinnick/ Getty Images

361 Library and Archives Canada PA-117267

362 Photo by Dave Sandford/ Getty Images/NHLI

363 BC Sports Hall of Fame & Museum

364 Grant-Mann Lithographers, Ltd. Of Vancouver (S-778)

365 © Bob Straith/GVSHofF

366 BC Sports Hall of Fame & Museum

368-369 Photo by Dave Sandford/Getty Images

372 (left) Library and Archives Canada C-001352; (right) Canadian Space Agency

373 (both) Glenbow Archives NA-964-4; NA-3835-14

374 (left) © Woodstock Public Library/Len Taylor; (right) Yukon Archives, Ernest Brown Fonds, #863

375 Yukon Archives, Ernest Brown Fonds, 88/25#1

376 (left) Library and Archives Canada nlc-5042; (right) Collection Particulière

377 (top) Taken from *Narrative of a Second Expedition to the Shores of the Polar Sea, in the years 1825, 1826 and 1827*, (Edmonton: M.G. Hurtig, 1971); (bottom) Glenbow Archives NA-1344-5

378 Courtesy of the Charter Community of Deline Rec Department Photograph by coach Ken Caine.

379 The Thomas Fisher Rare Book Library, University of Toronto, Joseph Tyrell Fonds, P10400

380 CP/Winnipeg Free Press (Fred Greenslade)

382 (clockwise from top left) Hockey Online; Boston Bruins; Detroit Red Wings; Boston Bruins; New York Rangers; Montreal Canadiens; New York Rangers; Photograph Ernie Fitzsimmons; New York Islanders; Rochester Americans

383 Photo by Doug Pensinger/ Getty Images

Sources

I found the following sources particularly useful in the creation of this book.

WEBSITES

The Backcheck hockey website
(http://www.collectionscanada.ca/hockey/index-e.html)

The Society for International Hockey Research website
(http://www.sihrhockey.org/public_news.cfm)

BOOKS

Abbott, Bill. *Herder Memorial Trophy: A History of Senior Hockey in Newfoundland and Labrador*. St. John's: Breakwater, 2000.

Beardsley, Doug. *Country on Ice*. Winlaw Press: Polestar Press, 1987.

Beddoes, Dick. *Greatest Hockey Stories*. Toronto: Macmillan Canada, 1990.

Beliveau, Jean with Chris Goyens and Allan Turowetz. *My Life in Hockey*. Toronto: McLelland & Stewart, 1994.

Bidini, Dave. *The Best Game You Can Name*. Toronto: McLelland & Stewart, 2005.

Boyd, Bill. *All Roads Lead to Hockey*. Toronto: Key Porter Books, 2004.

Boyd, Bill. *Hockey Towns: Stories of Small Town Hockey in Canada*. Toronto: Doubleday Canada, 1998.

Brewitt, Ross. *Into the Empty Net*. Toronto: Stoddart, 1996.

Brewitt, Ross. *Last Minute of Play*. Toronto: Stoddart, 1993.

Cherry, Don with Stan Fischler. *Grapes*. Toronto: Prentice Hall, 1982.

Cuthbert, Chris and Scott Russell. *The Rink: Stories From Canada's Hockey Towns*. Toronto: Viking, 1997.

Delisle, Tom and Gordie Howe. *And Howe!* Traverse City, MI: Power Play Publications, 1995.

Dowbiggin, Bruce. *The Stick*. Toronto: Macfarlane, Walter & Ross, 2002.

Dupuis, David. *Sawchuk: The Troubles and Triumphs of the World's Greatest Goalie*. Toronto: Stoddart, 1998.

Fisher, Red. *Hockey, Heroes and Me*. Toronto: McLelland & Stewart, 1996.

Flood, Brian. *Saint John, A Sporting Tradition: 1785-1985*. Saint John: Neptune Publishing, 1985.

Frayne, Trent. *Famous Hockey Players*. New York: Dodd, Mead & Company, 1973.

Frayne, Trent. *It's Easy All You Have To Do Is Win*. Toronto: Longmans Canada Limited, 1968.

Frayne, Trent. *The Mad Men of Hockey*. New York: Dodd, Mead & Company, 1974.

Germain, Georges-Herbert. *Overtime: The Legend of Guy Lafleur*. Toronto: Penguin Canada, 1990.

Goyens, Chris and Allan Turowetz. *Lions in Winter*. Toronto: Douglas & McIntyre, 1981.

Gretzky, Wayne with Rick Reilly. *Gretzky: An Autobiography*. New York: HarperCollins, 1990.

Hunt, Jim and Bobby Hull. *Hockey is My Game*. Toronto: Longmans, 1967.

Hunter, Douglas. *Yzerman: The Making of a Champion*. Toronto: Doubleday Canada, 2004.

Houston, William. *Ballard*. Toronto: Summerhill Press, 1984.

Irvin, Dick. *The Habs*. Toronto: McLelland & Stewart, 1991.

Irvin, Dick. *Now Back too You Dick*. Toronto: McLelland & Stewart, 1988.

Lapp, Richard M. and Alex MacAulay. *The Memorial Cup*. Madeira Park, BC: Harbour Pub Co., 1997.

McAllister, Ron. *Hockey Heroes*. Toronto: McLelland & Stewart, 1949.

McFarlane, Brian. *Proud Past, Bright Future: One Hundred Years of Canadian Women's Hockey*. Toronto: Stoddart Publishing, 1994.

McKinley, Michael. *Putting a Roof on Winter*. Toronto: Douglas & McIntyre, 2000.

McRae, Earl. *Requiem for Reggie*. Toronto: Chimo Publishing, 1977.

Mahovlich, Ted. *The Big M: The Frank Mahovlich Story*. Toronto: HarperCollins, 1999.

Mahovlich, Ted. *Triple Crown: The Marcel Dionne Story*. Toronto: HarperCollins, 2004.

Martin, Lawrence. *Mario*. Toronto: LesterPub, 1993.

Meeker, Howie with Charlie Hodge. *Golly Gee It's Me: The Howie Meeker Story*. Toronto: Stoddart, 1996.

Potvin, Denis with Stan Fischler. *Power on Ice*. Harper & Row, 1977.

Richards, David Adams. *Hockey Dreams*. Toronto: Doubleday Canada, 1996.

Roche, Bill. *The Hockey Book*. Toronto: McLelland & Stewart, 1953.

Sanderson, Derek and Stan Fischler. *I've Got to Be Me*. New York: Dodd, Mead & Company, 1970.

Savole, Mark. *Broken Time and Broken Hearts: The Maritimes and the Selection of Canada's 1936 Hockey Team*. M.A. thesis, University of New Brunswick, 1997

Taylor, Jim. *Wayne Gretzky*. Toronto: McLelland & Stewart, 1984.

Vaughan, Garth. *The Puck Starts Here: The Origin of Canada's Great Winter Game*. Fredericton: Goose Lane, 1996.

White, Gregory B. *Icing the Puck: the Origins, Rise, and Decline of Newfoundland Senior Hockey*. M.A. thesis. Memorial University of Newfoundland, 1997.

Whitehead, Eric. *Cyclone Taylor*. Toronto: Doubleday, 1977.

Whitehead, Eric. *The Patricks: Hockey's Royal Family*. Toronto: Doubleday, 1980.

Wilkins, Charles. *After the Applause*. Toronto: McLelland & Stewart, 1990.

Willis, Sheldon. *Putting it on Ice: A Social History of Hockey in the Maritimes (1880-1914)*. M.A. thesis. Saint Mary's University, 1996.

Young, Scott. *100 Years of Dropping the Puck: A History of the OHA*. Toronto: McLelland & Stewart, 1989.

Young, Scott. *The Boys of Saturday Night*. Toronto: Macmillan, 1990.

Young, Scott. *Scrubs on Skates*. Boston: Little Brown, 1952.

Zeman, Brenda. *Hockey Heritage: 88 Years of Puck-Chasing in Saskatchewan*. WDS Associates and the Saskatchewan Sports Hall of Fame, 1983.

Zeman, Gary W. *The History of Alberta Hockey Since 1893*. Edmonton: GMS Ventures, 1985.

And finally, I must acknowledge that I leaned every hour of every working day on Dan Diamond's invaluable *Total Hockey*, and Andrew Podnieks' *Players: The Ultimate A-Z Guide of Everyone Who Has Ever Played in the NHL*.

**THE CANADIAN HOCKEY ATLAS
IS AN ANGEL EDITION**

**CREATED UNDER THE EDITORIAL
AND CREATIVE DIRECTION
OF SARA ANGEL**

Book Design
Concrete Design Communications Inc.

Project Editor
Amy Hick

Editor
Joanna Freedman

Photo Research and Acquisition
Bao-Nghi Nhan

Copy Editor
Patricia Holtz

Index
Gillian Watts